SAP® Basis Administration Handbook, NetWeaver Edition

About the Author

Ranjit Mereddy has 12 years' experience in SAP NetWeaver/Basis technical architecture, enterprise architecture, and administration. He has led several successful SAP implementations as the SAP technical team lead and is an SAP-certified technical consultant. He has consulted for Fortune 500 companies and leading systems integrators, such as IBM, Accenture, and the federal government. He has his own SAP professional consulting practice. SAP consulting and outsourcing services provided by his professional firm can be accessed at www.wecollab.com. He can be reached at ranjit.mereddy@wecollab.com or sapert@yahoo.com. He can be followed on Twitter @RanjitMereddy (www.twitter.com/RanjitMereddy).

About the Technical Editor

Raj Patel is a senior managing consultant with IBM Business Consulting Services. Raj has over 20 years' experience in the IT industry, with the last 18 years focused on SAP Basis. He specializes in applying information technology expertise to deploy SAP systems to solve complex business problems. As an IT consultant, he has been providing SAP implementation and project management expertise to variety of clients. He has a bachelor's degree in electronic computer engineering from the University of Rhode Island.

SAP® Basis Administration Handbook, NetWeaver Edition

Ranjit Mereddy

New York Chicago San Francisco
Lisbon London Madrid Mexico City
Milan New Delhi San Juan
Seoul Singapore Sydney Toronto

The McGraw-Hill Companies

Library of Congress Cataloging-in-Publication Data

Mereddy, Ranjit.
SAP Basis administration handbook / Ranjit Mereddy. — NetWeaver ed.
p. cm.
Included index.
ISBN 978-0-07-166348-9 (alk. paper) — ISBN 0-07-166348-7 (alk. paper)
1. Management information systems. 2. SAP NetWeaver. I. Title.
T58.64.M46 2012
006.7'6—dc23

2011042740

McGraw-Hill books are available at special quantity discounts to use as premiums and sales promotions, or for use in corporate training programs. To contact a representative, please e-mail us at bulksales@mcgraw-hill.com.

SAP® Basis Administration Handbook, NetWeaver Edition

1 2 3 4 5 6 7 8 9 0 DOC DOC 1 0 9 8 7 6 5 4 3 2 1

ISBN 978-0-07-166348-9
MHID 0-07-166348-7

Sponsoring Editor
Wendy Rinaldi

Editorial Supervisor
Janet Walden

Project Management
Sandhya Gola,
Cenveo Publisher Services

Acquisitions Coordinator
Stephanie Evans

Technical Editor
Raj Patel

Copy Editor
Lisa McCoy

Proofreader
Claire Splan

Indexer
Jack Lewis

Production Supervisor
James Kussow

Composition
Cenveo Publisher Services

Illustration
Cenveo Publisher Services

Art Director, Cover
Jeff Weeks

Dedicated to my daughter, Divya Mereddy

Contents at a Glance

Contents

Part V SAP Monitoring and Troubleshooting

Part VI Database Management in SAP

Acknowledgments

I would like to thank my mother, Neeraja Devi Mereddy, and father, Satyanarayana Reddy Mereddy, for making all the sacrifices and sending me to great schools. I would like to thank all of my teachers at St. Paul's High School, Hyderabad, India, for providing me with an excellent education. I would not have been in a position to conceive and write a book without the sacrifices of my parents and patience of my teachers in providing me with a sound education.

I would like to thank McGraw-Hill Professional Editorial Director Wendy Rinaldi for sponsoring this book and Acquisitions Coordinator Stephanie Evans for guiding me through the initial writing and technical edits. I would also like to thank Senior Acquisitions Editor Lisa McClain for considering the initial book proposal and seeing the need for this book in the SAP education marketplace. I would like to thank Associate Acquisitions Editor Meghan Riley for guiding me through the initial chapters of the technical writing and edits. I would like to thank Project Manager Sandhya Gola, Editorial Supervisor Janet Walden, copy editor Lisa McCoy, and the entire production staff for helping with the publication process. This book would not have been possible without the financial and publishing support of McGraw-Hill Professional.

I would like to thank the technical editor, Raj Patel from IBM, for carefully reviewing the book chapters and offering suggestions to improve the quality of the book. His suggestions in the early chapters were particularly helpful in guiding the book in the right direction in terms of quality and content.

I would like to thank my daughter, Divya Mereddy, for putting up with my long periods of being at home during weekends but not available to help in school and homework activities. I would like to thank my wife, Srilekha Mereddy, for providing support while I was busy writing the book.

I would like to thank my sisters, Kavitha and Savitha, and my brother, Rajesh, for providing a safe and supporting environment growing up and helping me meet my educational and career goals. I would like to thank my brothers-in-law, Shekar Reddy and Uday Kumar Reddy, for helping me to come to the United States.

I would like to thank Dr. Kenneth E. Conway and Dr. Craig Liddell for providing advice, opportunities, and guidance for my career when I first came to the United States almost 20 years back.

I would like to thank my good friends, Prahalad Puranik, Srinath Devalapalli, Rakesh Kuruba, Vinod Raghavan, Vijayender Reddy, and PVS Ravi Kumar, for being positive influences in my career and life. I would like to thank my good friend and fellow SAP Basis colleague Sitapati Kalluri for countless deep technical discussions on SAP NetWeaver/Basis subject matter over the last 12 years. I would like to thank Philip Thilak for his friendship and deep Oracle database discussions in SAP environments. I would like to thank Prashant Nanga for giving me my initial break into SAP consulting. I would like to thank Prasad Rao and CyberTech International for providing my initial SAP training 12 years ago. I would like to thank Srinivas Garimella (Vasu) for encouraging me to go into SAP consulting.

I would like to thank Peter Van Avermaet for helping me to deepen my SAP basis skill during early part of my career. I would like to thank Srikanth Yelimati, Santhosh Jamandlamudi, Anand Kaliyamurthy, Raj Joshi, and Sunil Guditi, for checking in on me while writing this book.

Special thanks go to my neighborhood Starbucks!

Introduction

SAP Basis administration involves all system administration activities of the SAP applications running on ABAP and Java stacks. SAP Basis has evolved into a complex skill over time, and this book will serve as a handbook for all system administration activities. This book covers both ABAP and Java stack architecture and administration skills. This book is intended for the following audiences:

- University professors and lecturers who need a textbook to teach SAP system administration and SAP NetWeaver architecture to students
- New SAP Basis administrators
- SAP system administrators experienced in ABAP systems who need to develop Java administration skills
- SAP system administrators experienced in Java systems who need to develop ABAP administration skills
- Experienced SAP administrators who need to develop skills in advanced administration activities such as homogeneous and heterogeneous system copies and further understand NetWeaver internal architecture and administration activities
- SAP Basis professionals and prospective Basis administrators who are seeking information on SAP career trends, certification options, career progression options, and hot skills
- SAP and enterprise architects who are seeking to understand the internals of NetWeaver architecture
- SAP technology and IT managers who are seeking a broad understanding of Basis architecture and administration functions to make better decisions

How to Use This Book

The book is organized into nine parts and one appendix. Each of the nine parts of the book addresses a major SAP Basis administration activity. Each part is further organized into several chapters. There are 28 chapters in this book. The initial chapters are focused on architecture and installation aspects, and later chapters address all other system administration activities. If you are a new Basis professional it is recommended that you read the chapters in the order presented in the book. If you are an experienced professional, you can read the chapters in the order that meets your requirements or need. For university professors and lecturers teaching a class, it is recommended that you cover the initial architectural concepts first and then teach the material according to your schedule. At the end of each chapter additional resources are provided so that students can further enhance and develop their Basis skills. In general, the book starts with basics and fundamentals and then, as the chapters progress, more advanced topics in SAP Basis administration are covered. The appendix specifically focuses on SAP Basis career trends, certification requirements, training curriculum and career progression, and hot SAP Basis skills. An overview of the 28 chapters and appendix is provided here to further explain the content and value of the book to your skill and career development needs.

Chapter 1: SAP NetWeaver and Business Suite Introduction This chapter provides an overview of the evolution of SAP software and the Basis skill set, SAP NetWeaver stacks, SAP Business Suite, and its key capabilities.

Chapter 2: SAP NetWeaver Application Server ABAP Overview This chapter covers the architecture concepts of the SAP ABAP stack, such as the three-tier architecture of SAP applications, starting SAP applications based on the ABAP stack, verifying that the application started properly, and how to log in and move around in SAP applications using transaction codes and menu paths.

Chapter 3: SAP NetWeaver Application Server Java Overview This chapter provides a detailed discussion of Java programming language concepts and architecture. It covers the internals of the Java startup framework in SAP Java applications. The understanding gained from this chapter will help Basis administrators diagnose any SAP Java application startup issues in a methodical manner.

Chapter 4: SAP ERP Integration Overview with Other Systems This chapter discusses the integration of SAP ERP applications with other applications in the enterprise. Examples of such applications are SAP BW (Business Warehouse), SAP PI (Process Integration), SAP Solution Manager, and third-party enterprise tools such as Tivoli, Autosys, and Taxware. This chapter shows the complexity of the SAP application in terms of its integration with other enterprise applications and tools to serve a business purpose.

Chapter 5: SAP ABAP and Java Stack Installation Preparation This chapter describes the tasks necessary prior to installation, such as visiting the SAP software download location and checking the product availability matrix for SAP applications and tools for downloading the SAP software.

Chapter 6: SAP ABAP and Java Stack Installation This chapter covers the installation tools, the detailed steps involved in SAP ABAP and Java stack installation, and troubleshooting installation issues.

Chapter 7: SAP ABAP and Java Stack Post-installation This chapter discusses all the important post-installation activities in ABAP and Java stacks. These include SAP license installation and performing the kernel upgrade. Support package application is also discussed in detail.

Chapter 8: Installing SAP Stand-Alone Systems This chapter covers the installation of SAP stand-alone systems, such as SAProuter, SAP Live Cache, and SAP Web Dispatcher.

Chapter 9: SAP System Landscapes in ABAP and Java Stacks This chapter explains the software logistics of ABAP and Java systems. The SAP client concept, System Landscape concepts, and client instance strategy are discussed in detail.

Chapter 10: SAP Client Administration in ABAP Systems This chapter discusses all the client administration activities, such as creating the local client copy, remote client copy, client import, and client deletion.

Chapter 11: SAP Transport Management System in ABAP Systems This chapter discusses the internals of setting up SAP transport management concepts in ABAP systems, the internals of the transport control program, transport command options, and transport route configuration.

Chapter 12: SAP Software Logistics for Java Systems This chapter discusses the software logistics in Java systems, the four-System-Landscape in Java systems, the Java developmental lifecycle, and the NetWeaver development infrastructure.

Chapter 13: SAP Complex System Landscapes This chapter will cover topics such as SAP implementation approaches and complex System Landscapes, such as a five-System-Landscape.

Chapter 14: SAP Processes in an ABAP Stack This chapter discusses the core ABAP processes and administration activities in the system. Topics such as the concept of a SAP work process, the kinds of SAP work processes, profiles and profile management, locks and updates, operation modes, logon groups, and RFC server groups are covered in detail.

Chapter 15: SAP Processes in Java Stack This chapter discusses the key Java stack administration tools, such as Visual Administrator, the configuration tool, and NetWeaver Administrator.

Chapter 16: Structured Monitoring and Analysis This chapter discusses the techniques for structured monitoring and analysis. Both ABAP and Java systems startup troubleshooting processes are explained in detail in this chapter.

Chapter 17: Solution Manager Installation and Monitoring This chapter discusses the installation and configuration of Solution Manager. It also covers the installation and configuration of CCMS agents, Solution Manager Diagnostics, central performance history, and Wily Introscope.

Chapter 18: SAP Service Marketplace Administration This chapter discusses SAP Service Marketplace administration activities, such as searching OSS Notes, opening OSS messages, creating Service Marketplace users, downloading SAP software, and requesting developer and access keys.

Chapter 19: Database Installation and Configuration This chapter discusses Oracle Database internals and installation.

Chapter 20: Database Configuration and Administration Using SAP BRTOOLS This chapter discusses the internal workings of SAP and Oracle Databases and naming conventions used for the SAP standard tablespaces, data and logfiles. It also covers the administration of the SAP database using BRTOOLS.

Chapter 21: Database Backup and Restore This chapter discusses the concepts of database backup strategies, performing a complete backup using BRTOOLS, and performing a restore of a database using BRTOOLS.

Chapter 22: SAP Performance Tuning in the ABAP Stack This chapter discusses the memory management concepts in ABAP stacks, memory allocation sequence in dialog and background work processes, performance tuning transactions, performing SQL trace, and recommended performance tuning parameters.

Chapter 23: SAP Performance Tuning in the Java Stack This chapter discusses the key concepts of Java memory management, scalability of Java applications, and troubleshooting Java memory issues in SAP applications.

Chapter 24: SAP System Sizing Overview This chapter discusses the theory and practice of SAP sizing, the different types of sizing, user and throughput sizing, and using the SAP Quick Sizer tool to perform sizing projects.

Chapter 25: SAP Upgrade of an ABAP Stack This chapter discusses the ABAP system upgrade key concepts, upgrade strategy, upgrade tools, upgrade software logistics, and a complete end-to-end ABAP upgrade process.

Chapter 26: SAP Upgrade of the Java Stack This chapter discusses the Java system upgrade concepts and tools, dual-stack upgrade procedure, and a complete end-to-end Java upgrade process.

Chapter 27: SAP Homogeneous System Copies This chapter discusses the different homogeneous system copy options and provides details on each.

Chapter 28: SAP Heterogeneous System Copies This chapter discusses the end-to-end heterogeneous system copy or OS/DB migration using SAP standard tools.

Appendix: SAP Basis Career Trends and NetWeaver Certification This chapter discusses the SAP Basis career trends, certification requirements and options, training curriculum, hot SAP Basis skills, and career progression options for SAP Basis professionals.

PART

SAP NetWeaver Introduction and Architecture

CHAPTER

SAP NetWeaver and Business Suite Introduction

SAP is the world's largest business software company, headquartered in Walldorf, Germany. There are 121,000 SAP installations worldwide with more than 86,000 customers operating in 120 countries. SAP business applications are installed in 25 different industries, and more than 12 million users work every day with SAP solutions. SAP business applications run on the NetWeaver technology platform. Administering the SAP NetWeaver platform and its plethora of SAP business applications in a mission-critical environment is not only challenging, but also offers a rewarding career for IT professionals. A key resource in any new SAP implementation or production support organization is the Basis administrator of the SAP system. SAP Basis administration involves all of the system administration activities of the NetWeaver technology platform. A Basis administrator commands top salaries and a stable job with excellent career progression opportunities in an organization.

Objective

The main objective of this book is to provide a handbook for all major SAP Basis administration skills necessary to manage a SAP NetWeaver platform. I will be sharing practical Basis experience and best practices that I have accumulated over the last 12 years as SAP Basis administrator and technical architect. This objective will be accomplished by providing a high-level overview for each of the major SAP Basis system administration skill areas, followed by specific tools, techniques, and procedures for performing the activities.

Audience

This book is written for the following audiences:

- A new SAP Basis administrator assigned to work on a SAP implementation by the organization, or a prospective SAP Basis administrator.
- An experienced SAP Basis administrator needing a handbook to perform complex SAP Basis tasks, such as homogeneous and heterogeneous system copies, dual-stack SAP upgrades, performance tuning, performing SAP database redirected restores, and so on.

- A SAP Basis administrator who is strong in SAP ABAP (Advanced Business Application Programming) system administration and who would like to pick up SAP Java system administration skills.
- A SAP Basis administrator who is strong in SAP Java system administration and would like to pick up SAP ABAP system administration skills.
- A SAP technical architect who would like a handbook for planning and performing activities, such as SAP sizing and SAP application technical integration to enterprise backup software, such as Tivoli, and so on.
- A technical architect who would like to understand how SAP will integrate with the organization's data center operations and plan for sizing and architecting the needed infrastructure for rolling out the solution.
- An enterprise architect who would like to understand how a SAP infrastructure footprint could be integrated within enterprise architecture standards.
- A university professor or college lecturer who would like a reference book in SAP NetWeaver platform technology for teaching and training requirements.

Brief History of SAP

SAP was started in 1972 by five former IBM employees with a vision of creating a standard application software for real-time business processing. SAP stands for Systems Applications and Products in Data Processing. Since its inception SAP has issued several releases, such as SAP R/1, SAP R/2, and SAP R/3. The R in these releases stands for "Real-Time" data processing. The 3 in the R/3 stands for three-tier client-server architecture. The most current release of SAP is SAP Business Suite 7.

Table 1-1 lists the major SAP releases and the release year.

Year Released	SAP Release
1973	SAP R/1
End of 1970s	SAP R/2
1992	SAP R/3
1998	SAP R/3 Release 4.0B
1999	SAP R/3 Release 4.5B
1999	SAP R/3 Release 4.6B
2001	SAP R/3 Release 4.6C
2003	SAP R/3 Enterprise Release 4.70
2004	SAP ECC 5.0 ERP (mySAP ERP 2004)
2005	SAP ECC 6.0 ERP (mySAP ERP 2005)
2009	SAP Business Suite 7 (ERP 6, Enhancement Package 4)

Table 1-1 Major SAP Releases

SAP Basis Skill Set Evolution

With the evolution of the SAP releases over time, the skill set required to perform the SAP Basis job has also evolved. Table 1-2 lists the major SAP releases and skill evolution from a Basis administration perspective.

This book addresses the skill sets required for performing SAP Basis administration activities for the most current SAP Business Suite 7 release level. SAP Business Suite applications run on top of SAP NetWeaver Application Server. Both ABAP and Java system administration activities of the SAP NW AS will be covered in this handbook. This book will cover NW 7.0 and NW 7.1 releases.

SAP Releases	Architecture	Required Skills
SAP R/1 and R/2	Mainframe, IBM database systems	Basis administration in a mainframe environment with IBM database skills
SAP R/3	Client-server	Basis administration in a client-server environment with skills in multiple databases (Oracle, DB2, and SQL Server) and operating systems (UNIX flavors, Windows, and AS/400)
SAP R/3 4.6C and 4.7	Client-server, web application server	Addition of ITS (Internet Transaction Server) and web application server skills
SAP ECC 5.0/6.0	NetWeaver Application Server ABAP and Java, service-oriented architecture	Java skills become important, along with the skills listed for the previously mentioned releases
SAP Business Suite 7	NetWeaver Application Server ABAP and Java, service-oriented architecture, Business Process Platform, Composite Application Platform	SAP ABAP administration skills SAP Java administration skills SAP service-oriented architecture skills SAP business applications such as ERP (Enterprise Resource Planning) , CRM (Customer Relationship Management), SRM (Supplier Relationship Management), PLM (Product Lifecycle Management), SCM (Supply Chain Management) NetWeaver Stack administration skills such as Business Intelligence (BI), Process Integration (PI), NetWeaver portals, Master Data Management (MDM), Development Infrastructure (DI), Mobile Infrastructure (MI), etc. SAP BusinessObjects SAP Solution Manager and SAP NetWeaver Administrator

Table 1-2 SAP Basis Skill Set Evolution

SAP Business Suite 7

On May 5, 2009, SAP successfully completed the ramp-up of SAP Business Suite 7 and made it available to the general public. The SAP Business Suite 7 is composed of ERP 6.0 with Enhancement Package 4, SAP CRM 7.0, SAP SCM 7.0, SAP PLM 7.0, and SAP SRM 7.0. This release of SAP is service-oriented, with 2,800 enterprise services delivered. SAP Business Suite 7 applications run on top of the SAP NetWeaver 7.0 technology platform.

Major software updates to SAP Business Suite 7 are released in the form of Enhancement Packages (Figure 1-1). SAP delivers separate Enhancement Packages for the NetWeaver technology stack. SAP Business Suite 7 is delivered as a "synchronized release" for all major SAP applications that includes SAP CRM 7.0, SAP SCM 7.0, SAP SRM 7.0, and SAP PLM 7.0.

Table 1-3 identifies the key customer requests that SAP has addressed with the new release of SAP Business Suite 7.

Brief Overview of SAP NetWeaver Technology Stack

SAP Business Suite applications run on a NetWeaver application server ABAP, or Java, or both, depending upon the usage types (software units) that are needed to implement a given business scenario.

Table 1-4 lists the usage types (software units) that are available during the installation process.

NetWeaver usage types are software units that are to be installed and configured as per the requirement of a given business scenario. Usage types can be combined with others in one system or can be run separately in different systems. The AS ABAP and AS Java NetWeaver usage types are also used as a foundation for other units.

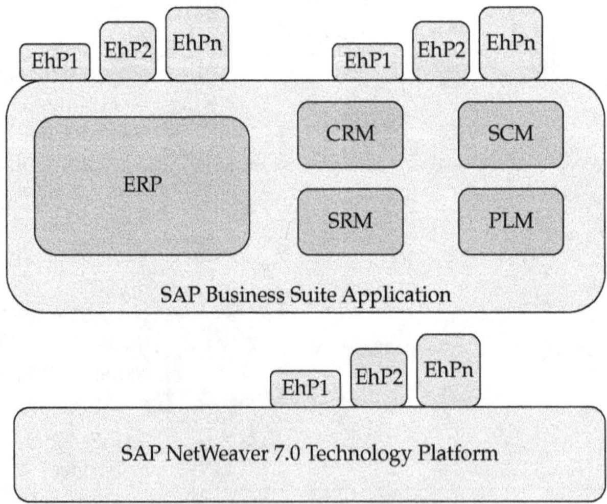

FIGURE 1-1 SAP Business Suite 7 with Enhancement Packages

Key Customer Request	SAP Business Suite Offering
Performing upgrades every other year is disruptive, expensive, and not sustainable for businesses running SAP software.	Offers "Enhancement Packages" for SAP Business applications that provide incremental innovations without business disruption. No major upgrades once customer is on SAP Business Suite 7.
5-1-2 maintenance strategy is short and expensive after five years. (Five years mainstream maintenance, with additional support through extended maintenance for one year with 2% fee increase, and an additional two years with 4% fee increases.)	SAP introduced 7-2 maintenance strategy starting November 2008. Offers seven years of mainstream maintenance and an additional two years of extended maintenance with 2% additional fee.
Installing and upgrading industry solutions is complicated in an ERP system.	SAP industry solutions are now integrated into the ERP core and do not require separate installation. Needed industry solutions can be activated in the ERP system with a concept called the "switch framework."
Use of service-oriented architecture is not clearly defined.	SAP Business Suite comes with 2,800 enterprise services. More bundles are under development and will be released in the near future.
Leveraging cross-application business processes is not clearly defined.	SAP is offering numerous "value scenarios" that increase business value to the customers by leveraging cross-system business processes.
More operational business intelligence and analytics for better decision making.	Delivers embedded analytics by integrating business objects into the SAP Business Suite.
Administration of SAP system is getting difficult and expensive with a complex portfolio of business applications.	Solution Manager is leveraged for monitoring and administering the entire SAP business suite.

Table 1-3 SAP Business Suite Key Value Propositions

Software Unit (Usage Type)	Description	Depends On
AS ABAP	NetWeaver Application Server ABAP	
AS Java	NetWeaver Application Server Java	
BI Java	NetWeaver Business Intelligence Java	AS Java, EP, EP Core
DI	NetWeaver Development Infrastructure	AS Java
EP	NetWeaver Enterprise Portal	AS Java
EP Core	NetWeaver Enterprise Portal Core	AS Java
MI	NetWeaver Mobile Infrastructure	AS ABAP, AS Java
PI	NetWeaver Process Integration	AS ABAP, AS Java

Table 1-4 Available Usage Types with NetWeaver Installation

Single-Stack System

A single-stack system is defined as a SAP system with either SAP NetWeaver AS ABAP or AS Java as the foundation usage type. Examples of single-stack systems are SAP Enterprise portal system running on NetWeaver AS Java as a foundation unit.

Dual-Stack System

A dual-stack system is defined as a SAP system where both SAP AS ABAP and AS Java are used as foundation units. An example of a dual-stack system is SAP Process Integration. A dual-stack system has one SID (System Identifier) and exactly one database with two different schema names (one for ABAP and one for the Java stack).

Dual Stacks vs. Separated Stacks

With the introduction of Business Suite 7 the official SAP recommendation is to install AS ABAP and AS Java capabilities as separate single-stack systems when the installation options support this. This is referred to as a "separated stack" install. The latest versions of installation tools starting with SAP NetWeaver 7 Enhancement Package 1 reflect this recommendation. For example, if a customer wants to install a business intelligence (BI) solution, then it is recommended to install BI ABAP components (BI Content) on a single system with AS ABAP and BI Java usage types in another separate system. Some solutions (Process Integration, Mobile Infrastructure, and Solution Manager) are mandatory dual-stack installations at this time. Starting with SAP NetWeaver Mobile Infrastructure 7.1, a dual-stack installation is no longer required. SAP is supporting existing systems with dual-stack installations, and will offer an upgrade path to move to separated stack architecture. SAP technical architects and enterprise architects should be aware of this new development and formulate the technical blueprint and capacity planning accordingly.

SAP Basis Administrator vs. SAP NetWeaver Administrator

"What's in a name? That which we call a SAP Basis administrator by any other name would be as challenging."

Since its inception SAP has considered the role "Basis administrator" to be the resource responsible for performing all system administration activities for an organization that is either implementing a new SAP solution or building a production support organization. With the release of the SAP NetWeaver technology platform a few years back, SAP has tried to brand the role as "SAP NetWeaver administrator." Despite SAP's best intentions, however, the name "SAP Basis administrator" seems to have stuck in terms of usage by the SAP world. The evidence is in the frequent usage of the term in all major job boards, usage by the project team and PMO (Project Management Office), and usage by corporate HR departments.

For discussion purposes, in this book we use the terms "SAP Basis administrator" and "SAP Basis administration" to include all system administration activities of a NetWeaver technology platform, including the newly released SAP Business Suite 7.

Summary

- SAP system administration and technical architecture work are challenging and yet provide a rewarding career for an IT professional.
- Business Suite 7 is the most current release of SAP.
- Business Suite 7 includes SAP ERP 6 with Enhancement Package 4, CRM 7.0, SCM 7.0, SRM 7.0, and PLM 7.0.
- The key benefits of Business Suite 7 are improved functionality, no major upgrades required, incremental innovation is delivered with the Enhancement Package concept, and 7-2 maintenance strategy.
- SAP NetWeaver usage types include AS ABAP, AS Java, BI, PI, EP, EP Core, DI, and MI.
- SAP ABAP and Java administration skills are needed to perform the job of a Basis administrator of the NetWeaver technology stack and business suite applications.
- Single-stack, dual-stack, and separated stack install options are available, depending upon the solution required.
- The SAP Landscape Governance Board is making a separated stack install recommendation where offered by the SAP installer for several SAP solutions.

Additional Resources

- **SAP NetWeaver Products overview** www.sdn.sap.com/irj/sdn/nw-products
- **SAP System Landscape Governance Board recommendations** www.sdn.sap.com/irj/scn/index?rid=/media/uuid/806c3398-a5ab-2d10-eb90-f364fa65c3b8#
- **SAP System Landscape Design Links** www.sdn.sap.com/irj/sdn/alm-landscape-design

CHAPTER

SAP NetWeaver Application Server ABAP Overview

SAP Business Suite applications run on top of SAP NetWeaver Application Server (SAP NW AS). SAP business applications could run on NetWeaver Application Server ABAP (NW AS ABAP), NetWeaver Application Server Java (NW AS Java), or both. SAP ERP 6 is one example of a SAP business application that predominantly runs on NW AS ABAP. The SAP NetWeaver Portal 7.0 application runs on NW AS Java. SAP PI 7.1 (Process Integration) runs on a dual stack that includes both AS ABAP and AS Java platforms.

This chapter covers the technical architecture foundation of SAP NW AS ABAP from a conceptual as well as practical perspective. This will help the SAP Basis administrator understand the internals of SAP NW AS ABAP and work on the various system administration activities of the SAP NW AS ABAP system and support all SAP business applications running on top of SAP NW AS ABAP. Chapter 3 will cover the technical architecture foundations of SAP NW AS Java.

Three-Tier Architecture

For best results, the SAP application should be installed as three-tier client-server architecture in production environments. The three-tier architecture is also referred to as a multitier architecture. In nonproduction environments and smaller business environments, a two-tier client-server architecture is acceptable as well. In a two-tier architecture both the SAP AS ABAP and database are installed on one physical machine and the SAP front end on the business user's desktop or a laptop. In a three-tier architecture the SAP AS ABAP and database are installed on separate systems and the front end is installed on the business user's desktop or laptop. This architecture offers excellent performance and scalability of the SAP solution for supporting demanding business needs.

The three tiers of the architecture are presentation tier, application tier, and database tier. The presentation tier includes the SAP front-end components, such as the SAP graphical user interface (GUI). The application tier includes SAP business logic and is executed on SAP NW AS ABAP. The database tier includes all SAP-supported relational database systems such as Oracle, DB2, and SQL Server. Figure 2-1 shows the three tiers of the SAP architecture.

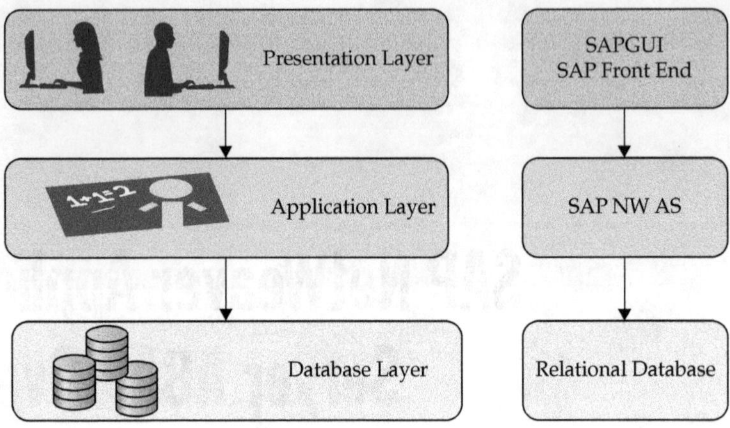

FIGURE 2-1 SAP three-tier architecture

SAP Presentation Tier

The SAP front end is a presentation layer tool. It is usually referred to as the SAPGUI. SAPGUI is an important interface from an end-user experience and productivity perspective. There are several variants of the SAPGUI, depending upon the operating system environment and browser-based usage. The primary front end for the ABAP-based transaction processing system (SAP ERP 6) is the SAPGUI for Windows. The primary front end for Java-based SAP applications is the browser. SAP NW Business Client is a new SAP front-end tool that will be available for general release along with the next Enhancement Package for NetWeaver (EhP2). SAP Business Client provides a single interface for both transaction-based ABAP systems and browser-based Java systems. The main method of network communication between the SAP front end and the application server is through TCP/IP network protocol standards. Table 2-1 lists the different variants of the SAPGUI, including the new SAP NW Business Client, along with the key benefits of choosing each of the tools as an enterprise-wide SAP front-end strategy.

SAP Front-End Variant	Operating System	Key Business Benefits
SAPGUI for Windows	Windows	Windows look and feel Stable and mature for executing business transactions
SAP GUI for Java	UNIX, MAC, and OS2	Supports businesses using non-Windows operating systems
SAP GUI for HTML	Windows and a standard Internet browser	Browser-based Fewer end-user training requirements
SAP NW Business Client	Windows	Support for both transaction-based ABAP systems and browser-based Java applications in a single front end

TABLE 2-1 SAPGUI Variants

SAP Application Tier

The application tier is referred to as SAP NW AS ABAP. This layer has the business rules and interacts with the underlying database via a database interface. SAP application server architecture is designed to provide services for tens of thousands of business users. Therefore, detailed understanding of this layer's architecture, processes, components, monitoring, and performance tuning is central to the administration activities of SAP Basis job. Figure 2-2 shows the different components of the SAP application layer.

The application tier consists of the components dispatcher, work process, message server, and gateway. Let us start by looking into the function of each application layer component and the configuration rules for each of the component.

Dispatcher

The dispatcher is a central process on an application server. The SAP dispatcher is responsible for initializing and reading profile parameters, starting work processes, logging on to the message server, and evenly distributing the transaction load across work processes.

Rule: One dispatcher for each application server.

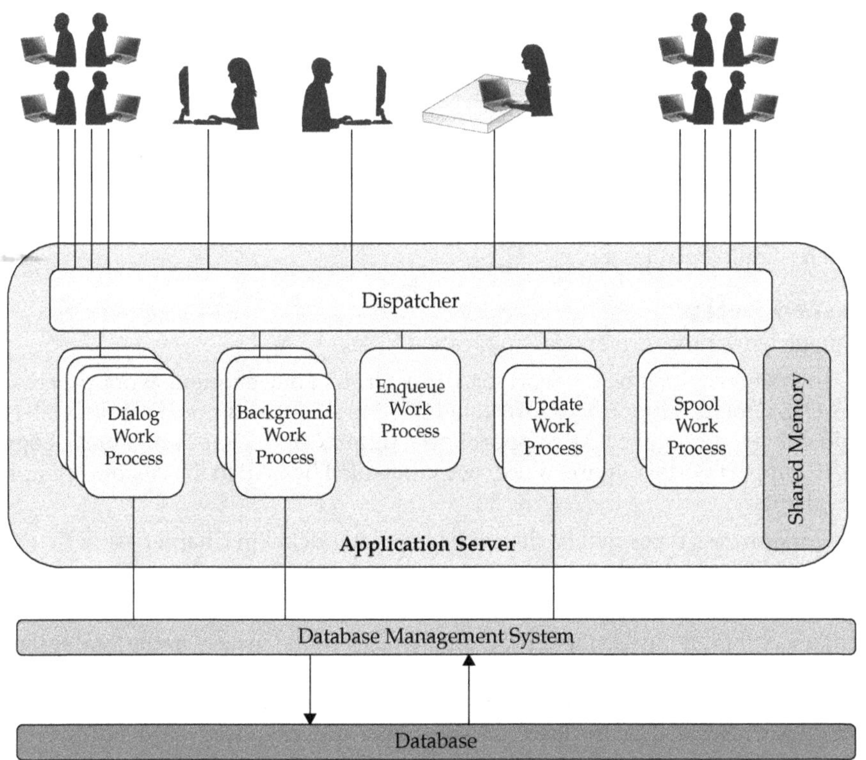

FIGURE 2-2 SAP NW AS ABAP application layer components

Work Process

The SAP work process executes the individual dialog steps of the SAP ABAP request. The architecture of the work process is designed so that limited numbers of work processes are capable of supporting many concurrent users. The dispatcher collects the requests from the SAP front end and forwards them to work processes for execution.

There are several different types of work processes in a SAP NW AS ABAP, and each work process type has a specific function. The following section identifies the different work process types and lists the responsibilities and configuration rules for each in an AS ABAP system.

Dialog Work Process

The dialog work process executes dialog programs.

Rule: There should be at least two.

Update Work Process

The update work process executes database updates. There are two kinds of update work processes: U1 and U2. The U1 type executes primary and time-critical updates, such as placing an order or moving material. The U2 type executes secondary and noncritical updates, such as statistical updates.

Rule: There should be at least one.

Background Work Process

The background work process executes background jobs submitted to the application server.

Rule: There should be at least one.

Spool Work Process

The spool work process executes spool requests submitted to the application server.

Rule: There should be at least one.

Enqueue Work Process

The enqueue work process manages application locks.

Rule: 1. In systems with a heavy workload, greater than one enqueue work process is possible. OSS (Online Support System) Note 127773 provides additional details. OSS Notes can be downloaded from the SAP Support Portal (http://service.sap.com/notes). Logging on to the SAP Support Portal requires a user account issued by SAP to the customer employees and consultants.

The work process types will be discussed in greater detail in Chapter 14.

Message Server

A message server is an independent program that lists all the servers in the SAP system. The message server decides which server a user logs on to (particularly in environments with multiple application servers). As shown in Figure 2-3, the message server communicates with the dispatcher based on the load statistics of the application server at any given time.

Rule: A SAP system with any number of application servers has one message server.

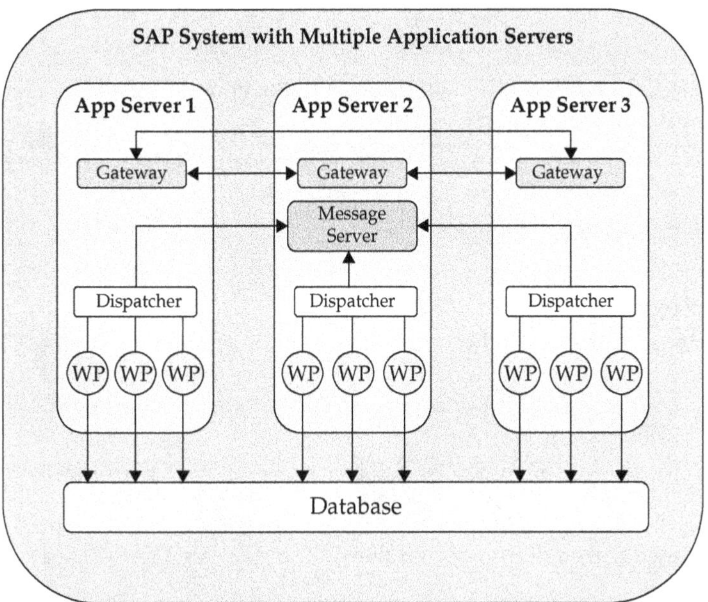

Figure 2-3 SAP message server and gateway

Gateway

The gateway service is responsible for communication between different SAP systems and external systems. Figure 2-3 shows a gateway service acting as a communication link between three application servers.

Rule: One gateway for each SAP instance.

Data Flow in a NW AS ABAP

SAP NW AS ABAP provides the technology for running ABAP applications. Select Java applications can now be run in the same ABAP work process with the new Virtual Memory Container (VMC) technology.

Data flow in a typical NW AS ABAP system (see Figures 2-2 and 2-3) for a SAPGUI request is as follows:

1. The end user will log in to the desired SAP system from SAPGUI.
2. Logon groups defined in the system will connect to the message server and, based on the load distribution, will direct the request to the appropriate dispatcher. Once the user is assigned to a dispatcher, the user remains with the same dispatcher until logged out.
3. The dispatcher will pick up the request and distribute it to the work process. If the work processes are all occupied, then they are gathered in a queue.

4. The work process executes ABAP or SAP-delivered select Java programs via VMC technology in the ABAP engine (see the section "VMC Technology").
5. If needed, the work process will connect to the underlying relational database via a database interface using Open SQL.
6. The database interface converts Open SQL to native SQL through the underlying relational database and gets the requested data.
7. The data is sent back to the end user.

VMC Technology

SAP has developed a new Java VMC architecture and integrated it with the ABAP work process for the purpose of executing SAP-developed Java programs. This is not intended for executing custom-developed Java programs. In such a case, customers are advised to use the SAP NW AS Java.

The SAP VMC architecture (Figure 2-4) allows an ABAP work process to use a pool of Java virtual machine from a preallocated virtual machine pool. VMC is already coded in the SAP standard kernel. However, it is not activated by default, and the following profile parameters need to be activated and configured to use the VMC in NW AS ABAP–based systems.

```
vmcj/enable = on
vmcj/option/maxJavaHeap = 200M
```

Activating the VMC requires significant memory and swap space resources. Make sure that you have adequate system resources before activating the VMC; otherwise, the system

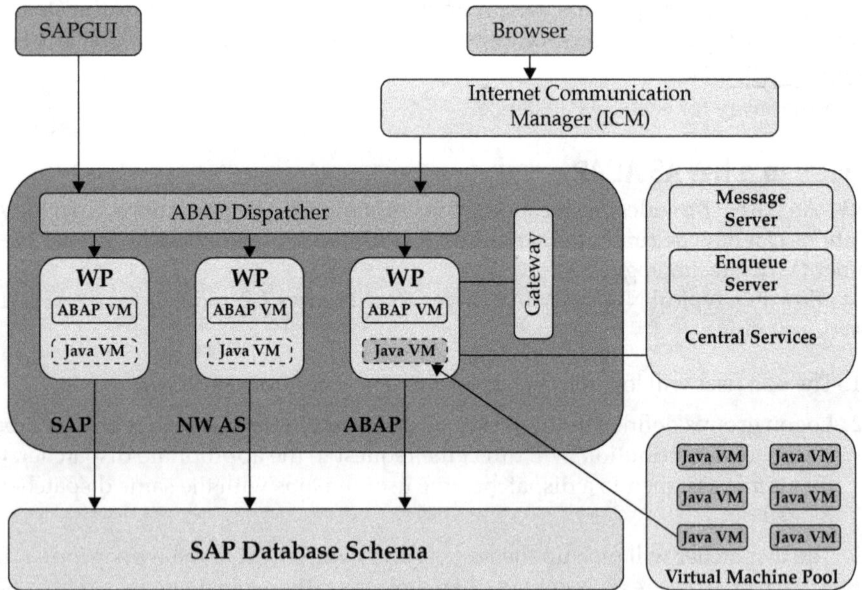

FIGURE 2-4 VMC architecture

may not start properly. OSS Notes 854170 and 863354 provide more details for activating the VMC and performing administration activities with it.

SAP also provides the following two transactions for administering the VMC:

- Transaction code SM52 provides an overview of configured Java VMC.
- Transaction code SM53 provides system administration of the Java VMC.

Data Flow in a Typical NW AS ABAP System for Browser Requests

For the browser-based end-user requests, the data flow is a little different. For browser-based requests, SAP NW AS ABAP can act as a web server or a web client. As a web server it can accept the incoming Hypertext Transfer Protocol (HTTP), Hypertext Transfer Protocol Secure (HTTPS), and Simple Mail Transfer Protocol (SMTP) requests and send the requested data. It can also act as a web client by sending HTTP, HTTPS, and SMTP requests to an external web server. This capability in the NW AS ABAP is implemented by Internet Communication Manager (ICM) and the Internet Communication Framework (ICF).

Internet Communication Manager

Internet Communication Manager is implemented as a stand-alone process and is started along with other components in the ABAP AS ABAP stack. It can be seen as a process icman for the UNIX system at the operating system level. Browser requests are received by ICM, and it determines if the requests need to be sent to an ABAP or a Java stack. If the request is determined to be for the ABAP stack, then it is sent to the work process and the ICF. If the request is determined to be for the Java stack, then it is sent to the Java server processes.

The main components of the ICM are threads, memory pipes, connection info, watch dog, and signal handler. Figure 2-5 shows the components inside ICM.

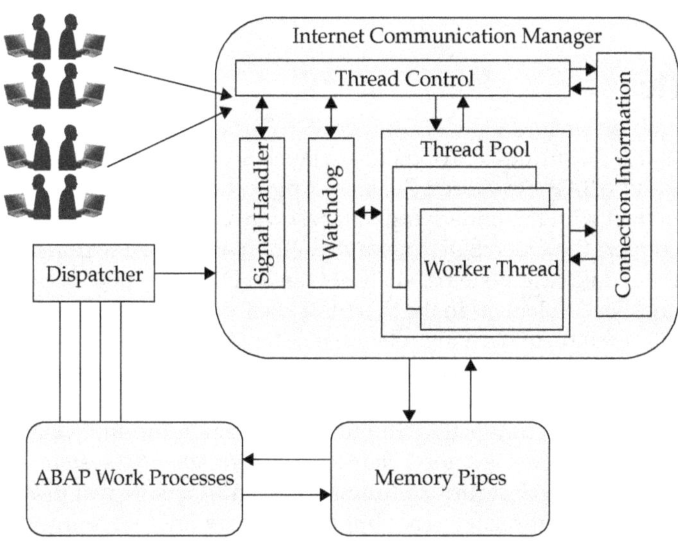

FIGURE 2-5 ICM components

The function of each of the ICM components is as follows:

- **Threads** Incoming HTTP requests from the browser are accepted by thread control and then passed to the worker thread.
- **Memory pipes** Help transfer data between the ICM worker thread and ABAP work process.
- **Connection info** Table with network connections information.
- **Watch dog** Frees up the waiting worker thread from timed-out connections and passes the information back to the worker thread when it eventually receives it for processing.
- **Signal handler** Processes operating system and SAP dispatcher signals.

Internet Communication Framework

ICF is part of SAP standard kernel delivery. Requests sent from the ICM are forwarded to one or more ABAP programs by ICF. Once the response is received, ICF sends the data back to ICM and eventually to the client. ICF performs this activity in the form of standard services. One example of such a service is the Internet Transaction Server (ITS).

Integrated ITS

Earlier SAP versions had an architecture that included an external ITS. The current version of ITS, however, is referred to as integrated ITS. Integrated ITS is needed for some scenarios of SAP usage—for example, access via SAPGUI for HTML. ITS will help automatically convert the SAP screen for the end user using SAPGUI for HTML.

- Transaction code SMICM is used to administer the ICM.
- Transaction code SICF is used to manage the ICF services.

SAP Database Tier

A relational database such as Oracle, DB2, or SQL Server, with several hundreds and thousands of tables, constitutes a SAP database layer. SAP application data is stored in the database tables and ABAP (Advanced Business Applications Programming) programs use Open SQL to interact with the underlying database via a database interface. The database interface will convert the Open SQL to native SQL. Even though SAP uses a number of different relational database systems, such as Oracle, DB2, and SQL Server as a data repository, the application logic is in the SAP data dictionary that sits on top of the database data dictionary. Therefore, underlying relational databases have to be managed as a "SAP database" using SAP-provided tools. It is not recommended to bypass this application layer to directly connect with and manipulate the database data using native database tools. If the database data is accessed directly without going through the application logic or SAP-provided database tools, there is a good chance of making the SAP system data inconsistent. Basis administrators and SAP security administrators must ensure that proper application security is in place so that the safeguards implemented by SAP are followed. Over the last three to four decades, the SAP ERP system has grown in terms of the number of tables. In the ERP6 release of SAP there are about 71,000 tables in an SAP application.

Now that we have looked into the architecture of SAP NW AS ABAP, let us start looking into how to start, stop, and verify a proper functioning of SAP systems. SAP installations will be covered in detail in Chapters 5 through 8.

Starting the SAP System

To start a SAP system, log on to your UNIX system as the SAP administrative user (<SAPSID>adm)—for example, devadm, where SAPSID= DEV—and enter the following command from your <SAPSID>adm user account home directory:

```
startsap        [DB|R3|ALL]
```

where:

DB starts the database system.

R3 starts the instances and associated processes of the R/3 system.

ALL starts both the database system and the R/3 system. ALL is the default and can be omitted.

Please note that in a two-tier setup the ALL option works, but in a three-tier setup, the database must be started prior to issuing `startsap`.

SAP Parameter Read Sequence During SAP System Start-up

The following sequence is used for reading the system parameters during SAP start-up:

1. SAP kernel code
2. Default profile
3. Instance profile

SAP Profiles

SAP profiles are operating system files that contain SAP instance setup information. These files are installed as a part of SAP system installation. The SAP system uses profile parameters at the system start-up. There are three types of profiles:

- **Start profile** This parameter file will define which SAP services will be started (for example, message server, dialog, gateway, or enqueue process).
- **Default profile** This parameter file will define the profile parameters applicable for all instances (application servers) in the system (for example, the name of the database host, or the host on which the message server is running).
- **Instance profile** This parameter file defines the profile for the specific instance, which allows individual application servers to be configured differently for specific tasks and users.

SAP profiles will be discussed in greater detail in Chapter 7.

Verifying the System Started Correctly

You can perform the following checks to ensure that the SAP system has started correctly:

1. startsap log (startsap.log) file in the <SAPSID>adm home directory should report that all the services and processes have started.
2. The database starts without any errors as per startdb.log in the home directory of <SAPSID>adm.
3. Check at operating system level for the SAP processes (dispatcher and work processes).
4. Check the last lines in the available.log file in the following location:

   `/usr/sap/<SID>/<instance name>/work/`

The last line in the available.log file will have a status entry saying the system is either available or unavailable.

SAP Operating System–Level Processes

When the SAP system is started, it starts several operating system–level processes, as explained in the architecture section of this chapter. Checking the operating system–level processes will ensure that the system has started correctly and is functioning properly. Check that the dispatcher and the work processes, message server, enqueue server, gateway, icman, and Oracle database processes are up and running. Figure 2-6 shows the different processes that should be available when the system is started correctly.

Now that we have looked into starting the SAP system and verifying its proper functioning, let us look into the user logon process and navigation aspects of the system.

```
DEVadm> ps -ef | grep sapDEV
DEVadm 15571 11242  0  May 28 ?     17:08   dw.sapDEV_DVEBMGS15 pf=/usr/sap/DEV/SYS/profile/DEV_DVEBMGS15_indus
DEVadm 13054 11242  0  May 28 ?      3:45   dw.sapDEV_DVEBMGS15 pf=/usr/sap/DEV/SYS/profile/DEV_DVEBMGS15_indus
DEVadm 11241 11215  0  May 22 ?      0:18   ms.sapDEV_DVEBMGS15 pf=/usr/sap/DEV/SYS/profile/DEV_DVEBMGS15_indus
DEVadm 11243 11215  0  May 22 ?      0:05   co.sapDEV_DVEBMGS15 -F pf=/usr/sap/DEV/SYS/profile/DEV_DVEBMGS15_indus
DEVadm 12067 11242  0  May 27 ?    186:10   dw.sapDEV_DVEBMGS15 pf=/usr/sap/DEV/SYS/profile/DEV_DVEBMGS15_indus
DEVadm 11267 11242  0  May 22 ?    225:08   dw.sapDEV_DVEBMGS15 pf=/usr/sap/DEV/SYS/profile/DEV_DVEBMGS15_indus
DEVadm 11268 11242  0  May 22 ?    154:24   dw.sapDEV_DVEBMGS15 pf=/usr/sap/DEV/SYS/profile/DEV_DVEBMGS15_indus
DEVadm 11280 11242  0  May 22 ?     45:41   dw.sapDEV_DVEBMGS15 pf=/usr/sap/DEV/SYS/profile/DEV_DVEBMGS15_indus
DEVadm 11285 11242  0  May 22 ?     12:01   dw.sapDEV_DVEBMGS15 pf=/usr/sap/DEV/SYS/profile/DEV_DVEBMGS15_indus
DEVadm 11244 11215  0  May 22 ?      0:01   se.sapDEV_DVEBMGS15 -F pf=/usr/sap/DEV/SYS/profile/DEV_DVEBMGS15_indus
DEVadm 11313 11242  0  May 22 ?      0:01   dw.sapDEV_DVEBMGS15 pf=/usr/sap/DEV/SYS/profile/DEV_DVEBMGS15_indus
DEVadm 18606 11242  2  Jun 03 ?    170:04   dw.sapDEV_DVEBMGS15 pf=/usr/sap/DEV/SYS/profile/DEV_DVEBMGS15_indus
DEVadm 12379 11242  0  Jun 02 ?      3:43   dw.sapDEV_DVEBMGS15 pf=/usr/sap/DEV/SYS/profile/DEV_DVEBMGS15_indus
DEVadm 29946 11242  0 15:42:23 ?    71:22   dw.sapDEV_DVEBMGS15 pf=/usr/sap/DEV/SYS/profile/DEV_DVEBMGS15_indus
DEVadm 13015 11242  0  May 28 ?      3:34   dw.sapDEV_DVEBMGS15 pf=/usr/sap/DEV/SYS/profile/DEV_DVEBMGS15_indus
DEVadm 16310 11242  0  Jun 03 ?      5:30   dw.sapDEV_DVEBMGS15 pf=/usr/sap/DEV/SYS/profile/DEV_DVEBMGS15_indus
```


FIGURE 2-6 SAP processes at the operating system level

Login Process to the SAP System

SAPGUI is installed on the desktops or laptops of the business users using the SAPGUI installation CD. The installation will create a SAP logon icon, shown below, as a shortcut on the desktop. Double-click the SAP logon program, and enter the application server information for the SAP system to which you would like to connect.

Copyright by SAP AG

Double-clicking the SAP logon icon will open the following window. You can create a new connection to the SAP application server by clicking the New Item button (shown in the following illustration) and then clicking the next button in the subsequent screen.

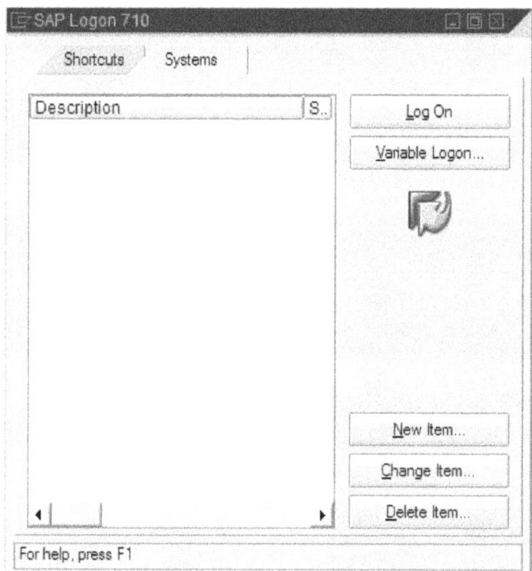

Copyright by SAP AG

Enter the description, application server, system number, and system ID; and click Finish as shown in the following illustration.

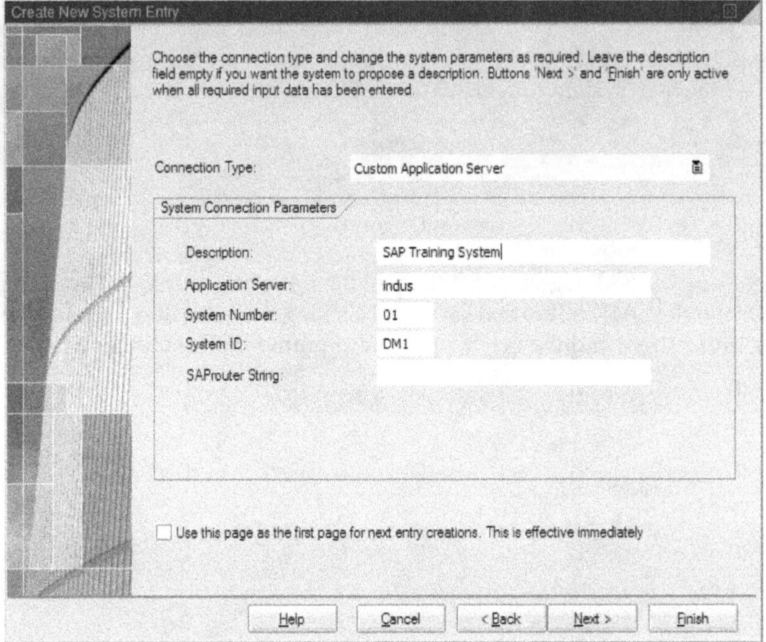

Copyright by SAP AG

Select the system you would like to connect to, and click the Logon button as shown:

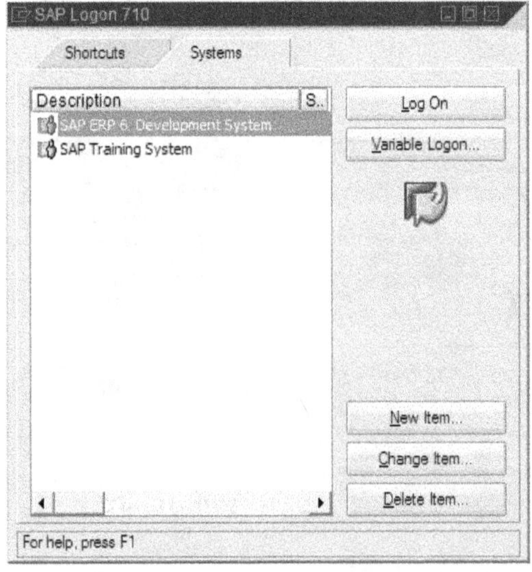

Copyright by SAP AG

Enter the user name and password in the next screen, and press ENTER:

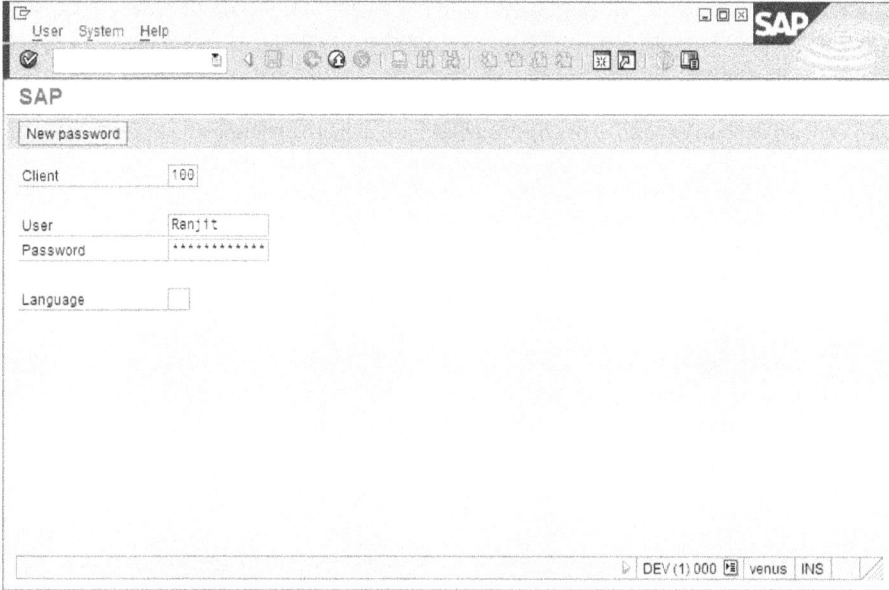

User System Help

SAP

New password

Client 100

User Ranjit

Password *************

Language

DEV (1) 000 venus INS

Copyright by SAP AG

You will see the following screen. You can either use the menu path or enter transaction codes in the command line to navigate and move around in the SAP system.

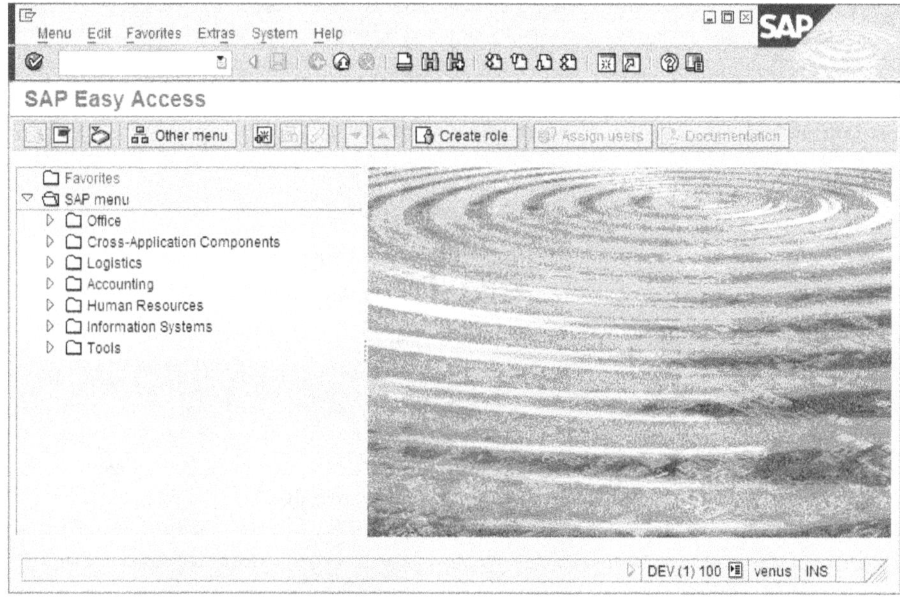

Copyright by SAP AG

Moving Around in a SAP System

Transaction codes and menu paths are two primary ways to navigate the SAP system. Transaction codes are alphanumeric codes that are assigned to the program. Execute transaction codes by entering them in the command field of the SAPGUI. The other way to navigate the system is through the menu paths. Transaction codes are quicker and more useful to quickly jump from one task to another. Most experienced SAP Basis administrators use transaction codes as a primary way to navigate the SAP system. Throughout the course of this book transaction codes will be used for explaining various SAP Basis tasks. SAP table TSTC lists all the transaction codes of a SAP system. The SAP ERP6 system has about 105,000 transaction codes. Don't panic! You will need only a handful of SAP transactions to perform important SAP Basis administration tasks!

Shut Down the SAP System

To shut down the SAP system, log on to UNIX as the SAP administrative user (<SAPSID>adm). Enter this command from <SAPSID>adm home directory with the following options:

```
stopsap        [DB|R3|ALL]
```

where:

DB stops the database system.

R3 stops the instances and associated processes of the R/3 system.

ALL stops both the database system and the R/3 system. ALL is the default and can be omitted.

Please note that in a two-tier setup the ALL option works, but in a three-tier setup, the database must be shut down separately after SAP processes have stopped.

Table 2-2 provides a list of the SAP Basis transaction codes used to check the SAP architecture and parameterization. Table 2-3 is a list of tables that are referred to in this chapter.

Transaction Code	Used for Accessing
SM50	SAP Work Process Overview
SM51	SAP Application Server Overview
SM52	Virtual Machine Overview
SM53	VMC Monitoring and Administration
SM66	Global Work Process Overview
SMICM	ICM Monitor
SICF	Administer ICF Services
SMGW	Gateway Monitor
SMMS	Message Server Monitor
SM01	Transaction Codes list
RZ10	Edit SAP System Profile Parameters
RZ11	Display SAP Profile Parameters

TABLE 2-2 Useful SAP Transactions for Reviewing SAP NW AS ABAP Architecture

Table Name	Description
TSTC	SAP Transaction Codes
DD02L	SAP Tables
DD02T	SAP Table Texts

Table 2-3 SAP Standard Tables Referred to in this Chapter

Summary

- SAP technology should be implemented as a multitiered architecture.
- The presentation layer is one of the variants of SAPGUI.
- Other SAPGUI variants include SAPGUI for Windows, SAPGUI for Java, SAPGUI for HTML, and SAP NW Business Client.
- The application layer is SAP NW AS ABAP.
- The SAP application tier includes the dispatcher, message server, gateway, work processes, VMC, ICM, ICF, and integrated ITS.
- The database layer is a relational database.
- Use Startsap to start the SAP system.
- Use Stopsap to stop the SAP system.
- The SAP logon program is used to configure and connect to multiple SAP systems.
- Transaction codes and menu paths are used to navigate SAP systems.
- Gaining a clear understanding of SAP system architecture will help a Basis administrator to troubleshoot SAP start-up issues.

Additional Resources

- **SAP NetWeaver product release information** www.sdn.sap.com/irj/sdn/nw-products
- **SAP landscape design and infrastructure** www.sdn.sap.com/irj/sdn/alm-landscape-design
- **SAP design and architecture** www.sdn.sap.com/irj/sdn/landscapelayout

CHAPTER

SAP NetWeaver Application Server Java Overview

SAP NetWeaver Application Server Java (NW AS Java) provides a robust infrastructure for building standards-based Java business applications for the enterprise. SAP recognized the growing significance of the Java programming language and started incorporating the Java infrastructure capability with SAP Web Application Server 6.10. SAP has further improved the capability to develop and execute industry-compliant Java business applications in its subsequent versions of the application server. NW 7.0 and NW 7.1 releases will be covered in this chapter. The most current NW release available for general use is NW 7.1. SAP Solutions Process Integration (PI) 7.1 and Mobile Infrastructure (MI) 7.1 run on NW 7.1.

Before we do a deep dive into the NW AS Java architecture, let us understand some important Java programming language concepts.

Java Programming Language Concepts

Java is an object-oriented programming language developed by Sun Microsystems in 1995. The main advantage of the Java programming language is its write once, run anywhere approach. Java applications are compiled to bytecode that can be executed on any Java Virtual Machine (JVM), regardless of the computer processor architecture. JVM is a software program that will emulate a computer processor and execute the bytecode. This allows Java applications to be platform-independent.

Unlike traditional compilers that generate machine code for a specific platform, Java compilers generate code (bytecode) for the JVM. The JVM acts as an interface between the Java and the physical hardware. Since execution of the bytecode requires an interpretation step as well, Java is considered both a compiled and an interpreted programming language. Because of this Java programs could run slow, and this is its main disadvantage. Just In Time (JIT) compilers and new performance optimization techniques are helping to mitigate some of the Java performance problems.

The Java compiler generates class files from the source code that are executed by the JVM. Multiple class files can be combined as an archive file and are referred to as jar files. JVM and the Java compiler can read the class files directly from the jar archive.

Sun Microsystems (acquired by Oracle) markets the Java Software Development Kits (SDKs) in three versions:

- J2EE (Java 2 Enterprise Edition)
- J2SE (Java 2 Standard Edition)
- J2ME (Java 2 Mobile Edition)

Now that we covered the basic concepts of the Java programming language, let us start looking into the three-tier architecture for the SAP Java applications.

SAP Three-Tier Architecture for Java Applications

SAP NW AS Java is based on the industry-standard three-tier architecture. The three tiers of the architecture are the Presentation layer, the Application layer, and the Database layer.

Presentation Layer

The Presentation layer for Java-based SAP applications are accessed with a standard web browser. Figure 3-1 shows the NetWeaver portal access with the help of the browser URL (http://<server name>:port number/irj/portal).

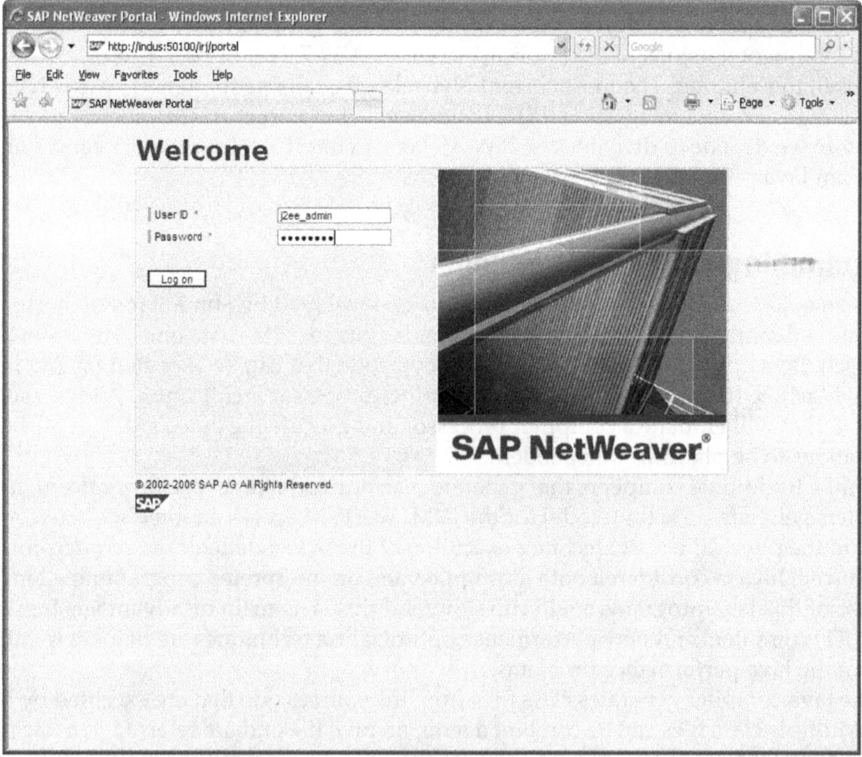

Copyright by SAP AG

FIGURE 3-1 Browser-based access to the SAP Java application

You can log in to the Presentation layer of the SAP NetWeaver portal shown in the figure by providing the user ID and the password and clicking the Log On button. This will show the NetWeaver Portal application as in Figure 3-2.

Application and Database Layers

The Application and Database layers in SAP NW AS Java are implemented as a Java cluster. Figure 3-3 shows the Java cluster architecture. The Java cluster architecture and startup control and framework are implemented differently in NW 7.0 and NW 7.1. Both cluster architectures will be discussed in this chapter.

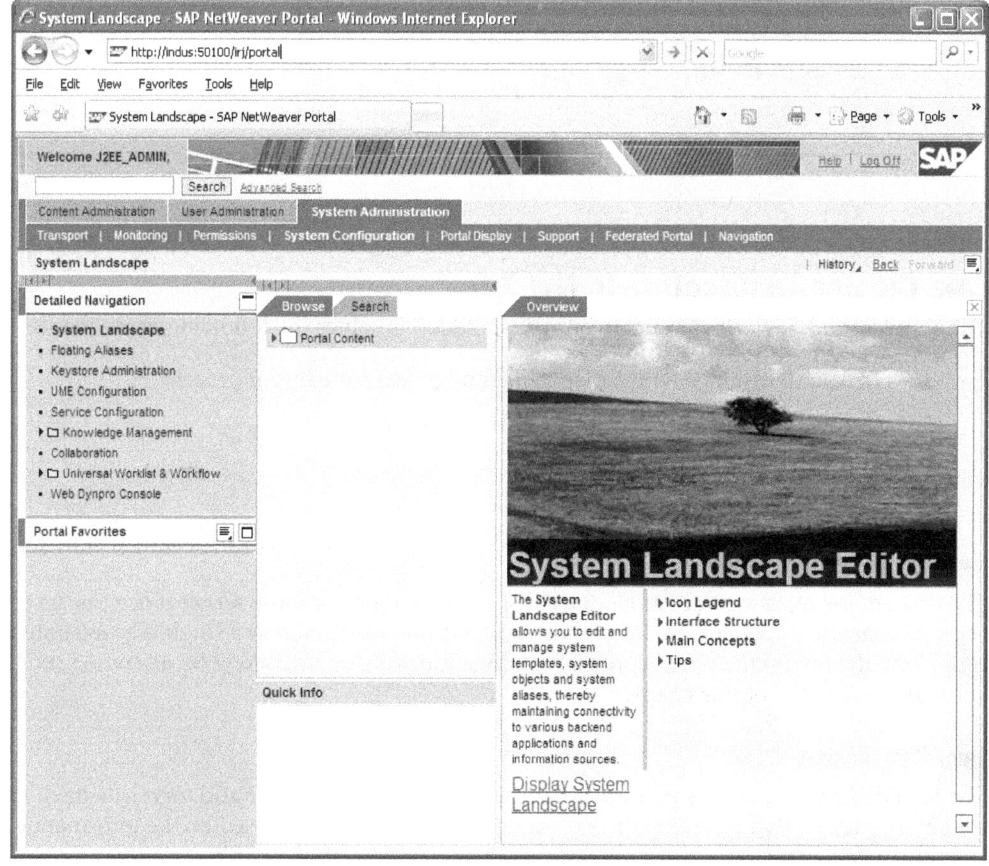

FIGURE 3-2 NetWeaver portal after the login

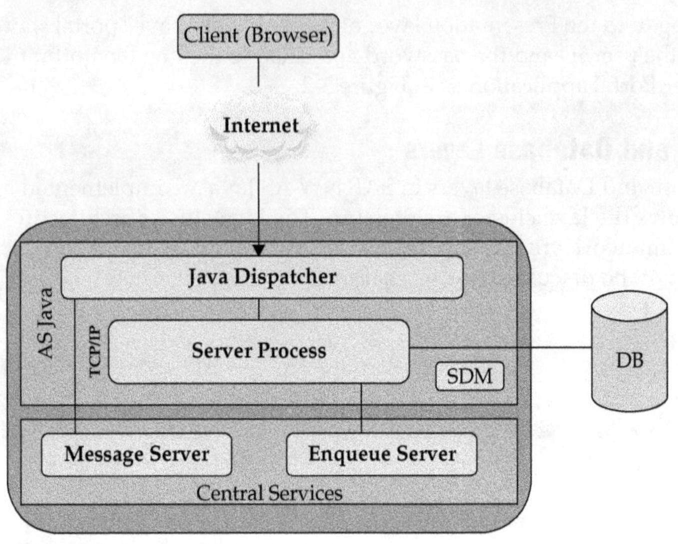

FIGURE 3-3 Java cluster architecture in NW 7.0

SAP Java Cluster Architecture in NW 7.0

The simplest SAP Java cluster architecture installation involves the following components:

- Java central instance with a dispatcher and at least one server process
- Software Deployment Manager (SDM)
- Central services instance
- Database

Java Central Instance

The Java central instance consists of a Java dispatcher and one or more server processes. Java central instance components can be started, stopped, and monitored as a single administrative unit using the Java startup and control framework, details of which will be discussed in subsequent sections of this chapter.

Java Dispatcher

The Java dispatcher receives requests from the browser or web server and forwards them to the server process that is having the lowest utilization at this time based on the information from the message server.

Java Server Process

The Java server process executes the J2EE application and returns the response to the web browser or the web server. The Java server process is multithreaded and, therefore, can execute multiple requests in parallel.

Software Deployment Manager

SDM helps in deploying SAP-delivered Java software packages in the form of software development archives (SDAs) and software component archives (SCAs).

Java Central Services Instance

A Java central service is a special instance and comprises the message server and the enqueue server. It is installed and runs on one physical machine. Java central services provide a mechanism for communication and synchronization within a Java cluster.

Message Server

The message server program provides message services, such as communication, between the Java cluster elements. The message server is responsible for the following key functions:

- Event notification in the Java cluster elements
- Load balancing
- Broadcasting messages in a Java cluster

Enqueue Server

The enqueue server program provides enqueue services, such as managing locks and cluster-wide synchronization. The enqueue server manages the lock table in the main memory. It is responsible for the following functions:

- Managing locks in the Java cluster
- Managing synchronization in the Java cluster

Java Database

This usually is a relational database supported by SAP. For Java-only SAP applications such as NetWeaver Portal there is a single database schema. For dual-stack SAP business applications such as Process Integration (PI), both Java and ABAP share the same database but have different schema names.

Constraints of the NW 7.0 Architecture

The NW 7.0 release is a stable and reliable platform for many of the SAP business applications. However, in certain situations it has constraints that could have an effect on the performance of the system. Following is a list of some of the constraints in the NW 7.0 architecture:

- In heavy workload situations, a Java server node that is incorrectly configured or lacks needed memory resources could crash or become frozen, resulting in the loss of yet-to-be-processed user requests.
- Lack of effective real-time monitoring tools can make it difficult to be proactive and plan for performance tuning on an anticipated workload ahead of time.
- Lack of easy troubleshooting tools can make it hard to identify the root cause of a crashed Java server process.
- There is a dependency on JVM that might no longer be supported by Sun Microsystems, or there could be different implementations of JVM from different vendors running on several different operating systems.

Motivation for the NW 7.1 Architecture

SAP was motivated to address these constraints in the NW 7.1 release. SAP PI 7.1 is one example of a SAP solution that is available for general use using NW 7.1 architecture. Some of the key new architecture improvements with the NW 7.1–based SAP business applications are as follows:

- Separation of yet-to-be-processed user requests from in-process user requests by using fast channel architecture (FCA).
- Real-time monitoring of Java processes with new and improved SAP Management Console (SAP MC).
- SAP Memory Analyzer tool to help better identify the root cause of the server process crashes.
- SAP developed its own Java SE 5–compliant JVM, referred to as SAP JVM.

Let us now study the SAP cluster architecture in NW 7.1, with an emphasis on the new improvements for making SAP NW AS Java more robust.

SAP Java Cluster Architecture in NW 7.1

In NW 7.1, the following changes were implemented by SAP:

- The SAP Java dispatcher has been replaced by Internet Communication Manager (ICM).
- SDM is no longer available.
- The fast channel architecture was introduced.
- Standard JVM has been replaced with SAP JVM.

Figure 3-4 shows the new Java cluster architecture in NW 7.1. The central services instance is not changed and provides the message and enqueue services to the Java cluster.

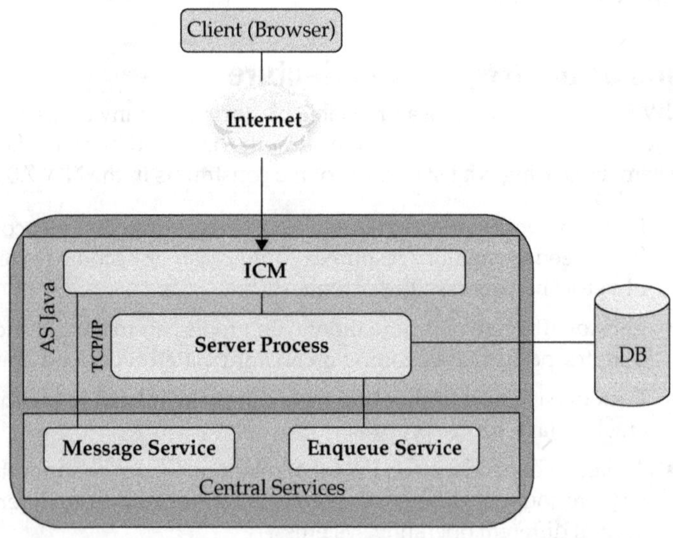

FIGURE 3-4 Java cluster architecture in NW 7.1

Fast Channel Architecture

Fast channel architecture (FCA) is an interprocess communication based on shared memory, allowing quick failover and redirection of user requests. Figure 3-5 shows the FCA and the SAP JVM in the Java instance.

Shared Memory (Now Part of Java Instance)

The Java instance now includes shared memory and is used to keep the yet-to-be-processed user requests in a queue. In the event the Java server process crashes, the pending queue is not lost along with the server process. Since shared memory is part of the Java instance, it will survive the crash and ICM will redirect the queue to another healthy Java server process in the cluster for execution. This will improve overall stability, dependability, scalability, and performance of the Java applications.

SAP JVM

SAP is using its own JVM, referred to as SAP JVM. SAP JVM is a Java SE 5–compliant virtual machine based on Sun's HotSpot Technology.

Robust Java Architecture

Because of the FCA, better use of shared memory to keep pending user request queues, ICM redirection capabilities, and SAP JVM, the overall robustness of the SAP NW AS Java platform has improved significantly. This should translate into a stable and reliable platform for customers using SAP Java business applications.

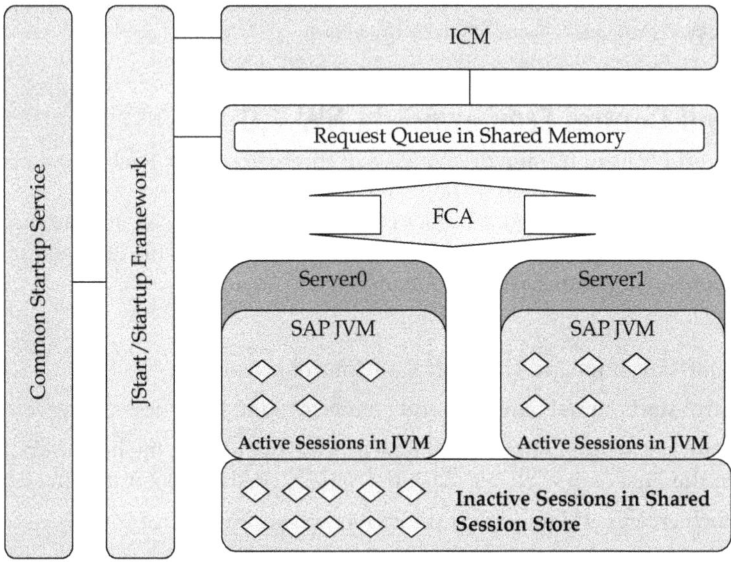

FIGURE 3-5 NW 7.1 fast channel architecture

Now that we have looked into the detailed architecture of the SAP NW AS Java, let us study the practical aspects of starting the SAP Java stack and also examine the internals of the startup process. This understanding will help us to troubleshoot any startup problems and quickly resolve the issues.

Starting a SAP NW AS Java System

Login as <sid>adm user (e.g., devadm for the SAP system where SAP SID=DEV) and issue the startsap command in the user's home directory. This will start the SAP NW AS Java system. There is a specific sequence in which the startsap script will start the system, which is explained in the next section.

Start and Shutdown Sequence

SAP Java–based systems will start in the following sequence:

1. Database is started.
2. Central services instance is started (Java message server and enqueue server).
3. Central instance is started (Java dispatcher, server process, and SDM).
4. Dialog instances are started (Java dispatcher and server process).

The shutdown sequence is the exact opposite of the startup sequence.

When the startsap command is issued, it will start the Java startup and control framework. It is the responsibility of the startup and control framework to start the rest of the components and processes of the SAP Java cluster. The startup and control framework is a little different in NW 7.0 and NW 7.1 releases. We will study both here.

Java Startup and Control Framework in NW 7.0

The Java start and control framework consists of three programs. Each of the programs has specific responsibilities, as shown in Table 3-1.

Since we now know the responsibilities of the three programs, let us examine the process steps of the start and control framework, as shown in Figure 3-6. This understanding will help you troubleshoot any system startup problems.

Step 1:

- The startsap command will start the JControl process.
- JControl starts signal handling and connects to the Java message server.
- JControl starts the JLaunch bootstrap process by reading the bootstrap.properties file in the /usr/sap/<SID>/<instance>/j2ee/cluster/bootstrap directory.
- JLaunch creates VM and loads it into its own address space.

Step 2:

The bootstrap program synchronizes the binary data from the Java database with the file system.

Java Program Name	Responsibility
JControl	Starts the JLaunch (Java dispatcher and Java server process). Starts signal handling to stop the instance. Monitors the Java cluster components to take actions such as restarting and terminating the processes.
JLaunch	Starts a Java program that starts and loads the JVM into its own address space and represents a Java cluster element. If JControl stops, all the JLaunch processes stop as well. For example: If the server is configured to have three server processes, then five JLaunch processes will be started. One JLaunch is for the Java dispatcher process. Three JLaunch processes represent the three server processes. One JLaunch is for the SDM process. JLaunch cluster elements read the offline configuration manager properties and store the information in the Java database hash tables. Shuts down the offline configuration manager, reads the properties, and starts the Java Enterprise runtime. Starts the service framework and all the services.
Bootstrap Java program	Synchronizes binary data from the Java database with the file system. Writes an Instance.properties file that is read by the JControl to start the configured Java cluster elements.

TABLE 3-1 JControl, JLaunch, and Bootstrap Java Programs

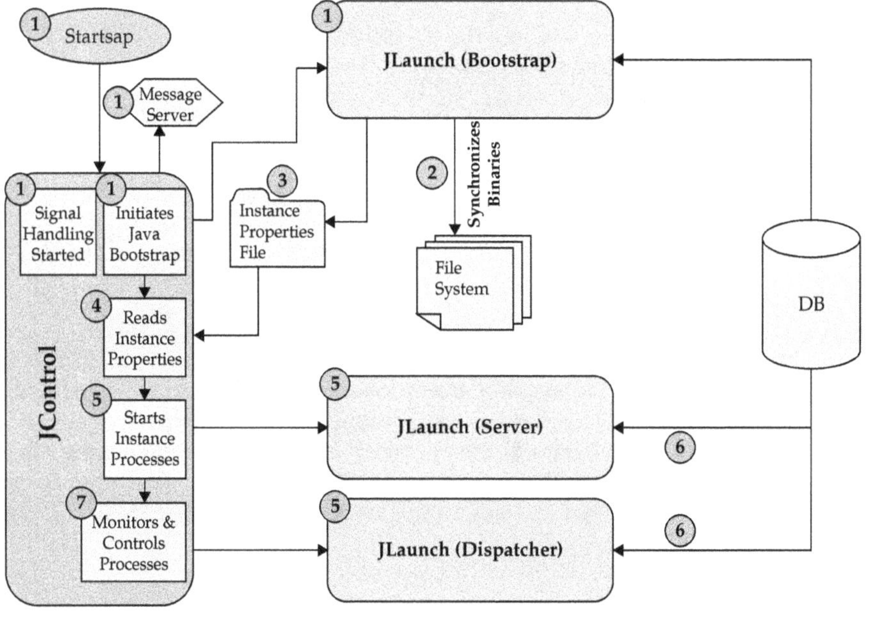

FIGURE 3-6 NW 7 Java start and control framework

Step 3:
The bootstrap program reads the database and writes the file instance.properties to the file system in directory /usr/sap/<SID>/JC00/j2ee/cluster. This file has information on the Java cluster elements (dispatcher and server processes) that need to be started.

Step 4:
JControl reads the instance.properties file.

Step 5:

- JControl starts the JLaunch for cluster elements defined in the instance.properties file.
- Each JLaunch starts VM and loads it in its address space and starts the cluster element.

Step 6:

- The JLaunch cluster element starts offline configuration manager to read the Java Enterprise runtime properties and saves it in database hash tables.
- JLaunch stops the offline configuration manager and reads the saved properties in the database and starts the Java Enterprise runtime.
- The service framework and all the configured services are started.

Step 7:
The JCMON process monitors the status of all the started cluster elements and takes actions such as restarting terminated processes.

Bootstrap Properties File

The following is an example of a typical bootstrap.properties file:

```
devadm> pwd
/usr/sap/DEV/JC00/j2ee/cluster/bootstrap
devadm> more bootstrap.properties
install.dir=/usr/sap/DEV/JC00/j2ee
secstorefs.lib=/sapmnt/DEV/global/security/lib
rdbms.driverLocation=/oracle/client/10x_64/instantclient/classes12.jar
rdbms.connection=jdbc/pool/DEV
instance.prefix=ID1543753
rdbms.initial_connections=1
secstorefs.keyfile=/sapmnt/DEV/global/security/data/SecStore.key
secstorefs.secfile=/sapmnt/DEV/global/security/data/SecStore.properties
rdbms.maximum_connections=5
system.name=DEV
```

It is possible to skip or force synchronization of the file system with the database (bootstrap process) by changing the bootstrap properties. Disabling the bootstrap process can help to start the Java instance faster. The bootstrap property element.resynch has three possible values to alter the behavior of the bootstrap process, which are detailed in OSS Note 710663. Please note that disabling bootstrapping should be considered only in a steady-state system. During Java updates and patching the application bootstrap process should be enabled, which it is by default.

Verifying the SAP Java System Started Properly

You can use the following ways to make sure your SAP Java system started correctly and is operational. The verification steps are explained in detail under subsequent sections.

- Verify if the JControl process is started at the operating system level.
- Verify if the JLaunch processes are started at the operating system level.
- Verify if the dispatcher, SDM, and Server 0 … n are in " Running" status in JCMON.
- Verify using the URL http://<server>:<port>/index.html (e.g., http://venus:50000/index.html) | System Information.
- For dual-stack systems, the Java system status can be verified by using SMICM transaction code (SMICM | Goto | HTTP Server | Display Data).
- The last entry in the /usr/sap/<SID>/<Instance>/work/available.log shows the current status of the server.

JControl

The JControl process can be verified by issuing the process command shown here. You should see one JControl process running at the operating system level.

```
devadm> ps -ef | grep jcontrol

devadm 11264 11242   0   May 22            1:34 jcontrol
pf=/usr/sap/DEV/SYS/profile/DEV_JC00_indus -DSAPSTART=1 -DCONNECT
```

JLaunch

The JLaunch process can be verified by issuing the process command as shown here. You should see one JLaunch for each of the Java cluster elements. In the example there are four JLaunch processes running at the operating system level. The first JLaunch is for the Solution Manager Diagnostic (SMD), the second JLaunch is for the Java dispatcher process, the third JLaunch is for the server process, and the fourth JLaunch process is for the Software Deployment Manager (SDM). You will notice more JLaunch processes if there are more Java server processes configured in the system.

```
devadm> ps -ef | grep jlaunch

smdadm   25644 25642  0 Jun24 ?        00:19:05 /usr/sap/SMD/J98/../exe/
jlaunch pf=/usr/sap/SMD/J98/../SYS/profile/SMD_J98_indus -DSAPINFO=SMD_98_
server -nodeId=0 -file=/usr/sap/SMD/J98/profile/smd.properties
-syncSem=884757 -nodeName=smdagent -jvmOutFile=/usr/sap/SMD/J98/work/
jvm_SMDAgent.out -stdOutFile=/usr/sap/SMD/J98/work/std_SMDAgent.out
-locOutFile=/usr/sap/SMD/J98/work/dev_SMDAgent -mode=JCONTROL pf=/usr/sap/
SMD/J98/../SYS/profile/SMD_J98_indus
```

```
devadm   30270 30166  0 Jun21 ?        00:20:26 /usr/sap/DEV/JC00/exe/
jlaunch pf=/usr/sap/DEV/SYS/profile/DEV_JC00_indus -DSAPINFO=DEV_00_dis-
patcher -nodeId=0 -file=/usr/sap/DEV/JC00/j2ee/cluster/instance.properties
-syncSem=196611 -nodeName=ID9016200 -jvmOutFile=/usr/sap/DEV/JC00/work/
jvm_dispatcher.out -stdOutFile=/usr/sap/DEV/JC00/work/std_dispatcher.out
-locOutFile=/usr/sap/DEV/JC00/work/dev_dispatcher -mode=JCONTROL pf=/usr/
sap/DEV/SYS/profile/DEV_JC00_indus

devadm   30271 30166  0 Jun21 ?        00:37:35 /usr/sap/DEV/JC00/exe/
jlaunch pf=/usr/sap/DEV/SYS/profile/DEV_JC00_indus -DSAPINFO=DEV_00_server
-nodeId=1 -file=/usr/sap/DEV/JC00/j2ee/cluster/instance.properties
-syncSem=196611 -nodeName=ID9016250 -jvmOutFile=/usr/sap/DEV/JC00/work/
jvm_server0.out -stdOutFile=/usr/sap/DEV/JC00/work/std_server0.out
-locOutFile=/usr/sap/DEV/JC00/work/dev_server0 -mode=JCONTROL pf=/usr/sap/
DEV/SYS/profile/DEV_JC00_indus

devadm   30272 30166  0 Jun21 ?        00:00:09 /usr/sap/DEV/JC00/exe/
jlaunch pf=/usr/sap/DEV/SYS/profile/DEV_JC00_indus -DSAPINFO=DEV_00_sdm
-nodeId=2 -file=/usr/sap/DEV/JC00/SDM/program/config/sdm_jstartup.
properties -syncSem=196611 -nodeName=sdm -jvmOutFile=/usr/sap/DEV/JC00/
work/jvm_sdm.out -stdOutFile=/usr/sap/DEV/JC00/work/std_sdm.out
-locOutFile=/usr/sap/DEV/JC00/work/dev_sdm -mode=JCONTROL pf=/usr/sap/DEV/
SYS/profile/DEV_JC00_indus
```

JCMON

This tool can be used to start, stop, and monitor the Java cluster elements. You can call the tool as shown here in the UNIX operating system. Note the status of the cluster elements (dispatcher, SDM, and Server0) as "Running." If you start the JCMON tool during the startup process you will see the status as "Starting Applications."

```
devadm> jcmon pf=DEV_JC00_indus
[Thr 01] MtxInit: -2 0 0
============================================================
JControl Monitor Program - Main Menu
============================================================
0  : exit
------------------------------------------------------------
10 : Cluster Administration Menu
------------------------------------------------------------
20 : Local Administration Menu
------------------------------------------------------------
30 : Shared Memory Menu (Solid Rock, experimental)
------------------------------------------------------------
command => 20
------------------------------------------------------------
SAP System Name    : DEV
SAP System         : 01
MS Host            : indus
MS Port            : 3606
Process Count      : 3
PID of JControl    : 11264
```

```
State of JControl : All processes running
State inside MS   : All processes running
Admin URL         :
------------------------------------------------------------
|Idx|Name                |PID     |State                |Error|Restart|
|---|--------------------|--------|---------------------|-----|-------|
|  0|dispatcher          |   11372|Running              |    0|yes    |
|  1|server0             |   11373|Running              |    0|yes    |
|  2|SDM                 |   11374|Running              |    0|yes    |
------------------------------------------------------------
============================================================
JControl Monitor Program - Administration Menu (Local)
Instance: JC_indus_DEV_01
============================================================
0  : exit
1  : Refresh list
2  : Shutdown instance
3  : Enable process
4  : Disable process
5  : Restart process
6  : Enable bootstrapping on restart
7  : Disable bootstrapping on restart
8  : Enable debugging
9  : Disable debugging
10 : Dump stacktrace
11 : Process list
12 : Port list
13 : Activate debug session
14 : Deactivate debug session
15 : Increment trace level
16 : Decrement trace level
17 : Enable process restart
18 : Disable process restart
19 : Restart instance
------------------------------------------------------------
40 : Enable bootstrapping for all processes with specified process type
41 : Enable bootstrapping for all processes excluding specified process type
------------------------------------------------------------
99 : Extended process list on/off
------------------------------------------------------------
```

Java Startup Framework in NW 7.1

Because of the architectural changes made in NW 7.1, the Java startup framework has changed as well. Let us look into the details of the Java programs involved in the startup framework and the exact steps the startup framework uses to start the SAP Java stack in a NW 7.1 release.

The Java start and control framework consists of the JSTART program. The JSTART program has twin roles, as shown in Table 3-2.

Java Program Name	Responsibility
JSTART in the role of Java instance controller	Starts, stops, and monitors ICM and Java server processes. Opens a local port for communication and starts signal handling for stopping the instance.
JSTART in the role of server process	In this role, JSTART connects to the Java instance controller and loads the JVM into its address space. Starts the Java code and performs as a Java server process. It receives communication and reports the instance status to the Java instance controller.

TABLE 3-2 JStart in NW 7.1

Since we now know the responsibilities of the JSTART program's two different roles, let us examine the steps of the Java start framework. This understanding will help you troubleshoot any system startup problems.

Step 1:

- The startsap command will start the JSTART process.
- JSTART takes the role of Java instance controller (JIC).

Step 2:

- JIC will read the instance profile and get Java SDK details.
- JIC starts signal handling and opens the control port to receive any system stop signals.

Step 3:

- JIC first starts reading the profile parameters jstart/startupNodeFiles and jstart/instanceNodeFiles from the instance profile, searching for runLevel = 1 property.
- "OFFLINE DEPLOYMENT" corresponds to runLevel = 1.
- jstart/startupNodeFiles profile parameter provides the name of the file that contains the node definitions for the bootstrap and offline deployment phases. The default value of this parameter is $(DIR_EXECUTABLE)/startup.properties.
- jstart/instanceNodeFiles profile parameter provides the node list that will constitute the Java instance. This is derived at runtime.

Step 4:

- JIC starts another JSTART process as a child process with parameters from the OFFLINE DEPLOYMENT node and waits.
- The child JSTART process performs as a Java process, creates JVM, and loads it into its address space and starts the OFFLINE DEPLOYMENT program.
- The OFFLINE DEPLOYMENT program executes the deployment steps in the database.

Step 5:

- JIC reads the instance profile again searching for runLevel = 2.
- "BOOTSTRAP" node corresponds to runLevel = 2.
- JIC starts another JSTART process as a child process with parameters from the BOOTSTRAP node and waits.
- The child JSTART process performs as a Java process, creates JVM, and loads it into its address space and starts the BOOTSTRAP program.
- The BOOTSTRAP process synchronizes the binary data from the Java database to the file system and updates the instance.properties file.

Step 6:

- JIC reads the recently updated instance.properties and startup.properties file searching for runLevel = 3 or without any runLevel.
- This corresponds to ICM and Java server processes.
- ICM is started.
- Java server processes are started.
- A child process is started in each of the cases, and similar JVM actions are carried over as in the preceding steps.

Step 7:

- The JIC process monitors the status of all the started cluster elements and takes actions such as restarting terminated processes.

JSTART

You can check the JSTART process at the operating system level with the following UNIX command:

```
indus:DEV >  ps -ef | grep jstart
devadm 21340 21126   0 16:06:45 pts/2       0:00 grep jstart
devadm  5292  5252   0   Jun 02 ?          66:06 /usr/sap/DEV/JC00/exe/
jstart -nodeId=2 pf=/usr/sap/DEV/SYS/profile/DEV_DVE
devadm  5252  5212   0   Jun 02 ?           0:01 /usr/sap/DEV/JC00/exe/
jstart pf=/usr/sap/DEV/SYS/profile/JC00_va2
```

JSMON

JSMON in NW 7.1 is similar to JCMON of NW 7.0. You should use JSMON in the NW 7.1 release instead of JCMON. If you call JCMON in a 7.1 system, you will see the following message:

```
dx1adm> jcmon pf=DX1_JC00_indus
JCMon is a tool for internal use only.
```

You can call JSMON by executing the following code. The JSTART Monitor Program is started by using the following command from the command line:

```
jsmon pf=<path to profile>
Example: dx1adm> jsmon pf=DX1_JC00_indus
```

The JSTART Monitor Program is started, and the output and interface looks as shown:

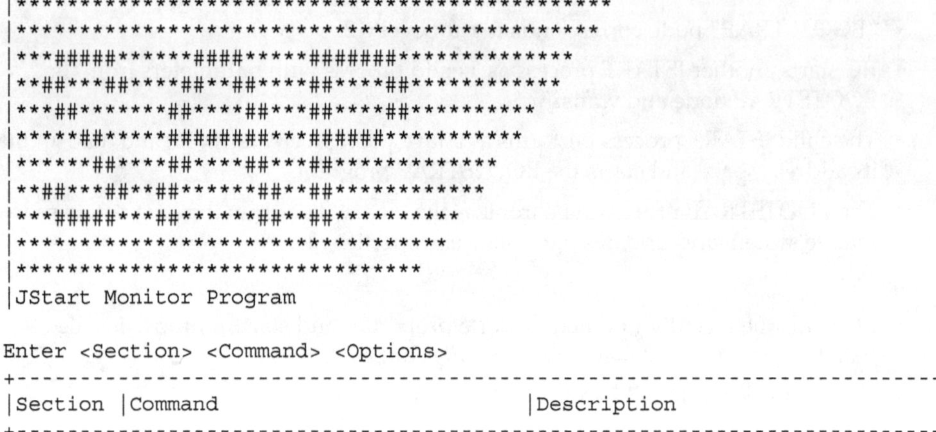

```
|*********************************************                  |
|********************************************                   |
|***####*****###****######************                          |
|*##***##****##*##****##****##**********                         |
|**##******##***##***##****##*********                          |
|****##****#######**#####**********                             |
|*****##****##*****##*************                              |
|**##***##*##*********##*##**********                            |
|***####**##******##**##**********                               |
|*********************************                              |
|*******************************                                |
|JStart Monitor Program                                         |
                                                                |
 Enter <Section> <Command> <Options>
 +--------------------------------------------------------------+
 |Section |Command                        |Description          |
 +-------------------------------------------------------------
 | jsmon  |exit/quit                      |exit JSMon program   |
 |        |help                           |show help            |
 |        |view                           |static instance data |
 |        |repeat <command>               |Timer repeats <command> |
 |        |trace <level>                  |set JSMon trace-level |
```

The syntax for entering commands in the JSMON tool is

```
<Section><Command><Options>
```

You can use the help command to get a list of all the sections, commands, and descriptions available for the JSMON tool.

```
>help
```

The following command lists the processes that are running at a given time:

```
>process view
Processes:
  +-----------------------------------------------------------------
---------------------------------------+
  |Idx      |Name           |PID |        State         |Err        |Run
  +-----------------------------------------------------------------
--------------------------------------+
   4         server2         30277        Running         0           1
   3         server1         30277        Running         0           1
   2         server0         30277        Running         0           1
   1         icm             30040        Running         0           1
   0         debugproxy      0            Initial         0           0
  +-----------------------------------------------------------------
---------------------------------------+
    Productive processes: 3
    Restricted processes: 0
    Applications: 401
    Shared caches: 0
```

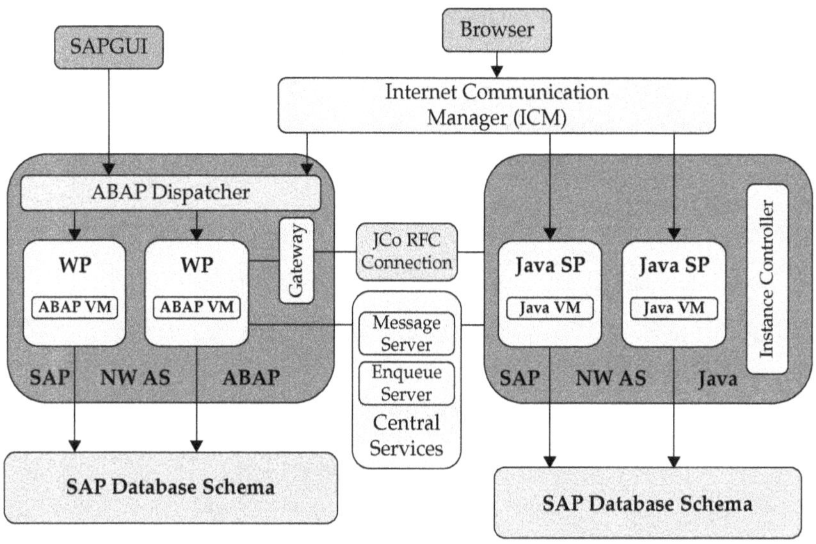

Figure 3-7 Dual-stack system (ABAP + Java)

Dual-Stack Systems

Dual-stack systems have both NW ABAP and NW Java stacks. A part of the SAP dual-stack application runs on the ABAP stack and the other part runs on the Java stack. The ABAP stack provides the stability and dependability of the SAP technology and depth in business applications, and Java stack offers the new technology and architecture for business applications. One example of a dual-stack system is the Process Integration solution. This has the Integration Server components running on the ABAP stack and the Integration Builder components run on the Java stack. The architectural diagram shown in Figure 3-7 illustrates a typical dual-stack system.

Starting a Dual-Stack SAP System

The command startsap is used to start a dual-stack system. The following shows the start sequence for the startsap command in a typical dual-stack SAP system:

```
devadm> startsap
Checking DEV Database
------------------------------
 ABAP Database is not available via R3trans
Starting SAP-Collector Daemon
------------------------------
 saposcol already running
 Running /usr/sap/DEV/SYS/exe/run/startdb
Trying to start DEV database ...
Log file: /home/devadm/startdb.log
DEV database started
```

```
 /usr/sap/DEV/SYS/exe/run/startdb completed successfully
Starting SAP Instance SCS01
------------------------------
 Startup-Log is written to home/devadm/startsap_SCS06.log
 Instance Service on host indus started
 Instance on host indus started
Starting SAP Instance DVEBMGS00
------------------------------
 Startup-Log is written to /home/devadm/startsap_DVEBMGS15.log
 Instance Service on host indus started
 Instance on host indus started
```

Shutting Down a Dual-Stack SAP System

The command stopsap is used to stop a dual-stack system. The following shows the stop sequence for the stopsap command in a typical dual-stack SAP system:

```
devadm> stopsap
Checking DEV Database
------------------------------
ABAP Database is running
Stopping the SAP instance DVEBMGS00
----------------------------------
 Shutdown-Log is written to home/devadm/stopsap_DVEBMGS00.log
 Instance on host indus stopped
 Waiting for cleanup of resources.........................................
Stopping the SAP instance SCS01
----------------------------------
 Shutdown-Log is written to /home/devadm/stopsap_SCS01.log
 Instance on host indus stopped
 Waiting for cleanup of resources.........
 Running /usr/sap/DEV/SYS/exe/run/stopdb
Trying to stop DEV database ...
Log file:/home/devadm/stopdb.log
DEV database stopped
 /usr/sap/DEV/SYS/exe/run/stopdb completed successfully
Checking DEV Database
------------------------------
 ABAP Database is not available via R3trans
```

SMICM Start and Shutdown Options

In a dual stack (ABAP + Java) system, the SMICM transaction code can be used to start and shut down the Java stack of the integrated system, as shown in Figure 3-8. In a dual-stack system the ABAP dispatcher controls the Java instances. The ABAP dispatcher sends a signal to the Java start and control framework.

- To stop the Java stack gracefully, you can call transaction SMICM and follow the menu path SMICM | Administration | Send Soft Shutdown | Without Restart.

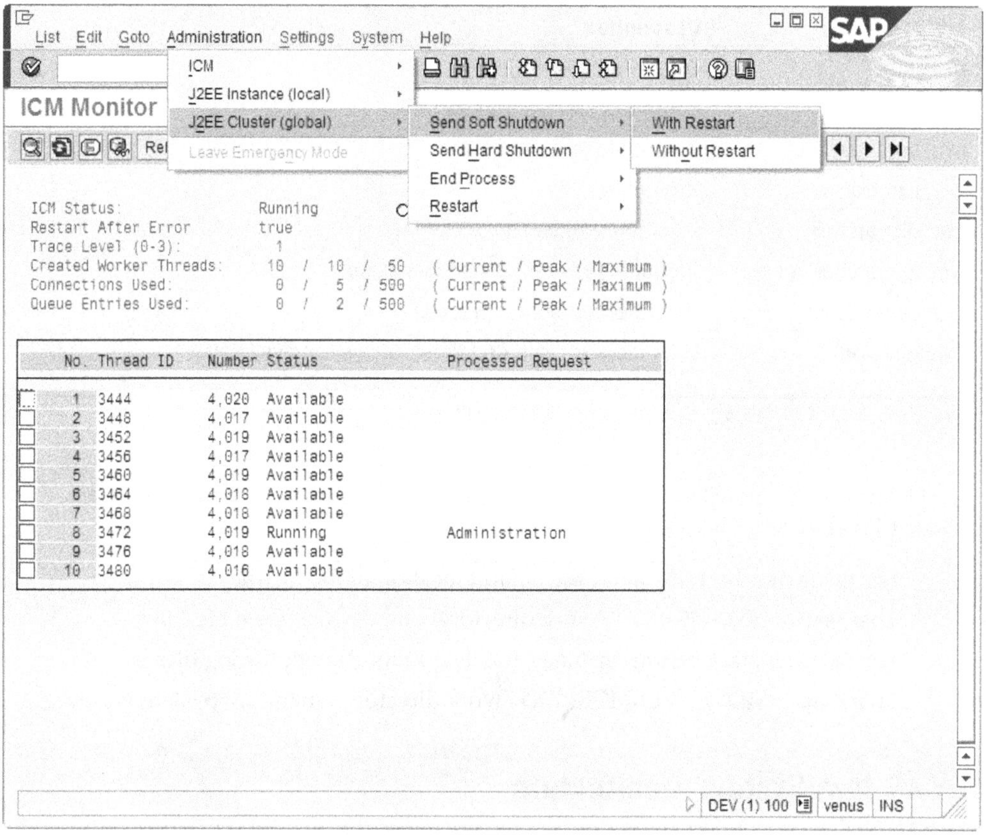

List Edit Goto Administration Settings System Help

ICM
J2EE Instance (local)
J2EE Cluster (global)
Leave Emergency Mode

Send Soft Shutdown
Send Hard Shutdown
End Process
Restart

With Restart
Without Restart

ICM Monitor

ICM Status: Running
Restart After Error true
Trace Level (0-3): 1
Created Worker Threads: 10 / 10 / 50 (Current / Peak / Maximum)
Connections Used: 0 / 5 / 500 (Current / Peak / Maximum)
Queue Entries Used: 0 / 2 / 500 (Current / Peak / Maximum)

No.	Thread ID	Number	Status	Processed Request
1	3444	4,020	Available	
2	3448	4,017	Available	
3	3452	4,019	Available	
4	3456	4,017	Available	
5	3460	4,019	Available	
6	3464	4,018	Available	
7	3468	4,018	Available	
8	3472	4,019	Running	Administration
9	3476	4,018	Available	
10	3480	4,016	Available	

DEV (1) 100 venus INS

FIGURE 3-8 Java system administration using SMICM

- To stop the Java stack immediately, you can call transaction SMICM and follow the menu path SMICM | Administration | Send Hard Shutdown | Without Restart.
- To restart the Java stack after stopping it gracefully, you can call transaction SMICM and follow the menu path SMICM | Administration | Send Soft Shutdown | With Restart.
- To restart the Java stack immediately, you can call transaction SMICM and follow the menu path SMICM | Administration | Send Hard Shutdown | With Restart.

Java System Logs

The following is the location and a list of important Java log files (Table 3-3) that need to be verified in case of problems with starting the SAP NW AS Java system. This will be covered in greater detail in Chapter 18.

Log File Name	Description
dev_jstart	Log file for JSTART
dev_bootstrap	Bootstrap startup framework log file
jvm_bootstrap.out	Output file for JVM
dev_jcontrol	JControl log file
dev_dispatcher	Dispatcher trace file
jvm_dispatcher.out	Output file for JVM dispatcher node
std_server0.out	Output of the server process
Available.log	Logs the start and end times of system availability

TABLE 3-3 SAP Java System Startup Log and Trace Files

The location of important log files for a single-stack Java instance and a dual-stack (ABAP + Java) instance is as follows:

- For the Java central instance, the default location of the log files is /usr/sap/<SID>/JC<XX>/work directory where XX=System Number
- For the dual-stack central instance, the default location of the log files is /usr/sap/<SID>/DVEBMGS<XX>/work directory where XX=System Number

SAP NW AS Java System Architecture

The SAP NW AS Java internal system architecture meets the Java EE (Enterprise Edition) 5 specification and consists of the following three logical layers, as shown in Figure 3-9:

- **Java Enterprise runtime** Java Enterprise runtime consists of several lower-level subsystems, referred to as managers. This group of managers provides core functions for runtime, such as class loading, port management, and so on.
- **Java system components** This includes interfaces, libraries and services, HTTP provider, security provider, and so on.
- **Applications** These are implemented as containers. Some of the examples are Web container (servlet and JSP), EJB container (EJB), and JDBC (Java Database Connectivity).

Java System Administration Tools

SAP provides several tools for administering the Java components. The most important tools are Visual Administrator, Configuration (Config) tool, and NetWeaver Administrator tool (NWA). Starting with the NW 7.1 release the Visual Administrator tool was phased out and its administration capabilities integrated into the NWA tool. This will be covered in more detail in Chapter 15.

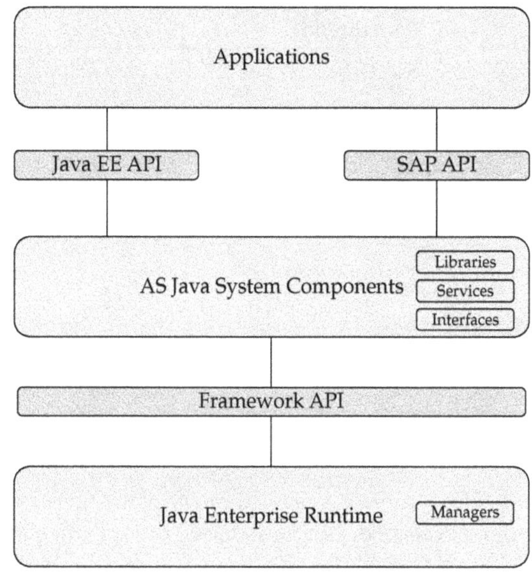

FIGURE 3-9 SAP Java system architecture internals

Java Application URLs

SAP Java–based applications are primarily accessed by URLs. Table 3-4 lists few Java-based applications that can be accessed using the provided URLs.

Verify SAP Usage Types

If you want to verify which active usage types are installed on a SAP system, you can use the following URL

```
http://servername:5<System Number>00/utl/UsageTypesInfo
```

e.g., http://indus:50100/utl/UsageTypesInfo

SAP Java Application	Generic URL	Example
SAP NetWeaver Portal	http://servername:5<System No>00/irj/portal	http://indus:50100/irj/portal
SAP Process Integration Integration Builder tool	http://servername:5<System No>00/rep/start/index.jsp	http://indus:50100/ rep/start/index.jsp
SAP SLD (System Landscape Directory)	http://servername:5<System No>00/sld/index.jsp	http://indus:50100/sld/index.jsp

TABLE 3-4 Common SAP Java Application URLs

Transaction Code	Description
SMICM	Starts up and shuts down Java instances
ST11	Log and trace files in the /usr/sap/<SID>/DVEBMGS<XX>/Work Directory
SXMB_IFR in PI/XI system	Starts PI/XI Integration Builder

TABLE 3-5 Java System Transaction Codes

Transaction Codes

Some of the useful transaction codes in a dual-stack (ABAP + Java) system are listed in Table 3-5.

Summary

- SAP provides a robust Java technology platform for running SAP-delivered as well as custom-developed standards-based Java applications.
- Java helps developers write the program once and run it everywhere.
- The Java cluster architecture in NW 7.0 includes Java central instance (java dispatcher and server processes), SDM, and Java central services instance (message server and enqueue server).
- The Java startup and control framework in NW 7.0 includes JControl, JLaunch, and Java Bootstrap programs.
- The Java cluster architecture in NW 7.1 includes Java central instance (ICM and server processes) and Java central services instance (message service and enqueue service).
- The Java startup framework in NW 7.1 includes the JStart program.
- SAP dual-stack systems have both ABAP and Java stacks.
- Startsap script and SMICM transaction can be used to manage dual-stack start procedures.
- SAP Java system architecture includes the Enterprise Java runtime; system components such as services, interfaces, and libraries; and the Java applications.

Additional Resources

- **SAP NetWeaver Application Server Java 7.1 Architecture Manual** www.sdn.sap.com/irj/scn/index?rid=/library/uuid/6016096b-aaf5-2910-1ebd-9fef2e14e983
- **SAP Application Server Infrastructure** www.sdn.sap.com/irj/sdn/server-infrastructure

CHAPTER

SAP ERP Integration Overview with Other Systems

So far in the first three chapters of this book we have studied an overview of SAP business suite applications and the NetWeaver Application Server ABAP and Java technology foundation that it runs on. In this chapter we will study the central role the SAP ERP system has in an organization and its network integration into the organization's enterprise infrastructure, as well as to the external systems outside the organization and the SAP support infrastructure. This chapter covers various communication and integration technologies that "bind" different SAP ABAP and Java-based applications, along with the third-party enterprise solutions, external vendors, and SAP support organization into an enterprise-wide SAP solution adding value and driving the business needs of an organization. This chapter is also intended to give an overview to enterprise architects as to how a SAP solution would fit into an enterprise-wide architecture.

Figure 4-1 illustrates the integration scenarios that could come into play with the implementation and operations of a SAP ERP system for a hypothetical SAP customer. The remaining sections of this chapter will use this hypothetical scenario to explain the common integration scenario groupings and the underlying communication protocol and standards used by SAP.

Basic Communication in SAP Business Solutions

SAP business applications use the following protocols and standards for communication and data transfer between different systems. One of the following basic network and communication standards is at the heart of the different integration scenarios with the SAP ERP system. Let us look into the details of each of the following protocols and standards.

TCP/IP

In SAP business applications, network communication is with the Transmission Control Protocol/Internet Protocol (TCP/IP) standards. During the system build phase, the required IP address is assigned to the host and necessary configuration is performed where a particular SAP business solution is planned to be installed.

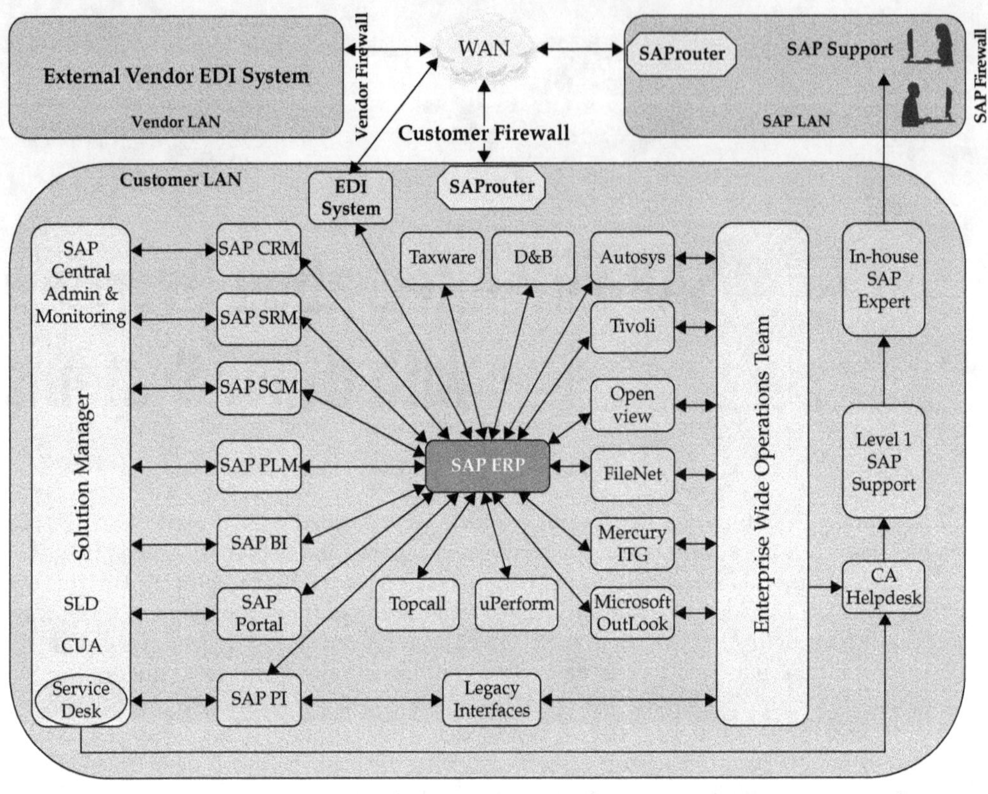

FIGURE 4-1 ERP integration scenarios

Network Ports

SAP business applications listen at clearly defined port numbers for incoming network connections. Table 4-1 lists the most important port numbers and the naming conventions and rules used for defining them for ABAP-based SAP applications.

Service	Default TCP Service Name	Default Port #	Range
Dispatcher	sapdp## where ## is the system number of the instance	3200	3200–3299
Message Server	sapms<SID> where SID = System Identifier	3600	Free
Gateway	sapgw## where ## is the system number of the instance	3300	3300–3399
ICM HTTP	80## where ## = system number of the instance	8000	Free
ICM HTTPS	443## where ## = system number of the instance	Not Active	Free
ICM SMTP	25	Not Active	25

TABLE 4-1 Network Ports in SAP ABAP Applications

Service	Default TCP Service Name	Default Port #	Range
HTTP	5##00 where ## is the system number of the instance	50000	50000–59900
HTTP over SSL	5##01 where ## is the system number of the instance	50001	50001–59901
Telnet	5##08 where ## is the system number of the instance	50008	50008–59908

Table 4-2 Network Ports in SAP Java Applications

SAP Java–based applications use a different set of network ports. Table 4-2 lists the most important ports and rules for using the SAP Java–based applications.

In UNIX operating systems, the services file maps port numbers to the named services.

This entry gets there during the time of the SAP installation of a given business solution. The services file location in a UNIX operating system is /etc/services. If, for any reason, the service file entry is missing, then the communication between the SAP applications will be lost and can be restored by adding an entry manually. Usually it requires a root user permission to make any changes to the etc/services file.

RFC

Remote Function Call (RFC) is SAP's communication interface. RFC communication between SAP business solutions involves an RFC client and an RFC server. The RFC server provides function modules. RFC clients call one of the function modules, pass on the data, and get a reply (value) back from the RFC server.

Setting Up an RFC Connection

Transaction code SM59 is used to create new RFC connections or to alter an existing connection. Several types of RFC connections can be set up in SAP systems using SM59 transaction code. RFC connection types "3" (connects to another ABAP system) and "T" (TCP/IP Connection) are most often used.

The following procedure is used to set up an RFC connection type "3" in SAP systems. Use transaction code SM59 in the SAPGUI command line (see Figure 4-2).

Select the connection type ABAP Connections, and click the Create icon. This will open the screen shown in Figure 4-3. Enter the following fields to complete the RFC destination configuration:

- **RFC Destination** Name of the RFC destination of the target ABAP system.
- **Description** Enter a text description.
- **Target Host** Enter the hostname or the IP address of the target ABAP system.
- **System Number** Enter the target ABAP system number.

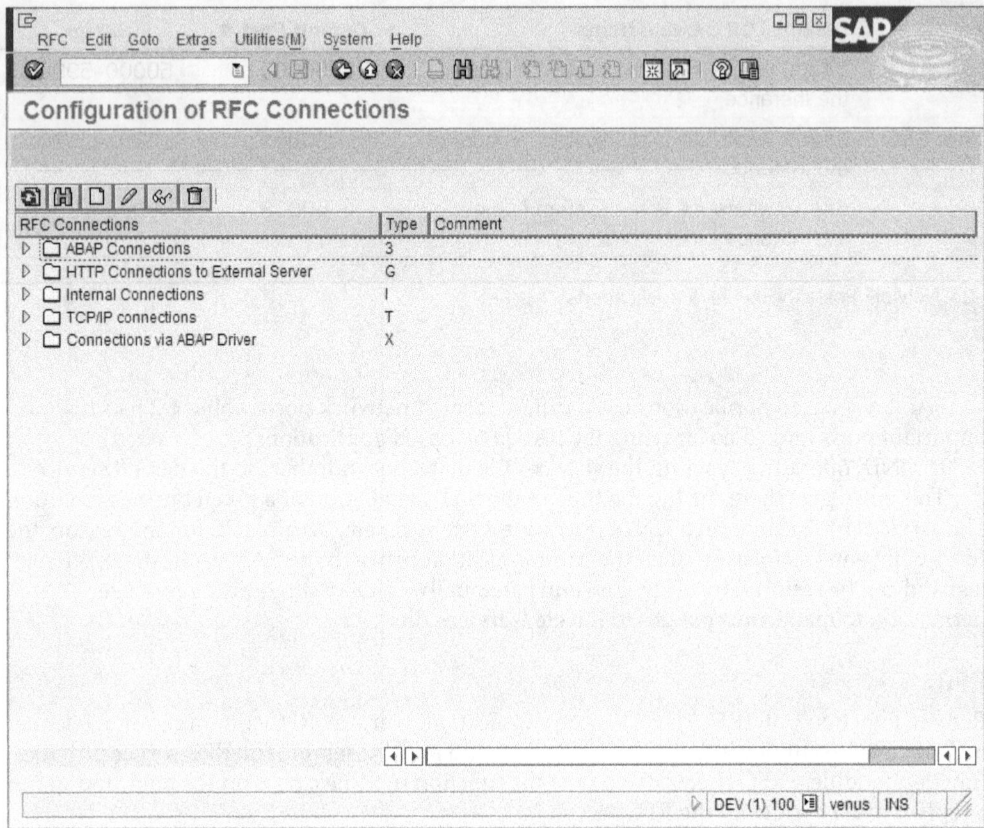

FIGURE 4-2 Initial RFC creation screen

Click the Logon & Security tab, and enter the logon information (Client, User, and Password).

After this, save your connection entries by clicking the Save button, as in Figure 4-4.

If you receive any message window saying the user can log in to the remote system, just click OK and continue. Your connection entries will be saved. The next step is to test if our RFC connection is working properly. Click the Connection Test button at the top of the screen. You will see the screen shown in Figure 4-5 if all of your connection entries are correct.

This is a basic connection test. This does not test the authorizations of the user who initiated the connection. In order to test if this user has the authorizations to initiate an RFC connection and successfully log in to the target system, go back to your RFC connection parameters screen and use the menu option Utilities | Test | Authorization Test.

This test should be successful as well before you can proceed with your work in the target ABAP system or use this connection for noninteractive login by application. You can use the similar procedure to create RFC connections to different ABAP systems in your SAP

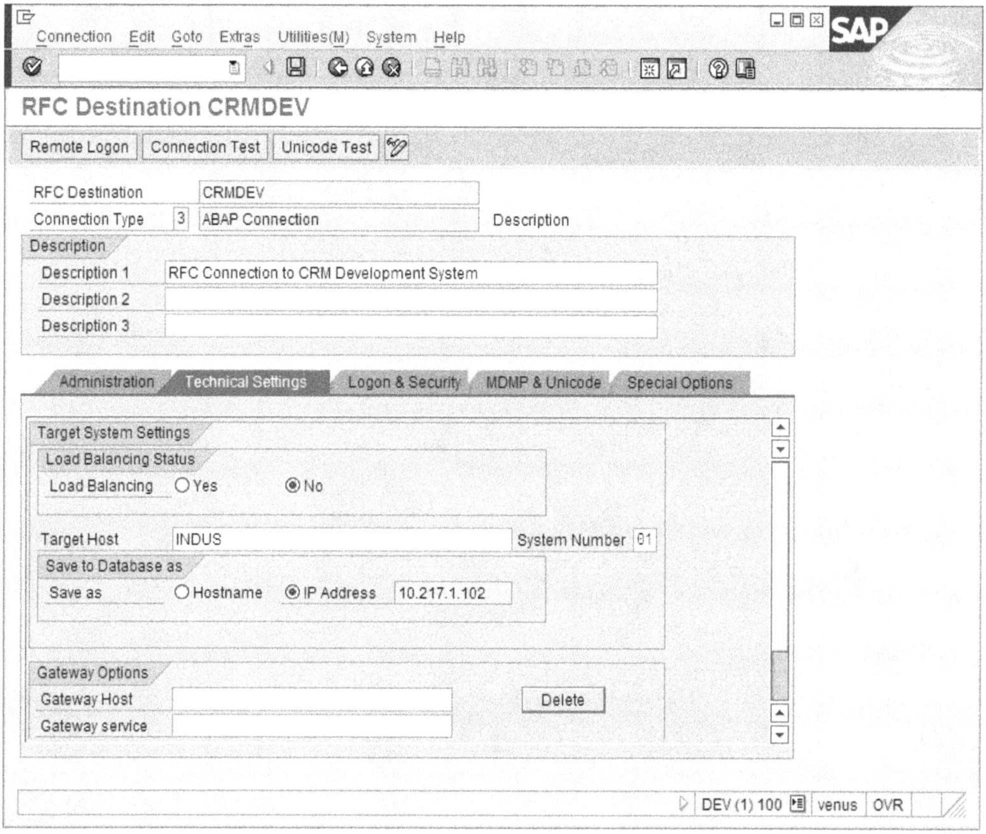

FIGURE 4-3 RFC connection entries

system landscape. Please note that a successful authorization test is mandatory, as this test executes a user login along with password verification and authorization test in the target RFC-connected system. A successful authorization test ensures that the RFC connection is completely ready for use in an application.

Several other RFC connection types are used to integrate the SAP system landscape. The RFC connection type "T" refers to starting an external program using TCP/IP. One example of such need in a SAP system landscape integration scenario is within the SAP Process Integration application. In this scenario the Process Integration (PI) ABAP components integrate with the SAP PI Java component using this connection type.

The SAP PI ABAP system integrates with the SAP Java–based PI component referred to as the System Landscape Directory (SLD) using an RFC connection called SAPSLDAPI. Figure 4-6 shows the details that have to be entered in setting up a TCP/IP RFC connection type. In this type of connection, a registered server program ID is entered in the RFC connection on the ABAP side, and the exact same entry is made in the JCO RFC provider service on the Java side. Once the settings are complete, the connection test can be executed.

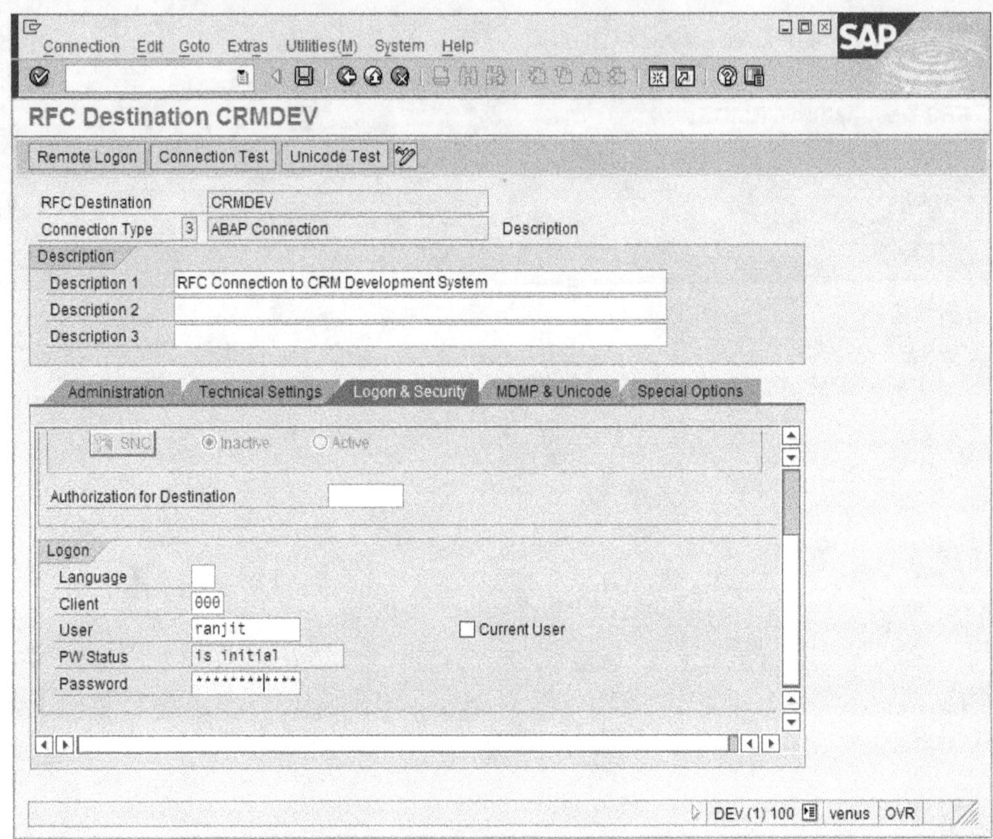

FIGURE 4-4 Login fields in maintaining an RFC connection

Table 4-3 lists all available RFC connection types that are used in the integration of SAP and different applications in an organization.

One of the common problems encountered while integrating older SAP releases with SAP releases starting with NW 7.0 is the changes to the password rules. Starting with NW 7.0, SAP supports a password length up to 40 characters and differentiates between uppercase and lowercase passwords. Earlier SAP releases supported a password length of eight characters and any lowercase passwords were automatically converted to uppercase. In order to resolve this issue easily, it is recommended to use an uppercase password of up to eight characters in length where you are integrating a newer SAP release into older SAP releases in a system landscape. OSS Notes 1023437 and 862989 provide additional details and recommendations for passwords that will help with integrating older SAP releases into the newer release landscape.

SAPconnect

SAPconnect allows a SAP ABAP system to send external communication to systems such as a SAP-certified fax, page, and e-mail solutions. SAPconnect can be set up using transaction code SCOT. The following procedure is used to set up a Simple Mail Transport Protocol

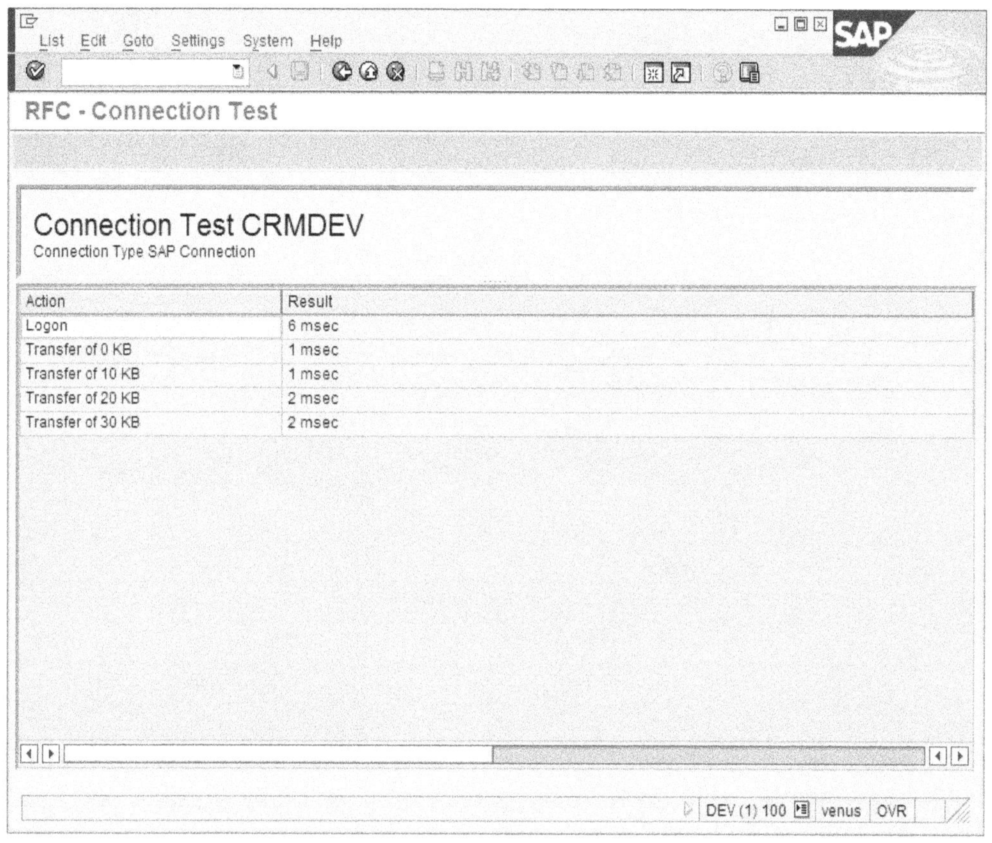

Copyright by SAP AG

FIGURE 4-5 Successful connection test

RFC Connection Type	Description
I	ABAP systems connected to the same database
3	Connection to other R/3-based ABAP system
2	Connection to other R/2-based ABAP system
L	Logical connection referring to other physical RFC connection
S	Start external program using IBM SNA (System Network Architecture)
X	Connection via ABAP driver routines or ABAP device drivers
M	Asynchronous RFC connections to ABAP systems using CMC (X.400 protocol)
H	HTTP connection to an ABAP system
G	HTTP connection to an external server

TABLE 4-3 SAP RFC Connection Types

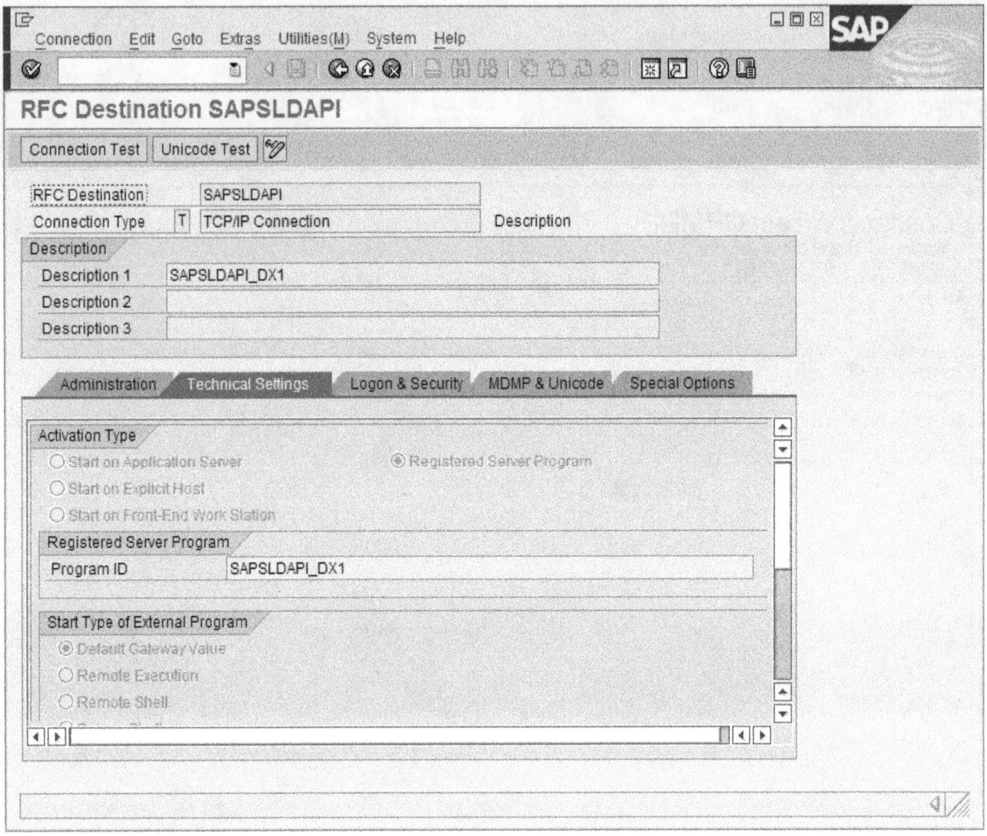

Copyright by SAP AG

FIGURE 4-6 SAP RFC connection type T

(SMTP) connection so that e-mails can be sent from SAP applications to external e-mail systems. The integration settings are performed in transaction code SCOT. Enter transaction code SCOT, double-click the SMTP node, and enter the configuration as per Figure 4-7.

Change the mail host for your environment. Click the Set button beside the Internet address type, type an asterisk (*) in the address area, and click either the check mark icon or Enter. After this step click Continue. Next, schedule a send job by clicking the Job icon on the top or pressing SHIFT–F7 and clicking and choosing the schedule job for all address types. Choose Schedule Immediately, leave the other defaults, and continue. This will schedule the send job. Next, make sure you maintain the e-mail address of the users in SU01 transaction. You can monitor the sent jobs by using the SOST transaction code.

Application Link Enabling/Electronic Data Interchange (ALE/EDI)

The basis of this ALE (SAP-to-SAP business data exchange) and EDI (SAP-to-EDI system business data exchange) communication mechanism is the Intermediate Documents (IDOC). An IDOC acts as a data container facilitating the exchange of business information between

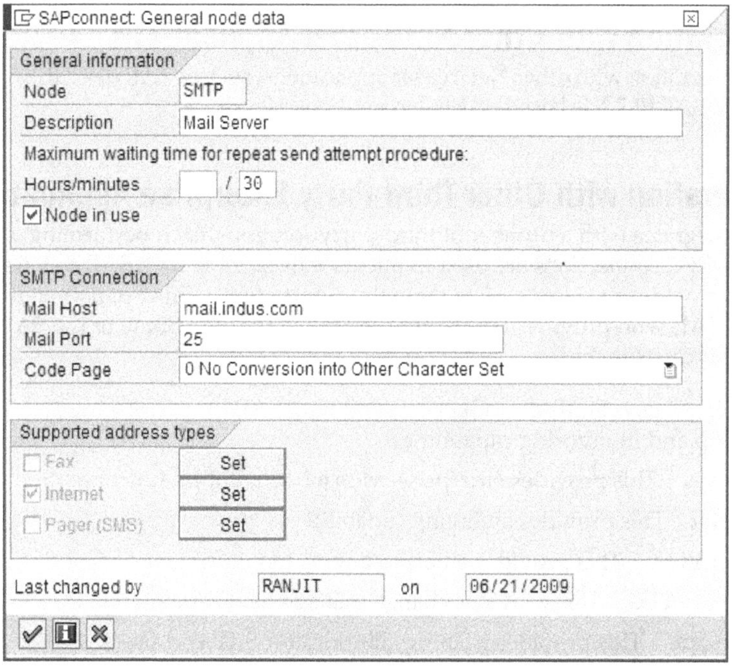

FIGURE 4-7 SCOT configuration

SAP systems and non-SAP systems. The basis of IDOC generation is the message types. Message types identify the usage of specific business data. One example of a SAP standard message type is "CREMAS." CREMAS is the vendor master data distribution message type. Transaction code WE81 shows all the message types that have been delivered along with the SAP standard install and customer-created ones as well.

SAProuter

SAProuter is an SAP program that is used to securely connect to the SAP support. There is a SAProuter program running on both the customer site and the SAP support organization site. The SAProuter program is installed inside the firewall and acts as an "application level gateway." This adds another layer of network security for both the SAP customer and SAP. More specific details will be discussed in Chapter 20.

SAP EPR Integration with Other Business Suite Applications

This group of SAP business applications includes SAP Business Suite 7 (SAP ERP 6 with EhP4, SAP SRM 7.0, SAP CRM 7.0, SAP SCM 7.0, and SAP PLM 7.0). SAP ERP 6 integrates with the other SAP Business Suite applications, primarily with the RFC connections. Each of the Business Suite applications in this group has special interfaces, but the underlying communication mechanism is via RFC connection over TCP/IP protocol.

SAP ERP Integration with Other NetWeaver Applications

SAP ERP 6 integration with other NetWeaver applications, such as SAP BW 7.0, SAP NetWeaver Portal 7.0, and SAP PI 7.1, is based on RFC connections as well.

SAP ERP Integration with Other Third-Party Enterprise Applications

SAP ERP 6 integrates with a number of third-party solutions, each performing an enterprise-wide service. RFC connections are used to integrate these tools with SAP ERP 6 systems, and SAP usually provides the interfaces to these third-party tools. Third-party vendors also work closely with SAP, who provides certification of their products. Some of the SAP-certified third-party products include

- **Tivoli** This is an IBM product certified with SAP for performing activities such as backup and monitoring capabilities.
- **Autosys** This provides enterprise-wide job scheduling functions.
- **FileNet** This provides archiving capabilities.
- **Open View** This provides enterprise-wide monitoring and reporting capabilities.
- **Mercury ITG** This provides change management capabilities.
- **uPerform** This provides training solutions for SAP end users.
- **Topcall** This provides faxing capabilities.
- **Taxware** This provides sales and use tax calculation for SAP systems.
- **D&B** This provides the business credit check capabilities for SAP systems.

This list is not comprehensive. Several hundreds of third-party enterprise-wide solutions are certified by SAP and can be integrated using one of the communication protocols discussed in this chapter. Table 4-4 provides the SAP certified partner directory link. This link will help SAP customers search for all SAP-certified third-party products. Some of the third-party tools require some additional configuration at setup before they can be used. Each of the third-party vendors publishes an install and configuration guide providing details of the third-party connector tool and the communication setup that is required before using the tool with the SAP solutions.

SAP URL	Description
www.sap.com/ecosystem/customers/directories/searchpartner.epx	SAP-certified third-party products
www.sdn.sap.com/irj/sdn/interface-certifications	SAP-certifiable integration scenarios

Table 4-4 Links to SAP-Certified Third-Party Products

SAP Business Suite Integration with Solution Manager

With the growing number and complexity of SAP business applications, it is becoming difficult to administer and operate the solution in an effective manner. SAP Solution Manager is recommended as a central system for all administration and monitoring activities of the SAP system landscape of an organization. SAP has delivered a number of capabilities in the SAP Solution Manager such as change and transport management, service desk functionality, monitoring and reporting capabilities, Central User Administration (CUA), hosting central System Landscape Directory (SLD), enterprise-wide NetWeaver administration, and end-to-end root cause analysis with tools such as Solution Manager Diagnostics (SMD) and Wily Introscope to help manage the entire landscape. More specific details will be discussed in Chapter 20.

SAP Solution Integration with Enterprise-Wide Operations

One of the key points from an operational perspective when integrating a complex system such as SAP is to integrate it effectively with existing enterprise solutions of a given organization so that the operations of the solution will be effectively managed by the enterprise-wide operations team. Different enterprise-wide third-party tools are integrated with the new SAP system, and the escalation procedures are documented and widely distributed so that the operations team can provide the agreed service level agreements (SLA) to the business side of the organization. Usually, the operations team is trained in the new SAP product's basic operations, such as taking backups, resetting user passwords, scheduling jobs, and addressing printing issues. The operations team will escalate the issue to an in-house expert to resolve a reported SAP issue.

SAP Solution Integration with SAP Support

SAP is a complex business solution and needs support from SAP resources from time to time. SAP Solution Manager is integrated into the SAP support organization via a SAProuter connection. SAP support resources can be granted access to the customer's SAP systems by the customer's system administrators using this SAProuter connection. Usually, the support process starts with an internal help desk ticket logged by an end user reporting an SAP issue. Solution Manager service desk functionality or a third-party enterprise-wide help desk solution such as Unicenter is used for logging the help desk tickets. Internal SAP experts at the organization will first try and resolve the reported problem. If this is not possible, an SAP message is logged by the customer at the SAP portal (http//service.sap.com/message). SAP resources log into client systems if required to resolve the reported issue.

SAP Solution Integration with EDI and Other External Vendors

SAP Solution Manager integrates and exchanges data with external vendors' EDI systems using integration products such as Gentran. Gentran is one of the leading EDI and data translation solutions.

SAP PI as an Enterprise Integration Hub

SAP Process Integration is intended as an integration hub for all of the organization's interfaces. PI 7.1 is the most current release and includes a number of performance improvements, with service-oriented architecture capabilities, and is well positioned to standardize and optimize all of the enterprise interface requirements. It avoids point-to-point interface connections and uses native integration capabilities between different SAP solutions, which helps reduce integration costs in a client's landscape.

Service-oriented architecture (SOA) is emerging as a standard for developing interfaces in an organization. In SOA, interfaces are developed as enterprise services so that they can be consumed by a number of other applications across the enterprise. SOA is an architectural standard that requires the functionality of the interfaces be published as a service in a platform-independent fashion.

SAP provides a methodology referred to as Enterprise SOA to implement SOA projects that includes additional capabilities that help clients build business solutions that have a lot of reuse capabilities within an enterprise. Enterprise SOA includes the following stages in a service interface development lifecycle:

- Business requirements gathering
- Service modeling
- Service definition
- Service implementation
- Service publishing
- Service consumption

SAP PI provides SOA tools for facilitating organizations to build and consume enterprise services. Different components of the SAP PI 7.1 systems are shown in Figure 4-8.

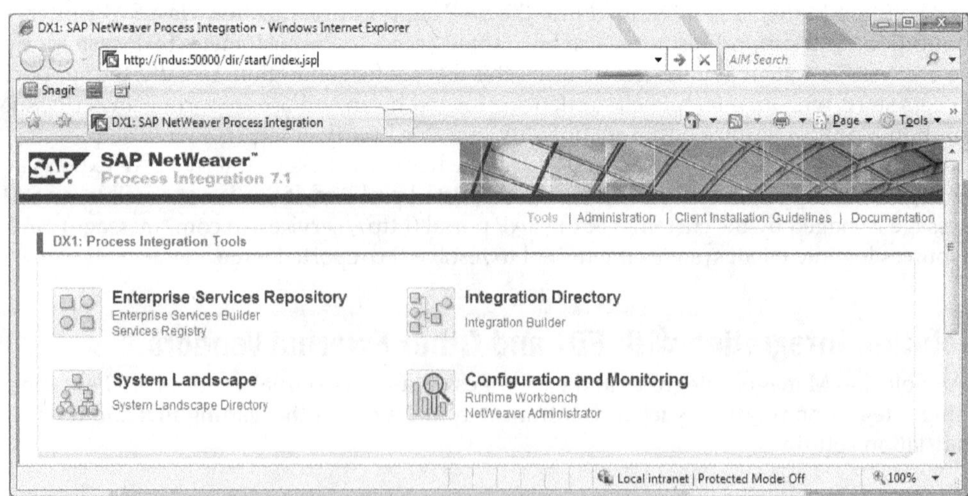

FIGURE 4-8 SAP PI 7.1 system and integration components

Enterprise Service Repository

Enterprise Service Repository (ESR) is a repository for the enterprise service inventory of assets built by an organization over time. This includes tools such as Enterprise Services Builder and Services Registry. Enterprise Services Builder helps to build enterprise services based on enterprise SOA standards. The services are then published in the Services Registry for enterprise-wide consumption.

System Landscape Directory (SLD)

System Landscape Directory (SLD) is a central provider of all software product and component definitions to the ESR. New software product and component definitions are created in SLD and are exported to the ESR to begin the development of the service interfaces.

Integration Directory

Integration Directory is the central configuration tool that helps in configuring message processing, communication and security, and routing rules for message flow.

Configuring and Monitoring

Runtime Workbench and NetWeaver Administrator (NWA) are two tools provided by SAP for monitoring and administering the PI solution. SAP is moving more monitoring and administration capabilities to the NWA tool, consistent with centralizing these activities across the entire SAP solution in a client landscape.

Integration Server

Integration Server is the runtime environment for the service interfaces and is installed as an ABAP component. Other PI components, such as ESR, SLD, and ID, are installed as Java applications.

Advanced Adapter Engine

This component consists of a number of adapters, such as the file adapter, IDOC adapter and JMS adapter. Theses adapters provide built-in mediation, mapping, queuing, and other capabilities between provider and consumer business applications. Advanced Adapter Engine can be installed as a central adapter engine along with Integration Server, or as a separate installation.

Enterprise Service Bus

Enterprise Service Bus (ESB) is an enterprise SOA environment combining the different service providers and consumers on a single communication infrastructure that provides functions such as runtime services, thereby enabling service-based communication.

The SAP PI solution with all the aforementioned capabilities is thus emerging as a central service interface hub for organizations.

Summary

- SAP ERP plays a central role in an organization's enterprise, integrating with several other SAP and non-SAP systems.
- Industry-standard TCP/IP and RFC communication is the basis of most of the SAP applications' network communication and integration.
- SM59 transaction is used to set up an RFC connection in SAP systems.
- The SAPconnect interface and SCOT transaction is used to set up communication services such as e-mail integration, faxing, and paging integration in SAP.
- ALE (Application Link Enabling) provides the basis for loosely coupling SAP business applications to exchange business data in different integration scenarios.
- EDI (Electronic Data Interchange) standards form one of the basis for exchanging data between SAP and outside vendors.
- The SAProuter program helps to establish a connection between customers' SAP systems and the SAP support organization using secure methods of network integration.
- The SAP PI system is emerging as an organization-wide integration hub in customer sites that have SAP as their main ERP system.
- The SAP PI system provides tools to develop enterprise services that enable SOA.

Additional Resources

- **SAP Process Integration** www.sdn.sap.com/irj/sdn/nw-pi71
- **SAP Solution Manager eLearning Catalog** www.sdn.sap.com/irj/scn/solutionmanager-elearning

PART

SAP Installation

CHAPTER

SAP ABAP and Java Stack Installation Preparation

Before we start looking into the chapters in this section related to SAP system installation, let us first understand the context of the SAP implementation project and the role of a SAP technical architect and SAP Basis administrator. Organizations invest in SAP software to achieve business capabilities deemed important as per a corporation's strategic planning priorities. There will be a sound business case and a financial sponsor for implementing a SAP project inside the organization. For example, SAP implementation projects for a Fortune 500 company could cost several million dollars and last for several years, depending upon the scope of the implementation effort. Because of the complexity of the business process and technology configuration involved, organizations usually partner with systems integrators such as IBM, Accenture, Deloitte, Capgemini, and SAP for implementing the SAP software. In recent years, international consulting firms such as Infosys, Tata Consulting Services (TCS), and Wipro are also helping to provide SAP implementation services to Fortune 500 companies in United States as well as in other parts of the world. Several smaller consulting firms provide SAP implementation services to the mid-market.

Stages of the SAP Implementation Project

SAP implementation projects follow a methodology for successfully managing the lifecycle of the program. Regardless of the specific implementation methodologies followed by the systems integrators and client organizations, different phases of the project more or less remain the same. Typical phases of SAP implementation projects include design, build, test, and deploy. These various phases are described in detail in the paragraphs that follow.

During the design phase of the SAP, project functional consultants will review the existing business processes and requirements and will identify any process gaps. Based on this understanding, functional resources will plan, design, and configure the SAP software. They will also develop functional specifications and pass them on to the SAP development team for writing the technical specifications and development of the Reports, Interfaces, Conversions, Enhancements, Forms and Workflow (RICEFW) inventory, which represents the needs of the SAP implementation project. From the SAP technology perspective, a technical architect will analyze the current organization's technical architecture and will develop a technology design blueprint. This document will lay out a detailed blueprint for all the technology components that would need to be installed and configured for the development, testing, and execution of the SAP software solution.

The next phase of the implementation project is the build phase. SAP Basis resources will help build the SAP development systems and establish naming conventions for software change management during this phase of the project. During the build phase, functional consultants will configure the SAP system to meet the requirements of the client's business processes and development consultants and integration consultants will build the RICEFW inventory.

After the build activities are completed, Basis administrators build the test systems and all the development and configuration performed is transported (export and import) to the test systems. In the test systems integration and user acceptance tests are performed, and after everything has been successfully tested the solution is ready for deployment.

Deployment of the software is the final phase of the SAP implementation. SAP Basis administrators build the production SAP systems and migrate all the changes to this system. The conversion team performs the data conversion activities from the old systems to the new SAP systems during a weekend before go-live, and then the new solution will be the system of record. After the new solution stabilizes in a week or two, the old systems are decommissioned.

As explained earlier, SAP Basis administrators play a key role in building the development, test, and production SAP systems and in setting up a transport mechanism for moving the configuration and development changes to different systems. SAP Basis resources also provide support activities to the project team in the areas of additional software installations, patch application, performance tuning, monitoring, backup and recovery, transport changes within the landscape, and so on. Subsequent chapters in the book will go into more detail regarding these activities.

In this chapter, we will look at the preparatory steps required before starting the actual SAP installation. This will include preparation and planning activities, such as how to translate SAP IT scenarios into installable SAP software usage types, checking the Product Availability Matrix (PAM) to verify the availability and compatibility of the SAP software release with regard to a given operating system and database, downloading the installation manuals, writing a build specification document for the UNIX team to create the file system, downloading the software using SAP Download Manager, and referring to SAP Online Support System (OSS) Notes for addressing any known issues with the installs. Now let us study each of these preparatory steps in detail.

Business Requirements Mapping to Technical Systems Installation

One of the key tasks of a SAP technical architect and a Basis administrator is to map the business requirements to the installable technical systems. SAP provides two guides to provide this mapping and identify the technical components that need to be installed. One is the master guide and the second is the technology infrastructure guide. The master guide is the starting point for planning any technical implementation of a SAP NetWeaver solution. The master guide helps map the business scenarios to be implemented to the technically installable components and how to lay out the SAP system landscape.

It identifies the business/IT practices that are available with the NetWeaver solution and the installable usage types that map to a given IT scenario implementation. The technology infrastructure guide is more focused on providing information with regard to distributing the SAP NetWeaver components to different physical hosts to provide a stable, robust, and high-performing SAP system.

Downloading the Master Guide and Technical Infrastructure Guide

The master guide and technology infrastructure guide can be downloaded at the following locations:

- https://service.sap.com/instguides | Installation | Master Guide
- https://service.sap.com/instguides | Installation | Technology Infrastructure Guide

IT Scenarios (Master Guide)

IT scenarios are groupings of SAP business processes delivered by SAP that give businesses an easy way of implementing a new capability into an organization in a structured way using reference models and implementation help. Several IT scenarios are delivered—for example, the enterprise data warehousing scenario gives a customer the capability to develop and operate a enterprise-wide data warehousing solution that includes capabilities such as designing and building business intelligence models, gathering and analyzing data from multiple sources in the enterprise and producing operational and strategic reporting, and implementing dashboards and data visualization options for decision makers.

A business process expert (BPE) working closely with the business leadership of an organization will decide which IT scenarios are in scope for a new SAP implementation. Once an IT scenario is decided upon to achieve a business goal by an organization, they will look to the technical team for help in mapping this business need to the actual physical build of the SAP infrastructure. A SAP technical architect or a Basis architect will map the identified IT scenario to the installable usage types.

Usage Types (Master Guide)

Mapping the identified IT scenarios to the installable software unit is done by usage types. SAP provides a master guide that maps the IT scenarios with the usage types. Master guide can be downloaded from the SAP portal at http://service.sap.com/instguides | SAP NetWeaver | SAP NetWeaver 7 | Installation | Master Guide. You will need a SAP Portal (SAP Online Service Marketplace) user account to gain access to the site. The following usage types are available for installation for different IT scenarios:

- AS ABAP (Application Server ABAP)
- AS Java (Application Server Java)
- BI Java (Business Intelligence Java)
- PI (Process Integration)
- EP (Enterprise Portals)

- EPC (Enterprise Portals Core)
- DI (Development Infrastructure)
- MI (Mobile Infrastructure)

For example, implementing the enterprise data warehousing IT scenario requires AS ABAP, AS Java, BI Java, EP, and EPC to be installed.

PAM

The Product Availability Matrix (PAM) is an online resource provided by SAP so that customers can check the availability of a given SAP product and supported operating systems and the databases. PAM can be accessed by using the SAP Portal URL: https://service.sap.com/pam. PAM also provides vital information, such as the other software dependencies and requirements, maintenance start and end dates, new product ramp-up release dates, and release-related OSS Notes. A Basis administrator uses this information to install the correct SAP release so that it is fully supported and compliant with SAP standard maintenance. Once the usage types and the product availability and release information are gathered, the Basis administrator can proceed to start planning for the actual physical installation of the SAP software.

Significance of SAP Sizing

SAP sizing helps to estimate the hardware resources that would be needed to install the system. Incorrect SAP sizing results in undersized systems that could affect the project implementation in terms of system growth, stability, and performance. SAP sizing should be done starting in the design phase and continue even after go-live to plan for capacity planning of the SAP system landscape. Usually, an initial SAP sizing effort is performed for budgeting purposes, and subsequent sizing efforts help to estimate the long-term needs of the SAP solution. Once the SAP sizing project is completed, the hardware vendor will provide recommendations. Since sizing is so important for the initial procurement of the hardware and for on-going capacity planning purposes, a whole chapter (Chapter 24) is devoted to studying this area in detail.

Hardware Procurement

Usually, the hardware vendor provides several configurations for the physical layout of the SAP systems. The systems integrator reviews these options and, working closely with the client, will make a recommendation for one of the configurations. After client sign-off on the final hardware recommendation, the order is placed and the physical servers are delivered to the clients or the hosting provider's data center and are installed by the data center and network team.

Download the SAP Installation Guides

SAP installation guides can be downloaded from the SAP Portal (SAP Service Marketplace at http://service.sap.com/instguides | SAP NetWeaver | SAP NetWeaver 7 | Installation | Installation Guide. You can download the specific guide you need, such as SAP NW AS ABAP or NW AS Java. The installation guide is generally divided into several sections. The planning and preparation sections are the most relevant for us in this chapter. These sections usually include activities such as hardware and software requirements and preparations, distribution of the usage types into one or more systems, creation of installation user accounts, and setting up the file system for the software. Usually, a Basis administrator compiles a list of activities from theses sections and translates this to a UNIX build specification document. This document forms the basis for preparing the hardware for the installation of the new SAP system. Let us now look into some installation definitions and a sample of the UNIX build specification used for an actual physical installation.

SAP Installation Definitions/Terminology Up to NW 7.0

An understanding of the following definitions will help you plan your build specification and perform the install for releases upto NW 7.0.

Central Instance

The central instance refers to the application services for the SAP system, including the enqueue and message services that are located on a single host machine. The central instance has multiple work processes for the dialog, update, and background services. The machine on which it runs is called the *central host.*

Database Instance

The instance associated with the underlying database of the SAP application is referred to as a database instance.

Central System Installation

If the SAP central instance and the database are installed on the same physical host, it is referred to as a central system installation. Usually, small SAP installations and nonproduction systems are installed with this type.

Distributed System Installation

In a distributed system installation, the central instance and database are installed on two different hosts. Usually, a distributed installation option is used for large SAP installations and for production systems.

Dialog Instance

Additional application server instances installed for scalability and load balancing purposes are referred to as dialog instances. Dialog instances have additional dialog, batch, spool, and update work processes. These are joined to the central system.

SID

The SID is a system identifier for the SAP system. It consists of exactly three alphanumeric uppercase characters; the first character must be a letter; and the SID should not include any of the reserved words, such as DBA, COM, and KEY. More reserve words are given in the install guide.

System Number

The system number is an identifier used for internal SAP processes. You are allowed to choose any two-digit number from 00 to 98. This number should be unique if more than one SAP system is to be installed on a single host.

SAPinst

SAPinst is the SAP install tool used to build the SAP application. The tool is delivered along with the downloaded SAP software or the SAP shipped software. SAPinst drives the entire installation based on the chosen install scenario.

SAP Installation Definitions/Terminology Starting from NW 7.1

The following terminology and component changes are seen starting with the NW 7.1 installation:

- The central instance (CI) is now called the "primary application server instance."
- The dialog instance (DI) is now called the "additional application server instance."
- The central system is now called the "standard system."
- The database instance term remains unchanged.
- The Software Deployment Manager (SDM) component is no longer available in the Java system. JSPM (Java Support Package Manager) performs all the activities of SDM as well.
- You no longer need to download JDK from another vendor. SAP JVM is shipped along with the install software in the master DVD, and is automatically installed by SAPinst.

SAP System Install Build Specifications

Now that we have reviewed the definitions that will be used in this and subsequent chapters related to SAP installations, let us look at a sample UNIX build specification. It is a best practice to write a formal build specification with all the naming conventions and provide it to the UNIX, storage, and database teams so that they can start allocating the needed storage space and building the underlying operating system (OS) file system (see Table 5-1) that is needed for the database and the SAP application installation. Please note that this is not a comprehensive build specification. Additional information such as swap space requirements, UNIX kernel parameters, OS patches, and swap information is included in the build specification as per the instructions and operating system–specific OSS Notes provided in the install guide. User accounts <SAPSID>adm (e.g., devadm) and ora<SAPSID> (e.g., oradev) can be created before the start of the installation as per instructions in the install manual and your organizations standards. Otherwise, the SAPinst program will create the accounts in the system during the course of the install.

Older installation program was buggy and used to give user account creation errors. To mitigate this situation it was recommended to create the user accounts outside the SAPinst tool. However, the newer release SAPinst install process has gotten significantly better and we are not seeing this to be an issue.

The next step in the installation preparation is to download the necessary SAP software.

File System	Size (MB)
/oracle	512
/oracle/stage	6144
/oracle/ DEV	6144
/oracle/DEV /origlogA	2048
/oracle/DEV/origlogB	2048
/oracle/DEV/mirrlogA	2048
/oracle/DEV/mirrlogB	2048
/oracle/DEV/oraarch	12288
/oracle/DEV/sapdata1	40000
/oracle/DEV/sapdata2	40000
/oracle/DEV/sapdata3	40000
/oracle/DEV/sapdata4	40000
/oracle/DEV/sapreorg	4096
/usr/sap	2048
/usr/sap/trans	12288
/usr/sap/DEV	4096
/sapmnt/DEV	4096

TABLE 5-1 Sample UNIX File System Layout with Estimated Size

Download SAP Software

For all licensed customers, SAP software can be shipped to their corporate offices to the designated recipient, or the software can be downloaded by the high-level administrator from the SAP software distribution center URL at http://service.sap.com/swdc or https://websmp201.sap-ag.de/swdc (see Figure 5-1). You can reach the software DVDs by using the following path for installing a NW 7.0. On the left side of the screen, expand the download option and follow the path |Installations And Upgrades | Installations And Upgrades - Entry By Application Group. Click SAP NetWeaver on the list on the right, and then choose SAP NetWeaver | SAP NetWeaver 7.0 | Installation And Upgrade | <Operating System> | <Database>. The software will now be available under Downloads. Select the DVDs or ZIP files that you would need as per the installation manual by selecting the check box beside each of the needed media, and click the Add To The Download Basket button at the bottom of the screen. This will place the selected software in the SAP download basket for approval. The software in the download basket needs approval from a SAP Solution Manager system installed at the client site. Use transaction code SOLUTION_MANAGER to approve the software in the download basket from the Solution Manager system. Once it is approved, it

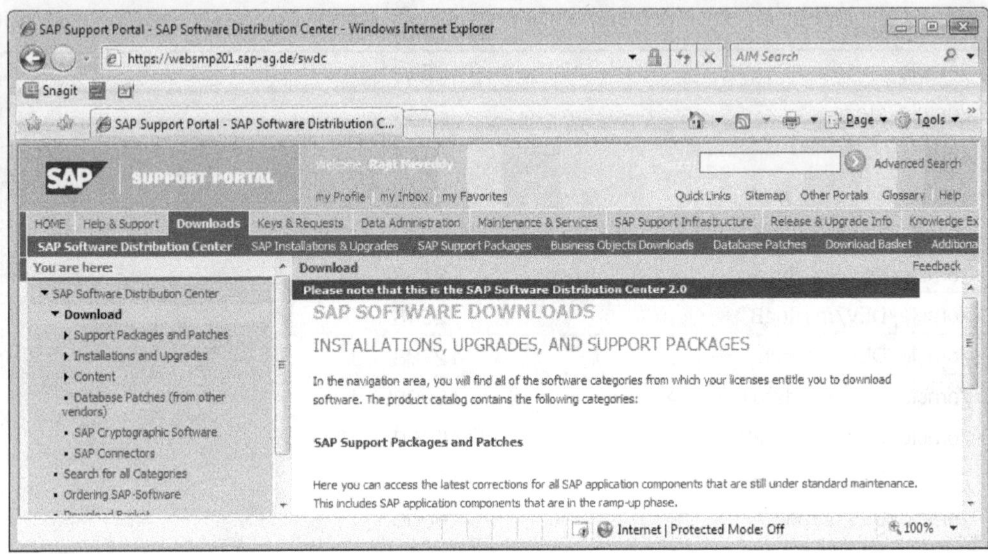

FIGURE 5-1 SAP download URL

is available for download using the SAP Download Manager. The SAP Download Manager is a front-end tool (see Figure 5-2) that will allow the downloading of approved SAP software to your laptop or desktop. Depending upon the number of DVDs or files that are in the download basket and the network speed, it could take anywhere from a few to several hours for the software download to complete. One best practice is to download the software directly to the UNIX operating system's SAP software download directory by installing a Java-based SAP Download Manager on the UNIX system. This will avoid multiple steps of downloading the software to your laptop and then to your server download location.

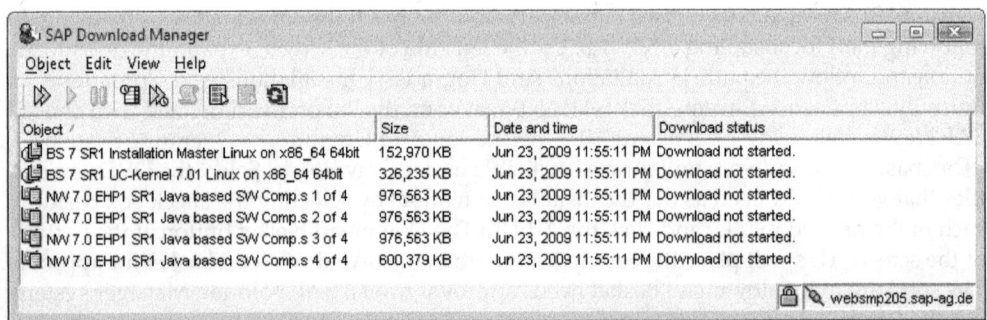

SAP Download Manager

Object Edit View Help

Object	Size	Date and time	Download status
BS 7 SR1 Installation Master Linux on x86_64 64bit	152,970 KB	Jun 23, 2009 11:55:11 PM	Download not started.
BS 7 SR1 UC-Kernel 7.01 Linux on x86_64 64bit	326,235 KB	Jun 23, 2009 11:55:11 PM	Download not started.
NW 7.0 EHP1 SR1 Java based SW Comp.s 1 of 4	976,563 KB	Jun 23, 2009 11:55:11 PM	Download not started.
NW 7.0 EHP1 SR1 Java based SW Comp.s 2 of 4	976,563 KB	Jun 23, 2009 11:55:11 PM	Download not started.
NW 7.0 EHP1 SR1 Java based SW Comp.s 3 of 4	976,563 KB	Jun 23, 2009 11:55:11 PM	Download not started.
NW 7.0 EHP1 SR1 Java based SW Comp.s 4 of 4	600,379 KB	Jun 23, 2009 11:55:11 PM	Download not started.

websmp205.sap-ag.de

FIGURE 5-2 SAP Download Manager

SAP System Naming Conventions

Before starting the SAP installations, it is very important to establish a naming convention for choosing the SID, system numbers for the SAP systems that are in scope. The naming conventions will help to standardize the SAP system identifier names and the network port numbers, and will make sure that the chosen names and numbers are unique and do not pose problems with port conflicts and multiple SAP systems with the same SID.

The following is an example of a naming convention that can be used for SAP systems:

- All development SAP systems have D as the first character.
- All quality assurance SAP systems have Q as the first character.
- All production SAP systems have P as the first character.
- All ECC systems have E as the second character.
- All BW systems have B as the second character.
- All portal systems have P as the second character.

The following is an example of the numbers that can be used for SAP systems:

- All development systems have a system number of 00.
- All quality systems have a system number of 01.
- All production systems have a system number of 02.

Table 5-2 shows how the SID and system number would appear when we apply these naming conventions. The naming conventions can be extended for all other SAP solutions at a given client site.

SAP System	SID	System Number
SAP ECC Development System	DE1	00
SAP ECC Quality Assurance System	QE1	01
SAP ECC Production System	PE1	02
SAP BW Development System	DB1	00
SAP BW Quality Assurance System	QB1	01
SAP BW Production System	PB1	02
SAP Portal Development System	DP1	00
SAP Portal Quality System	QP1	01
SAP Portal Production System	PP1	02

TABLE 5-2 Application of SAP System Naming Conventions

SAP Installation Planning Script

Before beginning the actual installation, it will help significantly from a planning perspective to write an installation script. This will not only help to enter the install parameters quickly during the course of the install, but also help to document the actual installation steps of the install. Table 5-3 shows a sample SAP installation script that can be used for planning the install. This script is not comprehensive and is intended to give you an idea for developing your own detailed customer-specific SAP install script.

Step Number	Install Step Description	Parameter for Install/ Needed Information	Result
1	Login as root.	Get root account from UNIX system administrator.	Successful login to the system.
2	Verify the SAP file system is built as per specification provided by Basis administrator.	Use OS commands to check the file system.	File system is built as specified in the build specification.
3	Set environmental variables.	For example, setenv JAVA_HOME /opt/java.	Java Home environmental variable is set.
4	Launch SAPinst tool.	Execute the SAPinst tool from the installation master CD as per install guide instructions.	SAP install tool is started successfully.
5	Drill down to the Install selection from the menu option.	For example, select the Central System Installation option for SAP NW 7 Java Install for Oracle Database.	The right NW ABAP or Java Install option for the intended database is chosen. You will notice a Next button on the SAP Installer.
6	Click the Next button and start feeding in the Install parameters. First choose between Typical and Custom.	For example, choose Typical for default parameter choices or Custom if you would like to change the default install parameters.	The install option is chosen and the Next button appears.
7	Continue feeding in parameters.	Enter parameters as per install guide instructions.	Click Continue.
8–200	Execute the service after parameter choices are completed.	All parameter selections are entered and the service is executed.	SAP install completed successfully.

TABLE 5-3 Sample SAP Installation Planning Script

Summary

- Design, build, test, and deploy are the four stages of a typical SAP implementation project.
- SAP provides a master guide and a technical infrastructure guide for mapping the business/IT scenarios to the physical installable software units (usage types).
- IT scenarios are the business process inventory delivered by SAP.
- IT scenarios map to one or several installable software units called usage types.
- SAP sizing will help to plan and procure the needed hardware.
- SAPinst tool is used to install usage types.
- Available usage types are NW AS ABAP, NW AS Java, BI Java, PI, EP, EP Core, MI, and DI.
- PAM (Product Availability Matrix) helps to check the product release, maintenance, and OS and DB support matrix and compatibility information for installation planning.
- Build specification document identifies and lists all the key preparatory steps for the installation planning.
- SAP Download Manager helps to download the software from the SAP software distribution center to the software hosting directory at the client site.
- Solution Manager is used to approve all the software downloaded to the download basket.
- Central system installation is performed for smaller, nonproduction installations.
- Distributed system installation is performed for larger, production installations.
- SAP naming conventions will help to standardize the systems in the customer's landscape.
- SAP installation planning script will help to plan and execute an installation in a smooth and effective fashion.

Additional Resources

- **Project Management Institute Website** www.pmi.org/Pages/default.aspx
- **SAP Sizing Information** http://service.sap.com/sizing
- **SAP Install Guides Information** http://service.sap.com/instguides
- **SAP Best Practices Information** http://service.sap.com/bestpractices
- **TCP/IP Ports Used by SAP Applications** www.sdn.sap.com/irj/scn/index?rid=/library/uuid/4e515a43-0e01-0010-2da1-9bcc452c280b&overridelayout=true

CHAPTER

SAP ABAP and Java Stack Installation

In the last chapter we studied the planning and preparatory steps that have to be done in order to perform a successful SAP system installation. In this chapter we will go into details of the actual SAP installation steps, such as usage of SAP and database installation tools, verifying the UNIX build before starting SAP installation tools, setting up the environment variables before starting the actual install, starting the installation process, entering the parameters in the SAP installation tool, executing the installation, troubleshooting any installation issues, restarting the installation after troubleshooting the issue, and uninstalling the SAP software when there is a need to delete a SAP system. In this chapter, one example of a SAP NW ABAP stack installation (NW 7.0 ABAP System) and one example of a SAP NW 7.0 Java stack installation (BI 7.0 Java System) will be covered in detail. In studying the installation procedures, Oracle Database and UNIX operating systems are used for examples in this chapter. Similar procedures can be used when installing SAP solutions in other operating systems and databases as well. In this chapter, practical aspects of performing an actual SAP installation are emphasized in detail, and a number of illustrations are included. The entire lifecycle of an installation process will be discussed in this chapter.

SAP software can be shipped to a customer location to a designated person or it can be downloaded to a central secure location at a customer data center from the SAP Portal (http://service.sap.com/swdc) by a Basis administrator with high-level user authorization. Most customers have moved to downloading the software on demand in recent years, because it is convenient and easy to get the most current versions of the SAP software. Usually, the software is downloaded to a shared network directory so that the same software inventory can be used to build all the SAP systems of the organization. The downloaded software is in a zipped format and needs to be unzipped before the installation media can be accessed.

Installation Tools

SAP media has the installation tools necessary to perform an SAP install. SAPinst and Oracle Universal Installer are the main tools used to perform SAP and Oracle Database software installations. Oracle Database software should be installed ahead of the SAP software installation. This will allow Basis administrators to install SAP software using

SAPinst without having to install the Oracle Database software during the course of the SAP install. SAPinst will create a new custom SAP database once the underlying Oracle Database software has been installed. Please download the Oracle software from the SAP software download location and not directly from the Oracle site. The reason is the SAP download location has the version of the Oracle package that has been tested with SAP and may include any needed dependencies and SAP relevant files as well.

SAPinst

The SAPinst tool is called from the SAP installation master DVD, which is downloaded from SAP Service Marketplace. The SAPinst tool (Figure 6-1) guides the Basis administrator

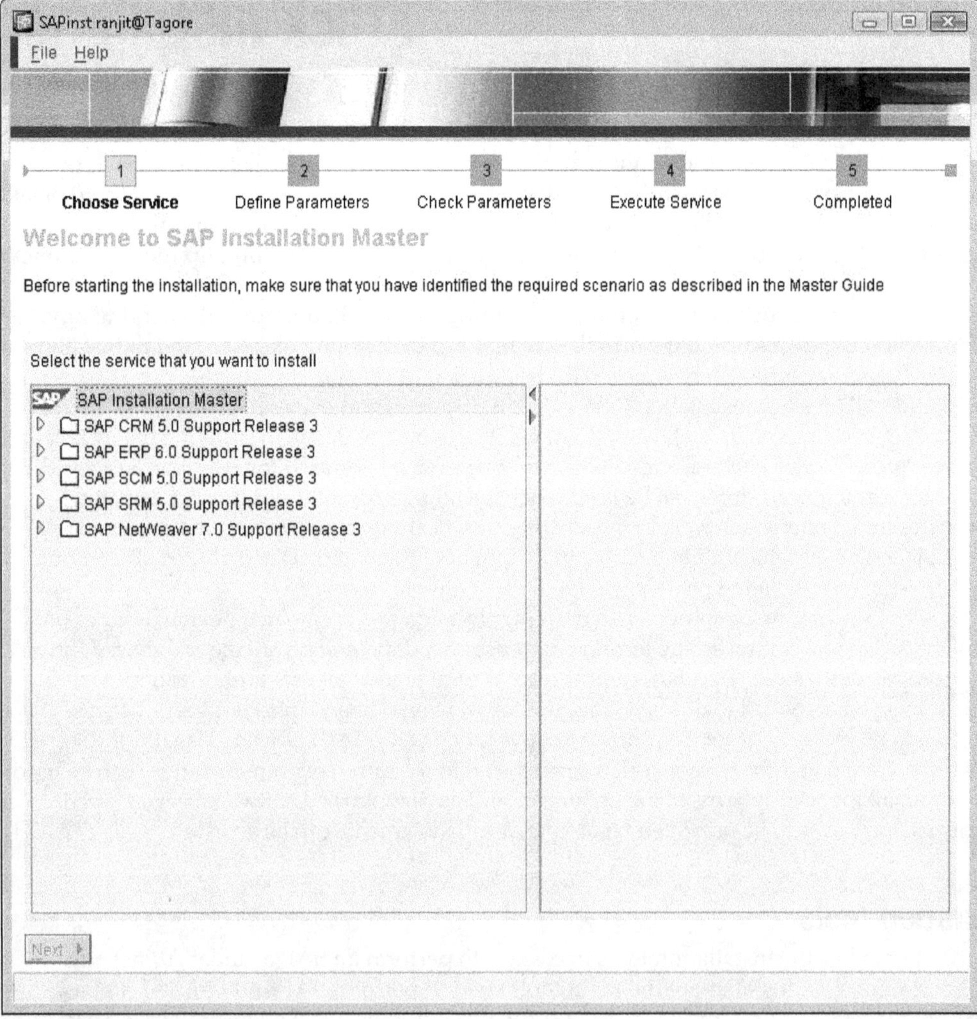

FIGURE 6-1 SAPinst tool initial screen

in choosing which solution needs to be installed and the different parameters that are needed for a successful installation. Over time, SAP has improved its software installation tools, and the current version of the SAPinst tool is effective and intuitive. The SAPinst tool performs the software installation in five phases, as shown in Figure 6-1. The details of each phase are explained in subsequent sections of this chapter.

Oracle Universal Installer (OUI)

Oracle Universal Installer is used to install the Oracle Database software. This installs only the Oracle binaries; the actual SAP database is created by the SAPinst tool. It is recommended to install the Oracle binaries ahead of the SAP software installation. If this is not done, SAPinst will stop the install at the Oracle Database software installation phase and prompt for its installation. After Oracle binaries are installed, SAPinst will continue the installation process. When installing the SAP NW 7.0 system, the Oracle Database version must be 10.2 or higher. Oracle Database software is installed with ora<SID> user id. Application of the most current Oracle patches is also recommended after the 10.2 software version is installed. The installation of Oracle Database software version 10.2 using the OUI is shown in Figure 6-2. Oracle Database software installation and Oracle patch application will be covered in detail in Chapter 19 of this book.

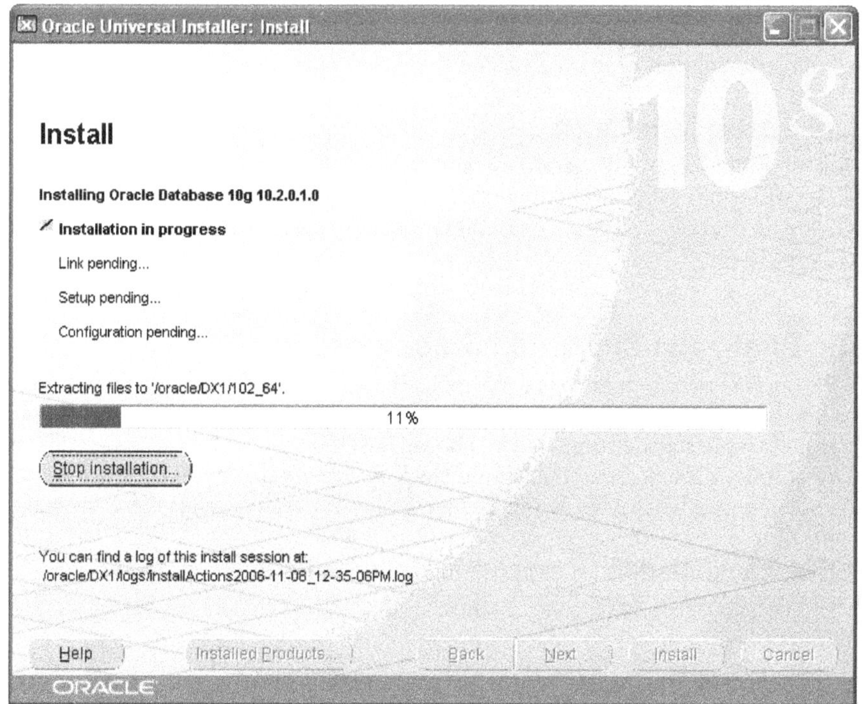

Copyright by SAP AG

FIGURE 6-2 Oracle Universal Installer tool

SAP Installation Options in NW 7.0–Based Systems

When installing NW 7.0–based systems, the following three options are available.

Central System Installation

In this install option, the SAP central instance and database instance are installed on the same host. This option is recommended for small installations and development and test systems.

Distributed System Installation

In this install option, the SAP central instance and the database instance are installed on two different hosts. This option is recommended for production systems.

High-Availability System Installation

In this install option, the SAP software is configured in a switchover group using high-availability software, such as Service Guard, provided by external vendors.

SAP Installation Options in NW 7.1–Based Systems

In NW 7.1–based installations, some of the terminology is changed. Otherwise, the installation options are more or less the same as in NW 7.0–based systems. The central system installation option is now called the standard system installation.

Standard System Installation

In this install option, , the SAP central instance and database instance are installed on the same host. This option is recommended for small installations and development and test systems. The distributed and high-availability install options are the same as in NW 7.0–based installs.

SAP Single-, Dual-, and Separated Stack Installs

During the "define parameters" phase of the installation process, the system will present the Software Units (Usage Types) selection screen. In this screen, single-stack, dual-stack and separated single stack options can be chosen based on the SAP solution architecture. Some SAP solutions are delivered on single-stack systems, some require a dual-stack system, and some are recommended to be installed as separated single-stack systems.

Single-Stack Installation (Example: Portal Installation)

The SAP NetWeaver Portal is a good example of the single-stack install option. Usage types AS Java, EP, and EP Core are chosen, as per Figure 6-3.

Dual-Stack Installation (Example: PI Installation and MI Installation)

Process Integration (PI) 7.0 and 7.1 systems are mandatory dual-stack systems. During the define parameter phase of the installation, AS ABAP, AS Java, and PI usage types are selected.

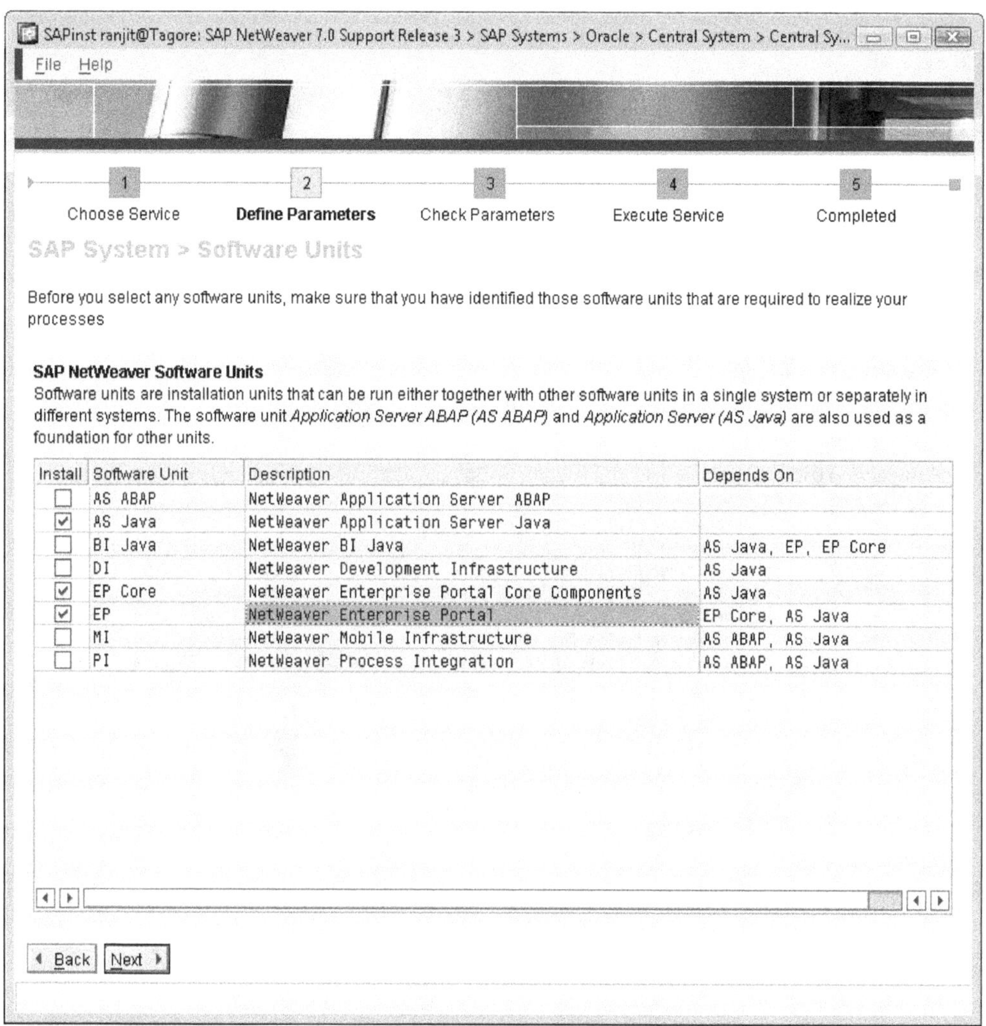

SAPinst ranjit@Tagore: SAP NetWeaver 7.0 Support Release 3 > SAP Systems > Oracle > Central System > Central Sy...
File Help
1 Choose Service
2 Define Parameters
3 Check Parameters
4 Execute Service
5 Completed
SAP System > Software Units
Before you select any software units, make sure that you have identified those software units that are required to realize your processes
SAP NetWeaver Software Units
Software units are installation units that can be run either together with other software units in a single system or separately in different systems. The software unit Application Server ABAP (AS ABAP) and Application Server (AS Java) are also used as a foundation for other units.
Install | Software Unit | Description | Depends On
AS ABAP | NetWeaver Application Server ABAP
AS Java | NetWeaver Application Server Java
BI Java | NetWeaver BI Java | AS Java, EP, EP Core
DI | NetWeaver Development Infrastructure | AS Java
EP Core | NetWeaver Enterprise Portal Core Components | AS Java
EP | NetWeaver Enterprise Portal | EP Core, AS Java
MI | NetWeaver Mobile Infrastructure | AS ABAP, AS Java
PI | NetWeaver Process Integration | AS ABAP, AS Java
Back Next

FIGURE 6-3 SAP single-stack Java installation usage type options

Mobile Infrastructure (MI) is installed as a mandatory dual-stack as well. Figure 6-4 shows the usage type selection of a PI 7.0 dual-stack installation.

Separated Stack Installation (Example: BI ABAP and BI Java Installation)

Starting with BI 7.0 EhP1 (Enhancement Package 1) installations, the official SAP recommendation for web reporting is a separated, single-stack installation option. It is recommended to install BI ABAP and BI Java as separate single-stack systems and integrate them afterward.

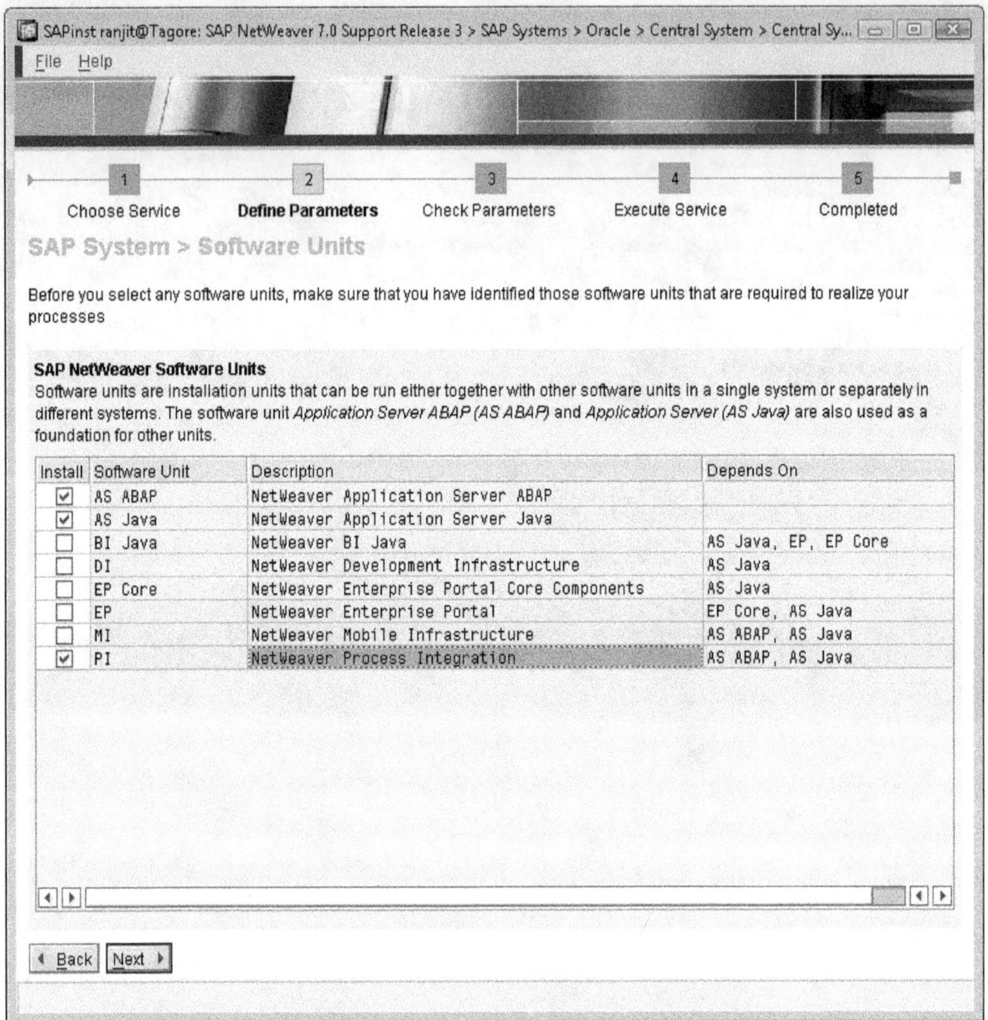

Figure 6-4 SAP dual-stack installation usage type options

Prerequisite Checker

SAPinst provides a tool called the Prerequisite Checker that will help Basis administrators check if the operating system environment is set up correctly and compatible for the SAP software installation. The path to call the Prerequisite Checker is SAP NetWeaver 7.0 | Software Life-Cycle Options | Additional Preparation Options | Prerequisites Check.

Prerequisite Checker will present the screen shown in Figure 6-5. Choose the services that you need it to check, and click the Next button.

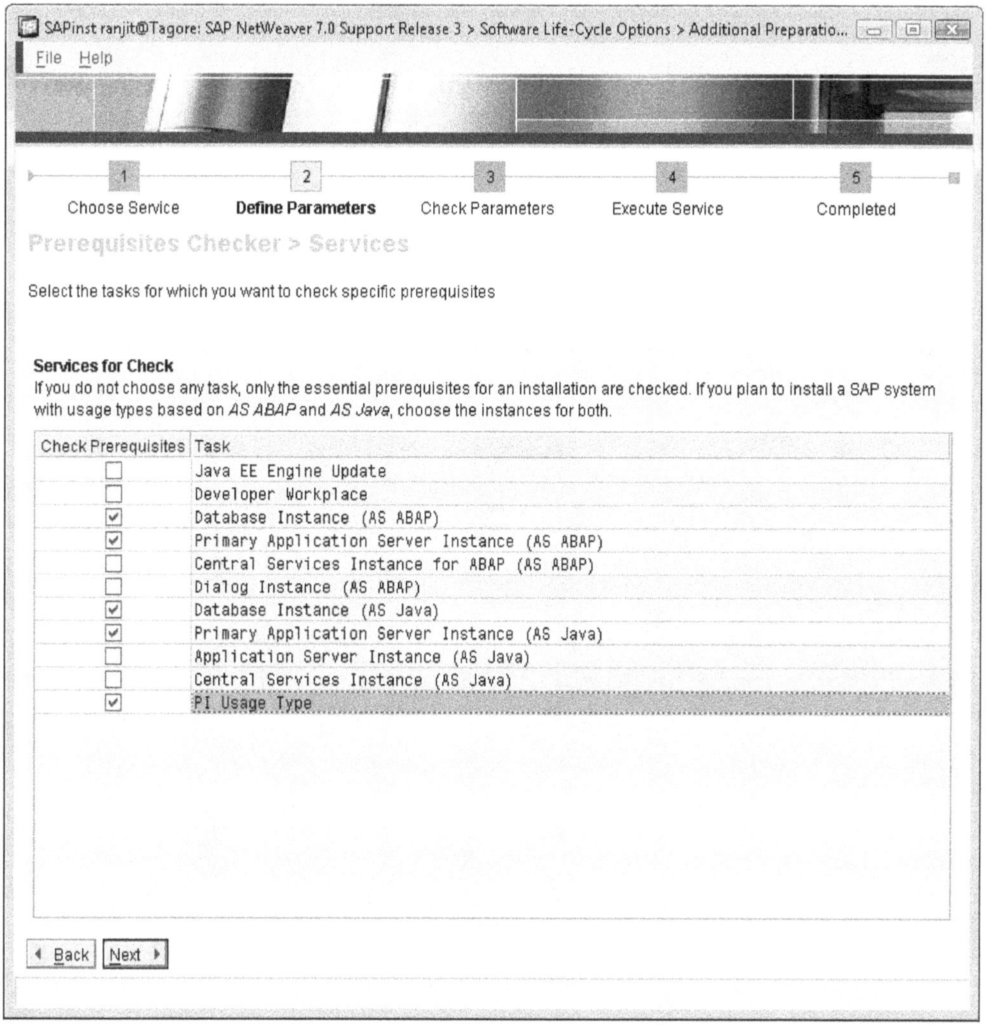

Figure 6-5 Prerequisite Checker services list

The results of the Prerequisite Checker, as shown in Figure 6-6, will identify issues such as software compatibility, memory requirements, and operating system support and will help the Basis administrator to address any issues that might arise before starting the actual install. Prerequisite Checker can be run in stand-alone mode or default integrated mode during the install. Running it in stand-alone mode ahead of the time will help to identify any issues early and remedy the situation before beginning the actual install, which saves time for the Basis administrator.

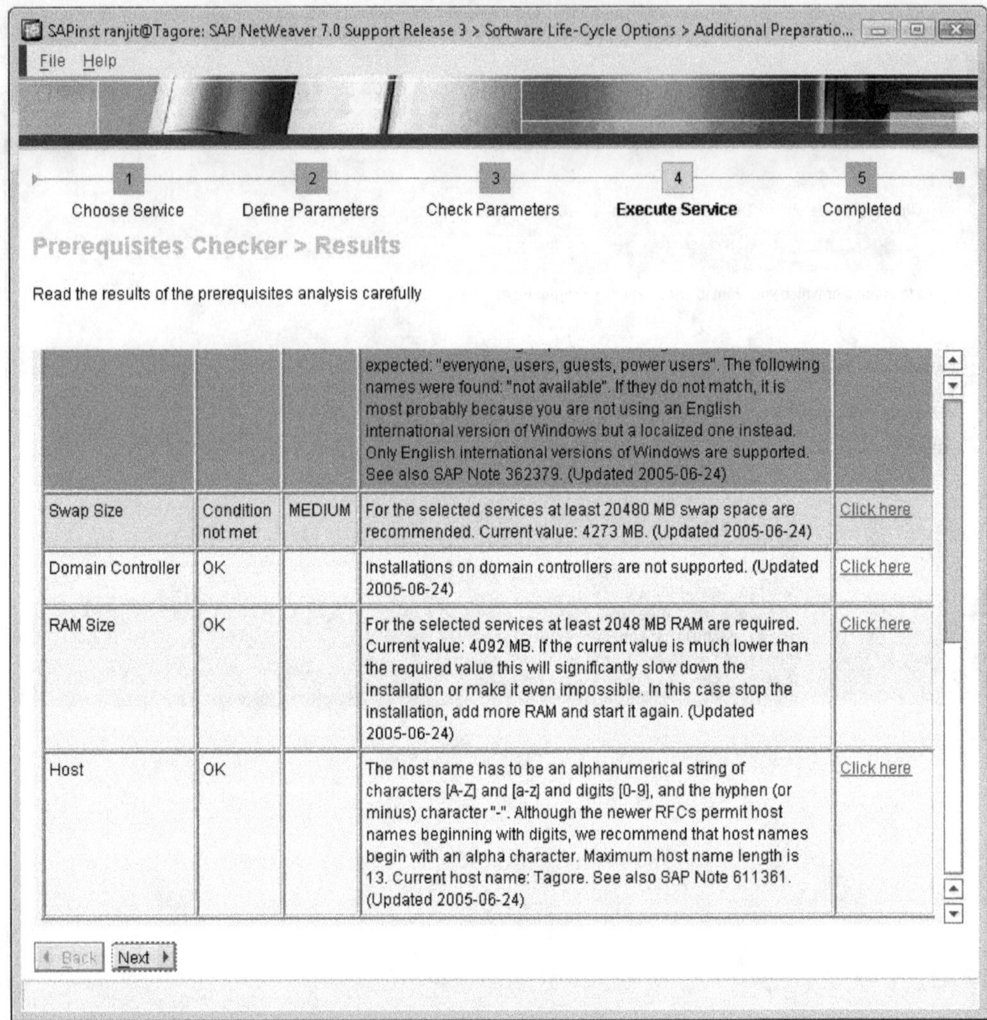

SAPinst ranjit@Tagore: SAP NetWeaver 7.0 Support Release 3 > Software Life-Cycle Options > Additional Preparatio...
File Help
1 Choose Service
2 Define Parameters
3 Check Parameters
4 Execute Service
5 Completed
Prerequisites Checker > Results
Read the results of the prerequisites analysis carefully
expected: "everyone, users, guests, power users". The following names were found: "not available". If they do not match, it is most probably because you are not using an English international version of Windows but a localized one instead. Only English international versions of Windows are supported. See also SAP Note 362379. (Updated 2005-06-24)
Swap Size
Condition not met
MEDIUM
For the selected services at least 20480 MB swap space are recommended. Current value: 4273 MB. (Updated 2005-06-24)
Click here
Domain Controller
OK
Installations on domain controllers are not supported. (Updated 2005-06-24)
Click here
RAM Size
OK
For the selected services at least 2048 MB RAM are required. Current value: 4092 MB. If the current value is much lower than the required value this will significantly slow down the installation or make it even impossible. In this case stop the installation, add more RAM and start it again. (Updated 2005-06-24)
Click here
Host
OK
The host name has to be an alphanumerical string of characters [A-Z] and [a-z] and digits [0-9], and the hyphen (or minus) character "-". Although the newer RFCs permit host names beginning with digits, we recommend that host names begin with an alpha character. Maximum host name length is 13. Current host name: Tagore. See also SAP Note 611361. (Updated 2005-06-24)
Click here
Back
Next

FIGURE 6-6 Prerequisite Checker results screen

Detailed ABAP Stack Installation (NW 7.0 ABAP Installation)

In this section of the chapter, the procedure for performing an NW 7.0 EhP1 ABAP stack installation is described in detail. It includes a number of illustrations and figures to aid in your understanding.

Installation Media

The following list of installation media is needed for a NW 7.0 EHP1 ABAP installation:

- SAP EHP1 for SAP NetWeaver 7.0 installation master DVD
- SAP EHP1 for SAP NetWeaver 7.0 installation export DVD
- SAP EHP1 for SAP NetWeaver 7.0 UC kernel for NW 7.01
- Oracle Database 10.2 and Client 10.2 software

Setting Up the Environmental Variables for the SAP Install

Begin the installation process by logging in as root and setting up the following environmental variables if you use Bourne and bash shells:

```
export JAVA_HOME=/opt/java1.4
export TEMP=/oracle/<SID>/sapreorg
export DISPLAY=<IP Address of your PC>:0.0
```

If you are using a csh (c shell), then the environmental variables are set using the following commands:

```
setenv JAVA_HOME  /opt/java1.4
setenv TEMP  /oracle/<SID>/sapreorg
setenv DISPLAY  <IP Address of your PC>:0.0
```

If the environmental variable TEMP is not set, the SAPinst tool will create an installation directory sapinst_instdir below the /tmp directory. Since installation logs and traces are important, it is recommended to change the default location of the installation directory files from /tmp to your chosen directory. In the previous example, TEMP is set to point to the /oracle<SID>/sapreorg directory. At least 300MB of free disk space should be allocated for the file system where TEMP is pointing and it should have 777 file permissions. The JAVA_HOME environmental variable should be set as per your company's Java installation path. The above path is given only as an example.

Starting SAP Installation with SAPinst

For SAP installations in UNIX environments, usually a client X terminal software such as WRQ Reflection X or Hummingbird Exceed is used to perform the installs. The preceding environmental variables should be set up after logging in as root to start the SAP system install. The SAPinst tool is called by executing the following command (./sapinst) from the installation master DVD. The following example is for a Linux operating system.

```
cd to the Installation Master DVD directory /downloads/SAP_DVD/
Installation_Master/Inst._Mast._7.01__NW_ERP_CRM_SRM_SCM/IM_UX_X86_64
root@ IM_UX_X86_64]#. /sapinst
```

When SAPinst is executed and started, it will start the GUI server and SAPinst GUI. The SAPinst GUI connects to the GUI server via a secure connection, which in turn connects to SAPinst. By default, GUI server uses port number 21212 and SAPinst uses port number 21200. If these port numbers are already taken by any other application, then it is possible to set a parameter in SAPinst to provide alternative port numbers. SAPinst can be executed with the following parameters:

```
./sapinst  SAPINST_DIALOG_PORT=<free_port_number_sapinst_to_gui_server>
Example: ./sapinst  SAPINST_DIALOG_PORT=  21218
./sapinst  GUISERVER_DIALOG_PORT=<free_port_number_gui_server_to_sapinst_gui>
Example: ./sapinst  GUISERVER_DIALOG_PORT =  21217
./sapinst -p  provides a complete list of parameters that are available for
sapinst.
```

This will launch the SAP installation tool. Figure 6-7 shows the initial screen of the SAP installation.

Phases of SAP Installation

SAP installation can be broken down into the following five distinct phases.

Choose Option

During this phase of the SAP installation, choose the SAP software option that you want to install using SAPinst.

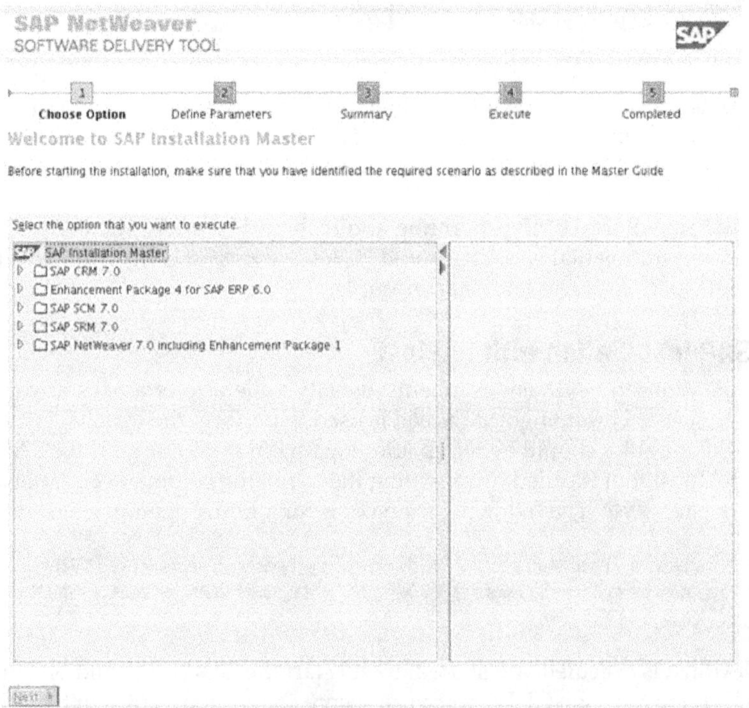

FIGURE 6-7 SAPinst initial screen

Define Parameters

During this phase of the SAP installation, choose the parameters required to perform a SAP installation. Detailed images of the parameters are provided later.

Summary

During this phase of the SAP installation, SAPinst provides a summary of all the installation parameters entered and will provide one final review and revise option before executing the install.

Execute

During this phase, SAPinst executes the selected option. This is the longest phase of the SAP installation.

Completed

This phase marks the completion of the SAP installation by SAPinst. Choosing the Typical install option means that minimal input is needed during the define parameter phase of the install, which simplifies the installation process. For most installations, this option is sufficient.

As shown in Figure 6-8, select a SAP system identifier (SID) and choose the Unicode system option. This SID will uniquely identify a SAP system in the landscape.

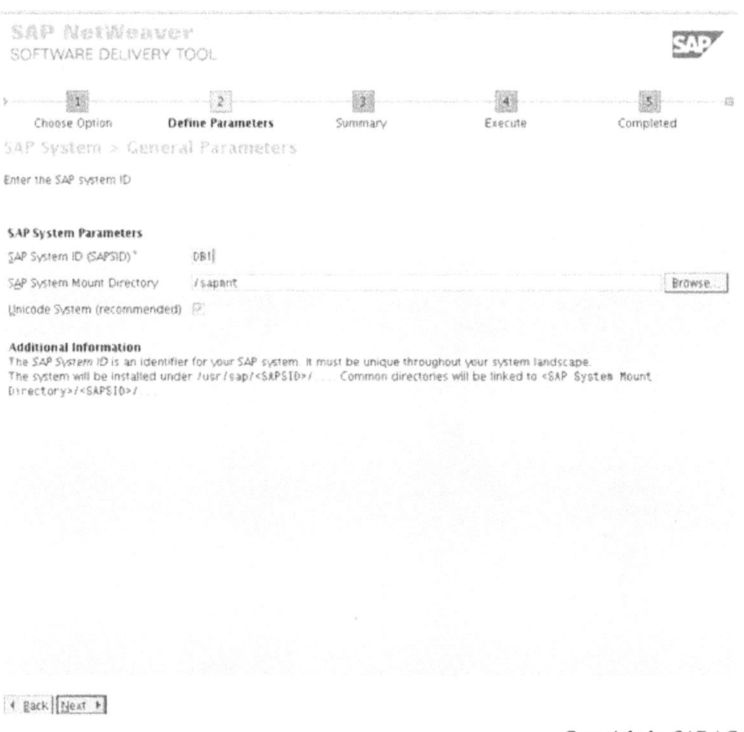

FIGURE 6-8 SAPinst parameter for choosing a SAP SID

SAP NetWeaver
SOFTWARE DELIVERY TOOL

SAP

1 Choose Option 2 Define Parameters 3 Summary 4 Execute 5 Completed

Parameter Summary

Choose 'Next' to start with the values shown. Otherwise, select the parameters you want to change and choose 'Revise'. If you change a parameter with 'Revise', the installer takes you to the screen where you can change the parameter. Depending on the changes, the installer might guide you through other screens that it has so far processed.

Database Statistics
Create statistics at the end of the import

SAP System > Central Instance
Central Instance Number
00

SAP System > Central Instance
ABAP Message Server Port
3600
Internal ABAP Message Server Port
3900

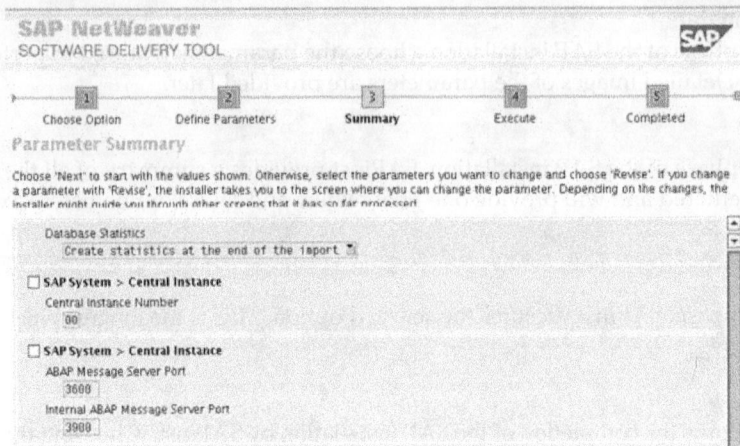

FIGURE 6-9 SAPinst parameter summary screen

In the subsequent two to three screens (not shown), SAPinst will prompt for the path to the installation media of the SAP and Oracle client software. You should enter the full path to the downloaded installation media. After clicking Next, SAPinst will check the software and will present an error if it cannot access or read the downloaded software.

After the summary screen shown in Figure 6-9 is validated and you click Next, SAPinst will request a Solution Manager key. This is mandatory, and the install will not proceed until the SAP Solution Manager key is provided. Please follow the procedure explained in the SAP OSS Note 811923 - Generating the SAP Solution Manager Key.

After verifying the Solution Manager key, SAPinst will start executing the install steps.

As shown in Figure 6-10, SAPinst executes the install steps, such as creating the SAP database using underlying Oracle tools and loading SAP-relevant data, configuring Oracle Database networking so that the SAP application will talk to the database, and starting the SAP instance.

The screen shown validates that SAPinst has successfully executed the chosen SAP installation option.

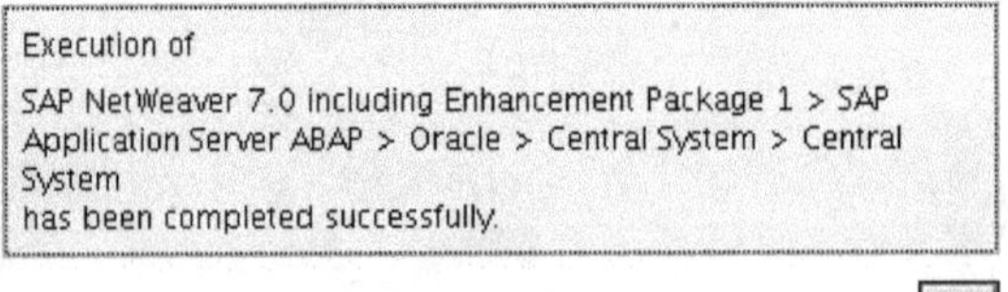

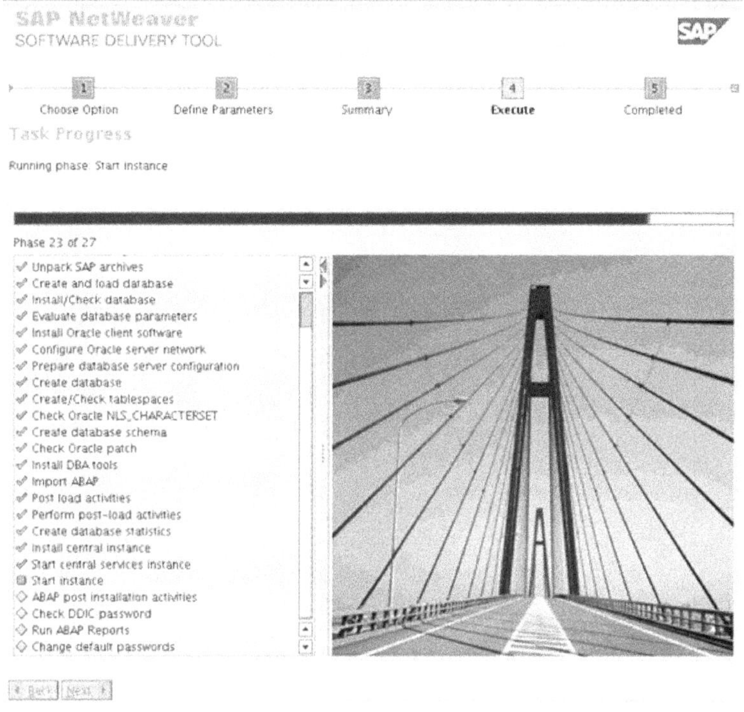

FIGURE 6-10 SAPinst executing the Start SAP Instance step

Detailed Java Stack Installation (BI 7.0 Java Installation)

The following detailed procedure shows the installation of the SAP Java stack. In this procedure, the Custom install option is chosen to demonstrate the difference between the typical install option chosen for an ABAP install. The Custom install option will prompt for more parameter input when executing the installation.

AS Java, BI Java, EP Core, and EP usage types are chosen for the installation of the BI Java system.

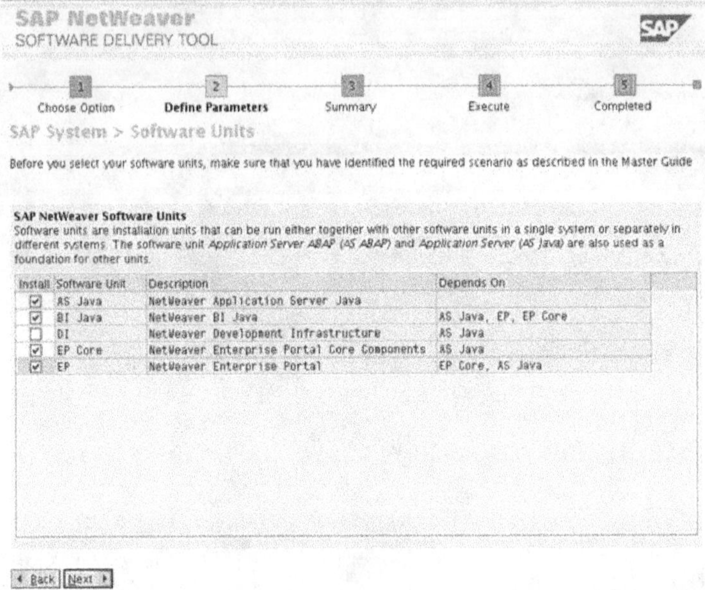

Copyright by SAP AG

1. As shown in the next illustration SAP SID parameters and the mount directory are provided to SAPinst.

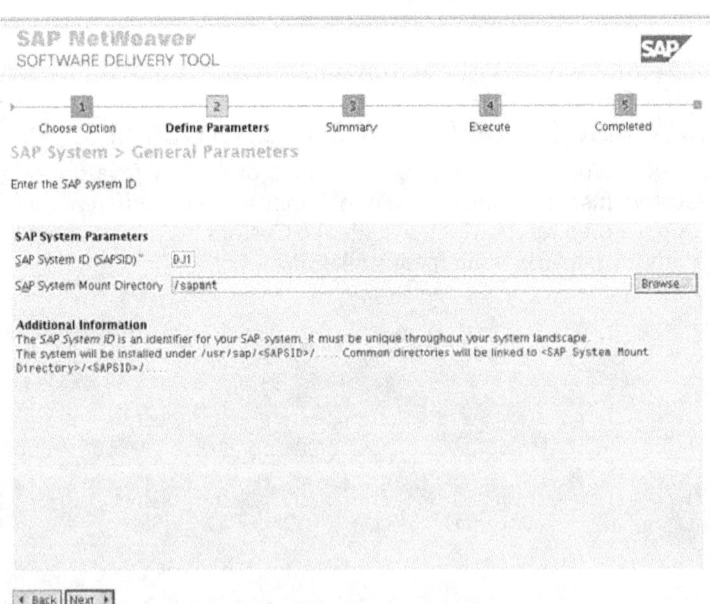

Copyright by SAP AG

2. Next, the master password and user account passwords are entered.
3. Then the Oracle Listener name and network port number are entered in the SAPinst. These are used to arrange the Oracle network configuration.

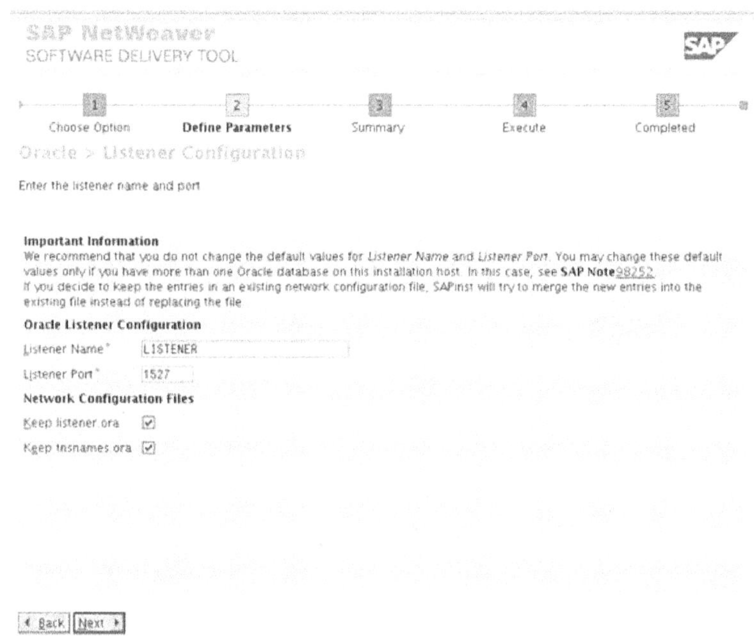

Copyright by SAP AG

4. Next, a key phrase is chosen for the secure store.

5. As the next illustration shows, database statistics are scheduled to be executed as part of the installation procedure.

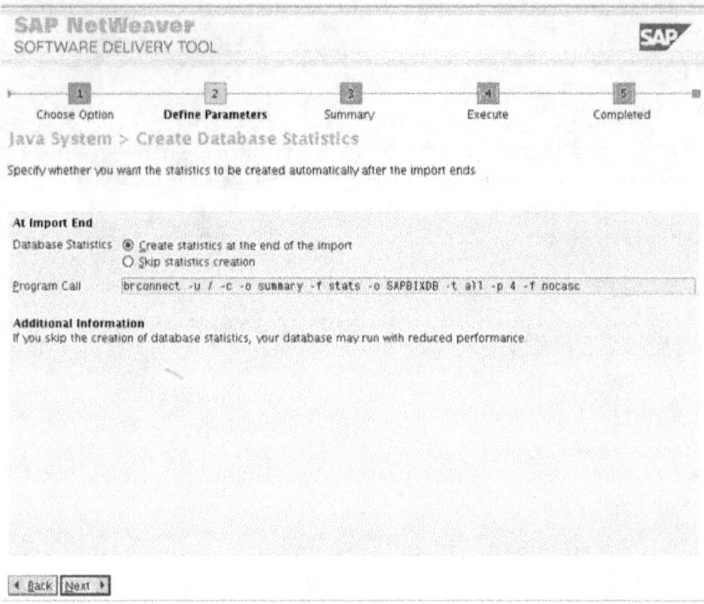

Copyright by SAP AG

6. System numbers for the central instance and SCS instance of the BI Java stack are provided to the SAPinst.

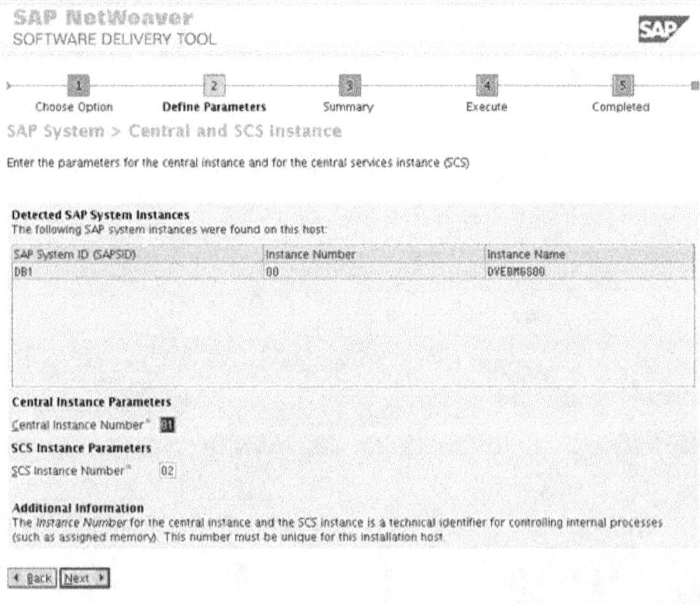

Copyright by SAP AG

7. The storage location of the user master accounts is entered in the SAPinst UME configuration option.

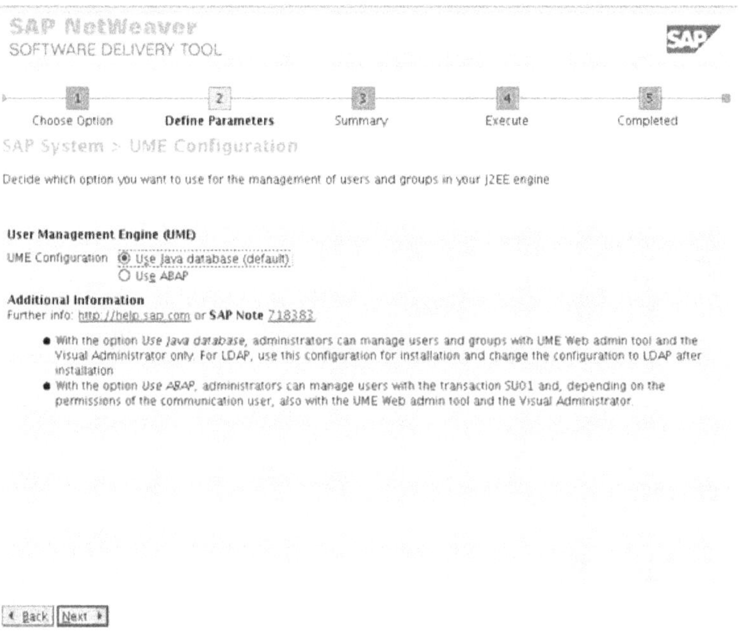

SAP NetWeaver
SOFTWARE DELIVERY TOOL
Choose Option
Define Parameters
Summary
Execute
Completed
SAP System > UME Configuration
Decide which option you want to use for the management of users and groups in your J2EE engine
User Management Engine (UME)
UME Configuration
Use Java database (default)
Use ABAP
Additional Information
Further info: http://help.sap.com or SAP Note 718383
With the option Use Java database, administrators can manage users and groups with UME Web admin tool and the Visual Administrator only. For LDAP, use this configuration for installation and change the configuration to LDAP after installation
With the option Use ABAP, administrators can manage users with the transaction SU01 and, depending on the permissions of the communication user, also with the UME Web admin tool and the Visual Administrator.
Back
Next

Copyright by SAP AG

8. Then passwords for the administrator account and user accounts are chosen in the SAPinst.

9. The SAP database-dependent and database-independent kernel archives are selected to be unpacked.

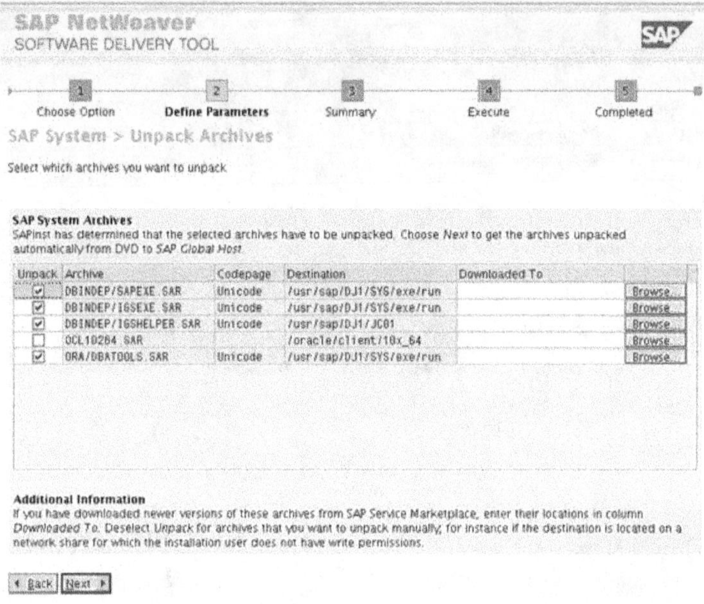

10. As shown in the illustration, the current installation is chosen to be registered in an existing central System Landscape Directory (SLD).

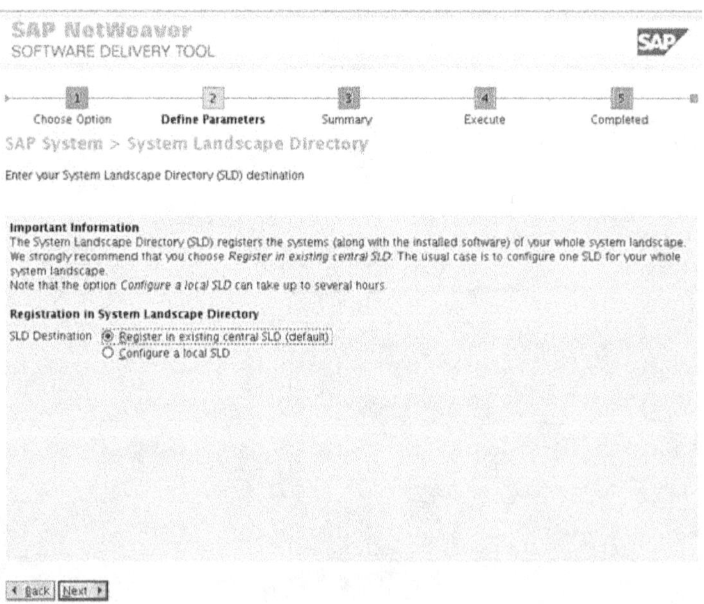

11. Next, a user account for the Solution Manager Diagnostic Agent is confirmed in the SAPinst.

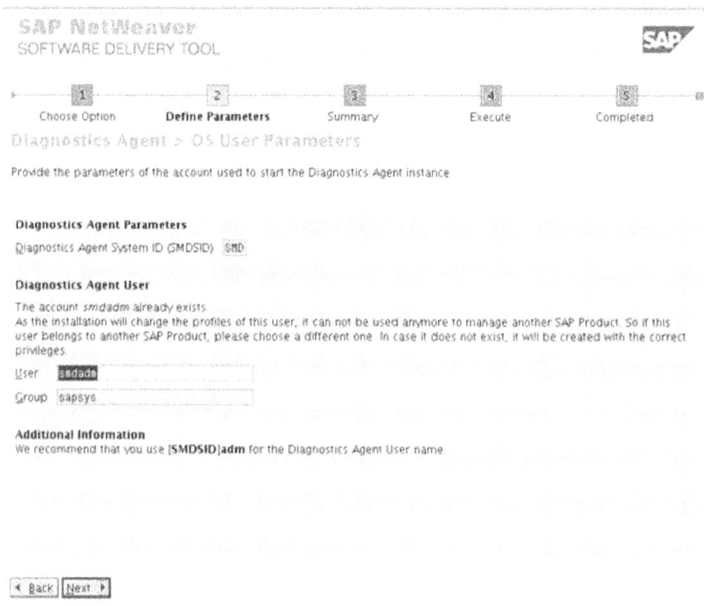

Copyright by SAP AG

12. A summary of all the entered parameters is presented for review and revision, as shown. After this is confirmed, click Next and the install will execute and be completed.

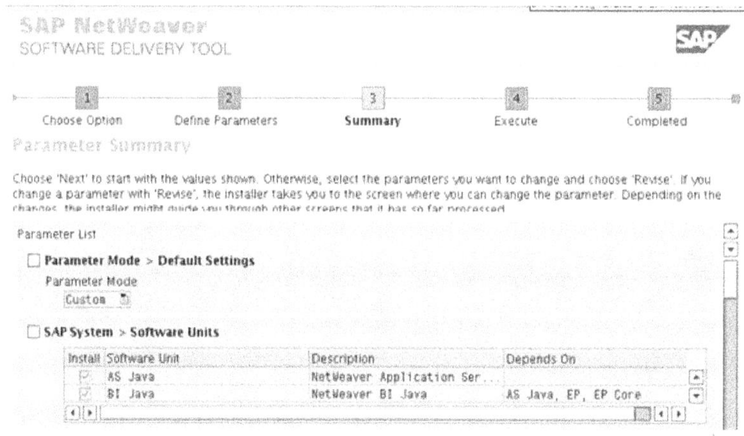

Copyright by SAP AG

13. As SAPinst is executing, the install steps will be marked off as complete.

14. The create database step of the install creates the SAP-customized Oracle Database and then loads data into it.

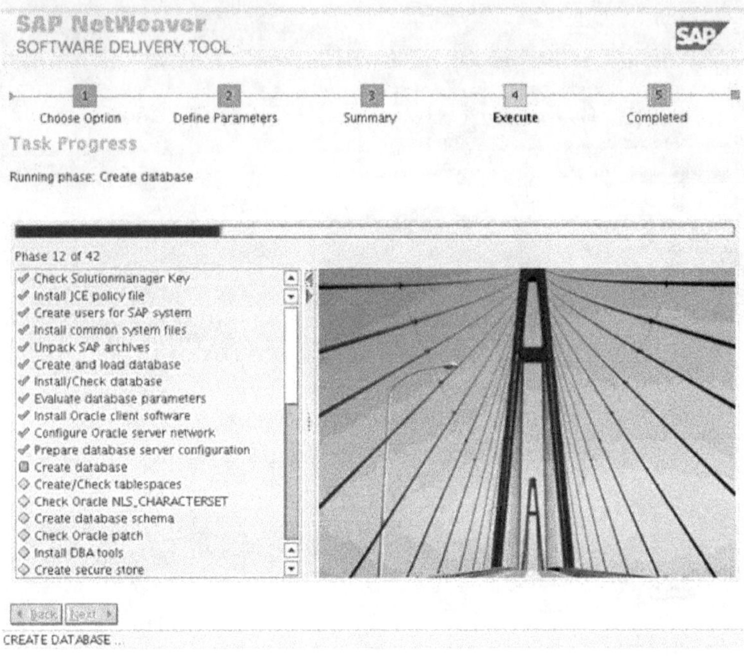

Copyright by SAP AG

15. Once SAPinst completes all the installation steps successfully, a message is shown confirming this.

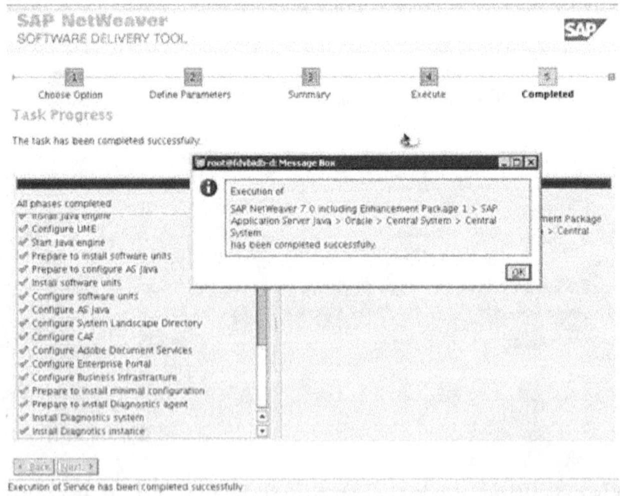

Copyright by SAP AG

SAP Installation Issue Category	Root Cause	Remedial Action
Disk Usage	One of the SAP file systems become completely full, causing the installation to stop because it could not write the files to the disk anymore.	Use operating system–specific disk usage commands, such as bdf, df, or du, to check the disk usage and add more space if any of the SAP install–relevant directories are full.
Memory Utilization	If memory utilization of the system reaches 100 percent, this causes either the system or a particular process to not start and the installation fails.	Provide the additional memory needed to start the SAP instance or the failing process and successfully complete the installation.
Network	SAP installs can fail because certain ports needed for SAP services are taken by other applications running on the same host. Incorrect network configuration.	The network ports needed for SAP systems should not be occupied by other applications. If they are used, this can be detected using the netstat command and the network ports released. Network configuration issues such as TCP/IP configuration, incorrect hostname, and IP address resolution have to be resolved.
Media	Sometimes the downloaded software or the media is corrupted.	Download the software again or order additional media as required.

Table 6-1 Typical SAP Installation Issues

Troubleshooting SAP Installation Issues

SAP installation can fail due to several reasons. The most common reasons for failure are listed in Table 6-1 along with the remedial actions that can be taken.

This list is not comprehensive; rather, as stated, it identifies the most common issues encountered during a typical SAP installation.

Restarting Failed SAP Installs

After fixing the installation issue, we can restart the install by calling the SAPinst again and choosing the Continue With The Old Option option.

Uninstalling SAP Software

SAP software can be uninstalled by choosing the relevant option from the software lifecycle menu of the SAPinst, as shown in Figure 6-11.

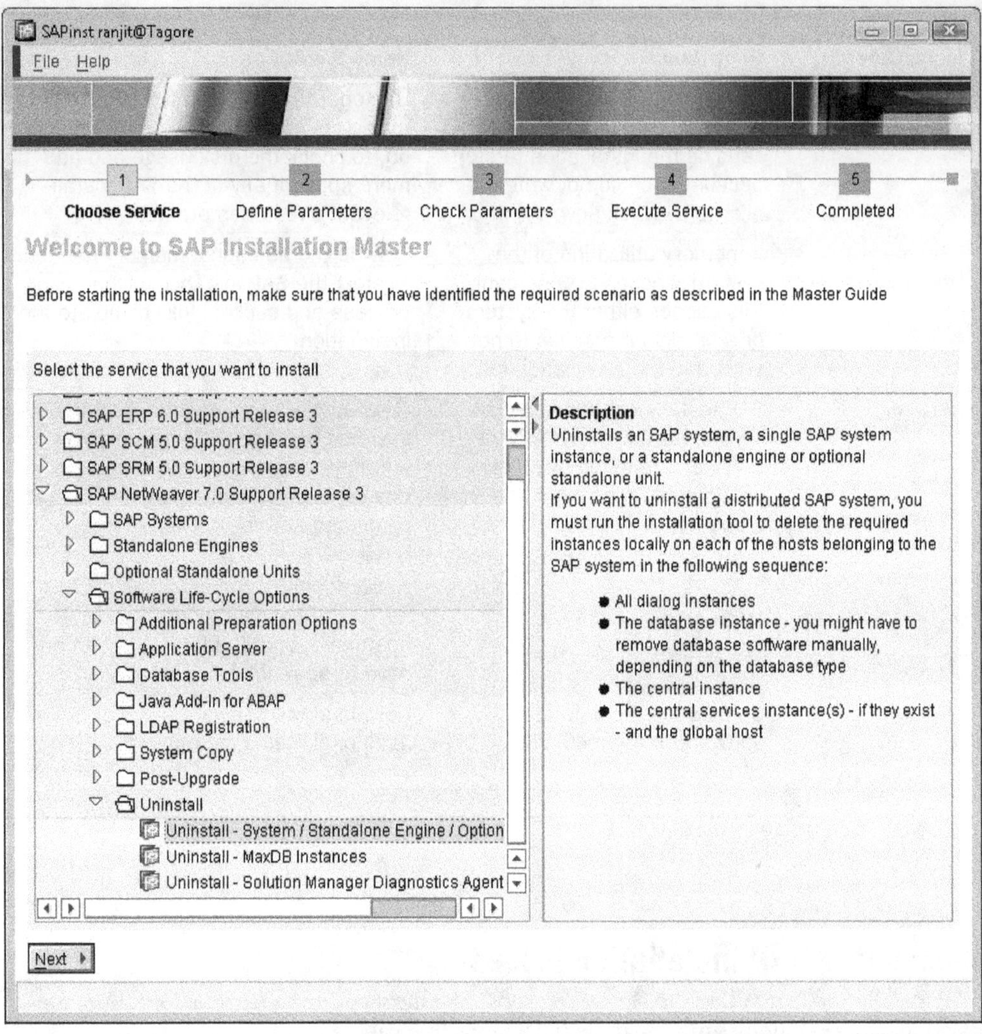

Figure 6-11 SAPinst SAP Software Uninstall option

Summary

- The SAPinst tool is used to install the SAP software solutions.
- The Oracle Universal Installer (OUI) tool is used to install Oracle Database software.
- SAP NW 7 install options include central, distributed, and high availability.
- SAP NW 7.1 install options include standard, distributed, and high availability.

- SAP solutions are installed as a single-stack, dual-stack, or a separated stack systems.
- SAP provides a Prerequisite Checker to verify the install requirements and compatibility.
- Installation media can be downloaded from the SAP Portal (SAP Service Marketplace) on demand.
- Installation media can also be ordered and shipped to the organization's data center site.
- SAPinst includes five phases for SAP software installation: choose service, define parameters, check parameters, summary and completed.
- Failed SAP installations can be restarted from where they failed after fixing the root cause of the problem.
- SAPinst can uninstall the SAP software if it is no longer needed and has to be removed from the server.

Additional Resources

- **SAP Software Distribution Center** https://service.sap.com/swdc
- **SAP Installation Tool - Features in Detail** www.sdn.sap.com/irj/sdn/installation?rid=/library/uuid/605aa73c-4164-2a10-fca6-b33e877fca19
- **SAP NetWeaver Installation Guides** https://service.sap.com/installnw70
- **SAP NetWeaver 7.0 general information** www.sdn.sap.com/irj/sdn/nw-70

- [illegible]

[illegible] Resources

- SAP NetWeaver 7.0 [illegible] installation [illegible]

CHAPTER

SAP ABAP and Java Stack Post-installation

In this chapter we will cover the post-installation steps that are performed for both ABAP and Java stack installations. With the addition of Java stack, dual-stack installation options, and enhancement packages, the time required to perform post-installation activities has increased significantly. It takes as much time to perform the post-installation tasks as it does to perform the actual install. ABAP and Java support package application and post-install configuration activities are the most time-consuming steps in the post-installation activities. Other post-installation activities include basic login checks at the application and operating system levels, initializing the SAP transport management system, setting up an initial printer, performing client copies, setting up online help, upgrading kernels, installing the permanent SAP license and any add-on packages, running ABAP load generation, and some initial performance tuning. After all the post-installation activities are completed, a complete offline backup should be performed.

ABAP Stack Post-installation Steps

The ABAP stack is accessed with the SAPGUI front-end tool, which can be called directly or from the SAPLogon program. The SAPGUI and SAPLogon programs are installed as part of SAP front-end installation. The SAPGUI tool allows you to connect to an individual SAP system, and SAPLogon allows you to configure connections to multiple SAP back-end systems. In the SAPLogon screen you can create a connection to the newly installed back-end SAP system by clicking the New Item button; entering the fully qualified hostname or IP address, system identifier, and system number; and clicking the Finish button, as shown in Figure 7-1.

After the entries are done, you can connect to the back-end system by double-clicking the newly entered system or by selecting the newly created system and clicking the Log On button as shown in Figure 7-2.

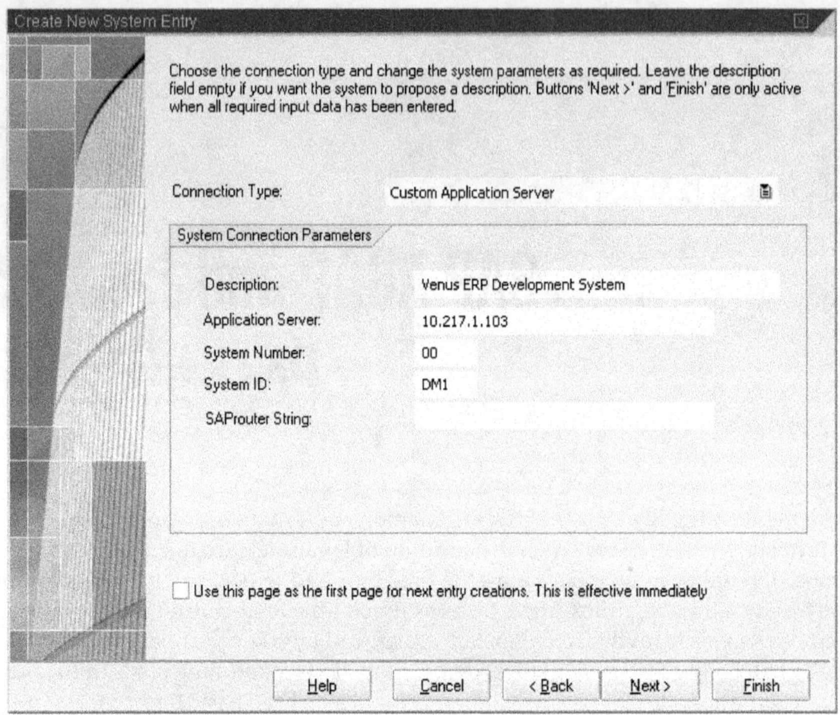

FIGURE 7-1 SAPLogon New Item properties screen

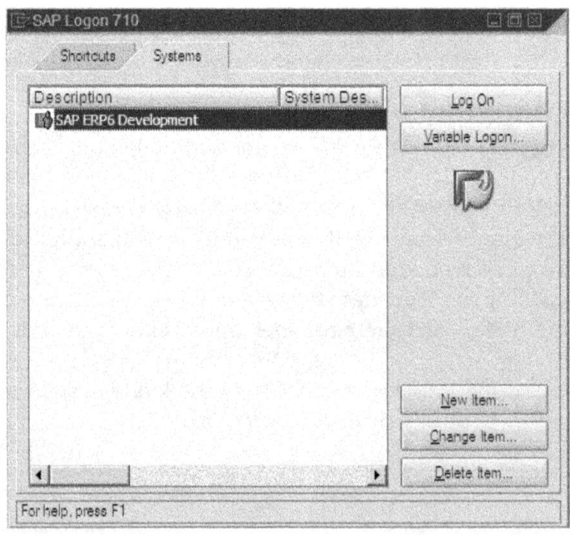

FIGURE 7-2 SAPLogon screen with one back-end entry

Client Number	Client Purpose	User Account	Default Password
000	SAP Reference Client	SAP*, DDIC	Master password chosen at install time
001	SAP Sample Client	SAP*, DDIC	Master password chosen at install time
066	Early Watch Service Client	EARLYWATCH	support
066	Early Watch Service Client	SAP*, DDIC	06071992

TABLE 7-1 SAP Standard Clients and Default Passwords

Most of the ABAP post-installation activities are done from the SAPGUI, and some activities, such as kernel upgrade, are done at the operating system level. When logging on to the system for the first time, SAPGUI will ask for a client number, user ID, and a password. A client in the SAP system is defined as a self-contained legal entity and data environment with its own set of master data and tables. Since the concept of a client and its administration activities are so important, Chapter 10 is devoted to this topic. SAP delivers default user accounts and clients with the standard SAP ABAP installation. The password for the default accounts was chosen during the time of the installation in the master password selection screen. Table 7-1 lists the SAP standard delivered clients and SAP standard user accounts.

Login Checks

Login checks should be done at the application level as well as at the operating system level. The goal of the login checks is to make sure that there are no errors or any serious warning messages after a new installation. If there are any issues, then they have to be corrected immediately. If necessary, log an online message with SAP support to get help in resolving the issue.

Login Checks at the Operating System Level

Log in at the operating system level as <SID>adm, and verify the start and shutdown of the recently installed SAP system. System startup and shutdown procedures have been discussed in detail in the earlier chapters of the book. As <SID>adm, verify that all SAP processes are up.

This can be verified by issuing the ps -ef | grep <SID>adm command. This will show all the SAP processes at the OS level.

As ora<SID>, verify that the the database is up and that Oracle processes are running by executing the following command:

```
orakb1> ps -ef | grep ora_
```

The output of the command should show that all Oracle processes are running.

```
orakb1    18976    Nov01        00:00:03 ora_pmon_KB1
orakb1    18978    Nov01        00:00:02 ora_psp0_KB1
orakb1    18980    Nov01        00:00:03 ora_mman_KB1
orakb1    18982    Nov01        00:02:06 ora_dbw0_KB1
orakb1    18984    Nov01        00:01:57 ora_lgwr_KB1
orakb1    18986    Nov01        00:00:25 ora_ckpt_KB1
orakb1    18988    Nov01        00:00:53 ora_smon_KB1
orakb1    18990    Nov01        00:00:00 ora_reco_KB1
orakb1    18992    Nov01        00:00:13 ora_cjq0_KB1
orakb1    18994    Nov01        00:00:02 ora_mmon_KB1
orakb1    18996    Nov01        00:00:06 ora_mmnl_KB1
orakb1    19000    Nov01        00:00:26 ora_arc0_KB1
orakb1    19002    Nov01        00:00:19 ora_arc1_KB1
orakb1    19006    Nov01        00:00:00 ora_qmnc_KB1
orakb1    19068    Nov01        00:00:00 ora_q000_KB1
```

Once you have verified that the SAP processes and Oracle processes are running properly, also verify that the Oracle Listener service is running properly. This is critical in the Oracle Database systems. As ora<SID>, verify that Listener is up and running by executing the following command. The output of the command shows that the Listener is up and listening for incoming database connections at port 1527.

```
orakb1> lsnrctl status
LSNRCTL for UNIX: Version 10.2.0.4.0
Copyright (c) 1991, 2007, Oracle.  All rights reserved.
Connecting to (ADDRESS= (PROTOCOL=IPC)(KEY=KB1.WORLD))
STATUS of the LISTENER
------------------------
Alias                     LISTENER
Version                   TNSLSNR for UNIX: Version 10.2.0.4.0
Start Date                11-SEP-2009 17:47:58
Uptime                    57 days 23 hr. 16 min. 50 sec
Trace Level               off
Security                  ON: Local OS Authentication
SNMP                      OFF
Listener Parameter File   /oracle/KB1/102_64/network/admin/listener.ora
Listener Log File         /oracle/KB1/102_64/network/log/listener.log
Listening Endpoints Summary...
  (DESCRIPTION=(ADDRESS=(PROTOCOL=ipc)(KEY=KB1.WORLD)))
  (DESCRIPTION=(ADDRESS=(PROTOCOL=ipc)(KEY=KB1)))
  (DESCRIPTION=(ADDRESS=(PROTOCOL=tcp)(HOST=venus)(PORT=1527)))
Services Summary...
Service "KB1" has 1 instance(s).
  Instance "KB1", status UNKNOWN, has 1 handler(s) for this service...
The command completed successfully
```

Login Checks at the Application Level

Log in to the newly installed SAP system using client number 000 and the DDIC user account. Once you log in to the system, execute the following transactions to check the

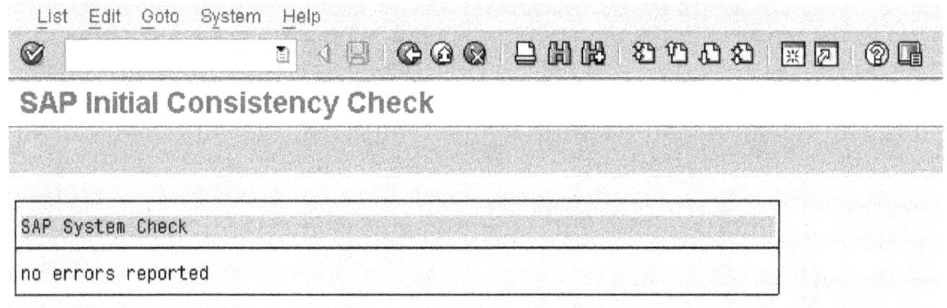

FIGURE 7-3 Checking SAP initial consistency

health of the newly installed system. Execute transaction SM28 or SICK to check the initial consistency of the system. Transaction execution should return the screen in Figure 7-3 showing that no errors are reported.

Next check the availability of the SAP server(s) that was newly installed with all the services, such as dialog, batch, update, enqueue, spool, ICM, and J2EE, by executing the transaction SM51 as shown in Figure 7-4. The output of the transaction should show that the server status is active with all the installed services.

Double-click the server name or execute transaction SM50 to verify that the status of the work processes is waiting, as shown in Figure 7-5, and there are no issues with the availability of the same. In some instances, such as kernel patch errors, there could be issues with the availability of the work processes; however, applying the newer kernel patch fixes usually takes care of the issue.

Once you have verified that you are able to log in to the system and confirm that the server has been installed correctly and all the core services are running properly, the next step is to check if there are any ABAP runtime errors in the newly installed system by executing the ABAP runtime analysis transaction code ST22. The output of the transaction in Figure 7-6 will show if there are any serious ABAP dumps in the newly installed system. Occasionally, there will be several serious ABAP dumps in a newly installed system. The ABAP dumps are usually because of a known error, such as bad system configuration or source code issues. Applying a support package patch usually resolves any issue.

SAP Servers

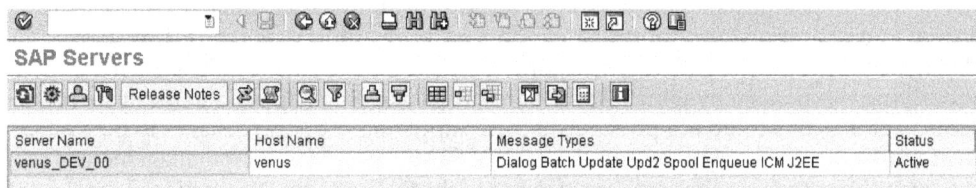

Release Notes

Server Name	Host Name	Message Types	Status
venus_DEV_00	venus	Dialog Batch Update Upd2 Spool Enqueue ICM J2EE	Active

FIGURE 7-4 Checking the SAP server list and available services

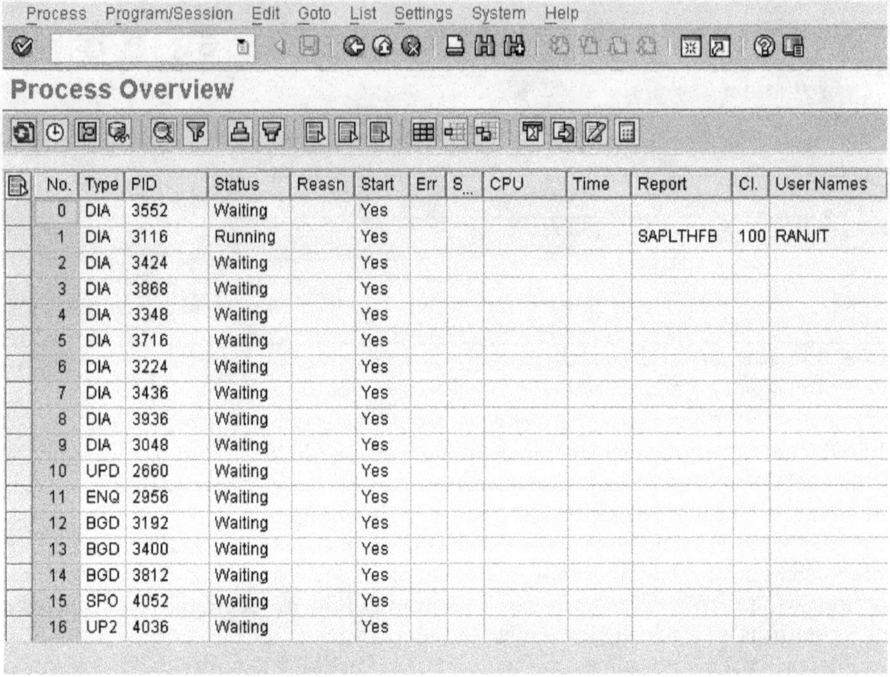

Process Program/Session Edit Goto List Settings System Help

Process Overview

No.	Type	PID	Status	Reasn	Start	Err	S...	CPU	Time	Report	Cl.	User Names
0	DIA	3552	Waiting		Yes							
1	DIA	3116	Running		Yes					SAPLTHFB	100	RANJIT
2	DIA	3424	Waiting		Yes							
3	DIA	3868	Waiting		Yes							
4	DIA	3348	Waiting		Yes							
5	DIA	3716	Waiting		Yes							
6	DIA	3224	Waiting		Yes							
7	DIA	3436	Waiting		Yes							
8	DIA	3936	Waiting		Yes							
9	DIA	3048	Waiting		Yes							
10	UPD	2660	Waiting		Yes							
11	ENQ	2956	Waiting		Yes							
12	BGD	3192	Waiting		Yes							
13	BGD	3400	Waiting		Yes							
14	BGD	3812	Waiting		Yes							
15	SPO	4052	Waiting		Yes							
16	UP2	4036	Waiting		Yes							

FIGURE 7-5 SAP server work process overview screen

The next transaction to verify proper system installation is SM21, which displays the system log. Study the system log particularly at the startup time of the newly installed system, as shown in Figure 7-7. The system log should show that the message server, gateway, and all the work processes started without errors and the initialization process is completed. This is a good indication that the newly installed system is installed properly and all the required services and processes started properly.

Initialize STMS

The next set of post-installation tasks involves setting up the basic transport management system in preparation for performing support package applications. SAP Transport Management System (STMS) helps in importing SAP objects, and also is used as an underlying mechanism by which ABAP support packages are applied to the system. Because of this, this setup is a prerequisite when applying support packages to the system. The following example shows a simple setup of STMS. Since transport management is so important for setting up the software logistics of the SAP systems, this topic will be covered in greater detail in Chapter 11. The following steps should be performed to set up basic STMS in the newly created SAP system. Execute transaction code SE06, and

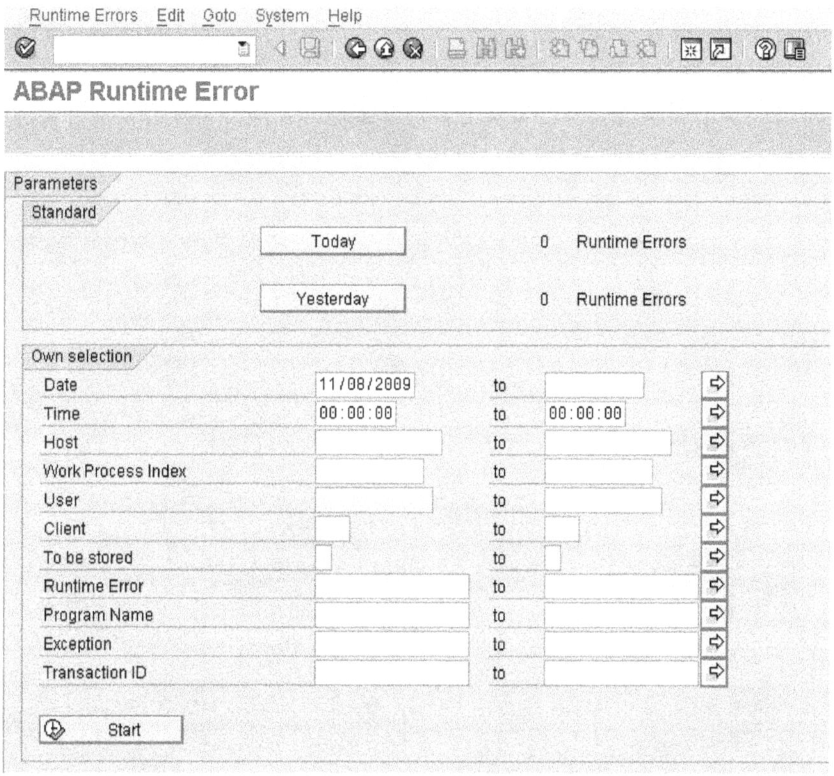

Figure 7-6 ABAP dump analysis

after verifying that the Standard Installation option is selected, click the Perform Post-installation Actions button.

This will perform the post-installation steps for Transport Organizer and prompt for Correction and Transport System (CTS)—an old name for STMS. Click Yes.

This completes the post-installation preparatory steps before configuring STMS. The system shows the following message: Processing after installation completed, configure TMS.

The next step when initially configuring the transport setup is to execute transaction code STMS. When you enter the STMS transaction in client 000, you will notice the screen in Figure 7-8. Verify the transport domain name, and click the Save button.

When the Save button is clicked, a series of initial configuration steps, such as transport profile configuration, transport directory verification, and other transport-related activities, are performed in the system. More details of the STMS setup will be discussed in detail in Chapter 11. At the end of the configuration, the security credentials of the transport management user are entered in the secure storage area, as shown in Figure 7-9, and a message appears notifying you that you are logged on to the domain controller.

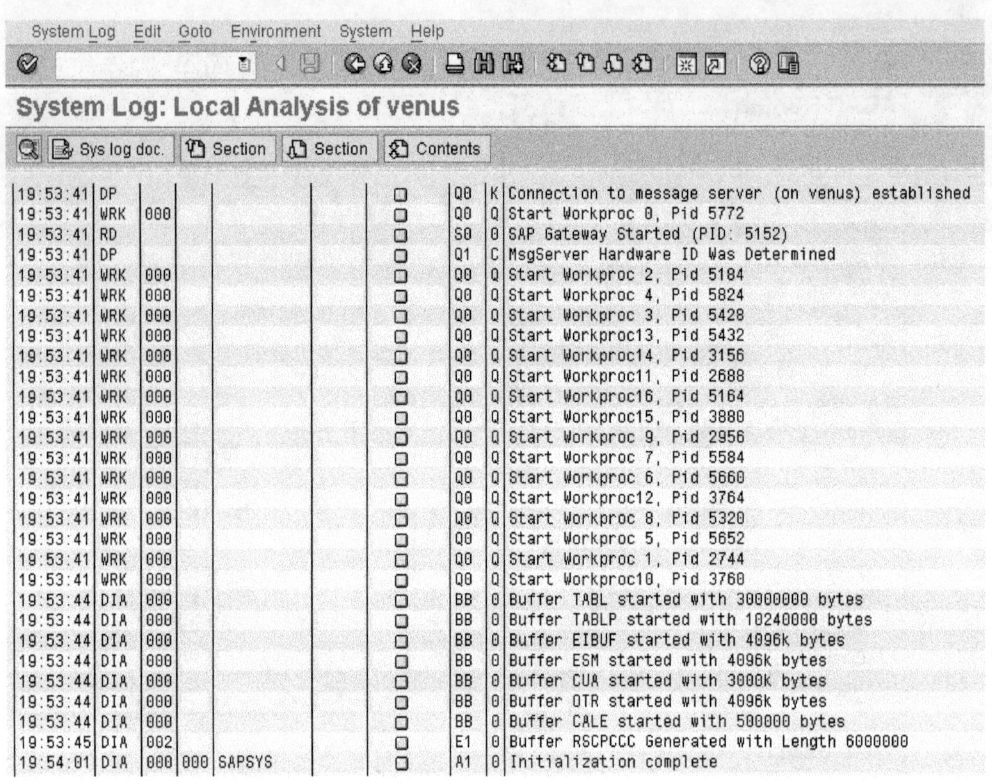

System Log Edit Goto Environment System Help
System Log: Local Analysis of venus
Sys log doc.
Section
Section
Contents
19:53:41 DP Q0 K Connection to message server (on venus) established
19:53:41 WRK 000 Q0 Q Start Workproc 0, Pid 5772
19:53:41 RD S0 0 SAP Gateway Started (PID: 5152)
19:53:41 DP Q1 C MsgServer Hardware ID Was Determined
19:53:41 WRK 000 Q0 Q Start Workproc 2, Pid 5184
19:53:41 WRK 000 Q0 Q Start Workproc 4, Pid 5824
19:53:41 WRK 000 Q0 Q Start Workproc 3, Pid 5428
19:53:41 WRK 000 Q0 Q Start Workproc13, Pid 5432
19:53:41 WRK 000 Q0 Q Start Workproc14, Pid 3156
19:53:41 WRK 000 Q0 Q Start Workproc11, Pid 2688
19:53:41 WRK 000 Q0 Q Start Workproc16, Pid 5164
19:53:41 WRK 000 Q0 Q Start Workproc15, Pid 3880
19:53:41 WRK 000 Q0 Q Start Workproc 9, Pid 2956
19:53:41 WRK 000 Q0 Q Start Workproc 7, Pid 5584
19:53:41 WRK 000 Q0 Q Start Workproc 6, Pid 5660
19:53:41 WRK 000 Q0 Q Start Workproc12, Pid 3764
19:53:41 WRK 000 Q0 Q Start Workproc 8, Pid 5320
19:53:41 WRK 000 Q0 Q Start Workproc 5, Pid 5652
19:53:41 WRK 000 Q0 Q Start Workproc 1, Pid 2744
19:53:41 WRK 000 Q0 Q Start Workproc10, Pid 3760
19:53:44 DIA 000 BB 0 Buffer TABL started with 30000000 bytes
19:53:44 DIA 000 BB 0 Buffer TABLP started with 10240000 bytes
19:53:44 DIA 000 BB 0 Buffer EIBUF started with 4096k bytes
19:53:44 DIA 000 BB 0 Buffer ESM started with 4096k bytes
19:53:44 DIA 000 BB 0 Buffer CUA started with 3000k bytes
19:53:44 DIA 000 BB 0 Buffer OTR started with 4096k bytes
19:53:44 DIA 000 BB 0 Buffer CALE started with 500000 bytes
19:53:45 DIA 002 E1 0 Buffer RSCPCCC Generated with Length 6000000
19:54:01 DIA 000 000 SAPSYS A1 0 Initialization complete

FIGURE 7-7 System log showing that the system start has no errors

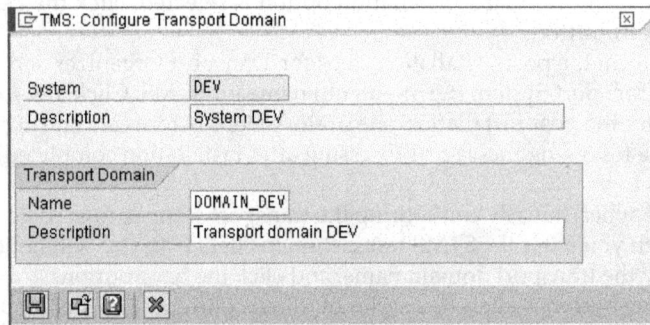

TMS: Configure Transport Domain

System	DEV
Description	System DEV

Transport Domain

Name	DOMAIN_DEV
Description	Transport domain DEV

FIGURE 7-8 Configuring the SAP transport domain in STMS

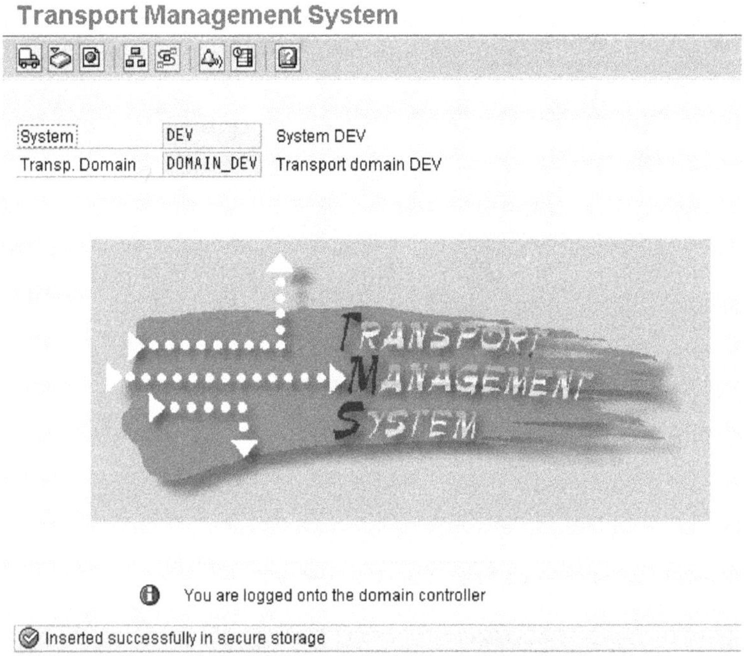

FIGURE 7-9 STMS initial configuration

ABAP Support Package Application

One of the most important post-installation tasks is applying ABAP support packages. ABAP support packages are bundles of source code corrections and bug fixes developed by SAP on an on-going basis, and are released to customers on a periodic basis. SAP releases the support packages as a stack, and they should be applied as such. The most current support package stack can be downloaded online from SAP Service Marketplace at http://service.sap.com/sp-stacks. ABAP support package stacks are downloaded as SAR files (SAP archive files) and use the transport mechanism setup noted earlier to import the source code corrections to the system. The following sections explain in detail the steps necessary to apply a support package.

Preparatory Phase

In the preparatory phase, SAR files are extracted by either uploading them from the front end or by manually extracting the SAR files placed in the /usr/sap/trans directory using the SAPCAR utility and uploading it from the application server. Since support package application generates lots of Oracle archive logs, it is recommended to turn off archiving during the course of the support package application. If support package application is done online, it is also recommended to turn off the maximum work process runtime parameter (rdisp/max_wprun_time) by entering the value **0**. This is a dynamic parameter and can be changed without restarting the SAP system. More details of SAP parameter changes will be discussed in Chapter 14.

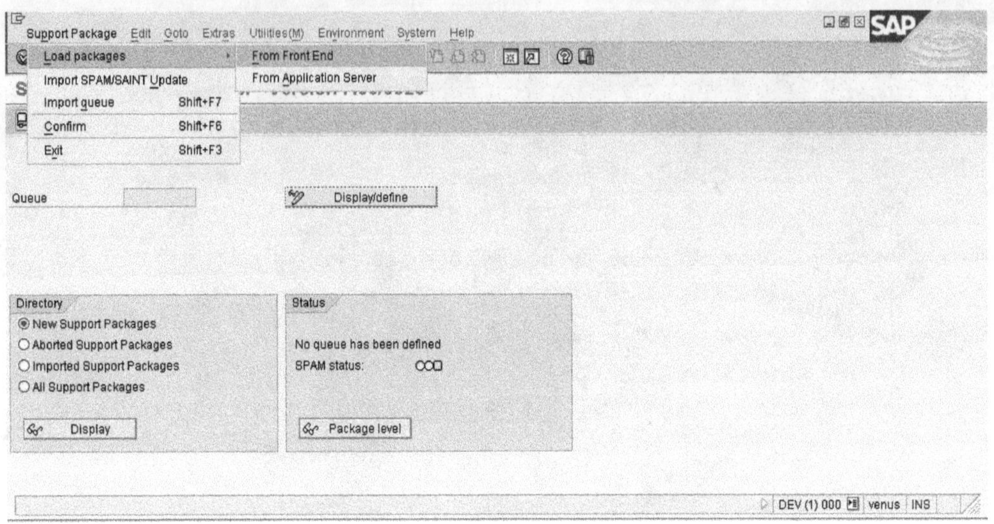

FIGURE 7-10 Loading SAP support packages from the front end

If there are few SAP support packages and they are small, they can be extracted easily using the menu path Support Package | Load Packages | From Front End option, as shown in Figure 7-10. This approach extracts the archive and places the files in the /usr/sap/trans/EPS/in directory. SAP Support Package Manager reads this directory for the application of any new support packages. It is recommended to log into client 000 with a user ID that has authorization similar to DDIC.

This will open a window requesting the location of the SAR files. Pointing the path to the location of the downloaded SAR files and clicking the Open button, as shown in Figure 7-11, will display the compressed files, which will be extracted when the Decompress button is clicked, as shown in Figure 7-12. The extracted files are transferred to the application server in the /usr/sap/trans/EPS/in directory. Once the files are extracted, they can be queued up in the Support Package Manager and imported into the system.

File successfully transferred, decompressed and then deleted indicates that the extraction has been completed successfully.

If there are several support packages and they are large, it is recommended to move the SAR files to the /usr/sap/trans directory of the SAP application server for extraction and loading. Figure 7-13 shows the location and extraction of a couple of SAP support package SAR file archives.

Once the archives are extracted, whether through the front end or through the application server, they are extracted to the Electronic Parcel Service (EPS) inbox at /usr/sap/trans/EPS/in directory. Once the files are extracted to the EPS inbox next step is to use the SPAM transaction menu path Support Package | Load Packages | From Application Server. This will show the confirm upload screen where you will click on Yes push button. This will result in the loading of the files from the application server as shown in Figure 7-14.

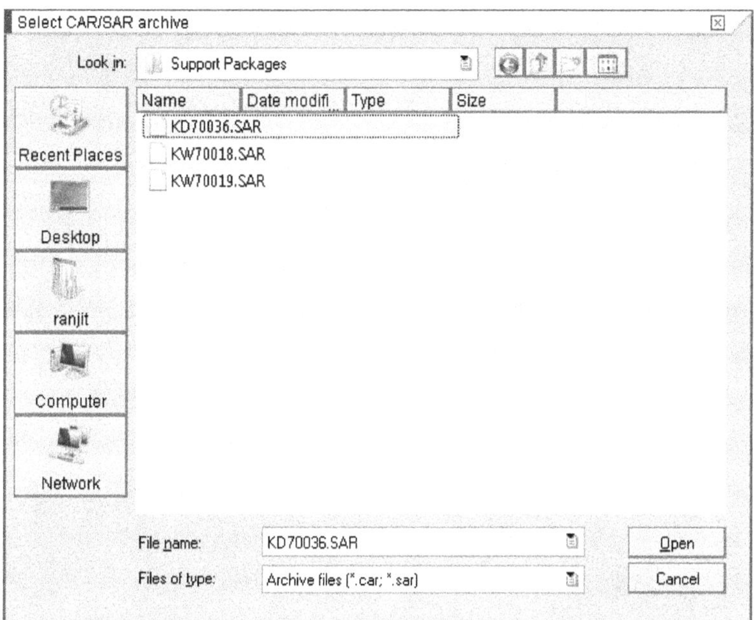

Copyright by SAP AG

FIGURE 7-11 SAP front end showing location to the downloaded SAR files

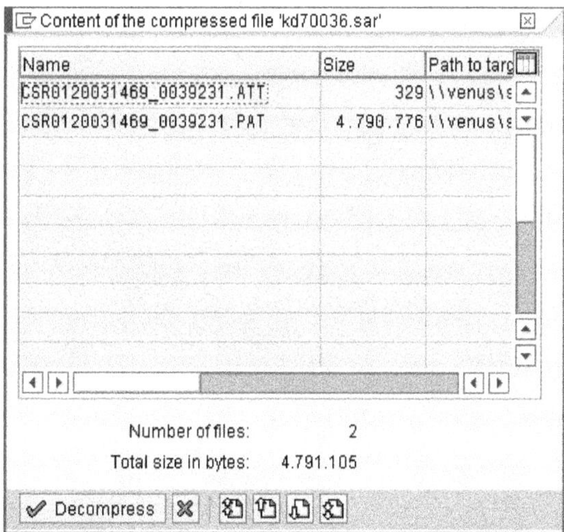

Copyright by SAP AG

FIGURE 7-12 Contents of the SAR files

```
C:\Windows\system32\cmd.exe

C:\usr\sap>cd trans

C:\usr\sap\trans>dir
 Volume in drive C has no label.
 Volume Serial Number is 40B4-6773

 Directory of C:\usr\sap\trans

11/08/2009  07:52 PM    <DIR>          .
11/08/2009  07:52 PM    <DIR>          ..
11/08/2009  06:33 PM    <DIR>          bin
03/21/2009  11:35 AM    <DIR>          buffer
03/21/2009  11:35 AM    <DIR>          cofiles
03/21/2009  11:35 AM    <DIR>          data
02/01/2009  11:38 PM    <DIR>          EPS
02/01/2009  11:38 PM    <DIR>          etc
11/08/2009  07:11 PM        31,577,391 KW70018.SAR
11/08/2009  07:14 PM        23,662,766 KW70019.SAR
11/08/2009  12:15 AM    <DIR>          log
04/29/2009  07:43 PM    <DIR>          sapnames
11/08/2009  07:28 PM    <DIR>          tmp
               2 File(s)     55,240,157 bytes
              11 Dir(s)  376,756,977,664 bytes free

C:\usr\sap\trans>SAPCAR -xvf KW70018.SAR
SAPCAR: processing archive KW70018.SAR (version 2.01)
x EPS/in/CSR0120031469_0029371.ATT
x EPS/in/CSR0120031469_0029371.PAT
x EPS/in/CSR0120031469_0031317.ATT
x EPS/in/CSR0120031469_0031317.PAT
SAPCAR: 4 file(s) extracted

C:\usr\sap\trans>SAPCAR -xvf KW70019.SAR
SAPCAR: processing archive KW70019.SAR (version 2.01)
x EPS/in/CSR0120031469_0032719.ATT
x EPS/in/CSR0120031469_0032719.PAT
SAPCAR: 2 file(s) extracted

C:\usr\sap\trans>_
```


FIGURE 7-13 Example using the SAPCAR -xvf command

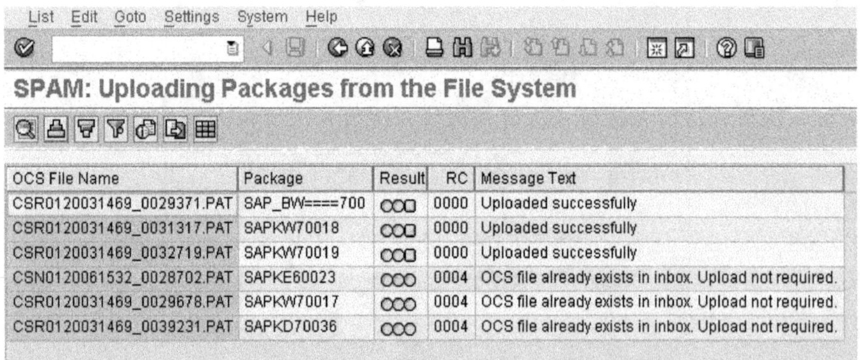

OCS File Name	Package	Result	RC	Message Text
CSR0120031469_0029371.PAT	SAP_BW====700		0000	Uploaded successfully
CSR0120031469_0031317.PAT	SAPKW70018		0000	Uploaded successfully
CSR0120031469_0032719.PAT	SAPKW70019		0000	Uploaded successfully
CSN0120061532_0028702.PAT	SAPKE60023		0004	OCS file already exists in inbox. Upload not required.
CSR0120031469_0029678.PAT	SAPKW70017		0004	OCS file already exists in inbox. Upload not required.
CSR0120031469_0039231.PAT	SAPKD70036		0004	OCS file already exists in inbox. Upload not required.

FIGURE 7-14 Output screen showing successful upload

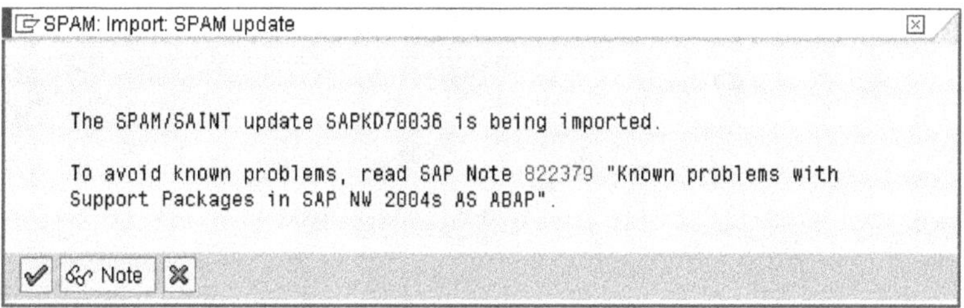

SPAM: Import: SPAM update
The SPAM/SAINT update SAPKD70036 is being imported.
To avoid known problems, read SAP Note 822379 "Known problems with Support Packages in SAP NW 2004s AS ABAP".
Note

FIGURE 7-15 Confirmation prompt for SPAM update

Application Phase

The first step when applying an SAP support package is to import the SPAM update, which is the patch for the Support Package Manager. The update can be started by calling transaction SPAM | Support Package | Import SPAM/SAINT update.The rest of the support packages should be applied only after applying the most current Support Package Manager update, as shown in Figure 7-15.

Clicking the green check mark starts the application of the SPAM update, and it runs to completion. You need to exit the SPAM transaction and restart it toward the end of the SPAM update application so that the system can confirm the changes. Figure 7-16 shows

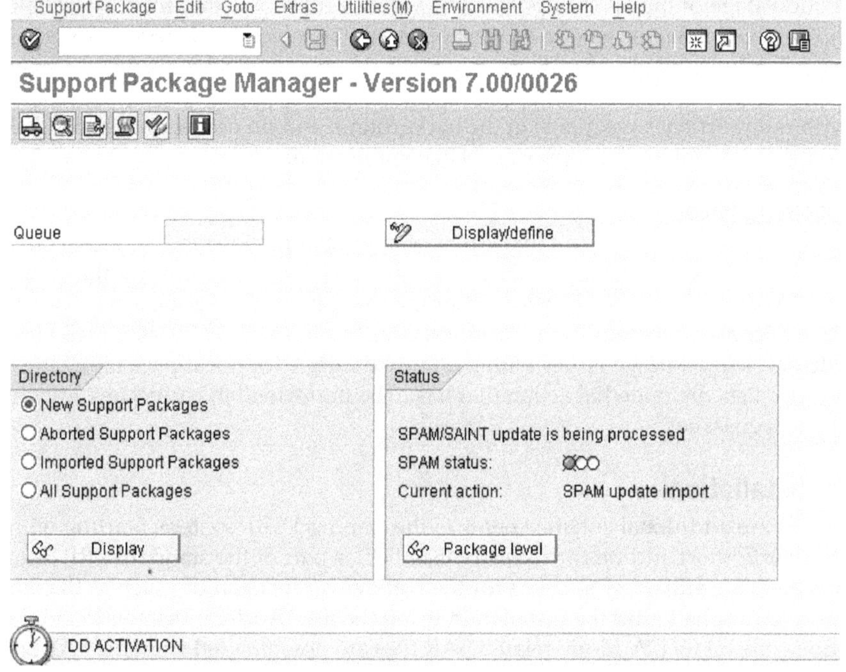

FIGURE 7-16 SPAM update application is in progress

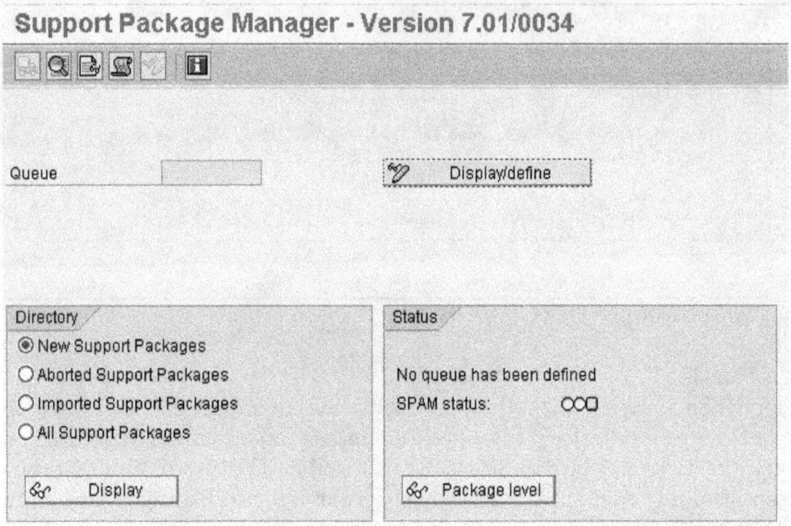

Copyright by SAP AG

FIGURE 7-17 Successful application of SPAM update

the execution stage of the SPAM update, and Figure 7-17 shows that the SAP update from Support Package Manager version 26 has been updated successfully to version 34.

After uploading and queuing all the support packages, the entire queue can be imported by selecting Support Packages | Import Queue (or by pressing SHIFT-F7). It is recommended to apply the support package queue in the background, and no user should be logged on the system for the duration of the support package application.

Troubleshooting Phase

Support package application can fail because of a number of reasons. The most common issues are with a lack of database space and known problems with some of the support packages. SAP provides a restart option after the root cause of the issue is resolved. OSS Note 822379: Known Problems with Support Packages in SAP NW 2004s AS ABAP should be used to check any known issues with the individual SAP support package or the queue. This note also lists the remedial action that has to be performed to correct any known support package issues.

Add-On Installation

SAP add-ons are additional enhancements to the standard SAP system. Starting with SAP Business Suite 7, most add-ons are already installed as part of the standard ERP install. However, there are still a few add-ons for the NetWeaver installation, such as BI content, that have to be applied after the installation using the SAP Add-On Installation tool with transaction code SAINT. Add-on–related SAR files are downloaded from the SAP Software Download Center and are extracted using the SAPCAR utility to the /usr/sap/trans/EPS/in directory, as described in the earlier section. Once extracted, the add-on files can be applied using the SAINT transaction code, as shown in Figures 7-18, 7-19, and 7-20.

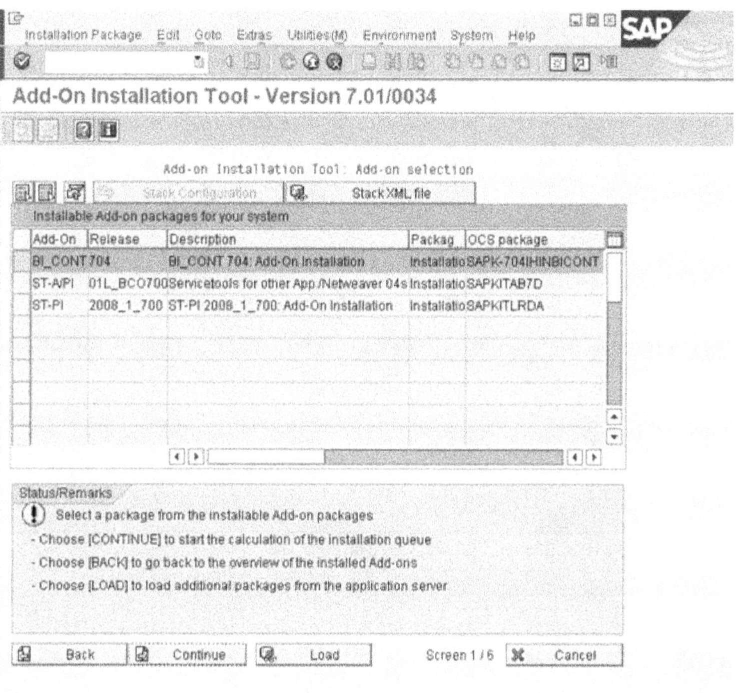

Copyright by SAP AG

FIGURE 7-18 Select the add-on and click Continue.

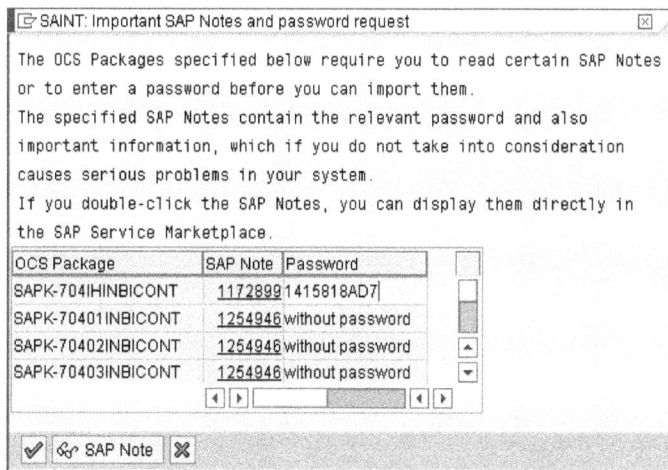

SAINT: Important SAP Notes and password request

The OCS Packages specified below require you to read certain SAP Notes or to enter a password before you can import them.
The specified SAP Notes contain the relevant password and also important information, which if you do not take into consideration causes serious problems in your system.
If you double-click the SAP Notes, you can display them directly in the SAP Service Marketplace.

OCS Package	SAP Note	Password
SAPK-704IHINBICONT	1172899	1415818AD7
SAPK-70401INBICONT	1254946	without password
SAPK-70402INBICONT	1254946	without password
SAPK-70403INBICONT	1254946	without password

SAP Note

Copyright by SAP AG

FIGURE 7-19 Confirm the installation by entering a password from the OSS note.

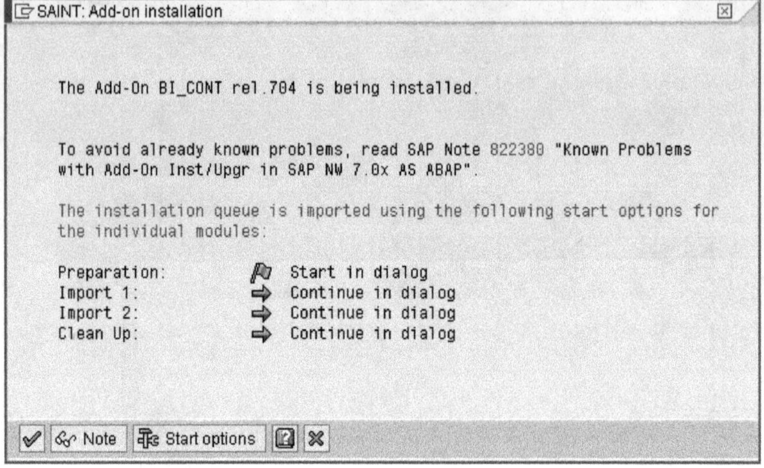

SAINT: Add-on installation
The Add-On BI_CONT rel.704 is being installed.
To avoid already known problems, read SAP Note 822380 "Known Problems with Add-On Inst/Upgr in SAP NW 7.0x AS ABAP".
The installation queue is imported using the following start options for the individual modules:
Preparation: Start in dialog
Import 1: Continue in dialog
Import 2: Continue in dialog
Clean Up: Continue in dialog
Note
Start options

FIGURE 7-20 Confirmation that the add-on will be installed

Kernel Upgrade

The SAP kernel is a group of both database-dependent and database-independent operating system binaries installed in the /sapmnt/<SID>/exe directory. Kernel executables perform functions such as memory management, database connections for performing imports, and process and task management. The kernel of the ABAP stack is coded in C/C++ programming language. The SAP kernel is installed as part of a standard SAP installation. However, the kernel becomes old as SAP releases newer versions of the kernel patches.

The following procedure can be used to perform a kernel upgrade in SAP systems. The first step is to download the following three SAR files from the SAP Software Download Center:

- SAPEXE_<Patch level>-<release date>.SAR
- SAPEXEDB_<Patch level>-<release date>.SAR
- DBATOOLS. _<Patch level>-<release date>.SAR

SAP kernel executables are located in the /sapmnt/<SID>/exe directory. The kernel upgrade procedure replaces the current set of kernel files with the newly extracted set. To complete this task:

1. Make a backup copy of the current kernel (sapmnt/<SID>/exe directory) and name it exeold.
2. Shut down SAP and SAPOSCOL (saposcol -k).
3. Make a new directory called /sapmnt/<SID>/exenew.

4. Extract the new kernel SAR files to a new exenew directory using the following syntax:

```
SAPCAR -xvf <filename.SAR>
```

5. Replace the kernel directory with the newly extracted kernel files.
6. Run the saproot.sh script using the root account to fix the authorizations of some kernel files as shown:

```
./saproot.sh <SID>
Example of the execution of the script is shown below:
./saproot.sh QB2
Preparing /usr/sap/QB2/SYS/exe/run/brbackup ...
Preparing /usr/sap/QB2/SYS/exe/run/brarchive ...
Preparing /usr/sap/QB2/SYS/exe/run/brconnect ...
Preparing /usr/sap/QB2/SYS/exe/run/brtools ...
Preparing saposcol ...
Preparing icmbnd ...
done
```

7. Start the SAP system and SAPOSCOL (saposcol -l).
8. Perform basic technical checks after the kernel upgrade.
9. Check the kernel release level using the command disp+work -v | more.
10. Check the kernel release and patch level using transaction code SM51 | Release Notes.

Please note that if it is not a complete kernel upgrade, you can shut down the SAP application, make a backup of the current kernel, and overwrite the extracted files with the newer extracted files. You can use the basic UNIX copy command with recursive option to perform this task.

SGEN (Generate the ABAP Loads)

Transaction code SGEN is used to generate the ABAP loads in the newly installed system after all of the post-installation tasks are completed. Execute transaction code SGEN, select the software components that need to be generated, and click Continue, as shown in Figure 7-21.

The next screen shows that the selected software components ABAP loads can be generated in the background. Select the Start Job Directly option, as shown in Figure 7-22. This will schedule the ABAP load generation in the background, and you can monitor the progress of the run, as shown in Figure 7-23. It is recommended to turn off Oracle archiving during SGEN execution.

Printer Setup

After the installation is completed, initially a SAP front-end printer is set up using transaction code SPAD (Spool Administration). Figures 7-24 and 7-25 show the device types and access method that has to be selected to successfully set up a local or front-end printer in SAP. This will allow users of the system to print to the default Windows printers.

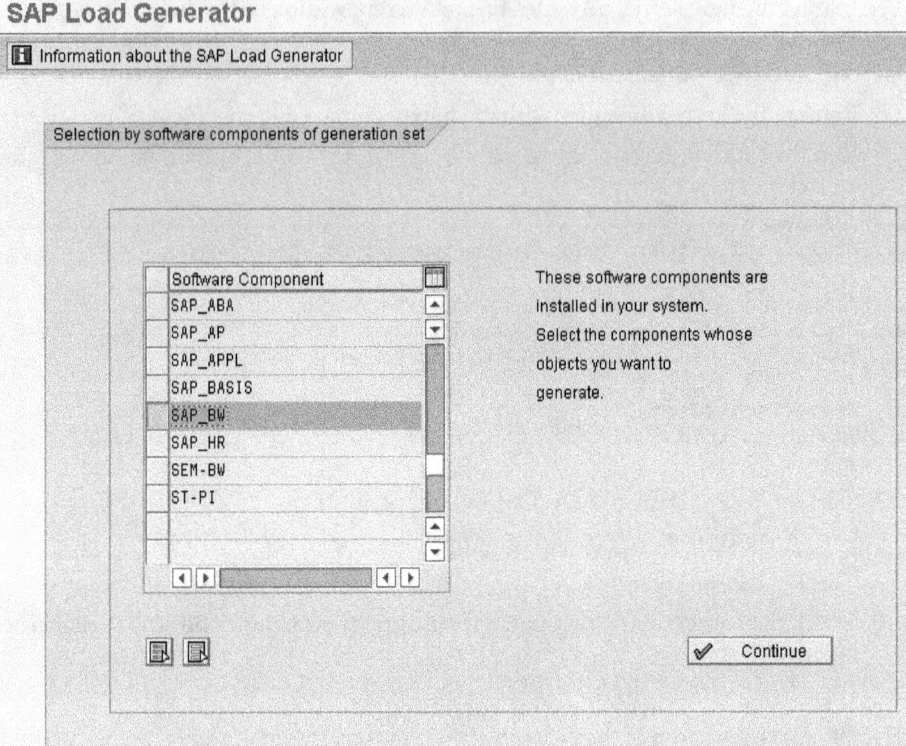

Figure 7-21 Software component selection screen in transaction SGEN

Installing the Permanent License

Every newly installed SAP system comes with a temporary license that is good for about four weeks. It is important to apply online at SAP Service Marketplace immediately after the installation for a permanent license. The SLICENSE transaction code is used to apply the permanent license to the SAP system. Execute transaction code SLICENSE, and get the active hardware key. Open the SAP URL http://service.sap.com/licensekeys, and select the Request Permanent License Key option from the Service Corner box. Follow the screens, enter the hardware key, and provide the e-mail address where the license file should be sent. Usually, SAP sends the license file about an hour after the online request is made. Once the permanent license file is received, use the following procedure to upload the file. Click the New Licenses button as shown in Figure 7-26.

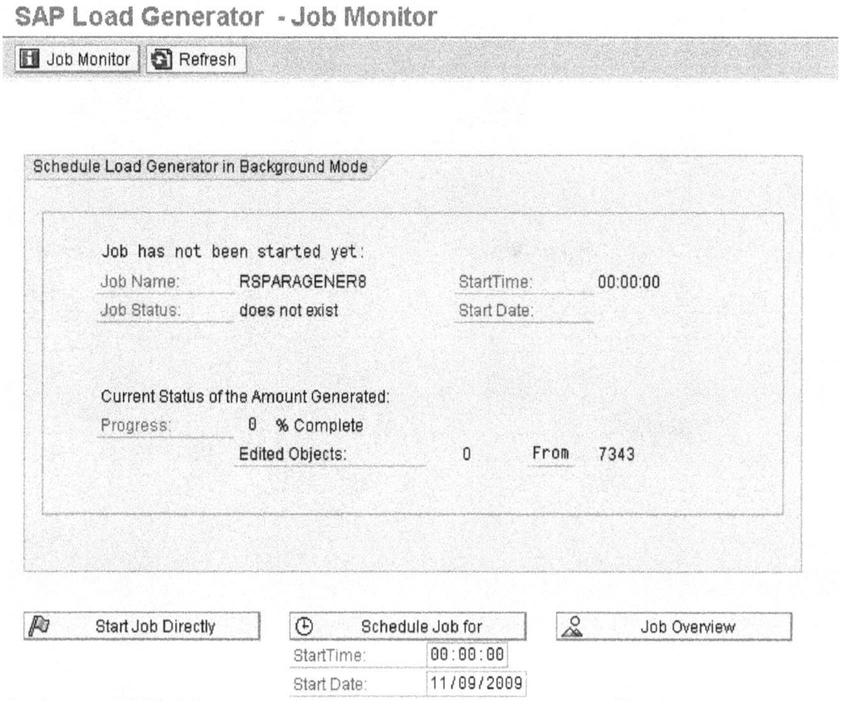

FIGURE 7-22 Starting the ABAP load generation

This will open another window asking for the location of the permanent SAP license file, as shown in Figure 7-27. Point the path to the downloaded permanent SAP license file, and click the Open button. This will install the permanent SAP license, as shown in Figure 7-28.

Client Copy

The client copy process allows a copy of the standard SAP delivered client 000 to a customer-specific client or to clients using various client copy tools. Since this topic is so important for setting up SAP software logistics, Chapter 10 is devoted to this topic.

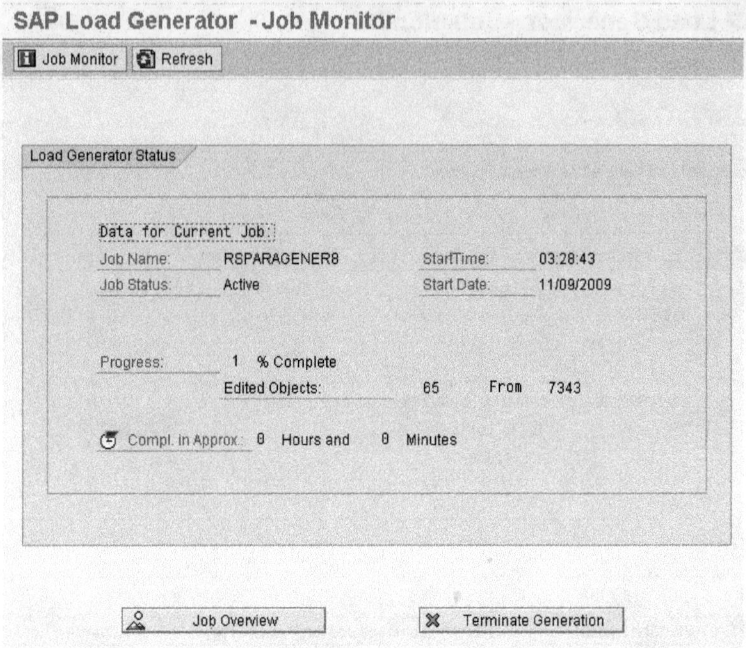
SAP Load Generator - Job Monitor
Job Monitor
Refresh
Load Generator Status
Data for Current Job:
Job Name: RSPARAGENER8
StartTime: 03:28:43
Job Status: Active
Start Date: 11/09/2009
Progress: 1 % Complete
Edited Objects: 65 From 7343
Compl. in Approx.: 0 Hours and 0 Minutes
Job Overview
Terminate Generation

Copyright by SAP AG

FIGURE 7-23 Progress of the ABAP load generation

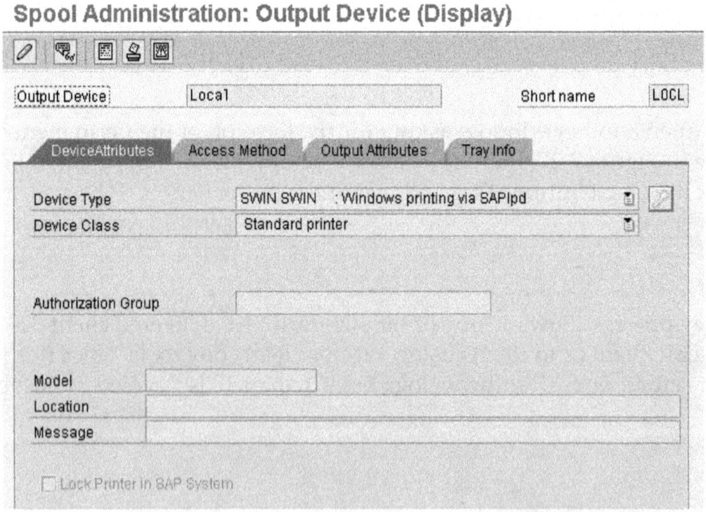
Spool Administration: Output Device (Display)
Output Device
Local
Short name
LOCL
DeviceAttributes
Access Method
Output Attributes
Tray Info
Device Type
SWIN SWIN : Windows printing via SAPlpd
Device Class
Standard printer
Authorization Group
Model
Location
Message
Lock Printer in SAP System

Copyright by SAP AG

FIGURE 7-24 Local printer setup with SWIN device type

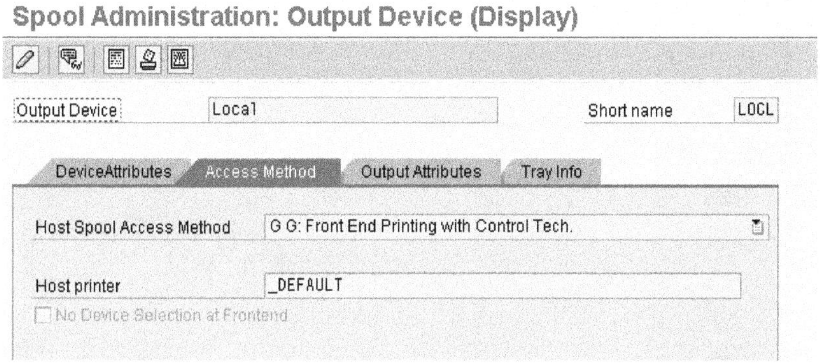

Spool Administration: Output Device (Display)

Output Device: Local — Short name: LOCL

DeviceAttributes | Access Method | Output Attributes | Tray Info

Host Spool Access Method: G G: Front End Printing with Control Tech.

Host printer: _DEFAULT

No Device Selection at Frontend

Copyright by SAP AG

FIGURE 7-25 Access method settings for a typical local printer in SAP

Profile Parameters

After a new SAP system is installed, it comes with a set of standard SAP parameters that are read at the start of the system. The parameters exist at the operating system level and have to be imported to the application using transaction code RZ10 and menu option utilities | Import Profiles | of active servers. Since profile parameter administration is very important, more details will be covered in Chapter 14.

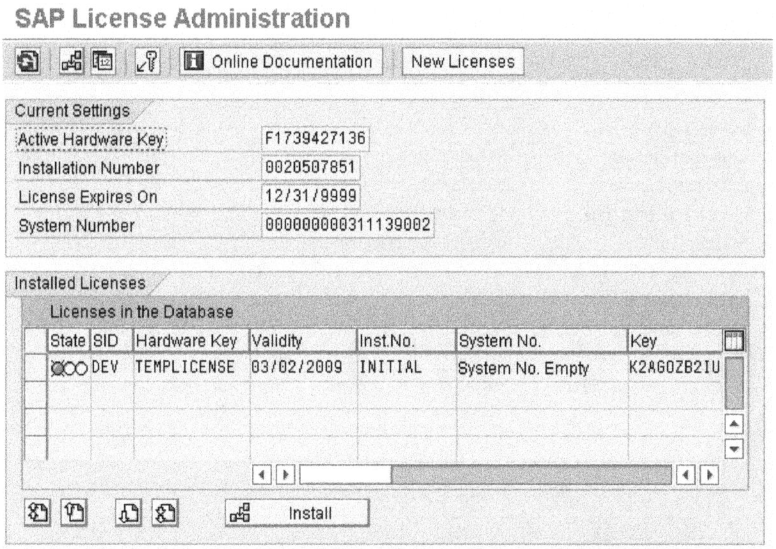

SAP License Administration

Online Documentation | New Licenses

Current Settings

Active Hardware Key	F1739427136
Installation Number	0020507851
License Expires On	12/31/9999
System Number	000000000311139002

Installed Licenses

Licenses in the Database

State	SID	Hardware Key	Validity	Inst.No.	System No.	Key
	DEV	TEMPLICENSE	03/02/2009	INITIAL	System No. Empty	K2AGOZB2IU

Install

Copyright by SAP AG

FIGURE 7-26 SLICENSE transaction showing the option to install the new licenses

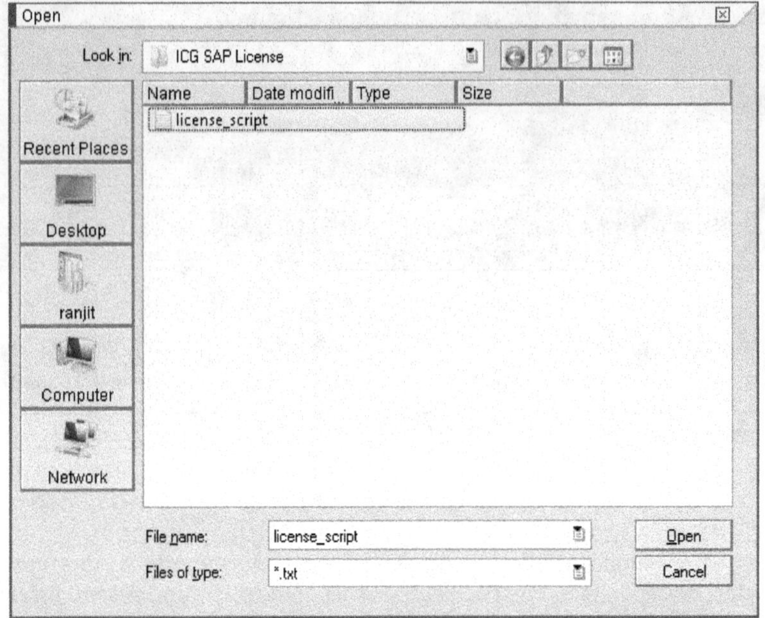

FIGURE 7-27 SAP license key script file

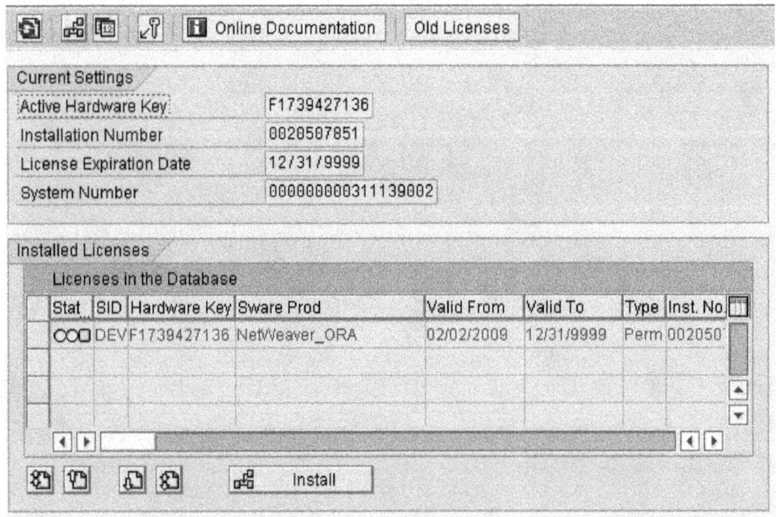

FIGURE 7-28 SAP permanent license

Setting Up SAP Online Help

The SR13 transaction code is used to configure and set up SAP online help, as shown in the illustration.

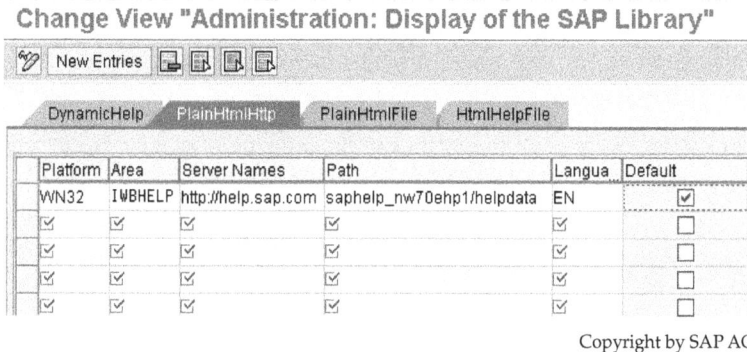

Change View "Administration: Display of the SAP Library"

New Entries

DynamicHelp | PlainHtmlHttp | PlainHtmlFile | HtmlHelpFile

Platform	Area	Server Names	Path	Langua	Default
WN32	IWBHELP	http://help.sap.com	saphelp_nw70ehp1/helpdata	EN	☑
					☐
					☐
					☐
					☐

Set Up the System Time Zone Setting

Use transaction code STZAC to set up and customize the time zone, as shown.

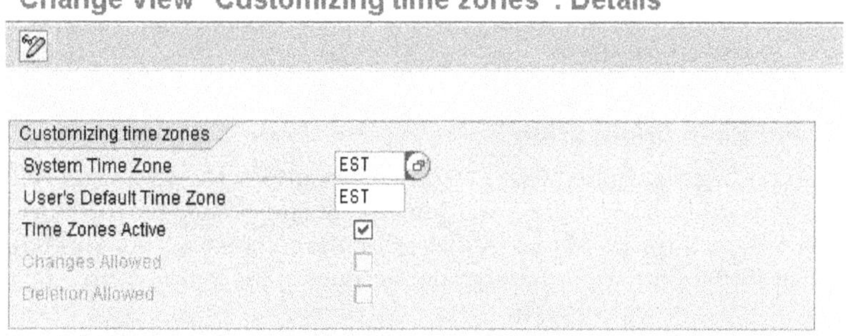

Backups

Make a complete offline backup of the system after all the post-installation tasks have been successfully completed.

Java Stack Post-installation Steps

Some of the key Java stack post-installation steps will be discussed in this section. After the installation is successfully completed, the first step is to log in at both the operating system and application levels, and check if everything is consistent and no errors are reported.

After this, some of the critical post-installation steps, such as installation of Java support packages and license key installation, will have to be performed.

Login Checks

After successfully installing the Java stack, execute the following tasks to check the system. The following procedures have been discussed in detail in earlier chapters of this book.

Log In and Check the System at the Operating System Level

1. As <SID>adm, check startup and shutdown of the SAP system.
2. As <SID>adm, check if all SAP processes are up.
3. As ora<SID>, check that the Oracle Database and Listener are up.
4. Check JCMON for Java systems up to NW 7.0.
5. Check JSMON for Java systems from NW 7.1.
6. Check the availability log in the work directory.

Log In and Check the System at the Application Level

1. Check the Index page.
2. Check the Portal Login page.
3. For dual-stack applications, transaction code SMICM can be used to check the availability of the Java stack.

Java Support Package Application

The Java support package is applied using the Java Support Package Manager (JSPM) tool. You have to log in as <SID>adm at the operating system and change the directory to the following location to start the JSPM tool by executing the command ./go. This will bring up the logon page for JSPM. Enter the administrator account at the login screen. The Java support package stack is downloaded from the SAP Software Download Center at http://service.sap.com/sp-stacks. After the stack is downloaded, save the list as an .xml file and include this file along with the Java SCA files in the /usr/sap/trans/EPS/in directory. Figure 7-29 shows the JSPM tool scanning the EPS inbox and showing the source and the target Java stack levels.

```
dk1adm> pwd
/usr/sap/DJ1/JC01/j2ee/JSPM
./go
```

You can get more details by clicking the Show Details button. After verifying the details, click Next to start deploying the Java patches.

JSPM first applies a patch to the Package Manager tool and restarts, similar to the SPAM tool. Once this is done, it will start scheduling and deploying the Java support packages by calling SDM internally. JSPM can also perform a kernel upgrade automatically if you include the kernel files in the usr/sap/trans/EPS/in directory. Figure 7-30 shows successful deployment of the Java support packages.

Deployment | Deployed Components | Logs

1 Select Package Type — 2 Specify Queue — 3 Check Queue — 4 Deploy Queue — 5 Completed

Support Package Stacks > Specify Queue

Select a support package stack to apply

Select	Product version / Enhancement Package	Target SP Stack	Details
◉	SAP EHP1 FOR SAP NETWEAVER 7.0	SAP EHP1 FOR SAP NETWEAVER 7.0 - 04 (05/2009)	Show Details

Back | Next | Cancel

Scan of inbox has finished.

FIGURE 7-29 JSPM showing target Java stack levels

Installing the Java Stack License

The Java license is applied using the Visual Administrator License Adapter tool. You can open the Visual Administrator tool by executing the following commands from the <SID>adm user account:

```
dj1adm> pwd
/usr/sap/DJ1/JC01/j2ee/admin
./go
```

This will start the Visual Administrator tool. Login to the tool and choose Server0 | Services | Licensing Adapter to install the license.

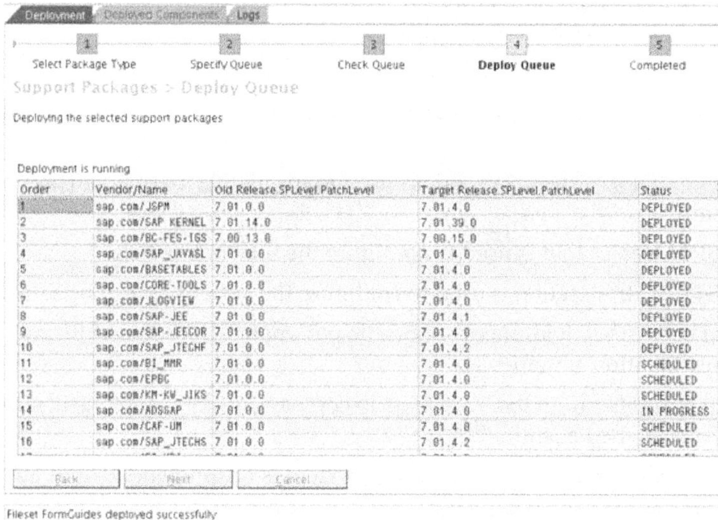

Order	Vendor/Name	Old Release.SPLevel.PatchLevel	Target Release.SPLevel.PatchLevel	Status
1	sap.com/JSPM	7.01.0.0	7.01.4.0	DEPLOYED
2	sap.com/SAP KERNEL	7.01.14.0	7.01.39.0	DEPLOYED
3	sap.com/BC-FES-IGS	7.00.13.0	7.00.15.0	DEPLOYED
4	sap.com/SAP_JAVASL	7.01.0.0	7.01.4.0	DEPLOYED
5	sap.com/BASETABLES	7.01.0.0	7.01.4.0	DEPLOYED
6	sap.com/CORE-TOOLS	7.01.0.0	7.01.4.0	DEPLOYED
7	sap.com/JLOGVIEW	7.01.0.0	7.01.4.0	DEPLOYED
8	sap.com/SAP-JEE	7.01.0.0	7.01.4.1	DEPLOYED
9	sap.com/SAP-JEECOR	7.01.0.0	7.01.4.0	DEPLOYED
10	sap.com/SAP_JTECHF	7.01.0.0	7.01.4.2	DEPLOYED
11	sap.com/BI_MMR	7.01.0.0	7.01.4.0	SCHEDULED
12	sap.com/EPBC	7.01.0.0	7.01.4.0	SCHEDULED
13	sap.com/KM-KW_JIKS	7.01.0.0	7.01.4.0	SCHEDULED
14	sap.com/ADSSAP	7.01.0.0	7.01.4.0	IN PROGRESS
15	sap.com/CAF-UM	7.01.0.0	7.01.4.0	SCHEDULED
16	sap.com/SAP_JTECHS	7.01.0.0	7.01.4.2	SCHEDULED

FIGURE 7-30 Successful deployment of the Java patches

Get the hardware key, and follow the same procedure for obtaining the SAP license script from SAP. Once you receive the SAP Java Stack permanent license, install the license script by using the Install License From File option in Visual Administrator.

Summary

- SAP login checks can be performed at the application level by connecting to the newly installed back-end SAP system using the SAPLogon program.
- Clients 000, 001, and 066 are standard SAP delivered clients.
- SAPGUI helps in connecting to an individual SAP system to perform application checks.
- Transaction codes SM28, SM51, SM50, ST22, and SM21 can be used to verify successful SAP installation.
- SAP operating system–level checks include successful startup and shutdown of the SAP system and the underlying database.
- SAP work processes and Oracle processes can be checked for successful verification of the newly installed SAP system.
- SE06 and STMS transaction codes are used to set up the initial SAP Transport Management system.
- STMS setup is a prerequisite for performing ABAP and Java support package application.
- SPAM transaction is used to apply the SAP ABAP support packages.
- SAINT (SAP Add-on Installation tool) is used to apply SAP add-ons.
- The SAP kernel upgrade procedure replaces the older version of the SAP kernel with the newer kernel executables.
- SGEN transaction is used to generate ABAP loads in the background.
- The SPAD transaction is used to set up an initial printer in the newly installed SAP system.
- The SLICENSE transaction code is used to install SAP permanent license keys in the system.
- The SR13 transaction is used to configure the SAP online help.
- The STZAC transaction is used to configure the system time zone settings.
- Client copy setup and import of profile parameters are some of the other important post-installation activities.
- Client administration tools are used to copy a SAP-delivered client, such as 000, to a customer-owned client.
- A complete offline backup of the SAP system is recommended after all the post-installation steps are completed.
- Java stack systems are verified at the application level by checking the index page of the Java stack.

- Java stack systems are verified at the operating system level by checking the SAP Java processes and Oracle processes.
- The JSPM tool is used to install Java support packages for Java stack–based systems.
- The URL http://service.sap.com/sp-stacks is used to download both ABAP and Java support package stacks.
- The URL http://service.sap.com/licensekeys is used to apply for the permanent SAP license.
- Visual Administrator License Adapter service is used to install the permanent license key in the Java stack systems.

Additional Resources

- **SAP NetWeaver Technology Software Developer Network** http://sdn.sap.com/irj/sdn/netweaver
- **SAP NW 7.0 Installation Guides** http://service.sap.com/instguidesNW70
- **SAP Release Notes** http://service.sap.com/releasenotes

CHAPTER

Installing SAP Stand-Alone Systems

In this chapter we will study the installation and configuration of some of the SAP stand-alone components. These components are not mandatory and are installed as part of meeting the requirements of a specific IT scenario. The SAPinst tool helps in the installation of most SAP stand-alone components. Some components, such as SAProuter, are installed by following a manual installation process.

The stand-alone components do not run on SAP AS ABAP or AS Java stack–based usage types. SAP Web Dispatcher and SAProuter installation and configuration will be discussed in detail in this chapter. SAP liveCache is a promising database technology, and installation of this technology will also be covered. SAPinst also provides an uninstall option if needed so that SAP software can be removed from the server in a structured manner. Table 8-1 lists some of the important SAP stand-alone components and their respective functions.

SAP Web Dispatcher

SAP Web Dispatcher can be installed using the SAPinst tool or by using the manual extraction and bootstrap process. In this chapter, the manual process is explained so that the reader has a detailed understanding of the process. A similar process is executed when the SAPinst tool is used to install and configure the SAP Web Dispatcher. This process can be broken down into the following four steps:

- SAP Web Dispatcher installation
- SAP Web Dispatcher bootstrapping
- SAP Web Dispatcher start and shutdown procedures
- SAP configuration file setup

SAP Web Dispatcher Installation

As the <SID>adm user account, create a directory called sapwebdisp under the /usr/sap/<SAPSID> path of the SAP server. Then download the latest version of the SAP Web Dispatcher SAR file (wdispadmin.sar) from the SAP Service Marketplace based on the

SAP Stand-Alone Component	Function	Installation Options
SAP Web Dispatcher	SAP Web dispatcher accepts incoming HTTP/HTTPS SAP requests and helps in load distribution to multiple customer application servers with the help of the message server.	SAPinst-based installation. Use the manual installation option by extracting the installation SAR file.
SAProuter	SAProuter acts as an "application-level gateway," meaning it will protect the customer SAP systems from outside connections, such as from the SAP support network.	Use the manual installation option by extracting the installation SAR file.
SAP liveCache Technology	SAP liveCache technology is a memory-resident database used in SAP supply chain management (SCM) solutions. Because it is memory-resident it delivers significantly better performance than the traditional database architectures.	SAPinst-based installation.
Stand-Alone Gateway	The stand-alone gateway allows a SAP system to be connected to external systems via a Remote Function Call (RFC) connection.	SAPinst-based installation.
Search and Classification (TREX)	This provides the search functions along with text mining and other related technologies.	SAPinst-based installation.

TABLE 8-1 Stand-Alone SAP Components

kernel release of your system. It is also possible to copy the older versions of the SAR file from the already installed SAP kernel directory to the newly created sapwebdisp directory. Once this step is complete, extract the wdispadmin.sar file in the sapwebdisp directory using the command SAPCAR -xvf wdispadmin.sar. Once the files are extracted, the next step is the bootstrapping process.

SAP Web Dispatcher Bootstrapping

When SAP Web Dispatcher is started for the very first time, it has to be bootstrapped using the following command. This will bootstrap the SAP Web Dispatcher and in the process generate a configuration file called sapwebdisp.pfl.

```
sbxadm> sapwebdisp -bootstrap
SAP Web Dispatcher Bootstrap
============================
```

```
This bootstrap will perform the following steps:
1. Create profile file "sapwebdisp.pfl"for SAP Web Dispatcher (if not
already existing)
2. Create user for web based administration in file "icmauth.txt"(if not
already existing)
3. Start SAP Web Dispatcher with the created profile
After the bootstrap you can use the web based administration
Generating Profile "sapwebdisp.pfl"
Hostname of Message Server (rdisp/mshost): tagore
HTTP Port of Message Server (ms/http_port): 8100
Checking connection to message server...OK
Unique Instance Number for SAP Web Dispatcher (SAPSYSTEM): 3
HTTP port number for SAP Web Dispatcher: 50000
Create configuration for s(mall), m(edium), l(arge) system (default:
medium): s
Profile "sapwebdisp.pfl" generated
Authentication file "icmauth.txt" generated
Web Administration user is "icmadm" with password "********"
Restart sapwebdisp with profile: sapwebdisp.pfl
sapwebdisp started with new pid 37575
Web administration accessible with "http://tagore:50000/sap/wdisp/
admin/default.html"
SAP Web Dispatcher bootstrap ended (rc=0)
```

SAP Web Dispatcher Start and Shutdown Procedures

In UNIX environments the following commands can be used to start and shut down the SAP Web Dispatcher:

- **Start command:**

  ```
  sapwebdisp pf=sapwebdisp.pfl  &
  ```

  and press the ENTER key
- **Shutdown command:**

  ```
  Kill -9 <PID of the SAP Web Dispatcher>
  ```

SAP Configuration File Setup

The SAP Web Dispatcher configuration file sapwebdisp.pfl can be further customized to suit the requirements of the system. The following is an example of the sapwebdisp.pfl file customized for a small scenario. The parameters can be increased to suit the requirements for a large productive installation.

```
sbxadm> more sapwebdisp.pfl
# Profile generated by sapwebdisp bootstrap
# unique instance number
SAPSYSTEM = 3
# add default directory settings
```

```
DIR_EXECUTABLE = .
DIR_INSTANCE = .
# Accessibility of Message Servers
rdisp/mshost = tagore
ms/http_port = 8100
# SAP Web Dispatcher Parameter
wdisp/auto_refresh = 120
wdisp/max_servers = 100
wdisp/shm_attach_mode = 6
# configuration for small scenario
icm/max_conn        = 100
icm/max_sockets     = 1024
icm/req_queue_len = 300
icm/min_threads     = 5
icm/max_threads     = 15
mpi/total_size_MB = 20
#maximum number of concurrent connections to one server
wdisp/HTTP/max_pooled_con = 100
wdisp/HTTPS/max_pooled_con = 100
# SAP Web Dispatcher Ports
icm/server_port_0 = PROT=HTTP,PORT=50000
icm/server_port_1 =
# SAP Web Dispatcher Web Administration
icm/HTTP/admin_0 = PREFIX=/sap/wdisp/admin,DOCROOT=./admin,AUTHFILE=icmauth
.txt
```

SAProuter

As mentioned, SAProuter acts as an "application-level gateway," meaning it controls access to the customer's SAP systems from the SAP support network and other external systems. Once installed and configured, the SAProuter program will allow network connections based on the configuration entries in the saprouttab table. SAProuter installation and configuration can be broken down into the following four steps:

- SAProuter installation
- SAProuttab configuration (Route Permission table)
- Starting and shutting down a SAProuter
- Important SAProuter options

SAProuter Installation

Create a directory called saprouter under the /usr/sap/ path of the SAP server. Then download the latest version of the SAProuter SAR file (saprouter*.sar) from the SAP Service Marketplace based on the kernel release of your system. It is also possible to copy the older versions of the SAR file from the already installed SAP kernel directory to the newly created saprouter directory. Once this step is complete, extract the saprouter*.sar file in the saprouter directory using the command SAPCAR -xvf saprouter*.sar. This will extract the SAProuter program and the niping program into the saprouter directory.

P * * *	Permits access to all ABAP systems in the network with no password.
P * * * pass	Permits access to all ABAP systems in the network using the password pass.
D hostx	Denies access starting from hostx.
P 10.2.*.* 176.1.*.*	Permits all connections from 10.2.2.11 to 176.1.1.116.

TABLE 8-2 Sample saprouttab Table

SAProuttab Configuration

After the saprouter installation is complete, the next step is to configure the saprouttab table. This is a file that needs to be created in the /usr/sap/saprouter directory. At startup, SAProuter will read the permitted network entries in the saprouttab file and thereby control access to the customer SAP systems outside the network, such as access by SAP support resources. The following syntax is used to maintain the saprouttab table:

```
P/S/D <source host> <dest host> <dest serv> <password>
```

where P = Permit, S = Secure, D = Deny, source host = connection originator, dest host = destination host, dest serv = port, and password = password.

Table 8-2 shows an example of a simple saprouttab table.

Starting and Shutting Down a SAProuter

The following command can be used to start a SAProuter in a UNIX environment. This command starts the SAProuter (-r option) with the logging option activated (-G option) and is using port 3299 (-S option). There are a number of other options for starting a SAProuter, and details can be obtained by referring to the SAProuter install and configuration guide.

```
nohup ./saprouter -r -G routerlog -S 3299  &
```

The saprouter -s option will stop the running SAProuter.

SAProuter Options

Table 8-3 lists some of the additional SAProuter options.

SAProuter Option	Means
saprouter -n	Re-reads a modified saprouttab without restarting the saprouter
saprouter -t	Allows change of trace level
saprouter -G<logfile>	Name and path of saprouter log file
saprouter -K <sncname)	If SNC (Secure Network Connection) is installed and configured

TABLE 8-3 SAProuter Options

SAP liveCache Technology

SAP liveCache technology is used in SAP SCM solutions. It is a memory-resident database technology based on MaxDB technology. This technology allows for real-time access of high data volumes with high performance. SAP liveCache can be installed using the SAPinst tool. From the list of SAPinst stand-alone engines, select the liveCache installation option, as shown in Figure 8-1. The other stand-alone install options are also discussed in this chapter.

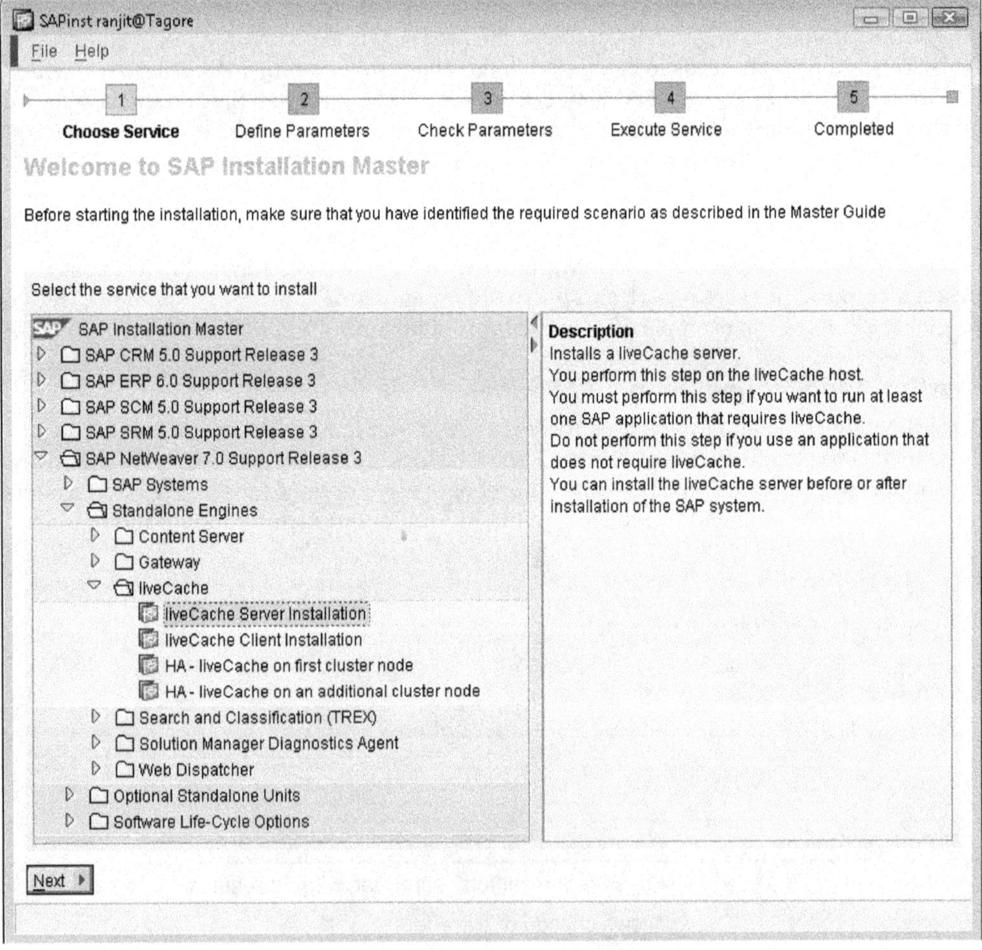

FIGURE 8-1 SAP liveCache installation option

1. Select the liveCache ID, as shown, and click Next.

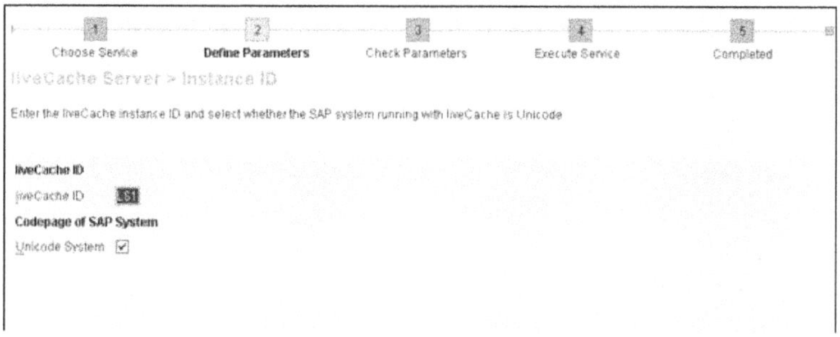

Copyright by SAP AG

2. Enter a password for the liveCache administrator, as shown, and click Next.

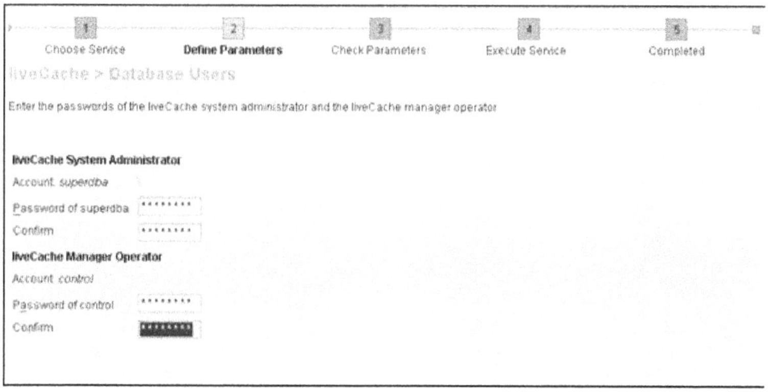

Copyright by SAP AG

3. Choose an SAP liveCache user, and click Next.

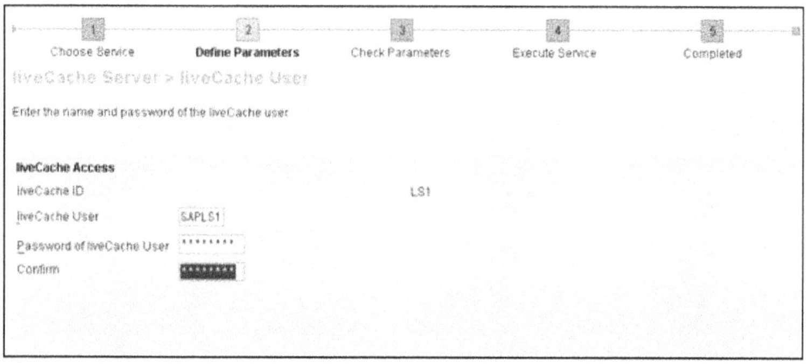

Copyright by SAP AG

4. Enter the liveCache instance parameters as shown, and click Next. You can change the instance parameters to suit your specific needs.

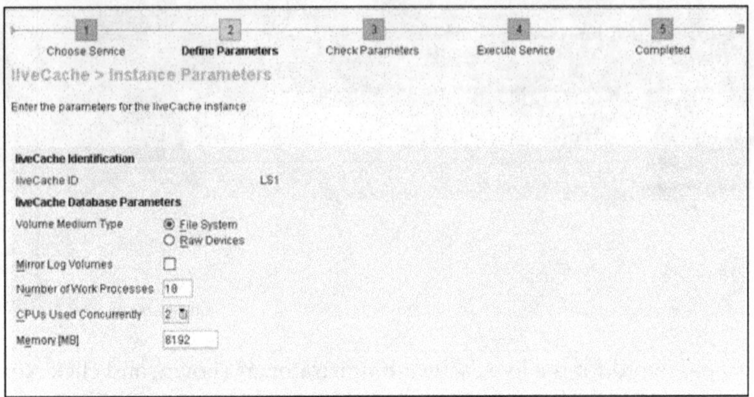

1 Choose Service
2 Define Parameters
3 Check Parameters
4 Execute Service
5 Completed
liveCache > Instance Parameters
Enter the parameters for the liveCache instance
liveCache Identification
liveCache ID LS1
liveCache Database Parameters
Volume Medium Type
File System
Raw Devices
Mirror Log Volumes
Number of Work Processes 10
CPUs Used Concurrently 2
Memory [MB] 8192

Copyright by SAP AG

5. Enter the path for the liveCache log volumes, and click Next.

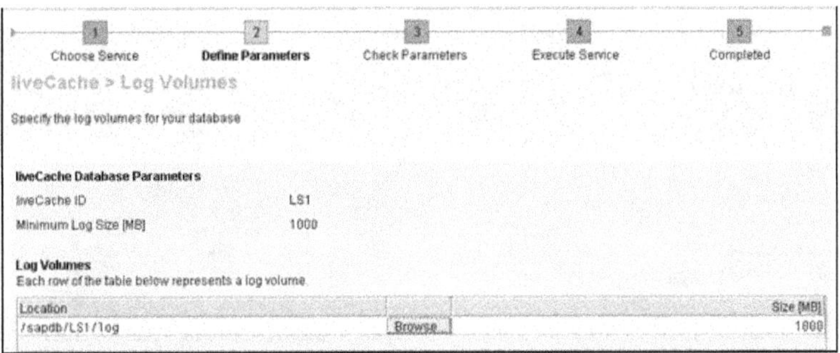

1 Choose Service
2 Define Parameters
3 Check Parameters
4 Execute Service
5 Completed
liveCache > Log Volumes
Specify the log volumes for your database
liveCache Database Parameters
liveCache ID LS1
Minimum Log Size [MB] 1000
Log Volumes
Each row of the table below represents a log volume.
Location
Size [MB]
/sapdb/LS1/log
Browse
1000

Copyright by SAP AG

6. Enter the path to the liveCache data volumes, and click the Next button as shown.

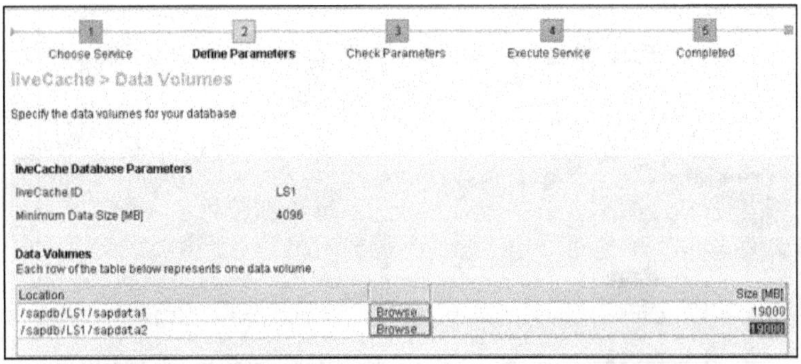

1 Choose Service
2 Define Parameters
3 Check Parameters
4 Execute Service
5 Completed
liveCache > Data Volumes
Specify the data volumes for your database
liveCache Database Parameters
liveCache ID LS1
Minimum Data Size [MB] 4096
Data Volumes
Each row of the table below represents one data volume.
Location
Size [MB]
/sapdb/LS1/sapdata1
Browse
19000
/sapdb/LS1/sapdata2
Browse
19000

Copyright by SAP AG

The SAPinst tool successfully installs liveCache utilizing the parameters entered.

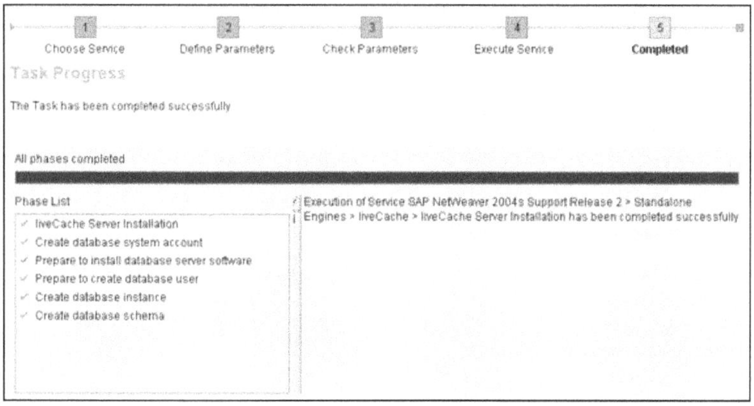

SAP Uninstall Option

SAP provides an uninstall option to remove the SAP software from the customer's systems in a structured manner. Use this tool if you need to remove an SAP install instead of manually deleting the SAP-related files from the system. The uninstall option can be accessed by calling the SAPinst tool and choosing the uninstall option from the Software-Lifecycle Options menu, as shown in Figure 8-2.

Summary

- The SAPinst tool provides options for installing stand-alone tools and engines such as SAP Web Dispatcher and liveCache technology.
- The SAP Web Dispatcher allows distributing HTTP/HTTPS SAP requests to several application servers via the message server.
- SAProuter acts as an application-level gateway and controls access to the client's SAP systems by SAP support resources logging in from remote locations.
- SAPinst provides an uninstall option to remove the SAP software in a clean manner instead of deleting the files manually.
- SAPinst provides several other installation options that can be used based on the client's IT scenario, such as SAP TREX (Search and Classification) and SAP stand-alone gateway installation.

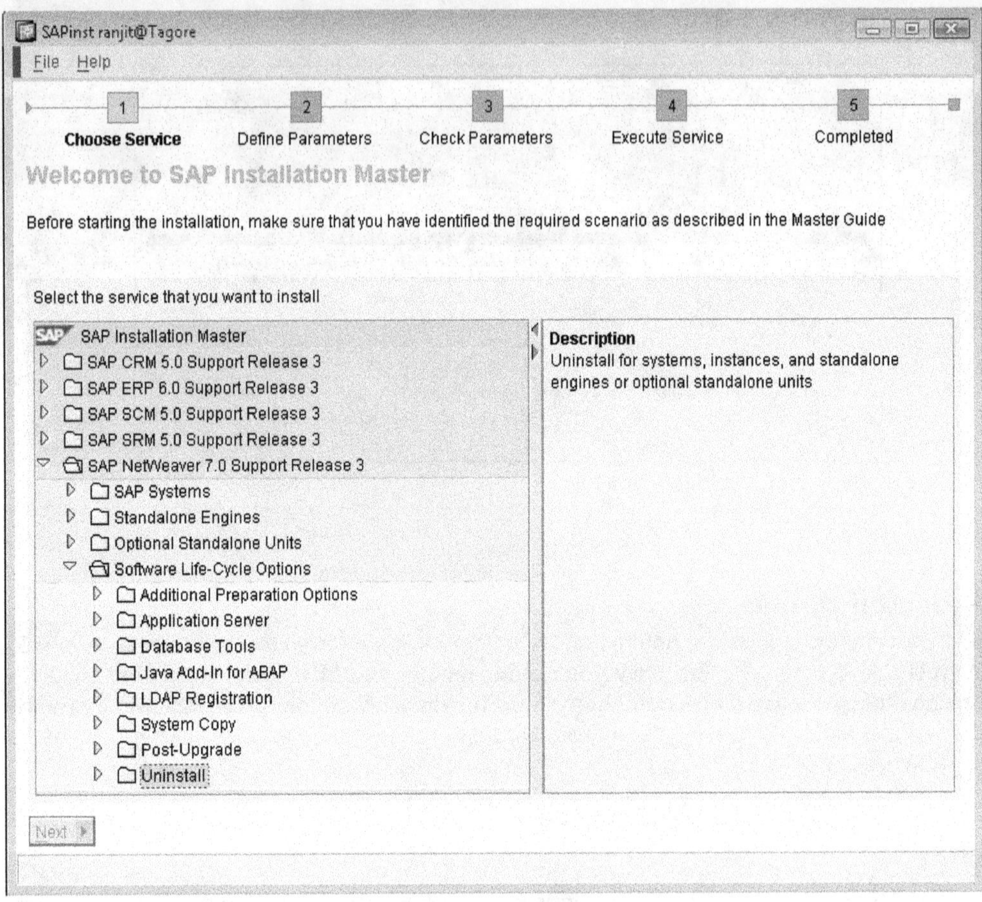

FIGURE 8-2 SAPinst showing the Uninstall option

Additional Resources

- **Additional information on SAProuter** http://help.sap.com/saphelp_nw04s/helpdata/en/4f/992ce8446d11d189700000e8322d00/frameset.htm
- **Detailed documentation on SAProuter 7.10** https://websmp207.sap-ag.de/~form/sapnet?_FRAME=CONTAINER&_OBJECT=011000358700003588172003E
- **SAP Web Dispatcher overview** www.sdn.sap.com/irj/sdn/go/portal/prtroot/docs/library/uuid/b0c9e490-0201-0010-e899-fd57db5e9a66;jsessionid=(J2EE3417600)ID1580467750DB10005911907367397718End

PART

SAP Software Logistics

CHAPTER

SAP System Landscapes in ABAP and Java Stacks

In this section of the book several chapters will be devoted to studying the software logistics of SAP systems in both ABAP and Java stacks. SAP software logistics provides a methodical way of developing and configuring SAP software in development systems and moving the changes in an orderly fashion to quality assurance systems for testing and eventually to the production system for final deployment. In order to accomplish this, SAP has provided a number of built-in software version and change management tools to ensure a smooth implementation of SAP software by the project team.

SAP software logistics includes such topics as SAP System Landscapes, SAP change management, SAP client concepts, SAP client instance strategies, SAP transport strategies, SAP transport management system, SAP multirelease strategies, and n and n + 1 architecture. For a successful SAP implementation, a well-thought-out SAP software logistics is important. Usually, a SAP technical architect or a Basis architect develops the software logistics strategy in cooperation with the team leads of the SAP project team. What a good urban plan is to a well-built city, a well-designed software logistics plan is to a smoothly functioning SAP implementation project.

Now let us look into some key activities and roles that come into play during this phase of SAP project implementation. During this phase, the development and quality assurance systems are built by the Basis team and the client instance strategy and software change management strategy is agreed on and implemented. We will focus on the details of the SAP System Landscapes and SAP client instance strategy in this chapter. Subsequent chapters will deal with the client administration activities, transport strategy, transport management system, and related topics. During this phase of the SAP implementation, the developers will start writing code that the standard software does not already include and that has been identified as a gap in supporting the requirements of the business. The SAP functional team will start creating the organizational structure of the business in the system and configuring the tables of the SAP software to support the business process.

It is the responsibility of the SAP Basis administrator to communicate and enforce the agreed-upon rules laid out for the SAP software logistics while both the developers and the configurators work on the development systems. Once all the development and configuration work is complete, the changes are moved to the quality assurance systems by the Basis administrators using SAP transport tools as per the SAP transport strategy. Once the changes are in the quality assurance system, the testing team will execute the test plan along with all the test cases. Any defects in the software identified in the quality assurance system are fixed in the development system and moved to the quality assurance system for retesting. Once all the testing is complete, the Basis team will move the changes to the production system for deployment.

Software Logistics in ABAP Systems

As mentioned, software logistics in an ABAP system includes a discussion of concepts such as SAP System Landscapes, SAP client concept, SAP client instance strategy, SAP version management, SAP client-dependent and client-independent data, SAP configuration changes using the Implementation Guide, and SAP change requests and transport management. Some of the examples of SAP ABAP systems are SAP ERP, SAP BW, and SAP SCM.

System Landscapes

The System Landscape is defined as a SAP server environment usually comprising of development, quality assurance, and production systems. Additional systems in a typical landscape may include servers for training and data conversion purposes as well. Recommendations for a System Landscape are based on the purpose, organization size, and scope of the implementation effort of the project.

In a one-System-Landscape, development, quality control, and production needs are met by a single system. This kind of landscape is usually used for demo and training environments only. It is not recommended for productive operation. In a two-System-Landscape, development and test are performed in one system and changes are then moved to a second production system. This landscape does not allow for an isolated test environment, and any changes to the development objects can have an immediate impact on the testing environment. This landscape is not recommended for productive operations. It is usually used in demo, training, and very small organizations where the scope is limited. SAP recommends a minimum of three System Landscapes consisting of development, quality control, and production systems. This is the most common SAP System Landscape, and it meets the needs of most mid-size to large organizations. The illustration shows a minimal three-System-Landscape environment consisting of development, quality assurance, and production system environments. Moving the code changes and configuration changes from the development system to quality assurance systems and then to production systems in an orderly manner, with proper testing and an approval process, is usually referred to as a "promote to production strategy." For some SAP implementation projects, the needs are more demanding than the typical three-System-Landscape, and in these cases the landscape is further extended into four or five System Landscapes. This is further discussed in detail in Chapter 13.

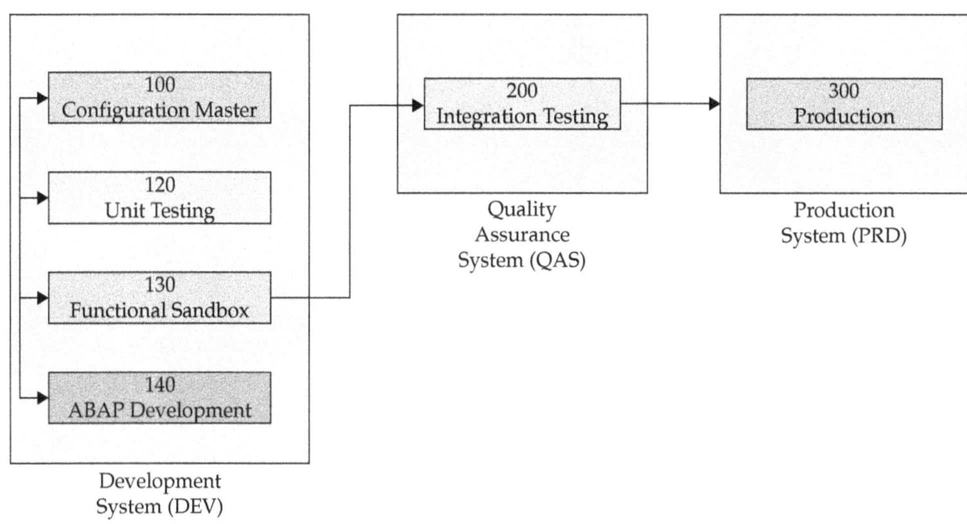

Client Concept

When we install a SAP system, it is usually referred to as an SAP instance. The SAP instance is identified by three alphanumeric characters referred to collectively as the SAP system identifier (SID). Examples of SID include DEV, QAS, DV1, PRD, and PR1. In addition, each SAP instance can have more then one logical data areas within it, referred to as clients. Clients are identified with a three-digit number such as 100, 320, or 500. SAP delivers three standard clients for every new ABAP system instance. They are SAP reference clients 000, 001, and SAP early watch client 066.

The SAP client is defined as a self-contained unit in an SAP instance with its own dataset and set of tables. This separation of data areas will allow SAP developers and functional configurators to work in different clients of the same instance without affecting each other's work and the on-going work of the other teams. The SAP client concept also allows for legal separation of data within an instance. Upon installing a new SAP system, the Basis team creates a copy of the SAP reference client 000 or 001 on to a new client with a unique three-digit identifier. The client copy process and different client administration activities will be discussed in more detail in Chapter 10.

SAP nonproduction systems usually have multiple clients and are created as per the client instance strategy of a given SAP implementation. We will study more about the client instance strategy in subsequent sections of this chapter. The SAP client number is entered when the user logs on to the system and will allow the logged-on user to view data belonging to this particular client. The following illustration shows the user entering a client number to log in to the system. The user can work in client number 100 while other users are working at the same time in other clients belonging to the same SAP instance.

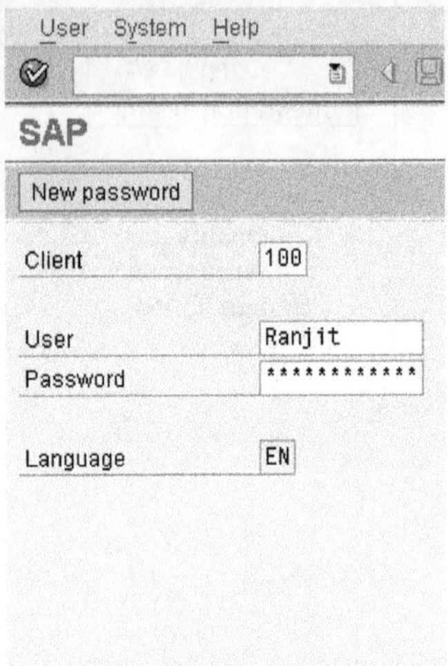

Copyright by SAP AG

Client-Dependent and Client-Independent Objects

SAP client data is divided into two categories: client dependent and client independent. Client-dependent data is specific to a particular client. Examples include master data, such as material master data and user master records. Client-independent data is accessible across all clients. Examples include ABAP programs and some cross-client customizing data. This separation of data is achieved by SAP at the database level by the use of the Mandt field in the client-specific tables. For client-dependent or client-specific tables, the first field is defined with the Mandt field (Mandt is client in German.) If we take the example of client-specific user master record table (USR02), you will notice that the first field of the table shown in Figure 9-1 has a field called Mandt.

Therefore, a good way to find out if a SAP table is client dependent or client independent is to check the first field of the table. For client-independent tables, the Mandt field is absent and, therefore, the data can be viewed from all the clients of the SAP instance. The SAP Data Dictionary Table with Text Description (DD02T) shown in Figure 9-2 is a good example of a client-independent table.

Client Instance Strategy

The SAP client instance strategy is a group of SAP systems in the landscape supporting implementation of the software in an orderly manner with rigorous built-in change management tools. Each system in the landscape will have one or more clearly defined clients. The System Landscape involves the following systems with clearly defined roles.

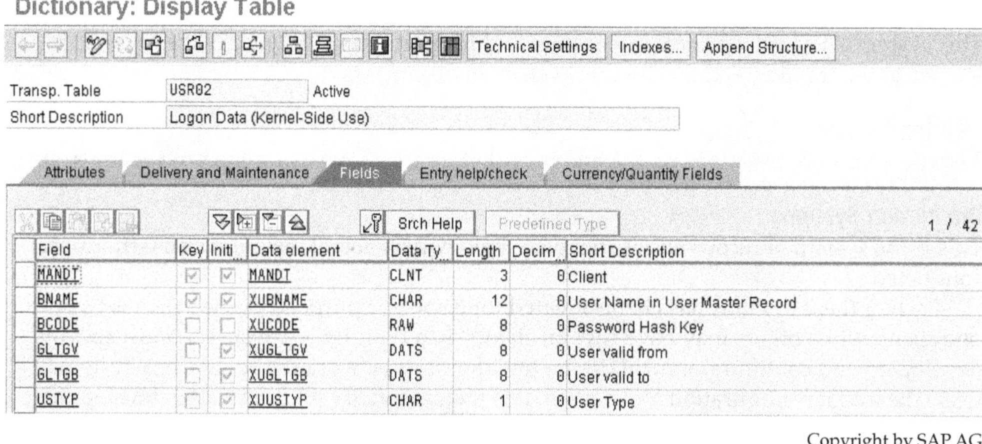
Dictionary: Display Table

Transp. Table USR02 Active
Short Description Logon Data (Kernel-Side Use)

Field	Key	Initi...	Data element	Data Ty...	Length	Decim...	Short Description
MANDT	☑	☑	MANDT	CLNT	3	0	Client
BNAME	☑	☑	XUBNAME	CHAR	12	0	User Name in User Master Record
BCODE	☐	☐	XUCODE	RAW	8	0	Password Hash Key
GLTGV	☐	☑	XUGLTGV	DATS	8	0	User valid from
GLTGB	☐	☑	XUGLTGB	DATS	8	0	User valid to
USTYP	☐	☑	XUUSTYP	CHAR	1	0	User Type

Copyright by SAP AG

Figure 9-1 Client-dependent user master table showing the Mandt field

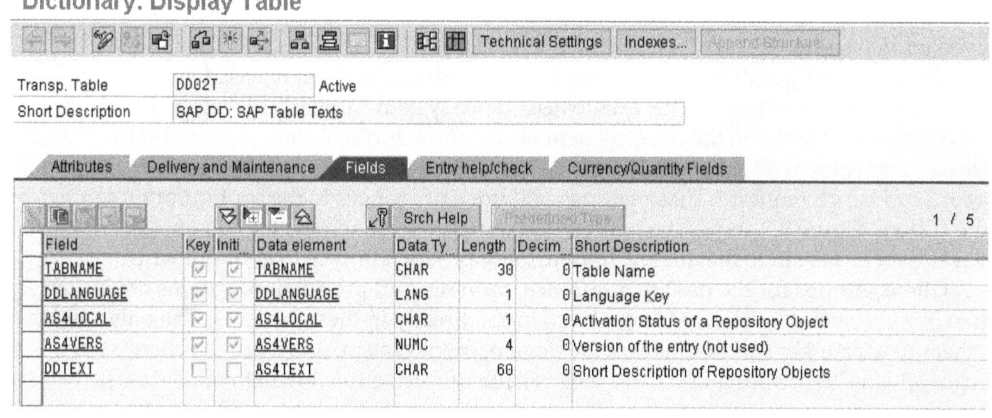
Dictionary: Display Table

Transp. Table DD02T Active
Short Description SAP DD: SAP Table Texts

Field	Key	Initi...	Data element	Data Ty...	Length	Decim...	Short Description
TABNAME	☑	☑	TABNAME	CHAR	30	0	Table Name
DDLANGUAGE	☑	☑	DDLANGUAGE	LANG	1	0	Language Key
AS4LOCAL	☑	☑	AS4LOCAL	CHAR	1	0	Activation Status of a Repository Object
AS4VERS	☑	☑	AS4VERS	NUMC	4	0	Version of the entry (not used)
DDTEXT	☐	☐	AS4TEXT	CHAR	60	0	Short Description of Repository Objects

Copyright by SAP AG

Figure 9-2 Client Independent Data Dictionary table showing no Mandt field

Sandbox System

This system helps functional teams and developers test new and high-risk scenarios without breaking the development system. Technical teams can also test patches and support packages in this system.

Development System

This system is the originator of all development and configuration objects of the SAP implementation. The development and configuration objects are moved from this system to the rest of the landscape using SAP Transport Management System. More details of the SAP Transport Management System (STMS) will be discussed in Chapter 11.

Quality Assurance System

This system is used to perform integration and regressions testing before the objects are moved to the training and production system environments.

Training Systems

These systems are used to train the end users before they start using the production system.

Production Systems

This is the system of record and is the live system where actual business transactions are conducted.

Each of these systems has clients created for a specific purpose. Some systems have only one client, while others may have several clients. In a typical SAP System Landscape, the developers and configurators will do the initial prototype work in the sandbox systems. Once the initial configuration looks good, it is then manually rekeyed in the development systems. The development system has several clients, each serving a specific purpose. There are at least three clients: the configuration master client, the development client, and the unit-testing client. Functional consultants configure the system in the configuration client. In this client, the settings will allow only client-specific configuration work and the changes are automatically saved in the change requests (data packages with a predefined number). (The details of the different client setting options and client administration activities are covered in Chapter 10.)

Once the configuration work is complete, the changes are then released and a Basis administrator moves them to the quality assurance system. Similarly, developers will create ABAP code and tables in the development client. The settings in this client will allow changes to the development objects, which are then are written to a change request usually referred to as a "workbench request." These settings will prevent changes to the configuration settings of the system. Figure 9-3 shows the path of the configuration and development objects from the development system to the quality, training, and production system environments.

Client settings for the quality assurance, training, and production systems are locked so that objects cannot be allowed to make changes directly in these systems. The only system where new changes can originate is the development system, and once the changes are released after the approval process, they will be moved to the downstream systems. Production systems usually will have only one client and it is prevented from making any direct changes. The training system will have several clients to support the on-going training classes. Additional training clients are set up using a copy process called a client copy. More details on the different client copy and transport processes will be discussed in subsequent chapters.

As shown in Figure 9-3, the transport path of the development object begins in Development System Client 210, and then it will be moved to Quality Assurance Configuration Gold Client 300 and to 310 for integration testing. Once the testing is successful the objects are imported to the training and production systems after securing the proper approvals from data owners. Similarly, the configuration changes originate from Client 200 of the development system and are imported to Client 300 of the quality assurance system. Once the integration testing is completed successfully, the objects are imported to the training and production systems after securing proper approvals from the data owners. In order to facilitate unit testing before releasing the configuration transports, Transaction Code SCC1 can be used to copy configuration changes to unit-testing Development Client 220 without releasing the transport request.

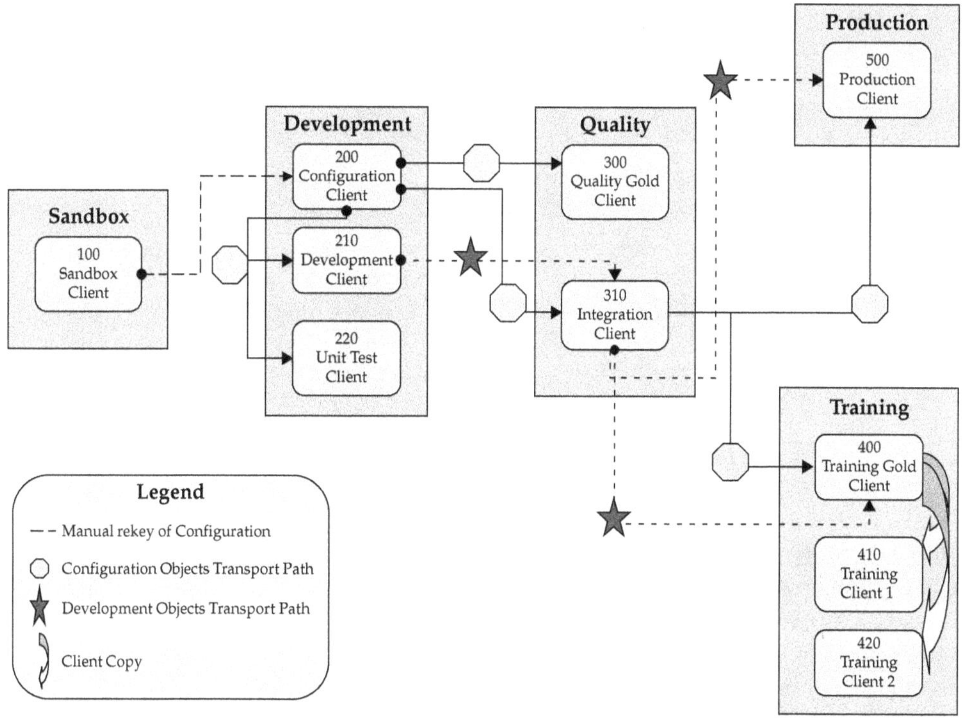

FIGURE 9-3 SAP client instance strategy

Change Requests and Transport Management

In the development system, the client settings are recorded automatically for the configuration and development clients. This results in SAP changes being saved in the development system in the form of change requests. A change request is a data package created by the system when changes are performed in the development system. Several tasks can be assigned to one change request number. All tasks should be released before releasing the change request. Releasing (exporting) the change request will create a data file and control file at the operating system level, resulting in transports. Each change request is assigned a unique number starting with the three-character SID of the development system. For example, if the SID is DV1, then the transport number will start with DV1K appended to a system and assigned number range starting with 9. In Figure 9-4 the transport number change request in a development system is DV1K922692. There is one task identified by the number DV1K922693 below this change request number. Usually, the team members save their respective work in the tasks and release the tasks as their work is completed. A team lead will verify the work of the team members and then will release the change request, therefore releasing the change request in the form of transports. All changes in the SAP system originate as transports in the development system and are imported to the target systems using SAP Transport Management System. More details on the SAP Transport Management System will be studied in subsequent chapters.

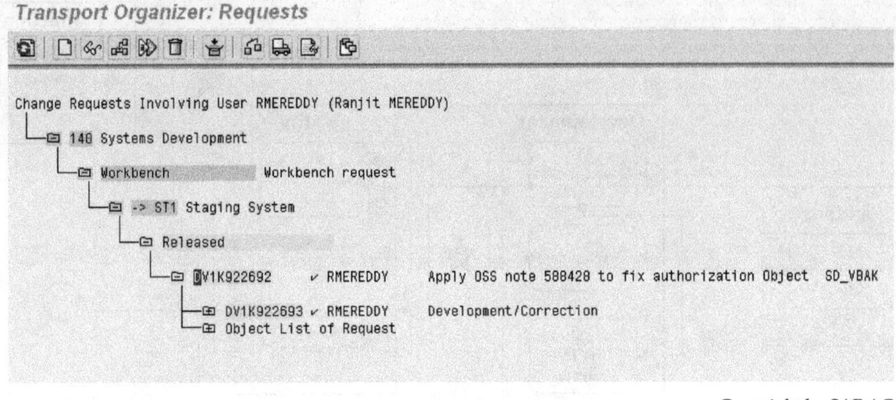

Copyright by SAP AG

FIGURE 9-4 SAP change requests

Software Logistics in Java Systems

Similar to ABAP systems, SAP provides a complete solution for developing and transporting Java-based applications. Some of the examples of SAP applications that are either completely Java-based or dual-stack are SAP NetWeaver Portal, SAP Process Integration, and SAP Development Infrastructure. SAP recommends four-System-Landscapes for the development of Java-based applications.

Four-System-Landscape for Java Applications

Unlike the SAP ABAP three-System-Landscape, in Java systems, the code is developed as a software component in the Java development system (e.g., .jar files) and it has dependencies, so a separate consolidation system is needed to consolidate and assemble the code. Once the code is assembled, it is actually ready to be moved to the test system for integration testing and finally delivered to the production system for final deployment. Figure 9-5 shows the four-System-Landscape of SAP Java NetWeaver Development Infrastructure (NWDI).

The following sections discuss the main components of the SAP NWDI.

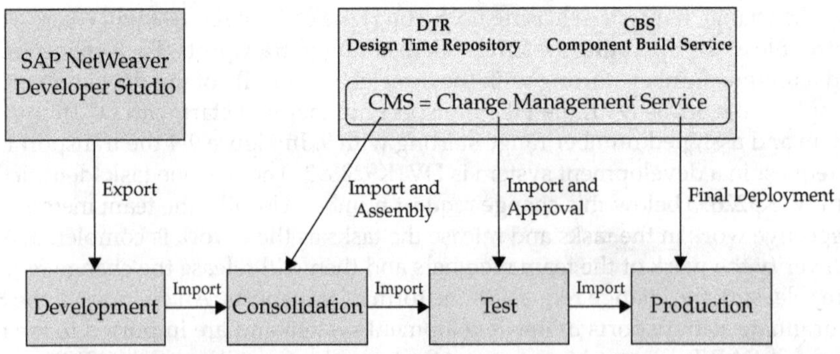

FIGURE 9-5 Java four-System-Landscape with NetWeaver Developer Studio

SAP NetWeaver Developer Studio

SAP NetWeaver Developer Studio is SAP's Java-based development environment. It is an open-source project based on the Eclipse platform.

Change Management Service (CMS)

Change Management Service is part of the NWDI and helps transport Java objects between the four systems of the Java landscape. It is similar to the SAP Transport Management System (STMS) of the ABAP systems.

Design Time Repository (DTR)

Design Time Repository is the part of the NWDI that acts as a central storage for all source files in different formats. DTR provides a check-in and check-out mechanism for source files so that developers can access the files from the repository.

Component Build Service (CBS)

Component Build Service is the part of NWDI that provides the central build environment. The build process is based on the SAP component model. The objects are ready to be imported to the test system after a successful build, and then will be moved eventually to the production environment for final deployment.

More details of SAP Java software logistics will be discussed in Chapter 12.

Summary

- The SAP System Landscape is a server environment comprising development, quality assurance, and production systems in an ABAP stack.
- Three-System-Landscapes are recommended for SAP ABAP development and configuration projects.
- Four-System-Landscapes are recommended for SAP Java development projects.
- The client concept in ABAP systems helps to isolate data environments where parallel activities can be organized within the same SAP instance.
- Client data can be categorized into client-dependent and client-independent.
- Client-dependent data is accessible within the same client.
- Client-independent data is accessible across all the clients in a SAP instance.
- SAP client instance strategy allows for orderly development and configuration in ABAP stacks providing a "promote to production" path for all the tested and approved changes.
- SAP Transport Management System (STMS) is used to move the change requests (transports) from the development environment to the quality, training, and production environments in an ABAP stack.
- SAP Change Management Service (CMS) of the NWDI is used to move Java object changes in the Java stack.

- NetWeaver Developer Studio is the Java application development platform used in the Java stack environments.
- The NWDI Design Time Repository (DTR) serves as a central repository for all source files.
- The NWDI Component Build Service (CBS) serves as a central build environment for Java applications.
- SAP NetWeaver Portal and Development Infrastructure usage types are good examples of a Java stack environment.
- SAP ERP (ECC) and SAP BW are good examples of an ABAP stack environment.

Additional Resources

- **SAP Software Logistics** www.sdn.sap.com/irj/sdn/softwarelogistics
- **SAP Landscape Design** www.sdn.sap.com/irj/sdn/landscapedesign
- **SAP NetWeaver Developer Studio** www.sdn.sap.com/irj/sdn/nw-devstudio

CHAPTER

SAP Client Administration in ABAP Systems

In this chapter we will cover all client administration activities of a typical ABAP system. One good example of an ABAP system where a lot of client administration activities such as client copies, client refreshes, and client deletions are performed is an ECC (ERP Central Component) system. New clients are created, refreshed, and deleted based on the client instance strategy of a given SAP implementation. In addition, testing strategy, conversion strategy, and training strategies call for the creation of additional clients, such as integration testing clients, conversion testing clients, and end-user classroom training clients. Out of all the client administration activities client copy is the most important and most of this chapter will go into considerable detail of this process. Other client administration activities are also covered to a fair extent in this chapter.

Proper setup of new clients and enforcement of correct client settings as per the client instance strategy are very important to protect the integrity of the change management process, distribution of custom code and configuration changes in a SAP landscape, and version management in an implementation project.

Client Copy (Local Client Copy)

The client copy process helps to create a new client as a copy of an existing client. After the installation a new client is created as a copy of client 000 or 001. Since this copy is performed on the local system, it is referred to as a local client copy. Whenever there is a reference to a client copy, by default, it means a local client copy. The following explains the prerequisites, best practices, and detailed procedure for setting up a new client using SAP standard tools. Client 300 will be created from SAP installation default client 000 in the example.

Prerequisites for Setting Up a New Client

The following prerequisites must be performed before setting up a new client. This will help ensure a smooth setup process.

Enable the sap* User

During the setup of a new client, the user account sap* is used during the initial copy process. By default, this account is disabled in a newly installed system. Since we need this account to perform a client copy, we have to enable it. This account status is governed by a SAP profile parameter login/no_automatic_user_sapstar. The account is enabled when the parameter value is set to 0. By default, the parameter value is 1. Transaction code RZ10 should be used to change the parameter value from 1 to 0 before starting the client copy process. More details on how to change SAP parameter values is explained in detail in Chapter 14. User account sap* is coded in the kernel and by default has all authorizations and has a default password of PASS. Once the parameter is enabled then the sap* user account can be used for performing a client copy.

Create a New Logical System

A logical system uniquely identifies a physical client in a SAP System Landscape and is used as an identifier for setting up communication between different SAP clients, systems, and external systems. Even though this is not mandatory for setting up a new client, it is highly recommended and is therefore listed as a prerequisite. Transaction code BD54 should be used to setting up a new logical system. Enter transaction code BD54 in the current client (client 000), which displays the following screen indicating that the logical systems table (TBDLS) is client-independent. Click the green check mark acknowledging this and continue.

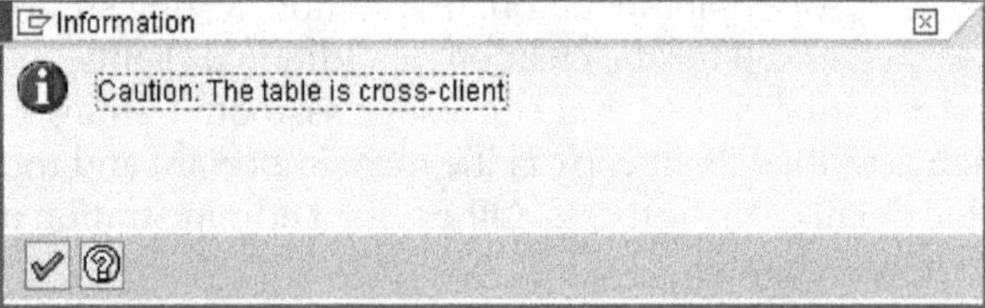

Copyright by SAP AG

The following screen will appear, where new logical system names can be maintained by clicking the New Entries button.

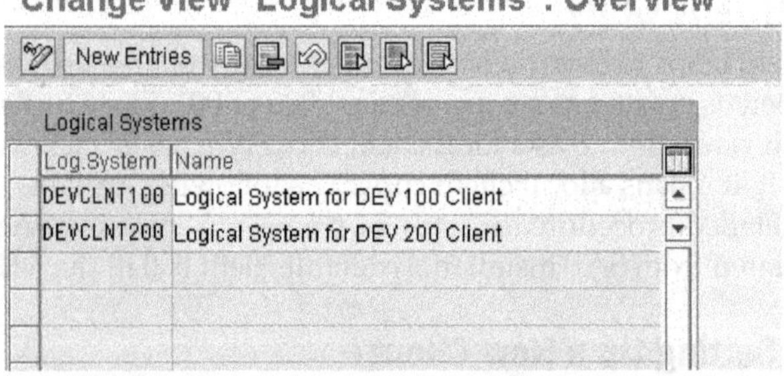

Copyright by SAP AG

This will present the following illustration where a new logical system name for client 300 is entered. The recommended naming convention for a new logical system name is <SID>CLNT<Client#>. For example, if you would like to create a new client in a SAP system with system identifier DEV and client number 300, this naming convention would translate to DEVCLNT300.

New Entries: Overview of Added Entries

Logical Systems

Log.System	Name
DEVCLNT300	Logical System for DEV 300 Client

Copyright by SAP AG

After the new logical system DEVCLNT300 is entered along with the text description, click the Save button (CTRL-S). You will be prompted to save the change in a data package number referred to as a transport request, as shown . Transport requests will be discussed in detail in Chapter 11. This data package will be used to export and import newly entered data from the development systems to all the downstream systems, such as quality assurance and production systems. In the illustration the system is prompting you to either enter an existing transport number or create a new transport request number. In our case, we will choose to create a new transport request by clicking the page icon (F8).

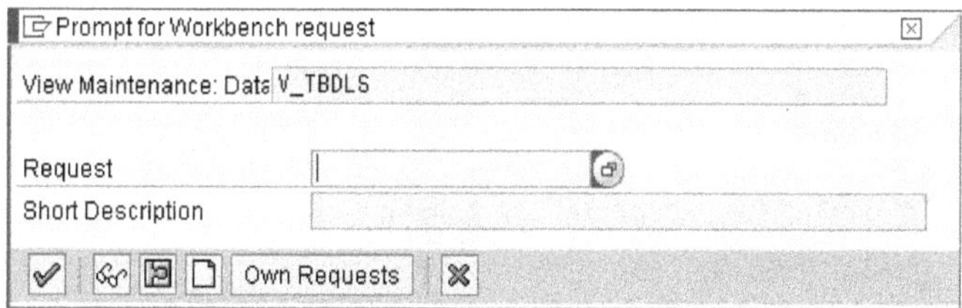

Copyright by SAP AG

This will show a create request window, as shown in Figure 10-1. Enter a text description in the Short Description field to properly identify the transport request.

Click the Save button. The following screen appears with an assignment of a new transport request number. In our case the system-assigned transport request number is DEVK900024. This number is uniquely identified in the entire SAP System Landscape and is used to move changes to all the downstream systems such as quality assurance and production systems.

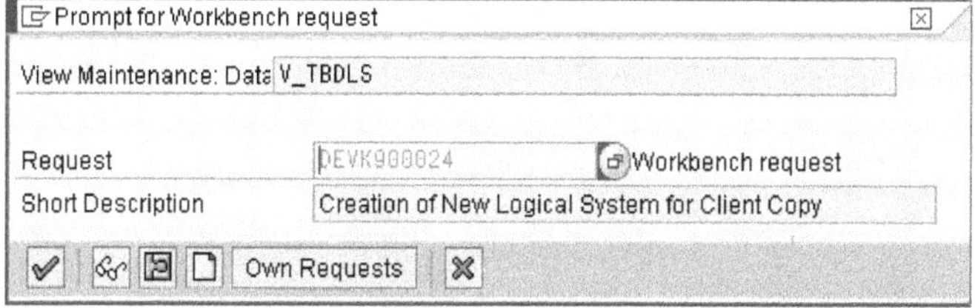

Copyright by SAP AG

Click the green check mark button or press ENTER. This will save the changes in the table and the uniquely identified transport request number. You will notice a message at the

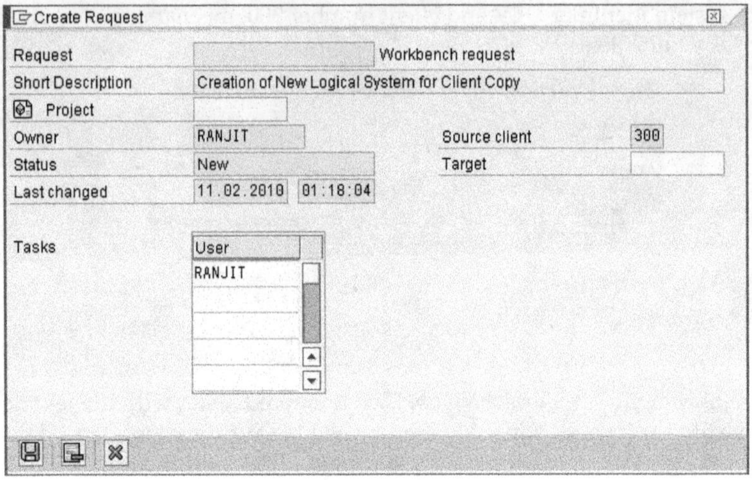
Create Request
Request
Workbench request
Short Description
Creation of New Logical System for Client Copy
Project
Owner
RANJIT
Source client
300
Status
New
Target
Last changed
11.02.2010
01:18:04
Tasks
User
RANJIT

Copyright by SAP AG

FIGURE 10-1 Create New Transport Request window

bottom of the screen notifying you that data was saved. This confirms that the newly created logical system DEVCLNT300 is saved in the database table.

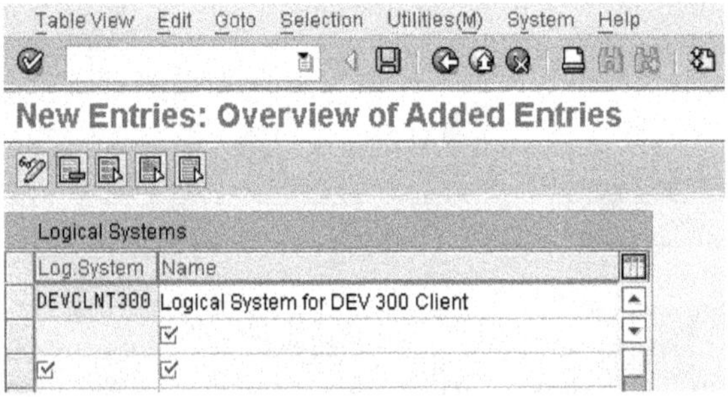
Table View Edit Goto Selection Utilities(M) System Help
New Entries: Overview of Added Entries
Logical Systems
Log.System
Name
DEVCLNT300
Logical System for DEV 300 Client

Copyright by SAP AG

When you press the BACK ARROW button (F3), you will notice that the newly entered logical system name is now showing in the table list.

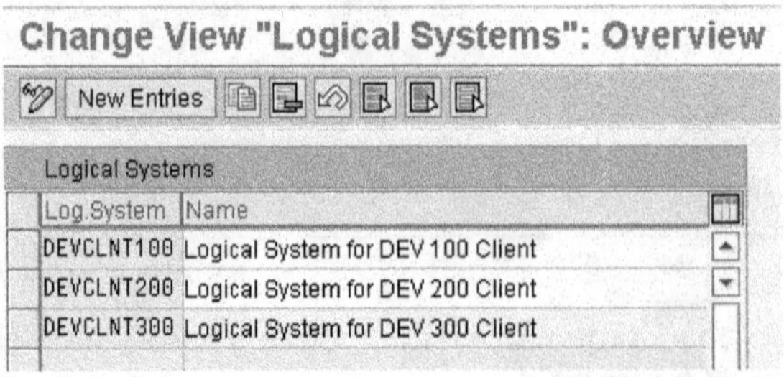
Change View "Logical Systems": Overview
New Entries
Logical Systems
Log.System
Name
DEVCLNT100
Logical System for DEV 100 Client
DEVCLNT200
Logical System for DEV 200 Client
DEVCLNT300
Logical System for DEV 300 Client

Copyright by SAP AG

Best Practices for Performing a Client Copy

The following best practices are recommended for performing a client copy. This will not only ensure a consistent setup of a new client with high data integrity, but also execute it with the highest performance with regard to client copy runtime.

Turn Off Oracle Archiving

If Oracle archiving is turned on, it will generate a lot of archive logs and can quickly fill up the archive directory and cause the client copy to stall. In order to avoid this scenario, it is recommended to turn off archiving for the duration of the client copy process.

Check Database Space

Check database space and, if needed, add sufficient space before the start of the client copy process so that a new client can be created successfully.

User Activity

Users should not be logged on to the source and target clients during a client copy run.

Additional Component Installs

Import all support packages, language installs, and add-ons before starting the client copy in the development system for the project team.

Client Copy Schedule

The client copy should be scheduled after regular working hours or over a weekend.

Test Run

Perform a test run for the client copy procedure to identify any potential problems up front.

Parallel Processing

Use parallel processing to reduce the runtime of the client copy.

Restart Option

After fixing a canceled client copy/refresh process, use the restart option.

Detailed Client Copy Procedure

The following provides a detailed procedure for performing a complete end-to-end client copy in a SAP system. In this example we will create a new client 300 as a copy of client 000. The first step in the client copy process is to log in to client 000 and enter transaction code SCC4; you will notice the following screen listing existing clients.

Display View "Clients": Overview

Client	Name	City	Crcy	Changed on
000	SAP AG	Walldorf	EUR	
001	Auslieferungsmandant R11	Kundstadt	USD	
066	EarlyWatch	Walldorf	EUR	21.07.2002
100	Test Client	Pittsburgh	USD	04.02.2009

Click the change button (the pencil icon or press CTRL-F1) and you will see the following window indicating that this is a cross-client table.

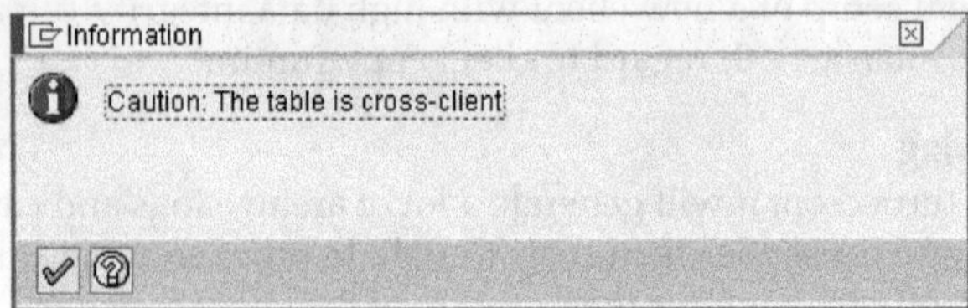

Copyright by SAP AG

Acknowledge the window by clicking the green check mark. This will show the client list in change mode with a New Entries button, as shown.

Change View "Clients": Overview

New Entries

Client	Name	City	Crcy	Changed on
000	SAP AG	Walldorf	EUR	
001	Auslieferungsmandant R11	Kundstadt	USD	
066	EarlyWatch	Walldorf	EUR	21.07.2002
100	Test Client	Pittsburgh	USD	04.02.2009

Copyright by SAP AG

Click the New Entries button, and you will see the following screen (Figure 10-2) for entering the new client information. Enter the information as shown. Please use the following guidelines for entering the information:

- **Client** Enter the client number as per the client instance strategy document. Enter a brief description of the purpose of the client as well.
- **City** The name of the city where the physical SAP system is located.
- **Logical System** In this field enter the unique logical system name that was created in the client copy prerequisite step, or use the down arrow (F4) to display the list of values from which to choose. Select DEVCLNT300.
- **Standard Currency** For United States installations, select USD. Otherwise, select the appropriate currency from the drop-down list (F4) for the country where SAP is being installed and implemented.
- **Client Role** Pick the relevant client role from the drop-down menu. In this example, we chose the client role Test.
- **Other Settings** This should be set as per client instance strategy client settings. Unless this is a development system, No Changes Allowed should be selected. More details will be covered in the section "Manage Client Settings."

Copyright by SAP AG

Figure 10-2 Client entries for a new client

Once all the entries are filled out, click the Save button or press CTRL-S. This following window will be displayed asking you to be careful when changing logical system names. Acknowledge the message by clicking the green check mark. This will save the new client information in table T000 and you will see a message saying data was saved.

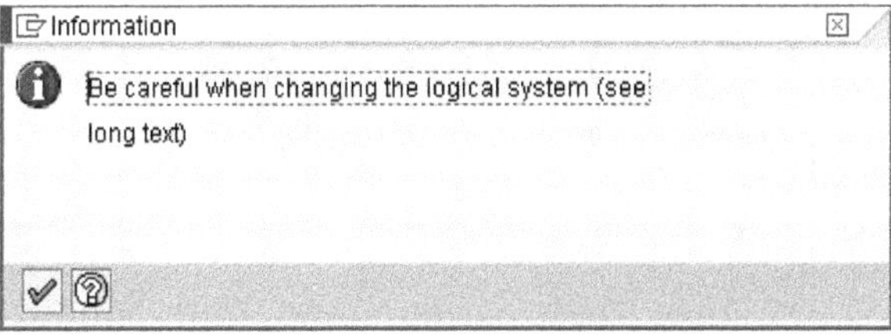

Information
Be careful when changing the logical system (see long text)

Copyright by SAP AG

The next step in the client copy process is to log in to the client that was newly entered into the client table, as shown. In this example the new client is 300. When logging in to the newly created client for the first time, use the sap* user account. The default password is PASS.

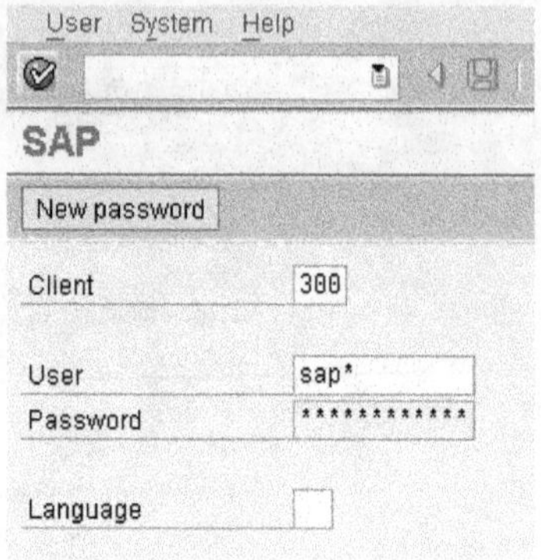

Copyright by SAP AG

Once the sap* user credentials are entered for client 300, press the ENTER key to complete the login process. After successful authentication, the system will present the copyright screen (Figure 10-3). Acknowledge the copyright by clicking the green check mark.

Once logged in, enter transaction code SCCL (Local Client Copy) to start the client copy. This will show the following screen. Enter the source client as 000. For client copy profile, choose SAP_CUST; this will copy all customizing data from client 000 to 300. One of the best practices is to select the test run to get an estimate of the runtime and to know if there are any issues or errors with the client copy. This option is recommended for large client copies, but can be skipped for smaller client copies. The test run option will execute the client copy, but actual database updates/commits will not happen. Running the test option will give important information, such as estimated runtime and the space requirements. This will help the Basis administrator plan the actual client copy run. In this example we will choose to skip the test run as it is a setup of the

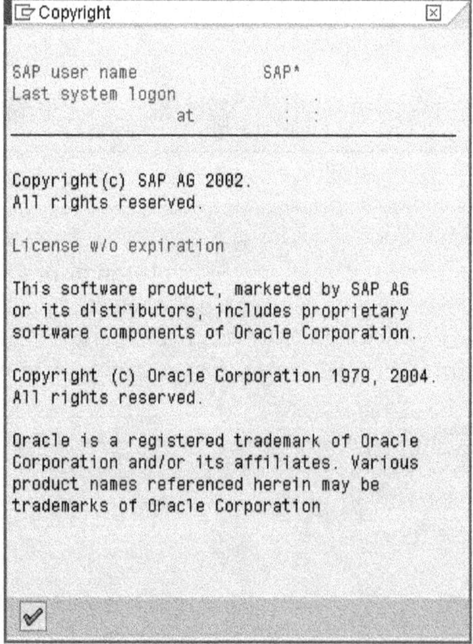

Copyright by SAP AG

FIGURE 10-3 Copyright screen

initial client with configuration data only. Configuration data client copies do not have a long runtime and a test run may not be useful for estimating the runtime.

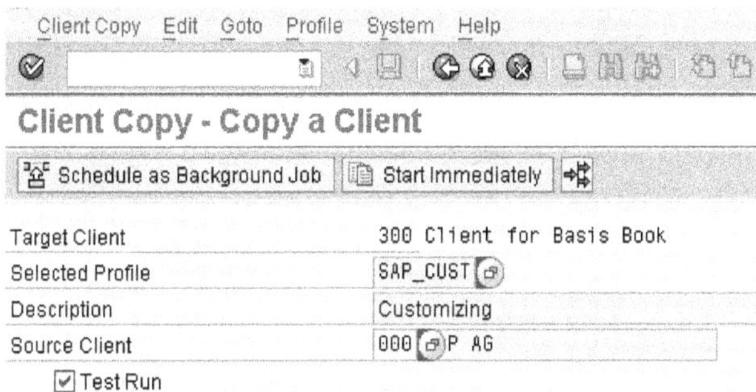

Copyright by SAP AG

The client copy tool (SCCL transaction) offers a list of expert options (Figure 10-4) that can be activated for the client copy run. Usually, the defaults are fine for most of the client copy jobs. However, under some special circumstances such as copying a large production client, some of the expert options can be activated. Select Edit from the menu, and then select Expert Settings. This will show the following screen with all the expert options. OSS note 446485 provides additional details for the special copying options for a client copy.

The next step in the client copy process is to configure parallel processing. Select Go To and choose Parallel Process (SHIFT-F1), and this will show the parallel process screen shown in

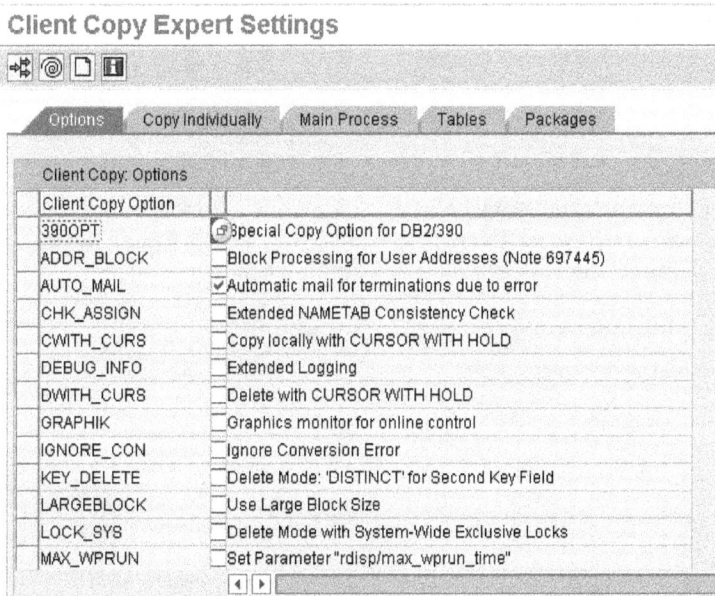

Client Copy Expert Settings

Options | Copy Individually | Main Process | Tables | Packages

Client Copy: Options

Client Copy Option	
390OPT	Special Copy Option for DB2/390
ADDR_BLOCK	☐ Block Processing for User Addresses (Note 697445)
AUTO_MAIL	☑ Automatic mail for terminations due to error
CHK_ASSIGN	☐ Extended NAMETAB Consistency Check
CWITH_CURS	☐ Copy locally with CURSOR WITH HOLD
DEBUG_INFO	☐ Extended Logging
DWITH_CURS	☐ Delete with CURSOR WITH HOLD
GRAPHIK	☐ Graphics monitor for online control
IGNORE_CON	☐ Ignore Conversion Error
KEY_DELETE	☐ Delete Mode: 'DISTINCT' for Second Key Field
LARGEBLOCK	☐ Use Large Block Size
LOCK_SYS	☐ Delete Mode with System-Wide Exclusive Locks
MAX_WPRUN	☐ Set Parameter "rdisp/max_wprun_time"

Copyright by SAP AG

FIGURE 10-4 Client copy expert options

the following illustration. Enter the number of parallel processes that you would like to use for the client copy, and select the server group by clicking the Logon/Server Group field drop-down menu. In our example we have chosen four parallel processes and the server group is Parallel_Load. You can create a new RFC server group for setting up parallel processing by clicking the Maintain RFC Server Groups button or by using transaction code RZ12. Once maintained here, the RFC server group can be used for client copy parallel process configuration. Click the Save button once the choices are complete.

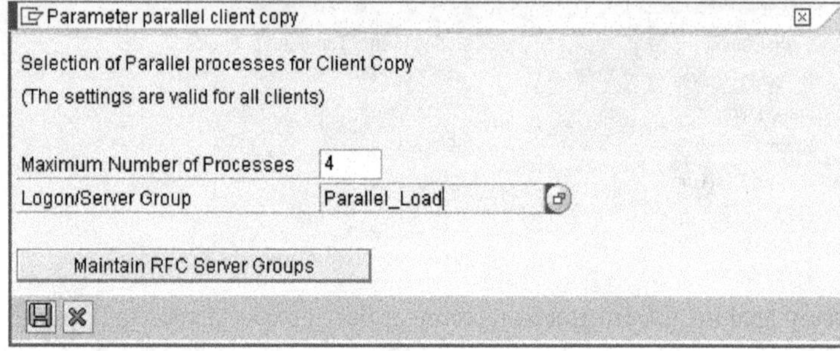

Copyright by SAP AG

The system will take you back to the local client copy screen with all the chosen entries as shown. Please note that the Test Run check box is not selected.

Client Copy - Copy a Client

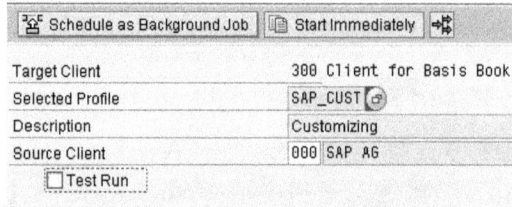

Schedule as Background Job | Start Immediately

Target Client 300 Client for Basis Book
Selected Profile SAP_CUST
Description Customizing
Source Client 000 SAP AG
Test Run

Copyright by SAP AG

Once the entries are completed, choose the Schedule As Background Job option, which will show the following screen. This will give an option of scheduling the client copy as a background job immediately or at a later date and time.

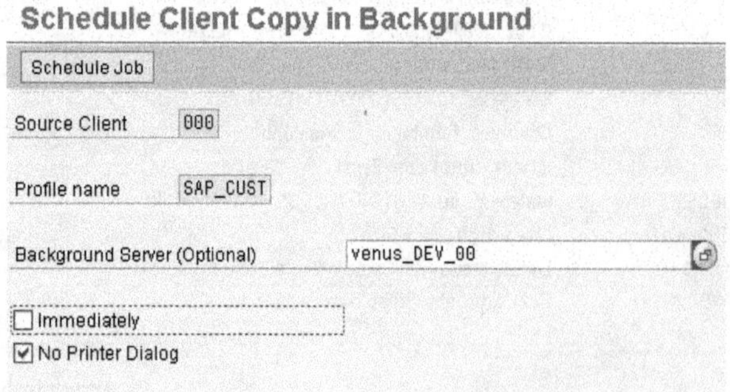

Copyright by SAP AG

Start Time

Immediate | Date/Time | After job | After event | At operation mode | >>

Date/Time
Scheduled start Date 09.02.2010 Time 20:45:00
No Start After Date Time

After job

At operation mode

After event

Periodic job

Check | Period values | Restrictions

Copyright by SAP AG

FIGURE 10-5 Client copy job showing the scheduling options

If you clicked the Schedule Job button, you see the screen shown in Figure 10-5 where you can schedule the client copy job either immediately or at a later date and time. If you select the Immediately check box the system will skip the scheduling options screen and jump directly to the client copy verification screen, as shown in Figure 10-6.

Click the Continue button and the following screen is displayed confirming that the client copy job has been successfully scheduled and the client copy logs can be verified using transaction code SCC3.

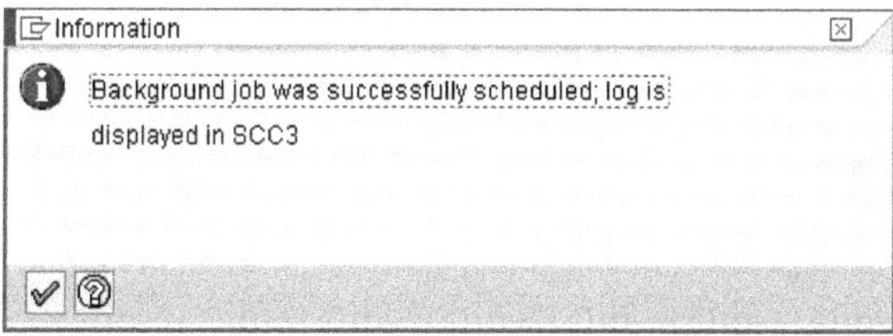

Copyright by SAP AG

The next step is to execute transaction code SM50 to verify that the client copy job started running. Figure 10-7 shows that the client copy has started with user account sap* in client 300 and four parallel processes are being executed as per the configuration.

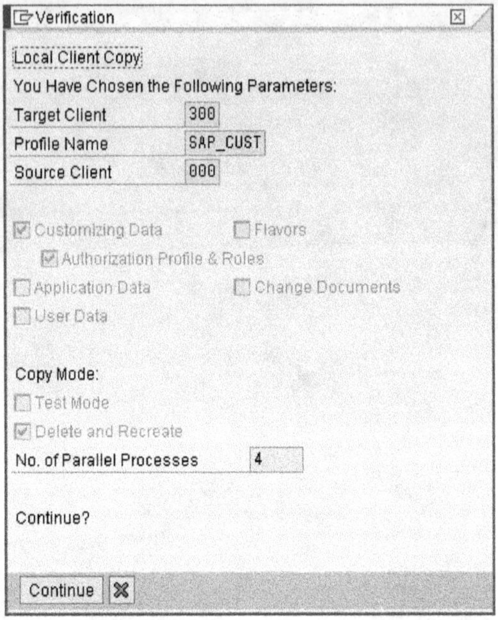

Verification

Local Client Copy

You Have Chosen the Following Parameters:

Target Client 300

Profile Name SAP_CUST

Source Client 000

☑ Customizing Data ☐ Flavors

☑ Authorization Profile & Roles

☐ Application Data ☐ Change Documents

☐ User Data

Copy Mode:

☐ Test Mode

☑ Delete and Recreate

No. of Parallel Processes 4

Continue?

Continue

FIGURE 10-6 Client copy verification screen

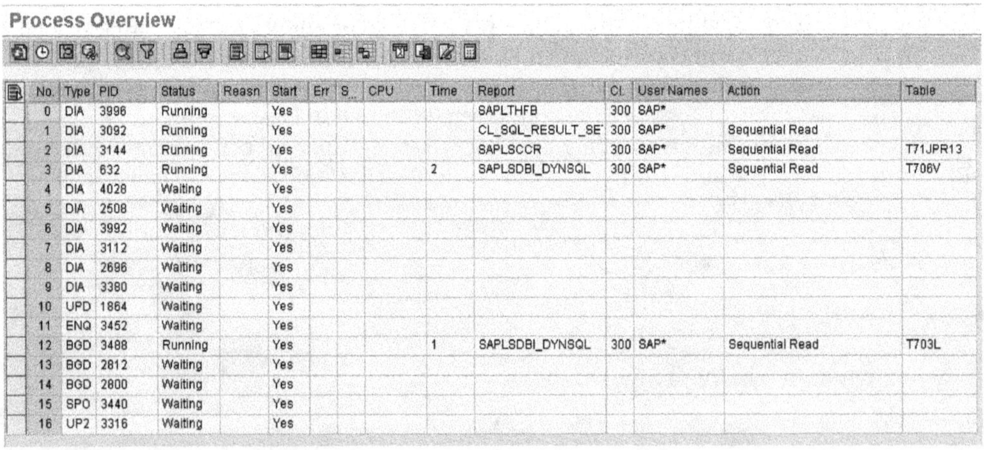

Process Overview

No.	Type	PID	Status	Reasn	Start	Err	S...	CPU	Time	Report	Cl.	User Names	Action	Table
0	DIA	3996	Running		Yes					SAPLTHFB	300	SAP*		
1	DIA	3092	Running		Yes					CL_SQL_RESULT_SE	300	SAP*	Sequential Read	
2	DIA	3144	Running		Yes					SAPLSCCR	300	SAP*	Sequential Read	T71JPR13
3	DIA	632	Running		Yes				2	SAPLSDBI_DYNSQL	300	SAP*	Sequential Read	T706V
4	DIA	4028	Waiting		Yes									
5	DIA	2508	Waiting		Yes									
6	DIA	3992	Waiting		Yes									
7	DIA	3112	Waiting		Yes									
8	DIA	2696	Waiting		Yes									
9	DIA	3380	Waiting		Yes									
10	UPD	1864	Waiting		Yes									
11	ENQ	3452	Waiting		Yes									
12	BGD	3488	Running		Yes				1	SAPLSDBI_DYNSQL	300	SAP*	Sequential Read	T703L
13	BGD	2812	Waiting		Yes									
14	BGD	2800	Waiting		Yes									
15	SPO	3440	Waiting		Yes									
16	UP2	3316	Waiting		Yes									

FIGURE 10-7 Process overview screen showing an active client copy run

Client Copy Logs

SAP provides tools to monitor the progress of the client copy in a systematic manner. Transaction code SCC3 will give the precise status of the client copy, and is the recommended client copy monitoring tool. When SCC3 transaction code is executed while a client copy is running, the system will show the following screen indicating that the client copy run is being processed.

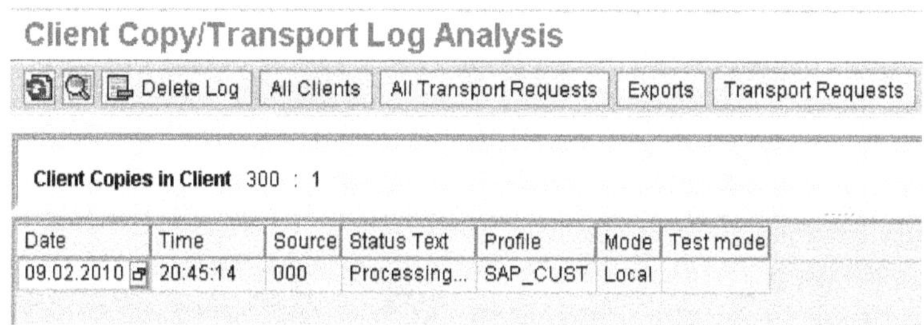

Date	Time	Source	Status Text	Profile	Mode	Test mode
09.02.2010	20:45:14	000	Processing...	SAP_CUST	Local	

Copyright by SAP AG

Details of the active client copy can be obtained by double-clicking the status line. This shows the detailed processing status of the active client copy, as shown in Figure 10-8. The detailed log shows the number of tables and lines copied in the client copy run at that time. You can click the refresh button on the top of the detailed log screen and notice that the

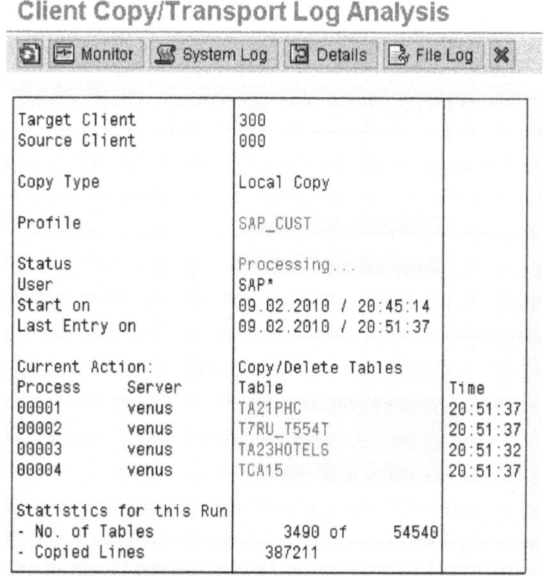


```
Target Client               300
Source Client               000

Copy Type                   Local Copy

Profile                     SAP_CUST

Status                      Processing...
User                        SAP*
Start on                    09.02.2010 / 20:45:14
Last Entry on               09.02.2010 / 20:51:37

Current Action:             Copy/Delete Tables
Process     Server          Table                    Time
00001       venus           TA21PHC                  20:51:37
00002       venus           T7RU_T554T               20:51:37
00003       venus           TA23HOTELS               20:51:32
00004       venus           TCA15                    20:51:37

Statistics for this Run
- No. of Tables               3490 of     54540
- Copied Lines              387211
```

Copyright by SAP AG

Figure 10-8 Detailed client copy run statistics

client copy is active and the table count is changing from time to time. The client copy process copies the table in an alphabetical sequence, and some of the larger SAP standard tables are copied toward the end of the client copy run. Transaction SCC3 can also be used to check the client copy logs of all the client copy runs that were performed in the system. This will help a Basis administrator analyze the history of different clients in a given system.

The following illustration shows that the client copy has been successfully completed.

Target Client	300
Source Client	000
Copy Type	Local Copy
Profile	SAP_CUST
Status	Successfully Completed
User	SAP*
Start on	09.02.2010 / 20:45:14
Last Entry on	09.02.2010 / 21:38:26
Statistics for this Run	
- No. of Tables	54540 of 54540
- Deleted Lines	3
- Copied Lines	5049341

Copyright by SAP AG

Client Copy Profiles

One of the main criteria for setting up a new client is the intended purpose of the target client. SAP client instance strategy defines the total number of clients that are called for in each system and the intended purpose of each. Depending upon the purpose of the target client, a Basis administrator creates a new client. The dataset that is copied from the source client to the target client will be based on the client copy profile. SAP provides the following client copy profiles for setting up the client copy. The client copy profile must be selected in the selected profile field, as shown in a previous illustration.

Profiles	Meaning
SAP_ALL	All Client-Specific Data w/o Change Documents
SAP_APPL	Customizing and Application Data w/o Change Docs
SAP_APPX	SAP_APPL w/o Authorization Profiles and Roles
SAP_CUST	Customizing
SAP_CUSV	Customizing and User Variants
SAP_CUSX	Customizing w/o Authorization Profiles and Roles
SAP_PROF	Only Authorization Profiles and Roles
SAP_UCSV	Customizing, User Master Records and User Variants
SAP_UCUS	Customizing and User Master Records
SAP_UONL	User Without Authorization Profiles and Roles
SAP_USER	User Master Records and Authorization Profiles

Copyright by SAP AG

SAP client copy profiles work on the basis of the different categories of data. Table 10-1 lists the main categories of SAP data.

SAP Data Category	Description
Master Data	Static/long-term data. Example: Vendor master data.
Transaction Data	Day-to-day transactions-related data. Example: Purchase order.
Application Data	Master data and transaction data.
Customizing Data	Data dealing with SAP application processing logic. Example: Customizing company codes, plants, and sales organizations for a given company.
User Master Data	Master data dealing with user account information.

TABLE 10-1 SAP Data Categories

SAP application data is dependent on customizing data. Thus, consistency of application data is based on customizing data. It is because of this reason that it is not possible to perform a client copy of only application data. Either you have to copy all data (customizing data and application data) using client copy profile SAP_ALL or copy only the customizing data using client copy profile SAP_CUST. When only customizing data, client copy profile (SAP_CUST) is used for performing a client refresh; the application data is deleted in the target client and only customizing data is copied from the source client.

Client Copy Restart Option

The client copy process can fail for any of the following reasons:

- Database space is filled up.
- File system is full and job logs cannot be written.
- Operating system has crashed.
- Database has crashed.
- There are network issues.

If any of these situations arises, the client copy is cancelled and SAP provides a restart option to continue the client copy after the problem has been rectified. To use the restart option, issue the SCCL transaction. This will result in the following screen indicating that the client copy was cancelled and a restart is required.

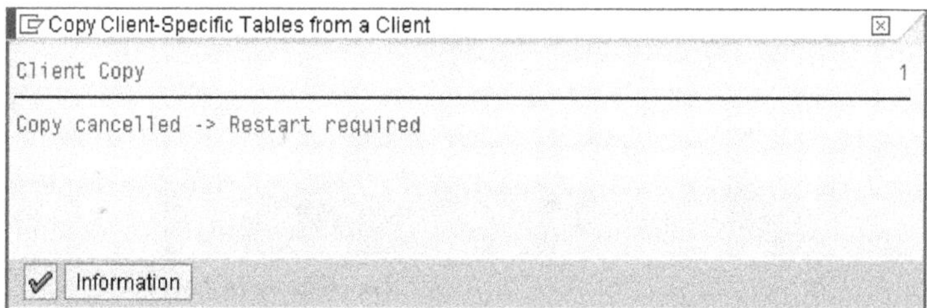

Copyright by SAP AG

Click the green check mark, and then the system will present the following screen with Restart Mode selected.

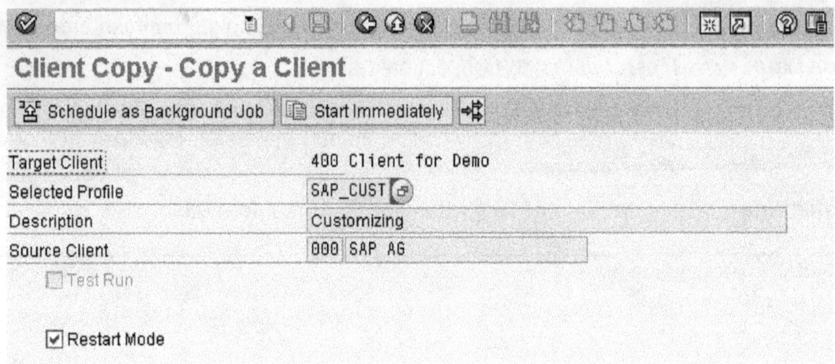

Choosing this restart option will present the verification screen shown in Figure 10-9. Click the Continue button, and the client copy will start from where it was cancelled and run to successful completion.

Verification

Local Client Copy

You Have Chosen the Following Parameters:

Target Client	400
Profile Name	SAP_CUST
Source Client	000

Customizing Data   Flavors

Authorization Profile & Roles

Application Data   Change Documents

User Data

Copy Mode:

Test Mode

Delete and Recreate

Restart

No. of Parallel Processes 4

Continue?

Continue

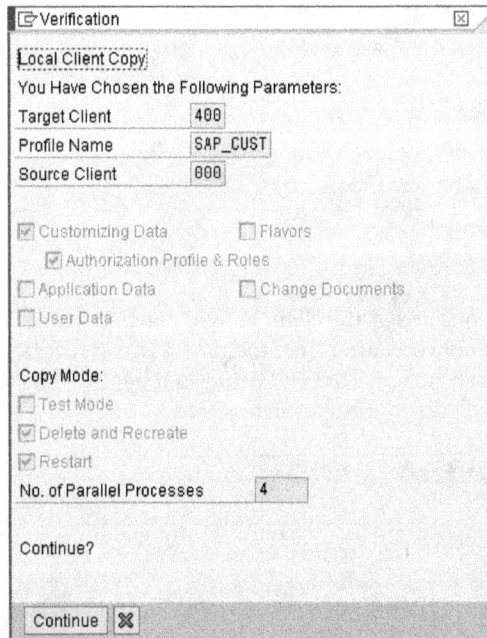

FIGURE 10-9 Client copy restart option verification screen

Remote Client Copy

A client copy performed between two different systems using an RFC connection is referred to as a remote client copy. When performing a remote client copy, an RFC connection for the source system must be set up between the source and target system client. Unlike a local client copy, a remote client copy performs a repository comparison as a prerequisite for the copy. If there are any data dictionary differences between the source and target system client, they have to be rectified before a successful completion of the remote client copy can take place. Data dictionary changes, such as adding a field to a table, can be transported from the source system to the target system to rectify the repository differences. SAP also provides an option of excluding certain tables from the copy process, but the customer has the responsibility for any inconsistencies as a result of this exclusion. A remote client copy performed over a WAN can have network-related performance bottlenecks as well. One other drawback of a remote client copy is that for the duration of the copy process, no user activity is allowed in the source client and therefore will not be available for general use. However, because of the ease of use and performance improvements made by SAP in recent releases, this is a viable option for Basis administrators who want to set up a target client from another SAP system. This procedure also takes care of all post-copy procedures that would have to be completed manually if another method such as a database copy were used for the copy process. Transaction code SCC9 is used to perform a remote client copy. The following illustration shows the initial screen for performing a remote client copy. Once the source system RFC connection is entered, the rest of the procedure is similar to that of performing a local client copy.

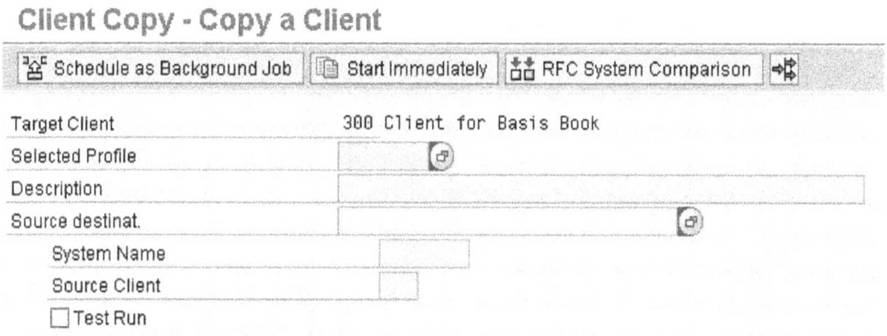

Client Copy - Copy a Client

Schedule as Background Job | Start Immediately | RFC System Comparison

Target Client	300 Client for Basis Book
Selected Profile	
Description	
Source destinat.	
System Name	
Source Client	
☐ Test Run	

Client Refresh

A client refresh involves refreshing the data of the existing target client and is based on the client copy profile used for the copy process. Instead of a two-step process of deleting the target client and then performing a client copy, the client refresh process can do it in one step. Usually, a gold client with clean data is maintained in each system as per the client instance strategy and is used as a source of the client refresh. The client refresh will delete and re-create data in the target client, depending upon the choice of the client copy profile. The runtime of the client refresh will depend upon several factors, including the data volume.

Client Copy of User Master Records

The client copy profile SAP_USER is used to copy only user master records from the source client to the target client. SAP user master records include the user accounts along with passwords and authorization-related information. The SAP security team usually invests a lot of time in creating user master records and developing appropriate authorizations for users in a given client over a period. When a client refresh is performed, this useful information could be lost and, therefore, it is a best practice either to save the user master records with a client copy of the user master records to another client before the client refresh or to perform a client export of user master records so that the same can be either copied back to any target client or imported back into any target client. This will save work for your security team who otherwise would be re-creating all the user master records with appropriate authorizations after the client refresh. The client export process is explained in subsequent sections of this chapter.

Client Copy of Transport Request

A client copy of data can be performed at a smaller dataset level between two clients of an SAP system. This is usually performed in the development system to quickly move smaller datasets using transport requests (data packages with unique numbers). Transaction code SSC1 is used to perform a client copy of transport requests. The following screen shows the client copy of transport request number DEVK900026 from client 300 to the logged-on client (400).

Copy by Transport Request

Schedule as Background Job | Start Immediately

Client Copy by Transport Request

Source Client 300

Transport Request DEVK900026

☑ Including Request Subtasks

☐ Test Run

This can be executed in a test run and as a background job. Since the dataset in a transport request is usually smaller, this is executed online by clicking the Start Immediately button without the Test Run check box selected. Click Yes, and the system will perform basic analysis and complete the copying of data that was specific to a given transport number.

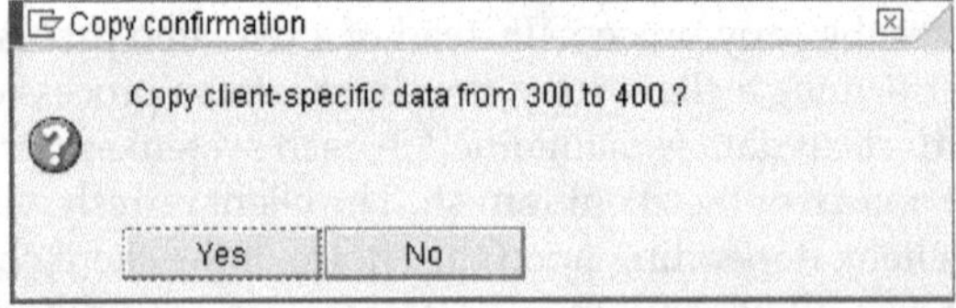

Client Deletion

Clients are deleted from the SAP system because they have served their purpose and the space needs to be released back to the system so that it can be used for other purposes. Clients are also deleted ahead of the time before a large client copy or refresh to improve the performance and runtime of the copy process. SAP transaction code SCC5 is used to perform a deletion of a client from a SAP system. The following illustration shows the initial screen of the client deletion transaction. Execute the transaction in the client that needs to be deleted. In the following example, client 300 needs to be deleted. Log on to client 300 and issue transaction code SCC5. Select the Delete Entry from T000 check box. This will remove the client entry from the list of clients in table T000 once all the client data is deleted from the system.

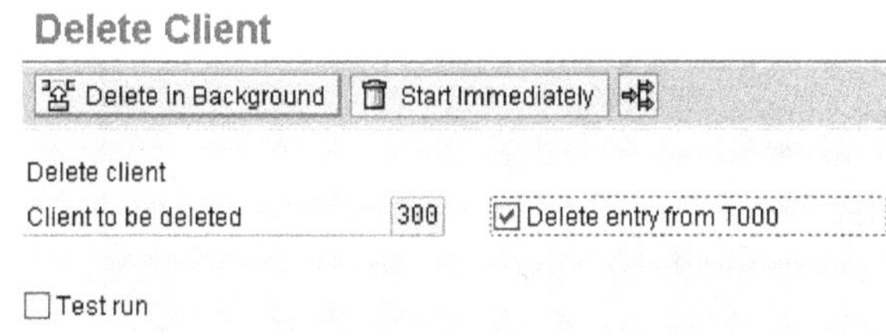

Copyright by SAP AG

Click the Delete in Background button, and you will see the following screen. Select the Immediately check box if you want the deletion to be executed in the background immediately, or click the Schedule Job button to schedule the client deletion in the background at a later date and time.

Schedule Client Copy in Background
Schedule Job
Profile name DELETE
Background Server (Optional) venus_DEV_00
Immediately
No Printer Dialog

Copyright by SAP AG

Once the scheduling option is selected, the system will present a verification screen as shown in Figure 10-10. To verify, click the Continue button. This will start the client deletion process. You can use transaction SCC3 to monitor the progress of the client deletion. The system will not release space automatically after the client is deleted. The database administrator has to perform a reorganization and release the space from the system for a different use.

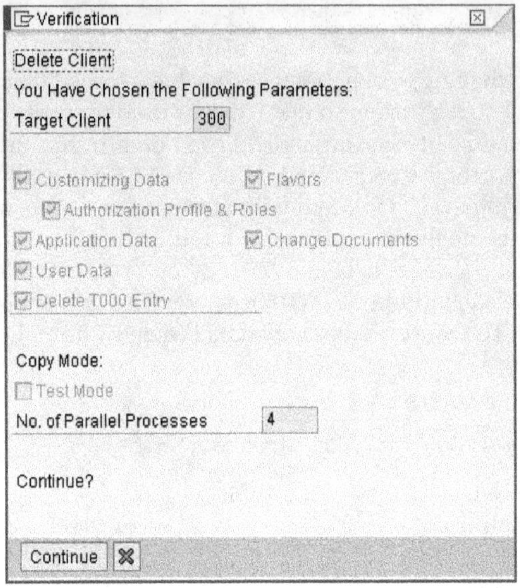

Verification

Delete Client

You Have Chosen the Following Parameters:

Target Client 300

Customizing Data / Flavors / Authorization Profile & Roles / Application Data / Change Documents / User Data / Delete T000 Entry

Copy Mode:

Test Mode

No. of Parallel Processes 4

Continue?

Continue

Copyright by SAP AG

FIGURE 10-10 Verification screen for client deletion

Client Transport

A client transport involves exporting client data from a source system and importing into a target system client. Client transport is a recommended option when there is no network connection between the two systems or if the source and target systems are not in the same local area network (LAN). Execute transaction code SCC8 to start the export process, as shown. There should be no user activity in the source system when the client export is scheduled. In the illustration client copy profile SAP_ALL is used and the target system SID is TST. Click the Schedule As Background Job button.

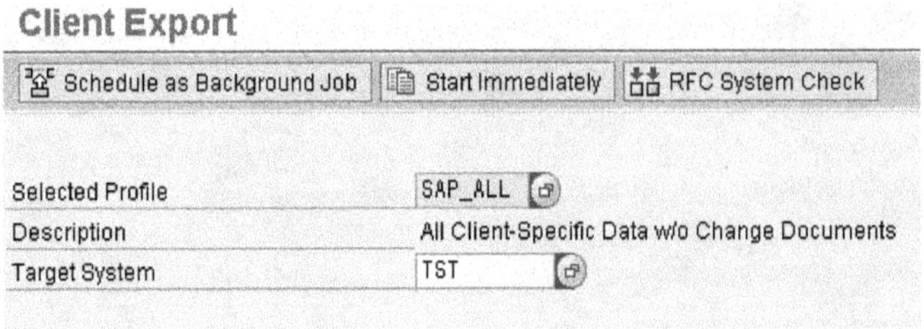

Client Export

Schedule as Background Job | Start Immediately | RFC System Check

Selected Profile	SAP_ALL
Description	All Client-Specific Data w/o Change Documents
Target System	TST

Copyright by SAP AG

Acknowledge subsequent screens by clicking Continue, check the verification screen as shown in Figure 10-11, and click Continue.

The system produces the following three transports (see Figure 10-12) as part of the client export process.

Verification

Client Export

You Have Chosen the Following Parameters:

Profile Name	SAP_ALL
Source Client	400
System Name	TST

☑ Customizing Data ☑ Flavors
☑ Authorization Profile & Roles
☑ Application Data ☐ Change Documents
☑ User Data
☐ Cross-Client Customizing

Continue?

Continue

Copyright by SAP AG

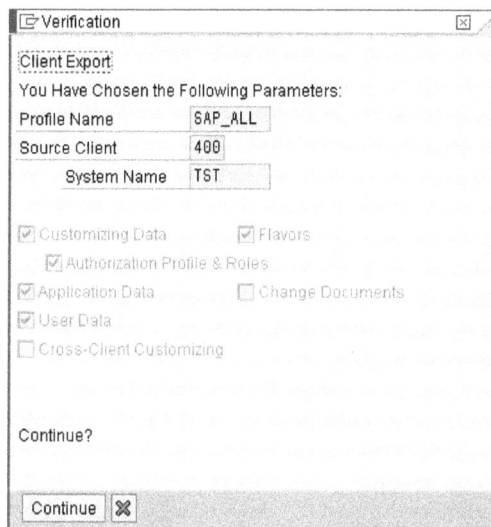

FIGURE 10-11 Client export verification screen

Press the ENTER key to continue the client export process. Subsequent screens will be similar to the client copy process. This will eventually lead to scheduling a background job for client export. You can use transaction code SCC3 and click the Export button to monitor the progress of the client export. Depending upon the needs of the target system client, the following three transports should be imported using SAP STMS in the target system:

- <SID>**KO** (Example: DEV**KO**00009) for cross-client data
- <SID>**KT** (Example: DEV**KT**00009) for client-specific data
- <SID>**KX** (Example: DEV**KX**00009) for client-specific texts

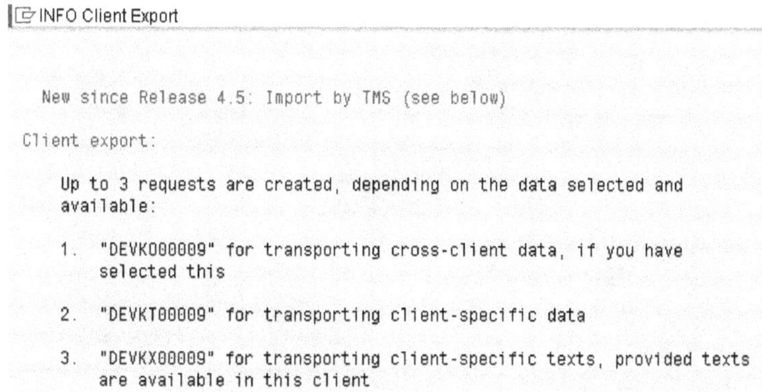

INFO Client Export

New since Release 4.5: Import by TMS (see below)

Client export:

Up to 3 requests are created, depending on the data selected and available:

1. "DEVKO00009" for transporting cross-client data, if you have selected this

2. "DEVKT00009" for transporting client-specific data

3. "DEVKX00009" for transporting client-specific texts, provided texts are available in this client

Copyright by SAP AG

FIGURE 10-12 Client export transports

If the target system client needs to get all data from the source system, then all three transports should be imported. The import sequence should be KO, KT, and KX. If only client-specific data is needed in the target system client, then only KT and KX transports should be imported. After the import is completed in the target system, transaction code SCC7 should be executed as a post-processing step in a client transport process.

Manage Client Settings

Enforcement of the client copy settings is an extremely important responsibility of a Basis administrator. The general rule of thumb is to allow changes only in the development system and to not allow any changes in other systems. Figure 10-13 shows the correct client settings for a SAP development client.

The configuration client settings should allow automatic recording of changes for client-specific configurations and no changes for repository objects, as shown in Figure 10-14.

For all systems other then development systems, the client setting should be closed and must not allow any changes for either client-specific or cross-client object changes. This will ensure that changes are always done in the development system and then moved to all the downstream systems, such as quality assurance, training, conversion, and production systems. Figure 10-15 shows the correct client setting for a production system environment. Similar settings are recommended for all nondevelopmental systems.

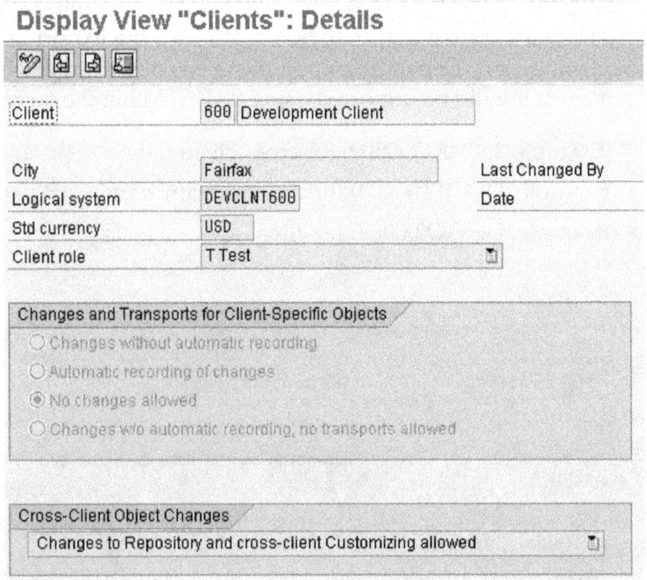

FIGURE 10-13 Recommended development client settings

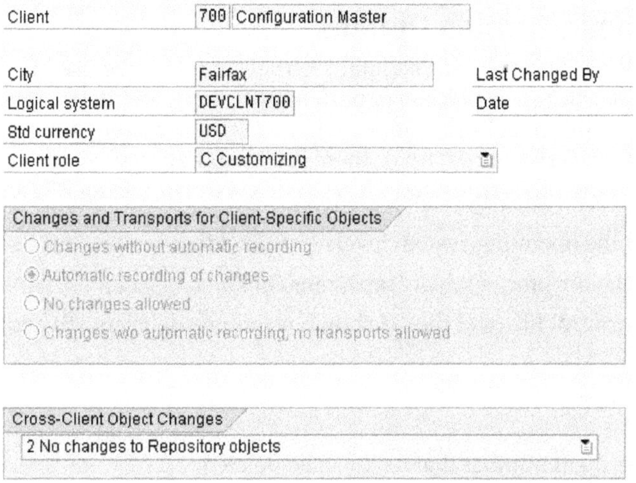

Client 700 Configuration Master

City Fairfax
Logical system DEVCLNT700
Std currency USD
Client role C Customizing
Last Changed By
Date

Changes and Transports for Client-Specific Objects
- ○ Changes without automatic recording
- ◉ Automatic recording of changes
- ○ No changes allowed
- ○ Changes w/o automatic recording, no transports allowed

Cross-Client Object Changes
2 No changes to Repository objects

FIGURE 10-14 Recommended client settings for the configuration master client

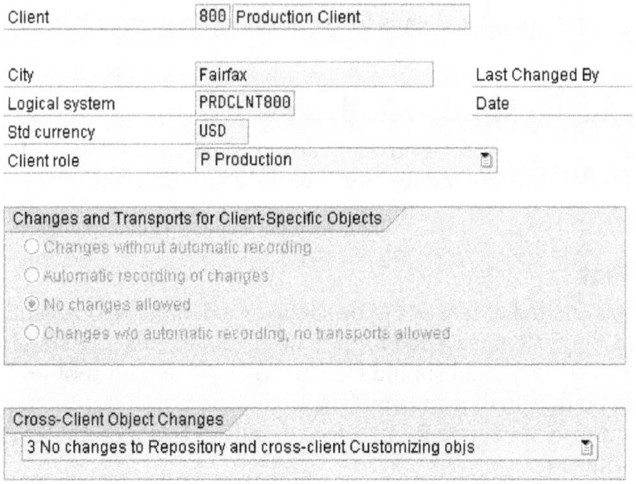

Client 800 Production Client

City Fairfax
Logical system PRDCLNT800
Std currency USD
Client role P Production
Last Changed By
Date

Changes and Transports for Client-Specific Objects
- ○ Changes without automatic recording
- ○ Automatic recording of changes
- ◉ No changes allowed
- ○ Changes w/o automatic recording, no transports allowed

Cross-Client Object Changes
3 No changes to Repository and cross-client Customizing objs

FIGURE 10-15 Recommended client settings for a production system client

R3trans Client Administration Options

SAP provides R3trans as part of the standard kernel, and it can be used to perform client administration activities such as client export, import, copy, and delete functions. Its use is generally not recommended, but the tool could be useful to administrators when transport management system is still not set up or there is a temporary issue with the transport system. The following procedure shows how to delete a client using R3trans.

1. Log in at the operating system level as <SID>adm user account (Example: devadm).
2. Change the directory to /usr/sap/trans/bin.
3. Create a control file (text file) as shown (example: delclient.ctl) and save it.

   ```
   clientremove
   client=<xyz>
   select *
   ```

   xyz is the client number that needs to be deleted.
4. Execute the following command to delete the client:

   Command syntax:

   ```
   R3trans -w <Log file> -u 1 <control file>
   ```

   Command example:

   ```
   R3trans -w delclient.log -u 1 delclient.ctl
   ```

SAP OSS Note 1942 provides details for performing additional R3trans options.

Additional Client Administration Activities

In addition to the previously discussed client administration activities, a few other activities are performed by a Basis administrator. Some of the common tasks are described in the following sections.

Set a Login Client

After a new client is created, if it needs to be set up as a default logon client, a parameter has to be changed and the system restarted for it to be effective. This SAP standard parameter is called as login/system_client and should be entered in the default profile. The value of the parameter should be the client number of the login client. SAP parameter changes are performed using transaction code RZ10. More details of SAP parameter changes will be discussed in Chapter 14.

Lock and Unlock Client

From time to time there will be a need to lock a client against any user logins. SAP provides the following functions for locking and unlocking clients.

Function SCCR_LOCK_CLIENT can be used to lock a client. Log in to client 000, and execute transaction SE37. Enter the function SCCR_LOCK_CLIENT in the Function Module field as shown and press F8.

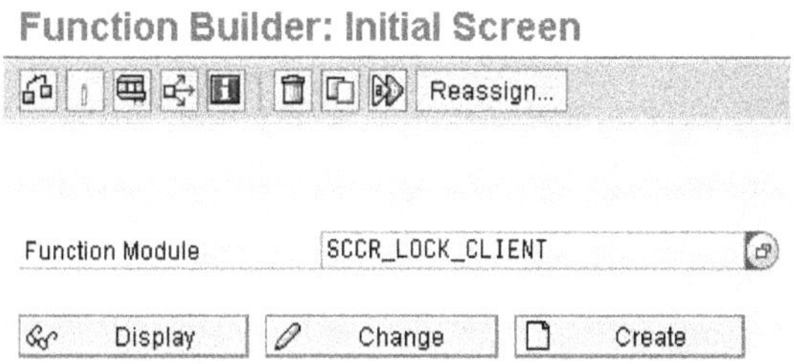

Function Builder: Initial Screen

Reassign...

Function Module SCCR_LOCK_CLIENT

Display Change Create

Copyright by SAP AG

This will bring up the following screen where the client number that needs to be locked should be entered in the Client field and then execute the function module by pressing F8.

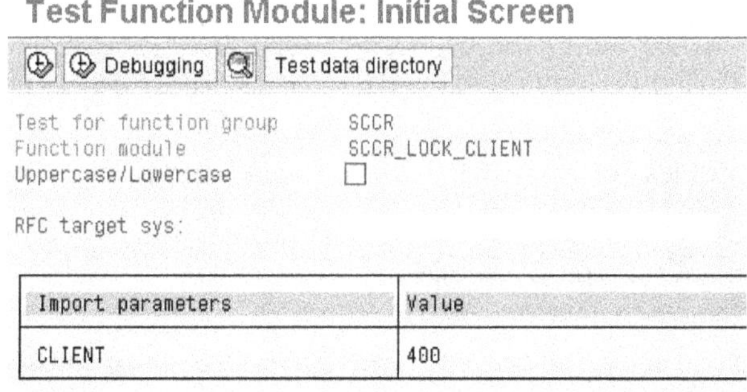

Copyright by SAP AG

Once the function module is executed, the following screen appears, notifying you that client 400 has been locked successfully.

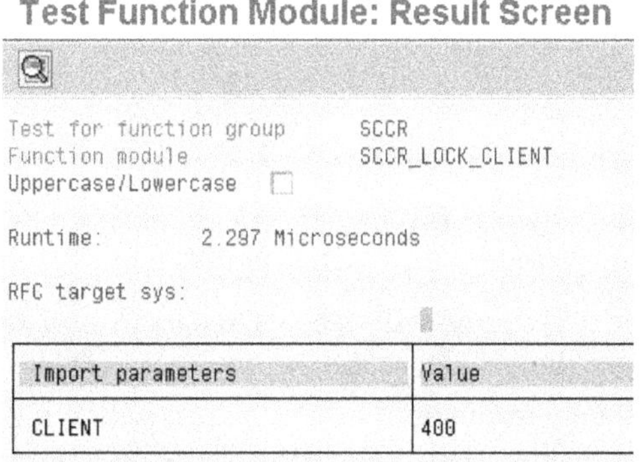

Copyright by SAP AG

After this is completed, if any end user tries to log in to client 400, the system will present this message: The client is currently locked against logon.

Once the client no longer needs to be locked, the administrator can unlock the client by using function module SCCR_UNLOCK_CLIENT.

Summary

- Client administration activities include performing a local client copy, a remote client copy, client transport, client deletion, setting and enforcing client settings, setting client parameters, and locking and unlocking clients.
- Transactions SCCL and SCC4 are used to perform a local client copy.
- Transaction SCC9 is used to set up a remote client copy.
- Transaction SCC3 is used to monitor client copies.
- Transactions SCC8 and SCC7 are used to perform client transports.
- Transaction SCC1 is used to perform a client copy of transport requests.
- Transaction BD54 is used to set up new logical systems.
- Parameter login/no_automatic_user_sapstar should be set to a value of 0 when using sap* kernel user account, with standard password PASS to perform a client copy.
- Client copy profiles determine what data is copied during client copies.
- SAP_ALL client copy profile copies all client data.
- SAP_CUST client copy profile copies only customizing data and deletes the application data in the target client.
- SAP_USER client copy profile copies only the user master records.
- Transaction code SCC5 is used to delete a client.
- The recommended client setting in a development system is to allow changes.
- The recommended client setting in all other systems is to not allow changes.
- R3trans can be used to perform client administration activities.
- Function SCCR_LOCK_CLIENT can be used to lock a client.
- Function SCCR_UNLOCK_CLIENT can be used to unlock a client.

Additional Resources

- **Client copy concept** http://help.sap.com/saphelp_nw70ehp1/helpdata/en/89/933d3c3a926614e10000000a11402f/frameset.htm
- **Client copy profile description with respect to data** http://help.sap.com/saphelp_nw70ehp1/helpdata/en/c2/17e73a86e99c77e10000000a114084/frameset.htm
- **Client copy and transport details** http://help.sap.com/saphelp_nw70ehp1/helpdata/en/69/c24c0f4ba111d189750000e8322d00/frameset.htm

CHAPTER

SAP Transport Management System in ABAP Systems

In this chapter we will study the theory and practice of SAP Transport Management in ABAP systems. First, a number of concepts will be covered, followed by practical Transport Management setup, use, and troubleshooting techniques. This chapter will also cover best practices for setting up Transport Management in SAP systems.

Transport Management Concepts

Transport Management in SAP ABAP systems includes concepts such as the data movement strategy between the three standard SAP System Landscapes (development, quality assurance, and production); data packaging of ABAP source code changes and configuration changes in the form of change requests or transport requests; exporting and importing the transport requests using the SAP transport control program (tp); and coordinating database updates and ABAP code generation by the tp program.

Data Movement Between SAP Systems

SAP development and configuration changes are done in the development system and then are packaged for orderly movement to quality assurance and production systems after thorough testing. During the installation of the SAP development system, a central transport directory referred to as /usr/sap/trans is created. This directory is NFS-mounted (Network File System mounted) to the quality assurance and production systems (Figure 11-1) so that data can be exported and imported using this as a central data area at the file system. The host, which has the central transport directory, is usually referred to as a saptranshost. SAP transport requests are exported out of the development system's database and are imported into the quality assurance and production system's databases using a transport program utility called tp.

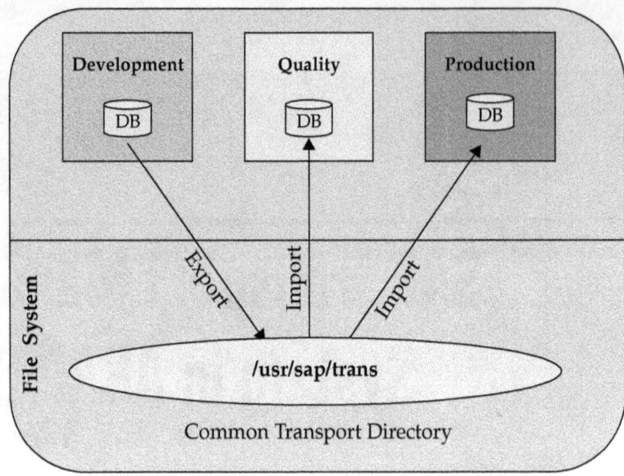

FIGURE 11-1 SAP Common transport directory

Change Request (Transport Request) and Task

The change request, or transport request, is a data package created by the system when changes are performed in the development system. Several tasks can be assigned to one change request number. All tasks should be released before releasing the change request. Releasing (exporting) the change request will create a data file and control file at the operating system level resulting in transports. Change requests and transport requests can be used interchangeably. The naming convention used to identify the change request or transport request is <SID>K9 followed by five digits. This number is generated by the system, and it usually assigns the next number that is available to track the changes. Please note that the creation of a new transport request number will only be noticed in the clients where automatic recording of this is turned on. In Figure 11-2, the change request number is DEVK900032 and the task number is DEVK900033. First, the task should be released (exported) by selecting the task number and then clicking the truck icon. The change request number is released by selecting the request and clicking the truck icon. When a change request is released (exported), the status changes from "modifiable" to "released." Once a change request is exported successfully, it writes the data to the common transport directory and is ready to be imported to the target system.

tp (Transport Control Program)

SAP provides a transport control utility called tp (transport control program or transports and programs) for importing the released change requests to the target systems. tp is a kernel executable and it helps in coordinating all activities associated with the export and import of transport requests. When the truck icon is clicked at the application level, as shown in Figure 11-2, tp is called at the operating system level and it exports the data. The following code using the usr/sap/trans file system directory shows the subdirectories that are created at the time of system installation under the common transport directory.

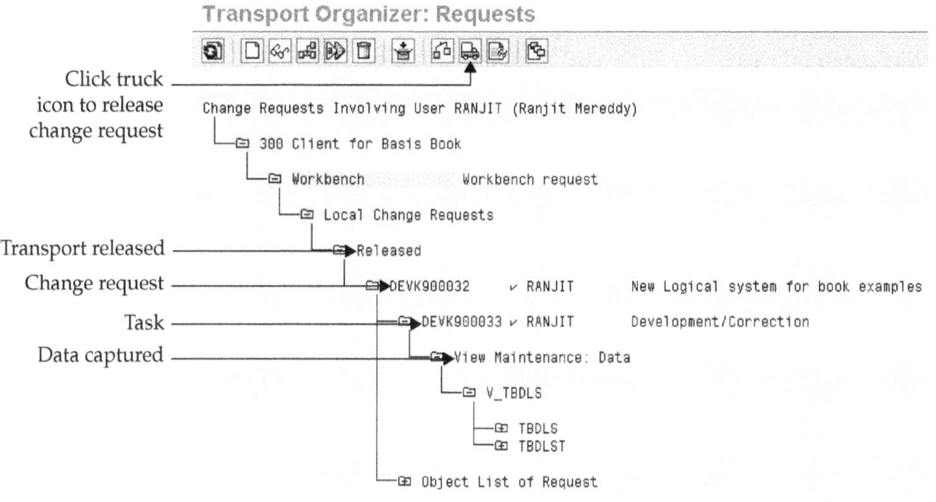

FIGURE 11-2 Change request and task

For every exported change request, tp writes one data file and one control file to the common transport directory data and cofiles subdirectories respectively.

```
devadm> pwd
/usr/sap/trans
devadm> ll
drwxrwxr-x   devadm sapsys   4096     Jan 21 15:35    bin
drwxrwxrwx   devadm sapsys   4096     Jan 6 11:56     buffer
drwxrwxr-x   devadm sapsys   53824    Feb 20 14:05    cofiles
drwxrwxr-x   devadm sapsys   57822    Feb 20 14:05    data
drwxrwxr-x   devadm sapsys   4096     Sep 1 20:32     EPS
drwxrwxrwx   devadm sapsys   237840   Feb 21 10:11    log
drwxrwxr-x   devadm sapsys   4096     Feb 20 14:05    sapnames
drwxrwxr-x   devadm sapsys   36864    Feb 21 17:00    tmp
```

Data file and cofiles have naming conventions. For example, transport request number DEVK900032, when released (exported), will create a data file R900032.dev and cofile K900032.dev. The transport subdirectories listed in Table 11-1 are part of the standard SAP installation.

tp Internals (Transports and Programs Internals)

The transport control program (tp) coordinates all transport-related activities in the system. When a developer or a customizing specialist (transport owner) completes his or her work in the development system, the changes are recorded as change request (transport requests). The transport owner releases the tasks and then the change request in the development system. When a transport is released, the transport control program (tp) executes an export command and writes a data file and a control file in the common transport directory at the

Transport Subdirectory	Purpose
/usr/sap/trans/bin	Global transport profile file
/usr/sap/trans/buffer	Target systems transport queue with sequence
/usr/sap/trans/cofiles	Transport request control file, including return codes
/usr/sap/trans/data	Transport data
/usr/sap/trans/EPS	Electronic Parcel Service (EPS) for support package application
/usr/sap/trans/log	Transport logs and trace files
/usr/sap/trans/sapnames	Transport requests for each user
/usr/sap/trans/tmp	Temporary files (set semaphores on currently executed transports)

TABLE 11-1 SAP Transport Subdirectories

operating system level. When the transport request is approved to be imported to the quality assurance system, the Basis administrator receives the transport request number and initiates a transport import into the target system, as shown in Figure 11-3. When the transport control program starts the import, it calls the kernel executable R3trans, connects to the database, and performs the needed database updates. It also starts an event-triggered

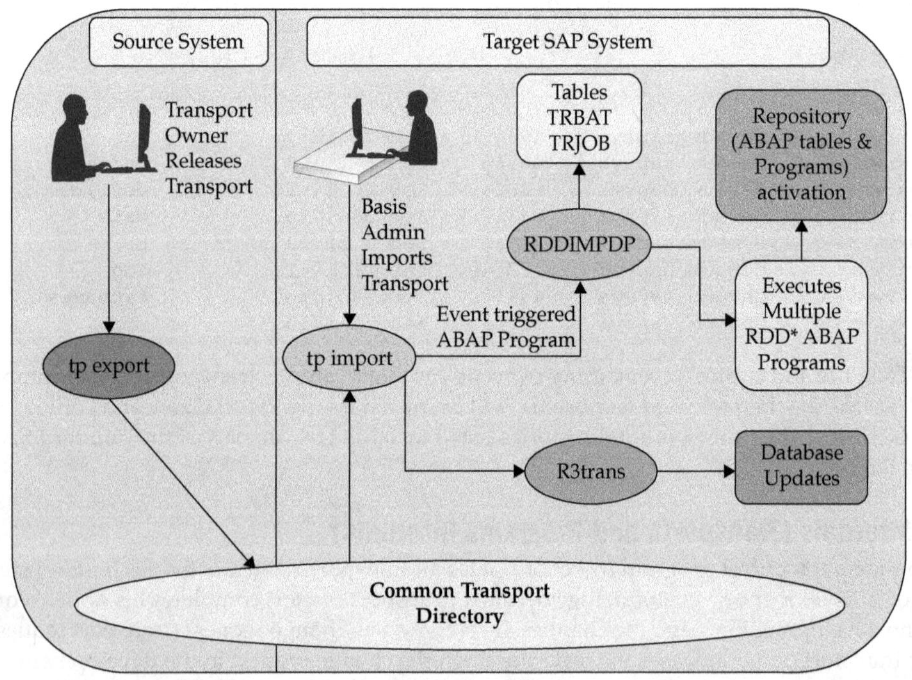

FIGURE 11-3 Transport control program internals (tp internals)

ABAP program called RDDIMPDP at the SAP application level. RDDIMPDP, in turn, starts several background jobs starting with RDD* and coordinates the statuses of these jobs by placing entries in the TRBAT and TRJOB tables. RDD* jobs execute all the conversion and activation steps of the ABAP programs and tables in the repository. When all the steps are complete, the table entries in the TRBAT and TRJOB tables are deleted until the next set of transports is imported to target SAP systems.

If event-triggered RDDIMPDP does not start for any reason, it can be scheduled in the target client by executing the report RDDNEWPP. While performing imports, sometimes the transport hangs, and one of the reasons for such a situation is the background job RDIMPDP may not be scheduled in the system. Please use OSS Note 71353 "Transports hang during background steps" to help troubleshoot different hanging and error conditions while performing imports in SAP systems.

tp Commands and Options

The transport control program command can be executed at the operating system level with the <SID>adm user account. It reads the following global transport profile file (TP_DOMAIN_GEN.PFL) for system GEN in the /usr/sap/trans/bin directory and executes the command with the options entered:

```
devadm> pwd
/usr/sap/trans/bin
TP_DOMAIN_GEN.PFL
devadm> more TP_DOMAIN_GEN.PFL
#TMS:0188:DOMAIN_GEN
#-------------------------------------------------------------------------
#Caution !
#This file was generated by the Transport Management System.
#Do not change this file using a text editor.
#For further information please see the online documentation of
#transaction STMS.
#If this file was destroyed, it can be regenerated in the TMS.
#To do this, log on to the domain controller (system GEN) and call
#Transaction STMS. In the System Overview, you can distribute the TMS
#configuration. This regenerates the file.
#STMS -> Overview -> Systems -> Extras -> Distribute TMS Configuration
#-------------------------------------------------------------------------
#
DEV/CTC             = 1
DEV/DBHOST          = venus
DEV/DBNAME          = GEN
DEV/DBTYPE          = ora
DEV/NBUFFORM        = 1
DEV/TP_VERSION      = 266
DEV/TRANSDIR        = /usr/sap/transGEN
```

The tp command has several options. You can get a list of all the possible options by executing the command tp help, as shown in Figure 11-4.

```
devadm> tp help

This is tp version 372.04.57 (release 701, unicode enabled)
usage:   tp <command> [argument(s)] [option(s)], where <command> may be one of:

------------------------------+-----------------------------+------------------
Exporting                     I Buffer Actions              I Disk Space
------------------------------+-----------------------------+------------------
EXPORT        I EXPWBO        I ADDTOBUFFER  I DELFROMBUFFERI CLEAROLD
R3E           I VERSE         I SETSYNCMARK  I DELSYNCMARK  I CHECK
SDE           I               I SETSTOPMARK  I DELSTOPMARK  I TESTOLD
TST           I               I MARK         I UNMARK       I
              I               I CLEANBUFFER  I              I
------------------------------+-----------------------------+------------------
Importing                     I Special Functions           I Information
------------------------------+-----------------------------+------------------
PUT           I               I LOCKSYS      I UNLOCKSYS    I SHOWBUFFER
IMPORT        I CHNTABS       I LOCK_EU      I UNLOCK_EU    I COUNT
CMD           I R3I           I WRITELOG     I GETPROTS     I SHOWPARAMS
              I MEA           I SAPSTART     I SAPSTOP      I GO
R3H           I MVREPOS       I GETTBATGENT  I GETTRBATENT  I CONNECT
ACT           I MVKERNEL      I GETDDXTTENT  I GETDDXTFENT  I CHECKIMPDP
TACOB         I SDI           I GETOPENCORR  I CREATECOFILE I SHOWINFO
GENTB         I GENT1         I PREPAREBUFFERI CREATEINFO   I GETOBJLIST
GENT2         I GEN           I CONTP        I EXPCHK       I EXTRDOCU
DIST          I XPA           I SHOWSEMAPHOREI SHOWSEMACLIENI GETCONVENT
MVNTABS       I VERSI         I SETSEMAPHORE I DELSEMACLIENTI EXPLAINRC
IMPSYNC       I DELIVER       I DELSEMAPHORE I GETTPSTATENT I
DEPLOY        I IMPORTPREVIEWI CHECKIN       I CHECKINMOVE  I CHECKOUT

For more details call tp with the desired command (and no other parameters)
```


FIGURE 11-4 Transport command options

Let us look into some specific examples of transport control program usage. The following command displays a count of the transports that are waiting in the system DEV queue:

```
devadm> tp count DEV pf=TP_DOMAIN_DEV.PFL
This is tp version 372.04.40 (release 701, unicode enabled)
Warning: Parameter DBLIBPATH is no longer used.
3 entries found in buffer DEV
tp finished with return code: 0
meaning:
Everything OK
```

The following transport commands add a new transport to the target system (QAS) buffer and import it to the specified client:

```
tp addtobuffer DEVK9000032 QAS client=100 pf=TP_DOMAIN_QAS.PFL
tp import DEVK9000032 QAS client=100 pf=TP_DOMAIN_QAS.PFL
```

Transports Script

tp commands can be used to create a UNIX script so that mass activities, such as adding hundreds and thousands of transports to the target SAP system buffer and importing them, can be done automatically. This will save a lot of time and minimize the errors in execution of the commands as well. The following is a sample UNIX script (go.sh) for adding transports to the buffer and importing them into the target QAS system. The script can be created in the /usr/sap/trans/bin directory of the target SAP system.

```
qasadm> more go.sh
#!/bin/sh
while read i
do
tp ADDTOBUFFER  $i QAS client100  pf=TP_DOMAIN_QAS.PFL
tp import $i QAS client100  pf=TP_DOMAIN_QAS.PFL
done <list.txt
```

The list of transports to be executed by the script should be entered in the list.txt file, and the file can be in the same directory as the script. A sample list.txt file is provided here:

```
qasadm> more list.txt
DEVK9000032
DEVK9000039
DEVK9000045
DEVK9000057
DEVK9000063
DEVK9000070
DEVK9000081
DEVK9000093
DEVK9000097
```

Now execute the script by issuing **./go.sh** with the user account qasadm, which will add the previous nine transports to the QAS transport buffer and import them one at a time.

It is also useful to check and see if the tp is able to connect to the database by issuing the following command before executing the script. The command should give a return code of 0.

```
devadm> tp connect DEV pf=TP_DOMAIN_DEV.PFL
This is tp version 372.04.57 (release 701, unicode enabled)
Connection to Database of DEV was successful.
This is R3trans version 6.14 (release 701 - 05.03.09 - 08:28:00).
unicode enabled version
R3trans finished (0000).
tp finished with return code: 0
meaning:
  Everything OK
```

Transport Command Options

Table 11-2 lists the most commonly used tp commands.

tp Command	Example	Description
tp count	tp count QAS pf=TP_DOMAIN_QAS.PFL	This will give a count of the transports that are in the QAS transport buffer.
tp showbuffer	tp showbuffer QAS pf=TP_DOMAIN_QAS.PFL	This will show all the transports that are in the QAS buffer, including the count.
tp addtobuffer	tp addtobuffer DEVK9000032 QAS client=100 pf=TP_DOMAIN_QAS.PFL	This will add transport number DEVK9000032 to the QAS buffer with target client number 100.
tp delfrombuffer	tp delfrombuffer DEVK9000032 QAS pf=TP_DOMAIN_QAS.PFL	This will delete the transport number DEVK9000032 from the QAS buffer.
tp import all	tp import all QAS pf= TP_DOMAIN_QAS.PFL	This will import all the transports in the QAS buffer to the QAS system. It is very important to validate the list of transports that are in the target system transport queue before executing this command. Depending upon the number of transports in the queue, this may take from several minutes to several hours to complete.
tp import	tp import DEVK9000032 QAS client=100 pf= TP_DOMAIN_QAS.PFL	This will import transport request number DEVK9000032 to client 100 in the QAS system.
tp connect	tp connect QAS pf=TP_DOMAIN_QAS.PFL	This will test the connection to the QAS system.
tp locksys	tp locksys QAS pf=TP_DOMAIN_QAS .PFL	This will lock the QAS system.
tp unlocksys	tp unlocksys QAS pf=TP_DOMAIN_QAS.PFL	This will unlock the QAS system.
tp cleanbuffer	tp cleanbuffer QAS pf=TP_DOMAIN_QAS.PFL	This deletes the already imported transports in the QAS buffer.
tp help	tp help	This will show all tp command options.

TABLE 11-2 Most Commonly Used tp Command Options

Transport Management in Practice

In the first section of the chapter we have covered the Transport Management concepts and the internals of the underlying transport control program. SAP has provided a more user-friendly tool for performing transports in the system using SAP Transport Management System (STMS). It is recommended to use STMS for performing all transport management activities. STMS tools will call the underlying transport control program to perform imports into the target systems.

Development and Customizing Work

In SAP systems, a developer creates new tables and ABAP programs to meet the requirements of the business that the standard software does not address. The functional expert will configure the system so that its business processes execute the business need. The changes performed by both the developers and configurators in the development system are collected as change requests or transport requests.

Workbench Requests

A developer creating either a new ABAP program or table triggers the capturing of this information in a change request referred to as a workbench request. Workbench requests are generally client-independent repository creation or change activities. All workbench requests can be displayed, changed, and released using transaction code SE09.

Customizing Requests

SAP provides a tree-like hierarchical structure referred to as an Implementation Guide (IMG) to the functional experts to configure the system. Transaction code SPRO is used to start the Implementation Guide. Tasks in the Implementation Guide, when executed, will direct the configurators in the maintenance of the relevant configuration table. Once the configuration table entries are maintained and saved, the system will trigger a change request referred to as a customizing request. Customizing requests can be displayed and released from transaction code SE10. Most of the customizing requests are client-dependent.

Release a Transport Request

A transport request or change request can be a workbench request or a customizing request, and can be released in the source system. When a change request is released using transaction codes SE09 and SE10, the underlying transport control program (tp) is called with the export option and a cofile and a data file are written to the common transport directory. STMS configuration will allow transports released from the development system to be routed and populated in the target quality assurance system, where they are ready for import. The next section of this chapter will cover the STMS configuration steps in detail.

STMS Configuration

After the development system is installed, it is usually designated as a primary transport domain controller in the STMS configuration in client 000. As a part of post-installation transport configuration, executing transaction code STMS for the first time in a development system client 000 with system identifier DEV will show the following screen proposing the transport domain name DOMAIN_DEV.

TMS: Configure Transport Domain

System DEV
Description System DEV

Transport Domain
Name DOMAIN_DEV
Description Transport domain DEV

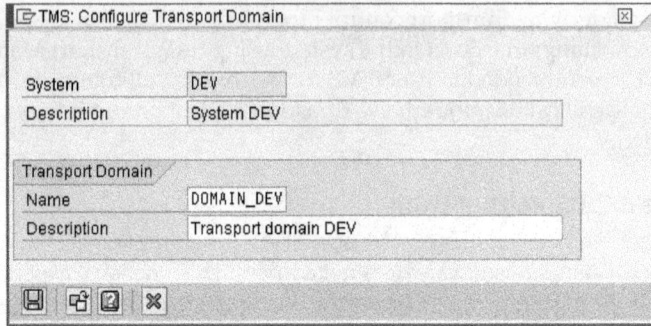

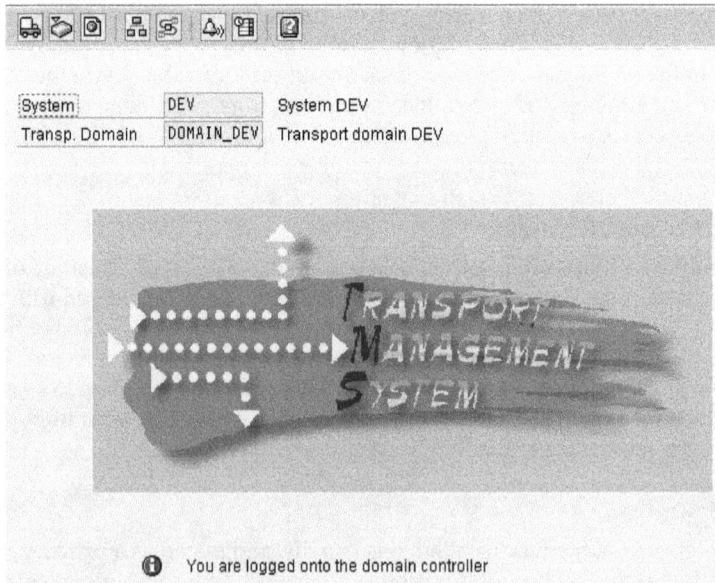

Click the Save button, and you will see the following message confirming that the basic configuration is completed. Figure 11-5 shows the completed domain controller configuration for system DEV.

FIGURE 11-5 STMS domain controller screen

Systems

If you click the systems overview icon (SHIFT-F6), you will see the following overview screen. Since this is the first and only installation in the landscape, we see only one system shown under the number of screens. As we install additional systems, such as quality assurance and production, they are added to the development primary transport domain controller to manage all the imports in the development, quality assurance, and production landscapes.

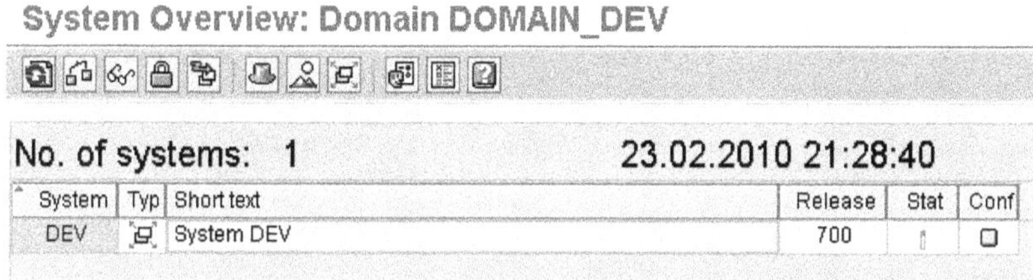

Copyright by SAP AG

Double-click the DEV system line, and you will notice the screens shown in Figures 11-6, 11-7, and 11-8.

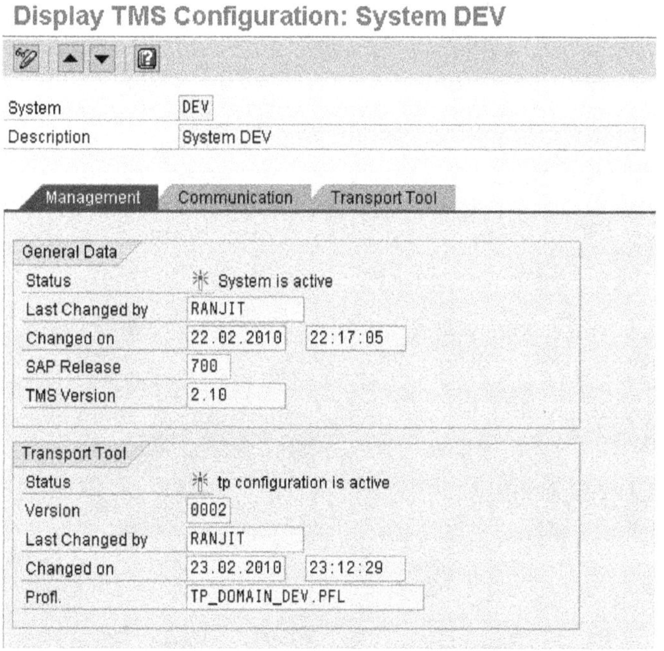

Copyright by SAP AG

FIGURE 11-6 STMS system overview screen (Management tab)

Display TMS Configuration: System DEV

System DEV
Description System DEV

Management | Communication | Transport Tool

Transport Domain
Name DOMAIN_DEV Transport domain DEV
Controller DEV
Backup
Workflow Engine

Transport Group
Name GROUP_DEV
Description Transport group DEV

RFC Address
System DEV
Target Host venus
System No. 00
User TMSADM
SNC Name
QoP
SNC Active

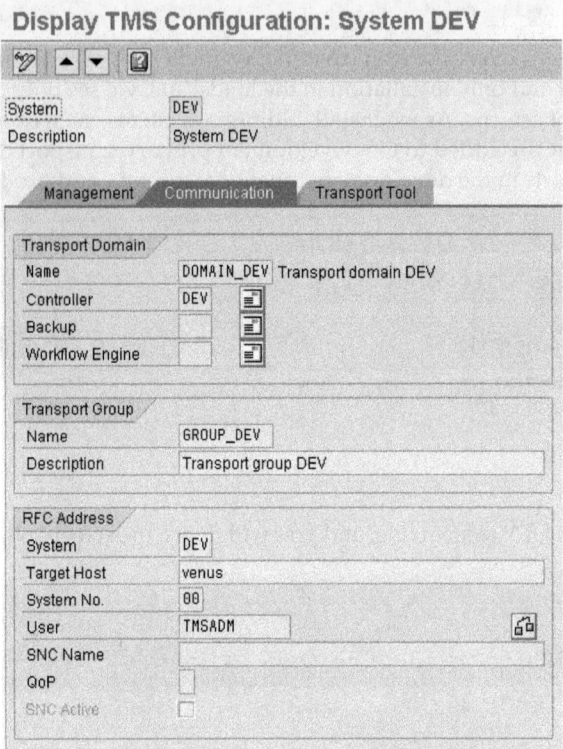

FIGURE 11-7 STMS system overview screen (Communication tab)

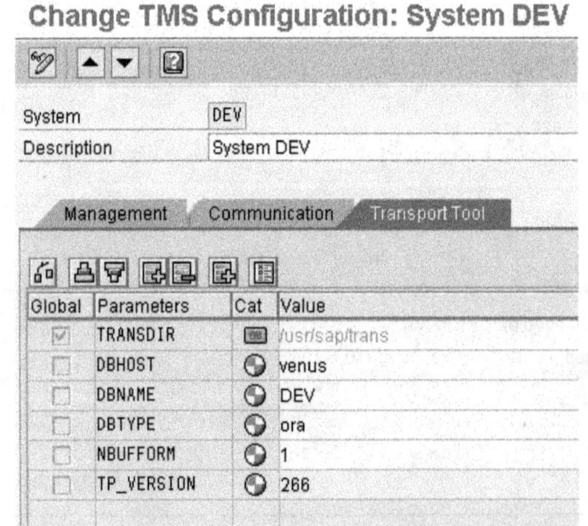

FIGURE 11-8 STMS system overview screen (Transport Tool tab)

Let us assume that we have three systems: DE2, SE2, and PE2. In this example, the primary domain controller is configured in the Solution Manager Development System and not in the DE2 system. In this instance, when DE2 is installed, it is added to the transport primary domain controller in Solution Manager and later on SE2 and PE2 will be added to it so that transports can be managed from STMS. The following procedure shows how to add a system to the primary domain controller. In the case of the DE2 system, execute transaction code STMS and click the other configuration icon (or press F6) on the initial screen. In this window enter the hostname, system number, and default user TMSADM; click the Save button; and you will see an informational message in the initial STMS screen of the DE2 system, indicating that this system is waiting to be included in the primary domain controller defined in the Solution Manager system, as shown in the illustration on the right.

SAP System waiting to be included in transport domain

Copyright by SAP AG

At this point, if you log in to the Solution Manager system that was defined as the transport primary domain controller, the newly added DE2 system will be shown in the status system, waiting for inclusion in domain as shown. This can be seen by executing transaction code STMS and clicking the system overview icon (SHIFT-F6).

DE2 GROUP_DE2 Domain DE2 700

Copyright by SAP AG

This newly added system must be approved by choosing the DE2 system and selecting SAP System | Approve. This will display the following screen, where you are prompted to accept the newly added DE2 system in the domain controller. Clicking the Yes button will complete the addition process. The same procedure should be used to add the other systems to the domain controller. Once the newly added systems are added to the domain controller, then the transport routes should be configured so that the flow of the transports can be managed in the landscape.

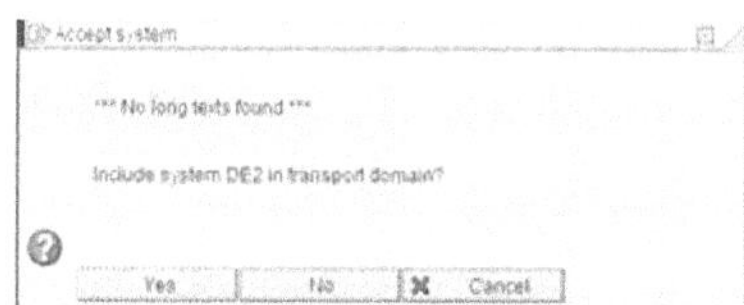

Copyright by SAP AG

Transport Routes

After the newly installed system is included in the primary domain controller, the next step is to configure the transport routes so that the change requests, when released in the development system, flow through to the consolidation (quality assurance) and then to the delivery system (production). To configure transport routes, you have to log in to the primary domain controller system client 000 and execute transaction code STMS. In the STMS screen click the Transport routes icon (SHIFT-F7). This will show following screen with no route configuration defined yet.

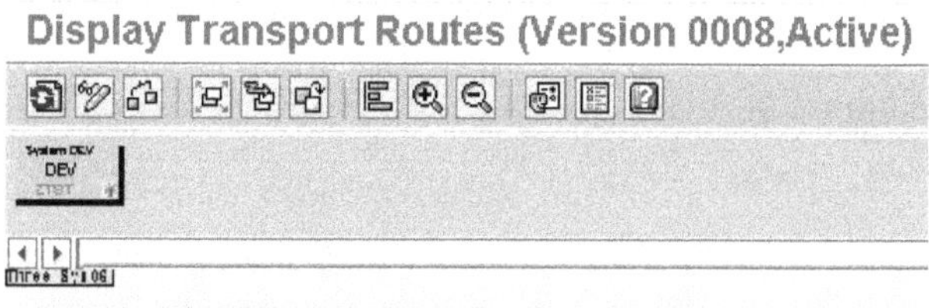

Copyright by SAP AG

Transport route editing can be performed in a graphical editor or a hierarchical editor. The following example uses a hierarchical editor; however, the default option for a newly installed system is a graphical editor. You can switch from a graphical to a hierarchical editor by selecting STMS | Transport Routes | Settings | Transport Route Editor.

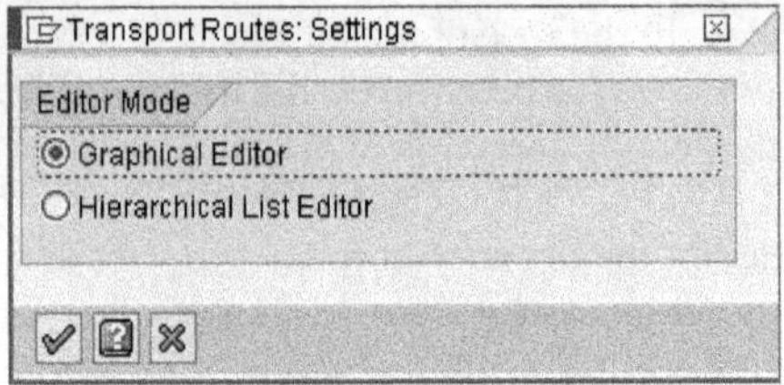

Copyright by SAP AG

Change the selection to Hierarchical Editor, and click the green check mark. There is still one more step to make the change.

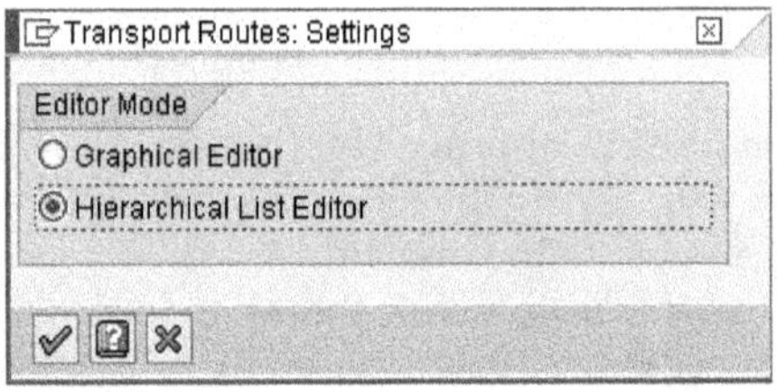

Copyright by SAP AG

In order to use the hierarchical editor, you have to use the Back button (press F3) and click the transports routes (SHIFT-F7) icon again. This will show the initial hierarchical editor screen shown in Figure 11-9.

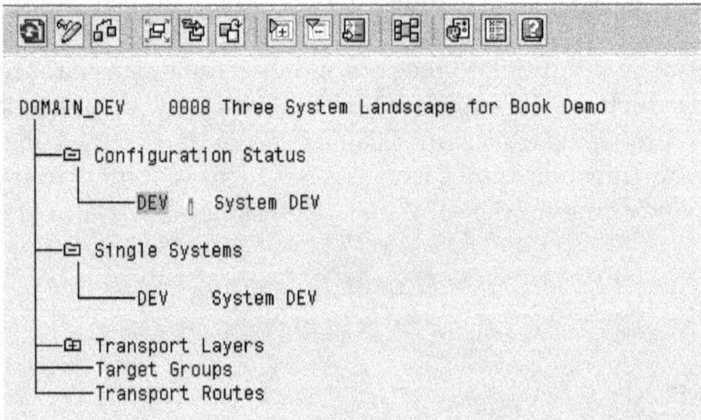

Copyright by SAP AG

FIGURE 11-9 Transport routes initial screen

By default, the initial screen is in display mode. To start configuring the transport routes, click the change icon (the pencil). This will put the editor in change mode. STMS transport route configuration includes three steps. First we create a transport layer; then we create the transport routes; and finally, the configuration is distributed and activated.

Transport Layer

The transport layer is assigned to development work and is a means of determining the target systems for the objects to be transported. When a new system is installed by default it is delivered with a standard transport layer 'SAP' as shown. This transport layer is used for any changes performed for SAP standard objects.

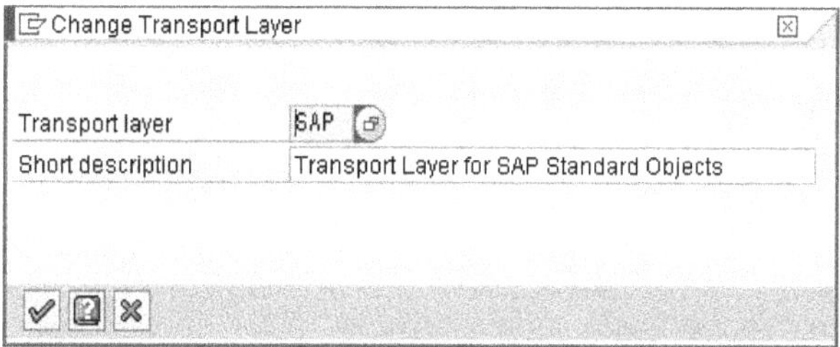

Copyright by SAP AG

Customers have to create their own transport layer as a first step in the configuration of the transport routes in the system. Once in change mode in the route editor, click the create button (F6). This will show the following screen where you enter the custom transport layer starting with the letter Z. Click the green check mark to save the newly created transport layer.

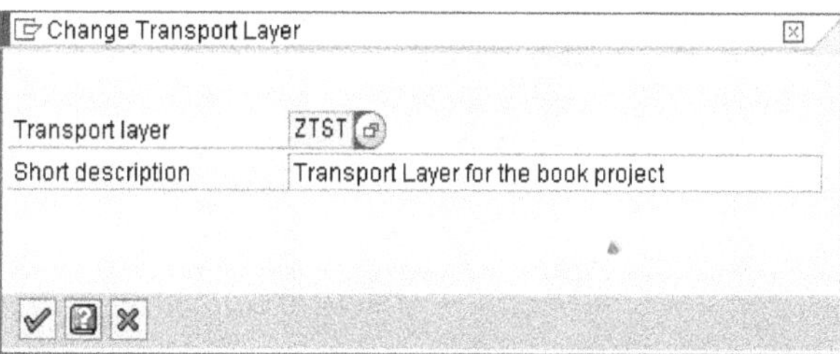

Copyright by SAP AG

Consolidation Route

Consolidation route configuration helps to move a released change request from a development system to a quality assurance system. You can create a new consolidation route by putting the cursor on the transport routes and clicking the create icon (F6).

You will see the following screen showing the entries that have to be made to create a consolidation route.

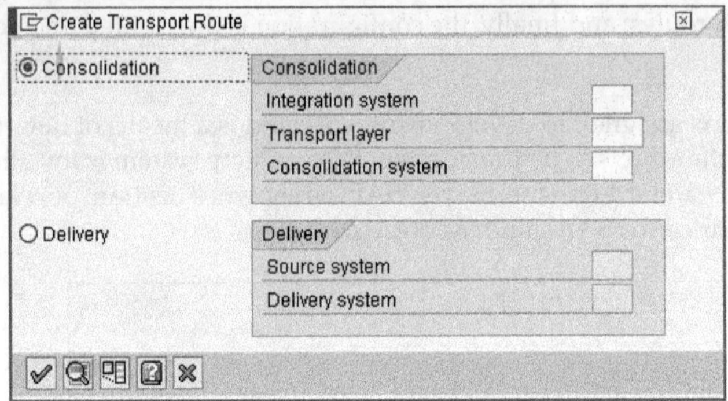

Enter the development source system in the integration system field, the custom-created Z transport layer under the transport layer screen, and the quality assurance system under the consolidation system field as shown. Then click the green check mark to complete the consolidation transport route configuration.

Create Transport Route
Consolidation
Consolidation
Integration system DEV
Transport layer ZTST
Consolidation system QAS
Delivery
Delivery
Source system
Delivery system

Delivery Route

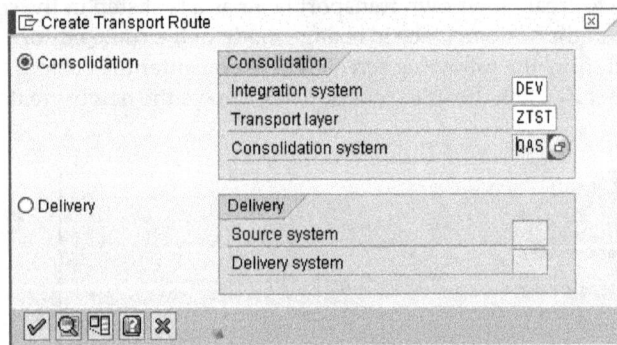

The delivery route will help flag change requests moved earlier to the quality systems that should now be moved to either a single or many target delivery systems, such as a production system. To create the delivery route with the editor in change mode, put the cursor on the transport routes and click the create icon (F6). This will show the following screen.

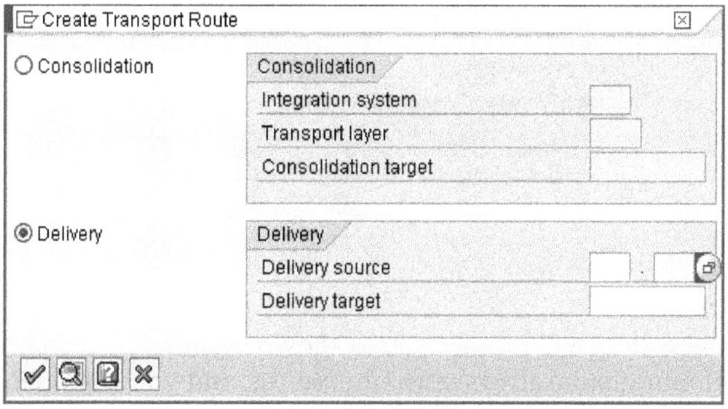

Create Transport Route

○ Consolidation

Consolidation	
Integration system	
Transport layer	
Consolidation target	

◉ Delivery

Delivery	
Delivery source	
Delivery target	

Copyright by SAP AG

Enter the delivery source field as quality assurance system (QAS) and the delivery target as production (PRD) as shown and click the green check mark.

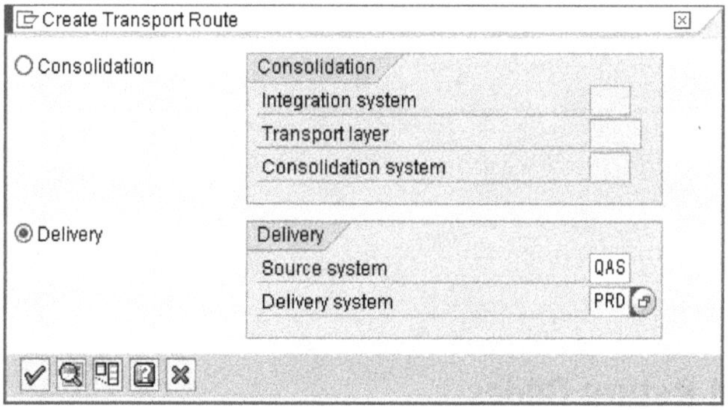

Create Transport Route

○ Consolidation

Consolidation	
Integration system	
Transport layer	
Consolidation system	

◉ Delivery

Delivery	
Source system	QAS
Delivery system	PRD

Copyright by SAP AG

Once the consolidation and delivery routes are configured, the transport editor screen looks as follows, showing the transport route configuration in a typical three-System-Landscape.

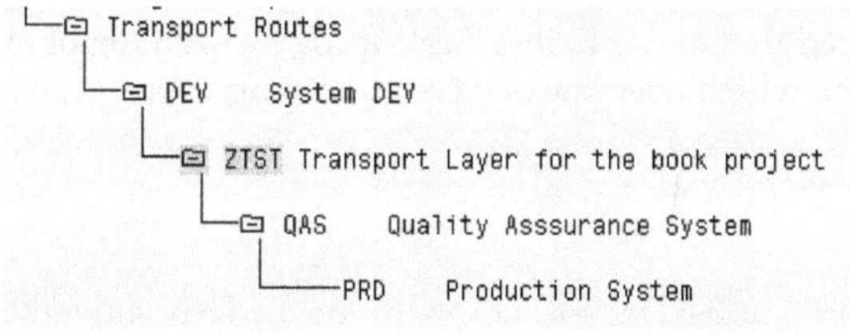

```
Transport Routes
  DEV    System DEV
    ZTST Transport Layer for the book project
      QAS    Quality Asssurance System
        PRD    Production System
```

Copyright by SAP AG

Once the route configuration is complete, click the Save button, and the following information screen appears. Click the green check mark to transfer the configuration.

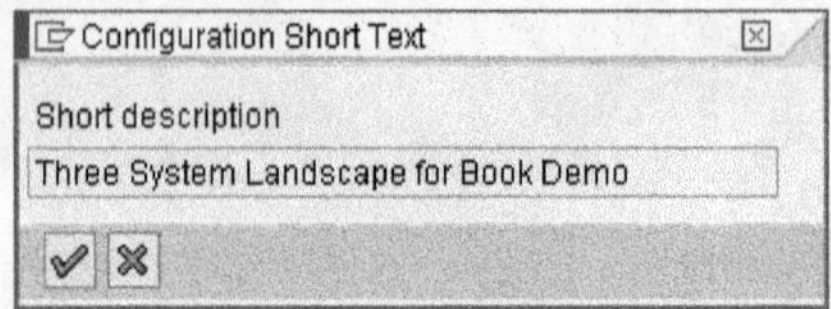

Copyright by SAP AG

Activation and Distribution

Once this is done, the system will prompt you as shown, asking if you want to distribute and activate the configuration to all systems. Choose Yes, and you will notice a confirmation screen.

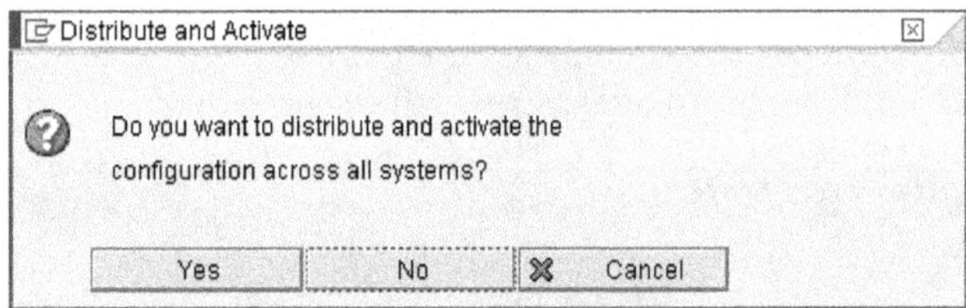

Distribute and Activate
Do you want to distribute and activate the configuration across all systems?
Yes
No
Cancel

Copyright by SAP AG

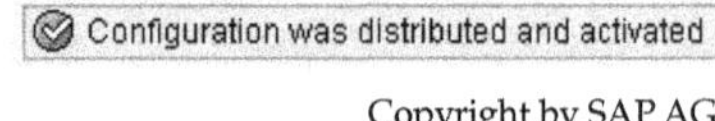

Copyright by SAP AG

Transport Logs and Return Codes

Transaction codes SE09 and SE10 can be used to check the transport logs. Enter one of these transaction codes, and click the display individually icon (F5). Enter the transport request number in the request field, and press ENTER. In the next screen, the transport logs can be seen by clicking the transport logs icon (CTRL-SHIFT-F2). You can drill down into the logs for additional details by double-clicking or keep pressing F5 to drill down up to four levels. The transport return code of 0 means a transport is successful, 4 is a warning, and 8 indicates that an error has occurred that needs fixing. Table tplog keeps a log of all transport activity and can be used to check which user performed a transport in the system.

Summary

- The three-System-Landscape will help with the orderly movement of SAP data from the development to quality assurance and then to production systems.
- Change requests help keep track of data changes as packages, which are imported into the target systems.

- The tp (Transports and Programs or Transport Control program) helps in coordinating all export and import activities in the system.
- STMS (SAP Transport Management System) is a graphical tool used to move the transports in the SAP landscape in an orderly fashion.
- Transport routes help direct transports to the correct target systems.
- Consolidation routes help move transports from the development system to a quality assurance system.
- Delivery routes help move transports to a production system.

Additional Resources

- **Change and transport system** www.sdn.sap.com/irj/sdn/cts
- **Transport Management demo link** www.sdn.sap.com/irj/scn/logon?redirect=https%3A%2F%2Fwww.sdn.sap.com%2Firj%2Fscn%2Felearn%3Frid%3D%2Flibrary%2Fuuid%2Fb0840131-efde-2910-80a2-e92825b1fb68 (link requires free SDN registration)
- **Change and transport system overview** http://help.sap.com/saphelp_nw70/helpdata/en/3b/dfba3692dc635ce10000009b38f839/frameset.htm

CHAPTER

SAP Software Logistics for Java Systems

SAP supports a robust software logistics solution for Java systems similar to the ABAP systems: NetWeaver Development Infrastructure (NWDI). NWDI consists of a local Java development and build environment on each developer's PC and a central development environment for managing versions, building, assembling the software components, and finally transporting the changes to the target environments. Let us start by looking into the Java application development steps and then go into topics such as the four-System-Landscape; Java development environment; NWDI components such as Design Time Repository (DTR), Component Build Service (CBS), Change Management Service (CMS), and System Landscape Directory (SLD); SAP CTS Plus; and SAP Central CTS.

Java Application Development Steps

Java application development requires a Java 2 Software Development Kit (J2SDK) that includes a JRE (Java Runtime Environment), Java compiler, and Java debugger. Table 12-1 lists the Java application development steps. First, the Java source code (.java files) is compiled into a platform-independent bytecode (class files) using the J2SDK in the development system. In the consolidation system, the class files and deployment descriptors are used to create .jar files, and this is usually known as the build activity. The next step is to create a Java application by integrating the .jar files with additional deployment descriptors in a process called an assembly. The last step is to deploy the application, either in the production system or at a customer installation. Since Java application development goes through development, build, assembly, and deployment phases. It is recommended to have a four-System-Landscape to support the process. In addition, a separate system is recommended for the NWDI components.

Environment	Steps
Development Environment	Development of Java source code (.java files) and compilation to Java bytecode (.class files).
Consolidation	Build Java archives (.jar files) and web archives (.war files) from the class files and deployment descriptor.
Test	Assembly of several .jar files and web archives, along with additional deployment descriptor, into enterprise archives (.ear files). Integration testing and approval for deployment to production.
Production	Enterprise archives (.ear files) deployed to production system or sent for deployment to a customer site.

TABLE 12-1 Key Java Application Development Steps

SAP Java Four-System-Landscape

A four-System-Landscape is recommended for Java application development. In ABAP systems, a three-System-Landscape consisting of development (DEV), quality assurance (QAS), and production (PRD) systems is recommended. ABAP programs can be developed fully in the DEV system and moved to QAS for testing. Once the testing is successful, they are approved to be imported into production. However, for Java systems, the development process is different and, therefore, a four-System-Landscape is recommended. In the Java development process, Java code is developed as software components (.jar and .ear files), which are transported to a build/consolidation system. In this system the software components are assembled into a working application, and this is then transported to a testing system. Once tested successfully, the application can be transported to production system.

The complete NWDI infrastructure with the four systems is shown in Figure 12-1. More details of the NetWeaver Developer studio and NWDI components such as DTR, CBS, and CMS will be discussed in more detail in subsequent sections of this chapter.

SAP Java Development Environment

SAP Java development uses an approach where individual developers work in their own local environments by checking out the code from a central environment and when the development is ready, they will check in the code version to be integrated with respect to version management in a central development system. This approach is supported by the SAP NWDI, which includes a local development environment installed on each developer PC called NetWeaver Developer Studio and central services such as DTR, CBS, and CMS. SAP NWDI helps in large-scale Java development projects where multiple developers are working in a coordinated manner to build Java applications that serve a particular business function.

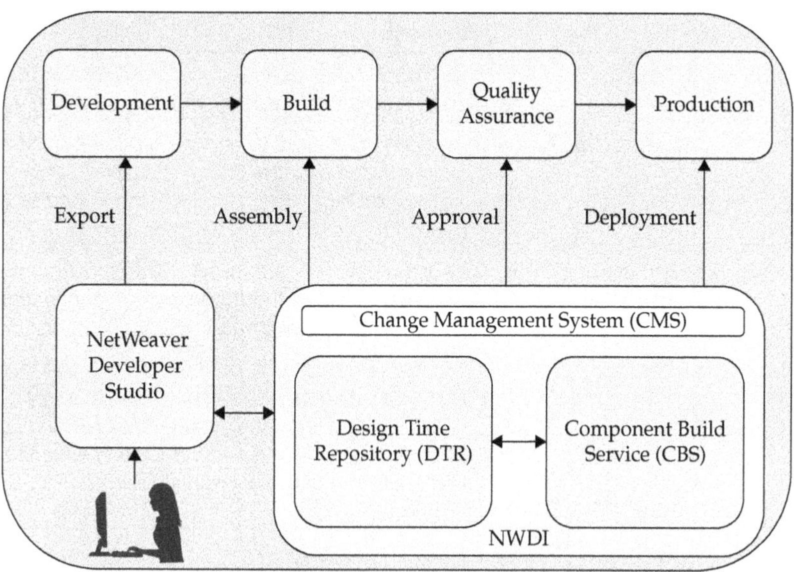

FIGURE 12-1 SAP Java four-System-Landscape

Each developer has NetWeaver Developer Studio installed on his or her laptop that includes a local J2EE environment. Each developer tests the Java code locally and ensures that the code is working before checking it in to the central environment.

SAP NWDI

NWDI is installed along with the Development Infrastructure (DI) and can be called using the following URL for a system with hostname saptst:

http://saptst:50100/devinf/main

This displays the start page of the NWDI environment, as shown.

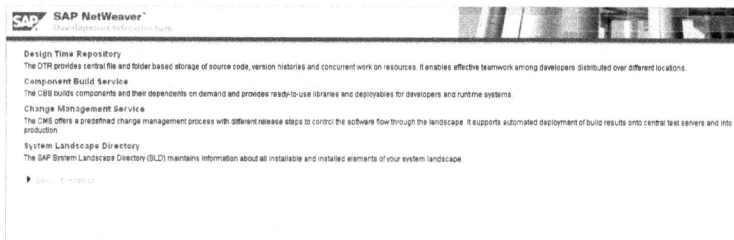

SAP NetWeaver

Design Time Repository

The DTR provides central file and folder based storage of source code, version histories and concurrent work on resources. It enables effective teamwork among developers distributed over different locations.

Component Build Service

The CBS builds components and their dependents on demand and provides ready-to-use libraries and deployables for developers and runtime systems.

Change Management Service

The CMS offers a predefined change management process with different release steps to control the software flow through the landscape. It supports automated deployment of build results onto central test servers and into production.

System Landscape Directory

The SAP System Landscape Directory (SLD) maintains information about all installable and installed elements of your system landscape.

NWDI Component	Purpose
Design Time Repository (DTR)	Its main function is to provide Java version management so that distributed development is possible.
Component Build Service (CBS)	Its main function is to provide a central build area synchronized with the DTR workspaces. After a successful build, the active version is placed in the active folders of the DTR workspaces.
Change Management Service (CMS)	Its main function is to provide transport management services between the development, consolidation, test, and production environments.
System Landscape Directory (SLD)	Its main function is to provide naming services to the software components that are being developed in a distributed environment. It prevents naming conflicts by providing a unique name for the new software component that is being developed.

TABLE 12-2 Central Services of NWDI

NWDI consists of several central services, such as DTR (Design Time Repository), CBS (Component Build Service), CMS (Change Management Service), and SLD (System Landscape Directory). The purpose of each is listed in Table 12-2.

SAP System Landscape Directory

The central idea of an SLD is to maintain the system information at one central location, which can be accessed by all applications in the SAP landscape. SLD uses an object-oriented model called CIM for SLD standard. Distributed Management Task Force (DMTG), located at www.dmtf.org, is a nonprofit organization that develops standards in the IT industry and has developed the CIM (Common Information Model). NWDI is linked to SLD so that the landscape information can be accessed from one central location. SLD is used by other SAP applications in the landscape as well.

SAP NetWeaver Developer Studio

SAP NetWeaver Developer Studio is a development and runtime environment installed on the local developer PCs. It is based on the open-source product Eclipse. SAP has included additional plug-ins and integration to the NW Java Application Server with the product so that developers can create robust SAP Java applications.

SAP Java Software Logistics in Process Integration Landscapes

The following section will provide an overview of installing CMS to support the transport of SAP PI (Process Integration) Java objects from development to test and production systems.

Installation and Configuration of CMS

Download the CMS software from the following location, and install it using Software Deployment Manager (SDM). The needed software components are listed in the illustration.

SCA	DICMS09_0-10003499.SCA	SP09 for DI CHANGE MGMT SERVER 7.00	0	Info	8314	11.08.2006
SCA	DICMS09P_2-10003499.SCA	Patch for DI CHANGE MGMT SERVER 7.00 SP09	2	Info	8316	25.01.2007

Copyright by SAP AG

Applicable JDI Component DI CHANGE MGMT. SERVER 7.00
Download Location www.service.sap.com/swdc | Download | Support Packages and Patches | Entry by Application Group | SAP NetWeaver | SAP NETWEAVER | SAP NETWEAVER 2004S | Entry by Component | Development Infrastructure | DI CHANGE MGMT. SERVER 7.00

Download these files, and place them in the download directory of the server.

1. Open SDM at /usr/sap/DM1/DVEBMGS01/SDM/program.
2. Call remotegui.sh (./RemoteGui.sh).
3. Click Connect, and provide login information.

The following illustration and Figures 12-2 and 12-3 provide an overview of the CMS software deployment steps using SDM.

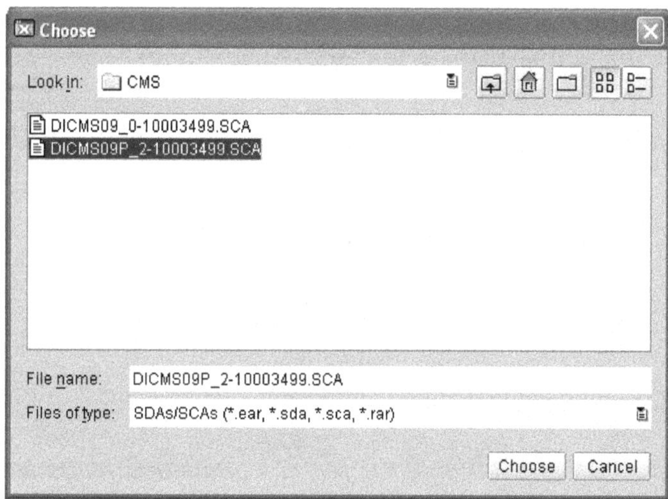

Copyright by SAP AG

PI Software Logistics with CMS

After the CMS software is deployed successfully, it can be called using the following URL:

http://saptst:50100/webdynpro/dispatcher/sap.com/tc~SL~CMS~WebUI/Cms

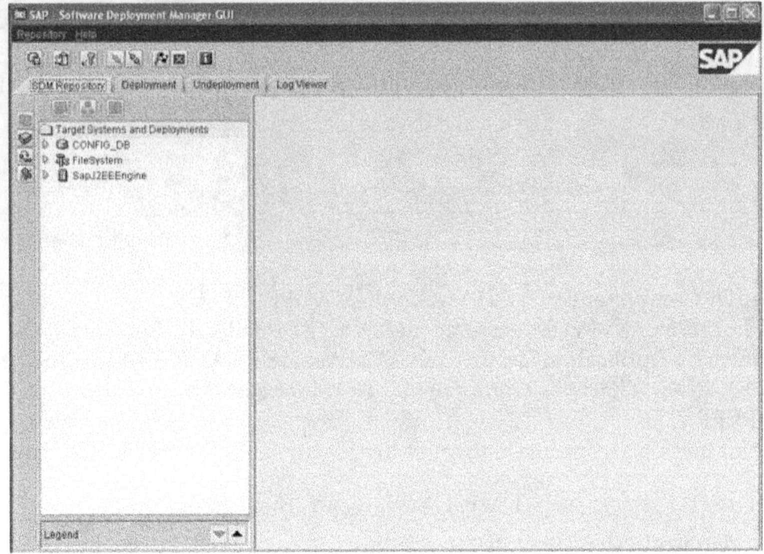

Copyright by SAP AG

FIGURE 12-2 SDM initial screen after login

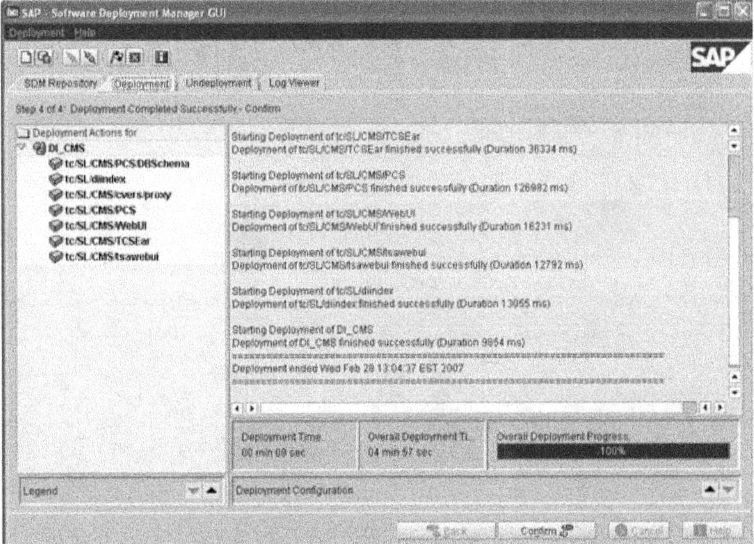

Copyright by SAP AG

FIGURE 12-3 SDM showing successful CMS software deployment

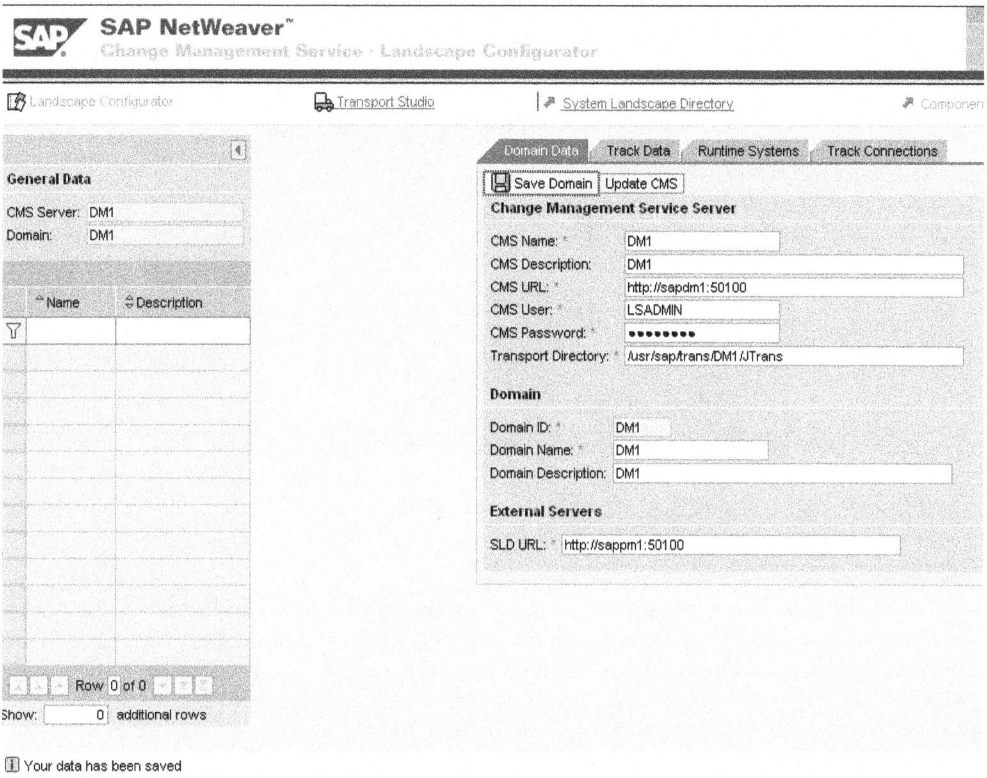

Copyright by SAP AG

FIGURE 12-4 CMS initial configuration screen

This will bring up the CMS configuration screen shown in Figure 12-4, where domains, tracks, and target URLs for transport are set up. The URL provides the screen for performing additional configuration steps. Detailed CMS configuration steps can be accessed by downloading a detailed CMS setup guide from the link provided at the end of the chapter under "Additional Resources."

SAP CTS+ and Integration of Java Software Logistics

CTS+ provides a way of integrating non-ABAP systems into the SAP Transport Management System. This will help the Basis administrator manage transports for both ABAP and Java systems from one central location. Figure 12-5 shows the critical configuration step of integrating a non-ABAP system into an existing STMS configuration. A more detailed CTS+ setup and configuration information link is provided in the "Additional Resources" section of this chapter.

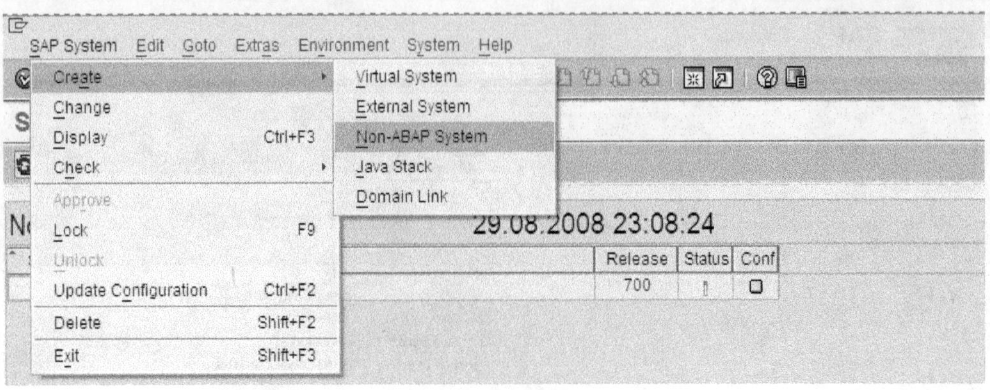

FIGURE 12-5 STMS configuration screen for including non-ABAP systems

SAP Central CTS

SAP landscapes are becoming more complex and managing change and software logistics is becoming more challenging. With the goal of further improving the software logistics in complex SAP landscapes, SAP is working on a concept called central CTS. This tool is intended to provide an easy means of configuring change management right in the CTS architecture. This will simplify the software logistics of heterogeneous landscapes and makes managing change more effective. A link to a detailed whitepaper for central CTS is provided in the "Additional Resources" section of this chapter.

Summary

- Java development is supported by SAP with NetWeaver Development Infrastructure (NWDI).
- Installation of SAP usage type Development Infrastructure (DI) provides most components of NWDI.
- NetWeaver Developer Studio provides a local Java development environment that works closely with the central services of NWDI.
- Central services include components such as DTR (Design Time Repository), CBS (Component Build Service), CMS (Change Management Service), and SLD (System Landscape Directory).
- DTR helps in version management in a distributed Java development environment.
- CBS helps in providing build service for the developed software components.
- DTR and CBS are synchronized and the active version is moved to DTR workspaces after the successful build activity is completed in the buildspaces of CBS.

- CMS helps in the transport management process between the different Java systems in a four-System-Landscape.
- SLD helps in providing naming services for the new software component development. This will ensure that there are no naming conflicts.
- CTS+ helps in integrating ABAP and Java System Landscape transport management.
- Central CTS is delivered by SAP with the intention of simplifying the change management in a complex SAP heterogeneous landscape.

Additional Resources

- **SAP NetWeaver Development Infrastructure overview** www.sdn.sap.com/irj/sdn/nw-di
- **Design Time Repository** www.sdn.sap.com/irj/sdn/nw-di?rid=/library/uuid/c0fcf2a5-1344-2a10-e7a7-cf6822697d40
- **Component Build Service** www.sdn.sap.com/irj/sdn/nw-di?rid=/library/uuid/403d2be9-1344-2a10-e492-c8a404da8552
- **Change Management Service** www.sdn.sap.com/irj/sdn/nw-di?rid=/library/uuid/80778622-1444-2a10-0283-a480e48acbfb
- **SAP SLD resources** www.sdn.sap.com/irj/sdn/nw-sld
- **NWDI development overview video demo (free registration is required to view the video)** www.sdn.sap.com/irj/sdn/nw-di?rid=/library/uuid/c0b1f2c8-54e0-2910-9ab3-b85f15093655
- **Best practices for implementing CTS+** www.sdn.sap.com/irj/sdn/cts?rid=/library/uuid/10456aac-44f7-2a10-1fbe-8b7bcd7bcd58
- **CMS setup guide** www.sdn.sap.com/irj/sdn/go/portal/prtroot/docs/library/uuid/f85ff411-0d01-0010-0096-ba14e5db6306
- **SAP Central CTS info** www.sdn.sap.com/irj/scn/index?rid=/library/uuid/5023ba03-25af-2c10-6191-99480554d90e

CHAPTER

SAP Complex System Landscapes

The implementation of SAP software by large organizations can take from six months to several years, depending upon the scope of the software deployment, the size of the organization, and the complexity of the business process that have to be set up in the new system. In this chapter we will discuss the different implementation scenarios, release management strategies for SAP software in a complex five-System-Landscape using N and N+1 architecture, and the best practices for managing SAP logistics and change management in complex SAP System Landscapes.

SAP Implementation Approach

SAP can be implemented in two main approaches: the big bang implementation approach and the phased implementation approach. Each of these has its pros and cons. One of the approaches is decided up-front during the release management planning.

Big Bang Implementation Approach

In the big bang implementation approach, SAP software is implemented all at once. End users will stop using the old legacy software and start using the new SAP software after the go-live. After a month of stabilization in the newly implemented SAP system, the old systems are retired. This approach is riskier, as change is introduced at once and the resource requirements are very high. If an implementation has any issues, this approach can cause business disruptions and cause lasting damage to an organization. This is the one of the main reasons why a phased implementation is recommended for deploying a SAP application in a systematic manner, thereby reducing business risk. A three-System-Landscape is sufficient for implementing SAP in a big bang approach.

Phased Implementation Approach

In a phased implementation, SAP software is implemented in several phases, which are referred to as releases. The standard SAP three-System-Landscape is not sufficient to address the needs of a phased multirelease implementation effort. In a phased implementation approach, after the first release goes live in the production system, there is a need for new development work and support packages application for the next release. If this is done in the existing development system, very soon this will be out of sync with the production system and cannot be used to create any production bug fixes. Because of this reason, SAP recommends a five-System-Landscape strategy to support a phased implementation approach with multiple releases over time.

SAP Five-System-Landscapes (N and N+1 Architecture)

The SAP five-System-Landscape is referred to as N and N+1 architecture, where N indicates the current release in the production system and N+1 is the new release development. Figure 13-1 shows the typical five-System-Landscape and the flow of transports.

Five-System-Landscapes have a production support path and a new release development path. In the previous example PSS | PSQ | PRD shows the production support path and DEV | QAS shows the new release development path. The following steps explain the detailed flow of activities in setting up a five-System-Landscape:

1. After the first release goes live and the production environment is stabilized, a transport freeze is established and a database copy is performed from DEV (new release development system) to PSS (production support development system).
2. At the same time a database copy is performed from PRD (production system) to PSQ (production support quality system) and a new transport path is established between PSS, PSQ, and PRD.

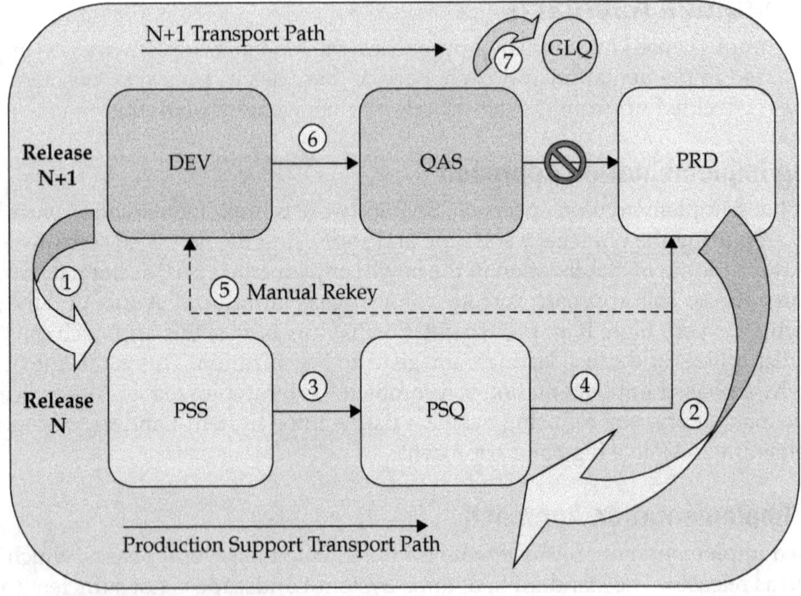

FIGURE 13-1 SAP five-System-Landscape

3. Production support transports are created in the PSS system and are imported to the PSQ system for testing.
4. Once production support break-fix transports are tested and approved they are imported to PRD.
5. All production support break-fix transports imported into PRD are manually rekeyed in the DEV system on a weekly basis.
6. New release development is performed in the DEV system and the transports are released to the QAS system. Manually rekeyed transports are released to QAS as well.
7. All transports that are imported to QAS will be queued up in a virtual holding buffer called GLQ (Go Live Queue). After integration and regression testing is successfully completed, all the GLQ transports are imported to the PRD system as part of the next release cutover activities. This cycle repeats for all the subsequent releases. When all the releases are deployed in production, the PSS and PSQ systems are retired.

SAP Best Practices in Complex System Landscapes

The following best practices are recommended in the complex System Landscapes for both the N and N+1 path:

- No transport is allowed to be deleted from the target import queues.
- If a bad transport is moved to a system, this should be followed up with a fix transport. This will help keep transports in the correct sequence.
- Preliminary transports moved to target systems must be left in the queue for subsequent mass import. This will ensure that the proper transport sequence is imported.
- Manual rekeying of all transports imported into production to the new release development system (DEV) on a weekly basis must be enforced.
- For every PSS transport there must be an equivalent manually rekeyed DEV transport.
- Use proper naming conventions for the production support and new release development transports.
- Use the Transport Documentation tab to enter details for a manually rekeyed transport in the new release development system. This information can be used for cross-reference purposes.
- Release all the manually rekeyed transports and new release transports to the QAS environment before a complete integration and regression testing effort.
- Minimize the number of change requests by limiting the transport release capability to select developers and configurators.
- Establishing transport windows or automatic transports every hour will cut down the administrative effort for performing transports.

Summary

- There are two kinds of SAP implementation approaches.
- The first approach is the big bang implementation approach, which poses a business risk.
- The second approach is the phased implementation approach. Since this approach mitigates the business risk, this is the recommended approach.
- The phased implementation approach is done with release planning.
- A five-System-Landscape is required for setting up and executing a multirelease phased SAP implementation project.

Additional Resources

- **SAP Landscape recommendation framework** www.sdn.sap.com/irj/sdn/go/portal/prtroot/docs/library/uuid/f0076ff1-a954-2b10-2a93-b2a63426e1e2
- **SAP software logistics** www.sdn.sap.com/irj/sdn/softwarelogistics

IV

PART

SAP Basis Services

CHAPTER

SAP Processes in an ABAP Stack

In this chapter we will study the different SAP processes in an ABAP stack. First we will look into how the SAP system can be technically configured with different profile parameters. Once we understand how to change the parameters, then we will study the different kinds of SAP processes, such as dialog, batch, update, lock (enqueue), and spool, that the SAP architecture provides for performing different user tasks, and how to configure the number of available processes by changing the required parameters. We will also study the special variation of configuring work process allocation based on set timetables (referred to as operation modes), load balancing (logon groups), work process quota allocations in an application server (RFC server groups), background job processing concepts, and printing in SAP systems.

SAP Profile Management

SAP profiles are operating system files set up during the time of installation by the SAP installation tool SAPinst. The profiles are written at the /sapmnt/<SID>/profile location in the file system. In a SAP system with an SID of BD1, for example, the files are written at /sapmnt/BD1/profile. The easiest way to access the profile is by logging on as <SID>adm (bd1adm) user account and issuing alias cdpro. This will take you directly into the profile directory, as shown. Three kinds of profile files are written by SAPinst at this location. They are start profile (START_DVEBMGS00_venus), instance profile (BD1_DVEBMGS00_venus), and default profile (DEFAULT.PFL). In the sample code, the SID is BD1, the hostname is venus, and DVEBMGS stands for D = Dialog work process, V = Update work process, E = Enqueue work process, B = Batch work process, M = Message server, G = Gateway, and S = Spool work process. The 00 toward the end of DVEBMGS**00** stands for

SAP Profile	Naming Convention	Actual Name	Function
SAP Start Profile	START<Instance><Instance Number>_<Hostname>	START_ DVEBMGS00_venus	The start profile lists the start processes, such as dispatcher and message server.
SAP Default Profile	DEFAULT.PFL	DEFAULT.PFL	The default profile lists applicable parameters for all instances.
SAP Instance Profile	<SID><Instance><Instance number>_<Host name>	BD1_DVEBMGS00_ venus	The instance profile lists parameters applicable to a specific instance.

TABLE 14-1 SAP Profiles

the system number. The .bak files are the backup files of the default and instance profiles. The different kinds of profiles will be discussed further in the next sections.

```
bd1adm> cdpro
bd1adm> ll
total 80
-rw-r--r-- 1 bd1adm sapsys 3406 Jan 22 10:15 BD1_DVEBMGS00_venus
-rw-rw---- 1 bd1adm sapsys 3406 Jan 22 10:15 BD1_DVEBMGS00_venus.BAK
-rw-rw---- 1 bd1adm sapsys 2394 Jan 22 10:14 DEFAULT.BAK
-rw-r--r-- 1 bd1adm sapsys 2394 Jan 22 10:14 DEFAULT.PFL
-rw-r--r-- 1 bd1adm sapsys 3827 Mar 10 18:10 START_DVEBMGS00_venus
```

SAP Start, Default, and Instance Profiles

Table 14-1 lists the three profiles and the function of each.

SAP Start Profile

The SAP start profile executes commands that start the main services, such as message server and dispatcher, and uses the keyword local. The following sample code of a Start profile shows the sequence of steps and executions of different commands at the start of the SAP system for SID BD1 on hostname venus. Usually, the start profile is set up once at the time of install and is not edited.

```
bd1adm> more START_DVEBMGS00_venus
#.*******************************************************************
#.*       Start profile START_DVEBMGS00_VENUS
#.*       Version                = 000009
#.*       Generated by user = Ranjit
#.*       Generated on = 22.01.2009 , 10:14:19
#.*******************************************************************
SAPSYSTEMNAME = BD1
SAPSYSTEM = 00
```

```
INSTANCE_NAME = DVEBMGS00
DIR_CT_RUN = $(DIR_EXE_ROOT)/run
DIR_EXECUTABLE = $(DIR_INSTANCE)/exe
DIR_PROFILE = $(DIR_INSTALL)/profile
_PF = $(DIR_PROFILE)/BD1_DVEBMGS00_VENUS
SETENV_00 = LD_LIBRARY_PATH=$(DIR_LIBRARY):%(LD_LIBRARY_PATH)
SETENV_01 = SHLIB_PATH=$(DIR_LIBRARY):%(SHLIB_PATH)
SETENV_02 = LIBPATH=$(DIR_LIBRARY):%(LIBPATH)
#-----------------------------------------------------------------------
# Copy SAP Executables
#-----------------------------------------------------------------------
Execute_00 = immediate $(DIR_CT_RUN)/sapcpe$(FT_EXE) pf=$(_PF)
#-----------------------------------------------------------------------
# Start SCSA administration
#-----------------------------------------------------------------------
Execute_01 = local $(DIR_EXECUTABLE)/sapmscsa pf=$(_PF) -n
#-----------------------------------------------------------------------
# Start SAP message server
#-----------------------------------------------------------------------
_MS = ms.sap$(SAPSYSTEMNAME)_$(INSTANCE_NAME)
Execute_02 = local rm -f $(_MS)
Execute_03 = local ln -s -f $(DIR_EXECUTABLE)/msg_server$(FT_EXE) $(_MS)
Start_Program_00 = local $(_MS) pf=$(_PF)
#-----------------------------------------------------------------------
# Start application server
#-----------------------------------------------------------------------
_DW = dw.sap$(SAPSYSTEMNAME)_$(INSTANCE_NAME)
Execute_04 = local rm -f $(_DW)
Execute_05 = local ln -s -f $(DIR_EXECUTABLE)/disp+work$(FT_EXE) $(_DW)
Start_Program_01 = local $(_DW) pf=$(_PF)
#-----------------------------------------------------------------------
# Start syslog collector daemon
#-----------------------------------------------------------------------
_CO = co.sap$(SAPSYSTEMNAME)_$(INSTANCE_NAME)
Execute_06 = local rm -f $(_CO)
Execute_07 = local ln -s -f $(DIR_EXECUTABLE)/rslgcoll $(_CO)
Start_Program_02 = local $(_CO) pf=$(_PF) -F
#-----------------------------------------------------------------------
# Start syslog send daemon
#-----------------------------------------------------------------------
_SE = se.sap$(SAPSYSTEMNAME)_$(INSTANCE_NAME)
Execute_08 = local rm -f $(_SE)
Execute_09 = local ln -s -f $(DIR_EXECUTABLE)/rslgsend $(_SE)
Start_Program_03 = local $(_SE) pf=$(_PF) -F
#-----------------------------------------------------------------------
# Start internet graphics server
#-----------------------------------------------------------------------
_IG = ig.sap$(SAPSYSTEMNAME)_$(INSTANCE_NAME)
Execute_10 = local rm -f $(_IG)
Execute_11 = local ln -s -f $(DIR_EXECUTABLE)/igswd_mt $(_IG)
Start_Program_04 = local $(_IG) -mode=profile pf=$(_PF)
```

Default Profile

The default profile has profile parameters that are applicable to all the application servers (system-wide parameters) of a SAP system. Some of the parameters that should be entered in the default profile are message server hostname, transport directory path, and default login client number. The following is an example of a default profile:

```
bd1adm> more DEFAULT.PFL
#.***********************************************************************
#.*       Default profile DEFAULT
#.*       Version             = 000004
#.*       Generated by user = Ranjit
#.*       Generated on = 22.01.2009 , 10:14:55
#.***********************************************************************
#parameter created                          by: Ranjit     30.08.2009 22:43:26
login/accept_sso2_ticket = 1
#parameter created                          by: Ranjit     30.08.2009 22:42:57
login/create_sso2_ticket = 2
SAPDBHOST = VENUS
j2ee/dbtype = ora
j2ee/dbname = BD1
j2ee/dbhost = VENUS
SAPSYSTEMNAME = BD1
SAPGLOBALHOST = VENUS
rdisp/bufrefmode = sendoff,exeauto
DIR_PUT = /usr/sap/$(SAPSYSTEMNAME)/put
#---------------------------------------------------------------------
# SAP Message Server for ABAP
#---------------------------------------------------------------------
rdisp/mshost = VENUS
rdisp/msserv = sapmsBD1
rdisp/msserv_internal = 3900
login/system_client = 100
```

Instance Profile

SAP profile parameters that are specific to a particular instance are entered in this profile. The following shows some of the parameters that are in the instance profile. Allocation of memory resources is one good example of a profile parameter that should be entered in an instance profile.

```
bd1adm> more BD1_DVEBMGS00_venus
#.***********************************************************************
#.*       Instance profile BD1_DVEBMGS00_VENUS
#.*       Version             = 000009
#.*       Generated by user = Ranjit
#.*       Generated on = 22.01.2009 , 10:15:21
#.********************************************************************
#parameter created                          by: Ranjit     30.07.2009 14:57:37
DIR_EPS_ROOT = /usr/sap/transBD1/EPS
#parameter created                          by: Ranjit     30.07.2009 14:57:01
```

```
DIR_TRANS = /usr/sap/transBD1
#parameter created                      by: Ranjit     28.07.2009 11:49:40
login/system_client = 100
#parameter created                      by: Ranjit     28.07.2009 10:20:55
#old_value: 0
changed: Ranjit 28.05.2009 09:10:21
login/no_automatic_user_sapstar = 1
SAPSYSTEMNAME = BD1
SAPSYSTEM = 00
INSTANCE_NAME = DVEBMGS00
DIR_CT_RUN = $(DIR_EXE_ROOT)/run
DIR_EXECUTABLE = $(DIR_INSTANCE)/exe
exe/saposcol = $(DIR_CT_RUN)/saposcol
rdisp/wp_no_dia = 10
#old_value: 3
changed: Ranjit 05.05.2009 08:15:12
rdisp/wp_no_btc = 5
exe/icmbnd = $(DIR_CT_RUN)/icmbnd
icm/server_port_0 = PROT=HTTP,PORT=80$$
#-----------------------------------------------------------------------
# SAP Message Server parameters are set in the DEFAULT.PFL
#-----------------------------------------------------------------------
ms/server_port_0 = PROT=HTTP,PORT=81$$
rdisp/wp_no_enq = 1
rdisp/wp_no_vb = 1
rdisp/wp_no_vb2 = 1
rdisp/wp_no_spo = 1
.....
```

Profiles Read and Override Sequence

Default parameters are in the source code (kernel) and are read first at the instance start. If a user makes any changes to the default parameter, either in the default profile or instance profile, then that overrides the source-code default parameter. The parameter read sequence is as follows:

1. Source code (kernel)
2. Default profile
3. Instance profile

Profile Maintenance (RZ10)

Profiles at the operating system level can be maintained by an editor such as vi. However, directly editing the profiles at the operating system level has many disadvantages, such as lack of parameter checks, lack of versioning, and any major parameter errors, if not checked, would result in the SAP system not starting. Because of these reasons, SAP provides a central profile maintenance tool with transaction RZ10. The tool performs basic consistency checks for parameter changes, provides version management, and creates a backup of the file at the operating system level. Before transaction RZ10 can be used to maintain the profile parameters, the profiles installed at the operating system level have to be imported to the database using the transaction code RZ10 menu path Utilities | Import Profiles | Of Active Servers. This will get the files copied from the file system to the database. Once the files are imported to the database, they are ready to be maintained using transaction code RZ10. The illustration shows the initial screen for transaction code RZ10.

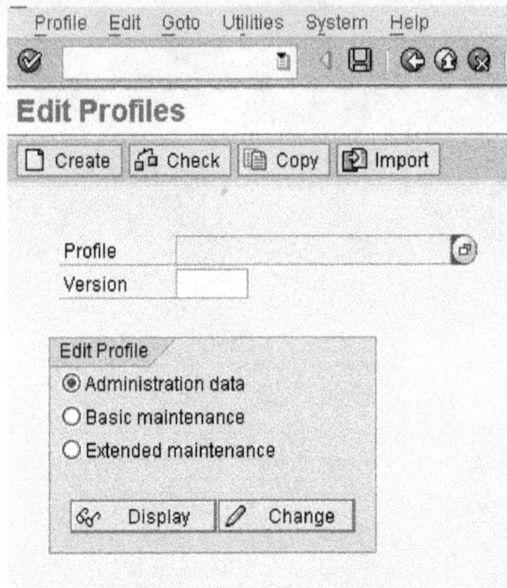

Copyright by SAP AG

In the screen use the Profile field drop-down menu, or place your cursor in the Profile field and press the F4 function key. This will provide a window with the three profiles, as shown.

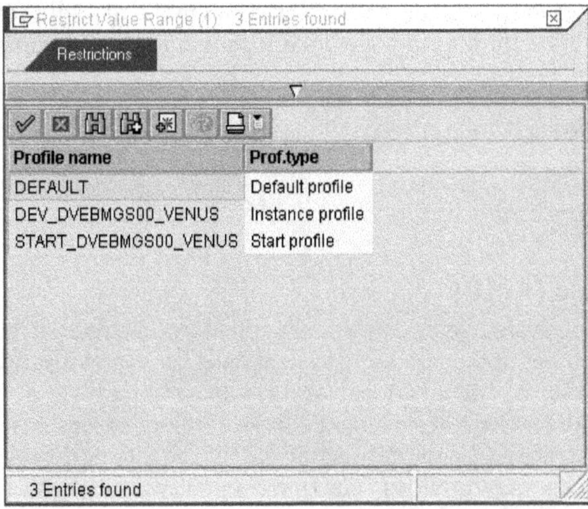

Copyright by SAP AG

Select the default profile, and the following screen will appear.

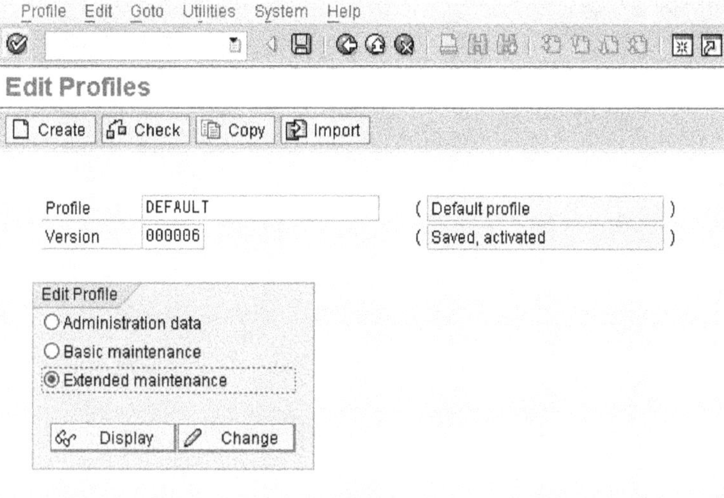

Copyright by SAP AG

Select the Extended Maintenance option, and click the Change button. This will show the following screen.

Maintain Profile 'DEFAULT' Version '000007'

Copy | Parameter | Parameter | Parameter

12.04.2010 Active parameters

Parameter Name	Parameter value
login/no_automatic_user_sapstar	0
SAPDBHOST	venus
j2ee/dbtype	ora
j2ee/dbname	DEV
j2ee/dbhost	venus
SAPSYSTEMNAME	DEV
SAPGLOBALHOST	venus
rdisp/bufrefmode	sendoff,exeauto
rdisp/mshost	venus
rdisp/msserv	sapmsDEV
rdisp/msserv_internal	3900
j2ee/scs/host	venus
j2ee/scs/system	01
j2ee/ms/port	3901
login/system_client	100

Copyright by SAP AG

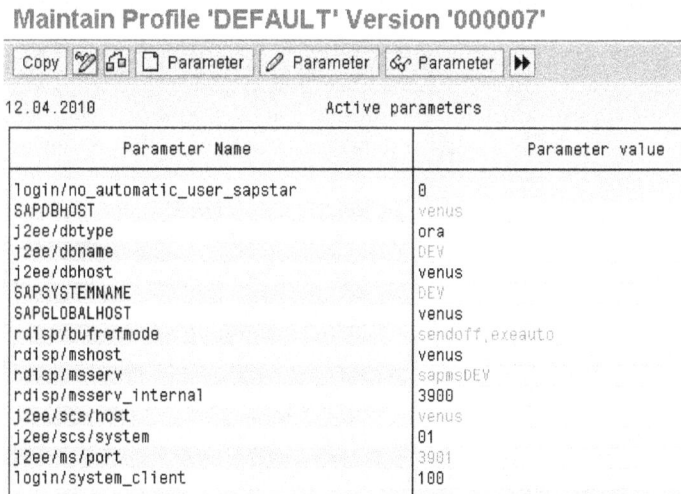

Click the Create button (F5 function key) to add a new profile parameter to the default profile. This will give you the screen shown in Figure 14-1, where a new profile parameter can be added. In the figure, a new profile parameter login/system_client with value of 100 is added.

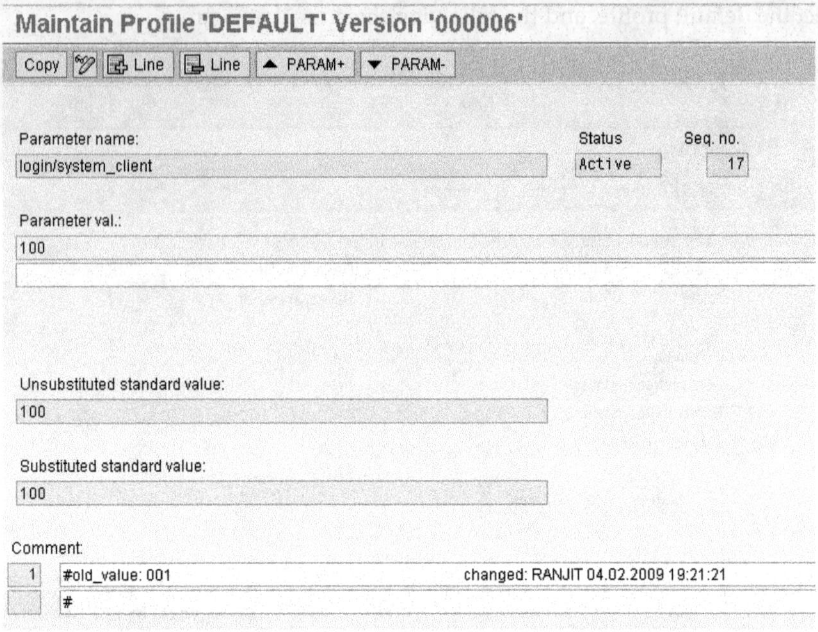

Copyright by SAP AG

FIGURE 14-1 Creation of a new parameter

Once a new parameter and its value is entered, click the Copy (SHIFT-F4) button and then use the Back button when you are done. Click the Copy button again. The "changed profile was transferred" message appears. Click the Back button one more time. At this point the profile is not saved. In order to save the profile in the database, click the Save button as shown.

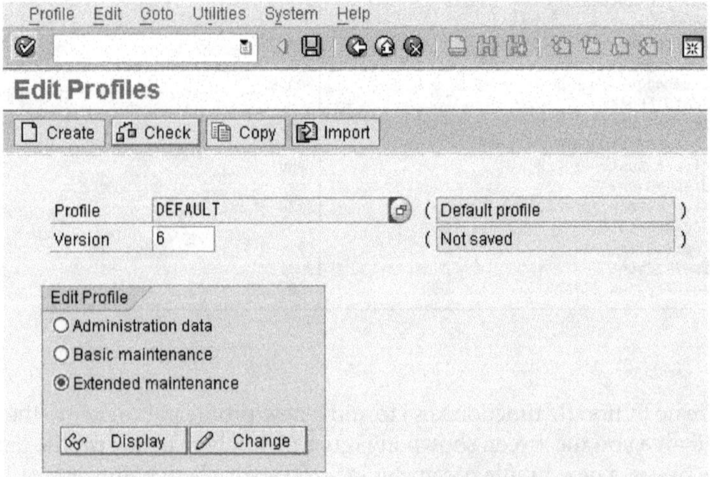

Copyright by SAP AG

This will show the following window, prompting you to click Yes or No to providing a list of incorrect parameter values, which are marked in red. Some of the parameters marked in red are not applicable to this version of SAP, however, and can be safely ignored.

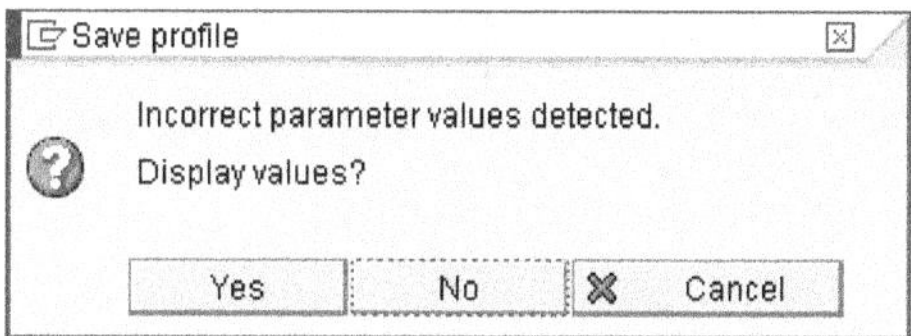

Copyright by SAP AG

Click Yes and verify the incorrect values. Once this is done, correct the values if they are relevant for this SAP release, or ignore the parameter if it is not relevant for this release. Once this is done, click the Back button and the following screen will be displayed, asking you to activate the profile. Successfully activating the profile creates a backup of the profile parameter file at the operating system level.

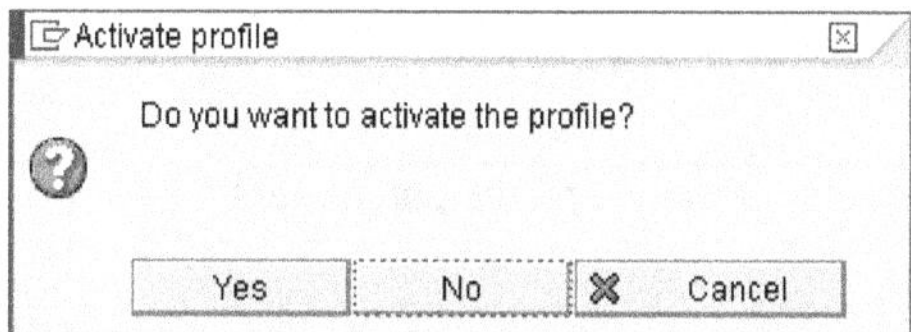

Copyright by SAP AG

Click Yes, and you will notice the following version information.

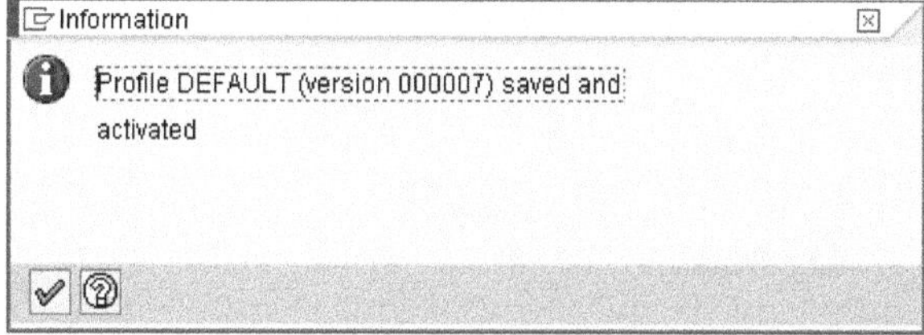

Copyright by SAP AG

Click the green check mark. In the next screen, click the green check mark again. The message shown in Figure 14-2 appears when we make changes to the profiles. Once the changes are complete, shut down and restart the system for the parameter changes to be effective.

Profile Parameter Check and Documentation

SAP transaction code RZ11 can be used to check the following:

- Current and default value of a profile parameter in the system
- Documentation of a profile parameter
- If the parameter can be switched dynamically

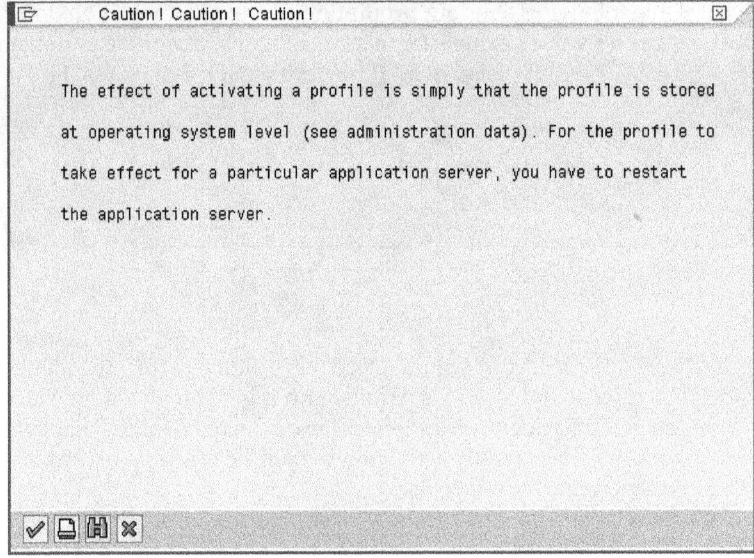

Caution ! Caution ! Caution !
The effect of activating a profile is simply that the profile is stored at operating system level (see administration data). For the profile to take effect for a particular application server, you have to restart the application server.

FIGURE 14-2 Caution message after activating profile parameters

The following illustration shows the initial RZ11 transaction screen. Enter the profile parameter **rdisp/gui_auto_logout** and click the Display button.

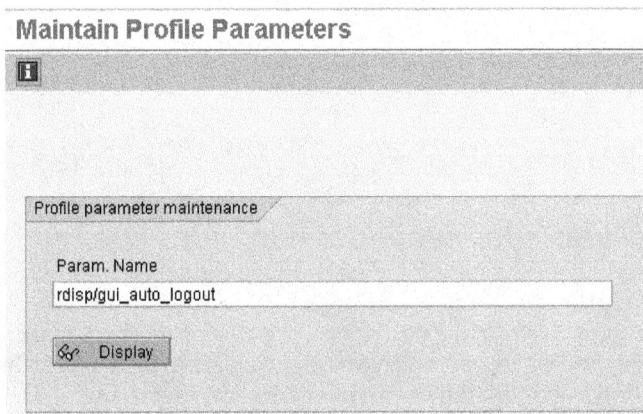

Maintain Profile Parameters

Profile parameter maintenance

Param. Name

rdisp/gui_auto_logout

Display

Figure 14-3 displays the default value, profile value, and the current value of the parameter in the system. We can also check if the parameter is dynamically switchable and read its documentation by clicking the Documentation button. You can change the value of

Display Profile Parameter Attributes

Documentation | Change Value

Param. Name

rdisp/gui_auto_logout

Short description(Engl)	Maximum Time of no Input at the GUI
Appl. area	Dispatcher and Task Handler
ParameterTyp	Character String
Changes allowed	Change permitted
Valid for oper. system	All operating systems
DynamicallySwitchable	☑
Same on all servers	☐
Dflt value	0
ProfileVal	0
Current value	0

FIGURE 14-3 Profile parameter details

the dynamically switchable parameter by clicking the Change Value button at the top of the screen and entering the desired value in the field below. The instance need not be bounced (restarted) for a dynamically switchable parameter to be effective. This group of parameters is effective immediately after you change the value and save it in the system.

SAP Work Processes

The SAP work process is a component of the application server that executes an ABAP application. SAP work processes are started as operating system processes, each with its own process ID (PID) when the system is started. The majority of the processing of the application is performed by the SAP work processes.

SAP Dispatcher

The SAP dispatcher is a central process on an application server and is responsible for the following actions:

- Reading SAP profile parameters
- Starting work processes
- Message server logon
- Connecting to presentation layer (SAP GUI)
- Distributing load evenly across all the configured work processes

Work Process Connection to the Database

The SAP work process runs at the operating system level with <SID>adm user account created at the time of the system installation. However, the underlying Oracle Database is owned by a user called SAP<SCHEMA-ID>. SAP work processes, therefore, while establishing a connection to the underlying Oracle Database retrieve the password for user SAP<SCHEMA-ID> from a SAP table called SAPUSER. After the SAP work process retrieves the password, it will go on to connect to the underlying Oracle Database. Once the work process establishes a connection to the database, it keeps it for the entire runtime of the SAP system. The connections are terminated only when the SAP system is shut down. The following shows the connection details of the SAP work process to the underlying Oracle Database for SAP<SCHEMA-ID> = SAPBDX and SAP SID = BD1:

```
  calling db_connect ...
  Oracle Client Version: '10.2.0.2.0'
  Client NLS settings: AMERICAN_AMERICA.UTF8
  Logon as OPS$-user to get SAPBDX's password
  Connecting as /@BD1 on connection 0 (nls_hdl 0) ... (dbsl 700 250407)
  Nls CharacterSet                  NationalCharSet
  C      EnvHp      ErrHp ErrHpBatch
  0 UTF8
  1 0x1fdc80a0 0x1fdcfb50 0x1fde02a8
  Attaching to DB Server BD1 (con_hdl=0,svchp=0x1fde01d8,srvhp=0x1fde3148)
  Starting user session (con_hdl=0,svchp=0x1fde01d8,srvhp=0x1fde3148,usrhp=
0x1fdd0368)
  Now '/@BD1' is connected (con_hdl 0, nls_hdl 0).
  Got SAPBDX's password from OPS$-user
  Disconnecting from connection 0 ...
  Closing user session (con_hdl=0,svchp=0x1fde01d8,usrhp=0x1fdd0368)
  Now I'm disconnected from ORACLE
  Connecting as SAPBDX/<pwd>@BD1 on connection 0 (nls_hdl 0) ... (dbsl 700
250407)
 Nls CharacterSet                  NationalCharSet
 C      EnvHp      ErrHp ErrHpBatch
 0 UTF8
 1 0x1fdc80a0 0x1fdcfb50 0x1fde02a8
 Starting user session (con_hdl=0,svchp=0x1fde01d8,srvhp=0x1fde3148,usrhp=0
x1fdd0368)
 Now 'SAPBDX/<pwd>@BD1' is connected (con_hdl 0, nls_hdl 0).
 Database NLS settings: AMERICAN_AMERICA.UTF8
 DB instance DB1 is running on venus with ORACLE version 10.2.0.4.0
 since MAR 19, 2009   Connection 0 opened (DBSL handle 0)
 Wp  Hdl ConName          ConId     ConState     TX
 PRM RCT TIM MAX OPT Date      Time    DBHost
 000 000 R/3              000000000 ACTIVE       NO
 YES NO  000 255 255 20090319 160040 venus
db_connect o.k.
```

Types of Work Processes

Several different categories of work processes are started when the SAP system is started:

- SAP dialog work processes
- SAP background (batch) work processes
- SAP update work processes
- SAP enqueue (lock) work processes
- SAP spool work processes

Dialog Work Processes

Dialog work processes will help in executing dialog programs. Dialog work processing is used for all interactive processing in the system. The number of dialog work processes is configured by modifying the rdisp/wp_no_dia profile parameter in the instance profile. Transaction code SM51 gives a list of all the application servers (Instances) for a SAP system. You can double-click the application server to get an overview of its particular work processes. Transaction code SM50 executed in a given application server provides an overview of all configured work processes for an instance. In Figure 14-4 the dialog work processes are seen as type DIA and are marked in a box.

In instances where there are multiple application servers, we can get an overview of global work processes by using transaction code SM66. This transaction code can be used to check the status of the work processes from different application servers of a single SAP

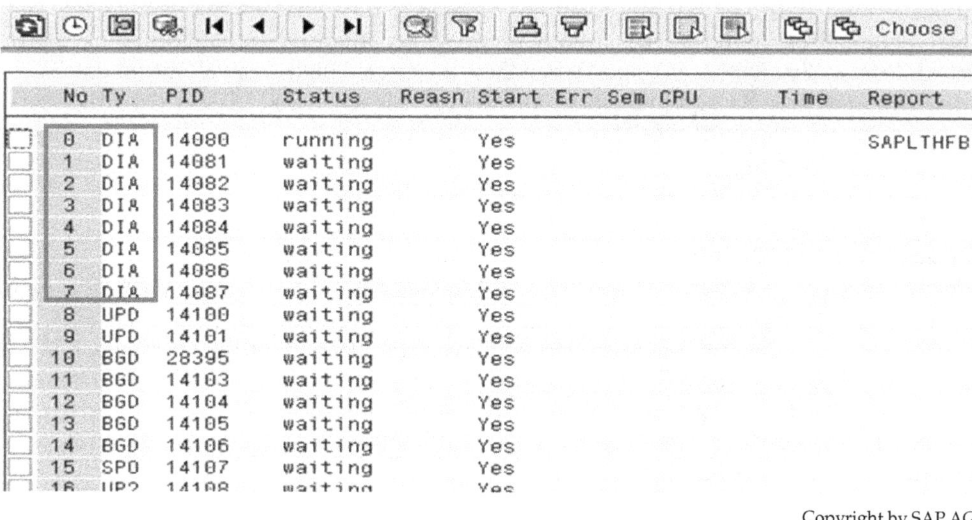

No	Ty.	PID	Status	Reasn	Start	Err	Sem	CPU	Time	Report
0	DIA	14080	running		Yes					SAPLTHFB
1	DIA	14081	waiting		Yes					
2	DIA	14082	waiting		Yes					
3	DIA	14083	waiting		Yes					
4	DIA	14084	waiting		Yes					
5	DIA	14085	waiting		Yes					
6	DIA	14086	waiting		Yes					
7	DIA	14087	waiting		Yes					
8	UPD	14100	waiting		Yes					
9	UPD	14101	waiting		Yes					
10	BGD	28395	waiting		Yes					
11	BGD	14103	waiting		Yes					
12	BGD	14104	waiting		Yes					
13	BGD	14105	waiting		Yes					
14	BGD	14106	waiting		Yes					
15	SPO	14107	waiting		Yes					
16	UP2	14108	waiting		Yes					

FIGURE 14-4 SAP work process overview (dialog work processes are highlighted)

system that are active at a given point of time. This transaction is particularly useful to check the execution of a online transaction or a background job in real time.

To summarize, the following three transactions help monitor and track SAP work processes:

- SM51 transaction lists all the application servers that belong to one SAP system.
- SM50 transaction lists work processes of an individual application server.
- SM66 transaction lists active work processes of all the application servers that belong to one SAP system.

By design, there are limited dialog work processes providing services to several hundred end users. If a long-running interactive ABAP program is executed, then this has the potential of tying up all the available dialog work processes, causing the system to hang. In order to prevent this from happening, SAP delivers a profile parameter rdisp/max_wprun_time that controls the maximum runtime of the dialog work process. The default value of the parameter is 600 seconds. The value can be increased to 1,200 seconds for an Online Transaction Processing System (OLTP) such as SAP ERP and 3,600 seconds for an Online Analytical Processing System (OLAP) such as SAP BW. In certain instances where only one long-running ABAP program is being executed, the parameter can be temporarily disabled by setting the value to 0. Since this a dynamically switchable parameter, it does not require a system restart. Because of the previously mentioned reasons, it is always recommended to run the long-running programs in the background and the background work processes, which are not restricted by any time limit.

Batch Work Processes

The background (batch) work process is responsible for executing background jobs in the SAP system. Background job processing is used for noninteractive processing. This is a collection of one or more ABAP or external programs ordered to run serially without any user intervention. Background work is usually very resource-intensive and long-running, and is scheduled usually after-hours (night) when there is expected high data volume for database updates and deletes. Background work processes provide scheduled job services to the users. The number of background work processes on a given application server is controlled by the rdisp/wp_no_btc parameter value entered in the instance profile. Figure 14-5 shows the SM50 transaction view with background work processes highlighted.

Update Work Processes

The update work processes perform the asynchronous database updates in the SAP system. There are two kinds of update work processes: Update (V1) and Upd2 (V2). There are usually several update processes configured for each application server. The number of update work processes on a given application server is controlled by the rdisp/wp_no_vb parameter value for V1 updates and the rdisp/wp_no_vb2 parameter value entered in the instance profile for V2 updates. Figure 14-6 shows SM50 work process overview with update work processes highlighted.

Enqueue (Lock) Work Process

The enqueue work process, or lock work process, will help in executing lock operations. The enqueue process is responsible for holding application locks. The processes are controlled by the rdisp/wp_no_enq parameter value entered in the instance profile. Figure 14-7 shows the enqueue work process.

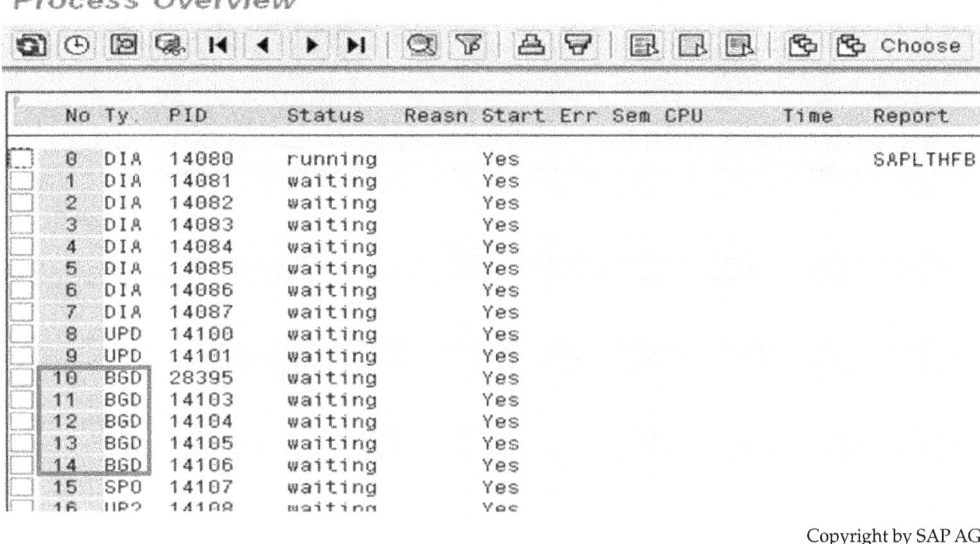

Process Overview

No	Ty.	PID	Status	Reasn	Start	Err	Sem	CPU	Time	Report
0	DIA	14080	running		Yes					SAPLTHFB
1	DIA	14081	waiting		Yes					
2	DIA	14082	waiting		Yes					
3	DIA	14083	waiting		Yes					
4	DIA	14084	waiting		Yes					
5	DIA	14085	waiting		Yes					
6	DIA	14086	waiting		Yes					
7	DIA	14087	waiting		Yes					
8	UPD	14100	waiting		Yes					
9	UPD	14101	waiting		Yes					
10	BGD	28395	waiting		Yes					
11	BGD	14103	waiting		Yes					
12	BGD	14104	waiting		Yes					
13	BGD	14105	waiting		Yes					
14	BGD	14106	waiting		Yes					
15	SPO	14107	waiting		Yes					
16	UP2	14108	waiting		Yes					

FIGURE 14-5 SAP work process overview with background work processes highlighted

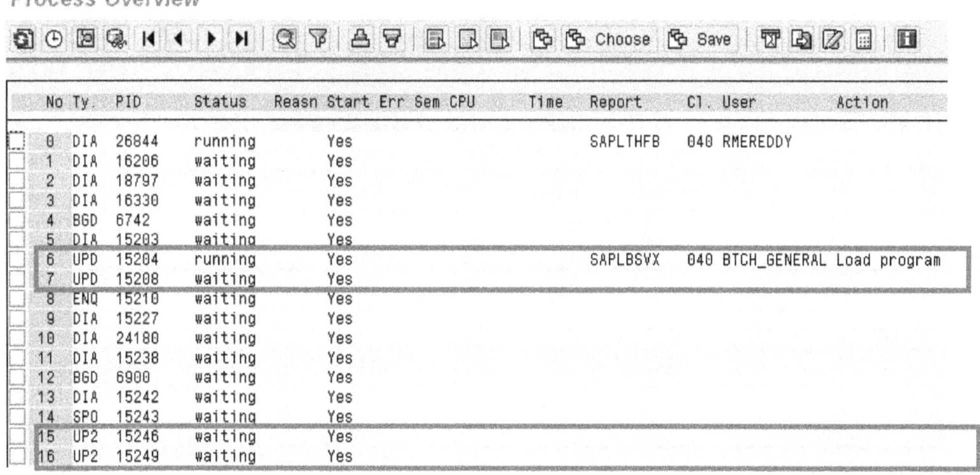

Process Overview

No	Ty.	PID	Status	Reasn	Start	Err	Sem	CPU	Time	Report	Cl.	User	Action
0	DIA	26844	running		Yes					SAPLTHFB	040	RMEREDDY	
1	DIA	16206	waiting		Yes								
2	DIA	18797	waiting		Yes								
3	DIA	16330	waiting		Yes								
4	BGD	6742	waiting		Yes								
5	DIA	15203	waiting		Yes								
6	UPD	15204	running		Yes					SAPLBSVX	040	BTCH_GENERAL	Load program
7	UPD	15208	waiting		Yes								
8	ENQ	15210	waiting		Yes								
9	DIA	15227	waiting		Yes								
10	DIA	24180	waiting		Yes								
11	DIA	15238	waiting		Yes								
12	BGD	6900	waiting		Yes								
13	DIA	15242	waiting		Yes								
14	SPO	15243	waiting		Yes								
15	UP2	15246	waiting		Yes								
16	UP2	15249	waiting		Yes								

FIGURE 14-6 Work process overview showing update processes highlighted

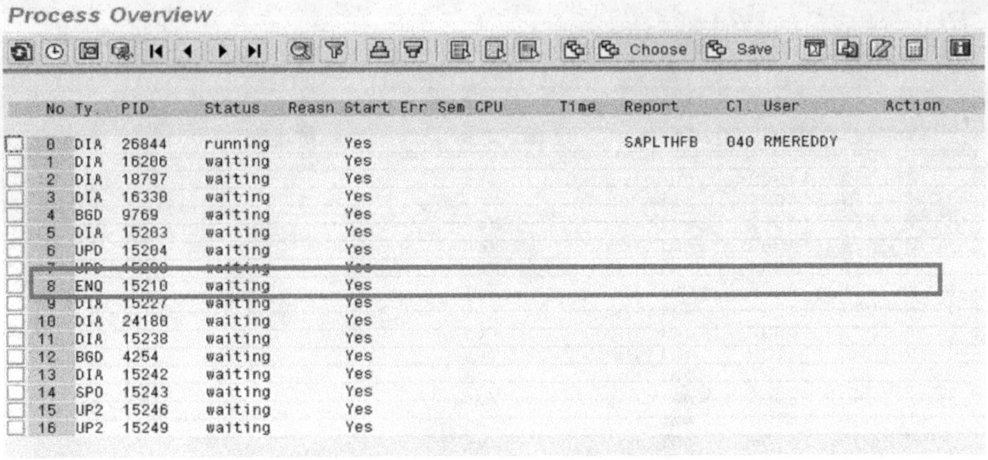

Process Overview

Choose Save

No	Ty.	PID	Status	Reasn	Start	Err	Sem	CPU	Time	Report	Cl.	User	Action
0	DIA	26844	running		Yes					SAPLTHFB	040	RMEREDDY	
1	DIA	16206	waiting		Yes								
2	DIA	18797	waiting		Yes								
3	DIA	16330	waiting		Yes								
4	BGD	9769	waiting		Yes								
5	DIA	15203	waiting		Yes								
6	UPD	15204	waiting		Yes								
7	UPD	[illegible]	waiting		Yes								
8	ENQ	15210	waiting		Yes								
9	DIA	15227	waiting		Yes								
10	DIA	24180	waiting		Yes								
11	DIA	15238	waiting		Yes								
12	BGD	4254	waiting		Yes								
13	DIA	15242	waiting		Yes								
14	SPO	15243	waiting		Yes								
15	UP2	15246	waiting		Yes								
16	UP2	15249	waiting		Yes								

FIGURE 14-7 Work process overview with enqueue work process highlighted

Spool Work Process

The spool work process helps in print formatting. More than one spool work process can be configured so that if one spool work process is hung then the other one can process the spool requests. The number of spool work processes on a given application server is controlled by the rdisp/wp_no_spo parameter value entered in the instance profile. Figure 14-8 shows the spool work processes in the work process overview screen.

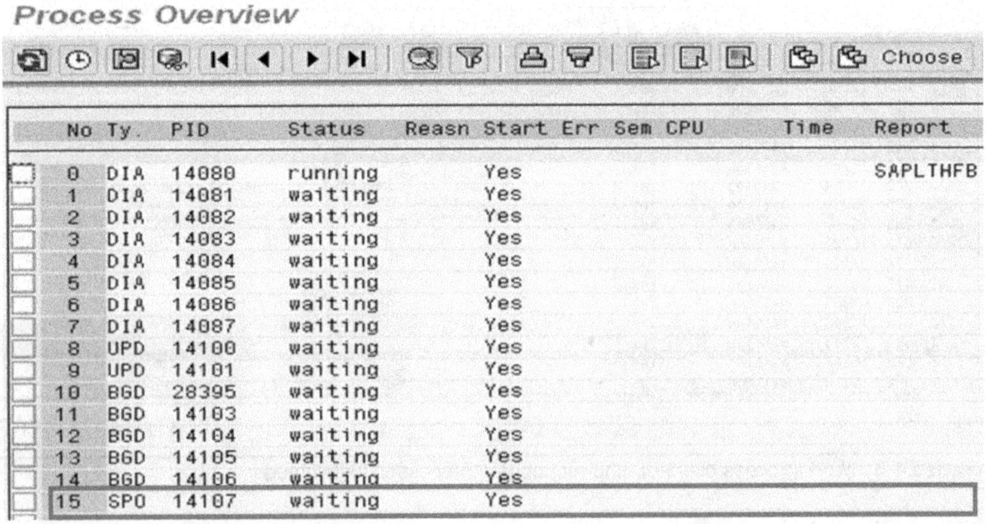

Process Overview

Choose

No	Ty.	PID	Status	Reasn	Start	Err	Sem	CPU	Time	Report
0	DIA	14080	running		Yes					SAPLTHFB
1	DIA	14081	waiting		Yes					
2	DIA	14082	waiting		Yes					
3	DIA	14083	waiting		Yes					
4	DIA	14084	waiting		Yes					
5	DIA	14085	waiting		Yes					
6	DIA	14086	waiting		Yes					
7	DIA	14087	waiting		Yes					
8	UPD	14100	waiting		Yes					
9	UPD	14101	waiting		Yes					
10	BGD	28395	waiting		Yes					
11	BGD	14103	waiting		Yes					
12	BGD	14104	waiting		Yes					
13	BGD	14105	waiting		Yes					
14	BGD	14106	waiting		Yes					
15	SPO	14107	waiting		Yes					

FIGURE 14-8 Spool work processes

Message Server and Message Server Monitor

There is only one message server, regardless of the number of application servers in a SAP system. The message server process starts and runs at the operating system level and can be checked by issuing the following command:

```
bd1adm>  ps -ef | grep db1adm | grep ms
bd1adm    7638  6893  0 19:09 pts/1    00:00:00 grep ms
bd1adm   18182 18158  0 Mar19 ?        00:01:49
ms.sapDB1_DVEBMGS00 pf=/usr/sap/BD1/SYS/profile/BD1_DVEBMGS00_VENUS
```

At the SAP application level, transaction code SMMS can be used to check the status and monitor a message server. The message server lists the available application servers, and its main responsibilities are as follows:

- Load balancing
- Deciding which application server the user will log into
- Providing communication between the application servers

Gateway Process and Gateway Monitor

The gateway process helps in communication with external applications using the CPI-C protocol. The gateway process starts and runs at the operating system level when the SAP system is started and can be checked by issuing the following command:

```
db1adm> ps -ef | grep db1adm | grep gwrd
db1adm    8965  6893  0 19:14 pts/1    00:00:00 grep gwrd
db1adm   18221 18183  0 Mar19 ?
00:01:59 gwrd -dp pf=/usr/sap/BD1/SYS/profile/DB1_DVEBMGS00_VENUS
```

At the SAP application level, transaction code SMGW can be used to check the status and active gateway connections of the system. A gateway process is installed along with the standard SAP installation in ABAP systems. In Java-only installations, the gateway is not installed as a part of a standard installation. If needed, a separate stand-alone gateway instance should be installed.

SAP Operation Modes (SM63, RZ04)

Businesses operating SAP systems need more dialog work processes during work hours and more background work processes during after hours. When a SAP system is initially configured, the static number of dialog and background work processes is set. This static setup does not allow us to use the system resources effectively in a 24-hour operation, where more dialog processes are needed during business hours and more background processes are needed during the night. SAP has provided us with a concept of operation modes where work processes are dynamically switched back and forth between dialog and background or other work process types based on a timetable referred to as the operation modes timetable. This allows businesses to utilize the system resources to a fuller extent by switching resources based on need. The total number of work processes remains unchanged after the operation mode switch, and only the work process types are switched. In order to set up operation modes, first we have to set up an operation mode timetable and then configure the work process distribution based on the operation mode timetable. The system will switch the work processes based on the operations modes timetable without shutting down the instance or changing the profile parameter values.

Operation Modes Timetable

The operation modes timetable can be maintained by using transaction code SM63. Choose the change option in transaction SM63, and maintain the operation modes timetable as shown. The start and end times can be marked for assignment to an operation mode name by double-clicking the start time row and double-clicking the end time row. The entire time range will be marked in black. Once the assignment is complete, the table will be as shown. This example has night and day operation modes defined in the operation modes timetable.

	Start/end time	Name of the active operation mode
	00.00 - 01.00	Night
	01.00 - 02.00	Night
==>	02.00 - 03.00	Night
	03.00 - 04.00	Night
	04.00 - 05.00	Night
	05.00 - 06.00	Night
	06.00 - 07.00	Night
	07.00 - 08.00	Day
	08.00 - 09.00	Day
	09.00 - 10.00	Day
	10.00 - 11.00	Day
	11.00 - 12.00	Day
	12.00 - 13.00	Day
	13.00 - 14.00	Day
	14.00 - 15.00	Day
	15.00 - 16.00	Day
	16.00 - 17.00	Day
	17.00 - 18.00	Day
	18.00 - 19.00	Day
	19.00 - 20.00	Night
	20.00 - 21.00	Night
	21.00 - 22.00	Night
	22.00 - 23.00	Night
	23.00 - 00.00	Night

Once the operation modes timetable setup is complete, the next step is to create new instance and operation mode assignments by using transaction code RZ04 and press the F6 button. This will bring up a screen where the hostname and the start and instance profiles must be entered. On saving this information, the system will prompt you to assign an operation mode to the instance and make changes to the work process distribution. Please note that changing the number of work processes is a little tricky in terms of working the interface. In order to increase or decrease the number of work processes of a given kind, put your cursor on the line where you want to increase the number of work processes and keep clicking the + button as shown. This will increase the number of work processes your cursor is in while simultaneously decreasing the number from the other work processes. You can decrease the number of work processes by using the – button.

Please remember that the starting point for these changes is based on the current configuration of the work processes in the instance profile and the total number of work processes will be unchanged. The following illustration shows the screen output when the assignment of an instance to a day and night operation mode and work process distribution is completed.

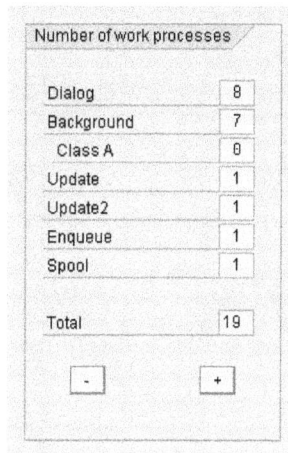

Number of work processes	
Dialog	8
Background	7
Class A	0
Update	1
Update2	1
Enqueue	1
Spool	1
Total	19

- +

CCMS: Maintain Operation Modes and Instances

Consistency check Profile view

Productive instances and their WP distribution

Host Name	Server Name	OP Mode	Instance Profile	Dia	BP	BPA	Spo	Upd	Up2	Enq	Sum
venus	venus_DEV_00		DEV_DVEBMGS00_VENUS								
		Day		10	3	-	1	1	1	1	17
		Night		3	10	-	1	1	1	1	17

After these two steps are completed, the operation modes will start executing based on the timetable. Please note that this switch does not work immediately and you have to wait for the next window for the operation mode cycle to kick in. You can start the operation mode manually by using transaction code RZ03. Operation mode switching is recorded in the system log transaction SM21, as shown. In the illustration, the system log is indicating that work processes are switched back to the daytime operation mode at 7 A.M. to more dialog work processes.

Time	Ty.	Nr	Cl.	User	Tcod	MNo	Text
06:59:06	SPO	21	000	SAPSYS		FAU	Connection to SAPLPD Broken
06:59:06	SPO	21	000	SAPSYS		FBM	Printer AX13 Temporarily Locked Due to Connection Problem
07:00:00	DP					Q0V	Work process 0 was switched from request type UPD to DIA
07:00:00	DP					Q0V	Work process 1 was switched from request type UPD to DIA
07:00:00	DP					Q0V	Work process 2 was switched from request type BTC to DIA
07:00:00	DP					Q0V	Work process 3 was switched from request type UP2 to DIA
07:00:00	DP					Q0V	Work process 4 was switched from request type UP2 to DIA

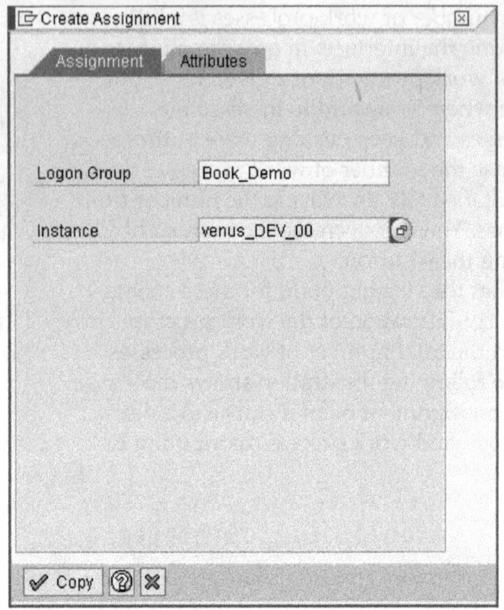

FIGURE 14-9 Logon group assignment screen

SAP Logon Group

Logon groups help to better balance the end-user requests across different application servers assigned to the same group. The message server will direct traffic to the least busy application server in the logon group. Transaction code SMLG is used to configure the logon groups. Multiple application servers can be assigned to one logon group. For example, three application servers can be assigned to a logon group called Sales Logon Group and all sales-related transactions can be directed to that particular logon group. In transaction SMLG, new logon groups can be created by pressing the F8 function key. This will display the screen shown in Figure 14-9, where you can create a new logon group and assign an application server to it.

SAP RFC Server Group (RZ12)

RFC server groups help in parallel execution of asynchronous RFC calls. Transaction code RZ12 is used to set up new RFC server groups. These consist of pools of application servers, each with its own setup of RFC server group quotas. New RFC server groups are configured by using transaction RZ12 and pressing the F8 function key. The following illustration shows an RFC server group being assigned to a particular application server and the resource determination on that particular application server will be based on the allocated RFC server group quotas.

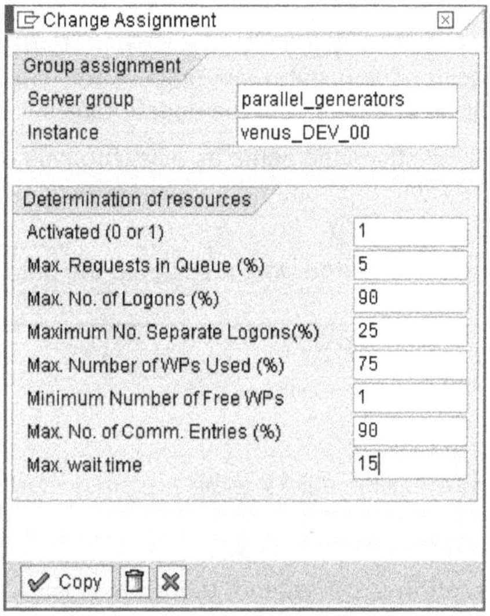

Change Assignment

Group assignment

Server group	parallel_generators
Instance	venus_DEV_00

Determination of resources

Activated (0 or 1)	1
Max. Requests in Queue (%)	5
Max. No. of Logons (%)	90
Maximum No. Separate Logons(%)	25
Max. Number of WPs Used (%)	75
Minimum Number of Free WPs	1
Max. No. of Comm. Entries (%)	90
Max. wait time	15

Copy

Update Concept

The SAP update concept can be better understood by examining the SAP logical unit of work (LUW) and database LUW. SAP LUW is a SAP transaction encompassing a business process that could include several screens. Each screen's data commit will constitute a database transaction or LUW. One SAP LUW may include several database LUWs.

When a screen commit is issued, the data is written to temporary update tables. The entries are not yet written to the application tables. Each SAP transaction has a dialog and an update component. The dialog component is executed by one or several dialog work processes. The update component is executed by the update work processes. At the end of the dialog part of the SAP transaction, the update part starts in the update work processes and data is written from the update tables to the permanent application tables.

Updates are processed in three different ways, depending upon the priority. Priority 1 updates are processed in time-critical U1 update work processes. One example of a priority 1 update is order creation. Priority 2 updates are processed in nontime-critical U2 update work processes. One example of such an update is statistical data. The third category of updates is referred to as a collective run. Collective run updates are collected and executed at a later time. A background job called RSM13005 is used for the collective run instead of the update work processes. Sometimes, the collective run updates are also referred to as U3 updates.

Update Mode	Update Description
Asynchronous Update	The most-programmed update mode in SAP transactions. Dialog work processes will not wait for the updates to be completed for application tables, thereby offering the best possible performance. At the end of the SAP transaction, the update work process will help in performing the update to the application tables from the update tables.
Synchronous Update	This update functions the same as asynchronous updates, except for the fact that the ABAP program waits for confirmation that the update has been completed successfully.
Local Update	Directs changes from the work process to the database.

TABLE 14-2 Update Modes in SAP Standard OLTP

In SAP, updates are programmed in ABAP to be executed in one of the following ways as shown in Table 14-2.

Table 14-3 lists the key temporary update tables where data is written by the screen data commits. After the SAP transaction is completed, the update work process will take the data in the update tables and post it to the permanent application tables.

Update Administration

Updates can be monitored with transaction code SM13. You can select the status of the update in the initial screen and press the F8 function key to get a list of updates with that status, as shown in Figure 14-10. Cancelled updates have to be managed carefully. Usually, these requests will be processed by working very closely with the owner of the transaction/ business process. Also, update work processes work closely with enqueue work processes. The locks are held in the lock table until the updates are processed successfully. When the updates are posted manually after working closely with the data owner, the locks will be released. It is not recommended to post the updates manually without checking with the data owner first. It is also not recommended to delete the locks from the lock table that are

Update Table Name	Update Table Description
VBHDR	This table has the update header information.
VBMOD	Update modules in V1 and V2 modules per update request.
VBERROR	When the update is cancelled the error information is saved in this table.
VBDATA	Update data.

TABLE 14-3 Update Tables

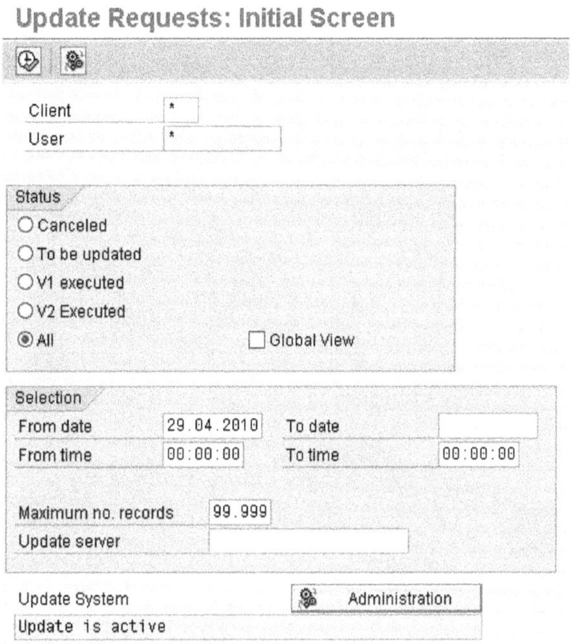

Update Requests: Initial Screen

Client *
User *

Status
Canceled
To be updated
V1 executed
V2 Executed
All
Global View

Selection
From date 29.04.2010 To date
From time 00:00:00 To time 00:00:00
Maximum no. records 99.999
Update server

Update System
Administration
Update is active

Copyright by SAP AG

FIGURE 14-10 The initial update status screen

created as a result of the updates. If the locks are deleted without properly posting the updates manually, then database inconsistencies may result. It is recommended to contact the data owner to determine if the cancelled or failed updates need to be posted manually after rectifying the underlying problem, such as database space issue, thereby releasing the locks after successfully posting the updates or deleting the updates and manually locking and reposting the transactions that were cancelled.

The update server toggles to an inactive status if there is a database space problem that is not addressed for some time. After the space is added, the status has to be activated manually using SM13 and the pending update requests will be posted automatically. Transaction code SM14 can be used to perform this activity as well, as shown in Figure 14-11. In this transaction you can carry out functions such as manually posting cancelled updates after the underlying issue is resolved; performing a reorganization of update records where incomplete update records are deleted from the database thereby releasing space; and setting up some additional advanced functions, such as update dispatching (for load balancing), resetting update statistics, and displaying and changing update profile parameters.

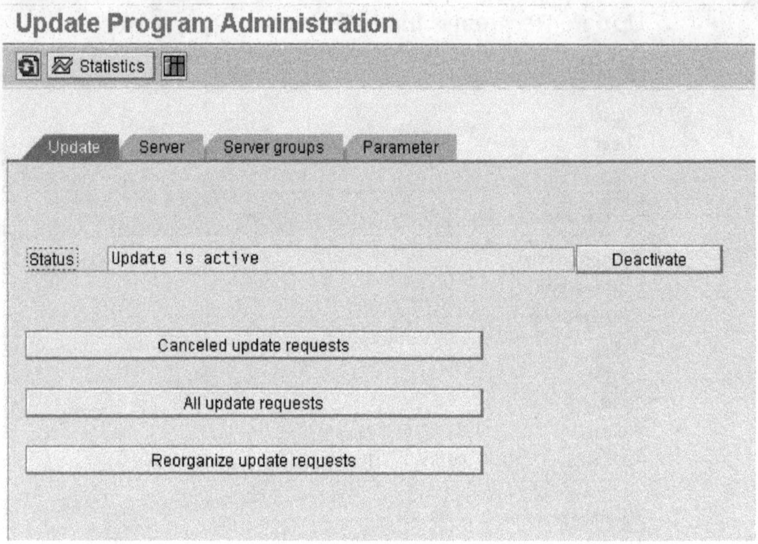

FIGURE 14-11 Initial update program administration screen

Lock Concept

SAP manages locks by using lock objects in ABAP programs. Lock objects are defined for the database objects in the data dictionary, and this creates two function modules. One is for locking the database object while a SAP transaction is being executed, and the second one is for unlocking a database object when the transaction is complete. Also, each SAP transaction or LUW may have many database locks. Database locks are usually held for a much shorter time compared to the application transaction locks. Transaction code SM12 is used to monitor and manage application locks.

Lock Modes

The four types of lock modes are described in Table 14-4.

Lock Mode	Description
Shared (S)	A shared lock for many transactions/users. A new exclusive lock request is rejected in this mode.
Exclusive (E)	No new locks are accepted by other users or transactions. The same lock owner can reset the lock.
Exclusive and Noncumulative (X)	This is a one-time lock and no additional lock requests can be made, even by the same owner.
Optimistic (O)	These are initially shared locks, but can be converted to exclusive locks.

TABLE 14-4 Types of Lock Modes in SAP Systems

Lock Table Profile Parameters (Regular Install and HA Install)

The lock table is not a physical table in the database, but is in the main memory of the enqueue server that records the current locks in the system. The size of the lock table is dependent on the allocated size of the profile parameter enque/table_size in kilobytes. Please note that in high-availability (HA) installations, the enqueue server is separated into a separate ASCS instance and, therefore, enque/table_size must be set directly in the ASCS profile (Example: BD1_ASCS01_venus) at the operating system level. Increasing the parameter value in either default or instance profile will not work.

Black and Blue Locks

SAP enqueue work processes and update work processes work closely. Blue locks in SM12 transaction code are locks carried over by the updates and will be released only when all the corresponding updates have been completed successfully. Since this group of locks is tied to updates and involves data integrity and consistency, these locks are also backed up at the operating system level and are reloaded into the lock table in the event of a system restart. Black locks in transaction SM12 are normal transaction locks and are associated with the dialog work processes.

Obsolete Locks

When user connectivity to the SAP system ends abruptly because of network issues, or if a transaction is canceled by the end user in a ungraceful manner, then the locks held for that particular transaction would still be present in the lock table and would prevent the same user or other users from accessing and making changes in the system. In these situations the obsolete locks can be deleted, but only after confirming this with the owner of the locks. It is never recommended to delete a lock table entry without performing due diligence with regard to the owner of the lock.

Lock Table Overflow

Lock table overflow is a condition when the SAP system demands more lock table entries than what it is currently configured for usage. Lock table overflow can be detected by using transaction SM12 or SM21. In transaction SM12, if you scroll down to the bottom of the screen you will see a message indicating that there was a lock table overflow. This is also recorded in the system log. The lock table overflow issue can be fixed by increasing the profile parameter enque/table_size value to a higher number.

Deadlocks

Deadlocks result when two or more users lock each other's data and are waiting for it to be released. Deadlocks can be resolved by releasing either the lock holder or lock waiter. Transaction code DB01 can be used to check if there is an active deadlock in the system.

Summary

- SAP profiles are installed at the operating system level by the SAP installation program SAPInst.
- SAP profiles include the start, default, and instance profiles.

- The start profile has all the start commands for the SAP system.
- The default profile includes all the parameters that are applicable to all application servers of an instance.
- The instance profile includes all the parameters that are applicable for a particular instance.
- Transaction RZ10 must be used to maintain SAP profile parameters.
- Transaction RZ11 must be used to display and check profile parameter documentation.
- SAP work processes help to execute ABAP programs in the system.
- Dialog work processes help to execute the interactive programs in the system.
- Background work processes help to execute noninteractive, long-running jobs.
- Enqueue work processes help in managing locks.
- Spool work processes help in formatting and printing.
- Update work processes help in managing updates in the system.
- SAP operation modes help to switch between dialog and background work processes, and vice-versa, based on a timetable.
- SAP logon groups help to perform logon load-balancing functions for the system.
- SAP RFC server groups help in parallelization of the tasks to be executed by the system.

Additional Resources

- **Configuring SAP logon groups** http://help.sap.com/SAPHELP_NW70/helpdata/EN/c4/3a64b4505211d189550000e829fbbd/content.htm
- **SAP lock concept** https://cw.sdn.sap.com/cw/docs/DOC-22824

CHAPTER

SAP Processes in Java Stack

In this chapter we will study the different SAP processes in the Java stack and the tools used to configure and administer the SAP NW AS Java. SAP configuration management primarily involves making parameter changes and administering the SAP Java cluster. SAP administration tools also support changes to the Java memory parameters, the starting and stopping of SAP cluster elements, and the starting and shutting down of the managers and services of the Java cluster elements. Additional administration activities include changes to the port numbers and implementation of secure protocols, such as HTTPS for secure communication.

The SAP Java cluster consists of one or more instances of SAP AS Java, a central services instance consisting of message and enqueue services, and the database. The SAP AS Java instance consists of at least a Java dispatcher and one or more server processes. Details of the SAP Java cluster and NW AS Java architecture and installation have been covered in previous chapters.

Java Administration and Configuration Tools

SAP provides three major tools for configuring and administering the SAP NW AS Java: the configuration tool (config tool), Visual Administrator, and NetWeaver Administrator tool (NWA). Table 15-1 provides a comparison of the three tools along with the prerequisites and intended purpose of each.

Configuration Tool (Config Tool)

The config tool connects to the database, scans the configuration information, and presents it in either a graphical user interface or a text interface. The config tool is XML-based and therefore allows an administrator to export and import all the system configuration parameters. It connects directly to the database and, therefore, does not need the Java engine to be running for its use. The config tool does not ask for a user name and password when logging into the tool. It just needs the operating system <sid>adm account user access to start the tool.

Tool	Prerequisites	Purpose
SAP configuration tool (config tool)	The database must be up, since the tool will make changes to the database settings.	Java virtual memory settings can only be maintained by this tool. Also used for configuration of managers and services. Only used for local configuration and administration. Any changes require a restart of SAP Web AS Java to become effective.
SAP Visual Administrator	The database and SAP AS Java must be up.	Starting and stopping services. Stopping the SAP Web AS Java. Configuration of managers and services. Remote configuration and administration tool. Changes become effective during runtime for selected parameters. No restart needed.
SAP NetWeaver Administrator (NWA)	The database and SAP AS Java must be up.	This tool replaced Visual Administrator starting with NetWeaver release 7.1. All Visual Administrator functions have been integrated into the NWA tool. Starting and stopping systems. Local NWA and landscape-wide monitoring and administration options (configured in central monitoring system of Solution Manager) available.

Table 15-1 Comparison of the Three SAP NW AS Java Tools

Starting the Config Tool

In order to start the configuration tool, log in as the <sid>adm user account at the operating system level, and go to the /usr/sap/<SID>/JC<SNo>/j2ee/configtool directory and locate the configtool.sh script. Start the configtool.sh script as shown after setting the display:

```
dk1adm> pwd
/usr/sap/DK1/JC01/j2ee/configtool
dk1adm> ./configtool.sh
```

This will bring up the following screen, asking you to acknowledge the use of the default database settings by clicking Yes or to verify/edit the settings by clicking No.

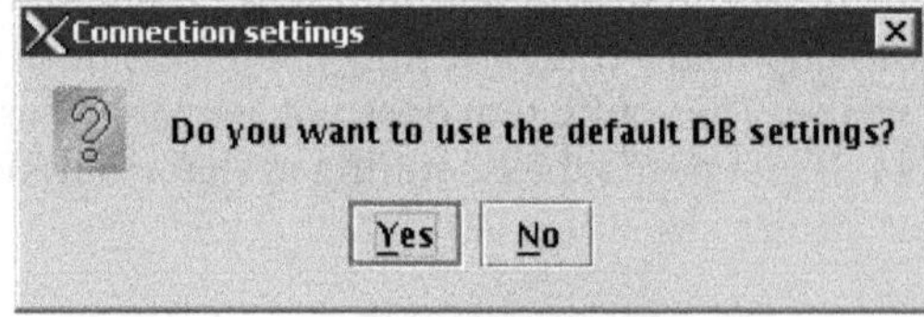

Copyright by SAP AG

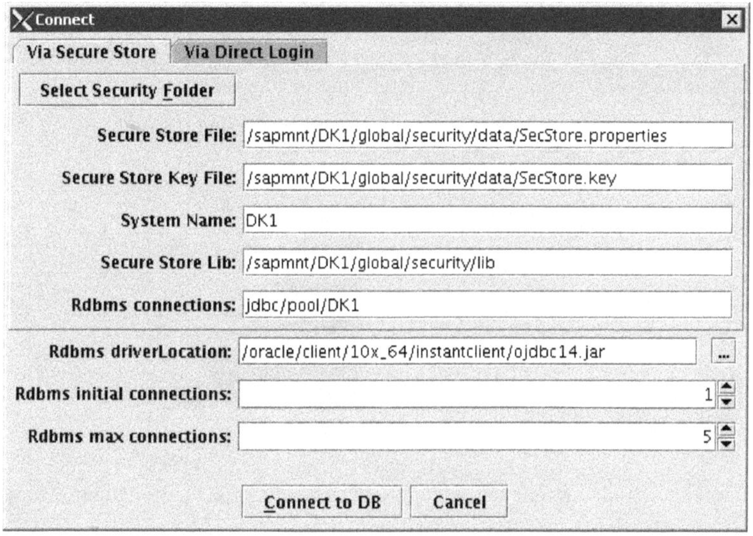

FIGURE 15-1 Database connection parameters and file paths

Choose No so that we can study and confirm the database settings. This will bring up the screen shown in Figure 15-1 showing the database parameters and file paths. Click Connect To DB to log in to the config tool. Clicking Yes as shown in the previous illustration will log you directly in to the config tool.

Once the database parameters are validated, the initial screen of the config tool is shown (see Figure 15-2).

When a Java cluster is configured and administered, a distinction is made between global and local configuration. In the previous figure, you will notice that the cluster data includes global sections (Global Dispatcher Configuration and Global Server Configuration) as well as instance-specific cluster element local configuration sections. In general, global configuration changes are effective for all the cluster elements when there is no explicit local parameter configuration and local configuration changes are effective for that particular cluster element only and override the global setting. The parameter evaluation sequence is more clearly defined in the next sections.

Global Parameter Configuration

Global configuration parameters fall into two categories. The first is the default parameter, and the second category is the custom value maintained by the customer. Custom values override the default values. Figure 15-3 shows the global properties view. Custom values can be set by clicking the parameter, entering a new parameter in the Value field, and clicking the Set button. The changes can be applied by selecting File | Apply or by clicking the Apply Changes icon (save icon). This will prompt the administrator to restart the cluster for the changes to become effective.

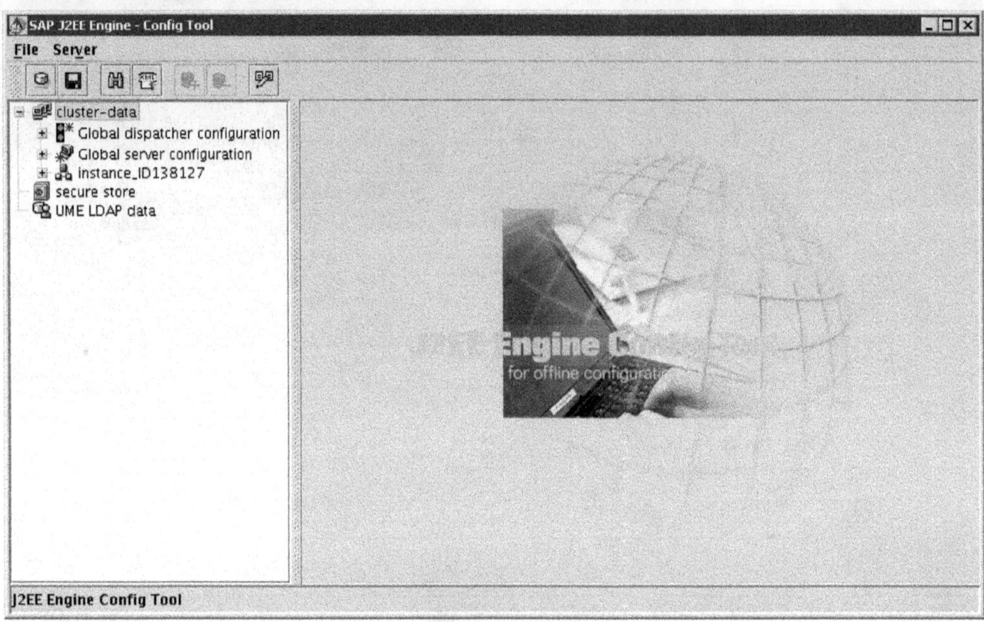

FIGURE 15-2 Initial screen of the configuration tool

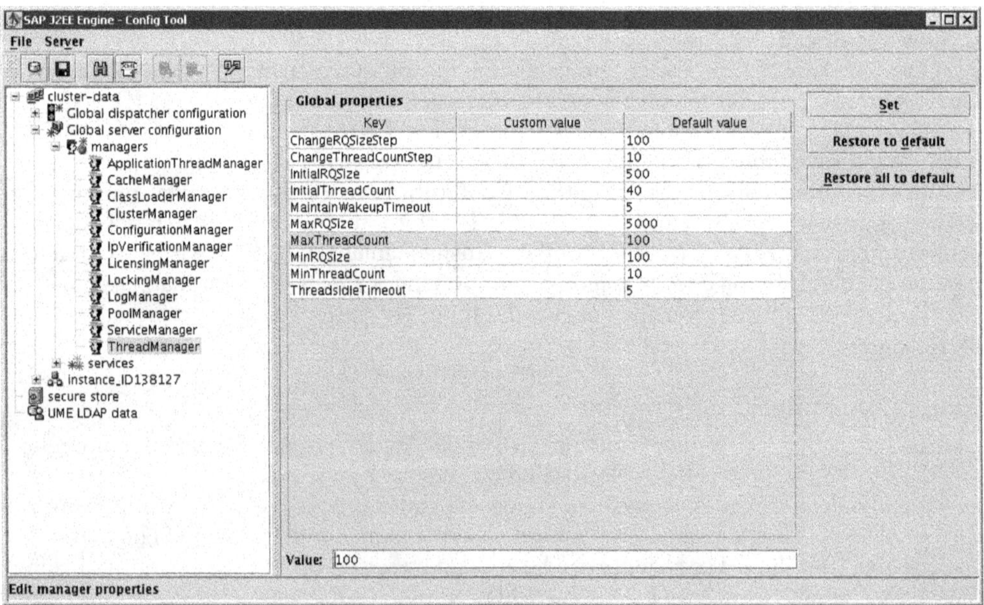

FIGURE 15-3 Configuration tool showing the global properties view

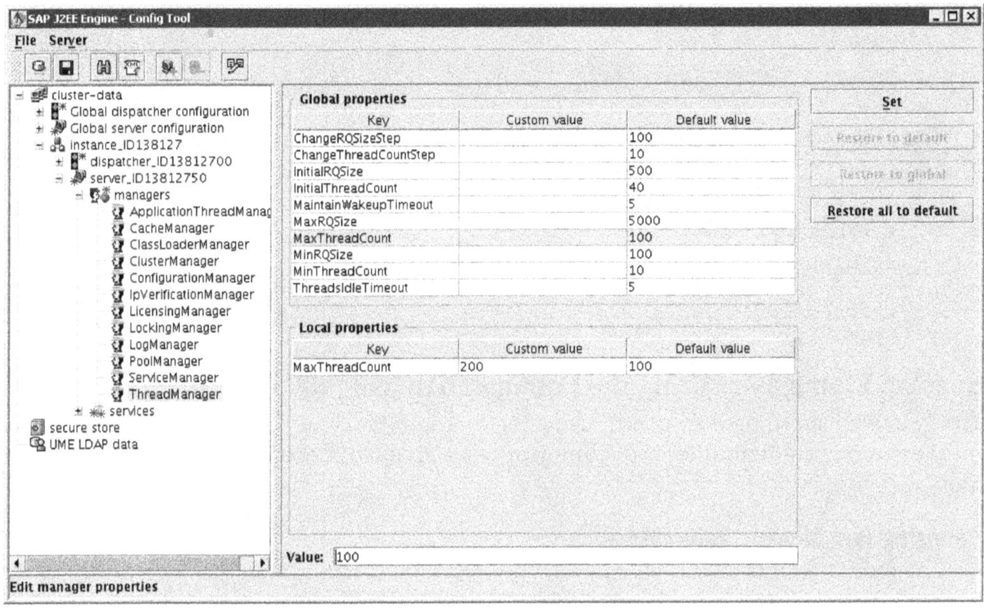

Copyright by SAP AG

FIGURE 15-4 Configuration tool showing local properties view

Local Parameter Configuration or Cluster Element Configuration

Local configuration parameters fall into two categories as well. The first is the default parameter, and the second is the custom value maintained by the customer. Custom values override default values. Also, local values override global values. If a local value is not set and is blank, then the global value is used by the local cluster element. In Figure 15-4, local properties of the Maximum thread count are set to a custom value of 200, and this will override the default value of the local properties as well as the global default value of the parameter. In this figure, only the global parameter view is displayed since it is in the local properties (individual cluster element view).

If a local value has to be added in the local properties view, select the parameter in the top section under Global Properties, and enter the new parameter in the Value field at the bottom of the screen. Then click the Set button. This will create a new entry in the local properties view. The illustration shows the options provided when the values are changed. These options are available at the top-right corner of the configuration screen in the local properties view. Explanations for the options are as follows:

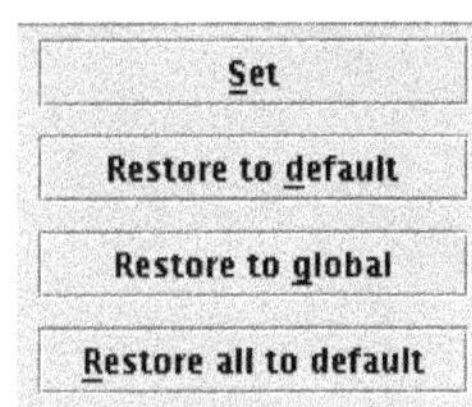

Copyright by SAP AG

- Set will update the custom value as per the configuration change.
- Restore To Default will remove the custom value in the local properties view.

- Restore To Global will completely remove the parameter from the local properties view.
- Restore All To Default will remove all the custom values in the local properties view.

The sequence of parameter evaluation in the configuration tool entries is as follows:

1. Local custom value
2. Local default value
3. Global custom value
4. Global default value

Specific Examples of Using the Configuration Tool

The following are some examples of using the configuration tool. These will demonstrate the main aspects of configuration and administration activities carried out by the configuration tool.

Changing Java Memory Parameters

Java memory parameters can only be changed with the configuration tool. After starting the configuration tool, select the cluster element that you would like to change the Java memory parameters for. This will present the screen shown in Figure 15-5 where the parameters can be edited or new parameters added under the Java Parameters section. The value of the maximum heap size can be changed in the Max Heap Size field.

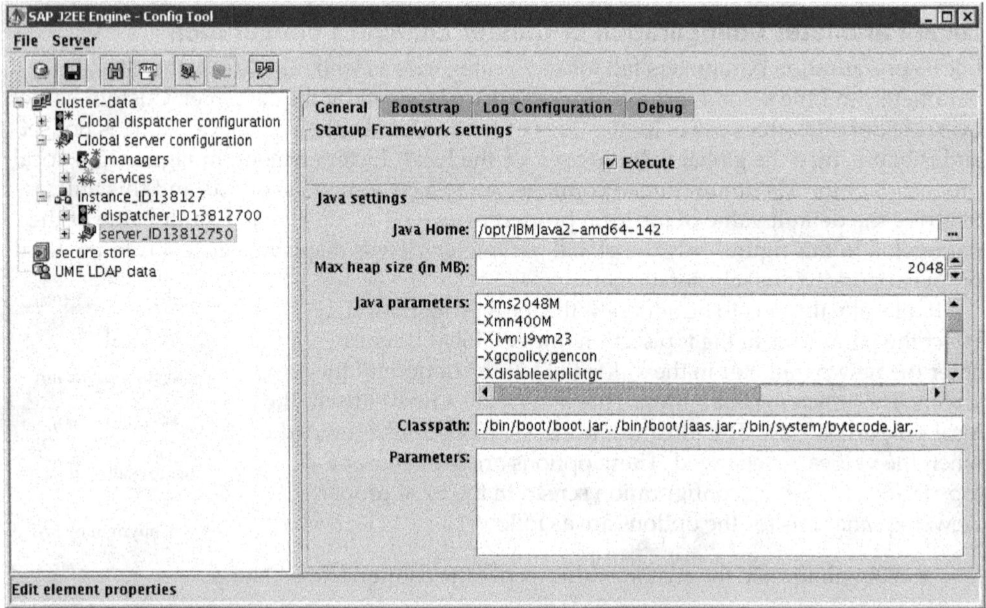

FIGURE 15-5 Changing Java virtual memory parameters using the configuration tool

Changing the System Numbers of the Java Instance After the Installation

The configuration tool can be used to change the port numbers of the central services instance after the installation is completed. Sometimes this needs to be performed to accommodate moving several Java instances to one partition of the UNIX system. In the following procedure, the system number is changed from 00 to XX. Execute the steps using the configuration tool and operating system commands.

1. Stop SAP by issuing the command stopsap r3 sap<sid>. The Oracle Database should be up and running.
2. Start the configuration tool.
3. As sidadm, run the config tool located at /usr/sap/DK1/JC01/j2ee/configtool/configtool.sh.
4. Choose Cluster-data | Global Dispatcher Configuration | ClusterManager.
5. Under Global Properties, select ms.port, and change the value from 3900 to 39XX.
6. Click the Set button.
7. Choose cluster-data | Global dispatcher configuration | LockingManager.
8. Under Global properties select enq.port and change value from 3200 to 32*XX*.
9. Click the Set button.
10. Click the Save button in the upper-left corner, or select File | Apply to save changes, and then quit the config tool.
11. Use the mv /usr/sap/<SID>/SCS00 /usr/sap/<SID>/SCSXX command to move the directory from SCS00 to SCSXX.
12. Change the directory to /sapmnt/<SID>/profile, and rename the default, instance, and start profiles with the new SCS number. Also edit the content of the files with the new number wherever it is needed.
13. Start SAP by issuing the startsap sap<sid> command. The system will now be started with the new SCS number.

JDBC Listener

The configuration tool uses Java Database Connectivity (JDBC) to connect to the underlying Oracle Database. Sometimes, a customer organization will need to change the Oracle Listener port, and when this is done if the port number is not changed in the configuration tool, then the tool will not be able to connect to the Oracle Database. The following procedure explains how to change the Listener port number from the default 1527 to 3781.

1. Start the configuration tool.
2. Go to secure store and change the key jdbc/pool/DK1/Url from jdbc:oracle:thin:@sapdk1:**1527**:DK1 to jdbc:oracle:thin:@sapdk1:<Listener Port Number>:DK1.
3. In this example the port number in Listener.ora is 3781. The setting should therefore be changed to jdbc:oracle:thin:@sapdk1:**37811**:DK1.

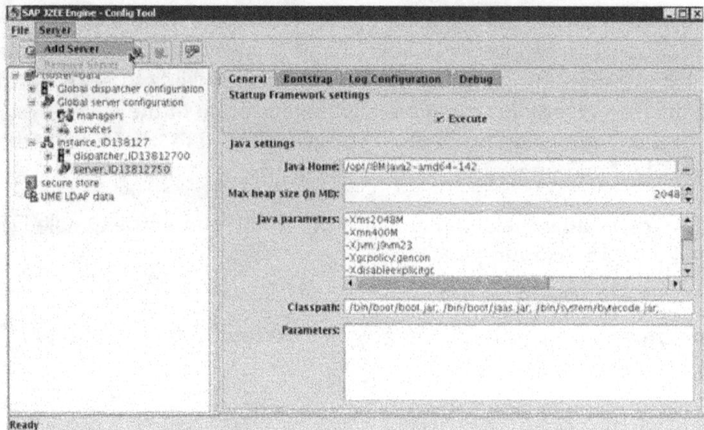

Copyright by SAP AG

FIGURE 15-6 Adding a new Java server node using the config tool

Adding Java Server Nodes

The configuration tool can be used to add new Java server nodes. These are added by starting the configuration tool and selecting Server | Add Server, as shown in Figure 15-6.

Click Yes to confirm the addition of the server node as shown.

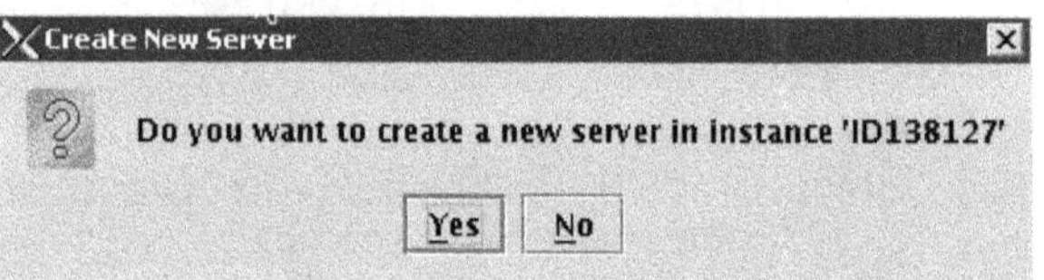

Copyright by SAP AG

Visual Administrator

Visual Administrator is a configuration and administration tool with a graphical user interface, and is a more comprehensive administration tool compared to the configuration tool. Visual Administrator allows you to configure and administer services, managers, interfaces, and libraries of the NetWeaver AS Java components.

Starting the Visual Administrator Tool

Visual Administrator is started by calling the go script under the /usr/sap/<SID>/JC<SNo>/j2ee/admin directory. The following commands show how Visual Administrator can be started in a UNIX operating system:

```
dj1adm> cd /usr/sap/DK1/JC01/j2ee/admin
dj1adm> pwd
/usr/sap/DK1/JC01/j2ee/admin
dk1adm> ./go
```

```
java version "1.4.2"
Java(TM) 2 Runtime Environment, Standard Edition (build 2.3)
IBM J9 VM (build 2.3, J2RE 1.4.2 IBM J9 2.3
Linux amd64-64 j9vmxa64142-20080923 (JIT enabled)
J9VM - 20080922_23329_LHdSMr
JIT  - 20080815_1845_r8
GC   - 200809_04)
```

This will display the initial connection screen showing the default connection. You can choose the default connection or create a new connection to log in to the Visual Administrator tool. Click the New button to create a new connection.

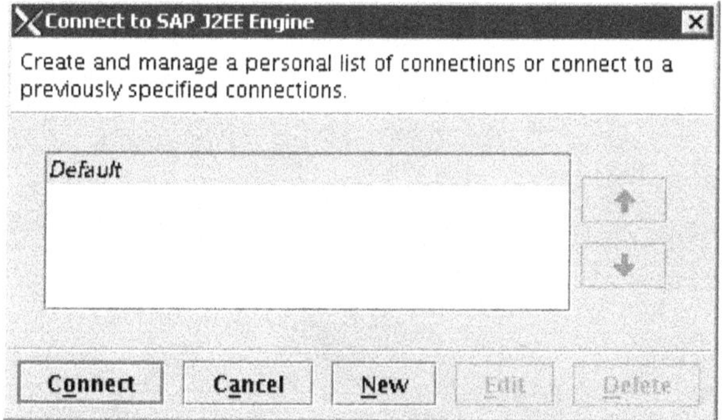

Copyright by SAP AG

When you click the New button the following screen appears. Enter the name of the new connection, and select the Direct Connection To A Dispatcher Node option.

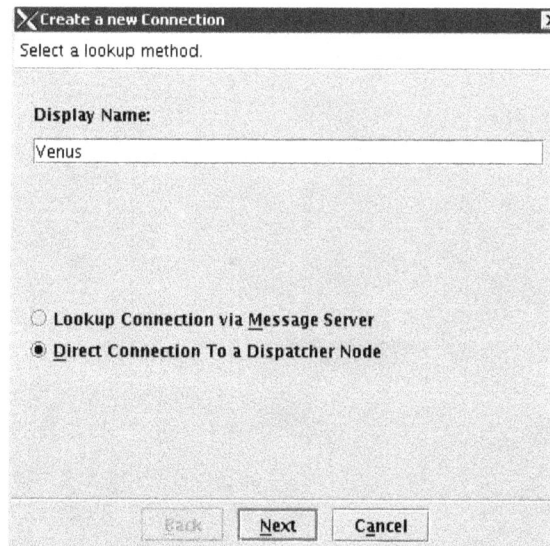

Create a new Connection
Select a lookup method.
Display Name:
Venus
Lookup Connection via Message Server
Direct Connection To a Dispatcher Node
Back
Next
Cancel

Copyright by SAP AG

Click Next and you will see the following screen. Enter the hostname and the port number for connecting to the Visual Administrator. Visual Administrator uses port number 50004 for an instance with system number 00. Once the entries are complete, click the Save button.

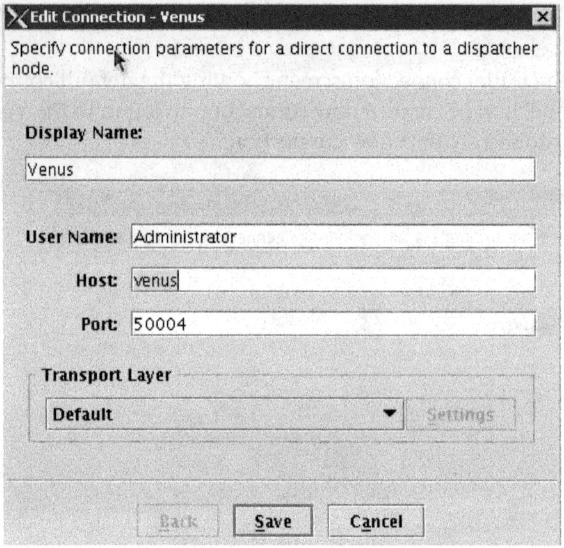

Edit Connection - Venus

Specify connection parameters for a direct connection to a dispatcher node.

Display Name: Venus

User Name: Administrator

Host: venus

Port: 50004

Transport Layer: Default | Settings

Back | Save | Cancel

Copyright by SAP AG

This will display a screen showing the newly added connection: venus.

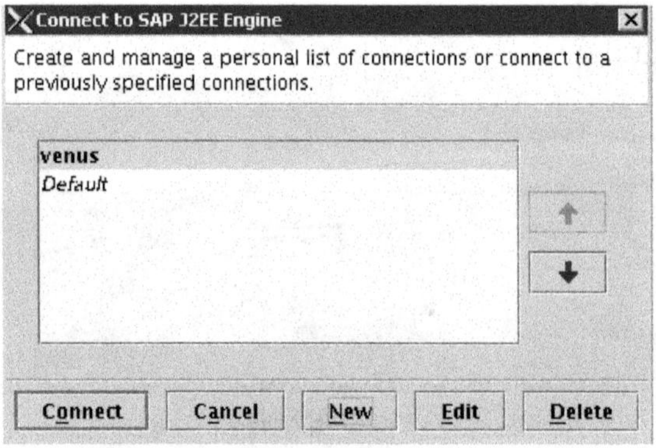

Connect to SAP J2EE Engine

Create and manage a personal list of connections or connect to a previously specified connections.

venus
Default

Connect | Cancel | New | Edit | Delete

Copyright by SAP AG

Select the newly created entry venus, and click the Connect button. This will display the following screen.

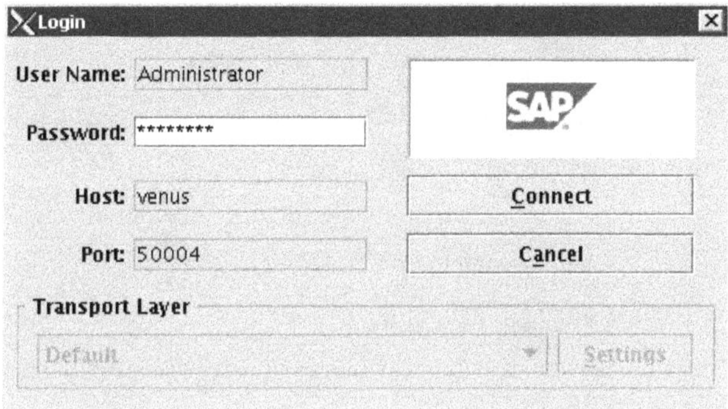

Copyright by SAP AG

Enter the password and click the Connect button. This will open the Visual Administrator tool as shown in Figure 15-7.

Three Kinds of Configuration in Visual Administrator

The following is a list of the three kinds of configuration options that are available with the Visual Administrator tool:

- Global configuration option only
- Global configuration with local maintenance option
- Local (cluster element level) configuration option only

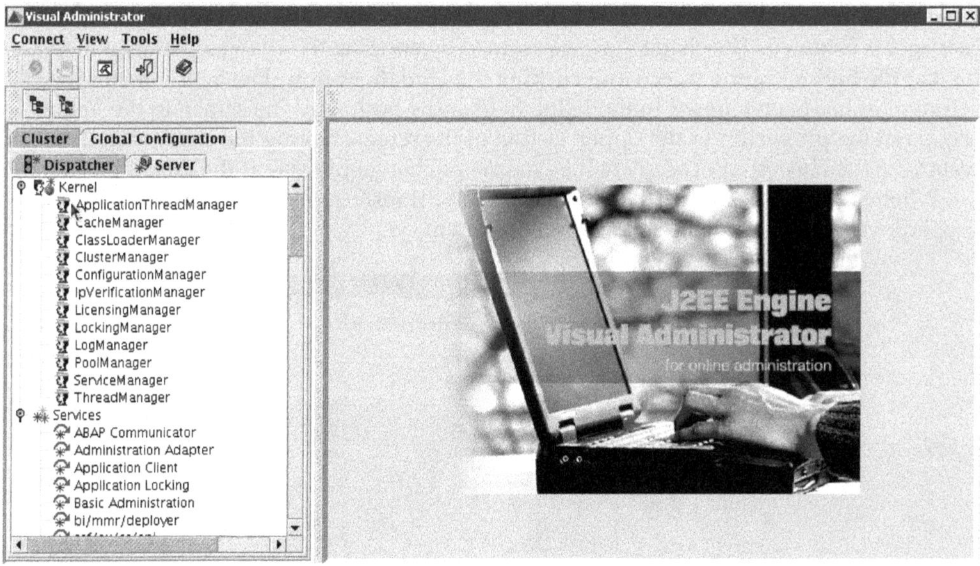

Copyright by SAP AG

FIGURE 15-7 Visual Administrator screen

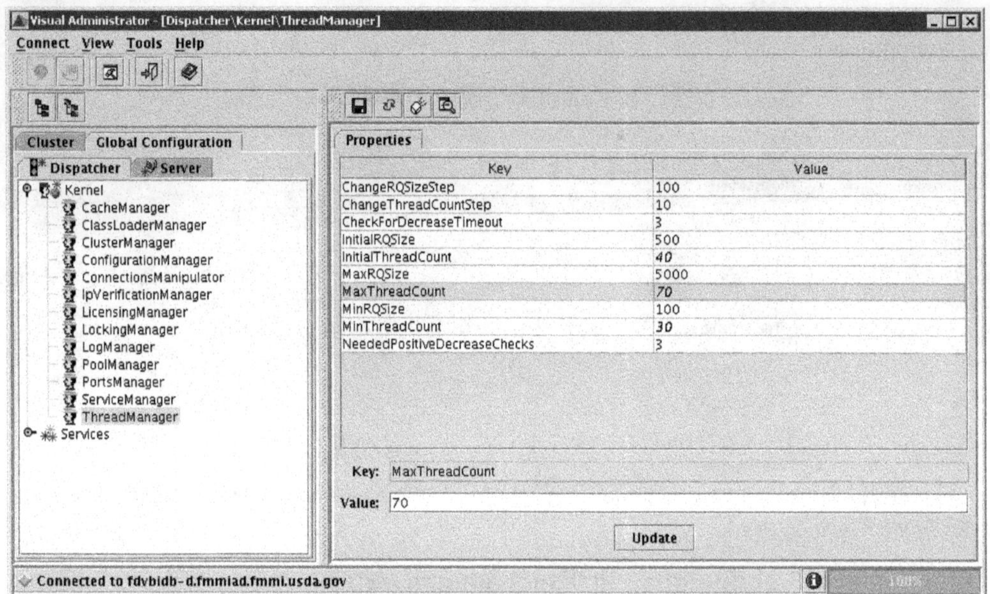

FIGURE 15-8 Global properties configuration without local transfer

Global Configuration Option Only

In this option the changes are performed at the global property level only, as shown in Figure 15-8. In this example the global server parameter Max Thread Count under Thread Manager is changed. The changes are performed by entering the changed value in the Value field at the bottom of the screen and clicking the Update button. This will transfer the setting that has been entered in the Value field at the bottom of the screen to the Value section in the properties in the upper section of the screen. Saving the changes and restarting the cluster will complete the parameter change process at the global level.

When the system asks if any settings have to be transferred to the local cluster properties section, you should choose No as shown.

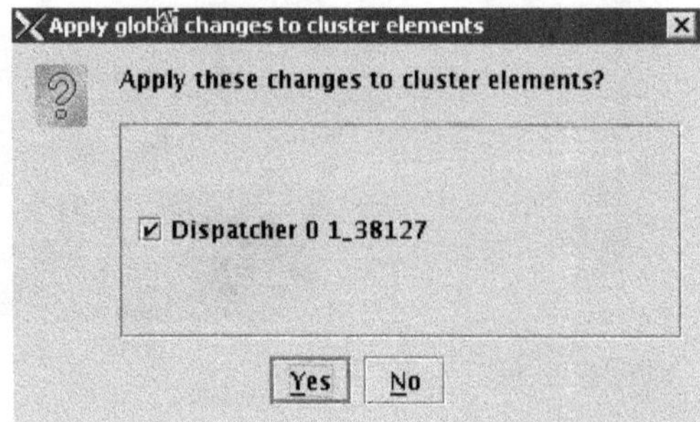

Global Configuration with Local Maintenance Option

In this option, the only difference is that we have to choose Yes. This will apply the changes to the cluster elements.

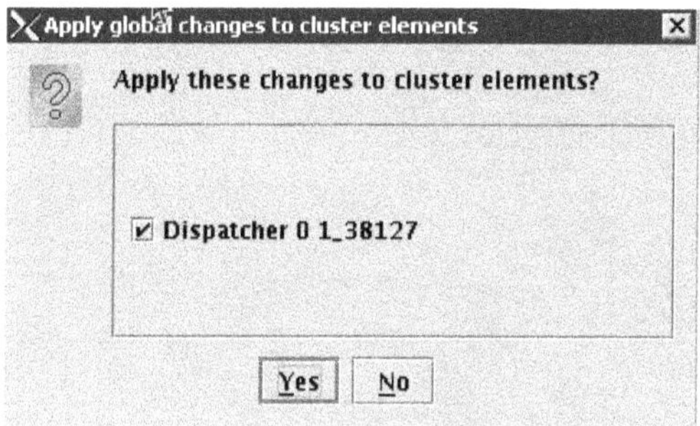

Copyright by SAP AG

Local (Cluster Element Level) Configuration Option Only

In this option, the individual cluster elements property Max Number Of Threads under Thread Manager is changed from 70 to 100 as shown in Figure 15-9. In order to change the parameter value, you have to select the row you would like to change. In the figure Max Thread Count has been selected and the value is changed to 100 in the Value field at the bottom of the screen. Then Update button was clicked. The new settings were saved and will be effective after NetWeaver AS Java is restarted.

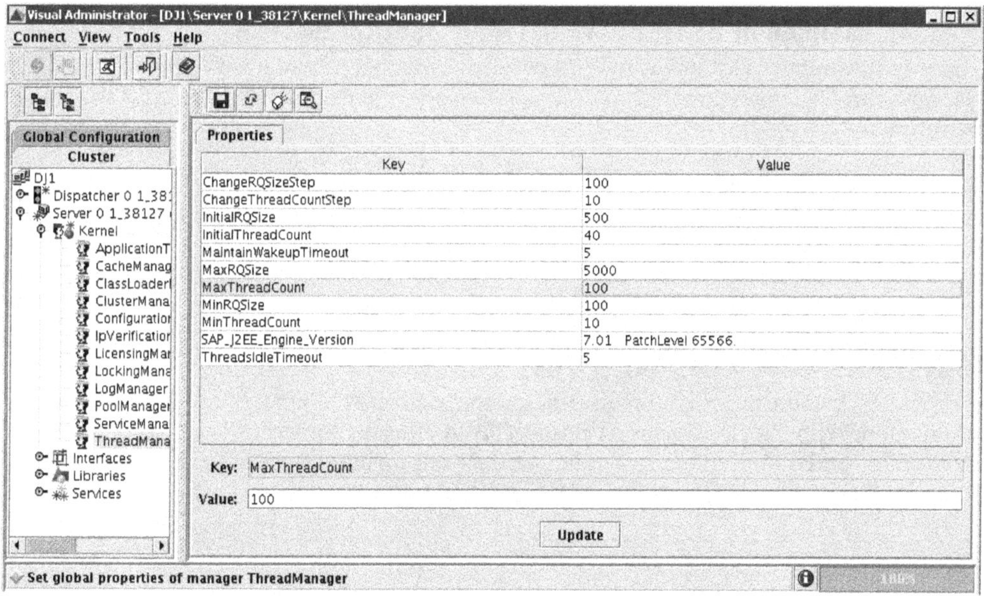

Copyright by SAP AG

FIGURE 15-9 Local properties configuration screen

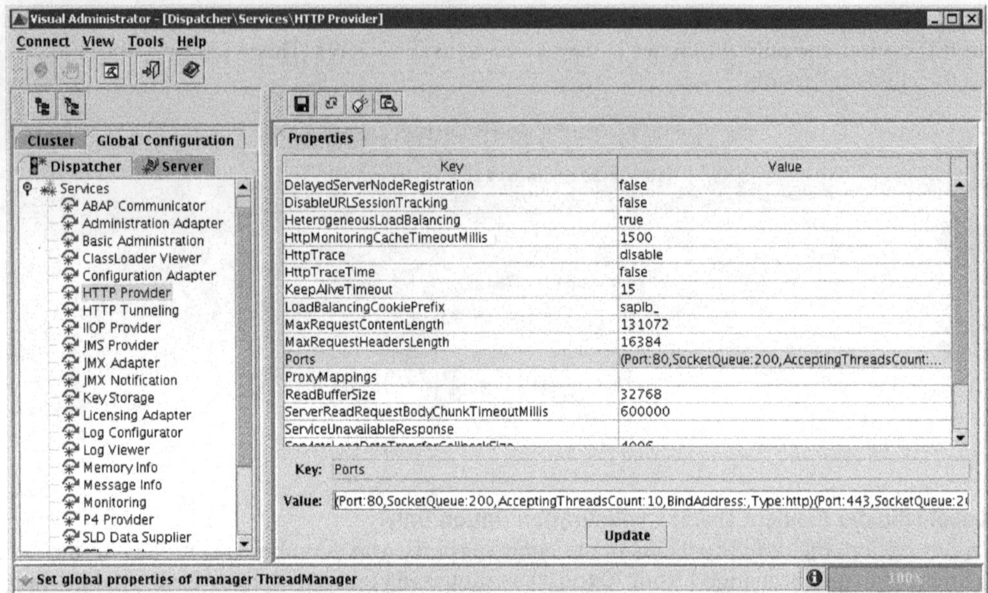

FIGURE 15-10 Changing the http port number using Visual Administrator

Specific Example of Using the Visual Administrator Tool

The Visual Administrator tool is used to perform a number of administration tasks in a Java stack system. The following section describes just one of the administrative tasks that can be performed.

Changing the HTTP Port

After the installation is completed, sometimes you need to change the http port number to overcome port conflicts at the customer sites. In Figure 15-10 the http provider service port number has been changed to 80. This will be effective after the Java cluster is restarted.

NetWeaver Administrator Tool (NWA)

NetWeaver Administrator is a browser-based tool delivered along with the SAP standard installation. With the NetWeaver 7.1 release, NWA officially replaces Visual Administrator. In addition, Software Deployment Manager (SDM) is no longer available; their respective functions have been integrated into NWA and JSPM, respectively.

The NWA tool is started by executing http://<hostname>:<port number>/nwa. For example, you can launch the starting page of the NWA tool for hostname venus with port number 50000 by using http://venus:50000/nwa as shown.

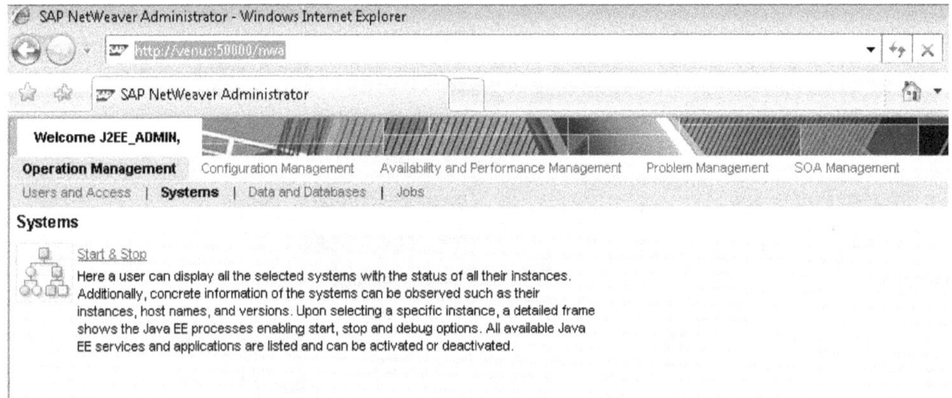
SAP NetWeaver Administrator - Windows Internet Explorer
http://venus:50000/nwa
SAP NetWeaver Administrator
Welcome J2EE_ADMIN,
Operation Management
Configuration Management
Availability and Performance Management
Problem Management
SOA Management
Users and Access | Systems | Data and Databases | Jobs
Systems
Start & Stop
Here a user can display all the selected systems with the status of all their instances. Additionally, concrete information of the systems can be observed such as their instances, host names, and versions. Upon selecting a specific instance, a detailed frame shows the Java EE processes enabling start, stop and debug options. All available Java EE services and applications are listed and can be activated or deactivated.

Copyright by SAP AG

NWA replaced all Visual Administration functions, and the equivalents can be easily accessed by using the NWA quick links. These, in turn, are accessed using http://<hosntname>:<port number>/nwa/quicklinks. For example, for hostname venus with port number 50000, the NWA quick links are accessed by calling http://venus.50000/nwa/quick links, as shown in Figure 15-11.

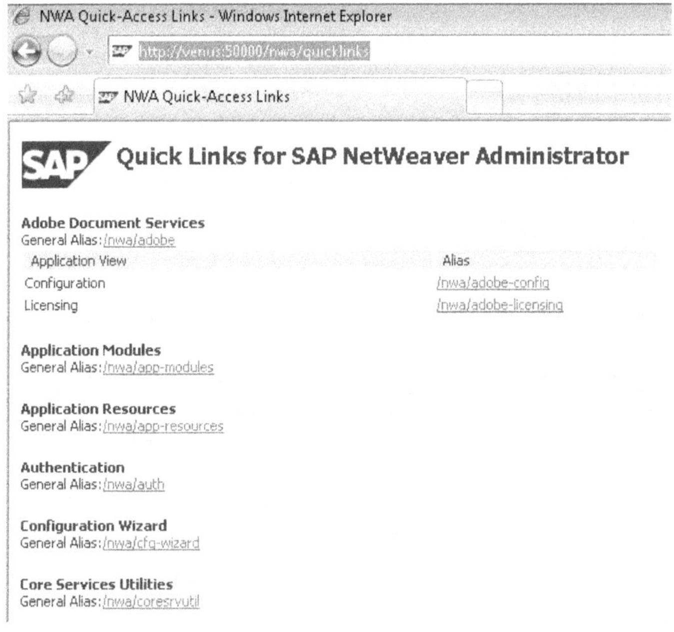
NWA Quick-Access Links - Windows Internet Explorer
http://venus:50000/nwa/quicklinks
NWA Quick-Access Links
SAP
Quick Links for SAP NetWeaver Administrator
Adobe Document Services
General Alias: /nwa/adobe
Application View
Alias
Configuration
/nwa/adobe-config
Licensing
/nwa/adobe-licensing
Application Modules
General Alias: /nwa/app-modules
Application Resources
General Alias: /nwa/app-resources
Authentication
General Alias: /nwa/auth
Configuration Wizard
General Alias: /nwa/cfg-wizard
Core Services Utilities
General Alias: /nwa/coresrvutil

Copyright by SAP AG

FIGURE 15-11 NWA quick links

NWA Administration Activity	Link
Configuration Wizard	/nwa/cfg-wizard
JCo RFC Destinations	/nwa/jco-destinations
Java HTTP Provider Configuration	/nwa/http
Logon Groups	/nwa/logon-groups
Java Scheduler	/nwa/scheduler
Jobs	/nwa/jobs
Java System Properties	/nwa/sys-config
Key Storage	/nwa/key-storage
Licenses	/nwa/licenses
Locks	/nwa/locks
Log Viewer	/nwa/logs
Message Server	/nwa/msg-server
Open SQL Data Browser	/nwa/databrowser
SQL Trace Administration	/nwa/sql-trace
SQL Connection Monitor	/nwa/sql-connections
Profile Management	/nwa/ProfileMgmt
SLD Data Supplier Configuration	/nwa/sld-config
Start and Stop	/nwa/start-stop
System Global Settings	/nwa/global-settings
System Info	/nwa/sysinfo
Trusted Systems	/nwa/trusted-systems
Web Services Administration	/nwa/WSAdmin

TABLE 15-2 NWA Quick Links and Descriptions

Table 15-2 provides a detailed list of the NWA quick links along with a text description of the available function.

The following illustrations show some of the quick links for starting and shutting down instances and processes, services, and log viewer options with the new NWA tool.

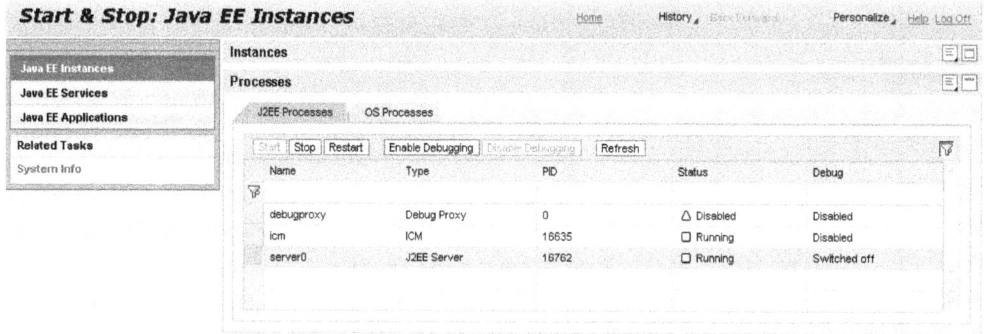

Copyright by SAP AG

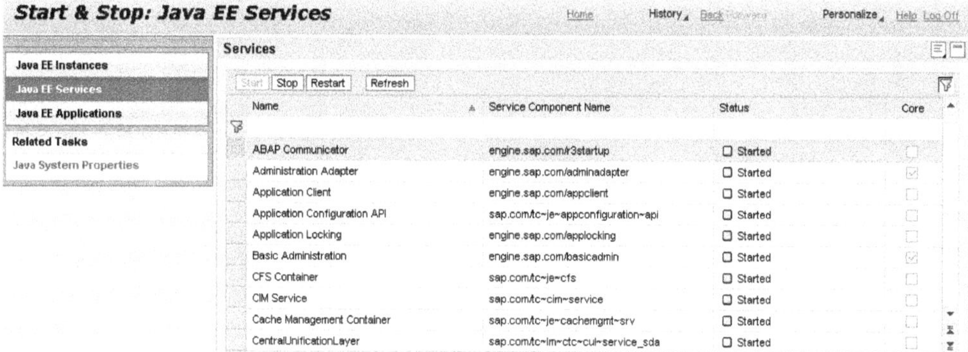

Copyright by SAP AG

The next illustration shows the quick link for system properties.

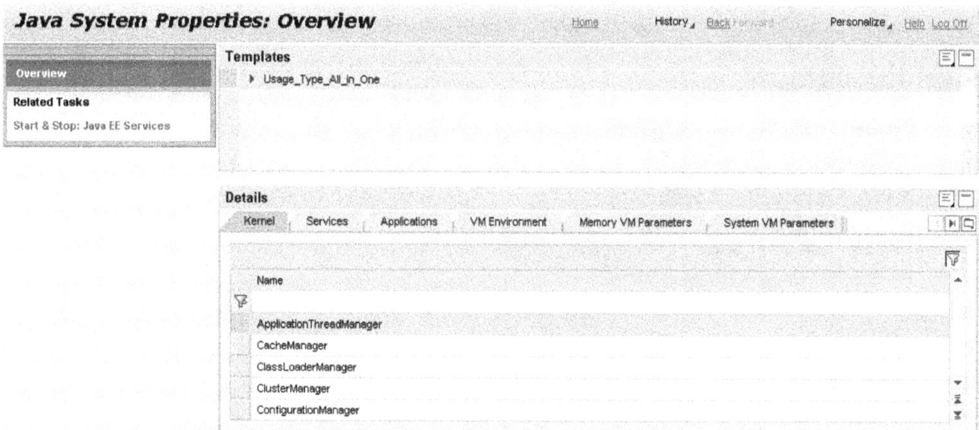

Copyright by SAP AG

And /NWA/logs quick link view is shown here.

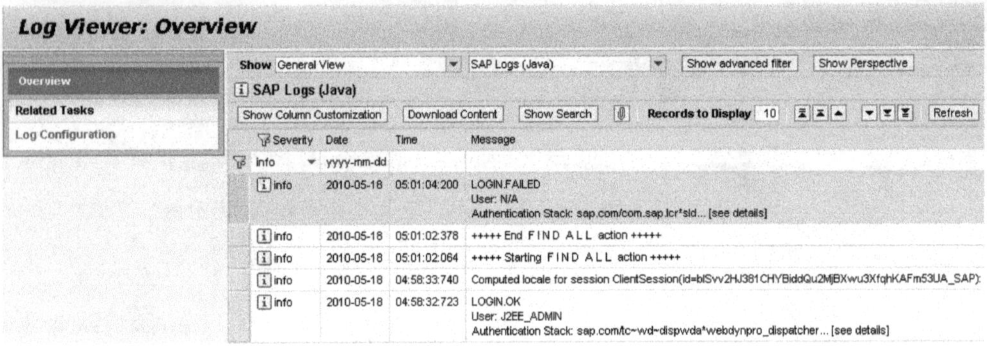

Summary

- SAP NW AS Java can be configured and administered using the configuration tool, Visual Administrator, or NetWeaver Administrator tool.
- The configuration tool is used to set up Java memory parameters. It directly connects to the database; therefore, the database needs to be up before you can use the tool.
- Visual Administrator is a graphical tool used for stopping the cluster elements and managing Java managers, services, and libraries.
- Visual Administrator connects to the Java engine; therefore, the system needs to be up before you can use the tool.
- NWA is the most current browser-centric tool delivered by SAP for configuring and administering the NW AS Java system, and it replaces Visual Administrator.

Additional Resources

- **NWA 7.1 for Visual Administrator users wiki link** http://wiki.sdn.sap.com/wiki/display/XI/NWA+7.1+%28for+VA+users%29
- **NWA tool in PI 7.1 weblog link** www.sdn.sap.com/irj/scn/weblogs?blog=/pub/wlg/17406

PART

SAP Monitoring and Troubleshooting

CHAPTER

Structured Monitoring and Analysis

In the first two chapters of this section we will study structured monitoring and troubleshooting approaches in both ABAP and Java stacks using classical as well as newer Solution Manager technologies such as Solution Manager Diagnostics and Wily Introscope. With the increased availability of technical information in the World Wide Web, SAP has moved all support activities online in the form of the SAP Portal referred to as SAP Service Marketplace. The last chapter in this section will cover different aspects of administration activities performed in the SAP Service Marketplace, such as creation of online SAP Service Marketplace user accounts, opening a support request, and searching for technical notes in SAP Online Support System (OSS) Notes.

Structured Monitoring and Analysis Approach

In this chapter we will focus on a structured monitoring and troubleshooting approach and will provide tools and techniques that will help a Basis administrator identify the root cause of the problem and provide a resolution to it.

Troubleshooting Is Both an Art and a Science

Troubleshooting is both an art and a science. The art part of it can be developed over time with practice and experience, and the science part of it can be applied by learning the application of tools, concepts, rules, and methods. Initially, it is recommended to start out with a good understanding of the concepts and then practice applying this knowledge to solve issues and gain more experience over time. With more practice, issues can be resolved intuitively, where you can narrow it down and resolve it quickly. The following section will cover a structured troubleshooting approach that can help you develop a plan for analyzing the issue in order to resolve it.

Problem Clustering Approach

There is no one standard approach to troubleshooting. Every system administrator will develop his or her own troubleshooting approach over time. The problem clustering approach is one of the structured analysis procedures that can be used in a methodical fashion to zero in on the problem. The idea behind this approach is to classify the reported problem under one of the groups of known problem areas as shown in Figure 16-1. This will help narrow down the problem to a particular problem area, and then you can focus on that particular area to further zero in on the specific issue and resolve it.

The tools and techniques covered in this chapter can be used to analyze the reported problem and categorize it into one of the problem clusters. The quicker a system administrator develops the skills to categorize the issue to a particular problem area, the faster he will be able to resolve the issue. Once the issue is categorized into a problem cluster, the same technique can be used in the identified problem area to further narrow down the problem.

Application Code Problem	Database Problem	Data Problem
• Source Code Corrections • Kernel Patch Issues • Support Package Issues	• SQL Error • Oracle Archiving Full • Tablespace Is Full	• Master Data Problem • Configuration Data Issue • Transaction Data Problem
Security Problem	**Operating System Problem**	**Network Problem**
• SAP Application Security • Oracle Database Security • Operating System Security	• Operating System Patches • Operating System Availability • Operating System Mounts	• IP Address Issues • DNS Issues • Firewall Issues
User Training Problem	**Storage Problem**	**Hardware Problem**
• User Data Entry Issues • New User • Introduction of New Functionality	• Storage Controller Issue • Storage Connection • Storage Configuration	• Backup Tape Issue • Network Card Issue

FIGURE 16-1 Problem clustering approach to structured troubleshooting and analysis

Troubleshooting Techniques

The following techniques will help the SAP Basis administrator to investigate the reported problem in a structured manner. Use these techniques along with the problem clustering approach to troubleshoot a problem.

Questioning Techniques

Asking the right question(s) is extremely important, and is a very effective tool to quickly understand the nature and origin of the reported problem. Some of the questions you can ask while investigating the problem are as follows:

- When was this problem first noticed?
- What changed recently before the problem started appearing?
- Do you notice the problem for every user in the system?
- Does the problem affect all systems or is it limited to only one system?
- Is the problem reproducible or does it occur sporadically?
- Do you get any specific error message when this issue is noticed?

Detective Work

To become successful in troubleshooting, you should develop the mind set of a detective. You should gather evidence in the system after asking relevant questions, and sometimes need to piece together information from different sources before you can get to the root cause of the problem.

Know What Is Normal So You Can Diagnose What Is Not Normal

Studying and understanding the concepts will help you understand what the normal behavior is in the system. If you know this, then it will become easy to spot an abnormal system behavior, aiding in quick resolution of the issue at hand.

Tool Choice

Spend a lot of time getting to know your tools and the location of the log and trace files. This will come in handy in enabling you to troubleshoot the issue quickly.

Search

It is truly amazing how much technical information is available on the Internet that is freely available to everyone. In the last few years the ability to search and qualify and use information, or piece together several sources of information, has become a vital skill in every SAP Basis administrator's tool kit. Searches can be performed using a variety of generic search engines, such as Google, Bing, and Yahoo!, as well as SAP-hosted specific site searches, such as SAP Developer Network (SDN) and SAP Service Marketplace. Online knowledge repositories such as Wikipedia and blogs also help significantly in troubleshooting the problem. Somewhere, someone likely has faced a similar issue, and there is a resolution posted in the online forums and discussion boards. With the exponential growth of software and hardware technologies, the ability to learn and apply knowledge dynamically is becoming an extremely important skill not only for a SAP Basis administrator but for every information technology professional.

Network Inside and Outside the Company You Work For

Sometimes the issue at hand is not in your domain expertise and you will need to discuss it with other domain experts inside and outside of your company. This is where your network will help. Develop a good network of professionals inside and outside of your company so that you can share your experiences and tap into this network when you need information.

Isolate the Problem

Sometimes the issue at hand is complex and even the problem clustering approach may not help to narrow down the issue. Under these situations, you can try to use the elimination technique.

Short-Term Workaround vs. Long-Term Fix

Sometimes you will be able to troubleshoot the problem but the long-term fix will need a lot of time. For example, you have found a bug in the SAP standard software and SAP needs some time to provide a patch to the problem. Under these circumstances it is a good idea to provide a short-term workaround to the end user instead of waiting for the long-term fix.

Log a Support Ticket with SAP

There will be times where there is no apparent solution to the issue at hand. You have tried everything you know and are not able to find a solution to the problem. It is recommended that you log a support ticket with SAP as soon as you find yourself in this situation. You can continue investigating the issue while SAP support is looking into it.

Structured Monitoring and Analysis in ABAP Systems

In this section we will cover the system startup problem scenarios and resolution, SAP standard monitoring transactions, and several ABAP system–specific problem scenarios and the troubleshooting steps that have to be taken.

Troubleshooting SAP ABAP System Startup Problems

One of the main job responsibilities of a SAP Basis administrator is to make sure that the system is available for the business during the hours established in the service levels of a given organization. SAP system availability in some industries is very demanding and is expected to be available 24/7/365. The following section discusses in detail the various scenarios in which a SAP system could hang and would not start up normally and where a Basis administrator has to find out the root cause and bring the system back up. Table 16-1 provides real-life scenarios that can happen with production and nonproduction SAP systems. The list is not comprehensive, but gives an overview of the problem scenarios that you could encounter and suggests possible approaches to resolving them.

Problem Scenario	Diagnosis	Resolution
You receive calls from several SAP users complaining that they are seeing an "hourglass" on the SAPGUI screen and the transactions are not getting processed.	The most likely reason for this behavior in the SAP system is that the "oracle archiving" directory is full and this has resulted in an archive-stuck situation.	Check the Oracle archive directory. If it is full, back up the Oracle Archive logs or temporarily move it to another location. This should help resolve the issue.
You receive calls from several SAP users complaining that they are not able to log in to the system, as it is showing an hourglass as soon as they enter their credentials and press ENTER.	The most likely reason for this behavior is that the SAP dialog work processes are exhausted by current user load/activity and no new users are able to log in to the system.	Check the dpmon tool (which is covered in the next section of this chapter) at the operating system level to confirm that all dialog work processes are busy. If this is the case, there are two options: Option 1: If there is a zombie process/processes that are causing the situation, check with the job owner and then kill the process. This will free up some of the dialog work processes. Option 2: If the jobs are mission-critical you may have to wait for their completion. This is not a desirable situation. You would have to focus on performance tuning the SAP application so that you would not have to be in this situation.
You receive a call from an end user complaining that he is not able to log in to the system. He is getting an NI error on his desktop when attempting to connect to the SAP system.	Check if this situation is for all users or if it is limited to only one user. If it is for all users, most likely your network connectivity in the LAN/WAN is an issue. If the issue is limited to an individual user, then most likely her SAP logon settings or services file configuration is an issue.	Report the issue to your network team immediately. The system should be accessible as soon as your TCP/IP connectivity is back. Log in remotely to the desktop/laptop of your business user and verify that all the application server settings in the user's SAP logon are correct, and also check the services and host files for proper port entries and hostname entries. This should resolve the issue.

Table 16-1 SAP ABAP System Startup Problem Scenarios (*Continued*)

Problem Scenario	Diagnosis	Resolution
Your get a call from the operations team saying that one of the SAP system start jobs failed and the server is down.	Log in as <sid>adm and issue R3trans -x to see if the SAP application can connect to the underlying database. You check the operating system level process and notice that the dispatcher and work processes are not up for that particular SAP instance. You also check the work directory, and the developer trace of the dispatcher has an entry that the system has inadequate memory and the dispatcher and work processes are dying.	Correct the resource issue, and the SAP will start up normally. Additional tip: Add "rdisp/TRACE = 2" in the instance profile at the OS level and recycle SAP. This will provide more details in various trace files in the work directory to help you identify the issues. Fix the issue and remove "rdisp/TRACE=2" from the instance profile and recycle SAP. Also, make sure that old trace files are deleted from the work directory, because they will be large and will take up extra space.
You get a call from the operations team saying that they are not able to start a SAP system. When startsap is issued, they are noticing messages that the system is already up when, in fact, it is not available.	You check the SAP processes at the operating system level and realize that the last shutdown of the system was not clean and there are still some SAP processes hanging.	Issue stopsap command. Then clean all the old SAP processes by using commands such as cleanipc <instance #> remove or kill command and restart the system. The system will start normally. Example: Issue cleanipc 00 remove command as <sid>adm user account to clean up all shared memory segments and processes that were hanging from the previous system shutdown.
You have performed a kernel upgrade and restarted the SAP system; however, it will not come up.	The new kernel patches are most likely causing the issues. Look for a known issues note with SAP Portal or temporarily replace the old kernel until you find a corrective kernel patch from SAP.	Replacing the old kernel or applying the corrective kernel patch and restarting the system should resolve the issue.
A junior Basis team member recently changed a number of SAP profile parameters to improve system performance and restarted the system. The system would not come up. He needs your expertise to resolve the issue.	The log files in the work directory indicate that the system was not starting, as the resources in the system are not sufficient.	Either go back to the backup profiles to startup the system or provides more resources to the system and restart the system.

TABLE 16-1 SAP ABAP System Startup Problem Scenarios (*Continued*)

Problem Scenario	Diagnosis	Resolution
Your production system went down during peak usage time and you are not able to track down the root cause based on your prior experience. An extensive search of SAP OSS Notes, SDN, (Google, and involvement of internal experts and your external contacts does not give any clues. The error messages in the system are not clear, and it is difficult to resolve the issue with this information.	Log a "very high" priority message to SAP so that you can get the SAP support resources involved as quickly as possible.	SAP support has determined that the issue was related to an OS patch that needs to be applied to the system. It is a bug! Applying the OS bug fix resolves the issue.

TABLE 16-1 SAP ABAP System Startup Problem Scenarios

Core System Monitoring Transactions in ABAP Systems

The transaction codes shown in Table 16-2 are the core of the SAP monitoring transactions. This list is not comprehensive, but will address the most important system components that have to be monitored.

Transaction Code	Description	What to Monitor
SM50	SAP Work Process Overview	Check the status of the work processes. They should be in waiting or running status. Other statuses, such as stopped or on hold, have to be investigated. Double-click the process to get additional details. Look for sections where the inserts, deletes, updates, and so on are changing.
SM51	SAP Server List	Status of the list of servers should be active. Any other status should be investigated.
SM28/SICK	SAP Initial Consistency Check	Should show no errors reported.
SM21	System Log	After system restart, look for the line "initialization complete." In day-to-day monitoring, check from any warning and error messages.
SM66	Global Work Process View	Look for any long-running processes and check if they are still active.

TABLE 16-2 Core System Monitoring Transaction Codes in an ABAP System (*Continued*)

Transaction Code	Description	What to Monitor
ST22	ABAP Dump Analysis	Look for any dumps. Open them by double-clicking and checking the error analysis section to investigate the problem.
SM13	SAP Updates	Check for any cancelled updates. Make sure that the update is active under Update Administration.
SM12	SAP Locks	Check for any old locks and lock table overflow condition. Old locks can be identified by the date and time stamp. Lock table overflow can be identified by looking for the message at the bottom of the screen.
SM58	Transactional RFC	Look for the status of the asynchronous RFCs. Status messages SYSFAIL and CPICERR indicate there is a problem that has to be further investigated. Status messages Recorded, Executed, Mailed, and Read are OK and do not need further investigation.
WE02/WE05	IDOC Monitoring	Look for IDocs with status message 63 (error-passing IDoc), and drill down to investigate the root cause of the issue.
SM37	Background Job Monitoring	Look for any cancelled messages and investigate the issue by drilling down into the job log.
SP01	Output Controller	Check for any error messages.
SP02	Display Spool Requests	Look for spool requests with a status error. Drill down to get more details and investigate the issue.
SM04	User List	Look for any old user sessions based on the date and time stamp.
AL08	Global User List	Look for proper distribution of the user load if there are application servers in the system.
SMLG	Logon Groups	Look for load distribution by pressing the F5 key in SMLG transaction.
SOST	Mail Transmission Requests	Check the mail status by looking in the msg (Message) field toward the right.
ST06	Operating System Monitor	Look for key operating system indicators, such as CPU utilization, memory utilization, and swap usage. Clicking the Detail Analysis button provides additional views for investigating any issues at the operating system level.

TABLE 16-2 Core System Monitoring Transaction Codes in an ABAP System (*Continued*)

Transaction Code	Description	What to Monitor
ST04	Database Overview	Look for key database usage indicators, such as database space utilization and data buffer quality.
ST02	Application Tune Summary	Look for key application performance indicators, such as extended memory utilization, application buffer swaps, and heap usage in the system.
DB12	Backup Logs	Look for the status of the backup jobs by clicking the Last Successful Backup and Overview Of Database Backup buttons. The return code of the jobs should be 0. If it is a non-zero return code, investigate the issue by clicking the Detail Log button in the top-left corner.
ST11	Error Log Files (Developer Traces)	SAP developer traces and logs can be accessed using this transaction. This can be used to drill down into the developer traces. Example: By drilling down into the developer trace dev_disp, you can check the developer traces for the dispatcher.
AL11	SAP Directories	You can drill down into the SAP directories and look for additional log and trace file details from the application level. Example: You can drill down into the DIR_TRANS directory to check the detailed transport log file information.
DB02	Database Space Overview	Check the database space utilization.
DB01	Oracle Lock Monitor	Check if there are any dead locks.
STMS	Transport Management System	Check the transport status and log files.
SE16N	Table Display	Display table data.
SM35	Batch Input Monitoring	Monitor batch input session status and logs.
ST03N	Work Load Monitor	Monitor work load statistics such as response times.
STAD	Business Transaction Analysis	Review business transaction analysis and detailed transaction statistics information.

TABLE 16-2 Core System Monitoring Transaction Codes in an ABAP System

Log File Name	Log File Location	Log File Provides Info On
Default log file location for a SAP ABAP system (Example: SID in this path is DM1)	/usr/sap/DM1/DVEBMGS00/work	All the log and trace files are written to this location.
dev_disp	/usr/sap/DM1/DVEBMGS00/work	Developer trace file for dispatcher.
dev_rd	/usr/sap/DM1/DVEBMGS00/work	Developer trace file for gateway.
dev_w<number>	/usr/sap/DM1/DVEBMGS00/work	Developer trace file for individual work processes.
dev_ms	/usr/sap/DM1/DVEBMGS00/work	Developer trace file for message server.
R3trans, DPMON, and other kernel executables	/sapmnt/DB1/exe	Kernel executables location that can be used for troubleshooting and monitoring purposes.
100JOBLG (Example: Job log directory for client 100) 100BDCLG (Example: BDC log for client 100)	/usr/sap/DB1/SYS/global	System logs, background job logs, and batch input logs.
ALOG*.<SID>, SLOG*.<SID> and individual transport log files	/usr/sap/transDM1/log	All the transport logs.
DM1arch1_532_695914865.dbf	/oracle/DM1/oraarch	Oracle offline archive log files.
alert_DB1.log	/oracle/DB1/saptrace/background	If there is any Oracle database issue, this is the most critical log file to check.

Table 16-3 Location and Purpose of Key ABAP System Log and Trace Files

Key Log and Trace File Location for ABAP Systems

Table 16-3 lists the key log and trace files and their location in an ABAP system.

Specific Tools for Troubleshooting Error Scenarios in the ABAP Stack

The following tools and methods are recommended to be used to troubleshoot specific ABAP stack error scenarios.

Troubleshooting SAP Application Connectivity to the Underlying Database

Sometimes a SAP system will not start because of application connectivity issues with the underlying database. However, the database has successfully started. SAP provides a tool called R3trans to check the connection of an application to the underlying database. Execute the following command at the operating system level with the <SID>adm user account. A successful connectivity check will give a return code of 0, as shown.

```
dt1adm> R3trans -d
This is R3trans version 6.14 (release 701 - 05.03.09 - 08:28:00).
unicode enabled version
R3trans finished (0000).
```

If there is an issue with the connectivity of the application to the underlying database, when you issue the same command you will see a higher return code, such as 12, as shown. At the same time the system will write a detailed connection log to a file called trans.log in the same directory. Read the trans.log file to identify the specific error information. Usually, connectivity issues are a result of an incorrect user account or password, issues with Oracle client shared libraries, and Oracle network configuration issues.

```
R3trans finished (0012).
```

dpmon (Work Process Overload/Hanging)

If all the SAP dialog work processes are occupied, the system will not be able to allow any new users to log in, including the system administrators. If you suspect this to be the case, you can use the dpmon tool at the operating system level to verify this and, if needed, free up some dialog work processes by killing some of them after checking with the owner. To avoid this situation, you have to add an adequate number of dialog work processes to the system based on the sizing and performance testing information.

The dpmon tool can be called by issuing the following command after you log in to the system as <SID>adm and change the directory to /usr/sap/SB2/SYS/profile for a system with SID = SB2:

```
sb2adm> pwd
/usr/sap/SB2/SYS/profile
sb2adm> dpmon pf=SB2_DVEBMGS00_venus
```

Structured Monitoring and Analysis in Java Systems

In this section we will cover the system startup problem scenarios and resolution with regard to SAP standard monitoring transactions in Java systems.

Troubleshooting SAP Java System Startup Problems

Understanding Java startup and the control framework and associated concepts is very important before you can successfully diagnose and resolve a Java system startup problem. It is recommended to review Chapter 3 for Java system architecture overview before proceeding with the following section. Table 16-4 provides real-life Java startup problem scenarios, and it explains the diagnosis and resolution steps that have to be performed to resolve an issue. The log and trace files noted in the scenarios are, by default, in the work directory located in the path /usr/sap/DJ1/JC<System Number>/work.

Problem Scenario	Diagnosis	Resolution
A junior Basis administrator has incorrectly diagnosed an Oracle archive full/ file system full issue and attempted to make the system available by restarting the system. The restart fails, and at this point he reaches out to you (the senior Basis administrator) to help resolve the problem.	When a Java system is failing to start, the following should be checked to see why: Check if the Oracle and SAP processes are running at the operating system level. If the processes are partially up, then the next step is to check and see which ones are up by using tools such as JCMON/ JSMON. When this scenario was investigated, it was found that the processes were partially up, and JCMON shows that it cannot connect to the shared memory and terminates. This indicates that the startup framework is having an issue. If some of the processes are not running, start looking into the work directory log and trace files. Checking the work directory files (bootstrap log files) indicates that the connection to the underlying database is an issue; therefore, bootstrapping is failing. Upon further investigation, you will find out that the Oracle archiving directory (/oracle/ DK1/oraarch) was full and this was the root cause of the issue.	First you will save and delete several Oracle archive log files, clearing space at the operating system level. Next you will shut down the system gracefully, as you have partially up processes. If needed, you will kill the processes at the OS level. Once the cleanup is completed you will issue the command to start the system. Since the underlying "Oracle archiving file system full" issue is resolved the system starts properly with the bootstrapping process completing successfully.
A junior Basis administrator has changed the heap parameters in the configuration tool. After making the changes, he restarts the system for the new parameters to take effect. He notices that the restart failed and reaches out to you (the senior Basis administrator) to help resolve the problem.	You will start investigating the problem as in the previous scenario, and this time you notice that one of the server nodes was in stopped status in the JCMON tool. This leads you to look into the work directory logs for further investigation. One of the work directory log files std_ server0.out has an error message saying that the initial heap size was configured more then the maximum allocated size. This is the root cause of the issue.	You will start the configuration tool and either increase the maximum heap size (2GB is the upper limit recommendation) to make it higher than the initial heap size or if it is already set at 2GB then reduce the initial heap size to a value less than this. After the changes are completed the system is restarted. This time the system will start properly.
One of your junior administrators did not diagnose a Java application issue properly and instead restarted the system repeatedly, and this has led to a situation where the system was not started properly.	You start investigating the issue and find out that the file system was full and the application was writing a number of very large heap dump files with a size as big as 2GB in the following location: /usr/sap/ DK1/JC01/j2ee/cluster/server0.	You move the heap dump files to another location or remove the files. Shut down the system and, if needed, clean the shared memory segments with the cleanipc command. You can also kill the hanging processes. Restart the system.

TABLE 16-4 SAP Java System Startup Problem Scenarios (*Continued*)

Problem Scenario	Diagnosis	Resolution
You have made a parameter change to improve the system performance and restarted the system in a maintenance window. You notice that the system restart was failing and all the processes were not getting started properly. You also notice that the Oracle Database starts properly and the issue is with the Java startup framework.	You start investigating the issue as per the earlier approaches, and you see that one of the bootstrap files/developer trace files has an error message indicating that the instance properties file could not be read. Upon further investigation you find out that the permissions have been changed in the following directory: /usr/sap/DK1/JC01/j2ee/cluster where the instance properties file is located. After checking with your UNIX group you find out that one of the junior UNIX system administrators has recently applied a security patch and made some changes to the file permissions, including the SAP file systems.	Change the file permissions by comparing them with the other functioning systems. Shut down and restart the system.
You apply some performance-tuning parameters to the Java system and restart the system during the weekly maintenance window. You notice that the Oracle Database comes up fine but the Java startup framework, bootstrapping, and application start are failing.	You start investigating the problem and notice that there are error messages in one of the developer traces/bootstrap logs saying that there are issues connecting to the underlying Oracle Database. Upon further investigation you find out that the JdbcCon.log file in the <SID>adm user account has error log messages indicating that the connect string is having issues with connecting to the database. You check with your Oracle Database administrator and find out that she recently changed the Oracle Listener port number in the listner.ora file while reconfiguring the Oracle network configuration to meet the organization's standards. This change is the root cause of the problem.	If a Listener port number is changed in the listener.ora file then the same port number must be entered in the secure store JDBC settings in the configuration tool. Log in to the configuration tool and change the Listener port number from the old number to the newly assigned number as in listener.log file. Go to secure store and change the key jdbc/pool/DK1/Url from jdbc:oracle:thin:@sapdb1:**1527**:DB1 to jdbc:oracle:thin:@sapdb1:<Listener Port Number>:DK1 Shut down and restart the system, and it will start properly.
You start the system after performing some maintenance work over a weekend and notice that the J2EE engine is not starting.	You start investigating the problem using the previous approach and notice that the logs in the work directory are showing that the jcontrol and jlaunch are not able to read any parameters for the Java system. Checking the parameter rdisp/j2ee_start is showing that the value is currently set to 1. Upon further investigation you notice that the j2ee parameters are missing in the instance profile. Upon researching the SAP OSS Note system online you find OSS Note: 741289 explaining the loss of parameters in some instances.	Adding the parameters back to the instance profile and restarting the system helps resolve the problem.

Table 16-4 SAP Java System Startup Problem Scenarios (*Continued*)

Problem Scenario	Diagnosis	Resolution
You get a call from your SAP process integration lead saying that they are processing a large message volume in the system and the system seems to be not processing the requests anymore.	You start investigating the issue and notice that Oracle Database and SAP Java processes are running properly. This issue seems to be related to an application-specific problem. You check the defaultTrace.trc file located at /usr/sap/DJ1/JC01/j2ee/cluster/server0/log. The log file shows that there are out-of-memory errors in the log.	Increase the heap size parameter in the configuration tool for the server node that was showing out-of-memory errors. Restarting the system resolved the issue.

Table 16-4 SAP Java System Startup Problem Scenarios

Core System Monitoring Components in Java Systems

Table 16-5 lists the core Java system monitoring tools and explains the areas that have to be monitored.

Tool/URL/Component	Description	What to Monitor
Index Page	Check the index page by typing in the URL in the browser http://<hostname>:<portnumber>/index.html and then click the System Information section. Enter the login information when prompted.	Check and make sure that all processes are running.
OS Processes	Log in as <SID>adm at the operating system level and issue ps -ef | grep ora_ and ps -ef | grep <sid>adm.	Check and make sure that all Oracle processes and SAP processes are running.
JCMON/JSMON	JCOMN/JSMON call with the instance profile at the operating system level.	A check should show that all the dispatcher, server, and SDM processes are running.
SMICM	For dual-stack systems, the SMICM transaction code can be used to check the status of the Java stack.	The Java stack status must show it is operational.
NWA	http://<hostname>:50000/nwa/quicklinks	Check all the monitoring links. The status of different processes and services should be operational.
CCMS	CCMS alerts will send an e-mail saying that a Java component is having issues or crossed a preset threshold.	Log in to the target system and verify the component that is causing the issues.

Table 16-5 Core System Monitoring in a Java System

Key Log and Trace File Location for Java Systems

Table 16-6 lists all the key log and trace files for a Java system.

Log Filename	Log File Location	Log File Provides Info On
In general, all the log and trace files are written in the work directory of the Java system.	In a single-stack Java system, the logs are at /usr/sap/<SID>/JC<Instance Number>/work Example: /usr/sap/DK1/JC01/work In a dual-stack system, the logs are at /usr/sap/<SID>/DVEMBGS<Instance Numbers>/work Example: /usr/sap/DM1/DVEBMGS00/work If there is a dialog instance, then the log files are located at /usr/sap/<SID>/J<Instance Number>/work Example: /usr/sap/DK1/J01/work	All the key log and trace files are located in the work directory.
dev_jcontrol	/usr/sap/DJ1/JC01/work/dev_jcontrol	Jcontrol process trace file
dev_bootstrap	/usr/sap/DJ1/JC01/work/dev_bootstrap	This is the log for the bootstrapping process. There are several other bootstrap log files, one for each process, and it is identified by the ID.
dev_server, (dev_server0), and dev_dispatcher	/usr/sap/DJ1/JC01/work/dev_server0 /usr/sap/DJ1/JC01/work/dev_dispatcher	These are the trace files for each of the jlaunch processes.
std_server0.out, std_dispatcher.out, and std_sdm.out	/usr/sap/DJ1/JC01/work/std_server0.out /usr/sap/DJ1/JC01/work/ std_dispatcher.out /usr/sap/DJ1/JC01/work/ std_sdm.out	JVM output log and trace files
Default trace file Example: defaultTrace.2.trc	/usr/sap/DJ1/JC01/j2ee/cluster/server0/log/ defaultTrace.2.trc	This captures all the log and trace information for the application.

TABLE 16-6 Location and Purpose of Key Log and Trace Files for Java Systems

Summary

- A problem clustering approach is recommended for structured monitoring and troubleshooting issues in ABAP and Java systems.
- A combination of problem clustering and specific troubleshooting tools will provide a basis for methodically diagnosing and resolving a problem.
- For both ABAP and Java systems, the key log and trace files are written to the work directory.
- In real-life troubleshooting scenarios, reviewing the work directory logs for error messages is one of the most important tools available to SAP Basis administrators.

Additional Resources

- **NetWeaver Server troubleshooting guide wiki** http://wiki.sdn.sap.com/wiki/display/TechTSG/%28JSTTSG%29Main+Page
- **NetWeaver Troubleshooting help** http://help.sap.com/saphelp_nw04/helpdata/en/a2/bb0a412a06f023e10000000a155106/frameset.htm

CHAPTER

Solution Manager Installation and Monitoring

SAP software solutions have evolved from a single ERP software solution (SAP R/2 and R/3) to a portfolio of business suite solutions such as SAP ERP, NetWeaver Portal, Business Intelligence, Customer Relationship Management (CRM), Supplier Relationship Management (SRM), Supply Chain Management (SCM), and Product Lifecycle Management (PLM). This has resulted in increased complexity in managing and monitoring the solution. SAP has invested considerable development effort into the Solution Manager software to address this complexity and help customers centrally manage and monitor the entire SAP software portfolio deployed at any given client site.

Solution Manager Overview

SAP has used Information Technology Infrastructure Library (ITIL) standards for the development of the SAP Solution Manager system. ITIL is the de facto standard for IT service management worldwide. It was developed by Central Computer and Telecommunications Agency (CCTA) in the United Kingdom in the 1980s and has been improved over time. At present, the ITIL standard is a collection of books, and its main focus and use by IT organizations fall under the categories of Service Support and Service Delivery. Table 17-1 lists the ITIL standards and the software components developed by SAP in Solution Manager to support the standard.

Most SAP customers use only a subset of the Solution Manager–delivered functionality. This chapter will cover the SAP Solution Manager installation process and the components that are mostly used by the clients such as SAP Solution Monitoring, Solution Manager Diagnostics, and Wily Introscope; getting the Solution Manager key to perform installation; central performance history; and brief use of end-to-end root cause analysis and monitoring tools. The main focus of the chapter will be on SAP monitoring using the different capabilities of the Solution Manager system.

ITIL Standard	SAP Solution Manager Component
Incident Management	Service Desk
Change Management	Change Request Management (ChaRM)
IT Monitoring	Solution Manager Monitoring (Alert Monitoring)
Service Level Management	Service Level and Solution Reporting
Capacity Management	Solution Management Assessment
Availability and Continuity Management	Solution Management Optimization, Early Watch Alert, and Going Live Services

TABLE 17-1 ITIL Standards and Equivalent SAP Solution Manager Components

Solution Manager Installation

SAP Solution Manager is a dual-stack system (ABAP and Java stacks). Installing Solution Manager is similar to installing SAP NetWeaver Application Server and uses the SAPinst tool. Call the SAPinst tool as per the directions given in the earlier installation chapters. The only difference is the SAPinst in this case must be called from the Solution Manager Installation Master CD. The screen in Figure 17-1 will appear when the CD is first run. Select Central System Installation and click the Next button.

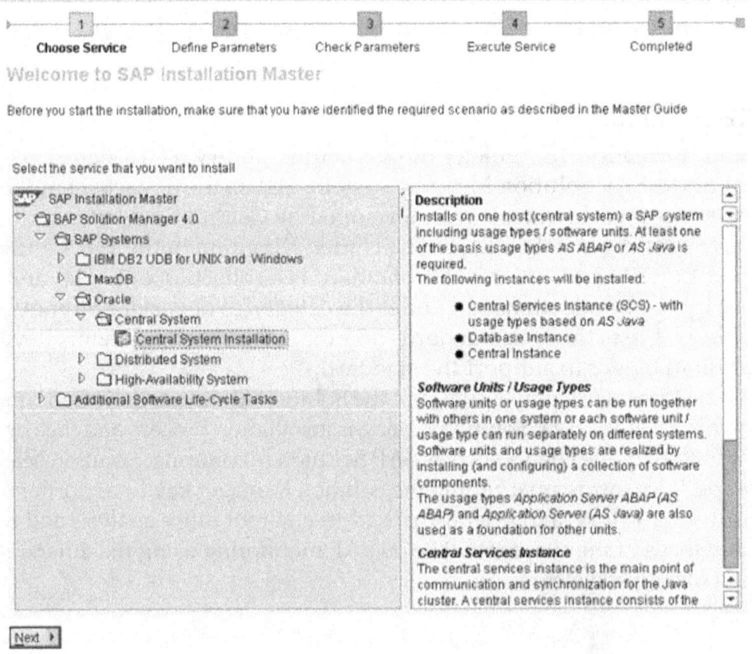

FIGURE 17-1 The initial Solution Manager installation screen

The SAPinst tool will start gathering the parameters that are needed to perform the installation. Provide the installation parameters in the SAPinst screens as per Table 17-2.

Parameter Name	Parameter Value
Java Component for Solution Manager CD	Path to the downloaded Java Component Solution Manager CD.
System ID, SAP system mount dir, and Unicode Flag	Choose the system ID (Example: DS1), the mount point is /sapmnt, and select the Unicode check box.
SAP System Master Password	Choose a master password.
Database ID (SID) and Database Hostname	Choose a database SID. (This is the same as the system ID.)
Installation Export CD for Solution Manager	The path to the downloaded export CD for Solution Manager.
Oracle RDBMS CDs	Path to the Oracle Database software CDs.
Kernel CD and Oracle Client Software	Path to the NW2004s kernel CD and Oracle Client software CD.
Unpack Archives	Choose all kernel components to be unpacked. (Both database-dependent and database-independent).
Choose System Landscape Directory Option	Choose to install and configure local SLD (Figure 17-2). Choose a unique SLD name and enter the user accounts in the next screen.
Parameter Summary Screen	Verify all the entered parameters, and click Start if they are correct. Click Revise if you need to change any parameter.
Installation of Oracle Database Software	It is recommended to install the Oracle Database software ahead of the SAPinst installation. If this is done, the installation will not stop in this step. If this is not done, SAPinst will stop at this step.
Execute Service Installation Phase of SAPinst	SAPinst will enter into an execute service phase once the check parameter phase is complete. In this Solution Manager installation 44 individual installation steps will be carried out.
Execute Service Installation Phase of SAPinst at SLD Creation	Figure 17-3 shows that the SAPinst tool is at the SLD creation and configuration step.
SAPinst Completed	Figure 17-4 shows that the SAP Solution Manager installation has been executed successfully.

TABLE 17-2 SAPinst Parameters During Installation of Solution Manager

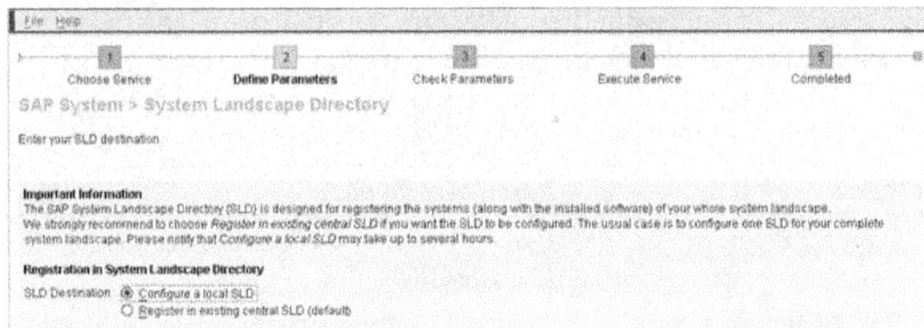

FIGURE 17-2 Selection screen for local SLD in Solution Manager

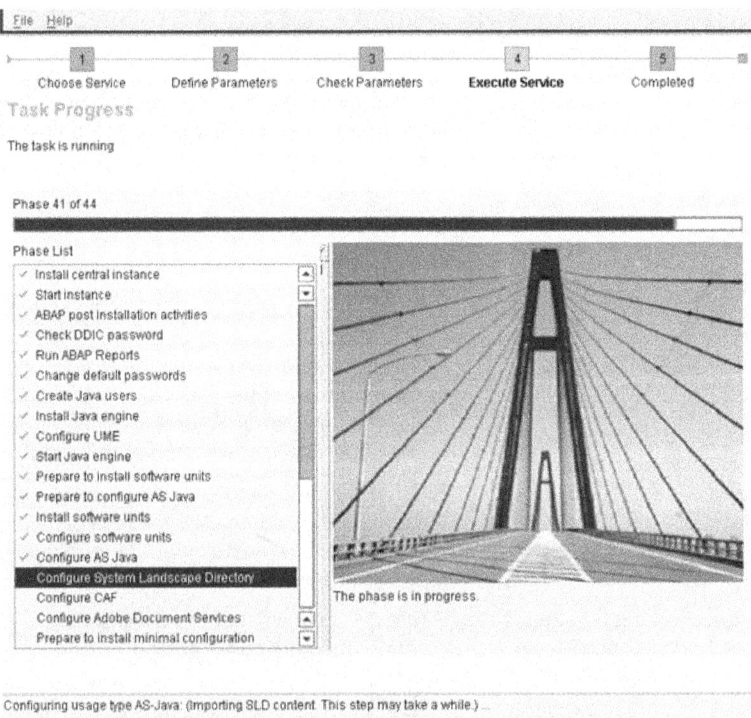

FIGURE 17-3 Solution Manager installation at the configure SLD step

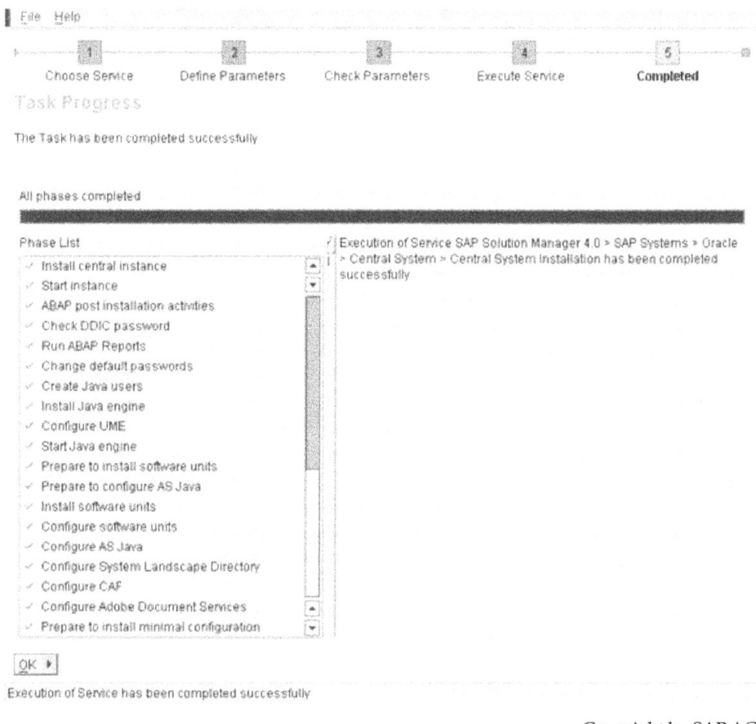

FIGURE 17-4 Successful completion of SAP Solution Manager System

Generating the Solution Manager Key

A Solution Manager key is required to perform SAP installations, and the following procedure should be used to generate it. Log in to your Solution Manager system, execute transaction code SMSY, and choose Systems, right-click, and select the Create New System option. The following screen appears. Enter the system identifier, product, and product version; and click the Save button.

Create New System

System DS1

Product 01200314690800000134 SAP NETWEAVER

Product Version 01200615320900001275 SAP NETWEAVER 7.1

Installation Number 0012317689

Create Product

This will present the next screen where you select the check boxes that are relevant to the current installation and click the Save button from the icon group at the top. Once this is done, select the "other object" icon (SHIFT-F5), as shown here.

In the next screen that appears, you enter the system (SID) information and click the Generate Installation/Upgrade Key button (CTRL-SHIFT-F10).

The next screen that appears is where you should enter the system ID, system number, and the message server hostname. Once this is done, click the Generate Key button, and the system will generate under the Installation/Upgrade Key section. Make a note of the Solution Manager key, and enter the same in the SAPinst Solution Manager Entry screen to continue the installation.

Generate Installation/Upgrade Key

System ID	QB1
System Number	00
Message Server (max. 15 chars)	venus

Generate Key

Monitoring with Solution Manager

Central monitoring is the most commonly used Solution Manager component. In this section we will go into the details of the central monitoring architecture and setting up of the agents in the satellite SAP systems.

Availability Monitoring

Availability monitoring, as the name implies, helps to monitor the availability of the SAP systems and sends an e-mail alert to the infrastructure team if any server is down. This will help the infrastructure team respond to the situation quickly, and they do not have to manually monitor the system availability. The CCMSPING agent is used for availability monitoring.

CCMSPING

CCMSPING is installed in the central monitoring system. It queries the message server of the configured SAP systems in the SAP Landscape and sends an alert if any system is not available.

Register the CCMS Agents

Download CCMSPING from the SAP Service Marketplace and register it in the central monitoring system using the following command:

```
REGISTER ccmsping -push -R pf=/usr/sap/DK1/SYS/profile/DK1_DVEBMGS01_venus
```

where DK1 is the SID and venus is the hostname.

The following command is used to check if the CCMSPING agent is running on the central monitoring system:

```
dk1adm> ps -ef | grep ccmsping
dk1adm    9128     1  0 May19        00:43:02 ccmsping -DCCMS -push -n00
```

Configuration of the CCMSPING

The following steps should be performed to configure the CCMSPING in the central monitoring system.

1. Edit the /etc/services file with all the message servers in all systems that will be part of availability monitoring.
2. Create a CSMREG user in the central monitoring system using transaction code RZ21 by choosing Technical Infrastructure | Configure Central System | Create CSMREG User.
3. Execute transaction RZ21 and then select | Technical Infrastructure | Availability Monitoring | Configure CCMSPING Availability Monitoring.
4. In the next screen, click the Monitoring down arrow, and select Create System.
5. The connection data and monitoring options screen is displayed. In this screen enter the connection information for both ABAP and Java stacks, as well as the RFC destination for the CCMSPING, to check the availability of the systems.
6. In the RZ20 transaction code systems that are in scope for availability monitoring can be assigned to the method for e-mail alert.
7. To configure the e-mail alert, copy the SAP-delivered method using transaction code RZ21 and selecting Technical Infrastructure | Configure Central System | Assign Central Autoreactions.
8. In Defined Central Autoreactions window, click the Create button and then click the Create With Template button to copy the CCMS_OnAlert_Email_V2 method to a custom ZCCMS_OnAlert_Email_V2 method, as shown.

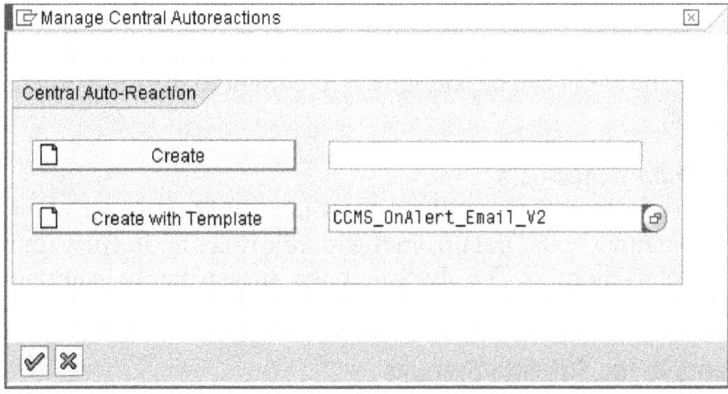

Copyright by SAP AG

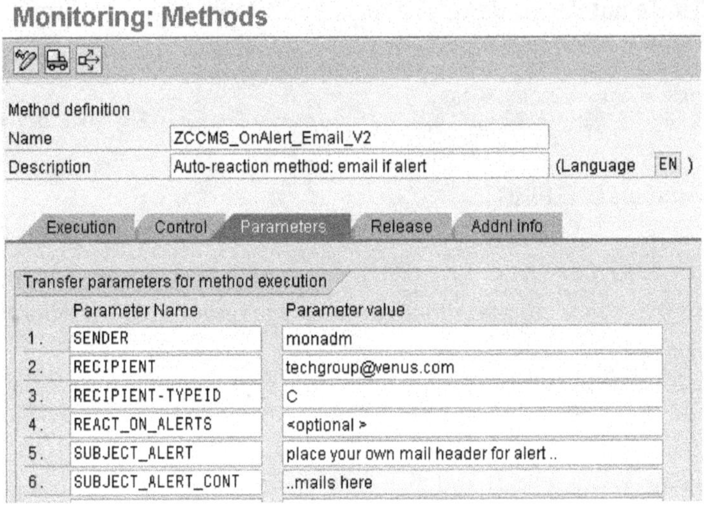

Monitoring: Methods

Method definition

Name	ZCCMS_OnAlert_Email_V2	
Description	Auto-reaction method: email if alert	(Language EN)

Execution | Control | Parameters | Release | Addnl info

Transfer parameters for method execution

	Parameter Name	Parameter value
1.	SENDER	monadm
2.	RECIPIENT	techgroup@venus.com
3.	RECIPIENT-TYPEID	C
4.	REACT_ON_ALERTS	<optional >
5.	SUBJECT_ALERT	place your own mail header for alert ..
6.	SUBJECT_ALERT_CONT	..mails here

FIGURE 17-5 Configuration of central e-mail autoreaction method

9. In the next screen, enter the ZCCMS_OnAlert_Email_V2 method, click the Parameters tab, and configure the entries as shown in Figure 17-5. In this example an e-mail notification will be sent to the techgroup@venus.com distribution list. OSS Note 176492 can be used for different configuration options. Once configuration is complete, an e-mail alert is sent to the distribution list when a system is not available.

Monitoring the Architecture

The monitoring architecture is built into SAP systems and is part of the standard installation. This helps the infrastructure team start monitoring the system right after the installation. However, it would be time-consuming to monitor each of the newly installed SAP systems. In order to monitor all the systems for a given customer, SAP provides a central monitoring infrastructure that uses the agents installed in the satellite systems to send monitoring data to the central system. The alerts can be configured to be sent to the infrastructure team via an e-mail distribution list.

Data Suppliers and Data Consumers

Data suppliers are programs that collect the data from individual systems and populate the monitor sets. Data consumers read data from the monitoring architecture (monitor sets) and produce alerts in the alert monitor. The alerts help the infrastructure team monitor the SAP systems proactively.

Installation of Agents in the Satellite Systems

The SAP central monitoring architecture consists of Computing Center Management System (CCMS) agents installed on the satellite systems. The agents push the monitoring

SAP CCMS Agent Name	System Type
SAPCM3X	Agent for SAP Basis 3.X release
SAPCCM4X	Agent for ABAP systems as of Basis 4.X, central monitoring system as of SAP Basis 4.6C
SAPCCMSR	Components with no SAP instance and SAP Web AS 6.2, central monitoring system as of SAP Basis 4.6B
SAPCCMSR -j2ee	Java instances as of NetWeaver 2004 and central monitoring system as of NetWeaver 2004

TABLE 17-3 CCMS Agent Types

data to the central monitoring system, which can be configured to send e-mail alerts to the infrastructure team so that corrective action can be taken in a prompt fashion.

Different Kinds of CCMS Agents

Several kinds of CCMS agents have to be installed in the satellite system, depending upon the target system. Table 17-3 lists the main CCMS agents and the target system they have to be installed on so that they send the monitoring data to the central monitoring system.

Register, Start, and Stop CCMS Agents

The following commands can be used to register, start, stop, and check the status of the CCMS agents.

Register commands:

```
sapccm4x -R pf=/usr/sap/KB1/SYS/profile/KB1_DVEBMGS10_venus

sapccmsr -R -j2ee -DCCMS pf=/usr/sap/KX1/SYS/profile/KX1_DVEBMGS01_venus
```

Start commands:

```
sapccm4x -DCCMS pf=/usr/sap/KB1/SYS/profile/KB1_DVEBMGS01_venus

sapccmsr -j2ee -DCCMS pf=/usr/sap/KB1/SYS/profile/KB1_DVEBMGS10_venus
```

Stop commands:

```
sapccm4x -stop pf=/usr/sap/KB1/SYS/profile/KB1_DVEBMGS01_venus

sapccmsr -j2ee -stop pf=/usr/sap/KB1/SYS/profile/KB1_DVEBMGS10_venus
```

Status commands:

```
sapccm4x -status pf=/usr/sap/KB1/SYS/profile/KB1_DVEBMGS01_venus

sapccmsr -j2ee -status pf=/usr/sap/KB1/SYS/profile/KB1_DVEBMGS10_venus
```

Configuration of Alert Monitoring from the Central Monitoring System

Once the CCMS agents are registered and started in the satellite systems, the next step is to configure the central monitoring system to monitor for alerts from the satellite systems. The following steps have to be configured in the central monitoring system to set this up.

1. Run background job SAP_CCMS_CENSYS_DISPATCHER in the central monitoring system.
2. Run background job SAP_CCMS_MONI_BATCH_DP in the central monitoring and the satellite systems.
3. Create the CMSREG user using transaction RZ21 and selecting | Technical Infrastructure | Configure Central System | Create CMSREG User.
4. Create two RFC connections for the monitored satellite system: one for data analysis and the other for data collection.
5. From RZ21 select | Technical Infrastructure | Configure Central System | Create Remote Monitoring Entry | Choose Component Type (ABAP, Java, or Dual Stack). Choose the SID and choose the two RFC connections.
6. Add the monitored system in RZ20.
7. Configure the autoreaction method so that alerts can be e-mailed to the infrastructure team.

Alert Monitor Example (Thresholds, E-mail Alerts)

Transaction RZ20 provides the alert monitors. Threshold values can be set to the monitored components, and alerts can be configured to be generated based on this information. Figures 17-6, 17-7, and 17-8 show a sample alert threshold, alert monitors, and an alert e-mail, respectively.

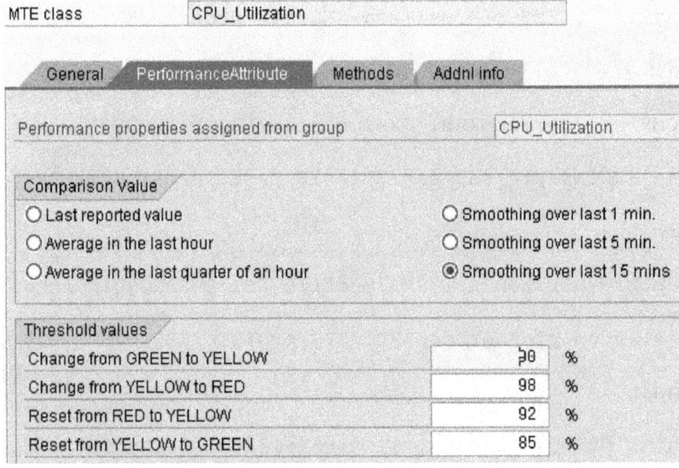

FIGURE 17-6 Alert threshold setting for CPU utilization

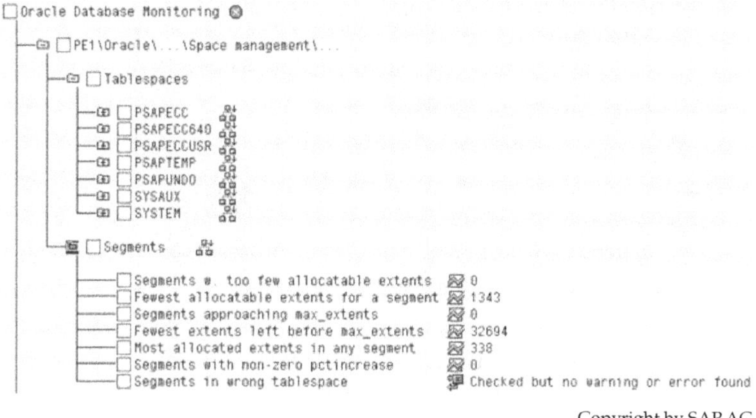

FIGURE 17-7 Alert monitoring (monitor sets) for Oracle Database monitoring

Central Performance History

CCMS alert monitors keep the performance data for a period of 24 hours. If you would like to analyze the data for a longer period, you can store the data in Central Performance History (CPH). You can define the storage period and granularity of the stored data to comply with the organization's service level agreements (SLAs). Transaction RZ23N can be used to configure the CPH. The illustration on the next page shows the initial screen of the CPH.

-----Original Message-----

From: CCMSADM [mailto:CCMSADM@VENUS.COM]
Sent: Sunday, Mar 03, 2010 5:08 AM
To: Mereddy, Ranjit; Peter Van Avermaet; Raj Patel
Subject: Project Skunk Works FILE SYSTEM ALERT

ALERT for KE1 \ jupiter_KE1_00 \ /oracle/kE1/sapdata1 \ Percentage_Used at 20100301 090811 (Time in UTC)
YELLOW CCMS alert for monitored object Percentage_Used
Alert Text:File system for 86 % full (threshold value: 85 %)
System:KE1
Segment:SAP_CCMS_jupiter_KE1_00
MTE:KE1\jupiter_KE1_00\/oracle/KE1/sapdata1\Percentage_Used
Client:000
User: SAPSYS

FIGURE 17-8 Sample e-mail alert from central monitoring system to distribution list

By clicking the Overview Of Available Data button in the data window you can see the available systems for the CPH.

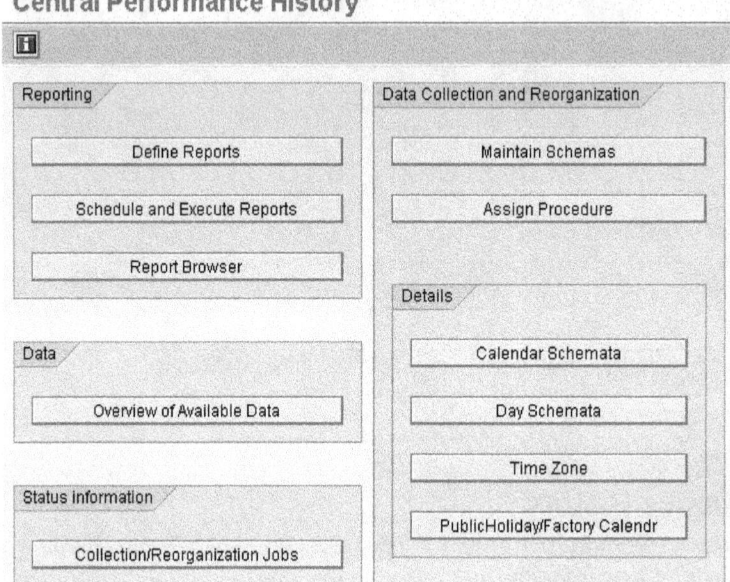

In the next screen you can select a system from the list of available systems and choose the category, such as CPU utilization, and generate a report that covers data for more than 24 hours. This reporting will be very useful for analyzing system-critical resource usage patterns, and could help resolve performance issues in the system.

Solution Manager Diagnostic

Solution Manager Diagnostic (SMD) and Wily Introscope are installed to enable end-to-end monitoring and root cause analysis. The SMD system is installed on the central monitoring system once in the landscape, and SMD agents are installed on the satellite systems that communicate to the central SMD system. SAPinst is used to install the SMD agent in all the satellite systems. The illustration shows the installation option for the SMD agent.

SAP SMD agent installation will install the following scripts to start and shut down the SMD agents at /usr/sap/SMD/J96/script, where 96 is the SMD instance number. You can

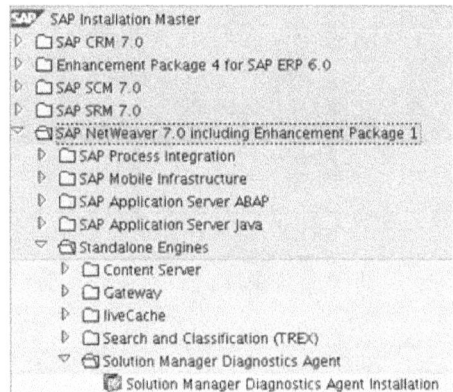

SAP Installation Master
SAP CRM 7.0
Enhancement Package 4 for SAP ERP 6.0
SAP SCM 7.0
SAP SRM 7.0
SAP NetWeaver 7.0 including Enhancement Package 1
SAP Process Integration
SAP Mobile Infrastructure
SAP Application Server ABAP
SAP Application Server Java
Standalone Engines
Content Server
Gateway
liveCache
Search and Classification (TREX)
Solution Manager Diagnostics Agent
Solution Manager Diagnostics Agent Installation

start and shut down the SMD agents by executing the following commands as the smdadm operating system user account:

```
./smdstart.sh command starts the SMD agent

./smdstop.sh command shuts down the SMD agent
```

Wily Introscope

Wily Introscope helps in monitoring and managing Java applications. It consists of a server component called the Introscope Enterprise Manager, and an Introscope Java agent is installed on the managed systems. A host-level Introscope agent is installed once per host. The host agent runs as part of the SMD agent to collect data at the operating system level.

Installing the Introscope Enterprise Manager

The following procedure demonstrates installing the Introscope Enterprise Manager.

1. Extract the SAR file downloaded from the SAP Service Marketplace:

```
monadm> SAPCAR -xvf SAPISEM8SP01_00-10007428.SAR
SAPCAR: processing archive SAPISEM8SP01_00-10007428.SAR (version 2.01)
x installer.properties
x introscope8.1.0.0linuxAMD64SAP.bin
SAPCAR: 2 file(s) extracted
```

2. Start the install by executing the following command:

```
monadm> ./introscope8.1.0.0linuxAMD64SAP.bin
Preparing to install...
Extracting the JRE from the installer archive...
Unpacking the JRE...
Extracting the installation resources from the installer archive...
Configuring the installer for this system's environment...
Launching installer...
Preparing SILENT Mode Installation...
Silent installer completed with status of: SUCCESS. For more details,
consult
install logs at: /usr/sap/ccms/wilyintroscope/install. Please wait
for the command
prompt to return...Installation Complete.
```

Starting the Introscope Enterprise Manager

The Wily Introscope Manager can be started as the central monitoring operating system user (example: monadm OS account for central monitoring system with SID MON) by executing the following commands:

```
monadm> pwd
/usr/sap/ccms/wilyintroscope/bin
```

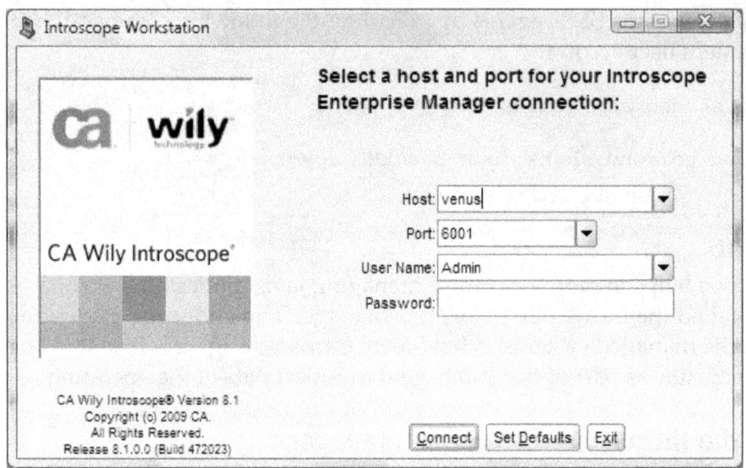

Copyright by SAP AG

FIGURE 17-9 Wily Introscope Enterprise Manager workstation view

Execute the command ./EMCtrl.sh to start the Introscope Enterprise Manager. Once the Enterprise Manager is started and the SMD agents and Wily agents are configured, the monitored systems start reporting to the Enterprise Manager. This can be viewed in either the Web view (browser-based) or the workstation view (swing-based client user interface with full functionality).

The workstation view can be accessed from the central monitoring system using the URL http://emhost:8081/workstation, where emhost is the central monitoring system host where the Introscope Enterprise Manager is installed.

The web view can be accessed from the central monitoring system using the URL http://emhost:8081/ webview, where emhost is the central monitoring system host where the Introscope Enterprise Manager is installed. Figure 17-9 shows the initial login of the web view.

Once you are logged on, you can see different views (dashboards) of the satellite systems. The following illustration and Figure 17-10 show the portal triage dashboard of one of the monitored Java systems.

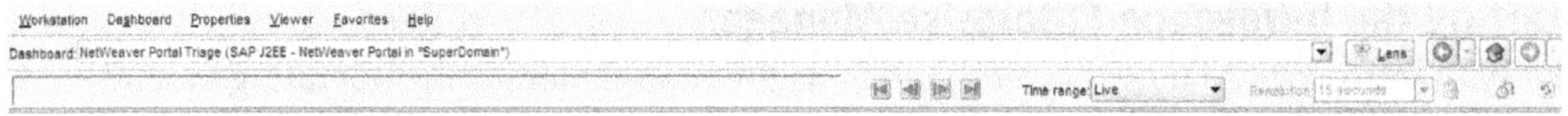

Copyright by SAP AG

You can also generate a report of the monitored system by choosing Workstation | Generate Report. Next choose one of the available templates. In this example, a J2EE overview template is chosen. Figure 17-11 shows the generated report.

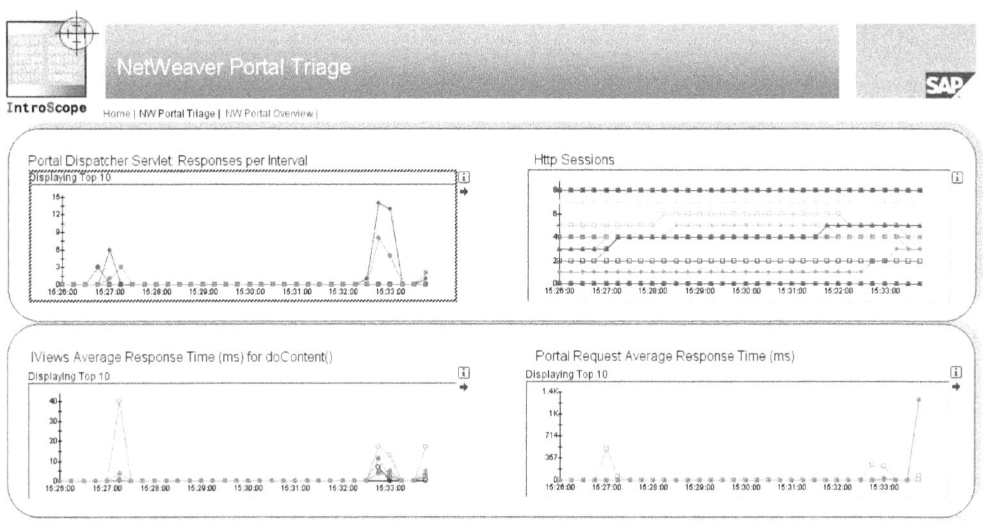

FIGURE 17-10 NetWeaver Portal triage real-time dashboard view

Summary

- The Solution Manager System is used to monitor and manage the complex SAP System Landscape from a central system.
- SAP has developed the Solution Manager System based on ITIL compliance.
- The SAPinst tool is used to install the Solution Manager System.
- Solution Manager System is primarily used by customers for monitoring the SAP landscape from one central system.
- Solution Manager System is used to generate the Solution Manager key that will be used during the installation of different kinds of systems in the client landscape.
- The CCMSPING agent is installed in the central monitoring system for availability monitoring.
- CCMS agents are used to monitor ABAP and Java systems, which report data back to the central monitoring system.
- SMD agents and Wily agents are installed in all monitored systems to enable end-to-end monitoring and root cause analysis.
- Wily Introscope provides dashboards to monitor and manage the SAP systems from one central system.

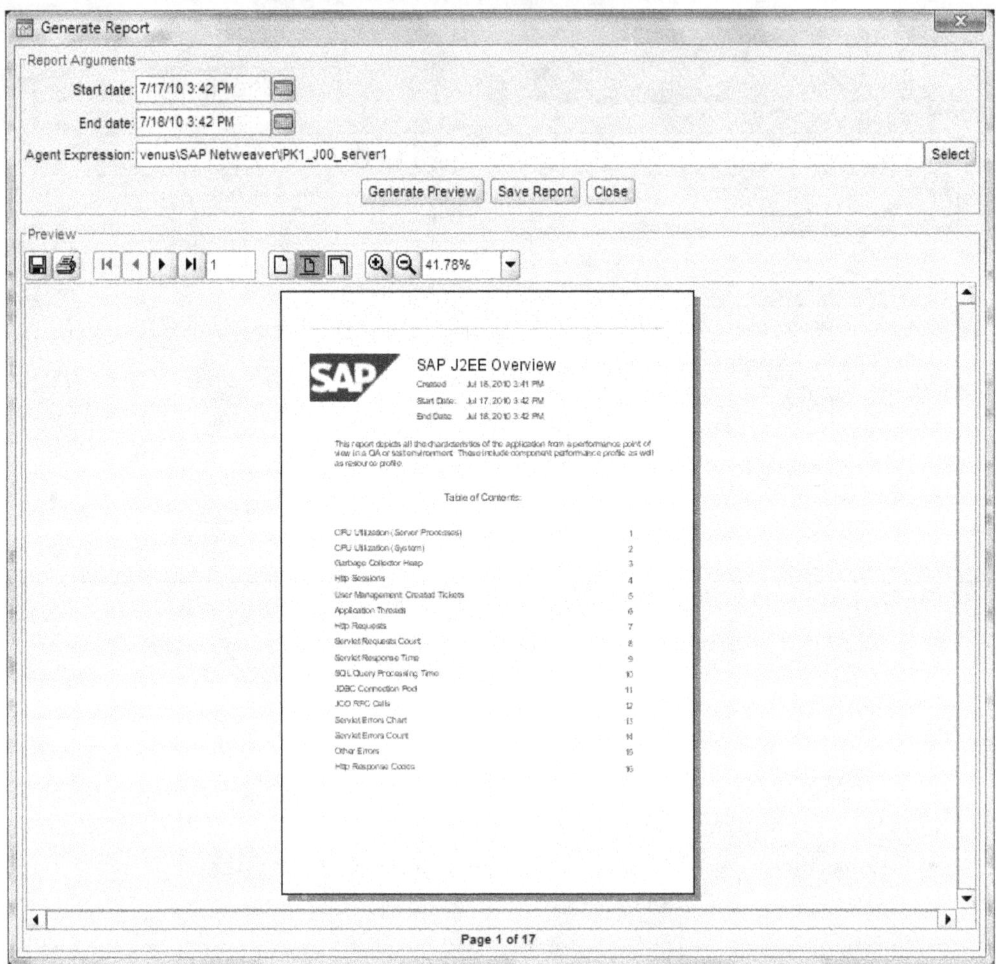

Figure 17-11 Report generation from Wily Introscope Enterprise Manager

Additional Resources

- **SAP monitoring overview** www.sdn.sap.com/irj/sdn/operations?rid=/webcontent/uuid/d05cab4b-f2c8-2a10-90aa-cfd6ad90f2dc
- **SAP monitoring setup guide** www.sdn.sap.com/irj/sdn/operations?rid=/webcontent/uuid/d012fc88-24cb-2a10-ae90-fdac28c595bd
- **SAP monitoring alert management** www.sdn.sap.com/irj/sdn/operations?rid=/webcontent/uuid/00c3b65b-5b22-2a10-628b-98c00a338f1c

CHAPTER

SAP Service Marketplace Administration

The SAP Service Marketplace is a support portal developed by SAP to provide support functions, such as searching for code fixes to the SAP standard code in the form of OSS (Online Service System) Notes; opening technical support requests (usually referred to as OSS messages); and getting different kinds of keys, such as developer keys and access keys, to make changes to SAP standard code when necessary, request licenses for newly installed systems, and download SAP software.

Service Marketplace Login

The SAP Service Marketplace (also known as the SAP Online Support Portal) can be accessed by customers with a user account usually referred to as an S user account by going to http://service.sap.com. When a customer purchases licenses from SAP, a super-user account (S user account with all privileges) is provided. Usually, it is the SAP Basis lead who initially has a super-user account. Additional user accounts with different levels of access are then created by the super-user and provided to the project team. Project team users can now log in to SAP Service Marketplace and perform different online activities, such as opening technical support messages or researching an OSS Notes database for any possible fixes for an issue. The illustration shows the initial login screen for SAP Service Marketplace.

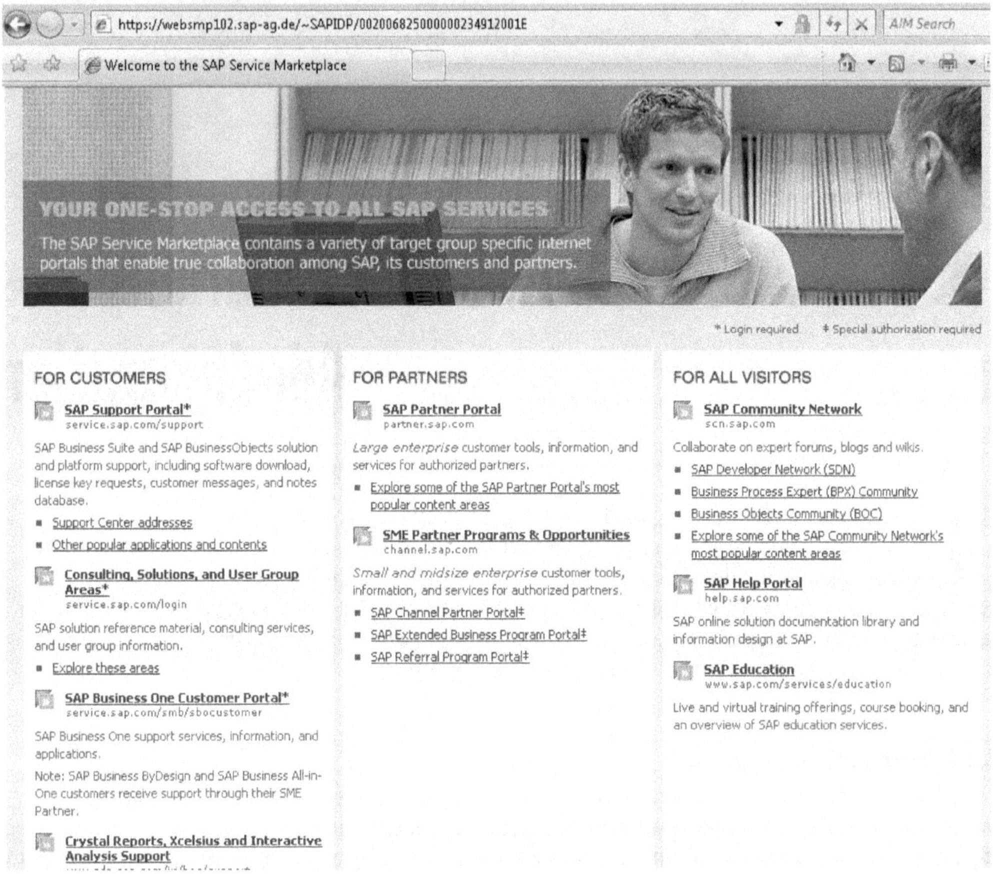

https://websmp102.sap-ag.de/~SAPIDP/002006825000000234912001E
AIM Search
Welcome to the SAP Service Marketplace
YOUR ONE-STOP ACCESS TO ALL SAP SERVICES
The SAP Service Marketplace contains a variety of target group specific internet portals that enable true collaboration among SAP, its customers and partners.
* Login required ‡ Special authorization required
FOR CUSTOMERS
SAP Support Portal*
service.sap.com/support
SAP Business Suite and SAP BusinessObjects solution and platform support, including software download, license key requests, customer messages, and notes database.
Support Center addresses
Other popular applications and contents
Consulting, Solutions, and User Group Areas*
service.sap.com/login
SAP solution reference material, consulting services, and user group information.
Explore these areas
SAP Business One Customer Portal*
service.sap.com/smb/sbocustomer
SAP Business One support services, information, and applications.
Note: SAP Business ByDesign and SAP Business All-in-One customers receive support through their SME Partner.
Crystal Reports, Xcelsius and Interactive Analysis Support
FOR PARTNERS
SAP Partner Portal
partner.sap.com
Large enterprise customer tools, information, and services for authorized partners.
Explore some of the SAP Partner Portal's most popular content areas
SME Partner Programs & Opportunities
channel.sap.com
Small and midsize enterprise customer tools, information, and services for authorized partners.
SAP Channel Partner Portal‡
SAP Extended Business Program Portal‡
SAP Referral Program Portal‡
FOR ALL VISITORS
SAP Community Network
scn.sap.com
Collaborate on expert forums, blogs and wikis.
SAP Developer Network (SDN)
Business Process Expert (BPX) Community
Business Objects Community (BOC)
Explore some of the SAP Community Network's most popular content areas
SAP Help Portal
help.sap.com
SAP online solution documentation library and information design at SAP.
SAP Education
www.sap.com/services/education
Live and virtual training offerings, course booking, and an overview of SAP education services.

FIGURE 18-1 Initial SAP Service Marketplace screen

When you log in to the SAP Service Marketplace, the screen shown in Figure 18-1 appears. You can access different sections of the SAP Service Marketplace by clicking the individual links and then drilling down into different sublevels, or you can access these items directly through a URL. Some of the SAP Service Marketplace options are shown in the illustration. In this chapter, the direct-access method via URLs is covered for all the important Basis administration SAP Service Marketplace online activities.

SUPPORT PORTAL
Advanced Search
my Profile my Inbox my Favorites
Quick Links Sitemap Other Portals Glossary Help
HOME Help & Support Downloads Keys & Requests Data Administration Maintenance & Services Application Life-Cycle Management Release & Upgrade Info Knowledge Exchange
Search for SAP Notes Request Help Report a Product Error Connect to SAP SAP BusinessObjects Support Look up Support Center Addresses

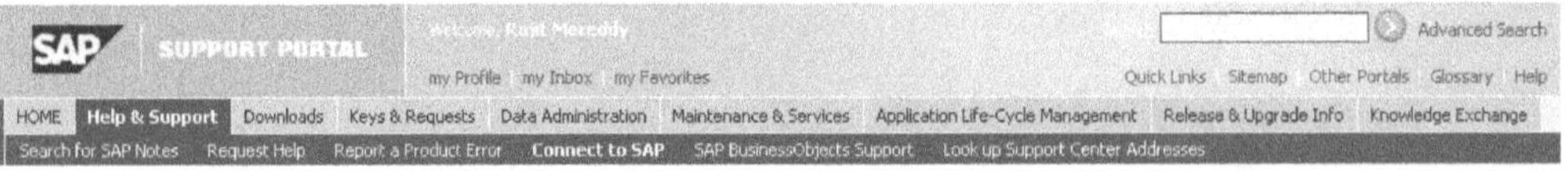

Creating S User Accounts

New S user accounts can be created by using the URL http://service.sap.com/user-admin, which displays the screen shown in Figure 18-2. You can request new S user accounts for your project team by clicking the Request New Users link. Once SAP receives the user account request, a new account is created and the login information (S user account and password) is available online. The Basis administrator can then provide this to the appropriate project team user. Once the user account is created by SAP, the necessary authorizations can be performed by the Basis administrator online. Several other options are available for administering the online user accounts, including a few mass maintenance options.

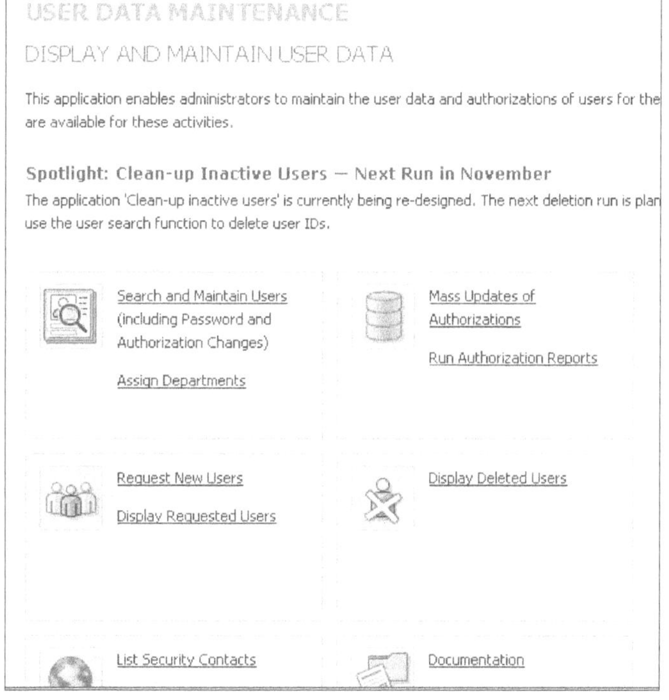

FIGURE 18-2 SAP online S user accounts administration screen

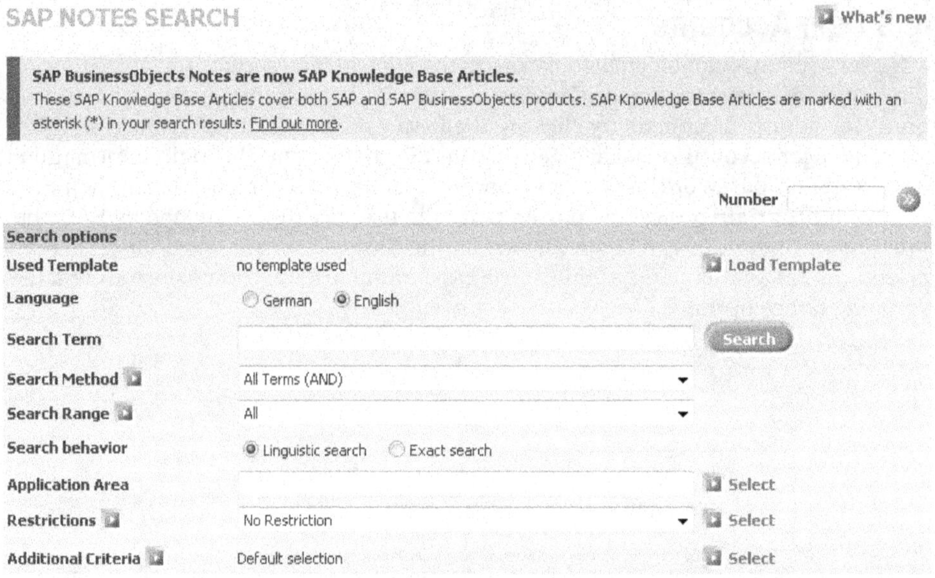

Copyright by SAP AG

Figure 18-3 Initial SAP OSS Notes search screen

Searching OSS Notes

One of the main benefits of SAP Service Marketplace is accessing the OSS Notes database. A Basis administrator and the project team members can search this database for any known code fixes or workarounds to software issues that are encountered during the course of implementation and for production support operations as well. The SAP OSS Notes database search screen can be accessed at https://websmp102.sap-ag.de/notes. The screen shown in Figure 18-3 appears, where you have the option of searching for a note based on a search keyword, or if you already know the note number, you can enter it in the Number field.

Opening Messages with SAP

Sometimes a SAP software issue is not resolved by even an extensive search of the OSS Notes database. Under these conditions you can log a technical support message with SAP. You can access the SAP message wizard directly at https://websmp102.sap-ag.de/message. This will bring up the SAP message wizard as shown in Figure 18-4. In this screen SAP requests users to search for a possible fix before opening a technical support request. You can follow the message wizard options sequentially (Choose System | Prepare Solution Search | Find Solution | Enter Message). If a customer is not able to find a relevant OSS Note, they are directed to send a technical support message. SAP will then look into the issue and will either provide a solution or ask the customer to open a service connection

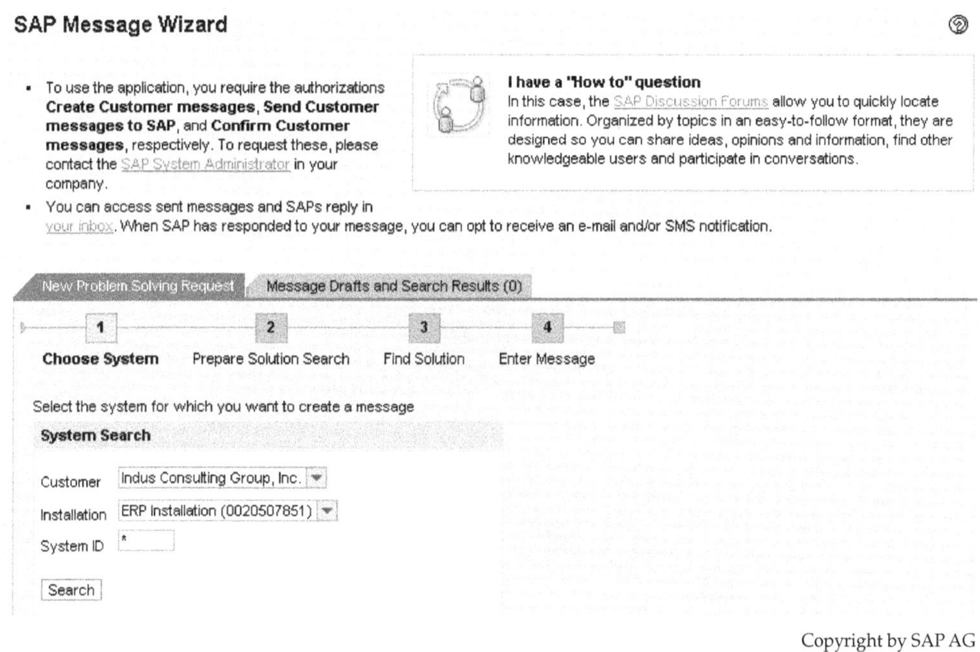

SAP Message Wizard
To use the application, you require the authorizations Create Customer messages, Send Customer messages to SAP, and Confirm Customer messages, respectively. To request these, please contact the SAP System Administrator in your company.
You can access sent messages and SAPs reply in your inbox. When SAP has responded to your message, you can opt to receive an e-mail and/or SMS notification.
I have a "How to" question
In this case, the SAP Discussion Forums allow you to quickly locate information. Organized by topics in an easy-to-follow format, they are designed so you can share ideas, opinions and information, find other knowledgeable users and participate in conversations.
New Problem Solving Request
Message Drafts and Search Results (0)
1
2
3
4
Choose System
Prepare Solution Search
Find Solution
Enter Message
Select the system for which you want to create a message
System Search
Customer
Indus Consulting Group, Inc.
Installation
ERP Installation (0020507851)
System ID
*
Search

FIGURE 18-4 Initial SAP message wizard screen

(secure network connection) so that a SAP support resource can log in to the customer's system and help resolve the issue.

Service Connections

SAP service connections are secure network connections between SAP and customer data centers. Sometimes, SAP needs to log in to customer systems to help resolve an issue and requests a service connection to the system. You can use the URL https://websmp102.sap-ag.de/serviceconnection to find the right system and open the service connection. Figure 18-5 shows the initial screen for maintaining service connections.

Download Software

One of the main benefits of SAP Service Marketplace is that you can download SAP software on demand. After the initial login, choose the Downloads option, as shown in Figure 18-6. The left side of the window will give download options based on application group, or you can choose to search individual software components. Once the correct software media is identified, it can be flagged for download and added to the download basket by clicking the Add To Download Basket button.

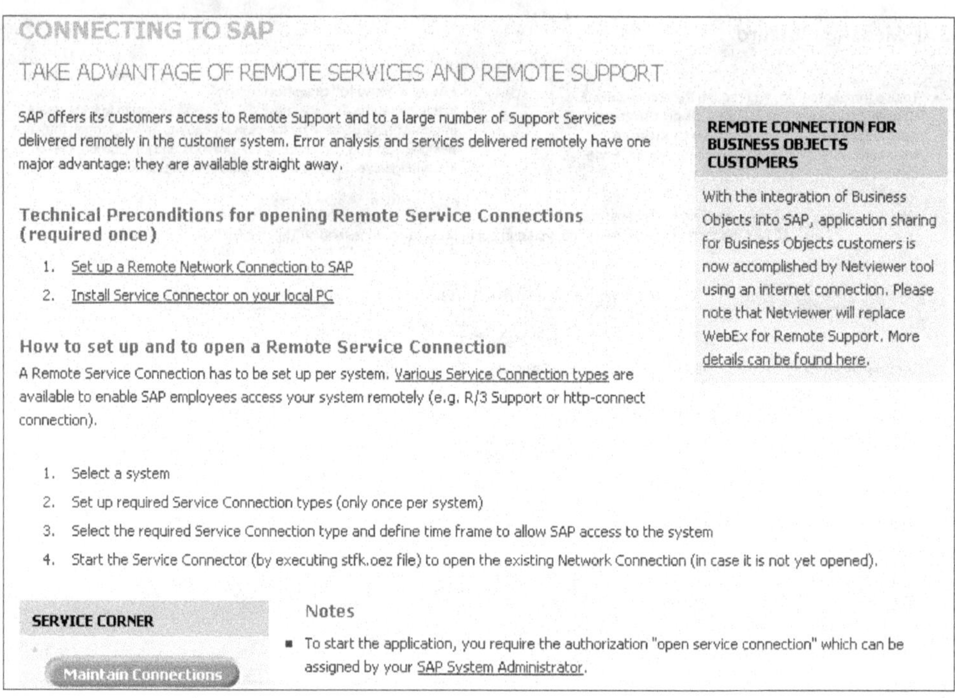

CONNECTING TO SAP
TAKE ADVANTAGE OF REMOTE SERVICES AND REMOTE SUPPORT
SAP offers its customers access to Remote Support and to a large number of Support Services delivered remotely in the customer system. Error analysis and services delivered remotely have one major advantage: they are available straight away.
Technical Preconditions for opening Remote Service Connections (required once)
1. Set up a Remote Network Connection to SAP
2. Install Service Connector on your local PC
How to set up and to open a Remote Service Connection
A Remote Service Connection has to be set up per system. Various Service Connection types are available to enable SAP employees access your system remotely (e.g. R/3 Support or http-connect connection).
1. Select a system
2. Set up required Service Connection types (only once per system)
3. Select the required Service Connection type and define time frame to allow SAP access to the system
4. Start the Service Connector (by executing stfk.oez file) to open the existing Network Connection (in case it is not yet opened).
REMOTE CONNECTION FOR BUSINESS OBJECTS CUSTOMERS
With the integration of Business Objects into SAP, application sharing for Business Objects customers is now accomplished by Netviewer tool using an internet connection. Please note that Netviewer will replace WebEx for Remote Support. More details can be found here.
SERVICE CORNER
Maintain Connections
Notes
To start the application, you require the authorization "open service connection" which can be assigned by your SAP System Administrator.

Figure 18-5 Use this screen to begin maintaining service connections.

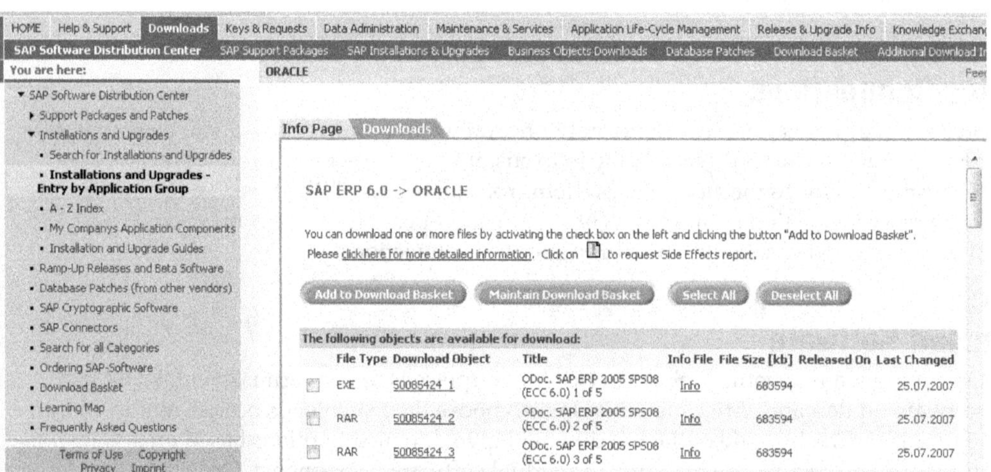

Figure 18-6 SAP software download

Download Manager

Once the SAP software is in the download basket, you can use the SAP Download Manager to download the software. You can install the SAP Download Manager either on your laptop or directly on one of the UNIX servers that serves as a media repository. The software can be obtained at https://websmp106.sap-ag.de/~sapidb/002006825000000233132001/.

Once the Download Manager is installed, it can accessed by choosing Start | Programs | SAP Download Manager. The following illustration shows the SAP Download Manager with several components ready to be downloaded.

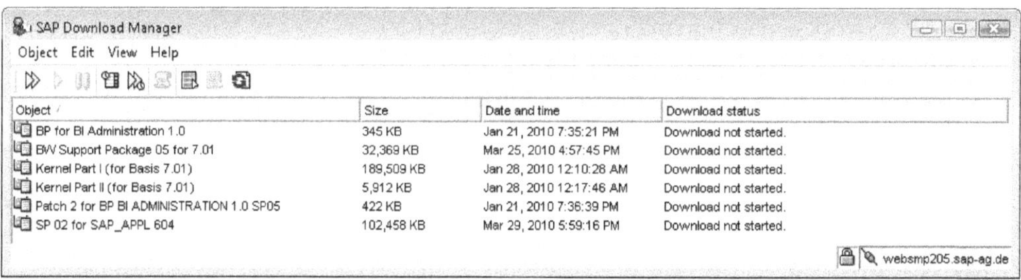

Copyright by SAP AG

Keys and Requests

If a developer or configuration resource has to change the SAP standard code or settings, SAP requires a developer key in addition to access keys. The developer key is issued by SAP for an individual developer user account, and access keys are issued for the development object that needs to be changed. The developer keys and access key sections of SAP Service Marketplace can be accessed at http://service.sap.com/sscr. The following illustration shows the initial screen for requesting a developer and access keys from SAP.

SSCR - SAP Software Change Registration

The SSCR (SAP Software Change Registration) is a procedure, valid from Re
SAP Dictionary objects. SAP matchcodes and tuning measures such as the s
With this procedure, the availability and reliability of productive R/3 installation

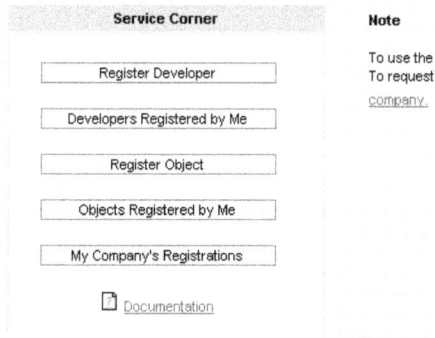

Service Corner

Register Developer

Developers Registered by Me

Register Object

Objects Registered by Me

My Company's Registrations

Documentation

Note

To use the
To request
company.

Copyright by SAP AG

Summary

- The SAP Service Marketplace can be accessed at http://service.sap.com.
- SAP online user accounts can be created by going to http://service.sap.com/user-admin.
- The SAP Notes database can be accessed at https://websmp102.sap-ag.de/notes.
- SAP technical support messages can be accessed at https://websmp102.sap-ag.de/message.
- SAP network connection maintenance requests for customer systems can be accessed at URL https://websmp102.sap-ag.de/serviceconnection.
- SAP Download Manager software and install instructions can be accessed at https://websmp106.sap-ag.de/~sapidb/002006825000000233132001.
- SAP developer keys and access keys can be obtained at http://service.sap.com/sscr.

Additional Resources

- **SAP Service Marketplace list of links** https://websmp205.sap-ag.de/quicklinks
- **SAP glossary link** http://help.sap.com/saphelp_glossary/en/index.htm

PART

Database Management in SAP

CHAPTER

Database Installation and Configuration

In this section we will cover different aspects of database management in SAP systems. Several relational database management systems are fully supported by SAP applications, and in this chapter we will use Oracle Database as an example to cover the database management concepts and tools provided by SAP to support the application install and maintenance. We will cover Oracle Database architecture and internals, database installation and configuration, and database patch application. In subsequent chapters we will cover the SAP BRTOOLS for administering the Oracle Database and database backup and restore concepts, tools, and procedures.

Oracle Database Internal Architecture

Oracle Database internals consist of two main components: the database and the Oracle instance. The database is the static part of the Oracle system, and the Oracle instance is the memory structures and the Oracle background processes that are started when the database is started. The Oracle Database internal architecture is shown in Figure 19-1.

Database

The Oracle Database includes all the files that constitute the dataset. This includes the datafiles, control files, online redo log files, and offline archive log files. When an Oracle system is started, the database files are associated with the Oracle instance, and any operations the user performs are recorded in the appropriate files at the operating system level. The following definitions will clarify the different files that constitute the Oracle Database.

Tablespaces

Oracle manages data in logical units referred to as tablespaces. A logical tablespace consists of one or several physical files referred to as datafiles. When a new database object, such as a table or an index, is created this occurs in an assigned tablespace. When the tablespace is

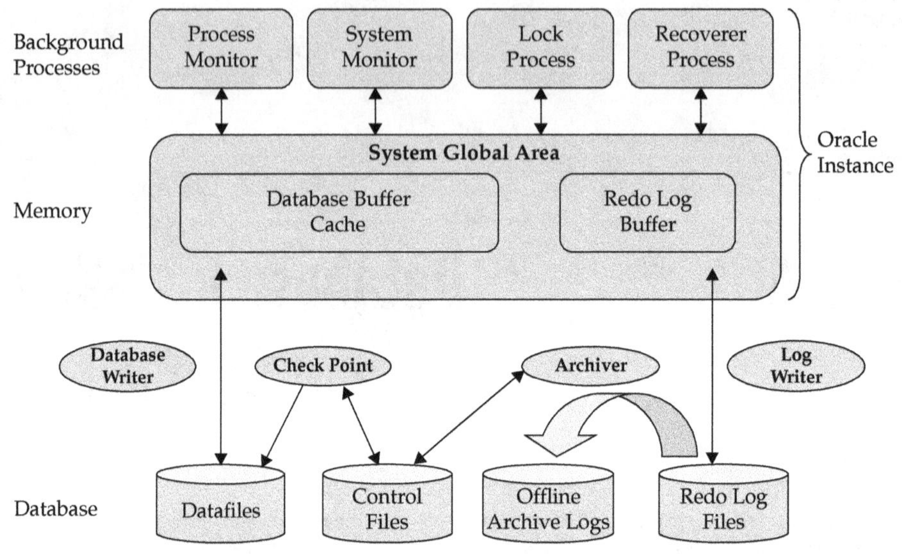

FIGURE 19-1 Oracle Database internal architecture

running out of space, it can be extended by adding datafiles. SAP follows specific naming conventions for the tablespaces.

Datafiles

Datafiles are actual physical files at the operating system level with set naming conventions to which the data is saved by database operations. Datafiles can be added to the tablespace as long as the mount point has space allocated and is available for such growth. In real-life production SAP systems, there will be tens and hundreds of datafiles depending upon the database growth of a given business operation.

Control Files

A control file has the list of physical datafiles and the paths where such files are located. When an Oracle instance is started, the system reads the control file to open the datafiles and redo log files and make it available for general database operations. Since the control file is such an important file, usually more than one copy exists at different locations at the operating system level.

Redo Log Files

When data is changed in the Oracle system, it is not permanently written to the datafiles right away. The data changes are written to the redo log files. In case there is a power failure, for example, data is applied back from the redo logs at instance start. In this way any data loss is prevented. Modified data is not written on a synchronous manner permanently to the datafiles immediately because of performance reasons. Instead, the data is written to the datafiles from time to time.

Offline Archive Log Files

The online redo log files are automatically moved to an offline device when the Oracle database is configured to turn on the archive log mode. When needed, offline archive log files can be used to perform a database point-in-time recovery.

Instance

When an Oracle Database is started it will start the background processes and open the memory structures configured for the database, and this is referred to as an Oracle instance. The Oracle instance is associated with the physical static database files to manage the database operations.

Memory Structures

Memory structures such as the system global area (SGA) are opened at the Oracle instance start and are based on the configuration parameter information. Refer to Figure 19-1 while studying the structures described in the following sections.

System Global Area

The system global area is a shared memory region allocated to an Oracle instance based on the configuration parameters. The SGA has two primary subareas: the database buffer cache and the redo log buffer. The Oracle SQL command "show sga" displays the current configuration of the SGA in the Oracle Database. This information can be obtained by using the following commands after you log in to the system at the operating system level as ora<sid> user:

```
oradxl> sqlplus '/as sysdba'

SQL*Plus: Release 10.2.0.4.0 - Production on Tue Sep 21 00:54:33 2010
Copyright (c) 1982, 2007, Oracle.  All Rights Reserved.

Connected to:
Oracle Database 10g Enterprise Edition Release 10.2.0.4.0 - 64bit Production
With the Partitioning, OLAP, Data Mining and Real Application Testing options

SQL> show sga

Total System Global Area 7962544640 bytes
Fixed Size                  2094544 bytes
Variable Size            3707767344 bytes
Database Buffers         4238002688 bytes
Redo Buffers               14680064 bytes
```

Database Buffer Cache The database buffer cache is a set of database buffers that keep the modified and unmodified blocks of data in the memory area to facilitate faster access to it.

Redo Log Buffer The redo log buffer keeps a log of changes to the data in the memory area. The size of the redo log is static.

Background Processes

When an Oracle instance is started a set of Oracle processes are started in memory and run in the background. Background processes are like jobs that perform common tasks to manage the proper functioning of the Oracle instance. Several kinds of background jobs are started at the instance start and perform a specific job function. Some of the examples of background processes are process monitor, system monitor, and lock process.

Process Monitor (PMON) For every end-user process there is a 1:1 Oracle shadow process. PMON monitors the Oracle shadow process. If a user process crashes, PMON cleans up the orphaned Oracle shadow process and makes sure the data consistency is maintained.

System Monitor (SMON) SMON performs recovery functions at instance start, writing an alert log when an instance process fails and conducting cleanup of temporary segments when not required.

Lock Process This background process works as a lock manager monitor.

Recoverer (RECO) Recoverer manages the in-doubt distributed transactions in distributed databases.

Other Processes

There are other critical background processes that operate in an Oracle database. The most important of these are covered in the following sections.

Database Writer (DBWR) The DBWR writes the data from the database buffer cache to the data files.

Log Writer (LGWR) The LGWR writes the redo log buffer to redo log files on the disk.

Archiver (ARC0) The archiver process will automatically write the online redo logs to archive log files at an offline storage location (initially, this is the local disk). This process does this when the Oracle Database is configured to run with archive mode on.

Checkpoint (CKPT) The CKPT process writes all modified database cache buffers in SGA to the datafiles.

The following command at the operating system level shows the Oracle background processes:

```
oradx1> ps -ef | grep ora_

oradx1    1527    1  0 Aug30        00:00:26    ora_pmon_DX1
oradx1    1533    1 0 Aug30         00:08:20    ora_dbw0_DX1
oradx1    1535    1 0 Aug30         00:10:27    ora_lgwr_DX1
oradx1    1537    1 0 Aug30         00:02:50    ora_ckpt_DX1
oradx1    1539    1 0 Aug30         00:04:57    ora_smon_DX1
oradx1    1541    1 0 Aug30         00:00:00    ora_reco_DX1
oradx1    1594    1 0 Aug30         00:02:47    ora_arc0_DX1
```

SAP Application Dataflow in the Oracle Database

In SAP applications, end-user requests are processed by the Oracle database as follows:

1. The end user logs into the SAP system via the SAP front end and executes a business transaction.
2. The user request is executed by the SAP dialog work process.
3. The Oracle server detects the incoming call, accepts the call, and sets up a dedicated server process.
4. There is a one-to-one relationship between SAP work processes and Oracle server (shadow) processes.
5. The user runs the SQL statement and commits the transaction.
6. The server process looks into the shared pool of the Oracle Database for any reusable SQL.
7. If it finds a reusable SQL, then it verifies authorization.
8. If it does not find reusable SQL, then a new, shared SQL area is allocated and is parsed and processed.
9. The server process then retrieves data from the SGA or the datafile.
10. The Oracle server process modifies the data blocks in the SGA and, when efficient, the database writer writes the changes permanently to the data files.
11. The log writer records committed transactions to the online redo log files.
12. A reply is sent back to the user regarding the status of the transaction call (success or error).

Oracle Database Installation

In the context of installing a SAP system underlying Oracle Database software, install (binaries/executables install) is required. This can be done ahead of the time or it can be done during the course of the SAP installation. In this chapter we will cover Oracle installation as part of a SAP install process. However, installing Oracle Database software ahead of time will save time on the SAP install. Regardless of the option chosen, basic installation and patching of Oracle Database is the same. When Oracle Database software is installed, a starter database should not be created, because the SAP install process will create a database for the application and will load data into the tables.

The following figures and illustrations show how Oracle software is installed. During the course of the SAP installation, the sapinst program will stop as shown in Figure 19-2 and ask the administrator to perform the Oracle install.

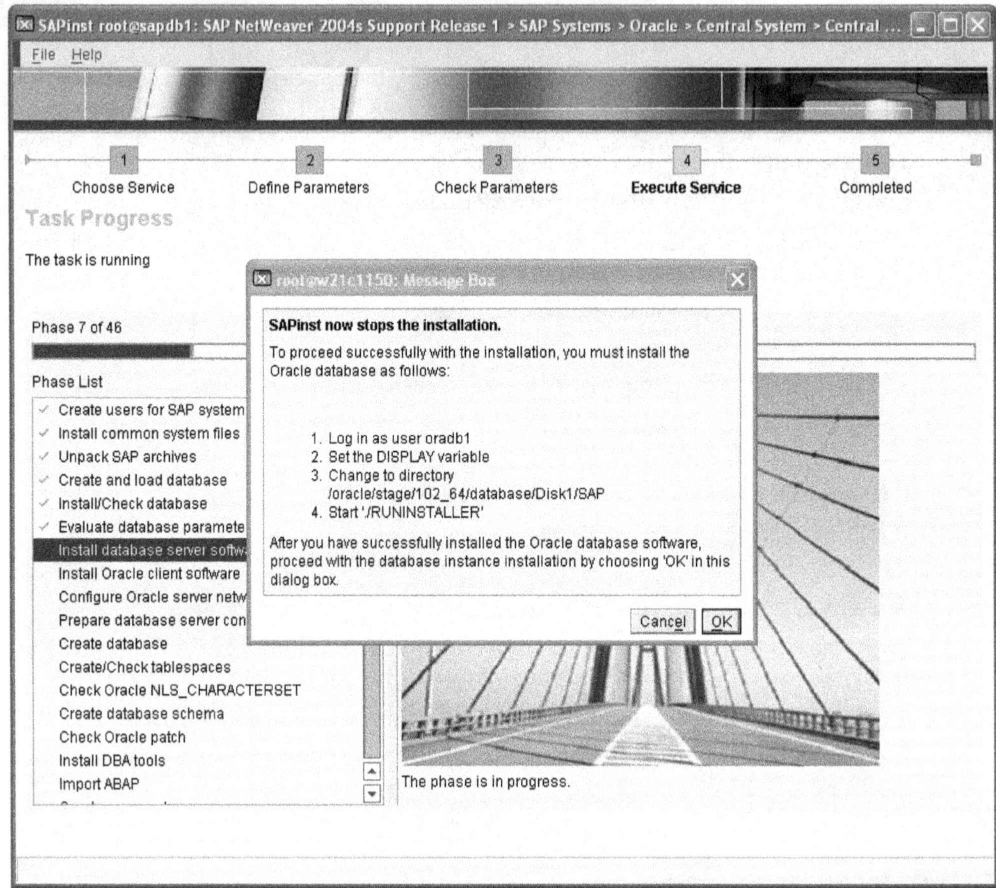

FIGURE 19-2 The SAPinst tool stops at the Oracle software installation step

When installing the Oracle software, the Oracle Universal Installer tool must be used. The following procedure should be followed before the Oracle Universal Installer tool is started.

1. Open another X term and set the DISPLAY variable for user ora<sid> (example: oradb1)

```
Setenv DISPLAY  <IP Address:0.0>
Setenv ORACLE_HOME  /oracle/DB1/102_64
Setenv ORACLE_SID  DB1

cd  to  /oracle/stage/102_64/database/SAP

./RUNINSTALLER
```

Figure 19-3 shows the initial screen of the Oracle Universal Installer.

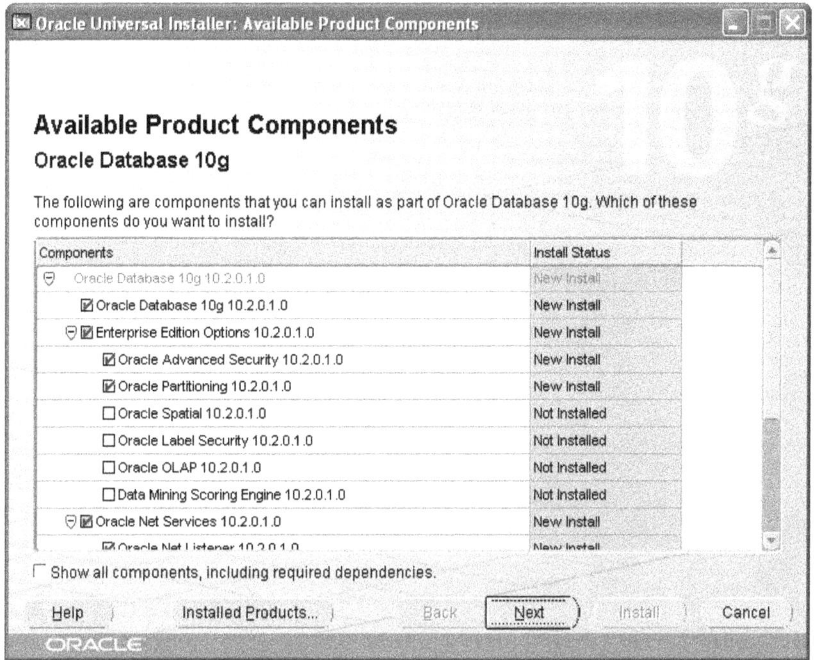

Copyright by SAP AG

FIGURE 19-3 Initial Oracle Universal Installer screen

2. Select the components as shown and then click the Next button to continue with the install. This will bring up the prerequisite check screen shown in Figure 19-4.
3. Verify the identified prerequisites, and click the Next button once these are met. This will display the summary screen shown in Figure 19-5.
4. Verify the summary screen and then click the Install button. This will start the Oracle software installation as shown in Figure 19-6 with a status indicator indicating the progress.

   After progressing through the different installation steps, the Oracle Universal Installer will stop at the screen shown in Figure 19-7 and ask the administrator to execute a script as root user.
5. As shown in Figure 19-7, open another terminal window, log in as root, and execute the root.sh script. The execution details of the root.sh script are as follows:

```
[sapdb1] /oracle/DB1/102_64 #./root.sh
Running Oracle10 root.sh script...
```

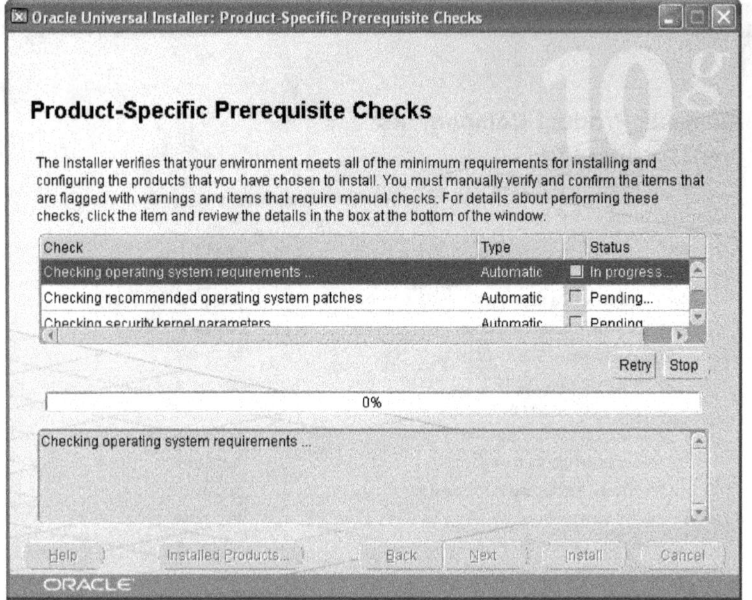

FIGURE 19-4 Oracle prerequisite checks

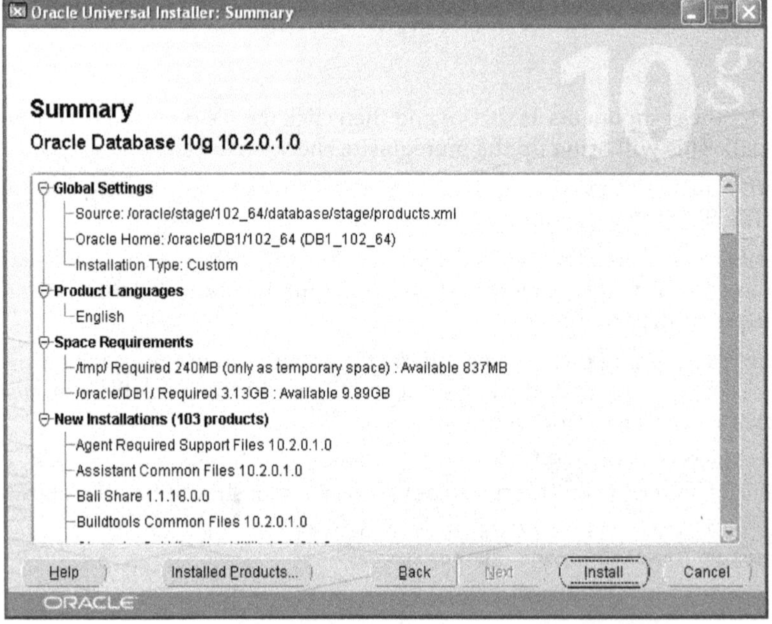

FIGURE 19-5 Oracle Universal Installer summary screen

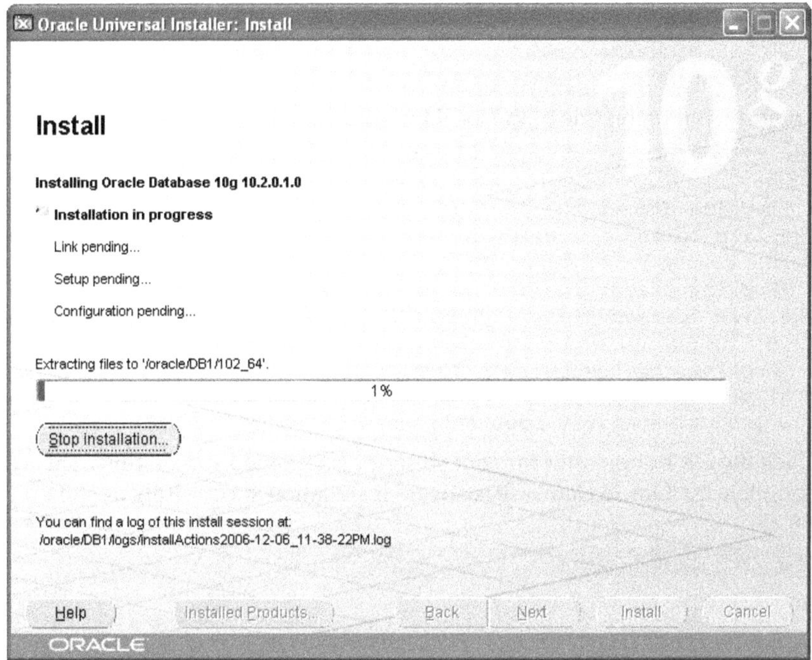

FIGURE 19-6 Oracle installation is in progress

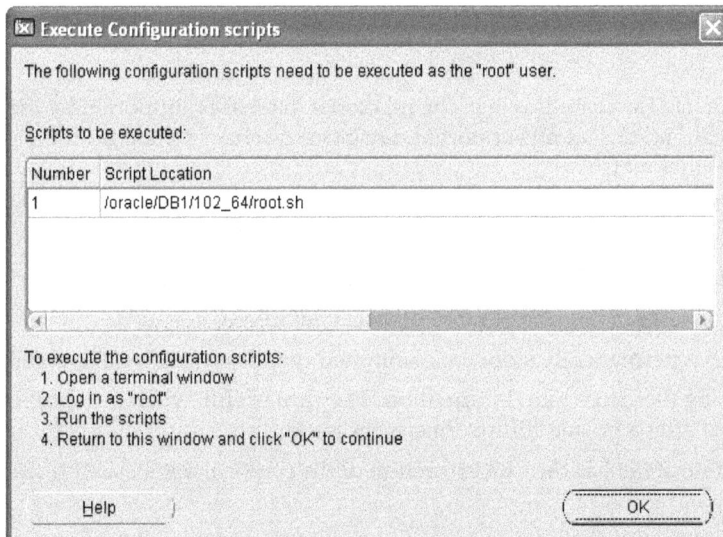

Execute Configuration scripts

The following configuration scripts need to be executed as the "root" user.

Scripts to be executed:

Number	Script Location
1	/oracle/DB1/102_64/root.sh

To execute the configuration scripts:
1. Open a terminal window
2. Log in as "root"
3. Run the scripts
4. Return to this window and click "OK" to continue

Help   OK

FIGURE 19-7 Oracle Universal Installer stopping for execution of root.sh script

The following environment variables are set as:

```
ORACLE_OWNER= oradb1
ORACLE_HOME=  /oracle/DB1/102_64
```

6. Enter the full pathname of the local bin directory: [/usr/local/bin]:

```
The file "dbhome" already exists in /usr/local/bin.  Overwrite it?
(y/n) [n]: y
   Copying dbhome to /usr/local/bin ...
The file "oraenv" already exists in /usr/local/bin.  Overwrite it?
(y/n) [n]: y
   Copying oraenv to /usr/local/bin ...
The file "coraenv" already exists in /usr/local/bin.  Overwrite it?
(y/n) [n]: y
   Copying coraenv to /usr/local/bin ...
Finished running generic part of root.sh script.
Now product-specific root actions will be performed.
```

7. Click the OK button after the root.sh script is executed successfully. This will complete the Oracle Database software installation successfully as shown.

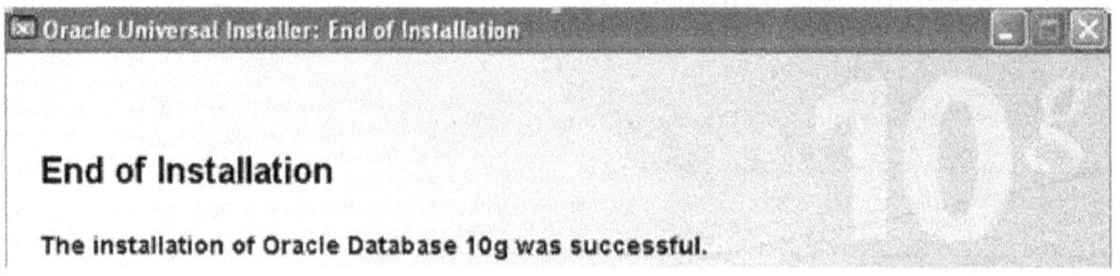

Oracle Universal Installer: End of Installation
End of Installation
The installation of Oracle Database 10g was successful.

Copyright by SAP AG

Summary

- The Oracle Database is one of the relational databases supported by the SAP application. A list of all supported databases can be obtained from the product availability matrix.
- The Oracle Database consists primarily of a passive database and an Oracle instance.
- The database consists of logical data units referred to as tablespaces.
- Each tablespace has one or more physical datafiles.
- Datafiles permanently store the committed data from database operations.
- Redo log files store redo information. They are useful when instance recovery is needed after a power failure or network issue.
- The control file has the exact structure of the physical database. It is read at instance start.

- The Oracle instance consists of the memory structures and background processes.
- Memory structures include a system global area (SGA) consisting of the database buffer cache and redo log buffers.
- The database writer writes the modified data from the database buffer cache to data files.
- The log writer writes the redo log buffers to the online redo log files on disk.
- The archiver process writes the online redo logs to offline archive log files.
- Oracle software installation is recommended to be performed ahead of SAP installation. However, Oracle software installation can also be performed during the course of the SAP installation.
- Oracle Universal Installer (OUI) is used to perform the installation. It can be used to perform the Oracle patch application as well.

Additional Resources

- **SAP on Oracle at SDN** www.sdn.sap.com/irj/sdn/ora?language=en
- **SAP online help administration guide for Oracle** http://help.sap.com/saphelp_nwpi71/helpdata/en/0b/5daf09b03344ad97338f838e09b9ee/frameset.htm

CHAPTER

Database Configuration and Administration Using SAP BRTOOLS

SAP uses a set of naming conventions for different database components, such as tablespaces, datafiles, and Oracle Database–related file systems. SAPinst also sets environmental variables, creates operating system and database user accounts, and creates configuration files as a part of the standard SAP installation. It is important to stick to the standard SAP naming conventions, as proper functioning of BRTOOLS will depend on such usage. The first half of this chapter will discuss the naming conventions, operating system (OS) and database user accounts, configuration files used by Oracle in SAP environments, and work process login and password control mechanisms, and the second half of the chapter will discuss the Oracle Database administration activities using BRTOOLS.

Naming Conventions for Tablespaces

The SAP default installation uses the classic Oracle Database tablespace naming conventions to separate the data and index tablespaces in older versions. With the advances in hard disk and memory technologies, these classic conventions have been changed as of SAP Web AS 6.10. Table 20-1 lists the tablespace naming conventions and a brief description of the purpose of the tablespace. In the new naming conventions, the entire SAP ABAP stack is in one tablespace PSAP<SCHEMA-ID> for ABAP systems and PSAP<SCHEMA-ID>DB for Java systems. New features in Oracle Database, such as system managed automatic segment space management, UNDO tablespaces, locally managed SYSTEM tablespace, and default temporary tablespaces, use the new tablespace format by default. Tablespaces SYSTEM, PSAPUNDO, and PSAPTEMP are locally managed upon creating, but with uniform extent size.

Tablespace Name	Description
SYSTEM	Oracle Dictionary tablespace
SYSAUX	Additional system-related tables and indexes
PSAPUNDO or PSAPROLL	Tablespace for undo or rollback segments
PSAPTEMP	Tablespace for database sort operations
PSAP<SCHEMA-ID Example: PSAPBIW	Tablespace for ALL SAP ABAP stack objects
PSAP<SCHEMA-ID>USR Example: PSAPBIWUSR	Tablespace for all customer objects
PSAP<SCHEMA-ID><REL> Example: PSAPBIW701	Tablespace for release-dependent data
PSAP<SCHEMA-ID>DB Example: PSAPBIWDB	Tablespace for ALL SAP Java stack objects

TABLE 20-1 Tablespace Naming Conventions

Naming Conventions for Datafiles

Datafiles are created under the subdirectory with the same name as the tablespace name, without the PSAP prefix and appended by an underscore and the <n>th datafile of the tablespace. Under the subdirectory, individual datafile naming conventions include the name of the tablespace without the PSAP prefix and with the extension .data<n>. Table 20-2 lists the tablespace names and the datafile naming conventions for SAP systems with SCHEMA ID DB1.

Naming Conventions for Redo Log Files

Redo log files are created at the time of the installation in the form of groups. Four redo log groups are created, each with a set of two redo log files. As shown in Table 20-3, the odd-numbered redo log files are grouped under origlogA and mirrlogA file systems, and even-numbered redo log files are grouped under origlogB and mirrlogB file systems.

SAP Tables and Their Relationship with Oracle Tablespaces

When a new SAP table is created, the logical storage parameters data class and size category are set in the technical settings of the table (transaction SE13).

Tablespace Name	Oracle Directory and Datafile Naming Conventions
SYSTEM	system_1/system.data1 system_2/system.data2 ... system_n/system.datan
SYSAUX	sysaux_1/sysaux.data1 sysaux_2/sysaux.data2 ... sysaux_n/sysaux.datan
PSAPUNDO or PSAPROLL	undo_1/undo.data1 undo_2/undo.data2 ... undo_n/undo.datan
PSAPTEMP	temp_1/temp.data1 temp_2/temp.data2 ... temp_n/temp.datan
PSAPDB1	db1_1/sapdb1.data1 db1_2/sapdb1.data2 ... db1_n/sapdb1.datan
PSAPDB1USR	db1usr_1/sapdb1usr.data1 db1usr_2/sapdb1usr.data2 ... db1usr_n/sapdb1usr.datan
PSAPDB1701	db1701_1/sapdb1701.data1 db1701_2/sapdb1701.data2 ... db1701_n/sapdb1701.datan
PSAPDB1DB	db1db_1/sapdb1db.data1 db1db_2/sapdb1db.data2 ... db1db_n/sapdb1db.datan

TABLE 20-2 Datafile Naming Conventions

Redo Log Groups	Redo Log Files
Group 1	/oracle/<SID>/origlogA/log_g11m1.dbf /oracle/<SID>/mirrlogA/log_g11m2.dbf
Group 2	/oracle/<SID>/origlogB/log_g12m1.dbf /oracle/<SID>/mirrlogB/log_g12m2.dbf
Group 3	/oracle/<SID>/origlogA/log_g13m1.dbf /oracle/<SID>/mirrlogA/log_g13m2.dbf
Group 4	/oracle/<SID>/origlogB/log_g14m1.dbf /oracle/<SID>/mirrlogB/log_g14m2.dbf

TABLE 20-3 Redo Log File Naming Conventions

Data Class	Description
APPLO	Master Data
APPL1	Transaction Data
APPL2	Organizing and Customizing Data

TABLE 20-4 Data Class Category

Data Class

The data class logically defines the tablespace where the newly created table will be stored. The data class is assigned to the data tablespace using the TAORA table and index tablespace using the table IAORA. With the new tablespace layout there is no separation of data and index tablespaces. Table 20-4 lists the main data classes and a brief description.

Size Category

The size category specifies the number of data records that are expected for this table. The range is from zero to nine. Table 20-5 lists the size categories with the expected number of data records.

Environmental Variables

Oracle environmental variables are initially set at the time of the installation. Operating system accounts <sid>adm and ora<sid> use the environmental variables to perform different SAP and database-related activities, such as starting up and shutting down the systems and administering the Oracle Database using BRTOOLS. Table 20-6 lists the key environmental variables and their purpose in SAP systems. OSS Note 830578 provides a complete list of environmental variables with their intended purpose.

Size Category	Expected Number of Data Records
0	0–1,100
1	1,100–4,700
2	4,700–19,000
3	19,000–76,000
4	76,000–300,000
5	300,000–610,000
6	610,000–1,200,000
7	1,200,000–2,400,000
8	2,400,000–4,800,000
9	4,800,000–190,000,000

TABLE 20-5 SAP Table Size Category

Environmental Variable	Variable Purpose/Description
ORACLE_SID	This is the system ID of the database. Example: DB1
ORACLE_HOME	This is the location of the Oracle software. Example: /oracle/DB1/102_64
SAPDATA_HOME	This is the directory for Oracle datafiles. BRTOOLS uses this environmental variable to administer the Oracle Database. Example: /oracle/DB1

Table 20-6 Key Oracle Environmental Variables

Oracle File System

During SAP installation, the Oracle Database instance is created and the data is loaded into the newly created database. Table 20-7 provides the Oracle file system used in SAP installations with a brief description of each. When troubleshooting an Oracle Database, a key file called

File System Name	Description
/oracle/<DBSID>	Oracle home directory for OS user ora<sid>
/oracle/<DBSID>/origlogA	Online redo log file (Original log A)
/oracle/<DBSID>/origlogB	Online redo log file (Original log B)
/oracle/<DBSID>/mirrlogA	Online redo log file (Mirror log A)
/oracle/<DBSID>/mirrlogB	Online redo log file (Mirror log B)
/oracle/<DBSID>/oraarch	Offline archive log files
/oracle/<DBSID>/sapreorg	BRSPACE logs are written in this location.
/oracle/<DBSID>/sapdata1 /oracle/<DBSID>/sapdata2 /oracle/<DBSID>/sapdata3 /oracle/<DBSID>/sapdata4 ...sapdatan	Datafiles are located in these directories.
/oracle/<DBSID>/saparch	BRARCHIVE logs are written in this directory.
/oracle/<DBSID>/saptrace	This has two subdirectories: /background and /usertrace. The /background subdirectory has an important Oracle alert file called alert<SID>.log. This file writes a detailed log of Oracle Database activities and should be checked if there are any issues with the database. The /usertrace subdirectory writes trace files for server processes.
/oracle/<DBSID>/sapbackup	BRBACKUP, BRRESTORE, and BRRECOVER logs are written in this directory.

Table 20-7 Oracle File System

File System	Description
/usr/sap/trans	This is the global transport directory.
/sapmnt/<SID>	This directory holds the system-wide files, such as executables, profiles, and global files.
/usr/sap/<SID>	This directory holds the instance-specific files for each dialog instance.

Table 20-8 SAP File System

alert<SID>.log is written to the location /oracle/<DBSID>/saptrace/background. This file has detailed Oracle Database information and can oftentimes help you to pinpoint the underlying problem.

SAP File System

During SAP installation, the SAP kernel is extracted and system profile files are written out at the operating system level. Table 20-8 lists the SAP file system that is created as part of a standard SAP install along with a brief description. The global transport directory is generally customized as /usr/sap/trans<SID> and is mounted on all the systems belonging to the same transport group so that the data and cofiles are available for import into any of the target systems.

Users and Groups in Operating Systems

The SAP installation will create two main users for the operation of the Oracle Database and the SAP system. Table 20-9 lists the two operating system–level user accounts with the correct group. The <SID>adm account must be used to start up and shut down SAP systems. The ora<SID> account must be used for any Oracle Database operation.

Database Users Created by Default SAP Install

During the standard SAP installation a number of database user accounts are created. Table 20-10 lists the accounts along with a brief description of each.

OS User	OS Group
<SID>adm	sapsys, oper, dba, and sapinst
ora<SID>	dba, oper, and sapinst

Table 20-9 Operating System Users

Database User Name	Description
SAP<SCHEMA-ID>	This account owns all ABAP application tables.
SAP<SCHEMA-ID>DB	This account owns all Java application tables.
OPS$ORA<SID>	This is a database administrator account. This account is granted the SAPDBA role.
OPS$<SID>ADM	This is an application administrator account and is the owner of the SAPUSER table. This account is granted the SAPDBA role.

TABLE 20-10 Database Users

SAP Schema ID and Password Control

In SAP systems, the work process connection to the underlying Oracle Database and the schema ID login mechanism is a two-step process. This method is used to protect the password of the SAP<SCHEMA-ID> in an encrypted form and retrieve it from the SAPUSER table while the work process is started. The two-step schema ID and password control mechanism is explained here for a hypothetical SAP system with DV1 as the SID and SAPBIW as the schema name.

1. The SAP work process logs in as OPS$-user account and retrieves the SAP<SCHEMA-ID> password from the SAPUSER table and disconnects.

```
Calling db_connect...
Logon as OPS$-user to get SAPBIW's password
Connecting as /@DV1 on connection 0
Attaching to DB Server DV1
Starting user session
Now '/@DV1' is connected
Got SAPBIW's password from OPS$-user
Disconnecting from connection 0...
Closing user session
Now I'm disconnected from ORACLE
```

2. The SAP work process now uses the retrieved password and logs in with the SAP<SCHEMA-ID>.

```
Connecting as SAPBIW/<pwd>@DV1 on connection 0
Starting user session
Now 'SAPBIW/<pwd>@DV1' is connected
Database NLS settings: AMERICAN_AMERICA.UTF8
DB instance DV1 is running on venus with ORACLE version 10.2.0.4.0
since NOV 07, 2010, 07:06:19
Connection 0 opened (DBSL handle 0)
db_connect o.k.
```

Configuration File Name	File Location	Description
init<SID>.ora	$ORACLE_HOME/dbs	Initialization parameter file for Oracle
init<SID>.sap	$ORACLE_HOME/dbs	SAP BRTOOLS parameter file
init<SID>.utl	$ORACLE_HOME/dbs	Third-party backup tool parameter file. Examples: Netbackup and IBM Tivoli Data Protector
spfile<SID>.ora	$ORACLE_HOME/dbs	Oracle Binary parameter file
listener.ora	$ORACLE_HOME/network/admin	Listener configuration file
tnsnames.ora	$ORACLE_HOME/network/admin	Oracle client configuration file

TABLE 20-11 Key Configuration and Parameter Files

Configuration and Parameter Files

During SAP installation, a number of critical Oracle configuration files are created. Table 20-11 lists the important Oracle configuration files along with a brief description of each. The files can be further configured and customized as per customer-specific requirements.

SAP Database Administration Using BRTOOLS

SAP provides a number of tools to administer the underlying Oracle Database. The combined group of tools is referred to as BRTOOLS. SAP recommends the use of BRTOOLS for performing all database administration activities, as the tool is application-aware and has several built-in mechanisms to work in an integrated way with the SAP application.

SAP BRTOOLS

BRTOOLS is a group of tools that help the administrator perform a specific database administration activity. The tools are provided as a character-based interface and are invoked at the operating system level by user account ora<SID>. The following sections discuss the BRTOOLS that are helpful for performing different database activities.

BRSPACE

This is called from within the BRTOOLS menu to perform instance, space, and segment management of the Oracle Database for the SAP system. The BRSPACE quick command option is also available for experienced SAP Basis administrators. This is explained in more detail in subsequent sections of this chapter.

BRBACKUP

This is called from within the BRTOOLS menu to perform database backups.

BRRESTORE

This is called from within BRTOOLS to perform database restores.

BRCONNECT

This is called to perform database tasks such as running update statistics, checking database consistency, cleaning up old logs, and monitoring the database in background during backups.

BRARCHIVE

This is called to perform a backup of Oracle archive logs.

BRGUI

BRGUI is a Java-based GUI used to perform all the BRTOOL activities. BRGUI calls underlying BRTOOLS to perform different database activities.

BRSTUDIO

BRSTUDIO is a browser-based tool that provides all the BRTOOLS database capabilities.

Database Administration Tasks Using BRTOOLS

BRTOOLS is the main tool for performing different Oracle Database activities in the SAP systems. It can be started at the operating system level with user account ora<sid> by calling the command shown in the illustration. Once executed, it shows the initial character-based BRTOOLS menu with all eight major database administration submenus.

```
orakb2> brtools
BR0651I BRTOOLS 7.00 (42)

BR0280I BRTOOLS time stamp: 2010-11-29 12.38.57
BR0656I Choice menu 1 - please make a selection
-------------------------------------------------------------------------------
BR*Tools main menu

1 = Instance management
2 - Space management
3 - Segment management
4 - Backup and database copy
5 - Restore and recovery
6 - Check and verification
7 - Database statistics
8 - Additional functions
9 - Exit program

Standard keys: c - cont, b - back, s - stop, r - refr, h - help
-------------------------------------------------------------------------------
BR0662I Enter your choice:
```


You can access the submenus by entering your choice (1–8) and selecting C (for continue). The following illustrations show each of the BRTOOLS submenus with several database administration capabilities. Each of these capabilities can be executed by selecting the appropriate number and choosing the continue option. In the illustrations that follow, a parameter choice is provided. In most cases, the defaults can be used, but if needed, the parameters can be changed to execute a particular database administration function.

```
BR0280I BRTOOLS time stamp: 2010-11-29 12.40.10
BR0663I Your choice: '1'
BR0280I BRTOOLS time stamp: 2010-11-29 12.40.10
BR0656I Choice menu 3 - please make a selection
-------------------------------------------------------------------------------
Database instance management
1 = Start up database
2 - Shut down database
3 - Alter database instance
4 - Alter database parameters
5 - Recreate database
6 - Show instance status
7 - Show database parameters
8 - Show database owners
9 - Reset program status
Standard keys: c - cont, b - back, s - stop, r - refr, h - help
-------------------------------------------------------------------------------
BR0662I Enter your choice:
```



```
BR0280I BRTOOLS time stamp: 2010-11-29 12.40.56
BR0663I Your choice: '2'
BR0280I BRTOOLS time stamp: 2010-11-29 12.40.56
BR0656I Choice menu 5 - please make a selection
-------------------------------------------------------------------------------
Database space management
1 = Extend tablespace
2 - Create tablespace
3 - Drop tablespace
4 - Alter tablespace
5 - Alter data file
6 - Move data file
7 - Additional space functions
8 - Reset program status
Standard keys: c - cont, b - back, s - stop, r - refr, h - help
-------------------------------------------------------------------------------
BR0662I Enter your choice:
```

```
BR0663I Your choice: '3'
BR0280I BRTOOLS time stamp: 2010-11-29 12.41.34
BR0656I Choice menu 7 - please make a selection
------------------------------------------------------------------------------
Database segment management
 1 = Reorganize tables
 2 - Rebuild indexes
 3 - Export tables
 4 - Import tables
 5 - Alter tables
 6 - Alter indexes
 7 - Additional segment functions
 8 - Reset program status
Standard keys: c - cont, b - back, s - stop, r - refr, h - help
------------------------------------------------------------------------------
BR0662I Enter your choice:
```



```
BR0663I Your choice: '4'
BR0280I BRTOOLS time stamp: 2010-11-29 12.42.13
BR0656I Choice menu 9 - please make a selection
------------------------------------------------------------------------------
Backup and database copy
 1 = Database backup
 2 - Archivelog backup
 3 - Database copy
 4 - Non-database backup
 5 - Backup of database disk backup
 6 - Verification of database backup
 7 - Verification of archivelog backup
 8 - Additional functions
 9 - Reset program status
Standard keys: c - cont, b - back, s - stop, r - refr, h - help
------------------------------------------------------------------------------
BR0662I Enter your choice:
```



```
BR0663I Your choice: '5'
BR0280I BRTOOLS time stamp: 2010-11-29 12.43.10
BR0656I Choice menu 11 - please make a selection
------------------------------------------------------------------------------
Restore and recovery
 1 = Complete database recovery
 2 - Database point-in-time recovery
 3 - Tablespace point-in-time recovery
 4 - Whole database reset
 5 - Restore of individual backup files
 6 - Restore and application of archivelog files
 7 - Disaster recovery
 8 - Reset program status
Standard keys: c - cont, b - back, s - stop, r - refr, h - help
------------------------------------------------------------------------------
BR0662I Enter your choice:
```



```
BR0663I Your choice: '6'
BR0280I BRTOOLS time stamp: 2010-11-29 12.43.38
BR0656I Choice menu 12 - please make a selection
------------------------------------------------------------------------------
Database check and verification
 1 = Database system check
 2 - Validation of database structure
 3 - Verification of database blocks
 4 - Reset program status
Standard keys: c - cont, b - back, s - stop, r - refr, h - help
------------------------------------------------------------------------------
BR0662I Enter your choice:
```



```
BR0663I Your choice: '7'
BR0280I BRTOOLS time stamp: 2010-11-29 12.44.03
BR0656I Choice menu 13 - please make a selection
------------------------------------------------------------------------------
Processing database statistics
 1 = Update database statistics
 2 - Collect missing statistics
 3 - Delete harmful statistics
 4 - Manage database statistics
 5 - Collect dictionary statistics
 6 - Collect system statistics
 7 - Reset program status
Standard keys: c - cont, b - back, s - stop, r - refr, h - help
------------------------------------------------------------------------------
BR0662I Enter your choice:
```



```
BR0663I Your choice: '8'
BR0280I BRTOOLS time stamp: 2010-11-29 12.44.31
BR0656I Choice menu 2 - please make a selection
------------------------------------------------------------------------------
Additional BR*Tools functions
 1 = Show profiles and logs
 2 - Clean up DBA logs and tables
 3 - Adapt NEXT extents
 4 - Change password of database user
 5 - Create/change synonyms for DBA tables
 6 - Reset program status
Standard keys: c - cont, b - back, s - stop, r - refr, h - help
------------------------------------------------------------------------------
BR0662I Enter your choice:
```


Database Administration Tasks Using BRSPACE Quick Mode

For experienced SAP Basis administrators, the BRSPACE quick mode command options will bring up the BRTOOLS submenu options directly, which can expedite administration activities. Table 20-12 lists the BRSPACE quick commands for different database administration activities.

BRSPACE Function	BRSPACE Quick Command
Database Instance Management Menu	
Start Database	brspace -f dbstart
Shut Down Database	brspace -f dbshut
Alter Database Instance	brspace -f dbalter
Alter Database Parameters	brspace -f dbparam
Recreating a Database	brspace -f dbcreate
Display Instance status	brspace -f dbshow -c dbstate
Display Database parameters	brspace -f dbshow -c dbparam
Display Database Owners	brspace -f dbshow -c dbowner
Space Management Menu	
Extend Tablespace	brspace -f tsextend
Create Tablespace	brspace -f tscreate
Drop Tablespace	brspace -f tsdrop
Alter Tablespace	brspace -f tsalter
Alter Datafile	brspace -f dfalter
Move Datafile	brspace -f dfmove
Show Tablespaces	brspace -f dbshow -c tsinfo
Show Datafiles	brspace -f dbshow -c dfinfo
Show Redo Log Files	brspace -f dbshow -c rfinfo
Show Control Files	brspace -f dbshow -c cfinfo
Show Disk Volumes	brspace –f dbshow –c dvinfo
Segment Management Menu	
Reorganizing Tables	brspace -f tbreorg
Rebuilding Indexes	brspace -f idrebuild
Exporting Tables	brspace -f tbexport
Importing Tables	brspace -f tbimport
Alter Tables	brspace -f tbalter
Alter Indexes	brspace -f idalter
Show Tables	brspace -f dbshow -c tbinfo
Show Indexes	brspace -f dbshow -c idinfo
Show Table Partitions	brspace -f dbshow -c tpinfo
Show Index Partitions	brspace -f dbshow -c ipinfo

TABLE 20-12 BRSPACE Quick Command Checklist

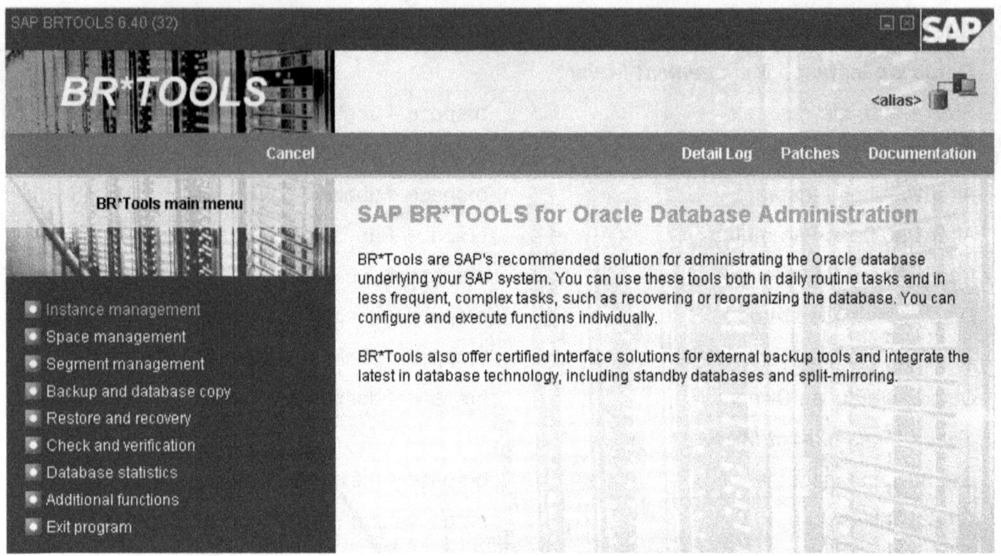

FIGURE 20-1 Initial BRGUI menu

Database Administration Tasks Using BRGUI

BRGUI provides a more user-friendly graphical user interface, and can be used to effectively administer a database. Figure 20-1 shows the initial menu option for BRGUI. This list is the same one that would be displayed when calling BRTOOLS. The BRGUI list will call the underlying BRTOOLS to execute a given database function.

Administering the Oracle Database Using SQL

Certain Oracle Database activities can be safely performed at the SQL level. One of these is switching the archive log mode. The following sections provide the commands used to toggle Oracle archiving modes in a SAP system.

Turning the Oracle Archive Log Mode ON

```
SQL> shutdown immediate
Database closed.
Database dismounted.
ORACLE instance shut down.
SQL> startup mount
ORACLE instance started.

Total System Global Area  272629760 bytes
Fixed Size                   788472 bytes
Variable Size             103806984 bytes
Database Buffers          167772160 bytes
Redo Buffers                 262144 bytes
```

```
Database mounted.
SQL> alter database archivelog;
Database altered.
SQL> alter database open;
Database altered.
```

Turning the Oracle Archive Log Mode OFF

```
SQL> shutdown immediate
Database closed.
Database dismounted.
ORACLE instance shut down.
SQL> startup mount
ORACLE instance started.

Total System Global Area  272629760 bytes
Fixed Size                   788472 bytes
Variable Size             103806984 bytes
Database Buffers          167772160 bytes
Redo Buffers                 262144 bytes
Database mounted.
SQL> alter database noarchivelog;
Database altered.
SQL> alter database open;
Database altered.
```

Summary

- Naming conventions and standards are very important for the database system tablespace names and file systems for the Oracle Database.
- BRTOOLS should be used to administer Oracle Databases in SAP systems.
- SQL commands can also be used to perform certain database activities.

Additional Resources

- **SAP Oracle Database tablespace naming conventions** http://help.sap.com/saphelp_nw70ehp1/helpdata/en/9f/4a56b2185851468b39b719daa2d3aa/content.htm
- **SAP BRTOOLS link** http://help.sap.com/saphelp_nw04/helpdata/en/0c/cd271365debc42bef96ac7fd907787/content.htm

CHAPTER

Database Backup and Restore

In this chapter we will discuss the significance of properly backing up the business data and restoring the data in the event of data loss or in case of a disaster in the data center. Topics such as significance of business data, development of a good organizational SAP database backup strategy, and the different backup and restore options that are available to the SAP Basis administrator are discussed. Emphasis is given on explaining the backup and restore concepts and tools first, followed by a real-life example of a detailed backup and restore scenario. This will help the Basis administrator develop his or her own organization's backup strategy and perform backups and restores as needed.

Significance of Business Data

Generally, SAP systems are categorized as mission-critical systems because they are used for performing online financial transactions and are the system of record for organizations. Depending on the business processes implemented at a given organization, these systems also perform critical business transactions involving manufacturing, sales, human resources and billing. When these systems are down for any length of time, it usually causes significant monetary losses to organizations and, therefore, protecting the systems against any data loss is of paramount importance. Brokerage firms, credit card companies, and online retail organizations are particularly impacted monetarily by any system downtime and business data loss to the tune of several million dollars in some instances. Thus, it is critical that the SAP Basis administrator work closely with the organization's Oracle Database administrator to develop a sound backup strategy and test it on a quarterly basis. This will ensure that if there is a situation where a system restore is needed this can be executed in as little time as possible without any business data loss to the organization.

Developing a Backup Strategy

The main factors that need to be taken into consideration before developing a sound backup strategy is to decide on the backup type and the tape cycle or backup cycle that will be used. The backup types and the tape cycle will depend on the size of the database, cost, and availability requirements of the SAP system to the organization.

Backup Types

The backup types are primarily online or offline categories, with each category having three subcategories (complete, incremental, and partial backups). The complete backup is further categorized into full and whole (all) backups. With the increased demands of availability of the business applications, most organizations look for an online backup to meet the requirements. Table 21-1 lists all the backup types and provides a brief description of each.

RMAN Integration with SAP Backup Tools

Oracle Recovery Manager (RMAN) is integrated with SAP BRBACKUP and BRARCHIVE tools and can be used to perform the backups. RMAN classifies the full backup as a level 0 backup and subsequent incremental backups as level 1 backups. If RMAN is used for the backups, BRRECOVER identifies this and applies the changes accordingly. If BRRECOVER

Backup Type	Description
Online backup	Database is open and operational with business transactions getting executed. Data changes are recorded in redo log files. Restore will include application of the log files followed by recovery of the database to get to the time stamp of the system at the end of the backup.
Offline backup	Database is shut down before the backup. Restoring the backup is sufficient to open the database to users.
Complete backup	Whole/All: All data without the catalog information is backed up. Other than this, there is no difference between the two backups. Full: All data and catalog information is backed up. The catalog information is needed to make any subsequent incremental backups.
Incremental backup	This is based on the catalog information of the full backup. An incremental backup will back up only the data blocks that have been changed since the last full backup. A restore will entail the application of the data files from the full backup followed by the application of the incremental backups. Incremental backups are *cumulative,* meaning in order to restore, you apply the full backup plus the last incremental backup. Incremental backups should be used to reduce the backup time where throughput of the backup infrastructure is low. This will help to make a backup of the system in less time.
Partial backup	The database is backed up in smaller units, such as individual datafiles. Partial backups are done when the time for a complete backup is very long. This is generally not a recommended approach, as recovery will be very time-consuming and there is lot of risk of missing online or offline archive log files. This backup method should never be implemented for production systems. The recovery process is also very time-consuming.

Table 21-1 Backup Types

has any issues, the RMAN tool can be used to perform the database recovery directly. The key advantage of using RMAN is that it will check for any Oracle block corruptions and therefore ensures the integrity of the backup. For backing up very large databases, a combination of RMAN and parallel backup of data and log files to several tapes is supported by SAP. This will cut down both the backup and recovery time of very large databases.

Backup Cycle (Tape Cycle)

A backup cycle or a tape cycle refers to the number of tapes that will be used for the backups and the cycle that will be used to reuse the tapes.

Backup Strategy

The following backup cycle strategy is recommended and is a best practice that can be used by SAP implementations:

- A 28-day tape cycle with a backup cycle of four weeks
- Complete online backup every day
- Complete offline backup once every 28-day cycle
- Backup of offline redo log files on ongoing basis
- Schedule backup verification (db verify) once weekly

Backup and Restore Tools

SAP provides BRTOOLS for performing backups and restores. BRTOOLS was explained in detail in the last chapter. In this chapter, the BRTOOLS will be covered that are specific to backup and restore/recovery activities.

BRBACKUP

The BRBACKUP tool helps the Basis administrator perform a backup of the SAP system. The tool can be called manually, or the backup job can be scheduled. One detailed real-life backup configuration and execution will be covered in this chapter. Based on this, you can plan and execute your own backups for your organization.

BRARCHIVE

The BRARCHIVE tool helps to back up the offline archive log files to either a disk or a tape.

BRRESTORE

The BRRESTORE tool helps to restore a database in the event of user error or a disaster.

BRRECOVER

The BRRECOVER tool calls BRRESTORE to restore the data and log files and then performs the recovery steps to get the database to a consistent status. One detailed real-life BRRESTORE and BRRECOVERY scenario will be covered in this chapter. Based on this, you can plan and execute a recovery when needed at your organization.

BRBACKUP Configuration

Before using the BRBACKUP tool, some basic configuration has to be performed. This is done in the initialization parameter file for BRTOOLS called init<SID>.sap. You can find the file in the /oracle/<SID>/102_64/dbs directory. For example, in a SAP system with SID KB2, the initialization parameter file initKB2.sap for BRTOOLS is located at /oracle/KB2/102_64/dbs. Figure 21-1 shows an example of the initialization file for BRTOOLS (initKB2_weekly.sap) that is configured for a weekly full, online backup to disk with the backups written to /oracle/KB2/sapbackup/weekly. You can change the parameter values to meet your requirements. When a new SAP system is installed, a sample parameter file is delivered, along with different parameters and detailed options. This file can be customized to meet the customer's specific requirements.

BRBACKUP to the Disk

When a new SAP system is installed, you have an immediate need to take a complete offline backup to save your installation, post-installation, and any additional configuration work that has been done. In the initial stages, the backups may have to be performed manually using BRTOOLS. Once the environment stabilizes the backups may be integrated with a third-party enterprise scheduling tool such as Autosys or Control-M. The following procedure will explain in detail how to take a complete offline backup manually using BRBACKUP. First, configure the basic BRBACKUP initialization parameter file as explained earlier. In this file

```
orakb2> more initKB2_weekly.sap

backup_mode = full
restore_mode = full
backup_type = online_cons
backup_dev_type = disk
# default: tape
backup_root_dir = /oracle/KB2/sapbackup/weekly
compress = yes
archive_function = save_delete
archive_copy_dir = /oracle/KB2/sapbackup/archive
tape_size = 100G
tape_address = /dev/nst0

volume_archive = (KB2A01, KB2A02, KB2A03, KB2A04, KB2A05,
         KB2A06, KB2A07, KB2A08, KB2A09, KB2A10,
         KB2A11, KB2A12, KB2A13, KB2A14, KB2A15,
         KB2A16, KB2A17, KB2A18, KB2A19, KB2A20,
         KB2A21, KB2A22, KB2A23, KB2A24, KB2A25,
         KB2A26, KB2A27, KB2A28, KB2A29, KB2A30)

volume_backup = (KB2B01, KB2B02, KB2B03, KB2B04, KB2B05,
         KB2B06, KB2B07, KB2B08, KB2B09, KB2B10,
         KB2B11, KB2B12, KB2B13, KB2B14, KB2B15,
         KB2B16, KB2B17, KB2B18, KB2B19, KB2B20,
         KB2B21, KB2B22, KB2B23, KB2B24, KB2B25,
         KB2B26, KB2B27, KB2B28, KB2B29, KB2B30)
```


FIGURE 21-1 BRBACKUP sample configuration file init<SID>.sap

```
orakb2> brtools
BR0656I Choice menu 1 - please make a selection
------------------------------------------------------------------------------
BR*Tools main menu
 1 = Instance management
 2 - Space management
 3 - Segment management
 4 - Backup and database copy
 5 - Restore and recovery
 6 - Check and verification
 7 - Database statistics
 8 - Additional functions
 9 - Exit program
Standard keys: c - cont, b - back, s - stop, r - refr, h - help
------------------------------------------------------------------------------
BR0662I Enter your choice:
4
```


FIGURE 21-2 Initial BRTOOLS menu

change the parameter backup_type to offline_force. Once this is done, the system is ready for a complete offline backup. Regardless of how the BRBACKUP job is scheduled, similar steps are executed and the datafiles, log files, control files, and parameter files are backed up.

Log in to the system as ora<SID> account, and execute the command brtools as shown in Figure 21-2. The initial BRTOOLS menu will appear. Choose option 4 (Backup And Database Copy) and press ENTER to go to the next screen.

From the Backup And Database Copy menu choose option 1, as shown in Figure 21-3. In the next screen, the backup mode can be changed from online to offline_force.

As shown in Figure 21-4, choose option 6 and press ENTER. This will help to change the backup type parameter from online to offline_force.

```
BR0681I Enter string value for "type"
```

```
BR0280I BRTOOLS time stamp: 2010-06-22 09.47.18
BR0656I Choice menu 9 - please make a selection
------------------------------------------------------------------------------
Backup and database copy

 1 = Database backup
 2 - Archivelog backup
 3 - Database copy
 4 - Non-database backup
 5 - Backup of database disk backup
 6 - Verification of database backup
 7 - Verification of archivelog backup
 8 - Additional functions
 9 - Reset program status
Standard keys: c - cont, b - back, s - stop, r - refr, h - help
------------------------------------------------------------------------------
BR0662I Enter your choice:
1
```


FIGURE 21-3 Backup And Database Copy menu

```
BR0280I BRTOOLS time stamp: 2010-06-22 09.47.59
BR0657I Input menu 15 - please enter/check input values
-------------------------------------------------------------------------------
BRBACKUP main options for backup and database copy

 1 - BRBACKUP profile (profile) ....... [initKB2.sap]
 2 - Backup device type (device) ...... [disk]
 3 # Tape volumes for backup (volume) . []
 4 # BACKINT/Mount profile (parfile) .. []
 5 - Database user/password (user) .... [/]
 6 - Backup type (type) ............... [online]
 7 # Disk backup for backup (backup) .. [no]
 8 # Delete disk backup (delete) ...... [no]
 9 ~ Files for backup (mode) .......... [full]

Standard keys: c - cont, b - back, s - stop, r - refr, h - help
-------------------------------------------------------------------------------
BR0662I Enter your choice:
6
```

Copyright by SAP AG

FIGURE 21-4 BRBACKUP menu for changing the backup type

Enter the parameter value offline_force in the new value for type field and press ENTER. This will take the new parameter value shown in Figure 21-5.

```
 (offline|offline_force|offline_standby|offline_split|offline_
mirror|offline_stop|
online|online_cons|online_split|online_mirror|online_standby|offstby_split|
offstby_mirror) [online]:offline_force
BR0280I BRTOOLS time stamp: 2010-06-22 09.48.16
BR0683I New value for "type": 'offline_force'
```

```
BR0280I BRTOOLS time stamp: 2010-06-22 09.48.16
BR0657I Input menu 15 - please enter/check input values
-------------------------------------------------------------------------------
BRBACKUP main options for backup and database copy

 1 - BRBACKUP profile (profile) ....... [initKB2.sap]
 2 - Backup device type (device) ...... [disk]
 3 # Tape volumes for backup (volume) . []
 4 # BACKINT/Mount profile (parfile) .. []
 5 - Database user/password (user) .... [/]
 6 - Backup type (type) ............... [offline_force]
 7 # Disk backup for backup (backup) .. [no]
 8 # Delete disk backup (delete) ...... [no]
 9 ~ Files for backup (mode) .......... [full]

Standard keys: c - cont, b - back, s - stop, r - refr, h - help
-------------------------------------------------------------------------------
BR0662I Enter your choice:
c
```

Copyright by SAP AG

FIGURE 21-5 BRBACKUP menu to change backup type to offline_force

```
BR0280I BRTOOLS time stamp: 2010-06-22 09.48.42
BR0657I Input menu 16 - please enter/check input values
-------------------------------------------------------------------------------
Additional BRBACKUP options for backup and database copy
 1 - Confirmation mode (confirm) ....... [yes]
 2 - Query mode (query) ................ [no]
 3 - Compression mode (compress) ....... [yes]
 4 - Verification mode (verify) ........ [no]
 5 - Fill-up previous backups (fillup) . [no]
 6 - Parallel execution (execute) ...... [0]
 7 - Additional output (output) ........ [no]
 8 - Message language (language) ....... [E]
 9 - BRBACKUP command line (command) ... [-p initKB2.sap -d disk -t offline_force -m
full -k yes -e 0 -l E]

BR0662I Enter your choice:
1
```

Copyright by SAP AG

Figure 21-6 BRBACKUP menu option to change the confirmation mode

Click C to continue with the parameter selection, and you will be presented with the screen shown in Figure 21-6, where the confirmation mode parameter can be changed from yes to no. This will ensure that BRBACKUP tool will not stop for any operator confirmation and will execute in an unattended mode.

```
BR0259I Program execution will be continued...
```

Change the value for confirm to no and press ENTER. This will change the confirmation mode as shown in Figure 21-7.

```
BR0681I Enter string value for "confirm" (yes|no|force) [yes]:
no
BR0280I BRTOOLS time stamp: 2010-06-22 09.49.01
BR0683I New value for "confirm": 'no'
```

```
BR0280I BRTOOLS time stamp: 2010-06-22 09.49.01
BR0657I Input menu 16 - please enter/check input values
-------------------------------------------------------------------------------
Additional BRBACKUP options for backup and database copy
 1 - Confirmation mode (confirm) ....... [no]
 2 - Query mode (query) ................ [no]
 3 - Compression mode (compress) ....... [yes]
 4 - Verification mode (verify) ........ [no]
 5 - Fill-up previous backups (fillup) . [no]
 6 - Parallel execution (execute) ...... [0]
 7 - Additional output (output) ........ [no]
 8 - Message language (language) ....... [E]
 9 - BRBACKUP command line (command) ... [-p initKB2.sap -d disk -t offline_force -m full -
c -k yes -e 0 -l E]
Standard keys: c - cont, b - back, s - stop, r - refr, h - help
-------------------------------------------------------------------------------
BR0662I Enter your choice:
c
```

Copyright by SAP AG

Figure 21-7 BRBACKUP menu with confirmation mode changed to no

Click C after acknowledging the command options so that BRBACKUP will continue program execution and will back up all the needed files. Study the complete flow of the BRBACKUP tool so that you will understand how the tool backs up files.

```
BR0259I Program execution will be continued...

BR0291I BRBACKUP will be started with options '-p initKB2.sap -d disk -t of-
fline_force -m full -c -k yes -e 0 -l E'
BR0280I BRTOOLS time stamp: 2010-06-22 09.49.04
BR0670I Enter 'c[ont]' to continue, 'b[ack]' to go back, 's[top]' to abort:
c
BR0280I BRTOOLS time stamp: 2010-06-22 09.49.10
BR0257I Your reply: 'c'
BR0259I Program execution will be continued...

##########################################################################

BR0051I BRBACKUP 7.00 (42)
BR0055I Start of database backup: bedmynhm.ffd 2010-06-22 09.49.10
BR0484I BRBACKUP log file: /oracle/KB2/sapbackup/bedmynhm.ffd
BR0477I Oracle pfile /oracle/KB2/102_64/dbs/initKB2.ora created from spfile /
oracle/KB2/102_64/dbs/spfileKB2.ora

BR0280I BRBACKUP time stamp: 2010-06-22 09.49.11
BR0057I Backup of database: KB2
BR0058I BRBACKUP action ID: bedmynhm
BR0059I BRBACKUP function ID: ffd
BR0110I Backup mode: FULL
BR0077I Database files for backup:
/oracle/KB2/origlogA/log_g11m1.dbf
/oracle/KB2/origlogB/log_g12m1.dbf
/oracle/KB2/origlogA/log_g13m1.dbf
/oracle/KB2/origlogB/log_g14m1.dbf
/oracle/KB2/origlogA/cntrl/cntrlKB2.dbf
BR0061I 20 files found for backup, total size 46955.135 MB
BR0143I Backup type: offline_force
BR0111I Files will be compressed
BR0130I Backup device type: disk
BR0106I Files will be saved on disk in directory: /oracle/KB2/sapbackup/bedmynhm
BR0126I Unattended mode active - no operator confirmation required

BR0370I Directory /oracle/KB2/sapbackup/bedmynhm created

BR0202I Saving init_ora
BR0203I to /oracle/KB2/sapbackup/KB2 ...

BR0202I Saving /oracle/KB2/102_64/dbs/initKB2.sap
BR0203I to /oracle/KB2/sapbackup/KB2 ...

BR0280I BRBACKUP time stamp: 2010-06-22 09.49.12
BR0198I Profiles saved successfully
```

```
BR0280I BRBACKUP time stamp: 2010-06-22 09.49.12
BR0307I Shutting down database instance KB2 ...

BR0280I BRBACKUP time stamp: 2010-06-22 09.49.43
BR0308I Shutdown of database instance KB2 successful

BR0201I Compressing /oracle/KB2/sapdata2/bix_1/bix.data1
BR0203I to /oracle/KB2/sapbackup/bedmynhm/bix.data1.Z ...

#FILE..... /oracle/KB2/sapdata2/bix_1/bix.data1
#SAVED.... /oracle/KB2/sapbackup/bedmynhm/bix.data1.Z  #1/1  6.7217:1  521038920

BR0280I BRBACKUP time stamp: 2010-06-22 09.51.44
BR0063I 1 of 19 files processed - 3340.008 MB of 46930.119 MB done
BR0204I Percentage done: 7.12%, estimated end time: 10:24
BR0001I ****______________________________________________

BR0201I Compressing /oracle/KB2/sapdata2/bix_2/bix.data2
BR0203I to /oracle/KB2/sapbackup/bedmynhm/bix.data2.Z ...

BR0280I BRBACKUP time stamp: 2010-06-22 09.55.48
BR0063I 3 of 19 files processed - 10820.023 MB of 46930.119 MB done
BR0204I Percentage done: 23.06%, estimated end time: 10:17

...........
...........
...........

BR0280I BRBACKUP time stamp: 2010-06-22 10.22.55
BR0063I 14 of 19 files processed - 46060.109 MB of 46930.119 MB done
BR0204I Percentage done: 98.15%, estimated end time: 10:23
BR0001I *************************************************_

BR0201I Compressing /oracle/KB2/sapdata1/system_1/system.data1
BR0203I to /oracle/KB2/sapbackup/bedmynhm/system.data1.Z ...

#FILE..... /oracle/KB2/sapdata1/system_1/system.data1
#SAVED.... /oracle/KB2/sapbackup/bedmynhm/system.data1.Z  #1/15  5.7143:1
122947324

BR0280I BRBACKUP time stamp: 2010-06-22 10.23.31
BR0063I 15 of 19 files processed - 46730.117 MB of 46930.119 MB done
BR0204I Percentage done: 99.57%, estimated end time: 10:23
BR0001I **************************************************

BR0201I Compressing /oracle/KB2/origlogA/log_g11m1.dbf
BR0203I to /oracle/KB2/sapbackup/bedmynhm/log_g11m1.dbf.Z ...

#FILE..... /oracle/KB2/origlogA/log_g11m1.dbf
#SAVED.... /oracle/KB2/sapbackup/bedmynhm/log_g11m1.dbf.Z  #1/16  2.5452:1
20599319
```

```
BR0280I BRBACKUP time stamp: 2010-06-22 10.23.35
BR0063I 16 of 19 files processed - 46780.118 MB of 46930.119 MB done
BR0204I Percentage done: 99.68%, estimated end time: 10:23
BR0001I **************************************************

BR0201I Compressing /oracle/KB2/origlogB/log_g12m1.dbf
BR0203I to /oracle/KB2/sapbackup/bedmynhm/log_g12m1.dbf.Z ...

#FILE..... /oracle/KB2/origlogB/log_g12m1.dbf
#SAVED.... /oracle/KB2/sapbackup/bedmynhm/log_g12m1.dbf.Z  #1/17  3.7548:1
13963350

BR0280I BRBACKUP time stamp: 2010-06-22 10.23.39
BR0063I 17 of 19 files processed - 46830.118 MB of 46930.119 MB done
BR0204I Percentage done: 99.79%, estimated end time: 10:23
BR0001I **************************************************

BR0201I Compressing /oracle/KB2/origlogA/log_g13m1.dbf
BR0203I to /oracle/KB2/sapbackup/bedmynhm/log_g13m1.dbf.Z ...

#FILE..... /oracle/KB2/origlogA/log_g13m1.dbf
#SAVED.... /oracle/KB2/sapbackup/bedmynhm/log_g13m1.dbf.Z  #1/18  3.0544:1
17165013

BR0280I BRBACKUP time stamp: 2010-06-22 10.23.43
BR0063I 18 of 19 files processed - 46880.119 MB of 46930.119 MB done
BR0204I Percentage done: 99.89%, estimated end time: 10:23
BR0001I **************************************************

BR0201I Compressing /oracle/KB2/origlogB/log_g14m1.dbf
BR0203I to /oracle/KB2/sapbackup/bedmynhm/log_g14m1.dbf.Z ...

#FILE..... /oracle/KB2/origlogB/log_g14m1.dbf
#SAVED.... /oracle/KB2/sapbackup/bedmynhm/log_g14m1.dbf.Z  #1/19  2.9265:1
17915460

BR0280I BRBACKUP time stamp: 2010-06-22 10.23.48
BR0063I 19 of 19 files processed - 46930.119 MB of 46930.119 MB done
BR0204I Percentage done: 100.00%, estimated end time: 10:23
BR0001I **************************************************

BR0280I BRBACKUP time stamp: 2010-06-22 10.23.50
BR0330I Starting and mounting database instance KB2 ...

BR0280I BRBACKUP time stamp: 2010-06-22 10.24.00
BR0331I Start and mount of database instance KB2 successful

BR0280I BRBACKUP time stamp: 2010-06-22 10.24.00
BR0530I Cataloging backups of all database files...

BR0522I 14 of 14 files/save sets processed by RMAN
```

```
BR0280I BRBACKUP time stamp: 2010-06-22 10.24.04
BR0531I Backups of all database files cataloged successfully

BR0280I BRBACKUP time stamp: 2010-06-22 10.24.04
BR0307I Shutting down database instance KB2 ...

BR0280I BRBACKUP time stamp: 2010-06-22 10.24.09
BR0308I Shutdown of database instance KB2 successful

BR0201I Compressing /oracle/KB2/origlogA/cntrl/cntrlKB2.dbf
BR0203I to /oracle/KB2/sapbackup/bedmynhm/cntrlKB2.dbf.Z ...

#FILE..... /oracle/KB2/origlogA/cntrl/cntrlKB2.dbf
#SAVED.... /oracle/KB2/sapbackup/bedmynhm/cntrlKB2.dbf.Z  #1/20  279.3570:1
93897

BR0280I BRBACKUP time stamp: 2010-06-22 10.24.09
BR0063I 1 of 1 file processed - 25.016 MB of 25.016 MB done
BR0204I Percentage done: 100.00%, estimated end time: 10:24
BR0001I **************************************************

BR0280I BRBACKUP time stamp: 2010-06-22 10.24.09
BR0304I Starting and opening database instance KB2 ...

BR0280I BRBACKUP time stamp: 2010-06-22 10.24.21
BR0305I Start and open of database instance KB2 successful

BR0280I BRBACKUP time stamp: 2010-06-22 10.24.21
BR0340I Switching to next online redo log file for database instance KB2 ...
BR0321I Switch to next online redo log file for database instance KB2 successful

BR0202I Saving space_log
BR0203I to /oracle/KB2/sapbackup/KB2 ...

BR0202I Saving /oracle/KB2/sapbackup/bedmynhm.ffd
BR0203I to /oracle/KB2/sapbackup/KB2 ...

BR0202I Saving /oracle/KB2/sapbackup/backKB2.log
BR0203I to /oracle/KB2/sapbackup/KB2 ...

BR0115I Compression rate for all files 4.5798:1

BR0056I End of database backup: bedmynhm.ffd 2010-06-22 10.24.22
BR0280I BRBACKUP time stamp: 2010-06-22 10.24.25
BR0052I BRBACKUP completed successfully

###########################################################################
BR0292I Execution of BRBACKUP finished with return code 0
###########################################################################
```

BRRESTORE and BRRECOVER

This section will show in detail how to perform a point-in-time recovery of a database that had issues with some data loss caused by a user error using BRRESTORE and BRRECOVER. The first step in the BRRESTORE and BRRECOVER process is to check the status of the database backups and verify the status of the datafiles and archive log files needed for a point-in-time recovery. Once this is done, the point-in-time recovery option must be chosen with a end recovery time so that the tool can restore and recover the needed backup set, including the datafiles and archive log files of that set. The figures will demonstrate the step-by-step process. If necessary, the same process can be used at your organization.

To start the process log in to the system that needs a restore and recovery as ora<SID> user and issue the brtools command as shown in Figure 21-8. The initial BRTOOLS menu appears. Choose option 4 (Backup And Database Copy) to start the verification process for the datafiles and archive log files of a chosen backup set.

Choose option 4 and press the ENTER key. The Backup And Database Copy menu option will appear as shown in Figure 21-9.

```
orakb2> brtools
BR0651I BRTOOLS 7.00 (36)

BR0280I BRTOOLS time stamp: 2010-12-26 19.26.24
BR0656I Choice menu 1 - please make a selection
-------------------------------------------------------------------------------
BR*Tools main menu

 1 = Instance management
 2 - Space management
 3 - Segment management
 4 - Backup and database copy
 5 - Restore and recovery
 6 - Check and verification
 7 - Database statistics
 8 - Additional functions
 9 - Exit program
Standard keys: c - cont, b - back, s - stop, r - refr, h - help
-------------------------------------------------------------------------------
BR0662I Enter your choice:
4
```


FIGURE 21-8 Initial BRTOOLS menu

```
BR0280I BRTOOLS time stamp: 2010-12-26 19.26.37
BR0656I Choice menu 9 - please make a selection
------------------------------------------------------------------------------
Backup and database copy

 1 = Database backup
 2 - Archivelog backup
 3 - Database copy
 4 - Non-database backup
 5 - Backup of database disk backup
 6 - Verification of database backup
 7 - Verification of archivelog backup
 8 - Additional functions
 9 - Reset program status

Standard keys: c - cont, b - back, s - stop, r - refr, h - help
------------------------------------------------------------------------------
BR0662I Enter your choice:
6
```

Copyright by SAP AG

FIGURE 21-9 BRTOOLS Backup And Database Copy menu

Choose option 6 and press the ENTER key. The back<SID>.log file will be read to check the status of the available backup sets and a list of available backups will be displayed, as shown in Figure 21-10.

```
BR0699I Reading log file /oracle/KB2/sapbackup/backKB2.log ...
```

```
BR0280I BRTOOLS time stamp: 2010-12-26 19.26.45
BR0658I List menu 20 - please select one entry
------------------------------------------------------------------------------
BRBACKUP database backups for verification

Pos. Log              Start                 Type      Files  Device   Rc

 1 = beewjquj.ind  2010-12-26 18.00.09   online     1/16   disk     0
 2 - beewetai.ind  2010-12-25 18.00.36   online     1/16   disk     0
 3 - beewalek.fnd  2010-12-24 21.00.30   online    15/16   disk     0
 4 - beevuxjs.ind  2010-12-23 18.00.24   online     1/16   disk     0
 5 - beevpzoi.ind  2010-12-22 18.00.16   online     1/16   disk     0

Standard keys: c - cont, b - back, s - stop, r - refr, h - help
------------------------------------------------------------------------------
BR0662I Enter your selection:
```

Copyright by SAP AG

FIGURE 21-10 BRBACKUP listing the available backups

```
BR0280I BRTOOLS time stamp: 2010-12-26 19.37.49
BR0656I Choice menu 9 - please make a selection
------------------------------------------------------------------------------
Backup and database copy

 1 = Database backup
 2 - Archivelog backup
 3 - Database copy
 4 - Non-database backup
 5 - Backup of database disk backup
 6 - Verification of database backup
 7 - Verification of archivelog backup
 8 - Additional functions
 9 - Reset program status

Standard keys: c - cont, b - back, s - stop, r - refr, h - help
------------------------------------------------------------------------------
BR0662I Enter your choice:
7
```


FIGURE 21-11 BRBACKUP verification of archive log backup menu option

The next step is to verify the availability of the needed archive log files. Choose option 7 as shown in Figure 21-11, and press ENTER.

The arch<SID>.log file will be read and the archive logs listed as shown in Figure 21-12.

```
BR0699I Reading log file /oracle/KB2/saparch/archKB2.log ...
```

Once the verification steps are complete, start the restore and recovery process by selecting the Back option and pressing ENTER. This will take you to the initial BRTOOLS

```
BR0280I BRTOOLS time stamp: 2010-12-26 19.38.03
BR0658I List menu 23 - please select one entry
------------------------------------------------------------------------------
BRARCHIVE archivelog backups for verification

Pos. Log          Start                  Device  Rc   Copy  First  Last

 1 = aeewjsfc.svd  2010-12-26 18.16.04   disk    0    1.     849    849
 2 - aeewiaek.svd  2010-12-26 10.00.02   disk    0    1.     848    848
 3 - aeewhewz.svd  2010-12-26 06.00.13   disk    0    1.     847    847
 4 - aeeweuiv.svd  2010-12-25 18.15.33   disk    0    1.     846    846
 5 - aeewdxsl.svd  2010-12-25 14.00.35   disk    0    1.     845    845

Press <Rtn> - scroll, <n> - select, 'c' - cont, 'h' - header, 's' - stop ...
```


FIGURE 21-12 BRBACKUP listing the available archive logs

```
BR0280I BRTOOLS time stamp: 2010-12-26 19.41.33
BR0656I Choice menu 1 - please make a selection
-------------------------------------------------------------------------------
BR*Tools main menu

 1 = Instance management
 2 - Space management
 3 - Segment management
 4 - Backup and database copy
 5 - Restore and recovery
 6 - Check and verification
 7 - Database statistics
 8 - Additional functions
 9 - Exit program
Standard keys: c - cont, b - back, s - stop, r - refr, h - help
-------------------------------------------------------------------------------
BR0662I Enter your choice:
5
```

Copyright by SAP AG

FIGURE 21-13 BRTOOLS Restore And Recovery menu option

menu again. Choose the Restore And Recovery option (option 5) as shown in Figure 21-13 and press ENTER to display the Restore And Recovery menu.

Choose option 2 (Database Point-In-Time Recovery) as shown in Figure 21-14 and press ENTER.

```
BR0280I BRTOOLS time stamp: 2010-12-26 19.41.44
BR0656I Choice menu 11 - please make a selection
-------------------------------------------------------------------------------
Restore and recovery

 1 = Complete database recovery
 2 - Database point-in-time recovery
 3 - Tablespace point-in-time recovery
 4 - Whole database reset
 5 - Restore of individual backup files
 6 - Restore and application of archivelog files
 7 - Disaster recovery
 8 - Reset program status

Standard keys: c - cont, b - back, s - stop, r - refr, h - help
-------------------------------------------------------------------------------
BR0662I Enter your choice:
2
```

Copyright by SAP AG

FIGURE 21-14 Database Point-In-Time Recovery menu option

```
BR0280I BRTOOLS time stamp: 2010-12-26 19.42.49
BR0657I Input menu 34 - please enter/check input values
-------------------------------------------------------------------------------
BRRECOVER options for restore and recovery

 1 * Recovery type (type) ............ [dbpit]
 2 - BRRECOVER profile (profile) ...... [initKB2.sap]
 3 ~ BACKINT/Mount profile (parfile) .. []
 4 - Database user/password (user) .... [/]
 5 - Recovery interval (interval) ..... [30]
 6 - Confirmation mode (confirm) ...... [yes]
 7 - Scrolling line count (scroll) .... [20]
 8 - Message language (language) ...... [E]
 9 - BRRECOVER command line (command) . [-p initKB2.sap -t dbpit -i 30 -s 20 -l E]
Standard keys: c - cont, b - back, s - stop, r - refr, h - help
-------------------------------------------------------------------------------
BR0662I Enter your choice:
c
```


FIGURE 21-15 BRRECOVER menu option showing the parameters

Accept the default parameter values as shown in Figure 21-15, type **c**, and press ENTER. The program will execute. Confirm the command parameters by typing **c** again and pressing ENTER.

```
BR0259I Program execution will be continued...

BR0291I BRRECOVER will be started with options '-p initKB2.sap -t dbpit -i
30 -s 20 -l E'

BR0280I BRTOOLS time stamp: 2010-12-26 19.43.48
BR0670I Enter 'c[ont]' to continue, 'b[ack]' to go back, 's[top]' to abort:
c
BR0259I Program execution will be continued...

###########################################################################

BR0701I BRRECOVER 7.00 (36)
BR0705I Start of database recovery: veewjzzs.dpt 2010-12-26 19.43.52
BR0484I BRRECOVER log file: /oracle/KB2/sapbackup/veewjzzs.dpt

BR0280I BRRECOVER time stamp: 2010-12-26 19.43.53
BR0707I Recovery of database: KB2
BR0708I BRRECOVER action ID: veewjzzs
BR0709I BRRECOVER function ID: dpt
BR0710I Recovery type: dbpit
```

The system will then prompt you as shown in Figure 21-16 with the Database Point-In-Time Recovery menu. Choose option 1 and press the ENTER key.

```
BR0280I BRRECOVER time stamp: 2010-12-26 19.43.53
BR0655I Control menu 103 - please decide how to proceed
-------------------------------------------------------------------------------
Database point-in-time recovery main menu

 1 = Set point-in-time for recovery
 2 * Select database backup
 3 * Check the status of database files
 4 * Restore control files
 5 * Restore data files
 6 * Restore split incremental control files
 7 * Restore and apply incremental backup
 8 * Restore and apply archivelog files
 9 * Open database and post-processing
10 * Exit program
11 - Reset program status
Standard keys: c - cont, b - back, s - stop, r - refr, h - help
-------------------------------------------------------------------------------
BR0662I Enter your choice:
1
```


FIGURE 21-16 Recovery menu option for choosing the time stamp for recovery

The screen shown in Figure 21-17 will appear. Choose option 4 and press ENTER.

Then the system will prompt you to enter the end point (time) for the point-in-time recovery. Type the necessary value and press the ENTER key. This will show the entered end time as the end point-in-time for recovery, as shown in Figure 21-18. Type **c** and press the ENTER key.

```
BR0280I BRRECOVER time stamp: 2010-12-26 19.49.46
BR0681I Enter string value for "end_pit" (<yyyy-mo-dd hh.mi.ss>) []:
2010-12-25 20.00.00
```

```
BR0280I BRRECOVER time stamp: 2010-12-26 19.49.33
BR0657I Input menu 104 - please enter/check input values
-------------------------------------------------------------------------------
Options for point-in-time recovery of database KB2

1 # Database instance of archivelog thread (instance) . []
2 ~ Last archivelog sequence to apply (last_seq) ...... []
3 ~ Last system change number to apply (last_scn) ..... []
4 ~ End point-in-time for recovery (end_pit) .......... []

Standard keys: c - cont, b - back, s - stop, r - refr, h - help
-------------------------------------------------------------------------------
BR0662I Enter your choice:
4
```


FIGURE 21-17 Menu option to choose the end-point time stamp for database recovery

```
BR0280I BRRECOVER time stamp: 2010-12-26 19.52.58
BR0657I Input menu 104 - please enter/check input values
-------------------------------------------------------------------------------
Options for point-in-time recovery of database KB2

1 # Database instance of archivelog thread (instance) . []
2 ~ Last archivelog sequence to apply (last_seq) ...... []
3 ~ Last system change number to apply (last_scn) ..... []
4 ~ End point-in-time for recovery (end_pit) .......... [2010-12-25 20.00.00]

Standard keys: c - cont, b - back, s - stop, r - refr, h - help
-------------------------------------------------------------------------------
BR0662I Enter your choice:
c
```

Copyright by SAP AG

FIGURE 21-18 Menu option showing the database recovery end time stamp

```
BR0280I BRRECOVER time stamp: 2010-12-26 19.52.58
BR0683I New value for "end_pit": '2010-12-25 20.00.00'
BR0259I Program execution will be continued...
```

Next step is the system will present a screen for choosing the database backup for the actual restore as shown in Figure 21-19. Choose option 2 and press the ENTER key.

```
BR0342I Database instance KB2 is open

BR0699I Reading log file /oracle/KB2/sapbackup/backKB2.log ...
```

```
BR0280I BRRECOVER time stamp: 2010-12-26 19.53.38
BR0655I Control menu 103 - please decide how to proceed
-------------------------------------------------------------------------------
Database point-in-time recovery main menu

1 + Set point-in-time for recovery
2 = Select database backup
3 * Check the status of database files
4 * Restore control files
5 * Restore data files
6 * Restore split incremental control files
7 * Restore and apply incremental backup
8 * Restore and apply archivelog files
9 * Open database and post-processing
10 * Exit program
11 - Reset program status

Standard keys: c - cont, b - back, s - stop, r - refr, h - help
-------------------------------------------------------------------------------
BR0662I Enter your choice:
2
```

Copyright by SAP AG

FIGURE 21-19 Menu option for database backup selection

```
BR0280I BRRECOVER time stamp: 2010-12-26 19.54.58
BR0659I List menu 105 + please select one or more entries
-------------------------------------------------------------------------------
Database backups for database point-in-time recovery
Pos. Log          Start                  Type     Mode    Device  Rc
 1 = beewetai.ind  2010-12-25 18.00.36   online   incr    disk    0
 2 - beewalek.fnd  2010-12-24 21.00.30   online   full    disk    0
 3 - beevuxjs.ind  2010-12-23 18.00.24   online   incr    disk    0
 4 - beevpzoi.ind  2010-12-22 18.00.16   online   incr    disk    0
 5 - beevlbsy.ind  2010-12-21 18.00.08   online   incr    disk    0
 6 - beevgdyq.ind  2010-12-20 18.00.28   online   incr    disk    0
Standard keys: c - cont, b - back, s - stop, r - refr, h - help
-------------------------------------------------------------------------------
BR0662I Enter your selection:
2
```

Copyright by SAP AG

FIGURE 21-20 Select the last full online database backup for recovery.

The system will then show the list of available backups. Choose option 2 (the last known good full backup) and press ENTER as shown in Figure 21-20.

```
BR0699I Reading log file /oracle/KB2/sapbackup/beewalek.fnd ...

BR0772I Checking the availability of archivelog files for database instance
KB2 ...

BR0699I Reading log file /oracle/KB2/saparch/archKB2.log for device type
'disk'...

BR0699I Reading log file /oracle/KB2/saparch/archKB2.log for device type
'tape/backint/rman'...

BR0699I Reading log file /oracle/KB2/saparch/archKB2.log for device type
'stage'...
```

The screen shown in Figure 21-21 appears so you can check the status of the database files for the chosen backup set. Select option 3 and press ENTER.

The following steps will continue the recovery process. Confirm each one, continuing with the process, and the system will restore and recover the database to the chosen point in time.

1. The data files that will be overwritten are displayed.
2. Confirm the default parameters and choose Continue.
3. The data files are restored.
4. Once data files are restored, click Continue.
5. The archive log files that need to be restored are displayed.
6. Confirm the default parameters and click Continue.
7. Archive log files will be restored based on the chosen time stamp.
8. Post database restore, Oracle recovery steps are executed and the database is opened.

```
BR0280I BRRECOVER time stamp: 2010-12-26 19.58.49
BR0655I Control menu 103 - please decide how to proceed
---------------------------------------------------------------------------
Database point-in-time recovery main menu
 1 + Set point-in-time for recovery
 2 + Select database backup
 3 = Check the status of database files
 4 * Restore control files
 5 * Restore data files
 6 # Restore split incremental control files
 7 # Restore and apply incremental backup
 8 * Restore and apply archivelog files
 9 * Open database and post-processing
10 * Exit program
11 - Reset program status
Standard keys: c - cont, b - back, s - stop, r - refr, h - help
---------------------------------------------------------------------------
BR0662I Enter your choice: 3
```


FIGURE 21-21 Menu option for checking the database file's status

9. A confirmation message is displayed indicating the restore and recovery completed successfully.
10. Restart the SAP system manually.

Summary

- When a business system is down, it can cost an organization millions of dollars.
- Developing and implementing an effective backup strategy is very important.
- The BRBACKUP tool helps to back up the database.
- A 28-day tape backup cycle is recommended.
- BRBACKUP can back up the data to disk or tape.
- BRBACKUP reads the BRTOOLS initialization file; therefore, the file needs to be customized as per the needs of your organization.
- The name of the configuration file is init<SID>.sap.
- BRRESTORE helps to restore the database.
- BRRECOVER helps to restore and recover the database.

Additional Resources

- **Backup strategy for Oracle databases** www.sdn.sap.com/irj/sdn/go/portal/prtroot/docs/library/uuid/6be4053a-0d01-0010-bfa7-bf9c2979a83c
- **Oracle backup and recovery page on SDN** www.sdn.sap.com/irj/sdn/ora?rid=/webcontent/uuid/1cc71b42-0d01-0010-7f91-f352b58078cf

PART

SAP Performance Tuning and Sizing

CHAPTER

SAP Performance Tuning in the ABAP Stack

This section consists of three chapters, and we will cover performance tuning of ABAP and Java stacks and SAP sizing. In this chapter we will focus on SAP performance tuning in the ABAP stack. We will first cover performance tuning concepts followed by discussing some common performance issues as well as tools and techniques that can be used to analyze performance issues. We will also cover specific examples of performance-tuning parameters to improve system performance. This chapter will conclude by discussing some of the implications of outsourcing SAP development work to distributed teams in the world and the importance of conducting performance tests and stress tests.

Significance of SAP System Performance

Good system performance is of paramount importance to the business users. For a newly implemented system, one of the main criteria for end-user acceptance is good response time. For a system that has been in productive operation for a while, good response times and availability are critical and have monetary implications if there is any adverse effect on system performance. Thus, one of the most important tasks of the Basis administrator is to monitor the system for any performance issues and take remedial actions as quickly as possible. The best way to provide good response times and meet or exceed system performance expectations are to incorporate system performance best practices and set up/tune parameters starting from the design and through the build, test, and deploy stages of the project. For example, if incorrect RAID technology is implemented in the initial stages of the project it will have an adverse effect on system performance throughout the project lifecycle as well as in the productive operations of the system. We will, therefore, cover performance tuning concepts such as dialog response times, memory management strategy, and SAP buffers and study how to incorporate these into SAP systems so that they provide optimal performance to business users.

Performance Tuning Concepts in the ABAP Stack

The main concepts relating to performance tuning in an ABAP stack are response times, memory management, allocation sequence of memory areas in dialog and background work processes, SAP buffers, and avoiding expensive SQL.

Response Times

Dialog response time is the time between when an end user initiates a request and receives the requested information from the system. The response time is measured at the application server (instance). Any time spent on network communication is not included in the dialog response time. Table 22-1 breaks down the steps performed by the end user, dispatcher, and work process and the different components of the dialog response times.

End-User Activity	Dispatcher Activity	Work Process Activity	Dialog Response Time Component
Executes a transaction or a program.	Receives the request and looks for a free work process.	A work process is assigned.	**Wait time** results if a free work process is not available.
		The work process copies the user context (user authorizations, variables, and pointers to data) from roll buffer to roll memory.	**Roll-in time** is the time required for the copy of the user context to be made.
		The work process cannot find the code in the program buffer and therefore calls the database and loads and generates the code.	**Load and generation time** results if the code needs to be loaded and generated from the database.
		If the work process cannot find the data in the SAP buffers, it makes a call to the database.	This results in **database request time**.
		The work process finds data in the SAP table buffer and gets the data.	This results in **buffer access time**.
		The work process acquires a lock.	This is **lock time** or **enqueue time**.
		The work process executes the program.	This is **processing time**.
The end user receives the data.	The requested information is dispatched to the end user.	The work process completes execution of the program and sends the data to the dispatcher.	This is the total dialog response time. (Note that this time is measured at the application server and the measurement stops at the dispatcher and does not include the network time.)

Table 22-1 Lifecycle of an End-User Request and the Components of Dialog Response Time

Of these listed components, processing times are not calculated directly. The following formula can be used to calculate the processing times:

> Processing time = Response time – (Wait time + Load/Generation time + Database Request time or Buffer access time + Roll-in time + Enqueue time)

SAP provides transactions that monitor the different components of the dialog response times and that can be used to isolate where the performance bottleneck is coming from and address the underlying issue. This will be discussed further in subsequent sections of this chapter. OSS Note 8963 provides more details on the different components of the response times.

SAP Memory Management Concepts

The following definitions need to be understood when discussing the memory management concepts for a SAP system. The different memory areas are shown in Figure 22-1:

- Virtual memory = Physical memory (Shared memory + Local memory) + OS swap space
- Shared memory = Allocated at instance start as per SAP extended memory parameter and related memory areas configuration in instance profile
- Local memory = Allocated on demand and released after use immediately as per SAP heap area related parameter/s configuration in instance profile

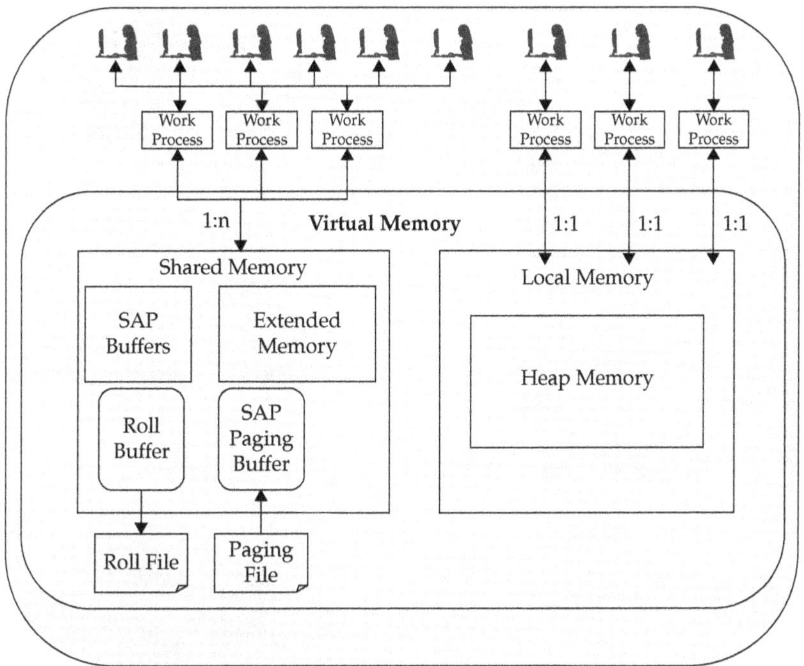

FIGURE 22-1 Memory areas in SAP systems

- Local memory is associated with individual work processes (1:1)
- Heap memory = Temporary memory is allocated out of local memory
- Heap memory is allocated when extended memory is full
- Local memory is used for ABAP load, data, local roll area, paging area and so on
- Shared memory is associated with all work processes (1:n)
- Shared memory has different SAP buffers, extended memory, roll buffer, and paging buffer
- SAP buffers contain global objects for all users and work processes such as programs and buffered table content
- Extended memory contains unfinished transaction data of application users (1:n relationship with work processes)
- Roll buffer contains initial user contexts (writes to roll file at file system level)
- Paging memory contains ABAP extracts and exports (writes to paging file at file system level)
- User context is defined as memory area that has individual user authorization data and variables that are associated with that specific user activity in the system

Now that we have looked into the definitions of different SAP memory areas, we will study the memory allocation sequence in the next section.

SAP Memory Allocation Strategy

By design, SAP serves more users with fewer dialog work processes. The dialog work processes achieve this design goal by moving the smaller user context and associated pointers to the actual transactional data (large memory areas) in the extended memory between the work processes called as rolling in and rolling out of the user contexts. This process allows the system to easily switch the smaller user contexts with pointers to extended memory with larger transactional data between different dialog work processes. The roll area and paging area, along with the roll file and paging file, respectively, are used for the roll-in and roll-out processes. Once the roll area and extended memory are used up by a user, the system is forced to use the on-demand local (heap) memory. If the entire heap memory is used up, the system will start using the swap space (swap file) at the operating system level, which results in degradation of system performance. Different profile parameters are used to set up the memory areas discussed here and will be covered in the subsequent sections of this chapter.

SAP Memory Allocation Sequence for Dialog Work Activity

The memory allocation sequence for a dialog work process is as follows. This allows the best utilization of memory for user context switching:

- **First** The roll area is used.
- **Second** Extended memory is used (user quota ensures no single user uses all of it).
- **Third** The rest of the roll area is used.
- **Fourth** The heap area is used.

If the dialog work process reaches the fourth stage and does not get completed, it reaches a stage referred to as PRIV mode. If many dialog work processes enter the PRIV mode system performance will seriously degrade for the rest of the users. The system parameters should be tuned so that this condition is minimized, particularly in the production systems.

SAP Memory Allocation Sequence for Background Work Activity

In the case of background work processes, the memory allocation sequence is a little different. Because of this allocation strategy, background work processes will not time out and will help execute long-running jobs:

- **First** The roll area is used.
- **Second** The heap area is used.
- **Third** The rest of the roll area is used.
- **Fourth** Extended memory is used (user quota ensures no single user uses all of it).

SAP Buffers

SAP buffers are allocated at the application level and are governed by profile parameters related to different kinds of buffers, such as table buffers and program buffers. Keeping the data at the application-level buffers and not having to go to the database level will provide significant performance benefits to the system. But at the same time, not all types of data should be buffered. For example, while it makes sense to buffer data that is static, it will not be helpful if the data gets changed frequently. In subsequent sections of this chapter a detailed list of SAP buffers and recommended parameters will be provided.

Performance Tuning Transactions

Performance tuning in the system can be done using a set of monitoring transaction codes for the application, database, and operating system. Table 22-2 lists the key performance tuning transactions and a brief description for each.

SQL Trace Overview

The following procedure can be used to get a SQL trace in a SAP system. SQL trace analysis will help us identify any expensive SQL statements and identify tuning/indexing opportunities to improve system performance.

Starting SQL Trace

The following procedure can be used to start a SQL trace for a program that is causing performance issues in the system:

1. Call transaction code ST05. Select either Activate Trace or Activate Trace With Filter. The Activate Trace option will start a SQL trace for the user who started the transaction. Activate Trace With Filter will provide different filtering options for capturing the SQL trace. Figure 22-2 provides the filtering options available for activating a SQL trace. Choose the user account under which the problem SQL is running and start the trace by clicking the green check mark.

SAP Transaction	Purpose
ST03N	This transaction can be used to check the response times. Different components of the dialog response times discussed earlier in this chapter can be checked in this transaction, and a Basis administrator can understand the root cause of the delay based on which component of the dialog response times is taking more time.
STAD	This transaction will provide statistical data on system performance.
ST02	This transaction provides tune summary of the SAP memory parameters and SAP buffer allocation and utilization. This is a very critical transaction and can be used to quickly diagnose a memory or an application-level buffering issue causing a performance bottleneck in the system. Increasing the affected memory parameter or SAP buffer will usually help resolve the performance issue.
SM66	This transaction code provides a global overview of the work processes of all the application servers in the system. This will allow the Basis administrator to get a quick snapshot of the current system usage.
SM50	This transaction helps the Basis administrator check the work process activity of the individual application server. This usually has more detailed drill-down information for providing additional clues to performance issues. It is recommended to start with SM66 to track a work process running on one of the application servers and then switch to that application server using SM50 or SM51 to get more details about the performance issue.
ST04	Checks database performance information.
ST06	Checks operating system performance information.
ST07	Checks application usage.
ST10	Checks table call statistics.
ST05	Performs a SQL trace. Since performing a SQL trace is a very important skill for a SAP Basis administrator, a detailed description of the procedure is provided in this chapter.

TABLE 22-2 SAP Performance Tuning Transactions

2. In most cases, this is the recommended SQL trace option. Enter the filtering criteria in the following screen and keep it ready. Open another SAP session and start executing the suspected transaction or report. Go back to the SQL trace filter options screen and press ENTER. This will start the trace. Let the trace run for few minutes and then turn off the trace by clicking Deactivate Trace.
3. Please note that trace file size is governed by the system parameter rstr/max_filesize_MB. The default size for an ECC (ERP Central Component) system is 16MB. During a trace, a lot of data is written; therefore, a long-running trace might overwrite older trace data.
4. Next, click the display trace. This displays the trace list, which will provide the SQL trace output for detailed analysis.

Set Restrictions for Writing Trace

User Name *

Transaction

NOR

Program Name

SAP R/3 Proc. No.

Table Names

Include

Exclude

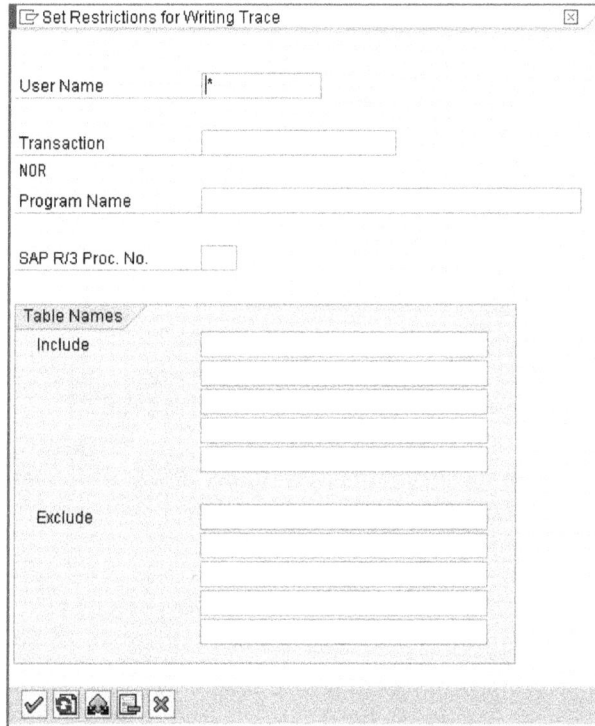

FIGURE 22-2 SQL trace filtering options

Analyzing the Trace File

Once the trace list is generated, the next step is to look for SQL statements that are taking significantly longer to execute. The following illustration shows the results of the SQL trace for further analysis.

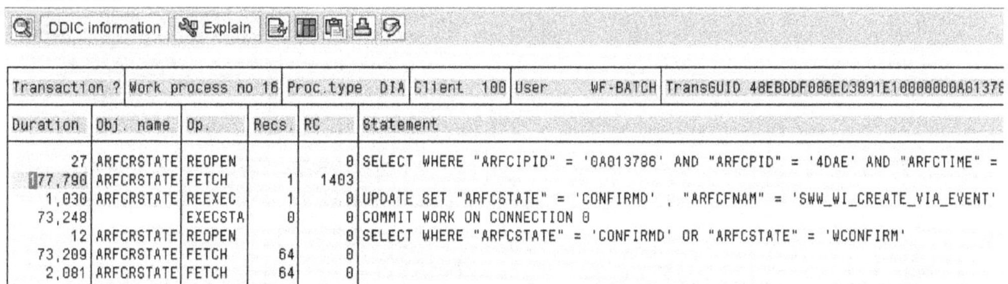

Trace List

DDIC information | Explain

Transaction ?	Work process no 16	Proc.type DIA	Client 100	User WF-BATCH	TransGUID 48EBDDF086EC3891E10000000A01378

Duration	Obj. name	Op.	Recs.	RC	Statement
27	ARFCRSTATE	REOPEN		0	SELECT WHERE "ARFCIPID" = '0A013786' AND "ARFCPID" = '4DAE' AND "ARFCTIME" =
177,790	ARFCRSTATE	FETCH	1	1403	
1,030	ARFCRSTATE	REEXEC	1	0	UPDATE SET "ARFCSTATE" = 'CONFIRMD' , "ARFCFNAM" = 'SWW_WI_CREATE_VIA_EVENT'
73,248		EXECSTA	0	0	COMMIT WORK ON CONNECTION 0
12	ARFCRSTATE	REOPEN		0	SELECT WHERE "ARFCSTATE" = 'CONFIRMD' OR "ARFCSTATE" = 'WCONFIRM'
73,209	ARFCRSTATE	FETCH	64	0	
2,081	ARFCRSTATE	FETCH	64	0	

- From the Trace List screen you could look into the SQL statements that are taking a long time to execute by noting the times in the first column. The unit of time is microseconds; thus, 1,000,000 microseconds is equal to 1 second. Usually, long SQL execution times (values greater than 100,000 microseconds) are marked in red, which provides us with our initial suspect list.
- The second column gives the name of the accessed database object.
- The third column gives the name of the database operation.
- The fourth column gives you the number of fetched records.
- The fifth column gives you the return code from Oracle Database.
- The sixth and final column gives you the SQL statement.
- Clicking the Explain button on the top of the trace list for a SQL row with reopened or open database operations will display a detailed plan.
- When the Explain Plan button is clicked, the screen will be divided into two halves, as shown in the illustration. The upper half of the screen will show the SQL statement and how it is executed in the Oracle Database. The lower half of the screen will give you the execution plan.

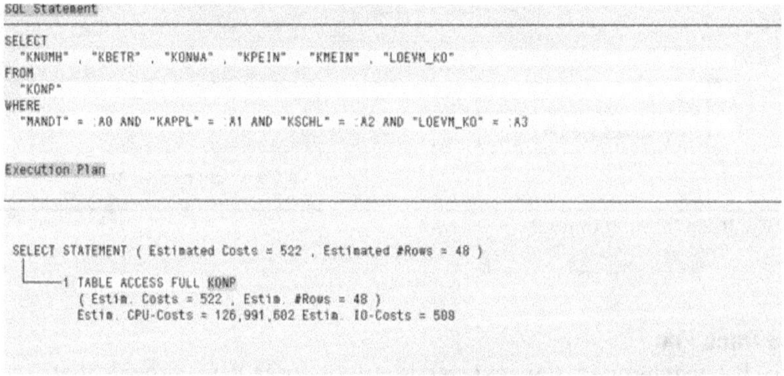

```
SQL Statement

SELECT
  "KNUMH" , "KBETR" , "KONWA" , "KPEIN" , "KMEIN" , "LOEVM_KO"
FROM
  "KONP"
WHERE
  "MANDT" = :A0 AND "KAPPL" = :A1 AND "KSCHL" = :A2 AND "LOEVM_KO" = :A3

Execution Plan

 SELECT STATEMENT ( Estimated Costs = 522 , Estimated #Rows = 48 )
  |
  └──1 TABLE ACCESS FULL KONP
       ( Estim. Costs = 522 , Estim. #Rows = 48 )
       Estim. CPU-Costs = 126,991,602 Estim. IO-Costs = 508
```


- The execution plan gives you the details on the processing of the selected SQL statements such as estimated costs and estimated rows.
- The estimated cost is the number based on the access optimization by the cost-based optimizer. Estimated costs are proportional to the number of blocks necessary to read to fulfill the request. Higher costs could indicate a problem. The estimated rows indicate how many rows might be found as a result of the select statement.
- In the same screen clicking the individual tables and indexes (Figure 22-3) will provide detailed information about the last analysis and the collected statistics for the object.
- Analyzing this information will show you the indexes that are currently being used and reveal if the creation of any new indexes is justified.

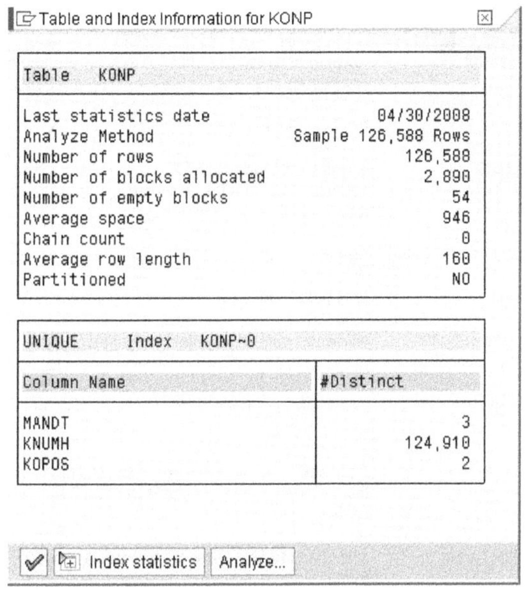

Table and Index Information for KONP
Table KONP
Last statistics date 04/30/2008
Analyze Method Sample 126,588 Rows
Number of rows 126,588
Number of blocks allocated 2,890
Number of empty blocks 54
Average space 946
Chain count 0
Average row length 160
Partitioned NO
UNIQUE Index KONP~0
Column Name #Distinct
MANDT 3
KNUMH 124,910
KOPOS 2
Index statistics
Analyze...

Copyright by SAP AG

FIGURE 22-3 Table usage statistics and index information

Performance-Tuning Parameters in ABAP Systems

The following section will cover tuning profile parameters to improve system performance. Usually, these parameters are changed in an iterative fashion as the system grows over time.

Performance-Tuning Parameter Recommendations for ABAP Systems

The following illustrations and Figures 22-4 and 22-5 show the most important performance-tuning parameter groupings for ABAP systems. Please check the most current version of the OSS Note that is provided in Figure 22-5 so that any new recommendations and information can be used while configuring your system.

Instance Parameters	SAP Parameter Technical Name	Parameter Details	OSS note	Value
	rdisp/wp_no_dia	# of Dialog Work Processes		30
	rdisp/wp_no_btc	# of Background Work Processes		10
	rdisp/wp_no_vb	# of Update Work Processes on CI/DB		8

Lock Table Parameters	SAP Parameter Technical Name	Parameter Details	OSS note	Value
	enque/table_size	This parameter defines the size of the lock table that is held in main memory by the enqueue server.	552289	20000

SAP Buffer Name	SAP Parameter Technical Name	Parameter Details	OSS Note	Value
Table Definition	rsdb/ntab/entrycount	Number of directory entries created for the "table definition buffer" and the "field description buffer".	670505	50000
Program	abap/buffersize	Program Buffer Size	103747	1000000
CUA	rsdb/cua/buffersize	Specifies the size of the CUA puffer. The CUA buffer holds objects from the GUI interface, such as menus, pushbuttons, and so on.	103747	8192
Screen	zcsa/presentation_buffer_area	Size of the buffer allocated for screens (dynpros)	103747	1.5E+07
Export/Import	rsdb/obj/buffersize	This parameter sets the size of the import /export buffer (KB).	103747, 702728	50000
	rsdb/obj/max_objects	Maximum number of objects in export / import buffer		40000
Partial Table	rtbb/buffer_length	Size of partial table buffers	103747, 146289	30000
Field Description	rsdb/ntab/ftabsize	Data area size for "Field descriptor buffer" to store the description of an R/3 table that is accessed at runtime.	103747, 146289	90000
Resident Table	zcsa/table_buffer_area	Specifies the size of the resident-table (100%) buffer.	103747, 146289	5E+07
	zcsa/db_max_buftab	Specifies the number of directory entries in the resident-table buffer. This is the maximum number of tables that can be buffered. Set the parameter to a large enough value to ensure that there are always free directory entries.	103747, 146289	10000
Presentation Buffer Entries	sap/bufdir_entries	Maximum number of entries in the presentation buffer.	103747, 146289	10000
Initial Record	rsdb/ntab/irbdsize	Data area size for the "Initial record buffer" to store the initial record layout of an R/3 table that is accessed at runtime.	103747, 146289	10240

FIGURE 22-4 SAP buffer parameters

SAP Parameter Technical Name	Parameter Details	OSS note	Value
sapgui/user_scripting	User scripting on the frontend	On-line Help	TRUE
rdisp/max_arq	Max. number of internal asynchronous messages		2000
rdisp/tm_max_no	This parameter limits the maximum number of users per instance.The dispatcher creates information about the connected users inthe structure tm_adm. RFC users are also counted towards this total.	384971	2000
gw/max_conn	This parameter specifies the maximum number of simultaneous activeconnections for Gateway	384971	2000
rdisp/max_comm_entries	Maximum number of communication entries for an application server. Each RFC or CPIC communication with a partner program requires an entry. If the initiator and the acceptor of an RFC/CPIC program are running on the same server, then two entries are required per communication. Every communication entry requires 100 Bytes in Shared Memory.	384971	2000
rdisp/appc_ca_blk_no	Specifies the number of shared memory blocks reserved for CPI-C communication for remote function calls and other CPI-C-based functionality	384971	2000
rdisp/wp_ca_blk_no	Number of the WPCA blocks of the dispatcher. The WPCA (Work Process Communication Blocks) blocks are used for communication between the GUI, the dispatcher, and the work processes.	384971	2000
gw/max_overflow_size	Size of local memory area for SAP gateway	384971	250000000
rdisp/accept_remote_trace_level	Not allow remote trace transfer		0

FIGURE 22-5 SAP gateway and RFC parameters to address heavy interface loads

SAPPFPAR Check

SAP profile parameter changes have to be done carefully. Incorrectly configured parameters may cause the system not to start. SAP provides a command called SAPPFPAR that can be called at the operating system level to verify the memory disposition of the SAP profiles that have been changed recently. Apply the system-wide performance-tuning parameters in the default profile and application server–specific performance parameters in the instance profile. The parameters will be effective after the system restart. The syntax for using the SAPPFPAR is as follows:

```
SAPPFPAR check pf=<path to the Instance Profile>
```

Effects of Outsourcing Projects and Performance Issues

In the last decade SAP development work has been outsourced to global teams. This trend has resulted in code work being shipped to different development centers in the world and assembled and quality-tested at the implementation site when all the pieces are ready. Because the code is developed by different teams distributed at different locations in the world, it is very important for the quality control development lead at the implementation site to perform a series of checks before the code goes to the production system. Often the code may work very well during initial roll-outs but may not perform well during subsequent roll-outs because of increased data volumes. Including a volume or stress test for critical programs and interfaces will help mitigate this issue.

Summary

- SAP response times are the most important criteria for measuring how well a system is performing.
- SAP memory and buffer parameters must be tuned to get optimal performance from the system.
- Expensive SQL statements are one of the most important contributors to poor system performance.
- The SQL trace tool can be used to tune expensive SQL statements.

Additional Resources

- **Performance analysis** www.sdn.sap.com/irj/sdn/performance-analysis
- **SAP NetWeaver Performance URL: Benchmark** www.sdn.sap.com/irj/sdn/go/portal/prtroot/docs/webcontent/uuid/10986f61-0a01-0010-bdad-cdd93247dbc1

CHAPTER

SAP Performance Tuning in the Java Stack

This chapter focuses on performance tuning concepts in the Java stack, such as memory allocation in the Java Virtual Machine (JVM); the garbage collection process in the JVM and its relationship to performance tuning; and scaling Java stack–based SAP applications by adding server nodes, threads, and, if needed, application servers. We will cover tasks such as configuring heap size and different memory areas using tools such as the configuration tool. We will also discuss common SAP Java performance issues, and toward the end of the chapter, specific examples will be provided for improving NetWeaver portal performance.

Java Memory Concepts

In order to configure and tune Java memory, it is important to understand the different memory areas of the Java Virtual Machine and the allocation and usage of the areas when a Java application is in use. This understanding will also help to troubleshoot issues with Java stack crashes as a result of memory-related issues. When a SAP Java stack is installed, it will take the installation defaults or configured values to start the Java engine and the application. After this the Basis administrator has to tune the Java stack memory parameters to cater to the needs of the individual Java application. SAP OSS Note 723909 provides detailed JVM recommendations for SAP NetWeaver releases 6.4 and 7.0. SAP Note 723909 includes references to several different OSS Note numbers for specific JDK vendors such as Sun, HP, and IBM. The appropriate OSS Note number should be used to get the recommended JVM parameters. SAP OSS Note 1248926 provides the details for NetWeaver 7.1–based products.

The maximum allocated memory (heap size) of one server node or the sum of the heap sizes of all the server nodes in a cluster must fit in the physical memory of the operating system. If this is not the case, then operating system swapping will occur with a serious degradation of system performance. For 32-bit operating systems and JDKs a maximum heap size of 1GB is recommended. For a 64-bit operating system and JDK a maximum heap size of 2GB is recommended. The maximum heap size for 64-bit operating systems and JDK can be increased up to 3.5GB, but the garbage collection process can take a little longer. Usually, it is better to add a server node that is configured correctly than to increase the heap size more than

Memory Area	Description	Technical Parameter Name
Young generation area	This is the memory area of the JVM that contains newly created objects by the SAP Java application.	Young Generation Initial Size (Minimum Size): **-XX:NewSize** Young Generation Maximum Size: **-XX:Max NewSize**
Tenured generation area	This is the memory area of the JVM that contains objects that have been in use for some time by the SAP Java application.	Tenured Generation Area = Maximum Heap Size (**-Xmx**) - Maximum New Size (**-XX:Max NewSize**)
Heap size (young generation area + tenured generation area)	This is the memory area allocated to the total heap size for the JVM.	Initial Heap Size: **-Xms** Maximum Heap Size: **-Xmx**
Permanent generation area	This is the memory area of the JVM that contains objects that are needed permanently, such as classes and methods.	Permanent Generation Area Initial Size: **-XX:PermSize** Permanent Generation Area Maximum Size: **-XX:MaxPermSize**

TABLE 23-1 Different Memory Areas of the Java Virtual Machine

the recommended values. SAP provides a configuration tool for making changes to the memory areas of the JVM, which require a restart of the J2EE engine. The three main areas of the JVM memory are the young generation memory area, the tenured (old) generation memory area, and the permanent generation memory area. The heap size is defined as the sum of the young and tenured generation memory area sizes. Table 23-1 lists the memory areas of the JVM with a brief description and technical name of the parameter. It is recommended to set the start heap size the same as the maximum heap size so that the system activity for any changes will be kept to the minimum with maximum performance benefit.

The Java heap size must be monitored using tools such as Wily Introscope. This tool will provide live as well as historical heap usage information. If the heap usage reaches the maximum allocated size, the configuration tool can be used to increase the heap size. The following illustration shows that the maximum heap size configured is 2GB and the peak usage of the heap size is around 1.5GB.

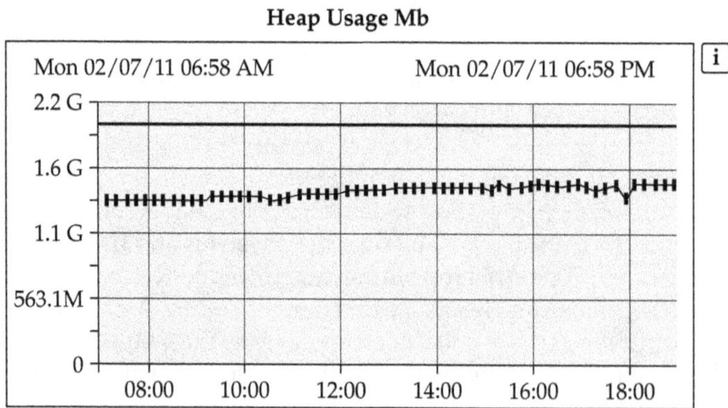

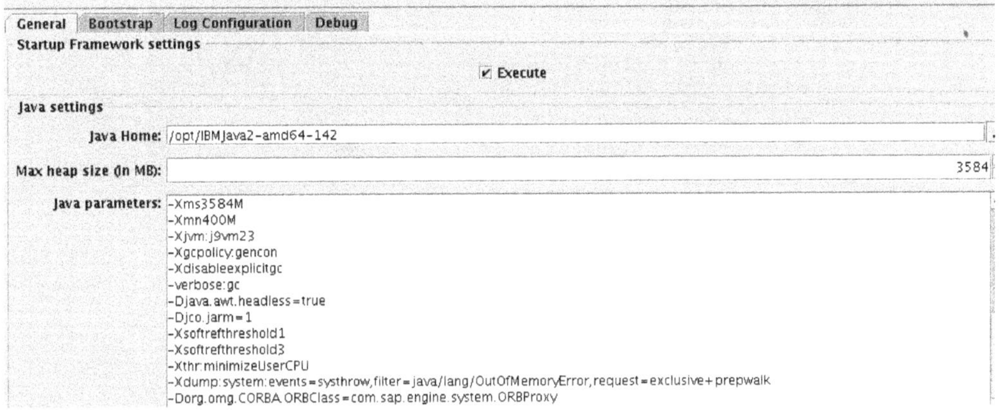

General | Bootstrap | Log Configuration | Debug

Startup Framework settings

Execute

Java settings

Java Home: /opt/IBMJava2-amd64-142

Max heap size (in MB): 3584

Java parameters:

```
-Xms3584M
-Xmn400M
-Xjvm:j9vm23
-Xgcpolicy:gencon
-Xdisableexplicitgc
-verbose:gc
-Djava.awt.headless=true
-Djco.jarm=1
-Xsoftrefthreshold1
-Xsoftrefthreshold3
-Xthr:minimizeUserCPU
-Xdump:system:events=systhrow,filter=java/lang/OutOfMemoryError,request=exclusive+prepwalk
-Dorg.omg.CORBA.ORBClass=com.sap.engine.system.ORBProxy
```


Figure 23-1 Configuration tool showing heap size configuration

The configuration tool must be used to configure different memory areas of the JVM. Figure 23-1 shows the configuration tool's Java memory settings. Please note that maximum heap size is configured the same as initial heap size of 3584MB. The configuration settings section can be reached by logging into the configuration tool and choosing Cluster Data | Instance ID | Server ID. The section on the right of Figure 23-1 shows where Maximum Heap Size (Xmx) and Initial Heap Size (Xms) can be configured.

Garbage Collection

In Java systems, the developer does not need to explicitly configure memory allocation and deallocation. Instead the system will automatically allocate the memory for the Java objects, and whenever the objects are terminated, the background process called the garbage collector (GC) will remove or destroy the memory area so that space is freed up for allocation to a new Java object. This way, the programmer does not have to worry about memory allocation and Java programming is more efficient and easy to use. Since GC is an automated process, the number of memory leaks caused by developer errors is also minimized. The following section will cover details of the GC process, types, and its effects on system performance. In order to explain the GC process in detail, different scenarios of memory allocation and deallocation are discussed so that the reader can get a good conceptual understanding of the GC process and how it can lead to situations such as Java system crashes in situations where either the memory is incorrectly configured or there is no adequate amount of physical memory available to the system.

Memory Areas in Garbage Collection

The two major memory areas that come into play during the GC process are the young generation memory area and the tenured (old) generation memory area. The sum of the young generation and tenured (old) generation memory areas is the maximum configured heap size. Figure 23-2 shows the different memory areas in the JVM and how the GC

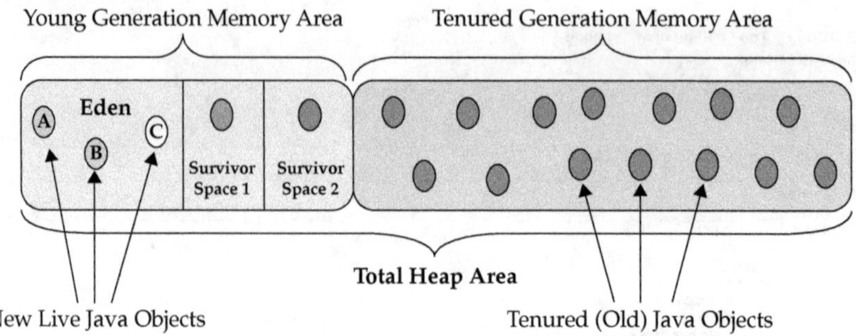

FIGURE 23-2 Different memory areas of the JVM during the garbage collection process

process works internally. The young generation area is further divided into the "Eden" and two "survivor spaces." New Java objects are allocated memory space in the Eden memory area of the young generation memory area. The survivor spaces are configured approximately to be one-eighth the size of the young generation area. In Figure 23-2 Java objects A, B, and C are new and are, therefore, allocated memory space in the Eden area of the young generation memory area. Survivor spaces 1 and 2 have Java objects that have been in use for sometime but are not still alive and are not yet ready to be moved to the tenured generation memory area.

Minor Garbage Collection

There are two kinds of GCs. One is the minor GC and the other is a full GC. In a minor GC scenario when a new Java object D tries to enter the Eden memory area it does not have enough memory to be allocated to this new object. This leads to memory allocation failure in the Eden memory area and results in a minor GC. The minor GC scans the entire young generation memory area so that unused memory can be freed up, as shown in Figure 23-3. Minor GC happens quickly and does not have any significant performance delays. From an end-user perspective the minor GC process is seamless and will not be noticed at all.

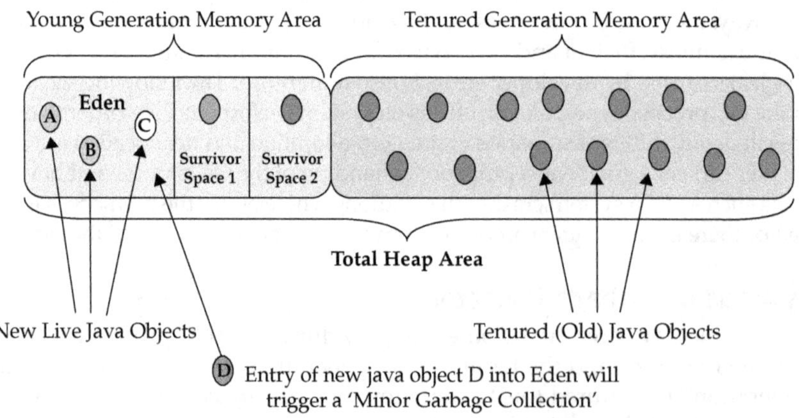

FIGURE 23-3 Minor garbage collection process initialization scenario

Please note that the minor GC process does not scan or clear any objects in the tenured memory area or the permanent memory area. Java objects that are still alive in the survivor memory space can be moved to the tenured memory area based on several criteria. It is also possible that the Java objects in the survivor spaces can be moved back and forth between the two spaces.

In Figure 23-4 a complete minor garbage collection scenario is discussed. A new Java object D needs memory to be allocated as per application usage. Since the Eden area already has three Java objects, A, B, and C, there is no additional memory for the new Java object D in the Eden memory area, and this results a memory allocation failure, which triggers the minor garbage collection process. This process scans the entire young generation memory area and finds that Java object A is not alive and is no longer needed. The minor GC process will destroy the memory area of Java object A, and this can now be allocated to the new Java object D. This is a very simplistic description of the minor GC process. In real-life scenarios far more objects will need memory space in the Eden memory area and far more objects will not live and their memory areas will be destroyed by the minor GC process. The memory allocation model assumes the "weak generational hypothesis," which states that a significant percentage of Java objects live for a very short period. Once usage is complete, the memory area is destroyed by the minor GC process and is freed up for the new Java objects.

In the example Java object C is still alive and is therefore moved to survivor space 1 and the Java object M in survivor space 1 is now moved to survivor space 2, as that is alive as well. Java object T in survivor area 2 has been alive for a long time and meets the criteria to be moved to the tenured (old) generation memory area. This increases the memory utilization of the tenured (old) memory area.

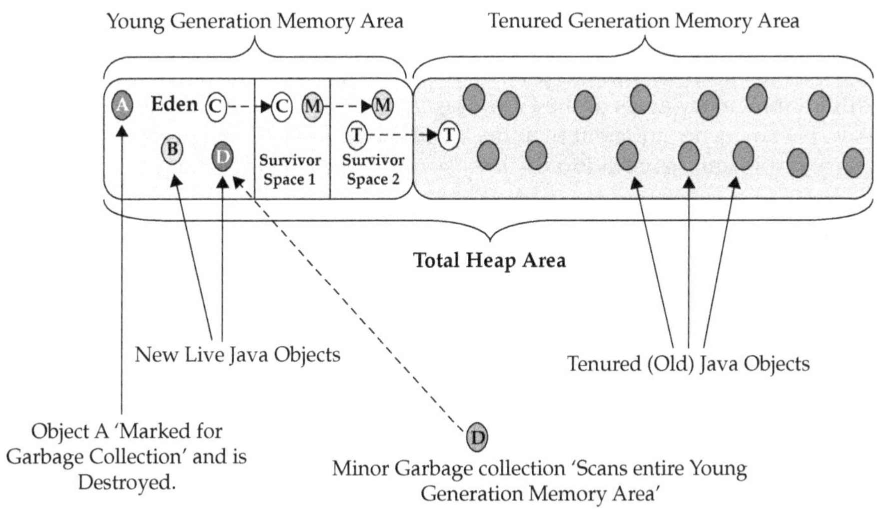

FIGURE 23-4 Minor garbage collection execution scenario causing the entire young generation area to be scanned

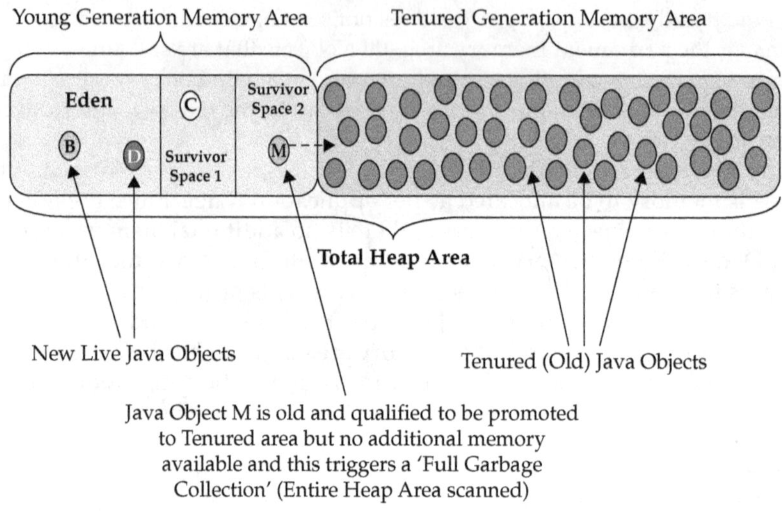

FIGURE 23-5 Full garbage collection scenario causing the entire heap area to be scanned

Full Garbage Collection

The next scenario we will discuss covers the full garbage collection. In this scenario, as shown in Figure 23-5, Java object M is qualified to be promoted to the tenured memory area, but this area is already full and a memory allocation error results. This leads to a full garbage collection scenario where the entire heap area is scanned, which could take a considerable amount of time. Full GC has some serious performance implications, and end users will start seeing the Java application hanging and becoming unresponsive. This situation will last until the full GC process is completed and additional memory is freed up in different memory areas of the JVM. It is ideal to tune the system to avoid full GC processes. If there is no sufficient memory available, a full GC will eventually lead to out-of-memory errors and may lead to the Java system ultimately crashing.

Out of Memory

This error is usually noticed in systems that are either incorrectly configured or there is no sufficient memory in the system for proper allocation. Table 23-2 describes the error messages can be seen in the server0 logs in the work directory depending upon which memory area is out of memory.

Scalability of Applications Based on the Java Stack

SAP applications based on the Java stack are highly scalable, and there are several ways to scale them. The following sections will list and discuss the different ways to scale the Java application. Scaling is important for provisioning, as it enables the system to handle increased concurrent user access or increased load.

Out Of Memory Error Message	Description
java.lang.OutOfMemoryError: Java heap space (failed to allocate '...' bytes)	This error message indicates that the heap size configuration is either incorrect or configured too small. Increasing the heap size and restarting the J2EE engine will help resolve the issue.
java.lang.OutOfMemoryError: PermGen Space	This indicates the permanent generation area is full. Increasing the permanent generation area and restarting the J2EE engine will help resolve the issue.
java.lang.OutOfMemoryError: Requested array size exceeds VM limit	Small heap size or Java program bug.
java.lang.OutOfMemoryError: Requested <size> bytes for <reason>. Example: Out of Swap Space	This error message indicates that the operating system swap size is configured too small.

TABLE 23-2 Out Of Memory Error Scenarios

Server Node

Server nodes in the Java stack are comparable to the work processes in the ABAP stack, with few differences. Unlike ABAP work processes, Java server nodes are multithreaded and are therefore capable of multitasking. ABAP work processes are single-threaded and perform one task at a time. The multithreaded server node architecture of the Java stack will allow few server nodes to process the load coming to the Java stack from the end users. Because of this key difference, there are far fewer Java server nodes compared to ABAP work processes. The number of server nodes to be configured will depend on the availability of the physical memory and CPU resources of the hardware. The addition of more server nodes will improve system performance as long as adequate resources are available at the operating system level. The configuration tool is used to add more server nodes. Select the instance to which a new node has to be added and choose Server | Add Server.

Application and System Threads

The server nodes are multithreaded, and the number of threads can be increased based on the workload and availability of system resources. Application and system threads are the most important ones that need to be configured to improve the system performance. Application threads accept end-user work, and system threads are used for performing generic system activities such as backups.

Configuration Tool to Increase the Thread Count

The configuration tool is recommended for increasing the application and system thread count. Specifically, Wily Introscope is recommended to monitor the use of the application and system thread usage and to increase these as needed to improve system performance.

The following illustrations show using application and system thread counts of a Java application.

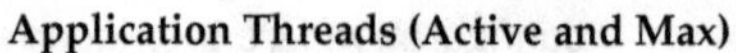

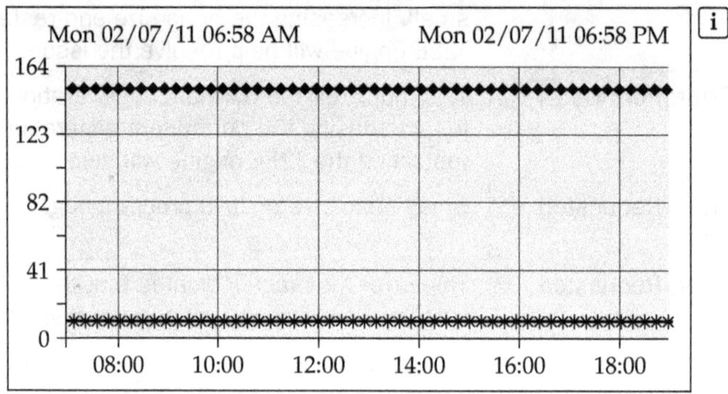

J2EE System Threads in Use

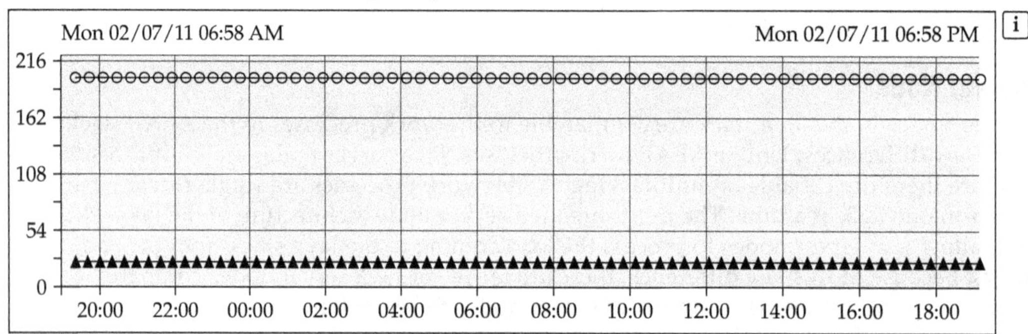

To increase the application thread count globally (for all server nodes), start the configuration tool at the operating system level, choose Global Server Configuration | Managers | Application Thread Manager, and change the values for Initial Thread Count, Maximum Thread Count, and Minimum Thread Count as shown in Figure 23-6.

- cluster-data
  - Global dispatcher configuration
    - managers
    - services
  - Global server configuration
    - managers
      - ApplicationThreadManager
      - CacheManager
      - ClassLoaderManager
      - ClusterManager
      - ConfigurationManager
      - IpVerificationManager
      - LicensingManager
      - LockingManager
      - LogManager
      - PoolManager
      - ServiceManager
      - ThreadManager

Global properties

Key	Custom value	Default value
DebugLogFileName		./log/managers/thread/DEBUG.log
InfoLogFileName		./log/managers/thread/INFO.log
InitialFOQSize		200
InitialThreadCount	40	40
MaintainWakeupTimeout		5
MaxFOQSize		5000
MaxRQSize		5000
MaxThreadCount	300	40
MinThreadCount	40	40
NoticeLogFileName		./log/managers/thread/NOTICE.log
ThreadsIdleTimeout		5
WarningLogFileName		./log/managers/thread/WARNING.log

FIGURE 23-6 Configuration tool usage to increase application thread count

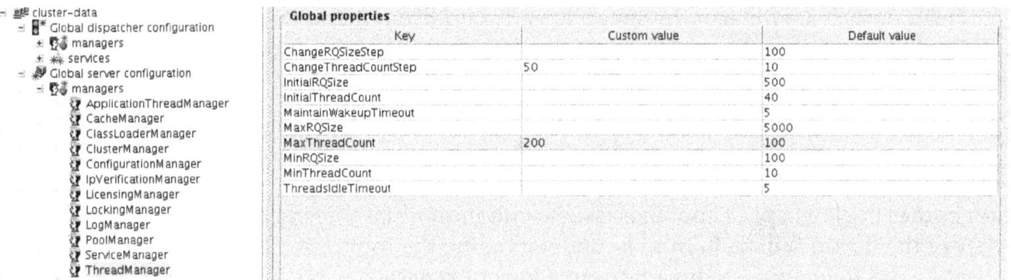

FIGURE 23-7 Configuration tool usage to increase system thread count

To increase the system thread count globally (for all server nodes), start the configuration tool at the operating system level, choose Global Server Configuration | Managers | Thread Manager, and change the values for Initial Thread Count, Maximum Thread Count, and Minimum Thread Count as shown in Figure 23-7.

Add More Java Application Servers

One other way to scale the Java stack is to add more application servers with their own server nodes and threads to improve the system performance. Usually, adding an application server requires more hardware resources.

Java Performance Troubleshooting Tools

SAP provides a number of tools for troubleshooting performance issues in the Java stack. Wily Introscope is one of the best tools to study the internals of the J2EE engine, and it captures and presents graphs on such important areas as heap utilization, garbage collection, thread count utilizations, and response times. In addition to this tool the following dump and memory analysis tools are helpful for diagnosing complex performance issues in the Java stack.

Heap Dump

Heap dump will allow you to understand the usage of the heap size in greater detail and will help to diagnose the root cause of an issue. In order to generate a heap dump, add the parameter -XX:+HeapDumpOnOutOfMemoryError to the Java parameter using the configuration tool. This will automatically write a heap dump file in out-of-memory situations at the following location:

```
/usr/sap/<SID>/<instance>/j2ee/cluster/server<N> directory
```

The heap dump files are extremely large and cause the Java system restart to hang as a result of disk space getting completely filled up. You can set an alternative path for the location of the heap dump file by setting the following Java parameter using the configuration tool:

```
-XX:HeapDumpPath=<directory where to save the heap dumps>
```

Heap dumps are binary profiles and need specialized memory analysis tools to perform additional troubleshooting activities. Heap dumps contain a snapshot of all the Java objects that are active or alive at the time of the dump. The file can be sent to SAP for additional analysis to identify the root cause of the issue.

Thread Dump

Sometimes the Java application has issues with individual threads hanging, and an internal view of the thread will be helpful in understanding the root cause of the issue. There are several ways to generate a thread dump. One of the easiest ways is to use the JCMON tool. Call the JCMON tool at the operating system level, and choose menu path 20 (Local Administration Menu). Next choose the option dump stacktrace menu by entering the number, selecting the server process by entering the value from the Idx column, and confirming the server process by choosing Yes.

For Sun and HP JVMs, the thread dump file is written at the following location:

```
/usr/sap/<SID>/<Instance>/work/std<node name>.out_'
```

For IBM JVMs the thread dump file is written at the following location:

```
/usr/sap/<SID>/<Instance>/j2ee/cluster/serverX/javacore.<timestamp>.<PID>.txt
```

Memory Analyzer

The memory analyzer tool is an open-source product that will help to analyze large productive heap dumps. The tool will help identify which Java objects are hogging large chunks of memory and will be helpful in identifying the root cause of the heap dumps in your system. The location to download the tool is provided in the additional resources section of this chapter.

Summary

- The primary SAP Java memory allocation areas in JVM are young generation memory area, tenured (old) generation memory area, and permanent generation memory area.
- The young generation memory area keeps the newly created Java objects.
- The tenured (old) generation memory area keeps the Java objects that are in use for a while and are still needed by the system.
- The permanent memory area keeps central classes and methods permanently.
- Garbage collection is a process of automatic memory allocation and deallocation by the system using garbage collector algorithms.
- A heap size of 1GB is recommended for 32-bit systems.
- A heap size of 2GB is recommended for 64-bit systems.
- A heap size up to 3.5GB can be configured for 64-bit systems.

- Minor garbage collection is quick and does not have any major performance implications.
- Full garbage collection is triggered when there is not enough memory to be allocated in the tenured memory area, and it has major performance implications.
- Out-of-memory errors could result if there is no more memory available for tenured memory area needs.
- Java server nodes are equivalent to ABAP work processes.
- Java server nodes are multithreaded and therefore can perform multiple tasks at a time.
- ABAP work processes are single-threaded, performing one task at a time.
- Application and system thread counts can be increased for each server node using the configuration tool.
- Heap dumps and thread dumps will help to understand the underlying issue in the JVM with regard to utilization of heaps and threads.
- The memory analyzer tool can be used to analyze the heap dump.

Additional Resources

- **Heap dump analyzer tool** www.sdn.sap.com/irj/sdn/wiki?path=/display/Java/Java+Memory+Analysis
- **Garbage collection tuning** www.oracle.com/technetwork/java/javase/gc-tuning-6-140523.html
- **Performance analysis** www.sdn.sap.com/irj/sdn/performance-analysis
- **SAP NetWeaver performance benchmark** www.sdn.sap.com/irj/sdn/go/portal/prtroot/docs/webcontent/uuid/10986f61-0a01-0010-bdad-cdd93247dbc1
- **Java memory analyzer** www.eclipse.org/mat

CHAPTER

SAP System Sizing Overview

In this chapter we will study the significance of SAP sizing and explore an overview of the entire SAP sizing process. We will also study SAP sizing theoretical concepts; tools provided by SAP to aid the customer in the sizing process, such as Quick Sizer; different kinds of sizing approaches; and some specific examples of sizing SAP solutions, such as ERP, BW, and network sizing. SAP sizing projects are started in a new SAP implementation and are updated throughout the lifecycle of the SAP projects from the blueprint design stage to the post-go live and upgrade stages of the projects. SAP recommends using different sizing approaches depending upon the stage of the project. When a new SAP project is in the design stages the infrastructure team is charged with performing an initial budget sizing to get an understanding of the costs of the servers and related technology that would be required for the project. This is followed up with iterations of sizing by closely working with the business teams until realistic user and expected volume information is provided to the sizing tool to calculate the needed hardware for the project.

Significance of SAP Sizing

Performing a SAP sizing at the beginning of the project is very important for several reasons. Foremost is to make sure that the performance and response time expectations of the business users are met by planning and providing adequate system resources before the projects goes live. Since ERP projects are major changes in an organization, it is very important to provide the data availability to the end users for a system that is being implemented as a system of record. This will make the end users embrace the system and champion it to the remaining business users inside the organization. Other reasons for performing a sizing project and to keep it updated are to not overspend on infrastructure that would not be utilized and would sit idle. A good sizing effort will help the infrastructure team to plan and procure the appropriate amount of system resources (CPU, memory, and disk) on time, considering that the lead times for the procurement process and vendor delivery could be considerable.

Sizing Theory and Practice

SAP sizing is based on a theoretical concept called the queuing model (or queuing theory). In this kind of modeling the queuing systems are studied mathematically to estimate the performance criteria such as response times. A SAP three-tiered software architecture is studied as a queuing model with one service center (CPU). In this three-tiered SAP architecture, all the major system resources, such as memory, disk, and network load, can be spread out in such a way that any queuing can be significantly reduced. However, the CPU of the database server is the single most-limiting factor in a three-tiered SAP software architecture and is, therefore, looked at first as being responsible for any major queues, which could cause delays in system response time and performance bottlenecks. A combination of theoretical models and performance load tests are used to understand the bottlenecks of the system.

Sizing Definition

SAP sizing is defined as a process of converting the business requirements into hardware requirements. SAP provides tools and benchmark standards for estimating the hardware requirements that would be needed for the business.

SAPS (SAP Application Performance Standard)

SAP, working closely with its hardware partners, has developed a hardware (platform)-independent benchmark referred to as SAP Application Performance Standard (SAPS) to help size SAP applications.

100 SAPS = 2,000 fully processed order line items per hour **(OR)**
6,000 dialog steps (screen changes) with 2,000 postings **(OR)**
2,400 SAP transactions

SAP Quick Sizer Tool

SAP provides a web-based online tool to customers for performing a sizing project. The SAP Quick Sizer tool has an online questionnaire that takes the user and throughput numbers provided by the customer's business and calculates the SAPS value. The SAPS value will help the hardware vendor to size and landscape the system for the customer.

Hardware Vendor Role in Sizing

Hardware vendor plays a critical role in taking the customer's SAPS value generated from the SAP sizing project and providing proposals (with different options) for the needed server hardware and the way the solution should be landscaped in the customer data center. Because of the importance of this activity, many hardware vendors such as IBM and HP have dedicated experts in sizing activities and help their customers in providing a suitable solution. Many customers will run a Quick Sizer sizing project and then share the information with multiple hardware vendors. The hardware vendors then will provide customized scalable solutions to their customers, and the customer will evaluate different proposals and will decide on a hardware vendor based on several criteria, such as business requirements, cost, and support services.

Benchmarking

SAP works closely with the hardware vendors to perform different benchmarks by running a simulated load in a theoretical machine and publishing the results. Usually SD (Sales and Distribution) transactions are executed for the benchmark standards. SAP customers can compare the SAPS values generated by the Quick Sizer project to the published benchmark numbers to get a good idea of the kind of hardware that they would need to run their business. SAP customers can access the benchmark information at the following URL: www.sap.com/solutions/benchmark/index.epx.

Kinds of Sizing

There are several different kinds of sizing. The sizing type will depend on the intended purpose. Table 24-1 lists different types of sizing with a brief description of each category, a sample scenario, and recommended tool for performing the sizing.

Sizing Type	Description	Example
Initial sizing	This type of sizing is done at the beginning of the project for budget purposes and to procure the initial hardware for the implementation of the SAP solution.	A new ERP implementation is started by an organization. Recommended tool: Online Quick Sizer
Resizing (type of productive sizing)	This type of sizing is done when no new business processes are added to the existing solution or no new SAP solutions are added to the existing solution. Only the **volume/load** of the users or the business data is increased.	Addition of 200 users to the existing business processes used in productive operation. Recommended tool: Use SAP monitors for the database (Transaction DB02), operating system (Transaction ST06), and front-end network load (Transaction ST03n). **DO NOT** use the SAP Quick Sizer tool for resizing purposes.
Delta sizing (type of productive sizing)	This type of sizing is done when a **new business function** is added to the existing production system.	Addition of a CRM or SCM solution to existing ERP operations in production. Recommended tool: Use SAP monitors to calculate any additional load for this roll-out. Use SAP Quick Sizer, expert sizing, or sizing templates to get the additional SAPS required for the CRM or SCM solution. Delta sizing = Additional load for new roll-out + Additional SAPS for CRM or SCM solution.

Table 24-1 Different Sizing Types (*Continued*)

Sizing Type	Description	Example
Upgrade sizing (type of productive sizing)	This type of sizing is done when a production system is upgraded to a newer release.	Upgrade an older release of SAP from version 4.7 to the most current SAP release Business Suite 7. Recommended tool: Use SAP monitors to calculate any additional load for the upgrade. SAP Notes listing the impact on CPU, memory, and disk as a result of an upgrade. (Note 901070 - Resource Requirements for SAP Enterprise Core Component 6.0)
T-shirt sizing	This type of sizing is mostly used for new applications. These applications are not yet integrated into the SAP Quick Sizer tool and use simple algorithms and assumptions to calculate the SAPS value/ hardware requirements.	T-shirt sizing for SAP Supply Network Collaboration (SNC). The guidelines can be downloaded from the following location: http://service.sap.com/sizing | Sizing Guidelines | Solutions & Platform.

TABLE 24-1 Different Sizing Types

Performing Sizing with SAP Quick Sizer Tool

In order to perform a sizing project using the Quick Sizer tool two pre-requisites must be met. The first one is to have a customer number and the second one is to have a valid user (S number) account to SAP Service Marketplace. The following procedure will explain how to create a new sizing project.

1. Start the web-based online SAP Quick Sizer tool by using the following URLs: https://websmp207.sap-ag.de/sizing or https://service.sap.com/sizing.
2. In the subsequent screen click Start The Quick Sizer as shown in Figure 24-1.
3. If pop-ups are not allowed, the system will notify you of this. Right-click the yellow bar at the top and select Allow Pop-Ups For This Site Temporarily Or Permanently and repeat steps 1–2. The following screen will appear in a separate window. Enter the customer number and a project name, and click the Create Project button as shown.

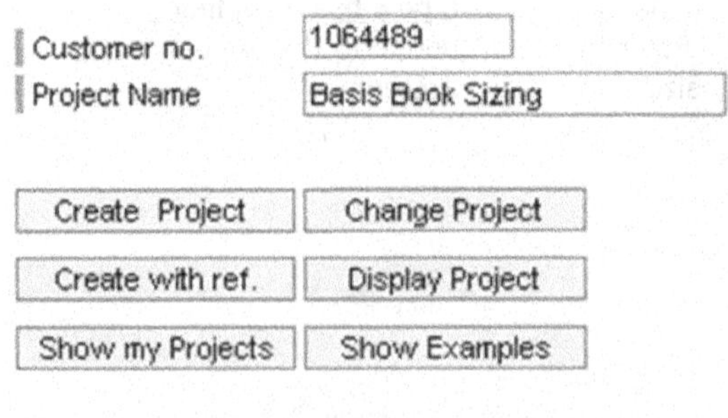

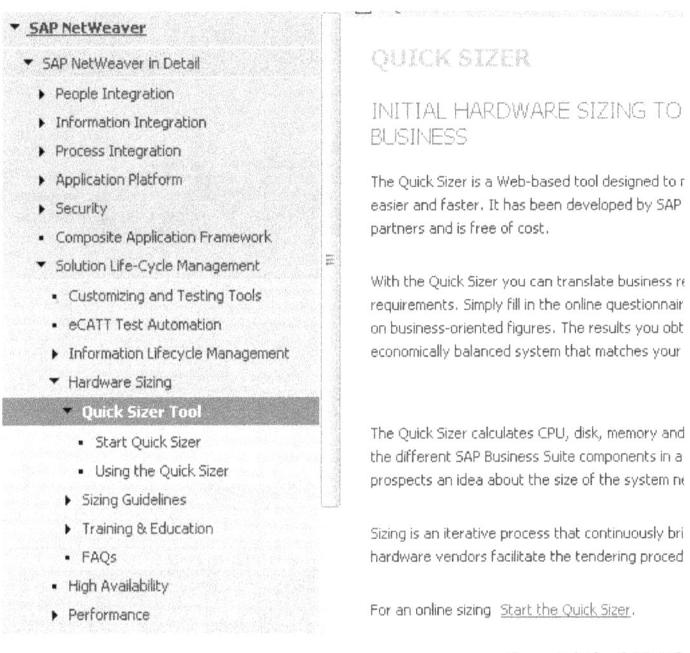

SAP NetWeaver
SAP NetWeaver in Detail
People Integration
Information Integration
Process Integration
Application Platform
Security
Composite Application Framework
Solution Life-Cycle Management
Customizing and Testing Tools
eCATT Test Automation
Information Lifecycle Management
Hardware Sizing
Quick Sizer Tool
Start Quick Sizer
Using the Quick Sizer
Sizing Guidelines
Training & Education
FAQs
High Availability
Performance
QUICK SIZER
INITIAL HARDWARE SIZING TO
BUSINESS
The Quick Sizer is a Web-based tool designed to r
easier and faster. It has been developed by SAP
partners and is free of cost.
With the Quick Sizer you can translate business re
requirements. Simply fill in the online questionnair
on business-oriented figures. The results you obt
economically balanced system that matches your
The Quick Sizer calculates CPU, disk, memory and
the different SAP Business Suite components in a
prospects an idea about the size of the system ne
Sizing is an iterative process that continuously bri
hardware vendors facilitate the tendering proced
For an online sizing Start the Quick Sizer.

FIGURE 24-1 SAP Quick Sizer start screen in the browser

4. The screen shown in Figure 24-2 appears. The main options for expanding the sizing element tree on the left and the collapse tree on the right are boxed and circled respectively in the figure. Clicking the arrow in front of the sizing element (Example: SAP ERP) will expand the hierarchy so the details of the sizing data can be entered in the tables. As shown on the right side of the figure the tree collapse control (circled) can be used to expand and collapse the project information, customer data, platform, communication, and other sections. Click the collapse trees, fill in the required information, and save the information by clicking the Save button on the top.
5. Expanding the SAP ERP section on the left will give the sizing tables for user- and throughput-based sizing on the right. The next step is to fill in the user count information and throughput information gathered from business teams and click the Save button.

User-Based Sizing

In user-based sizing, user count information is entered in the active user sizing table as shown in Figure 24-3. Three categories of users are defined in user-based sizing. SAP

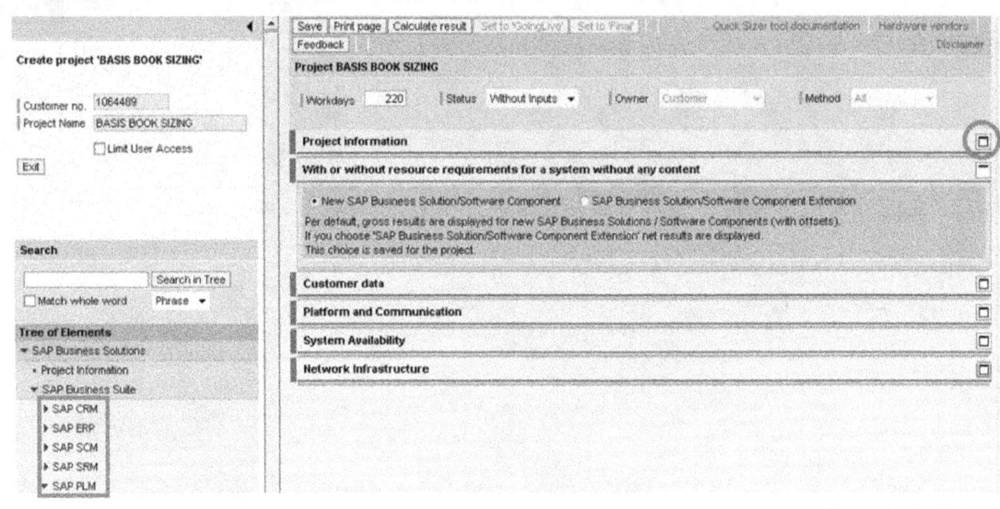

Copyright by SAP AG

FIGURE 24-2 The initial screen when using SAP Business Suite Sizing

recommends a distribution of high, medium, and low (10%, 15%, and 75%) user distribution if actual distribution is not known.

- **Low activity users** Number of concurrent users with a think time of about 300 seconds.
- **Medium activity users** Number of concurrent users with a think time of about 30 seconds.
- **High activity users** Number of concurrent users with a think time of about 10 seconds.

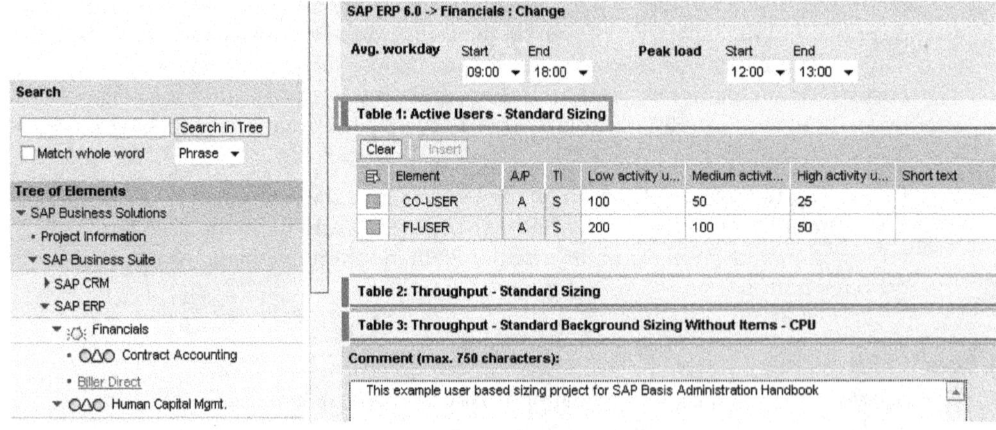

Copyright by SAP AG

FIGURE 24-3 Example of a user-based sizing table in Quick Sizer

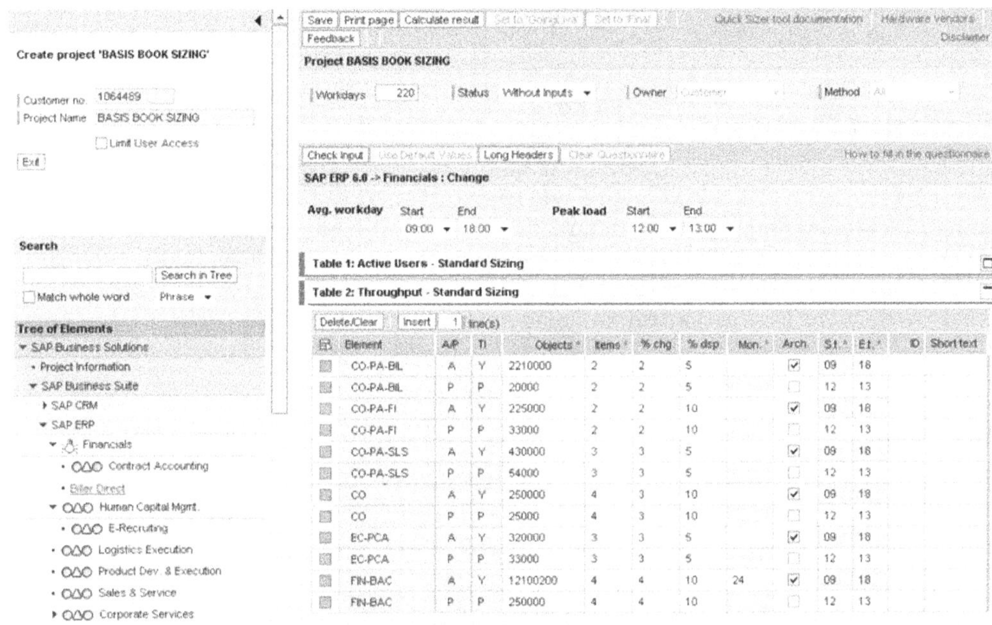

FIGURE 24-4 Example of a throughput-based sizing table in Quick Sizer

Throughput-Based Sizing

In throughput-based sizing, the volume data is gathered from the business teams and entered in the Quick Sizing project as shown in Figure 24-4.

Likewise, expand all the relevant sections of the SAP ERP sizing elements on the left section of the screen and fill in the user count and throughput data in different tables on the right side. Once the data entry is complete, click the Save button and then click the Calculate Result button to get the SAPS value of the sizing project, as shown in Figure 24-5. The sizing

All | SAPS | Memory and disk

Active Users Results for SAP Business Solutions

Solution	Release	CPU cat.	SAPS (total)	DB SAPS	App. SAPS (ABAP)
ERP	6.0	S	2.000	500	1.700

All | SAPS | Memory and disk

Throughput Results for SAP Business Solutions

Solution	Release	CPU cat.	SAPS (total)	DB SAPS	App. SAPS (ABAP)
ERP	6.0	M	8.200	800	7.400

FIGURE 24-5 Quick Sizer results screen showing the SAPS value

project name is then shared with your hardware vendor so that they can give a hardware recommendation based on the calculated SAPS value.

Specific Sizing Examples

This section will cover some specific SAP solution sizing examples. Sample sizing questionnaires and related information will be discussed as well. The SAP Quick Sizer tool sizing tables/questionnaire are online, and there is no download option for the questionnaire. However, SAP does provide offline questionnaires to its hardware partners. Customers can also prepare a user-friendly version using the online questionnaire as an example. The following sections have some sample sizing questionnaires that can be used to build your own. Once the questionnaires are ready, they can be shared with the business teams along with the sizing online documentation.

ECC Sizing

Figure 24-6 shows a sample ECC sizing questionnaire. The sizing questionnaire has tables for user sizing as well as throughput-based sizing. User sizing is based on concurrent user counts for low-, medium-, and high-activity users in the systems. The throughput sizing is based on the number of business documents that are created per each sizing element on a yearly basis or based on peak load. The shorter the peak load times, the higher the CPU utilization of the system. If there is a business requirement for processing a peak volume of business postings in narrower windows of time, then the SAPS value usually is quite high, indicating the high CPU requirements necessary to support the system.

BW Sizing

BW sizing can also be performed based on concurrent user counts as well as throughput (Info Cube metrics) information. Figure 24-7 shows a sample completed BW sizing questionnaire with concurrent user counts and Info Cube key figure, characteristics, initial, and periodic load information. Recent versions of Quick Sizer include the BW-Java components (web templates), and the resulting SAPS value is more accurate than the earlier versions. If the BW system is expected to be integrated into the corporate SAP NetWeaver portal, then additional portal sizing for the increased user load should also be performed.

Enterprise Resource Planning -> Financials Workdays = 250

Table 1: Active Users - Standard Sizing	Element	A/P	TI	Low activ user	Medium activ user	High activ user	Start Time	End Time
	FI-USER (Financial Transaction User)	Average	Snapshot	100	40	50	7	17

Table 2: Throughput - Standard Sizing	Element	A/P	TI	Objects	Items (Sub-Object of the Object)	Object Changes %	Object Display %.	Retention Period in Months	Start Time	End Time
	FIN-BAC (FI Documents)	Average	Yearly	14,763,548	4	5	10	24	7	17
	FIN-BAC (FI Documents)	Peak Load	Period	312,384	4	5	10		7	17

FIGURE 24-6 Sample SAP ECC sizing questionnaire

Table 2: Throughput - User Groups: Reporting & Analysis	Element	A/P	TI	# of Concurrently Active BW Users)	% predRep	% OLAP	% Explor	Start Time	End Time
	BW-INFO	Average	Snapshot	20	80	20		9	18
	BW-Busin	Average	Snapshot	100	40	60		9	18
	BW-EXPERT	Average	Snapshot	20	20	80	100	9	18

Table 4: Throughput - Definition of Infocubes	Element	A/P	TI	Dimensions	IC Key Figu	Initial Load	Periodic Lo	Periods
	INFOCUBE	Average						
	(ZFAGL_C10) New GL - Transaction data	Average		6	4	260000	12000	Month
	(ZFAGL_C11) New GL - Line Item Data	Average		13	3	3500000	140000	Month
	(ZFAAR_C02) FIAR: Transaction Data	Average		6	4	36000	1200	Month
	(ZFAAR_C03) FIAR: Line Item	Average		11	4	640000	45000	Month
	(ZI_C01) Material Batch Stock	Average		8	13	300000	120000	Daily Refresh
	(ZI_C03) Material Stocks/Movements	Average		11	24	2500000	150000	Month
	(ZS_C01) Sales Order Analysis Detail	Average		8	13	9200000	700000	Month

FIGURE 24-7 Sample sizing questionnaire for BW systems sizing

Network Sizing

When the application user count increases, the network bandwidth requirement also goes up. SAP provides certain sizing guidelines for calculating the SAP network bandwidth so that the organization's network team can plan for any needed network upgrades ahead of going live with the new users. The following formula can be used to calculate the needed network bandwidth for additional active users that will be added to the system:

$$C = X * N * D * 0.25$$

where:

C = Bandwidth in kbps needed for SAP GUI
X = Amount of data per dialog step in kilobytes
N = Number of active users
D = Average # of dialog steps per minute per user
0.25 = Numerical factor (includes conversion, protocol overhead, and safety factor)

Example:
C = 4.6 * 30 * 4 * 0.25
C = 138 kbps

Pitfalls to Avoid in Sizing SAP Projects

SAP sizing projects could run into some of the common pitfalls listed here. For each of the pitfalls a mitigation plan is offered so that these can be avoided while running a sizing project at your organization.

Customers Do It Themselves

Sizing projects are sometimes performed by customers themselves with inexperienced resources, and this can lead to inaccurate sizing estimates and affect the credibility of the project, as the system is either undersized or oversized. Undersized systems could experience serious performance issues, and oversized systems will make organizations incur unnecessary cost up-front and a significant amount of the system resources could be idle. This situation can be mitigated by assigning this task to an experienced consultant who has experience helping customers with performing several SAP sizing projects.

Incorrect Understanding of Sizing Elements

The next common pitfall is incorrect understanding of the sizing element by the business team member. The gathered throughput data is incorrect, and this renders the SAP sizing project inaccurate. This situation can be mitigated by an experienced SAP sizing consultant explaining the sizing element in detail using the sizing help document. This way, the gathered throughput data is correct and will yield more accurate sizing results.

Incorrect Peak Sizing

One other common pitfall is incorrect interpretation of the peak load and peak period. The business requirements for peak loads for some industries such as utilities are very high. A lot of volume is processed in a very short period. If the peak load time is estimated incorrectly, this will give an incorrect estimate of SAPS value, causing performance issues in the system. An experienced business team member inside the organization with a deep understanding of the business processes and volumes processed should be consulted in gathering peak load and peak period information so that the sizing results are accurate.

Sizing vs. Landscaping

Usually, customers assume that SAP Quick Sizer will help them not only size the solution that would be implemented, but also distribute the application components to different servers (landscaping). It is responsibility of the hardware vendor, in consultation with the customer, to properly landscape the system to maximize the resource utilization and minimize the downtime. Experienced SAP technical architects and Basis architects can also help landscape the solution so that requirements such as high availability, disaster recovery, and business continuity can be ensured. One other point that is important is to install the SAP servers in a package or virtualization environment so that they can be moved around between different servers to model the landscaping to suit the on-going requirements of the organization.

Other Considerations

ERP sections of the sizing tool/tables do not account for system activities such as printing and business workplace activities. This activity can be sized by filling up the sizing elements BC-PRINT and BWP, covered under the tables listed under the SAP NetWeaver sections of the sizing tool.

Summary

- SAP sizing is done initially for the purpose of budget allocation and procurement of servers.
- The web-based online SAP Quick Sizer tool is recommended to perform initial sizing.
- SAP sizing is based on the theoretical concept of queuing modeling (queuing theory).
- SAP sizing is the process of getting hardware requirements from business requirements.

- The SAPS (SAP Application Performance Standard) value is used as a benchmark by hardware vendors to provide an estimate of the hardware requirements needed for the customer.
- Customers can compare the SAPS value generated by the Quick Sizer project with the benchmark numbers published by SAP for different vendors and server configurations.
- Different types of sizing are available based on the stage of the SAP project, from blueprint to post go-live and upgrade stages.
- Resizing is done when load is added to the system.
- Resizing is done by gathering data from different SAP monitors.
- Delta sizing is done when new functionality is added to the project.
- Upgrade sizing is done for SAP upgrade projects, and usually SAP provides an OSS Note on the impact of the upgrade for system resources.
- T-shirt sizing is used for newly developed solutions.
- Network sizing can be performed by using a SAP-provided formula.
- Common SAP sizing project pitfalls are use of inexperienced resources to perform sizing, incorrect interpretation of the sizing elements, and mistakes in choosing the peak load volume and period in the Quick Sizer.
- Common pitfalls can be mitigated by assigning an experienced SAP sizing consultant to work closely with the business teams in arriving at accurate SAP sizing numbers.
- The hardware vendor is ultimately responsible for providing a scalable hardware solution to its customers.

Additional Resources

- **Sizing decision tree** https://websmp209.sap-ag.de/~sapidb/011000358700000970192010E/ebene1.htm (An S user account is required to log in to the SAP Service Marketplace.)
- **SAP benchmark** www.sap.com/solutions/benchmark/index.epx
- **SAP benchmark results interpretation** www.sap.com/solutions/benchmark/benchresults/benchresults.html
- **SAP benchmark glossary** www.sap.com/solutions/benchmark/glossary.epx

PART

SAP Upgrades

CHAPTER

SAP Upgrade of an ABAP Stack

In this part we will study the SAP upgrades in ABAP and Java stacks. In this chapter, in the initial sections we will study general upgrade topics, such as upgrade concepts, upgrade strategy, software logistics for performing successful upgrades, evolution of SAP upgrades, and upgrade tools. Subsequent sections will cover ABAP upgrades with a focus on upgrade to ERP 6 and Enhancement Package 4 to show how a technical upgrade would be planned and executed in a typical ABAP stack-based application. We will also study the most common technical upgrade issues that are encountered when performing an ABAP technical upgrade and in upgrade projects in general. The next chapter will focus on Java upgrades, and we will upgrade a dual-stack Process Integration (PI) system by way of example. A dual-stack application such as SAP PI is chosen so that we have an opportunity to study the synchronized upgrade procedure used to perform a dual-stack (ABAP + Java) upgrade along with learning how a Java stack–based SAP application would be upgraded.

Upgrade Concepts

Some of the key upgrade concepts that will be discussed before diving deeply into the upgrade tools and the actual planning and execution of the upgrade include the definition of technical downtime compared to business downtime, system switch upgrade, deciding on an upgrade strategy, and upgrade software logistics. The following sections will discuss these topics in detail. The upgrade concepts discussed here are applicable to both ABAP and Java stacks.

Technical Downtime vs. Business Downtime

The duration of time the system is not available as a result of the upgrade of the technical components of the SAP system is referred as technical downtime. Technical downtime is defined from the point of view of the technology team and particularly the Basis administrator's perspective. Business downtime is defined as the total duration of time the system is not available to the end user, from the beginning of the technical upgrade downtime until all the post-upgrade mandatory steps are executed in the system. This includes the time needed to perform post-upgrade and business validation steps. Business downtime is defined from the point of view of the end business user and, in general, from the business sponsor of the upgrade project inside the organization.

The goal of SAP as a vendor and as a Basis administrator is to reduce the business downtime for the upgrades as much as possible by deploying the best practices, tools, and when necessary, SAP services so that the upgrade is completed with minimum business downtime and delivers the new release functionality to the business. Depending upon the downtime needs of a given organization, different strategies can be deployed to minimize the business downtime. Strategies available vary from normal weekend scheduled downtime with either resource minimized or downtime-minimized strategies all the way to advanced upgrade technologies that support near zero downtime (NZDT). We will discuss these concepts in the next section.

System Switch Upgrade

In a system switch upgrade, the upgrade program creates a target release shadow instance (second instance) in parallel to the source release in the same database. The target release is built during production operation of the source release, except for certain steps that require a downtime. During downtime, the remaining steps are completed in the shadow instance and the upgrade program switches the shadow instance with the target release as the production system and deletes the source release. The key steps performed during downtime are: application tables are converted during the PARCONV_UPG phase, the kernel is switched to a newer level during KX_SWITCH_1 phase, and the EU_SWITCH phase executes the switch to the new system. If incremental table conversion (ICNV) is used, tables are converted during productive operation, further reducing the downtime. Over time, SAP has improved the upgrade to a point where the underlying complexity is hidden during the process and the downtime has been reduced significantly because of better technology, such as system switch upgrades and better tools such as ICNV. We will discuss the details of different upgrade tools in subsequent sections of this chapter.

Upgrade Strategy (Preconfiguration Mode)

The upgrade strategy is primarily based on availability of the resources and utilization of the downtime minimization tools and techniques during the upgrade. The strategy is executed based on one of the following preconfiguration modes delivered by SAP (Table 25-1).

Upgrade Software Logistics

The choice of upgrade software logistics primarily depends on the availability of additional system resources and the production support and downtime needs of a given business. For businesses where minimal production support is needed during the upgrade process in the standard three-System-Landscape of development, test, and production systems, the upgrade can follow the same promote-to-production path of Development | Test | Production. However, for the majority of businesses, production support would still be needed while an upgrade is executed. The most commonly used option in this scenario is the five-System-Landscape shown in Figure 25-1.

The key steps of the upgrade in a five-System-Landscape are explained here. Refer to Figure 25-1 as you follow the steps.

1. The development system (DEV) is copied to a production support system (PSS).
2. The quality assurance (QAS) system is copied to a production support QA system (PSQ).

Preconfiguration Mode	Brief Description	Implication of Choice
Low resource use	This choice should be made when the availability of system resources is a constraint. This choice maps to the upgrade strategy parameter **resource-minimized**.	Long downtime Slow import Archiving off ICNV not possible
Standard resource use	This choice should be made when you have some additional system resources. This choice maps to the upgrade strategy parameter **downtime-minimized**.	Minimal downtime Slow import Archiving off
High resource use	This choice should be made when availability of system resources is not a constraint and adequate resources can be provisioned during the upgrade. This choice maps to the upgrade strategy parameter **downtime-minimized**.	Minimal downtime Fast import Archiving on
Manual parameter selection	Control over selection of parameters manually and is intended for experts.	Upgrade can be further customized More expertise

TABLE 25-1 Preconfiguration Mode Choices During Upgrades

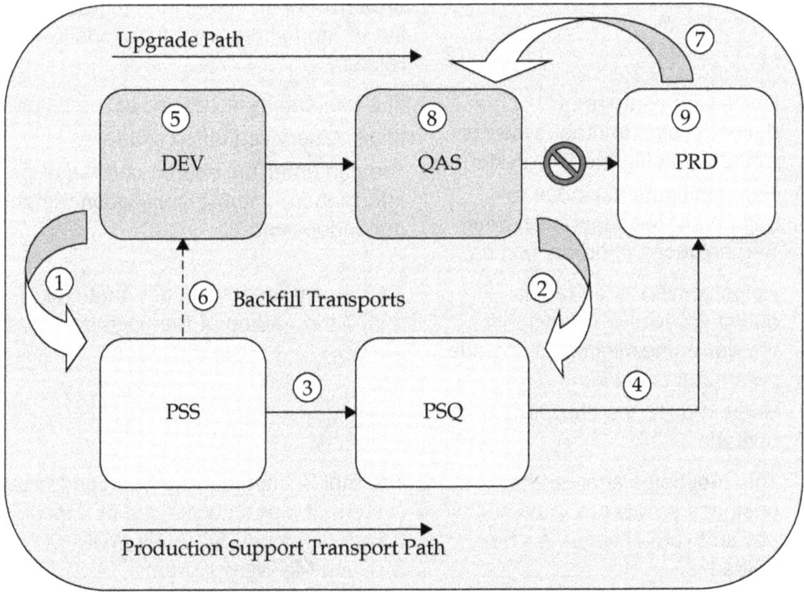

FIGURE 25-1 Upgrade software logistics

3. A transport path is set up between PSS and PSQ.
4. A transport path is set up between PSQ and the production system (PRD).
5. The DEV is upgraded to the target release.
6. Production support transports are backfilled to DEV from PSS.
7. The QAS system is refreshed from PRD (database copy from PRD).
8. The QAS is upgraded to the target release.
9. The PRD is upgraded to the target release.

Upgrade Tools

As the complexity and diversity of SAP applications has increased over time, the upgrade tools have evolved to meet the new business requirements. Table 25-2 lists the key tools that are used during different phases of the upgrade project.

Upgrade Tool or Service	Value Proposition	How to Access or Use the Tool or Service
Solution Browser (business value of new functions)	Shows the target release delta functionality for the business. Helps to build a business case for upgrading to the target release.	The tool can be accessed at the following URL: www.sapsolutionbrowser.com You can enter the source release, target release, and the key capability or application area (Example: Financials) to get a detailed list of the delta or new functionality in the new release.
Upgrade Dependency Analyzer	Helps with analysis of dependencies to other systems while upgrading the ERP system. Helps mitigate risks due to upgrade dependencies on other SAP solutions in production use.	The tool can be accessed at the following URL: https://service.sap.com/uda You can enter the source and target product information, and the application will show any dependencies.
ICNV	Helps convert large tables during productive operation if the downtime-minimized upgrade parameter is chosen. Helps reduce the downtime of the upgrade.	ICNV is a transaction code that can be executed during the uptime of the upgrade process.
Business Process Change Analyzer (BPCA)	This tool helps analyze the business processes impacted by any software changes such as upgrades. Helps plan for building test scripts for the upgrade project.	The tool is built into the Solution Manager system. It can be accessed by executing transaction code SOLMAN_WORKCENTER in the Solution Manager system.

TABLE 25-2 Upgrade Tools (*Continued*)

Upgrade Tool or Service	Value Proposition	How to Access or Use the Tool or Service
NZDT	This technique helps to clone a production system that will be upgraded during uptime. Record business transactions during productive operation from the source production system. Transfer the "recorded production" to the cloned system, and it will be used as the new production system.	New service from SAP. Requires more resources and expertise. Contact SAP by sending an e-mail to mds@sap.com.
Combined Upgrade and Unicode Conversion (CU & UC)	Helps convert from non-Unicode to Unicode systems while performing the upgrade.	Special procedure. Can be integrated along with the regular SAP upgrade. Requires more expertise. The CU & UC guides can be downloaded from the following location. This location has an OSS Note number listed. The guides are attached to the OSS Notes. The current OSS Note number is 928729. www.sdn.sap.com/irj/sdn/i18n?rid=/webcontent/uuid/c09cb763-f841-2a10-bcb1-d4cc8973e1eb More information can be obtained from the following URL: www.sdn.sap.com/irj/sdn/i18n
SAP Enhancement Package Installer	ERP 6 to ERP 6.4 is not supported by the upgrade program. Use the Enhancement Package Installer (64-bit systems), SAINT, or JSPM for 32-bit systems.	Enhancement Package Installer and the needed packages can be downloaded from SAP Service Marketplace. SAINT is a transaction code in ABAP systems.
Upgrade Sizing	Target release will need more resources.	Upgrade sizing is covered in the sizing chapter (Chapter 24) of this book.

TABLE 25-2 Upgrade Tools

Upgrade the GUI

Before you start the actual upgrade, the following items should be downloaded and a detailed upgrade script should be prepared for planning and executing the upgrade:

- Download the upgrade master guide and technical upgrade guide from http://service.sap.com/instguides.

- Download upgrade OSS Notes (Central Upgrade Note 1293744, Application-specific Upgrade Note 1292069, and Database-specific Upgrade Note 819655).
- Get the upgrade keyword from OSS Note 1292069.
- Download the upgrade master DVD and needed media as per the upgrade guide for your operating system and the database.
- Download the JCE Policy ZIP file as per OSS Note 1240081.

The main tool to execute the SAP upgrades is the Upgrade GUI. The tool is called from the upgrade master DVD downloaded from the SAP Service Marketplace.

Start the Upgrade GUI for the First Time

The following procedure can be used to start the Upgrade GUI for the first time.

1. Mount the upgrade master DVD.
2. Log in as <sid>adm user account at the operating system level.
3. Change to directory <path to upgrade master dvd>/upgrade master dvd, and execute the following command:

```
<Path to upgrade master DVD>/STARTUP jce_policy_zip=<path to the
downloaded jce policy zip file>
```

4. Next open an Internet Explorer (or any standard browser) window, enter the URL http://<hostname>:4239, and click Start Upgrade Front-end (SDTGui). This will start the Upgrade GUI.

Restarting the Upgrade GUI

Upgrade GUI can be restarted by executing the startup script from the upgrade directory located at /usr/sap/<sid>/upg/STARTUP.

Upgrade Roadmap Steps

SAP has simplified the upgrade user interface and has divided the processes into several roadmap steps. The following illustration shows the eight roadmap steps the upgrade process executes.

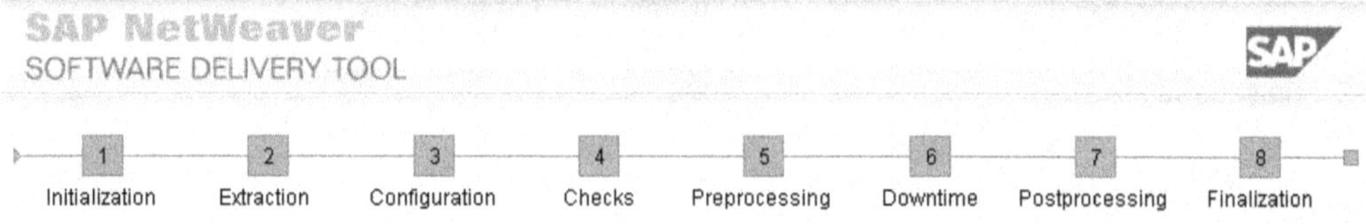

Copyright by SAP AG

When the Upgrade GUI is started, it will display the initialization step; by providing the requested information on the screen and clicking Next, you can proceed with the subsequent steps. Table 25-3 gives a brief overview of the eight roadmap steps.

Roadmap Step	Roadmap Step Name	Roadmap Step Description
1	Initialization Step	The upgrade program analyzes your system, and the progress status is shown on the screen. The Monitor tab indicates the status. Since it is a single-stack system, there will be a tab for ABAP as well.
2	Extraction Step	The upgrade program gathers the upgrade keyword, DDIC password, mount points for the upgrade software (DVD for export, RDBMS, upgrade master, RDBMD client, and kernel), and Solution Manager key.
3	Configuration Step	The upgrade program gathers information about the preconfiguration mode, support packages and add-ons, and shadow instance information.
4	Checks Step	The upgrade program checks if the operating system, database releases, and patch-level pre-requisites are met. It also checks the JDK version.
5	Preprocessing Step	The upgrade program builds the shadow instance. This step will be quick if a resource-minimized upgrade strategy is used because the longer-running steps are executed during downtime. This step will take a long time if the downtime-minimized upgrade strategy is used because the longer-running steps are executed during system uptime. When you click Next at the end of this step the actual downtime starts.
6	Downtime Step	The upgrade program creates the shadow instance and executes all the necessary steps to target release, and the system switches to the target release. A kernel switch is also executed and conversion of application tables to target release takes place.
7	Postprocessing Step	The upgrade program executes the postprocessing steps, such as rescheduling the suspended background jobs, sending the upgrade evaluation to SAP, and saving the upgrade logs.
8	Finalization Step	The upgrade program executes cleanup and closing activities and finalizes the upgrade; toward the end of the upgrade, it issues a "successful upgrade" message.

TABLE 25-3 Upgrade Roadmap Steps

Upgrade Key Planning Steps

The key planning steps for the upgrade are listed here. The complete list of planning steps must be obtained from the upgrade guide.

- Download the upgrade software.
- Download the upgrade guides (upgrade master guide, technical upgrade guide, and upgrade OSS Notes).

- Download the target release support packages and any add-ons.
- Download the JCE policy file.
- Allocate 25GB of disk space for the upgrade directory where all the logs and upgrade information are written. Ensure that the allocated space is local and is not NFS-mounted. Using NFS-mounted space may cause the upgrade to run slower.
- Extend the file systems to meet target release needs.
- Generate a Solution Manager key.
- Obtain the upgrade keyword.
- Decide on the upgrade strategy.
- Decide on the backup and recovery strategies during upgrades.
- Prepare any operating system and database-specific pre-requisites.

Upgrade Execution

Upgrade GUI helps in executing the eight roadmap steps. The following figures and illustrations demonstrate each of the upgrade roadmap steps.

Figure 25-2 shows execution of the initialization roadmap step during an upgrade process.

Figure 25-3 shows execution of the extraction roadmap step during an upgrade process.

Figure 25-4 shows successful completion of the extraction roadmap step during an upgrade process.

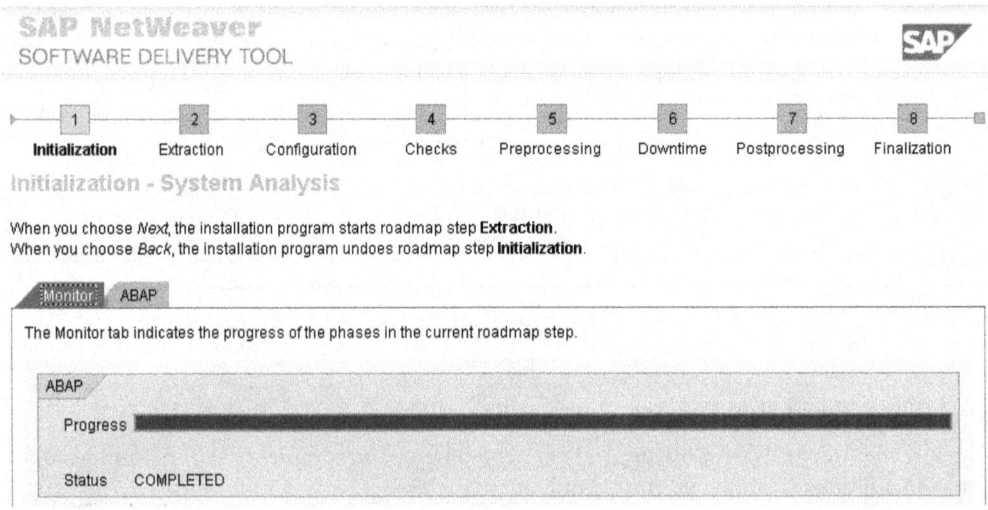

FIGURE 25-2 Initialization upgrade roadmap step

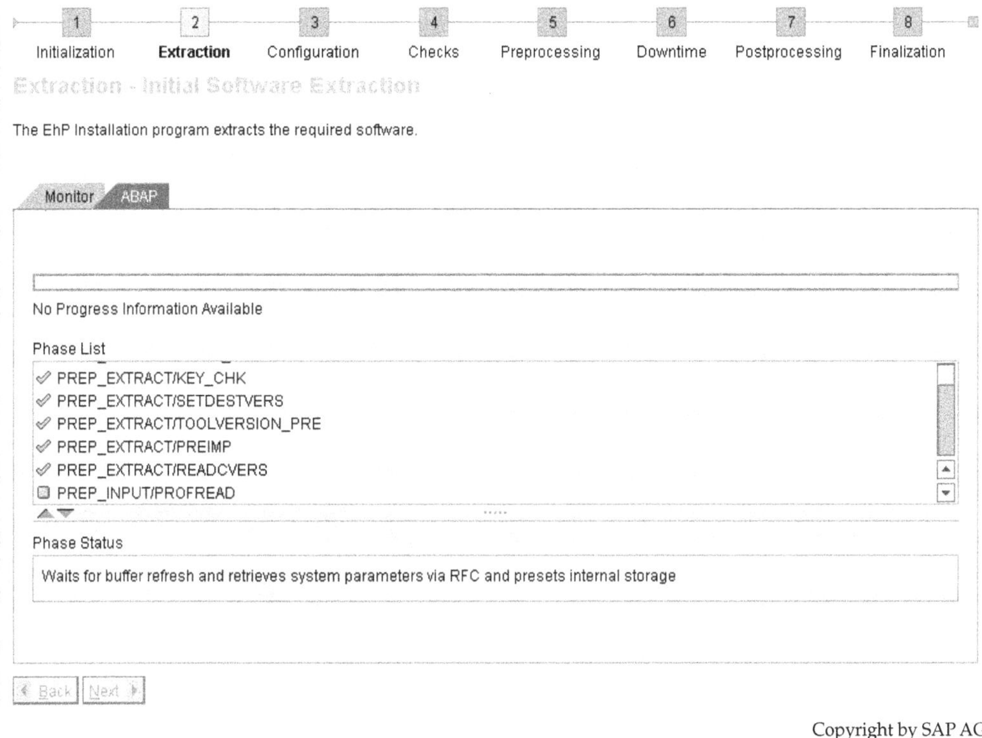

Copyright by SAP AG

FIGURE 25-3 Extraction upgrade roadmap step

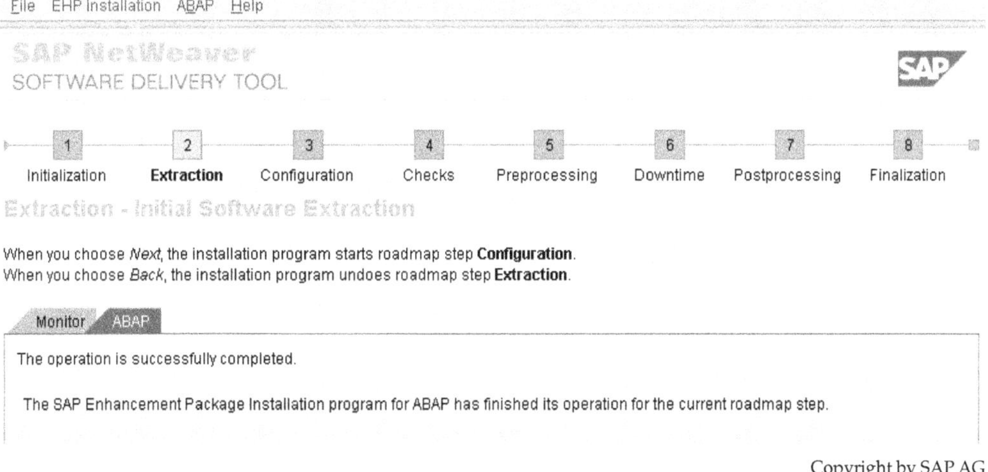

Copyright by SAP AG

FIGURE 25-4 Successful completion of extraction roadmap step

This illustration shows execution of the configuration roadmap step during an upgrade process. In this example, the standard resource use (downtime-minimized) upgrade strategy is chosen.

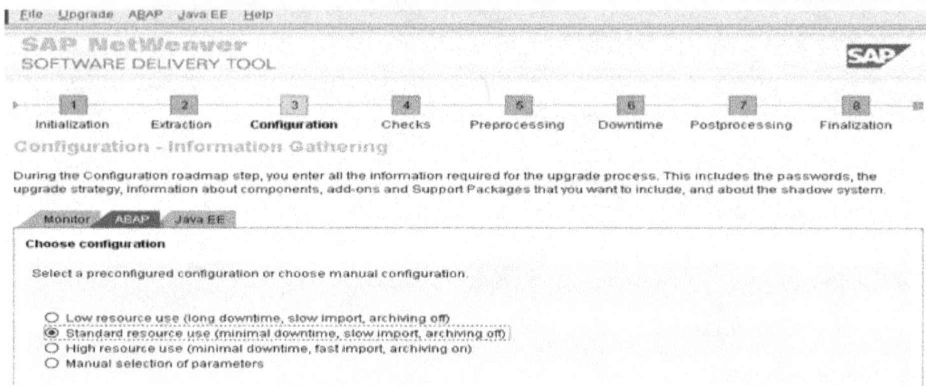

Copyright by SAP AG

The next illustration shows successful execution of the checks roadmap step during an upgrade process.

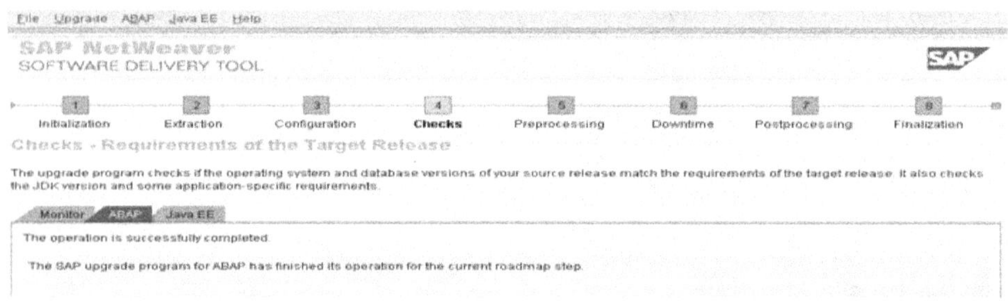

Copyright by SAP AG

Figure 25-5 shows execution of the preprocessing roadmap step during an upgrade process. At the end of this step, the upgrade program will show this screen in preparation for the downtime. After all the recommended steps are completed and you click OK, the actual downtime of the system starts.

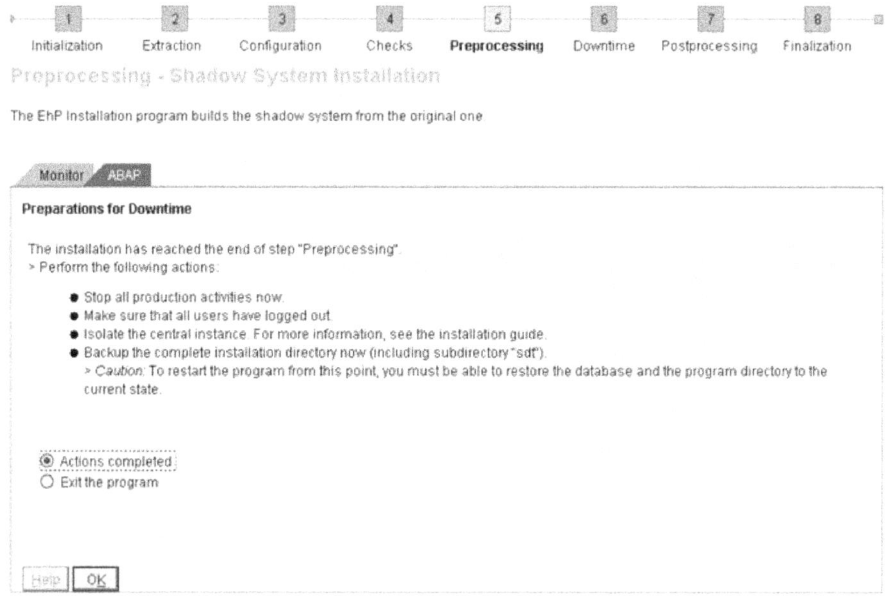

Copyright by SAP AG

FIGURE 25-5 Successful completion of the preprocessing roadmap step

The next illustration shows execution of the downtime step during an upgrade process. In this step, the upgrade program is checking if a backup was done.

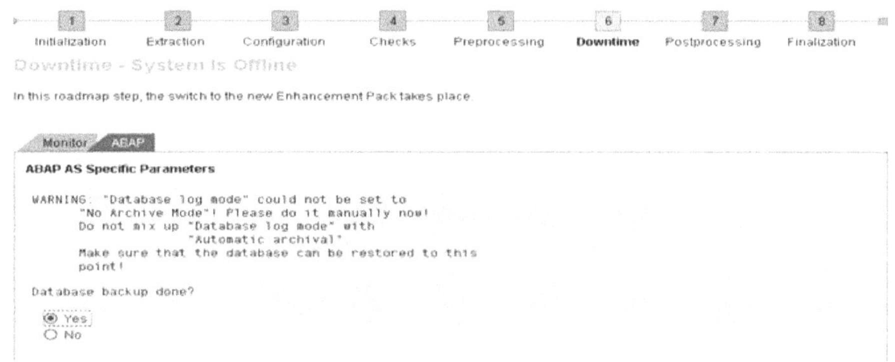

Copyright by SAP AG

Figure 25-6 shows execution of the postprocessing upgrade roadmap step during an upgrade process. The upgrade program is recommending starting the background jobs as per the needs of the organization. The jobs were suspended at the beginning of the upgrade process.

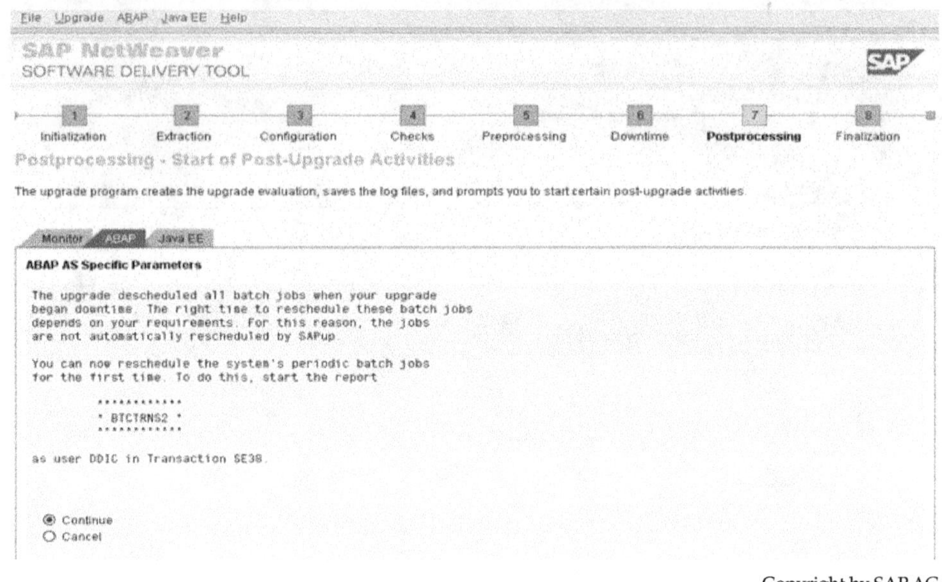

FIGURE 25-6 Successful completion of postprocessing upgrade roadmap step

This illustration shows execution of the finalization upgrade roadmap step during an upgrade process.

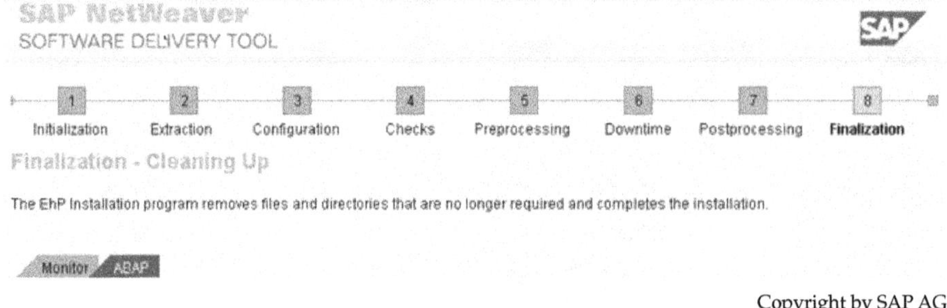

At the end of the successful SAP upgrade you will see the following message. This will show that all the upgrade roadmap steps have been successfully completed.

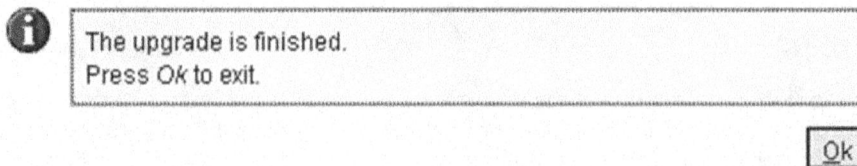

Upgrade Key Post-Steps

The following are some of the key post-steps after the technical upgrade is completed successfully:

- Stop and start the SAP system to make sure it is coming up without problems.
- Schedule the background jobs.
- Import the correct profiles in transaction code RZ10.
- Execute SGEN to generate all the ABAP loads. Set parallel processes so that SGEN will run faster.
- Perform post-steps as per the upgrade guide.
- Perform any customer-specific steps.
- Take a complete offline backup.
- Release the system for productive business use.

Summary

- The SAP upgrade is performed using the Upgrade GUI program.
- Technical downtime includes time required for performing the technical upgrade.
- Business downtime includes the technical downtime plus the additional downtime needed for performing post technical upgrade steps. It is also the time the application is not available to the end business user.
- The goal of effective upgrade projects should be to reduce business downtime.
- A system-switch upgrade creates a parallel shadow instance in the same database.
- The shadow instance is for the target SAP release.
- The resource-minimized strategy consumes fewer system resources but has a longer downtime.
- The downtime-minimized strategy consumes more system resources but has a shorter downtime.
- SAP provides a number of upgrade tools to help the customer plan and execute the upgrades.
- The upgrade program executes the upgrade in eight roadmap steps.
- The upgrade master guide, technical upgrade guide, and upgrade OSS Notes must be downloaded before starting the upgrade.
- Upgrade software must be downloaded before starting the upgrade.
- Upgrade software logistics must be planned ahead of the time for the upgrade project.
- Successful execution of SAP upgrades involves a lot of planning and practice runs before the final production upgrade is executed.

Additional Resources

- **Upgrade technology** www.sdn.sap.com/irj/sdn/upgradetech
- **Upgrade to ERP 6.0** www.sdn.sap.com/irj/bpx/index?rid=/webcontent/uuid/70a24e6f-de25-2b10-bdba-cd1affa226e3
- **Business rationale and perspective for SAP upgrades** www.sap.com/services/more/erpupgrade/index.epx
- **Getting started with upgrades to SAP ERP** www.sap.com/solutions/business-suite/erp/getting_started_upgrading.epx
- **SAP Solution Browser tool** www.sapsolutionbrowser.com
- **SAP upgrade dependency analyzer** https://service.sap.com/uda
- **SAP upgrade info center** https://service.sap.com/upgrade
- **SAP upgrade experience database** https://service.sap.com/upgradedb
- **SAP upgrade planning** https://service.sap.com/upgraderoadmap

CHAPTER

SAP Upgrade of the Java Stack

In this chapter we will focus on upgrading the Java stack. There are several SAP solutions that run on SAP NetWeaver Application Server Java. One good example is SAP NetWeaver Portal. However, some of them run on dual-stack (both ABAP and Java) application servers. Good examples of dual-stack applications are SAP Customer Relationship Management (CRM) and SAP Process Integration (PI). In this chapter we will use the SAP PI application upgrade as an example so that we have an opportunity to study not only the Java stack upgrade but also the synchronized upgrade procedure used to perform a dual-stack (ABAP + Java) upgrade.

Java Upgrade Concepts

SAP has standardized the upgrade procedures between ABAP and Java stacks. The upgrade concepts discussed in the last chapter are applicable to the Java stack upgrade as well. In general, Java stack upgrades are less complex and take a shorter time to complete as compared to an ABAP-based ERP upgrade. The reason is that the ERP application has more than 70,000 tables and has lot of interfaces and will add to the time and complexity of the upgrade. Regardless of the complexity, a clear understanding of the upgrade concepts will help to plan the upgrade well and therefore reduce the business risk of upgrading a Java application.

Upgrade Strategy

Similar to the ABAP stack upgrade, the Java upgrade has the same options available as part of the upgrade. Depending upon resource availability and downtime requirements, you can choose an upgrade strategy that is either resource minimized or downtime minimized.

System Switch Upgrade

SAP creates a shadow instance similar to ABAP upgrades in the Java stack upgrades as well. Toward the end of the Java upgrade, the shadow instance is kept as the new instance and the old instance is deleted. This technique helps to reduce the downtime, as many upgrade steps that were executed during downtime can now be executed during uptime. The original instance is replaced with the shadow instance, keeping the original system number.

Dual-Stack Synchronized Upgrade

In SAP solutions that are based on both ABAP and Java, SAP offers a synchronized upgrade approach. In this approach the ABAP and Java upgrades are synchronized. First, the upgrade tool will detect if a given SAP application is single stack or dual stack. If it determines that it is a dual-stack application, the upgrade tool will execute the eight roadmap steps for ABAP and Java in a sequential manner. The upgrade tool will automatically synchronize the roadmap steps and complete the upgrade.

Integrated GUI for Both ABAP and Java

Starting with the NetWeaver 7.1 release SAP is providing a new tool called the Upgrade GUI to perform upgrades. In older releases, upgrades used SAPUp for ABAP stack upgrades and SAPJup for Java stack upgrades. In a dual-stack upgrade the Basis administrator would have to use the two tools separately, and SAPUp and SAPJup would wait for each other at the three synchronization points during the upgrade. This not only made it difficult for the Basis administrator to plan and execute a dual-stack upgrade but was also introducing a number of potential errors during the upgrade. With the new Upgrade GUI tool, dual-stack upgrades are "integrated" and a Basis administrator no longer has to execute two upgrade programs in parallel. The integrated Upgrade GUI tool will gather parameters and other information for both ABAP and Java stacks, and will perform the upgrade following the eight roadmap steps in a single interface. The Upgrade GUI tool will show three tabs for dual-stack upgrades.

Additional Upgrade Tools and Services

In addition to the upgrade tools discussed in the last chapter SAP provides more tools and services that will help improve the customer's experience. Some of the additional upgrade tools and services are discussed in Table 26-1.

Upgrade Tool or Service	Value Proposition	How to Access or Use the Tool or Service
SAP Upgrade Experience Database	Database gathers upgrade experiences of customers and shares them with the customer base. Upgrade statistics such as runtime and so on can be obtained by the customers so that they can plan their own upgrades.	The tool can be accessed at the following URL: http://service.sap.com/upgradedb One example of a Java stack application that SAP is gathering information on at this time is the CRM system.
SAP Safeguarding for Upgrades	Service provided by SAP for customers with complex upgrade environments. Reduces the business risk by engaging SAP consulting expertise for complex upgrades.	The service information can be accessed at the following URL: www.sap.com/services/support/servicedetail.epx?context=%5B%5Bt=49e74de%5D%5D%7C
JLin test tool	Helps test Java source and syntax. After checks are completed, the system presents the test results that can be used to validate the upgrade of the Java application during testing phase of the project.	The tool is built into the SAP NetWeaver Developer Studio.

TABLE 26-1 Upgrade Tools

Upgrade Key Planning Steps

The key planning steps for the upgrade are listed in Table 26-2. There will be additional planning steps that you might have to perform. The list provided here is intended to cover the most important planning steps performed ahead of the upgrade execution. A complete list of planning steps must be obtained from the upgrade guide.

Upgrade Planning Step	Brief Description
Download the upgrade guides.	Upgrade guides can be downloaded from the following location: https://service.sap.com/instguides
Download the general upgrade note and database-specific upgrade note. The note numbers will change based on the solution and should be obtained from the most current upgrade guide downloaded as per the first step.	For this particular example upgrading to PI 7.1, the general upgrade note is 1061649 and the database (Oracle)–specific note is 960790. They can be downloaded from the following location: https://service.sap.com/notes
Download additional SAP Notes for upgrade as per the upgrade guide.	The complete list is given in the upgrade guide. Not all notes pertain to your upgrade. Please review the listed notes and download them from the following location: https://service.sap.com/notes
Ensure that the Oracle directory has adequate space at the operating system level.	The recommended Oracle archiving directory size is 25GB.
Ensure that the disk space requirements for the upgrade directory are met.	Create the following upgrade directory with a minimum of 10GB of free space: /usr/sap/<SID>/upg
Ensure adequate space is added to the sapdata directory mount points.	Add 32GB of disk space to each of the sapdata directories for the upgrade.
Ensure adequate space for the /usr/sap/<SID> directory.	Make sure at least 10GB of free disk space is available for the /usr/sap/<SID> directory.
Download the upgrade software, and copy it to a location that is available to the upgrade program.	Create a software download location on the server, and make sure that it is readable and available for the upgrades. Upgrade software can be downloaded from https://service.sap.com/swdc. Solution Manager Maintenance Optimizer will need to approve the software that is downloaded by the SAP Download Manager. Use the media list for the needed inventory of DVDs for the upgrade. The media list can be downloaded at the same location as the upgrade guides. A typical upgrade involves the following media list: Upgrade master DVD Upgrade export DVDs Upgrade kernel DVD Upgrade language DVDs (if needed) Upgrade Java DVD Database DVDs (if database upgrade or patching is needed)

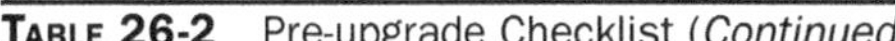
TABLE 26-2 Pre-upgrade Checklist (*Continued*)

<table>
<tr><th>Upgrade Planning Step</th><th>Brief Description</th></tr>
<tr><td>Download the target release support packages and any required add-ons.</td><td>Support packages and enhancement packages software can be downloaded from https://service.sap.com/swdc under the Support Packages And Patches section. Solution Manager Maintenance Optimizer will need to approve the software that is downloaded by the SAP Download Manager.
Once downloaded, the support packages SAR and CAR files are extracted to the following directory:
/usr/sap/trans/EPS/in</td></tr>
<tr><td>Generate a Solution Manager key.</td><td>Use transaction code SMSY in the Solution Manager system, as explained in Chapter 6, to get a Solution Manager key.</td></tr>
<tr><td>As per OSS Note 1154961, execute the database data checks.</td><td>Execute the following on the server to perform the checks as explained in OSS Note 1154961:
http://<server>:<port>/<appln>/support/CheckService
where <appln> = rep or dir</td></tr>
<tr><td>Download the JCE jurisdiction policy files from the SAP Service Marketplace.</td><td>Download these at https://service.sap.com/swdc. Then choose Installations And Upgrades | Browse Our Download Catalog | SAP Cryptographic Software.
OSS Note 1240081 provides more details.</td></tr>
<tr><td>Check the Oracle Database version pre-requisite for the upgrade.</td><td>Should be at least Oracle version 10.2.0.2.</td></tr>
<tr><td>Check the PI source release level.</td><td>It should be at least XI 3.0 SP 9 or PI 7.0 SP 5.</td></tr>
<tr><td>Create the Software Deployment Manager (SDM) temporary directory.</td><td>Create a temporary directory sdm under /tmp as follows:
cd /usr/sap/<SID>/JC00/SDM/program
./StopServer.sh (Stops SDM)
./sdm.sh jstartup mode=standalone (Starts SDM in standalone mode)
./sdm.sh filetransferdir "dir=/tmp/sdm" (Changes the directory for SDM)
./sdm.sh jstartup mode=integrated (Changes SDM mode to integrated)
./StartServer.sh (Starts SDM)</td></tr>
<tr><td>Change the event timeout in the configuration tool.</td><td>Start the configuration tool and choose Cluster Data | Global Server Configuration | Managers | Service Manager | Global Properties. Set the custom value of the EventTimeout property to 120. This will avoid errors during the upgrade deployment steps.
Restart the Java instance after the changes are completed.</td></tr>
<tr><td>Avoid authorization errors in Java components after the upgrade by applying OSS Note 1349854.</td><td>Create a ZUPGRADE user account in the PI ABAP system as a service user type. This account is an internal user used during the upgrade. It can be deleted after a successful upgrade.
In the User Management Engine (UME) assign the Administrator role to the SAP* account and to the ZUPGRADE account.</td></tr>
<tr><td>Download the most current SAP upgrade program (SAPUp).</td><td>The most current SAR file can be downloaded from the SAP software download location.</td></tr>
</table>

TABLE 26-2 Pre-upgrade Checklist

Upgrade Execution

The upgrade execution steps are performed by Upgrade GUI. When the upgrade program is executed from the upgrade master DVD, it starts an HTTP service in the background. Upgrade GUI connects to the back-end HTTP service with a browser at port 4239.

Start the Upgrade GUI for the First Time

The following procedure can be used to start the Upgrade GUI for the first time.

1. Mount the upgrade master DVD.
2. Log in as <sid>adm user account at the operating system level.
3. Change to directory <path to upgrade master dvd>/upgrade master dvd, and execute the following command:

```
<Path to upgrade master DVD>/STARTUP jce_policy_zip=<path to the
downloaded jce policy zip file>
```

4. For performance reasons, copy the upgrade master DVD to a local file system. If NFS mount is used, the upgrade performance may suffer, so this is not recommended.
5. Next open an Internet Explorer (or any standard browser) window, enter the URL http://<hostname>:4239, and click Start Upgrade Front-end (SDTGui) as shown in Figure 26-1.

This will start the Upgrade GUI, which helps in executing the eight roadmap steps. Figure 26-2 shows that it has started the initialization roadmap step and completed it successfully. When you click Next, it moves to the extraction roadmap step.

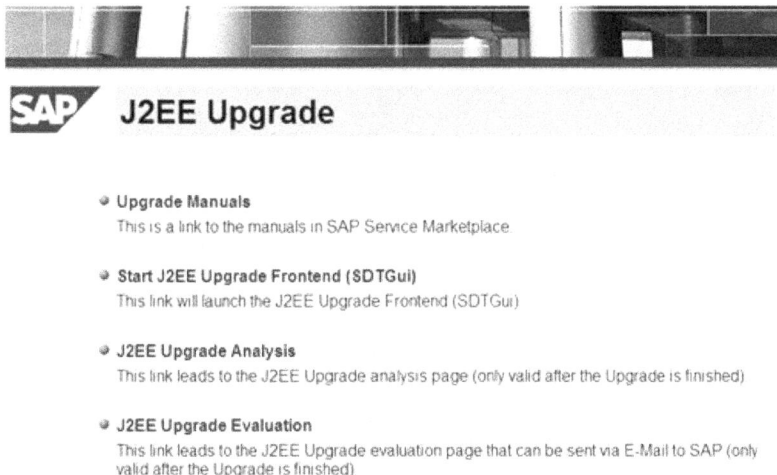

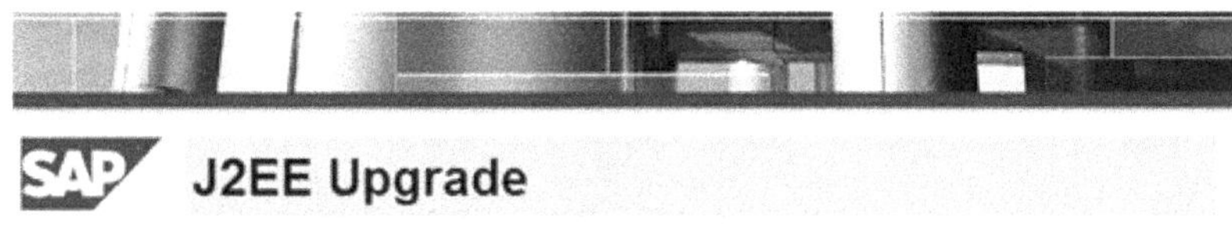
SAP
J2EE Upgrade
Upgrade Manuals
This is a link to the manuals in SAP Service Marketplace
Start J2EE Upgrade Frontend (SDTGui)
This link will launch the J2EE Upgrade Frontend (SDTGui)
J2EE Upgrade Analysis
This link leads to the J2EE Upgrade analysis page (only valid after the Upgrade is finished)
J2EE Upgrade Evaluation
This link leads to the J2EE Upgrade evaluation page that can be sent via E-Mail to SAP (only valid after the Upgrade is finished)

FIGURE 26-1 Starting the Upgrade GUI

Initialization Extraction Configuration Checks Preprocessing Downtime Postprocessing Finalization

Initialization - System Analysis

When you choose *Next*, the upgrade program starts roadmap step **Extraction**.
When you choose *Back*, the upgrade program undoes roadmap step **Initialization**.

Monitor Java EE ABAP

The Monitor tab indicates the progress of the phases in the current roadmap step.

Java EE
Progress
Status COMPLETED

ABAP
Progress
Status COMPLETED

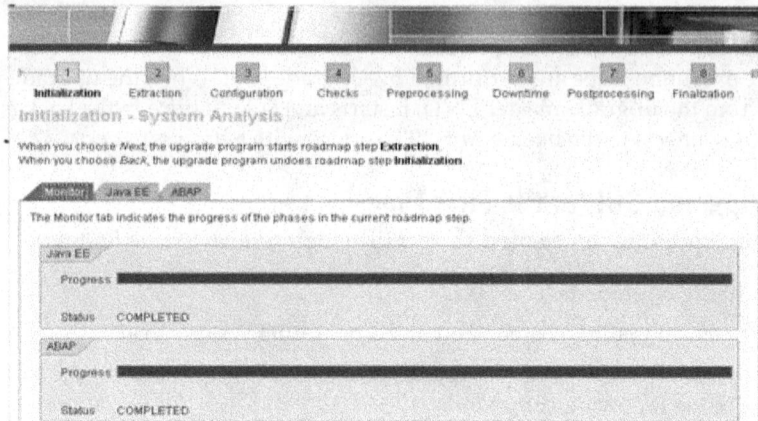

FIGURE 26-2 Upgrade GUI in extraction roadmap step

Restarting the Upgrade GUI

Upgrade GUI can be restarted by executing the startup script from the upgrade directory located at /usr/sap/<sid>/upg/STARTUP.

The following figures and illustrations will provide a sample of each of the upgrade roadmap steps in a dual-stack upgrade. The upgrade program will switch between the two stack upgrades, and synchronization of upgrades between the ABAP and Java stacks is performed automatically by the Upgrade GUI tool.

Figure 26-3 shows the extraction phase of the upgrade. The Upgrade GUI is asking for the DDIC password.

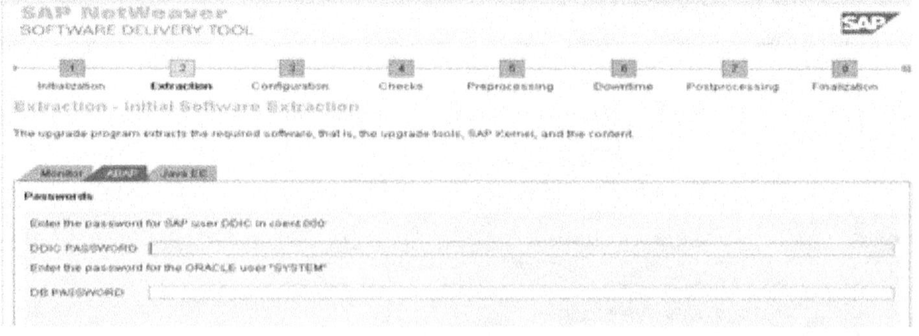

FIGURE 26-3 Upgrade GUI in extraction roadmap step

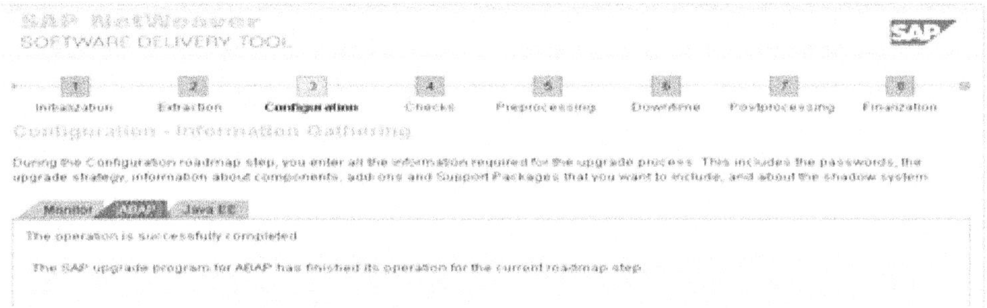

FIGURE 26-4 Configuration roadmap step successfully completed for ABAP stack

Once this is entered, click Next and the Upgrade GUI will request for the following in subsequent screens. Enter the requested information and keep clicking the Next button.

- Upgrade keyword
- Mount points of the upgrade software downloaded earlier
- Solution Manager key

Figure 26-4 shows that the ABAP stack configuration steps have been completed successfully.

Once this is completed, the Upgrade GUI tool will start the configuration steps for the Java stack. Figure 26-5 shows the start of the Java configuration roadmap step. You are prompted for the password for the J2EE_ADMIN account. Enter the password and click Next.

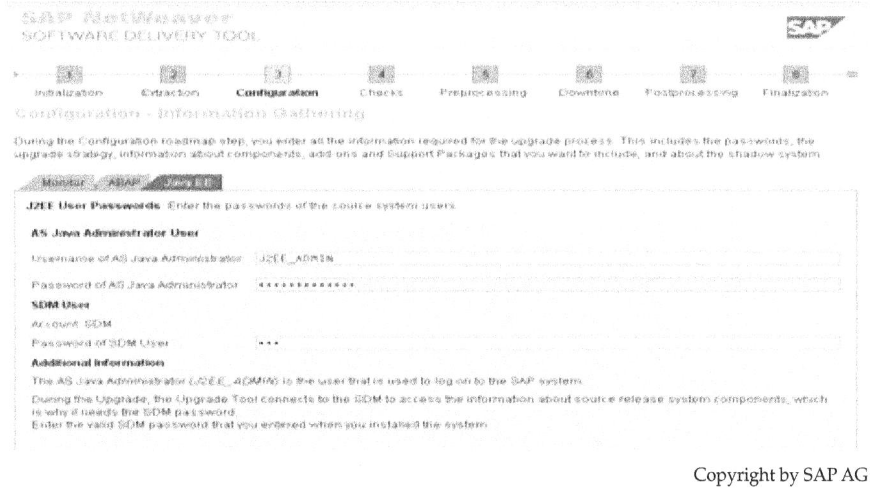

FIGURE 26-5 Configuration roadmap step for the Java stack

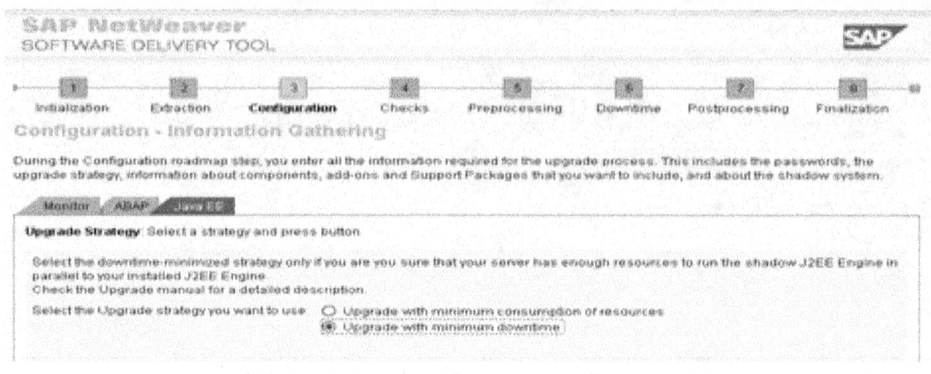

Copyright by SAP AG

FIGURE 26-6 Java configuration roadmap step for choosing an upgrade strategy

Figure 26-6 shows the selection of the upgrade strategy. Choose Upgrade With Minimum Downtime, and click Next.

In Figure 26-7 the system is requesting for the support package binding during the upgrade. Choose the support package stack and click Continue.

In Figure 26-8 the upgrade program is requesting to select the target Java support package level that was unpacked into the /usr/sap/trans/EPS/in directory in the planning stages of the upgrade.

Figure 26-9 shows the successful completion of the Java stack configuration step.

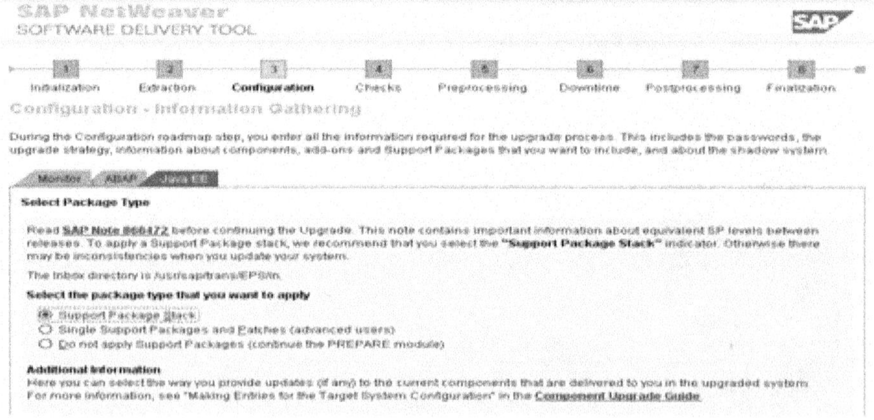

Copyright by SAP AG

FIGURE 26-7 Support package stack selection in Java configuration roadmap step

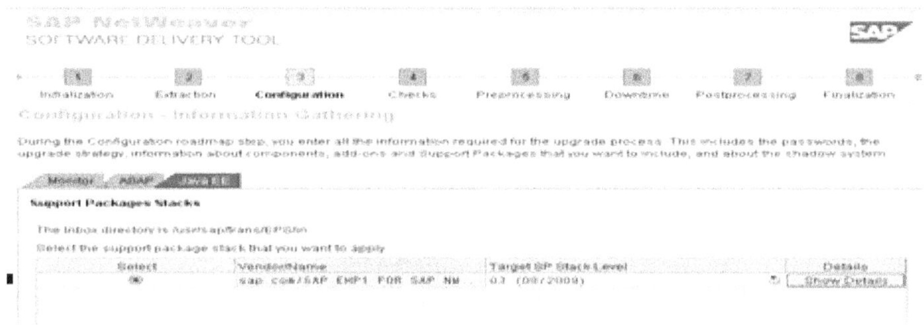

Copyright by SAP AG

FIGURE 26-8 Selection of target support package level in Java configuration step

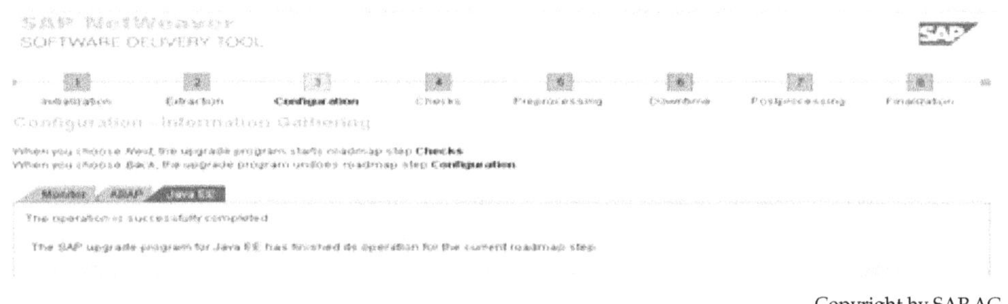

Copyright by SAP AG

FIGURE 26-9 Successful completion of Java stack configuration step

After continuing to execute the upgrade roadmap steps by entering the requested information and clicking Next, the system will enter into the downtime step. The following illustration shows a sample error during this step. The error logs are written in the log sub-directory of the upgrade directory. In this particular case, the message server internal port number was an issue, causing the system not to start toward the end of the downtime roadmap step. Changing the profile parameter value of j2ee/ms/port =3901 and restarting the upgrade helped resolve the issue.

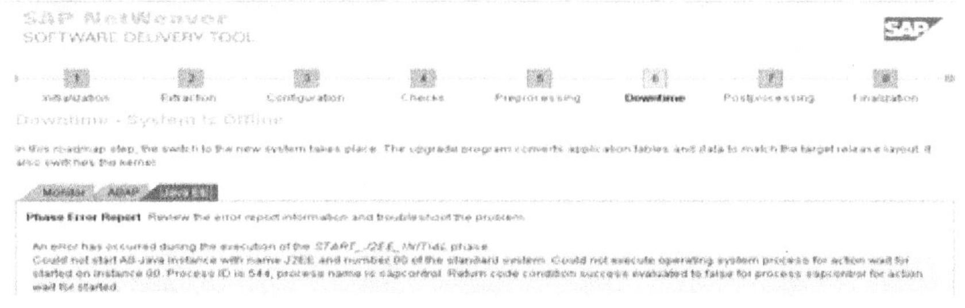

Copyright by SAP AG

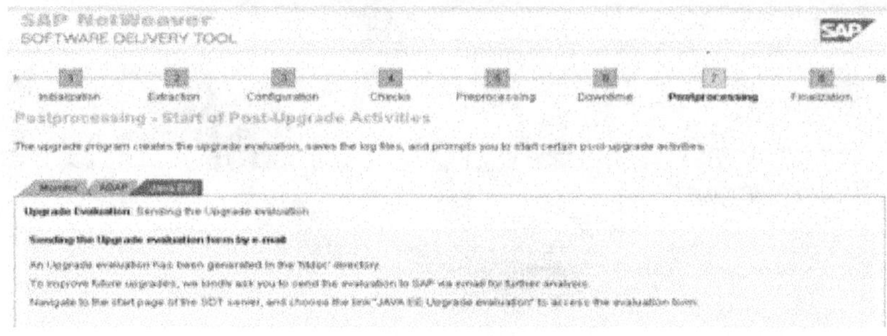

Figure 26-10 Upgrade evaluation screen in postprocessing roadmap step

After resolving this issue click Continue and keep clicking Next as you move through the subsequent roadmap steps. This will eventually lead to the end of the postprocessing roadmap step and the upgrade program will show the upgrade evaluation screen shown in Figure 26-10. The evaluation information can be sent to SAP. SAP uses this information to gather statistics and issues from real upgrades performed by customers, which helps them further improve the upgrade tool and help customers.

Click Next and the upgrade program will show that the Java postprocessing roadmap step is completed successfully, as shown in Figure 26-11.

Toward the end of the finalization roadmap step, the upgrade program will issue the following confirmation message notifying you of the successful execution of the dual-stack upgrade.

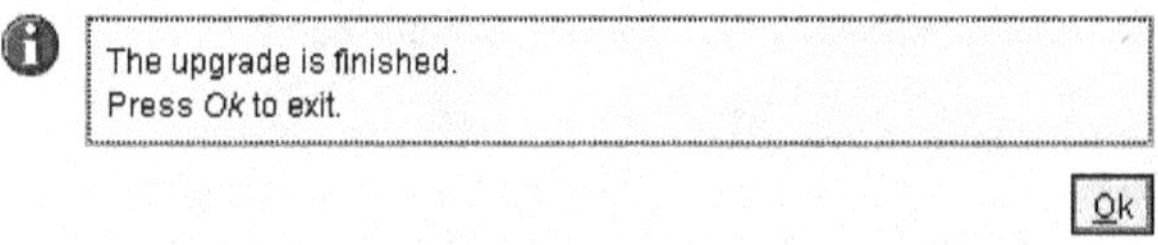

The procedure described here is not comprehensive. In the "Additional Resources" section of this chapter an e-class demo link is provided. This demo will provide additional details about the upgrade process.

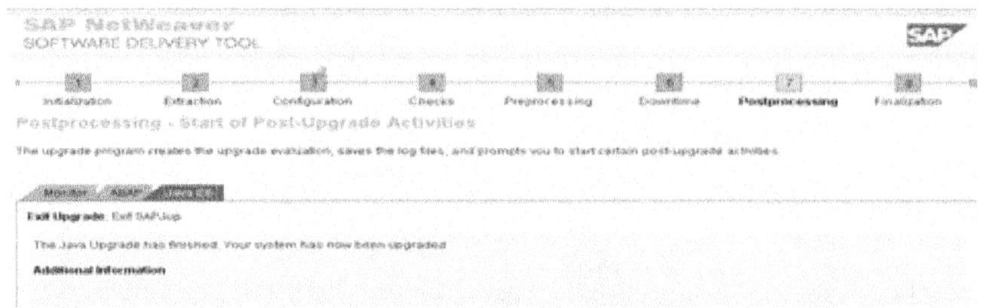

Figure 26-11 Successful completion of Java postprocessing upgrade roadmap step

Upgrade Key Post-Steps

The following are some of the key post-steps after the technical upgrade is completed successfully:

- Stop and start the SAP system to make sure it is working properly.
- Schedule the background jobs.
- Import the correct profiles in transaction code RZ10.
- Execute SGEN to generate all the ABAP loads.
- Perform post-steps as per the upgrade guide.
- Perform any customer-specific steps.
- Take a complete offline backup.
- Release the system for productive business use.

Summary

- An SAP Java stack upgrade and a dual-stack (ABAP and Java stacks) upgrade can be performed using the new upgrade program Upgrade GUI.
- The Upgrade GUI tool integrates both ABAP and Java stack upgrades into one single tool.
- Careful planning will help with successful execution of the upgrade.
- The Upgrade GUI tool synchronizes the ABAP and Java stack upgrades.
- The upgrade directory log directory and troubleshooting section of the upgrade guide are the key resources needed to resolve any upgrade issues.
- SAP provides services such as safeguarding to reduce the business risk of the upgrades.

Additional Resources

- **SAP installation and upgrade guides** https://service.sap.com/instguides
- **PI upgrade guides download location** https://service.sap.com/upgradenwpi71
- **Dual-Stack Upgrade to PI 7.1 e-class demo** www.sdn.sap.com/irj/sdn/go/portal/prtroot/docs/media/uuid/504f6de3-2cbd-2a10-ce87-86e0c5b5c573

PART

SAP System Copy

CHAPTER

SAP Homogeneous System Copies

In this part we will study the system copy types and how to perform system copies using SAP and database vendor–provided tools and techniques. System copies are categorized into homogeneous system copies and heterogeneous system copies. In a homogeneous system copy, neither the underlying database nor operating system is changed during the copy procedure. In a heterogeneous system copy, the underlying database and/or the operating system is changed during the copy procedure. In this chapter we will study homogeneous system copies in detail, and in the next chapter we will cover heterogeneous system copies.

Reasons for Performing a Copy

There are several reasons for performing a system copy. The main reasons for a client/customer to plan and execute a system copy are as follows:

- To build a test system with the data as in the production system
- To accelerate the build times for initial builds of test and production systems
- To build conversion testing/mock systems before going live
- To build a second system for testing upgrades
- To build a production-like system for performance testing projects
- To move systems to remote datacenters for auditing, security, and compliance with the Sarbanes-Oxley Act (SOX)
- To move the systems to the outsourcing provider's hosting location
- To change the underlying database and/or operating system

Please note that most of the time the system copy is performed primarily for the ABAP system that hosts the transactional data for the ERP system. A Java stack of a single stack system such as NetWeaver Portal does not need a system copy; instead, the data can be exported and imported to the target system. This will save a lot of time in setting up target systems in a Java stack without performing a full system copy procedure.

Types of System and Database Copies

While performing system and database copies, several terms and procedures are used. Table 27-1 lists the most important terms and provides a brief description of each. More details on the procedures will be covered in this and the next chapter.

Terminology	Brief Description
System copy	It duplicates the source system using the SAPinst tool. The SAPinst tool uses the database files of the source system to build the target system. Please note that the export DVDs used for a regular SAP installation are not used for a system copy procedure.
Database copy	The database-specific copy component of the system copy. Each database has specific copy method. In this chapter we will use the Oracle offline backup procedure to study an end-to-end system copy procedure.
Homogeneous system copy	System copy procedure in which the database and/or operating system is NOT changed during the copy.
Heterogeneous system copy (migration)	System copy procedure in which the database and/or operating system is changed during the copy. This procedure is also referred to as migration.
Single-stack database copy	The system copy involves either an ABAP- or a Java-based application. An example of an ABAP-based application is a system copy of an ERP system. An example of a Java-based application is a system copy of a NetWeaver Portal system.
Dual-stack database copy	The system copy involves both ABAP and Java stack applications. An example is SAP Process Integration.
Database-specific copy method	SAP recommends using the database-specific copy method for performing the copy steps specific to a particular database of the system copy. If database-specific copy method is not used then the system copy tools will perform this activity as well. Using a database-specific method helps reduce the time needed to complete the system copy.
Database-independent copy methods	In some instances, such as when a database and operating system are changed during the system copy, it becomes necessary to use database-independent copy procedures. SAP provides the R3Load tool for performing a database-independent copy method. This will be discussed in detail in the next chapter.

TABLE 27-1 Common System Copy and Database Copy Terminology

Business Scenario for a Homogeneous System Copy

In this chapter we will study an end-to-end system copy procedure using a real-life business scenario. You have been requested to plan and set up a quality assurance system by the SAP project team as a copy of the most recent ERP production system. Your database is Oracle, and it runs on a UNIX operating system. After some analysis of different copy options, you have reached the conclusion that the Oracle offline backup method should be used. This procedure is chosen because of limited downtime available for the production system and faster database copy time in building the target quality assurance system. Where it is applicable, the copy steps important to a Java system and a dual system are covered in this chapter.

Process Flow of a Homogeneous System Copy

The process flow in a homogeneous system copy can be divided into three main categories. Each category will be explained in detail in later sections of this chapter:

- Steps executed in the source system (export steps)
- Steps executed in the target system (import steps)
- Steps executed in the target system after the copy (post-copy steps)

System Copy Export Steps

Export steps are carried out in the source system. It is recommended to keep users off the source system while the export steps are executed. It usually takes about one to two hours to complete all the export steps, which are described in the following sections.

Generating the Control File for the Target Database

Log in as the ora<sid> user account at the operating system level, and create an export directory (/oracle/KB1/sapreorg/export) under the sapreorg directory with 777 permissions. Next copy the OraBRCOPY.SAR file from the installation master DVD located at .../<OS>/COMMON/INSTALL/ORA/ to the /oracle/KB1/sapreorg/export directory. Extracting the OraBRCOPY.SAR file as shown will give four files. One of the files is the ora_br_copy.sh shell script. Execute the shell script as indicated, and this will generate the control file (CONTROL.SQL) and the target Oracle initialization parameter file (initKB2.ora). These files will be copied to the target system so that SAPinst will use them during the import step of the homogeneous system copy procedure. Please note that when the ORABRCOPY.SAR file is extracted it will also write an OraBRCopy.pdf file. This file can be referred to for additional information and options.

```
orakb1> pwd
/oracle/KB1/sapreorg/export

orakb1> SAPCAR -xvf ORABRCOPY.SAR
SAPCAR: processing archive ORABRCOPY.SAR (version 2.01)
orabrcopy.jar
ora_br_copy.sh
ora_br_copy.bat
OraBRCopy.pdf

SAPCAR: 4 file(s) extracted
```

The following is the generic command syntax for generating the control file:

```
./ora_br_copy.sh -generateFiles -forceLogSwitches -targetSid <TARGET_DBSID>
-password < oracle user system's password> -listenerPort <listener port>
```

For SID = KB2 and listener port = 1527, this command syntax will be as follows:

```
orakb1> ./ora_br_copy.sh -generateFiles -forceLogSwitches -targetSid KB2
-password <password of source system Oracle user System> -listenerPort 1527
```

When this command is executed, the database is restarted, log switches are performed, and a control file and init<SID>.ora file are written to the extract directory as shown. Please change the parameters, such as SID, listener port numbers, and password, as per your system. For some of the UNIX flavors, such as Linux, the password may need to be enclosed in single quotes for the command to be executed successfully.

```
SQL*Plus: Release 10.2.0.4.0 - Production on Fri Mar 19 15:51:24 2010
Copyright (c) 1982, 2007, Oracle.  All Rights Reserved.

Connected.
Database closed.
Database dismounted.
ORACLE instance shut down.
Disconnected from Oracle Database 10g Enterprise Edition Release 10.2.0.4.0 -
64bit Production
With the Partitioning, OLAP, Data Mining and Real Application Testing options

SQL*Plus: Release 10.2.0.4.0 - Production on Fri Mar 19 15:51:48 2010
Copyright (c) 1982, 2007, Oracle.  All Rights Reserved.
Connected to an idle instance.
ORACLE instance started.

Total System Global Area 9110028288 bytes
Fixed Size                  2098656 bytes
Variable Size            4563405344 bytes
Database Buffers         4529848320 bytes
Redo Buffers               14675968 bytes
Database mounted.
Database opened.
Disconnected from Oracle Database 10g Enterprise Edition Release 10.2.0.4.0 -
64bit Production
With the Partitioning, OLAP, Data Mining and Real Application Testing options


orakb1 12> pwd

/oracle/KB1/sapreorg/export

orakb1 13> ll
total 336
-rw-r--r--      orakb1 dba    1797     Mar 19 16:11 CONTROL.SQL
-rw-r--r--      orakb1 dba    3670     Mar 19 16:11 CONTROL.TRC
```

```
-rw-r--r--      orakb1 dba   1951     Mar 19 16:11 initKB2.ora
-rwxrwxrwx      orakb1 dba   1305     Jun  1  2008 ora_br_copy.bat
-rw-r--r--      orakb1 dba   2483     Mar 19 16:12 OraBRCopy.console.log
-rwxrwxrwx      orakb1 dba  91233     Jun  1  2008 orabrcopy.jar
-rw-r--r--      orakb1 dba   2467     Mar 19 16:12 ora_br_copy.log
-rw-r--r--      orakb1 dba      0     Mar 19 16:11 ora_br_copy.log.lck
-rwxrwxrwx      orakb1 dba  49039     Jun  1  2008 OraBRCopy.pdf
-rwxrwxrwx      orakb1 dba 117577     Mar 19 13:05 ORABRCOPY.SAR
-rwxrwxrwx      orakb1 dba   1107     Jun  1  2008 ora_br_copy.sh
```

Executing the SAPinst Export Steps for Java-Based Systems

For ABAP-based systems, this step is not needed. However, for Java-based systems such as SAP NetWeaver portal this step is needed. In this step the SAPinst tool will write an export dump for the Java component of the application. This will be copied to the target system and SAPinst will use Software Deployment Manager (SDM) to import the dump file during the import process. In newer dual-stack system releases this step is not needed, as SAP is storing everything in the database and the offline Oracle backup method will copy everything from the source system to the target system. The export dump can be written to the same directory created earlier on the source system at /oracle/KB1/sapreorg/export. Ensure at least 2GB of free space before starting the export process. The following procedure explains the details for executing the export step using the SAPinst tool. This will take approximately 30 minutes.

1. Log in as root and start the SAPinst tool from the installation master DVD by running ./sapinst.
2. In the welcome screen choose the path to start the export process shown in Figure 27-1.
3. Choose SAP NetWeaver 7.0 Enhancement Pack 1 | Software Life-Cycle Options | System Copy | Oracle | Source System Export | Central System | Based On AS Java | Database And Central Instance Export, and click Next.

In the next screens the system will ask for several parameter choices, as shown in Table 27-2. Enter the requested parameter values, and keep clicking Next as you work through the export process.

The SAPinst tool will complete the export steps and write an export dump file that needs to be copied to the target system import location. The SAPinst tool in the target system will read the export dump file and perform the import steps. The following illustration shows the successful completion of the export steps.

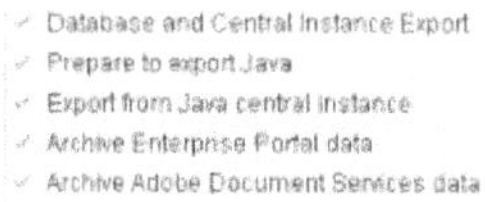

Copyright by SAP AG

Execute an Offline Backup of the Source System

You can use the last complete offline backup that was performed as a part of daily or weekly backups of your system. This has the advantage of not requiring any additional downtime to take an offline backup.

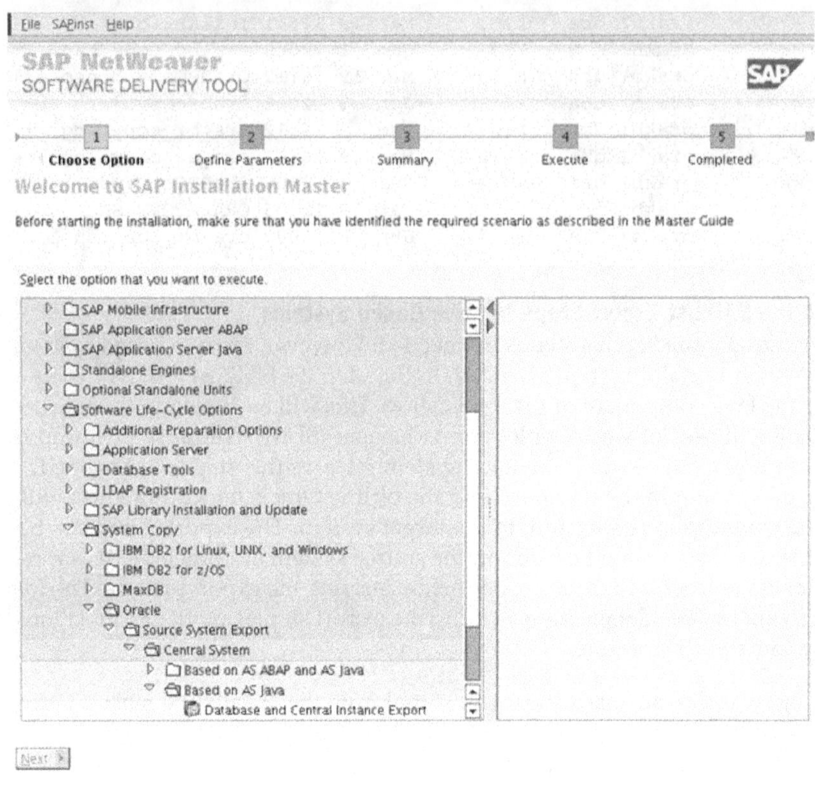

FIGURE 27-1 SAPinst screen showing the homogeneous system copy export selection

Parameter	Parameter Value
Path to the profile directory	Provide the path. Example: /sapmnt/KB1/profile for a source system SID KB1
Path to the Java runtime environment	Enter the JRE directory path.
Choose the system copy method	Select the Use Database Specific Tools check box.
Database export location	Enter the path where the export dump file will be written (Example: /oracle/KB1/sapreorg/export). If you select the Stop Running System check box, the system will prompt you to stop the system if it is not shut down at the time of the export. Select the check box.
Parameter summary screen	Verify the parameters selected, and click Start.

TABLE 27-2 SAPinst Homogeneous System Copy Export Parameters

System Copy Import Steps

The import steps in the target system will depend upon if the target system does not already exist and needs to be installed as part of the system copy procedure, or if a target system already exists and the data files of the target system have to be overwritten by the data files from the source system. In this section we will cover both options and will explain how to use SAPinst, BRTOOLS, and manual data file copy options for completing the homogeneous system copy.

Import Procedure If the Target System Is Already Installed

If the target system is already installed, then the process flow for the import steps will be as follows.

1. Use the Oracle offline backup copy method to complete the homogeneous system copy.
2. Delete or overwrite the target system datafiles and logfiles with the source system datafiles and logfiles, either manually or by using the BRTOOLS restore and recovery option.
3. Complete the database copy by starting the target database using the generated control file and copied source database files.
4. In case of Java-based systems, instead of performing a homogeneous system copy, export and import the content.
5. Perform any manual post-copy steps to complete the copy. (See the section on common post-copy steps in Chapter 25.)

Import Procedure If the Target System Is New

If the target system is not yet installed, then the process flow for the import steps will be as follows. This procedure applies to both ABAP and Java systems.

1. Install the target system database software.
2. Install the target system SAP software using the SAPinst tool but under the homogeneous system copy path.
3. Choose the homogeneous system copy option during the SAPinst tool execution.
4. SAPinst stops and requests to copy source database datafiles to the target system during the course of the homogeneous system copy.
5. Copy the datafiles manually from the source to the target, and continue the homogeneous system copy.
6. Perform any manual post-homogeneous system copy steps. (See the section on common post-copy steps in Chapter 25.)

Detailed Import Procedure When Target System Is Already Installed

The following steps must be performed in the source and target systems using the Oracle offline backup method.

Target System Steps In the target system, make sure that there is enough disk space to copy the source system database files. If needed, request more disk space ahead of time. Execute the following preparatory steps in the target system.

1. Stop the SAP system by issuing stopsap with the <sid>adm user account.
2. Log in as ora<sid> and issue sqlplus / as sysdba.
3. Get a control file list by issuing the following SQL command: select name from v$controlfile;.
4. Get the datafiles list by issuing the following SQL command: select file_name from v$datafile;.
5. Get the logfile list by issuing the following SQL command: select group#, member from v$logfile;.
6. Shut down the Oracle Database by issuing the command shutdown immediate;.
7. Take a full offline backup of the database in case you need to restore it later.
8. Stop the listener by issuing the command LSNRCTL stop.
9. Delete all the control files, datafiles, and logfiles listed in these commands at the operating system level.

Prepare the Source System and Generate the Control File The following steps have to be executed in the source system by copying the database files, logfiles, and the generated control file to the target system and restarting the database in the target system with the new control file.

1. Complete any open updates in the source system using transaction code SM13.
2. Work closely with the project team to perform any transports to the source system that would be needed in the target system after the copy.
3. Note the logical system names in transaction code SCC4. This information will be useful in executing the BDLS (conversion of logical systems) post-database copy step.
4. Stop the SAP application by issuing the stopsap R3 command as <sid>adm.
5. Generate the control file using the ora_br_copy.sh shell script, as explained earlier in this chapter, or generate a control file using the Oracle trace method.
6. The Oracle method of generating the control file is as follows:

```
cd    /oracle/<SID>/saptrace/usertrace
sqlplus / nolog
connect as sysdba
ALTER DATABASE BACKUP CONTROLFILE TO TRACE;
```

7. Shut down the database and take a full offline backup.
8. The control file generated in this way needs to be edited before it can be used in the target system.
9. The control file generated using the ora_br_copy.sh shell script has target system information already in it, so it does not need to be edited.

Editing the Control File Generated by the Oracle Trace Method The following changes have to be done to the control file generated by the Oracle method.

1. All occurrences of the source SID have to be replaced with the target SID.
2. Delete all the lines starting from the top of the file up to the second STARTUP NOMOUNT. (Do not delete the second STARTUP NOMOUNT line.)
3. Change the CREATE CONTROLFILE REUSE DATABASE "SSID" statement to CREATE CONTROLFILE SET REUSE DATABASE "TSID".

   Example: CREATE CONTROLFILE SET REUSE DATABASE KB1, where KB1 is the target SID.
4. Delete the RECOVER DATABASE USING BACKUP CONTROLFILE line completely.
5. Add the following lines to the control file and save the file so that certain post-database copy steps are taken care of at the start of the database in the target system where the target SID = KB1:

```
CREATE user ops$orakb1 identified externally;
CREATE user ops$kb1adm identified externally;

GRANT sapdba to ops$kb1adm;
GRANT sapdba to ops$orakb1;
GRANT sapconn to ops$kb1adm;
GRANT sapconn to ops$orakb1;

ALTER user SAPECC account unlock;

GRANT unlimited tablespace to ops$orakb1;
GRANT unlimited tablespace to ops$kb1adm;

CREATE table ops$kb1adm.sapuser as select * from ops$pk1adm.sapuser;

GRANT connect, resource to ops$orakb1;
GRANT connect, resource to ops$kb1adm;

DROP user ops$pk1adm cascade;
DROP user ops$orapk1 cascade;
```

Editing the Control File Generated by ora_br_copy.sh Shell Script
The previous SQL lines can be added to the CONTROL file generated by ora_br_copy shell script, or they can be executed after it is executed. A sample of the control file generated by ora_br_copy shell script for a target SID = KB1 is shown here:

```
REM ====================================================================
REM CONTROL.SQL
REM
REM       SAP AG Walldorf
REM       Systeme, Anwendungen und Produkte in der Datenverarbeitung
REM
REM       (C) Copyright SAP AG 2010
REM ====================================================================
```

```
REM Generated at:
REM Fri Jul 09 12:16:50 EST 2010
REM for target system KB1


CONNECT / AS SYSDBA

STARTUP NOMOUNT

CREATE CONTROLFILE REUSE
SET DATABASE "KB1"
RESETLOGS
ARCHIVELOG
MAXLOGFILES 255
MAXLOGMEMBERS 3
MAXDATAFILES 1022
MAXINSTANCES 50
MAXLOGHISTORY 19864
LOGFILE

GROUP 1 (
'/oracle/KB1/origlogA/log_g11m1.dbf',
'/oracle/KB1/mirrlogA/log_g11m2.dbf'
) SIZE 355M,

GROUP 2 (
'/oracle/KB1/origlogB/log_g12m1.dbf',
'/oracle/KB1/mirrlogB/log_g12m2.dbf'
) SIZE 355M,

GROUP 3 (
'/oracle/KB1/origlogA/log_g13m1.dbf',
'/oracle/KB1/mirrlogA/log_g13m2.dbf'
) SIZE 355M,

GROUP 4 (
'/oracle/KB1/origlogB/log_g14m1.dbf',
'/oracle/KB1/mirrlogB/log_g14m2.dbf'
) SIZE 355M

DATAFILE
'/oracle/KB1/sapdata1/system_1/system.data1',
'/oracle/KB1/sapdata1/system_2/system.data2',
'/oracle/KB1/sapdata1/undo_1/undo.data1',
'/oracle/KB1/sapdata1/sysaux_1/sysaux.data1',


'/oracle/KB1/sapdata2/ecc_1/ecc.data1',
'/oracle/KB1/sapdata2/ecc_2/ecc.data2',
'/oracle/KB1/sapdata2/ecc_3/ecc.data3',
```

```
'/oracle/KB1/sapdata2/ecc_4/ecc.data4',
'/oracle/KB1/sapdata2/ecc_5/ecc.data5',
'/oracle/KB1/sapdata2/ecc_6/ecc.data6',
'/oracle/KB1/sapdata2/ecc_7/ecc.data7',
'/oracle/KB1/sapdata2/ecc_8/ecc.data8',
'/oracle/KB1/sapdata2/ecc_9/ecc.data9',
'/oracle/KB1/sapdata2/ecc_10/ecc.data10',
'/oracle/KB1/sapdata2/ecc_11/ecc.data11',
'/oracle/KB1/sapdata2/ecc_12/ecc.data12',
'/oracle/KB1/sapdata2/ecc_13/ecc.data13',
'/oracle/KB1/sapdata2/ecc_14/ecc.data14',
'/oracle/KB1/sapdata2/ecc_15/ecc.data15',
'/oracle/KB1/sapdata2/ecc_16/ecc.data16',

'/oracle/KB1/sapdata3/ecc701_5/ecc701.data5',
'/oracle/KB1/sapdata3/ecc701_6/ecc701.data6',
'/oracle/KB1/sapdata3/ecc701_1/ecc701.data1',
'/oracle/KB1/sapdata3/ecc701_2/ecc701.data2',
'/oracle/KB1/sapdata3/ecc701_3/ecc701.data3',
'/oracle/KB1/sapdata3/ecc701_4/ecc701.data4',

'/oracle/KB1/sapdata4/eccusr_2/eccusr.data2',
'/oracle/KB1/sapdata4/eccusr_1/eccusr.data1',
'/oracle/KB1/sapdata4/eccusr_3/eccusr.data3',

'/oracle/KB1/sapdata5/ecc_17/ecc.data17',
'/oracle/KB1/sapdata5/ecc_18/ecc.data18',
'/oracle/KB1/sapdata5/ecc_19/ecc.data19',
'/oracle/KB1/sapdata5/ecc_20/ecc.data20',
'/oracle/KB1/sapdata5/ecc_21/ecc.data21',
'/oracle/KB1/sapdata5/ecc_22/ecc.data22',
'/oracle/KB1/sapdata5/ecc_23/ecc.data23',
'/oracle/KB1/sapdata5/ecc_24/ecc.data24',
'/oracle/KB1/sapdata5/ecc_25/ecc.data25',
'/oracle/KB1/sapdata5/ecc_26/ecc.data26',
'/oracle/KB1/sapdata5/ecc_27/ecc.data27',
'/oracle/KB1/sapdata5/ecc_28/ecc.data28',

'/oracle/KB1/sapdata6/ecc_29/ecc.data29',
'/oracle/KB1/sapdata6/ecc_30/ecc.data30',
'/oracle/KB1/sapdata6/ecc_31/ecc.data31',
'/oracle/KB1/sapdata6/ecc_32/ecc.data32',
'/oracle/KB1/sapdata6/ecc_33/ecc.data33',
'/oracle/KB1/sapdata6/ecc_34/ecc.data34',
'/oracle/KB1/sapdata6/ecc_35/ecc.data35',
'/oracle/KB1/sapdata6/ecc_36/ecc.data36'
;

ALTER DATABASE OPEN RESETLOGS;

ALTER TABLESPACE PSAPTEMP ADD TEMPFILE '/oracle/KB1/sapdata1/temp_1/temp.data1'
  SIZE 10000M REUSE AUTOEXTEND ON NEXT 20M MAXSIZE 10000M;
```

Copy the Source Database Files and Control File to the Target Server Location The next step is to copy the database files (datafiles, logfiles, and control file) from the offline backup location or from the source system directly using different copy methods, such as FTP, Secure FTP, or Secure Copy, from one server to another. The following provides an example of copying a control file and datafiles using the scp command:

```
Login as ora<target SID> (orakb1) and issue cd $ HOME

scp /oracle/<Source SID>/saptrace/usertrace/control.sql ./control.sql
```

Executing the following commands in the target system will copy the logfiles and datafiles recursively from the source to the target system:

```
scp -rp ora<source SID>@<source host>:/oracle/<SSID>/origlog*    /
oracle/<TSID>
scp -rp ora<source SID>@<source host>:/oracle/<SSID>/mirrlog*    /
oracle/<TSID>
scp -rp ora<source SID>@<source host>:/oracle/<SSID>/sapdata*    /
oracle/<TSID>
```

After all the files are copied, delete the temp.data1 file. This will be created when the target system is started using the new control file.

Starting the Target Database Log in to the target server as ora<sid> and issue the following commands to start the database:

```
cd $HOME
sqlplus /as sysdba
@./control.sql
```

This will execute the following steps as given in the control file.

1. New control file is created.
2. Source SID is changed to target SID.
3. Database is opened.
4. OPS$ user accounts for the target system are created and needed authorizations are granted.
5. The sapuser table is created.

Import Procedure When the Target System Is New

The following procedure must be used to perform the import if the target system is not installed and is a new system. In this scenario you have to install the database software on the target server. Then you have to use the SAPinst tool and perform a homogeneous system copy. This procedure installs a new SAP system and uses the database files copied from the source system to create the new system. The export DVDs are not requested by the SAPinst tool while performing a homogeneous system copy.

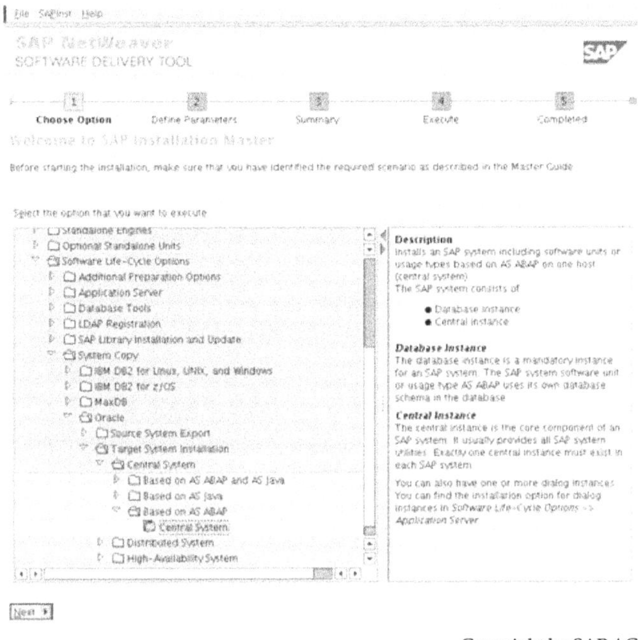

Copyright by SAP AG

FIGURE 27-2 SAPinst screen showing the homogeneous system copy selected

Installation of the Database Software The first step is to install the Oracle Database software in the target system as explained elsewhere in this book. This step will ensure that the Oracle binaries are installed ahead of the time and will cut down on the overall system copy procedure.

Creating a SAPinst Homogeneous System Copy Start the SAPinst tool as explained earlier in this book. However, at the welcome screen choose the system copy option instead of the new install option, as shown here and in Figure 27-2, clicking Next when finished.

SAP NetWeaver 7.0 Enhancement Pack 1 | Software Life-Cycle Options | System Copy | Oracle | Target System Import | Central System | Based On AS ABAP | Central System.

In the next screens, the system will ask for several parameter choices, as described in Table 27-3. Enter the requested parameter values, clicking Next as needed, until the import process is complete.

Copying Database Files from the Source to the Target System SAPinst will start the import steps, and during the course of the process will stop and present the following screen. Copy the database files from the source system to the target system as per the secure copy procedure discussed earlier. Once the copy is done, click the OK button. The remaining steps of the homogeneous system copy will be completed, and you will see a message notifying you that the copy is complete.

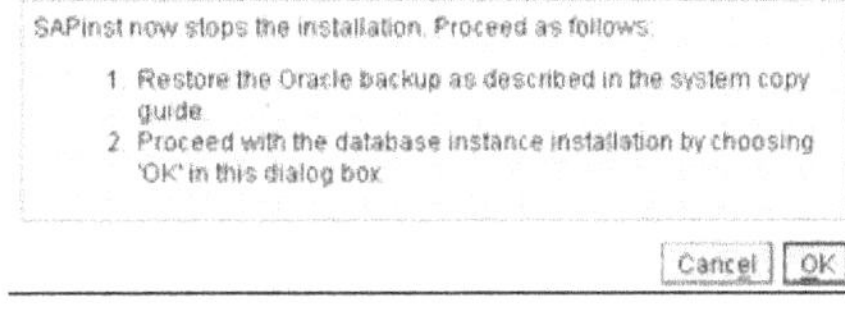

Copyright by SAP AG

Parameter	Parameter Value
Under the default settings screen, choose either Typical or Custom.	Choose typical for simplified copy process. If you choose custom option then you will be prompted for all parameters.
Java Development Kit	Enter the JRE directory path for your operating system.
Target system SID and SAP system mount directory	Enter the target system SID and /sapmnt as mount directory.
Master password parameter	Enter the password. Entering a single password is recommended, and it will be used for all the user accounts created by the SAPinst tool.
For the Database Installation parameter, choose the system copy method.	Choose Homogeneous System Copy (Backup/Restore).
Database parameters for Database SID and Database Hostname	Enter the database SID the same SAP SID, and enter the hostname of your target system.
Instance memory parameters and database schema parameters	Enter the instance memory as per your system allocation (Example 8GB). Enter the database schema name. It is recommended to keep the database schema names the same throughout your landscapes, as this will make database copies much simpler to perform. (Example: SAPERP or SAPECC)
Parameter asking for package location. This is the location of the dump files (particularly for Java systems) that were copied from the source system export location.	Enter the path where the export dump file will be copied to in the target system (Example: /oracle/KB1/sapreorg/export). The system will use the dump file during the import process. This is the case for Java-based systems. The SDM reads the dump file and deploys it as per the requirement.
For Java systems, the password used in the source system is required.	Enter the source system Java administrator user account.
Location for the kernel and Oracle client software DVDs	Enter the path for the kernel and Oracle client software DVDs.
Copy the CONTROL.SQL file to the SAPinst installation working directory. This file was created in the source system using the ora_brcopy.sh shell script in the section of this chapter that discussed exports.	<working directory>/sapinst_instdir/NW701/LM/COPY/ORA/SYSTEM/ CENTRAL/AS-JAVA OR AS-ABAP
Copy the Oracle initialization parameter file init_targetSID.ora to the /oracle/<DBSID>/102_64/dbs directory. This file was created in the source system by ora_brcopy.sh shell script.	Example: Copy initKB1.ora (SID=KB1) file to the /oracle/KB1/102_64/dbs directory.
Parameter summary screen	Verify the parameters selected, and click Start.

TABLE 27-3 SAPinst Homogeneous System Copy Import Parameters

Post-System Copy Steps

After the system copy is completed you will be able to start the target SAP system with the new SID, but you still need to perform additional post-copy steps before you can release the system to the end users. Some of the more important steps are discussed in Table 27-4. Most were explained in detail in Chapter 25. The list provided here is not comprehensive; for the complete steps, refer to the homogeneous system copy guide.

Post-Copy Step	Transaction Code or Procedure
Install the SAP license.	Use the SAPLICENSE transaction to install a new SAP license. The new license has to be requested as per the procedure explained in earlier chapters of this book.
Check the system for initial consistency.	Use transaction SM28 or SICK. You should not see any errors reported when this transaction is executed.
Convert logical system names from the source to the target system.	Use transaction code BDLS to convert all the logical system names from the source system to the target system. The logical source system names were captured at the beginning of the homogeneous system copy procedure prior to beginning the process.
Perform post-database copy steps for object directory entries and transports.	Execute transaction code SE06, choose database copy, and follow the subsequent screens by clicking Next/Continue. This will delete the old transport configuration and change the object directory entries ownership to the target SID.
Configure transport management for the newly copied system.	Use transaction code STMS and configure the transport management and transport route configuration.
Delete all cancelled and finished jobs.	Use transaction code SE38 and execute report RSBTCDEL2 to delete all the cancelled and finished jobs.
Delete all the source system jobs that are no longer needed, and schedule SAP standard housekeeping jobs.	Use transaction code SM37 to delete unwanted jobs. Use transaction code SM36 to define new SAP standard housekeeping jobs.
Adjust RFC connections.	Use transaction code SM59 to adjust the RFC connection hostnames and port numbers.
Set up logon groups.	Use transaction code SMLG to adjust the logon groups.
Generate the ABAP loads.	Use transaction code SGEN to generate the ABAP loads after the system copy.

TABLE 27-4 Post-Homogeneous System Copy Steps

BRTOOLS Restore and Recovery Option

BRTOOLS can be used effectively to restore and recover the SAP system from source to target systems using the redirected restore method. This procedure will help to automate a number of copy tasks and save the Basis administrator time when performing the copy. Refer to OSS Note 1003028.

Split Mirror Copy Option (SAP ATG)

System copies can be performed using certain advanced technologies from hardware vendors such as EMC, IBM, HP, and Hitachi. One of the most effective methods for copying the systems is referred to as a split mirror copy. SAP teams up with the hardware vendors and provides storage-based solutions to customers. The URL http://service.sap.com/atg provides additional information about these technologies.

Summary

- The system copy procedure helps to copy a source SAP system to a target SAP system using tools and techniques provided by SAP.
- The database copy contains the database components of the system copy.
- In a homogeneous system copy, the underlying database and/or operating system are NOT changed.
- In a heterogeneous system copy, the underlying database and/or operating system IS changed as part of the copy process.
- The heterogeneous system copy is also referred to as migration.
- There are three basic components to the copy procedure: export steps, import steps, and post-copy steps.
- Advanced techniques such as BRTOOLS redirected restore and recovery procedure and Advanced Technology group–related storage tools and techniques will help perform the system copies in an effective manner.

Additional Resources

- **System copy and migration** www.sdn.sap.com/irj/sdn/systemcopy
- **System copy export steps demo** www.sdn.sap.com/irj/scn/elearn?rid=/library/uuid/801eba00-ec8a-2a10-eca6-c7f38bdd4d19
- **System copy import steps demo** www.sdn.sap.com/irj/scn/elearn?rid=/library/uuid/207ac87d-e28a-2a10-9caa-ac5d69dc9302

CHAPTER

SAP Heterogeneous System Copies

In this chapter we will study the second type of system copy: the heterogeneous system copy. A heterogeneous system copy is also called an OS/DB migration, or operating system/database migration. Because of the complexity and importance of the migration project, SAP recommends that the migration be performed by a SAP-certified OS/DB migration consultant. This is particularly applicable for production system migrations.

Heterogeneous System Copy

During a system copy, if the underlying database, or operating system, or both are changed it is referred to as a heterogeneous system copy. The complexity of the heterogeneous system copy will depend on several factors, namely the size of the database, if both operating system and database are changed, and if the physical location of the systems is also moved during this process. An experienced migration-certified consultant who has performed several projects will be able to help guide you through the project and reduce the business risk.

Reasons for Performing a Heterogeneous System Copy

The following are the main reasons for performing a heterogeneous system copy. Sometimes a combination of reasons will justify or mandate a migration project.

- Enterprise operating system or database standards have been changed for strategic reasons by the information technology business leadership, and all SAP systems have to be migrated to the new operating system.
- In some instances, both the operating system and database standards have changed and a SAP migration effort is needed.
- Sometimes the datacenter-hosting location or contracting terms are changed or new hosting deals are negotiated for strategic reasons. The hosting provider may need a one-time migration of SAP systems so that it meets support standards.

- Compliance with Sarbanes-Oxley (SOX) can initiate a SAP migration project, particularly in the financial services industry.
- Performance and scalability issues can initiate SAP migration projects as well.

Business Scenario for Performing a Heterogeneous System Copy

You work for a financial services industry, and your corporate datacenter SAP systems operations are to be moved to a systems integrator's global datacenter such as IBM. This move has been initiated by your organization's business leadership to comply with SOX regulations. However, the current operating system is Windows and the systems integrator has standardized their operations around a UNIX-based operating system. In order to migrate current systems to the systems integrator's datacenter, and to comply with the SOX regulations, your corporation has initiated a migration project, and it will be performed using heterogeneous system copy.

Process Flow of a Heterogeneous System Copy

The key steps when performing a heterogeneous system copy are generating the migration key, exporting the source system, and installing and importing data into the target system. Each of these steps will be discussed in detail in the following sections.

Generating the Migration Key

When performing SAP migrations, you need to register and get a migration key from https://service.sap.com/migrationkey. Then click the Request Migration Key button as shown in Figure 28-1.

Migration Keys
Request Your Key For The SAP OS/DB Migration Tools Here
OS/DB Migration
Request migration key
Migration keys requested by me
Migration Keys Requested by Customer
Each OS/DB Migration of a SAP System requires its own migration key. This migration key is assigned on the basis of the installation number and additional system-specific information.
When an SAP System is exported or imported for the purpose of performing a heterogeneous system copy (SAP OS/DB Migration), a migration key must be entered into the migration tool. You will find information on OS/DB Migration and on the SAP OS/DB Migration Check service here.
This application enables SAP customers to request migration keys for their SAP Systems online. It also offers a detailed overview of all systems for which migration keys have been requested.

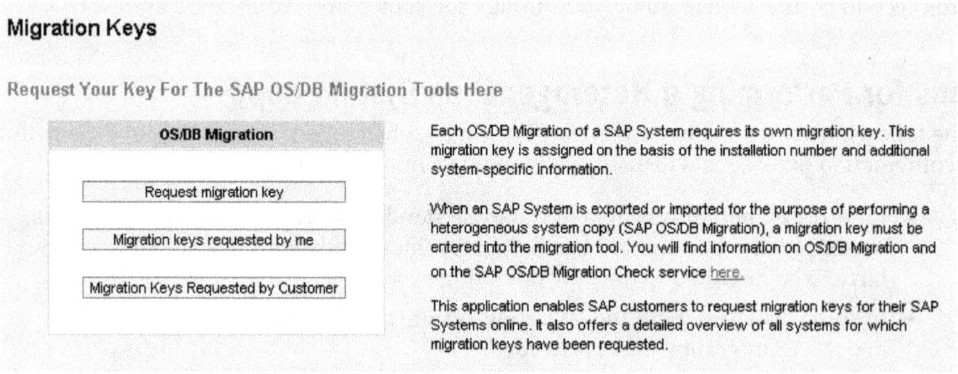

FIGURE 28-1 SAP migration key request

Source System

System ID DK1

Release Release 7.10

Operating system NT/INTEL/WIN2003

Database ORACLE 10.2.0.2

DB Server Hostname venus (case sensitive)

Target System

System ID DK1

Operating system AIX 7

Database ORACLE 10.2.0.2

DB Server Hostname ncrsap01 (case sensitive)

All fields are required

Submit Reset Cancel

Copyright by SAP AG

FIGURE 28-2 SAP migration key request form

You will have to navigate through a few more screens. Click I agree. At the installation overview screen, pick your installation number (Example: ERP installation), and then choose Migration Keys - Create Keys. The screen shown in Figure 28-2 appears. Fill out the form, and click Submit. SAP will generate a migration key for your installation. You will enter this information during the migration execution using SAPinst.

Export the Source Database

The source database export is performed in a database-independent form at the file system level. This will allow the data to be imported into the target environment with a different database by copying the export content to the target system. SAPinst drives both the export and import procedures. The following sections will describe the export tools, key export preparatory steps, and the detailed export steps that have to be performed for the heterogeneous system copy.

Export Tools

SAPinst is the main tool for performing both the export and import process in a heterogeneous system copy. Internally, SAPinst calls R3load for ABAP systems and Jload for Java systems when performing the export and import steps.

Export Directory

An export directory must be created before starting the SAPinst tool. The export directory will hold all the export files and will have to be copied to the target system to complete the import steps. For example, create an export dump destination at the operating system level, such as /usr/sap/DK1/export, where source SID = DK1.

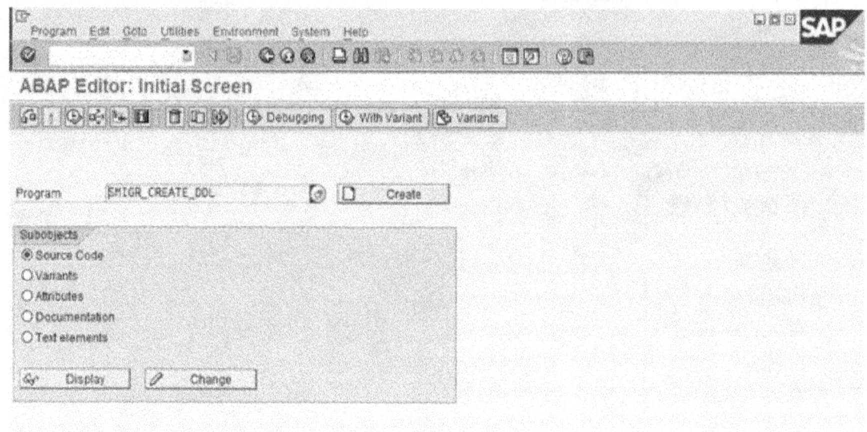

FIGURE 28-3 Execution of SMIGR_CREATE_DDL program in source system

Generate the DDL Statements

Before starting SAPinst you have to run the ABAP report SMIGR_CREATE_DDL in the source system. This will generate the Data Definition Language (DDL) SQL statements that need to be created in the target system during the import process. Figure 28-3 shows executing the report using transaction code SE38.

Executing this report will show the screen shown in Figure 28-4. In this screen choose the target system database, database version, and if unicode migration, mark the check box Unicode Migration under additional parameters. Also provide the export directory that was created in the earlier step. The DDL statements are generated and written to the export directory.

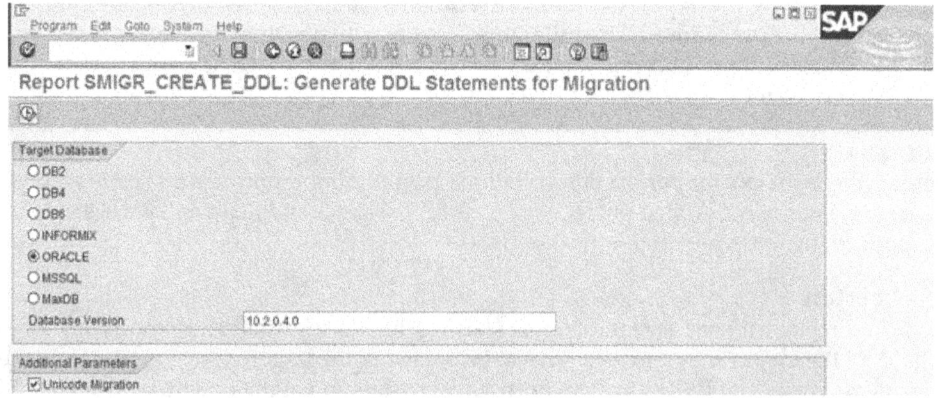

FIGURE 28-4 SMIGR_CREATE_DDL select options screen

Execute the program after selecting the relevant options, and once the program is complete you should see the following line indicating that the DDL statement generation completed successfully.

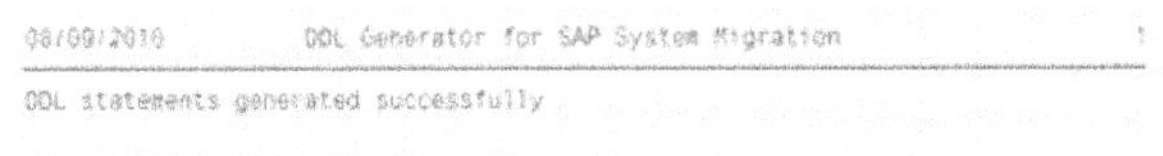

08/09/2010 DDL Generator for SAP System Migration 1
DDL statements generated successfully

Export Execution

Before starting the export step from SAP, the application has to be stopped. You can do this by issuing the command stospap R3 with the <sid>adm user account.

The database must be up while the export steps are executed with the SAPinst tool. The SAPinst tool can be started from the installation master DVD as root user account. Expand the System Copy, Oracle, Central System, Based On AS ABAP, and Database Instance Export sections as shown in Figure 28-5. Click Next.

SAPinst will prompt you for a series of parameters. Table 28-1 identifies the key parameters that need to be entered during this process.

Splitting STR files will improve performance of the heterogeneous system copy. During the export parameter entry phase, SAPinst will present the screen shown in Figure 28-6 for splitting STR files. Enter the parameters as shown. The parameter values can be adjusted to optimize the performance of your database and operating system.

Next, some of the target system database export parameters are presented. Figure 28-7 shows a sample parameter selection for a heterogeneous system copy. The choice between big-endian and little-endian is primarily based on the target operating system and how memory allocation is handled in that system. In big-endian systems the most significant byte is stored first, and in little-endian systems the least significant byte is stored first. Linux

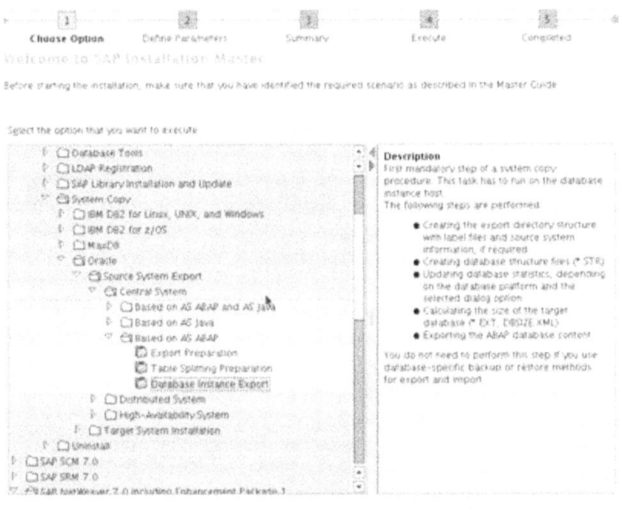

FIGURE 28-5 SAPinst selection of database export

Parameter Name	Parameter Value
Enter the profile directory of the source system	/sapmnt/<SID>/profile Example: /sapmnt/DK1/profile where SID = DK1
Enter the Java Runtime Environment (JRE)	Enter the path to the installed/supported JRE. Example: Path to the installed JRE Version 1.4.2
Database export location	Example: /usr/sap/DK1/export where source SID = DK1
Stop Running System check box	Selecting this check box indicates that SAPinst will prompt you if the SAP application is not shut down.
Confirmation screen for executing the ABAP report SMIGR_CREATE_DDL.	Click OK if this was done. If not, you have to execute the step as explained earlier in this chapter.
Export parameters for target system	Choose the target database (Example: oracle) and select the Split STR Files check box.
Splitting the STR files: large SAP tables can be split into smaller packages (STR files)	Choose split STR files and example configuration parameters as shown in Figures 28-7 and 28-8.

TABLE 28-1 Key SAPinst Export Parameters

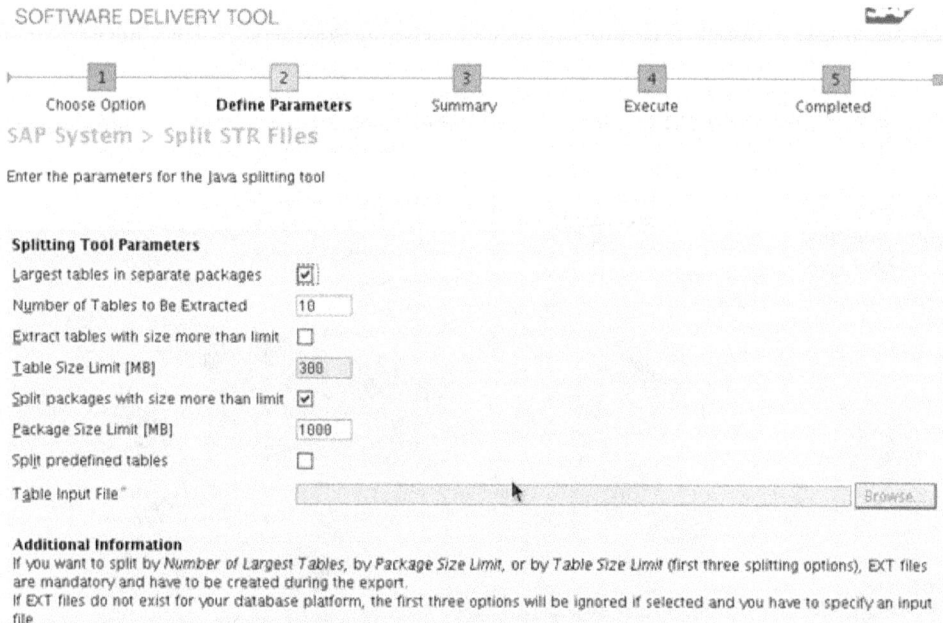

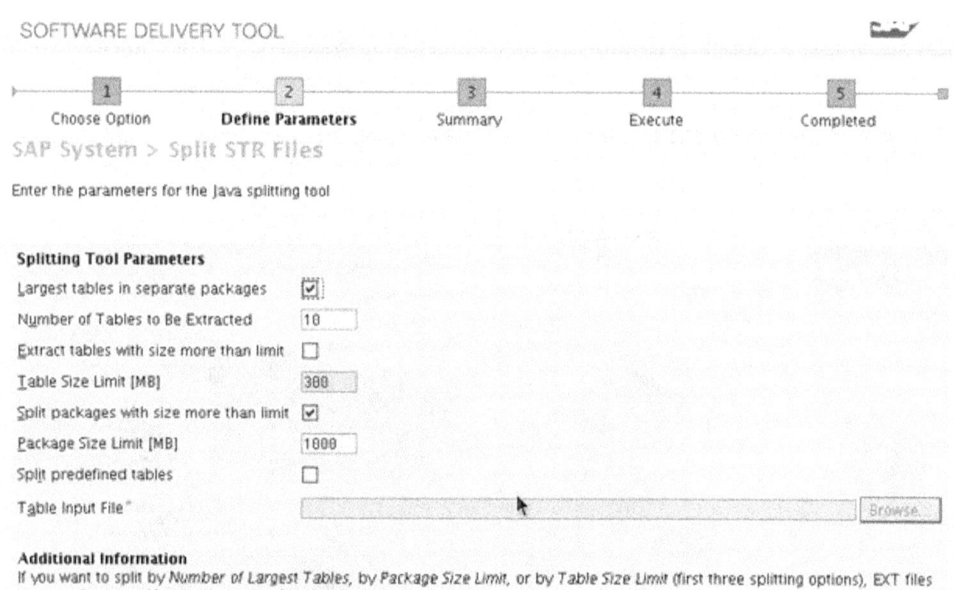

FIGURE 28-6 STR files splitting parameters

FIGURE 28-7 SAPinst database export options

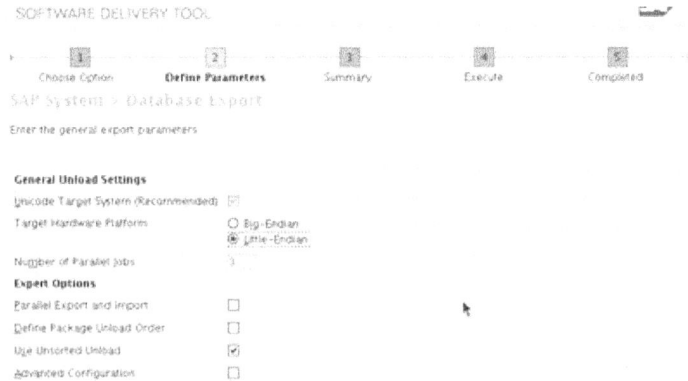

Copyright by SAP AG

on x86 and Windows on x86 are good examples of little-endian systems. AIX on PowerPC, Solaris on SPARC, and HP-UX on itanium are examples of big-endian systems. In the figure, the number of parallel jobs is 3 and the Use Unsorted Unload option is selected to improve the performance of the export.

Table 28-2 lists the most important OSS Notes for export options, such as table splitting, unsorted unload, and Oracle database parameter settings for heterogeneous system copy export. SAP also started supporting unloading the database from one operating system such as HP-UX to AIX using redirected restore instead of the R3Load procedure. Keep in mind that this is supported as long as the source and target operating systems belong to the same endian.

Once all the parameters have been entered, SAPisnt will present a summary screen where you can verify the parameters, and then click Start to initiate the execution of the SAPinst. This starts the execution of the export phase of the heterogeneous system copy, as shown in Figure 28-8.

If the SAP application is still running, SAPinst will prompt you as shown in the illustration so that the application can be stopped.

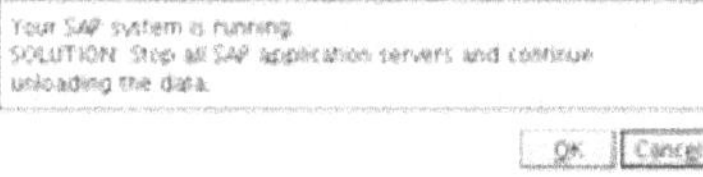

Your SAP system is running.
SOLUTION: Stop all SAP application servers and continue unloading the data.
OK
Cancel

Copyright by SAP AG

OSS Note Number	Description
952514	Using the table splitting feature
936441	Oracle settings for R3load-based system copy
1043380	Efficient table splitting for Oracle databases
954268	Optimization of export: Unsorted unloading
855772	Distribution monitor

TABLE 28-2 Export Options-Related OSS Notes

FIGURE 28-8 SAPinst executing the export steps

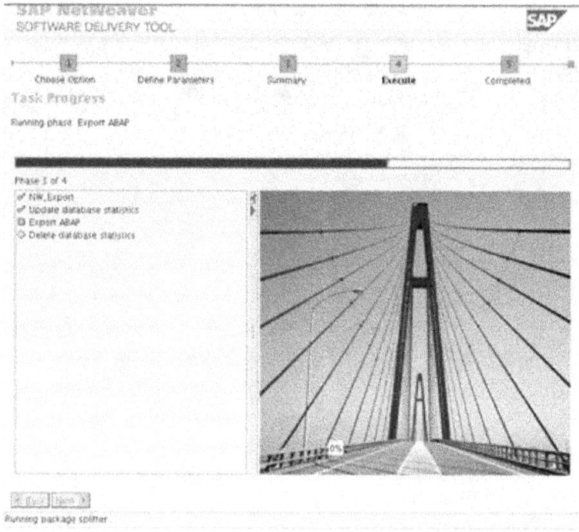

Copyright by SAP AG

The dump files are written to the export path location, and the EXPORT CD image/files have to be copied to the target system via network protocols such as FTP, or you can also burn a DVD image at the source system and ship it to the target location for copying and completing the import steps of the heterogeneous system copy.

Installing the Target System and Performing the Import Steps

Log in to the target system as root user account, and execute SAPinst from the installation master DVD as explained in earlier chapters of this book. This will start the SAPinst tool. Expand the System Copy, Oracle, Target System Installation, Central System, and Based On AS ABAP sections as shown in the following illustration.

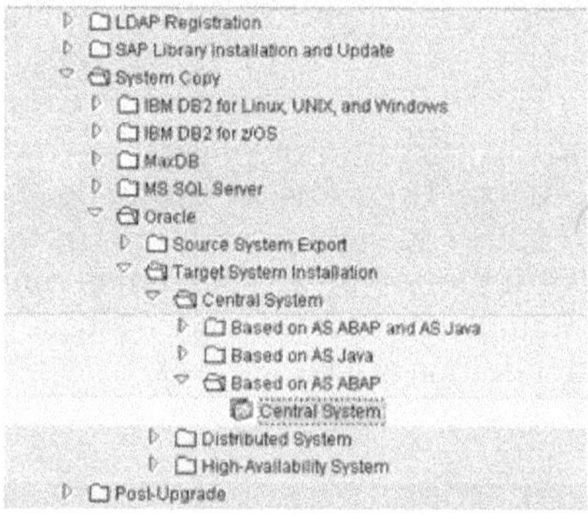

Copyright by SAP AG

Clicking Next will show the following screen, where you choose either Typical or Custom. If you choose Typical you will be prompted for the minimum number of parameters. If you choose Custom SAPinst will prompt for the complete set of parameters. Choose Typical and click Next as shown.

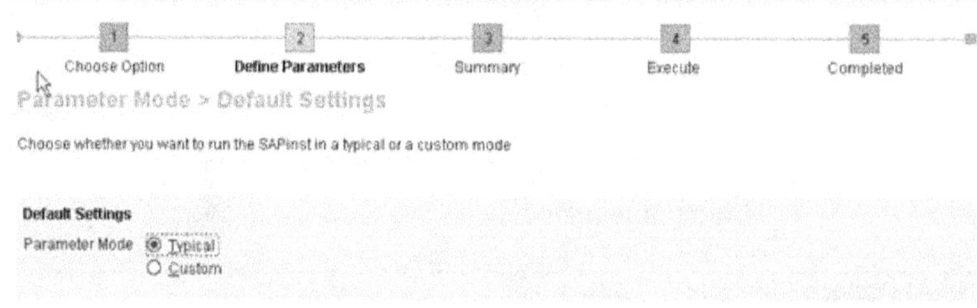

Copyright by SAP AG

SAPinst will present you with a series of parameter entry screens. Enter the requested parameters, and keep clicking Next until you reach the summary screen. Table 28-3 identifies the key parameters that SAPinst prompts you for during the target system installation and importing of the source system data.

The following figures and illustrations from SAPinst will provide an overview of some of the key parameter selection options and the final execution of the target system install and import steps while performing a heterogeneous system copy.

SAPinst Parameter	SAPinst Parameter Value
Enter the target system SID and select the Unicode system check box.	Enter the chosen identifier for your target system that is unique in your landscape (Example: DK1), and select the Unicode check box.
Choose master password for all user accounts created by SAPinst.	Choose a password. This will be used for logging into the target system at the operating system level after the system copy is completed.
Database installation method	Choose the Standard System Copy/Migration (Load Based option only). Do not select the Start Migration Monitor Manually check box.
Database SID and database hostname	Choose the database SID and hostname. The database SID is usually the same as the SAP SID (Example: DK1).
Pre-requisite checker results	The system will present the conditions that are not met in order to perform the install/system copy. Sometimes the conditions are of low priority and can be ignored. If that is the case, click Cancel. If not, meet the requirements as necessary, click Continue, and the checks are performed one more time.
Software packages (migration export) location	Enter the path to the location of the export files/export image copied from the source to the target system, and click Next.
Oracle installation check	SAPinst will check and see if Oracle database software (binaries) are installed. If not, you will be prompted to do this.
DDIC user account password in source system client 000	Enter the password of the source system DDIC user account in the client 000. This will be used by SAPinst to create an RFC connection to complete the import steps of the system copy.
Software packages location	Enter the location (path) to the following software packages: Unicode kernel DVD location Oracle client software DVD location
SAP Cryptographic software	Select the Install The SAP Cryptographic Library check box, and enter the path to the cryptographic library SAR file downloaded from the SAP software download location.
Summary screen	Verify that all the parameters were entered. If this looks accurate, click Start. Otherwise, click Edit to correct the parameter entries, and then click Start to execute the system copy steps.

TABLE 28-3 SAPinst Parameter Options for SAPinst Target System Installation and Import

FIGURE 28-9 Choosing the database installation method

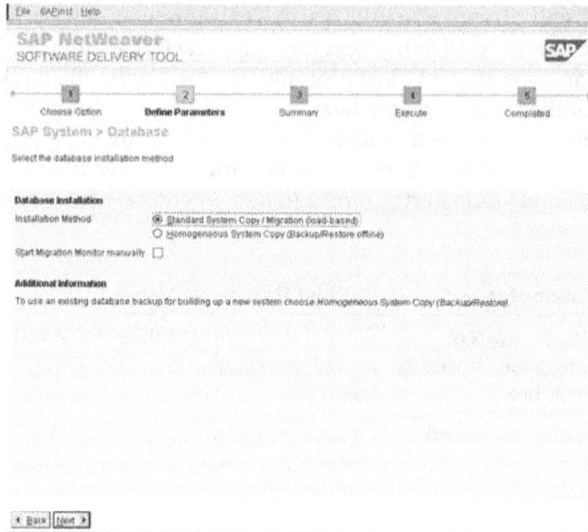

File SAPinst Help
SAP NetWeaver
SOFTWARE DELIVERY TOOL
Choose Option | Define Parameters | Summary | Execute | Completed
SAP System > Database
Select the database installation method
Database Installation
Installation Method
Standard System Copy / Migration (load-based)
Homogeneous System Copy (Backup/Restore offline)
Start Migration Monitor manually
Additional Information
To use an existing database backup for building up a new system choose Homogeneous System Copy (Backup/Restore).
Back Next

For the screen database installation method, choose Standard System Copy/ Migration (Load Based) as shown in Figure 28-9.

SAPinst will present the following screen if the Oracle software (binaries) is not installed.

Oracle software not installed. Install Oracle software before continuing.
OK

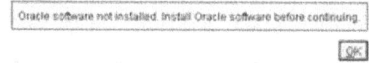

Figure 28-10 shows the execution steps for the heterogeneous system copy. Once all the steps are complete, SAPinst will display a message indicating that all the copy steps are completed successfully.

FIGURE 28-10 SAPinst execution phase of the heterogeneous system copy

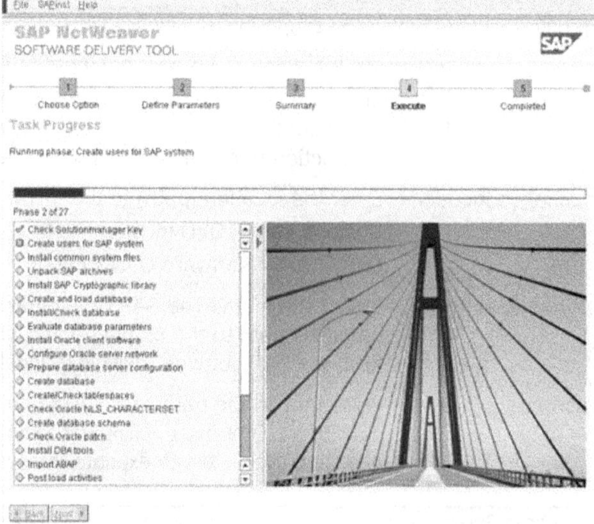

Summary

- In a heterogeneous system copy, the database, or operating system, or both are changed during the system copy process.
- Obtain a migration key before starting the heterogeneous system copy.
- The export phase of the copy will write the DDL statements and create a database dump file.
- The import phase of the copy reads the export dump and loads the data to the target system in a database-independent format.

Additional Resources

- **SAP migration (OS/DB migration)** https://service.sap.com/osdbmigration
- **SAP migration key** https://service.sap.com/migrationkey
- **Incremental migration of large databases** www.sdn.sap.com/irj/sdn/systemcopy?rid=/library/uuid/500b38f2-0711-2a10-7bb6-c4daf8439309

APPENDIX

SAP Basis Career Trends and NetWeaver Certification

I am writing this chapter from the vantage point of someone who has been working with SAP Basis/NetWeaver, technical architecture, and technology management for the last 12 years. Over the years I have been studying Basis/NetWeaver career trends and certification options closely so that I can reshape and adjust my own skill sets based on the evolving needs of the industry. One of the main goals of this appendix is to provide SAP Basis/NetWeaver career options for young professionals graduating from colleges and universities and also for experienced professionals who want to advance their careers. This chapter will cover a broad spectrum of issues faced by a prospective SAP Basis/NetWeaver professional as well as experienced professionals, such as what does a SAP Basis/NetWeaver and technical architecture career offer, why is it a valuable skill for the individual and for the organizations that hire them, how does one break into different career options, how does one get certified, what are the approaches for learning and developing the skill in depth, what career paths are available for Basis/NetWeaver professionals and how does one keep a balance between work and life. Hopefully, after reading this chapter, you will be better able to decide if SAP Basis/NetWeaver is a career choice for you or, if you are an experienced Basis/NetWeaver specialist, how to advance your career.

SAP Basis/NetWeaver Career

Over the years SAP Basis/NetWeaver administration and technical architecture have evolved into a highly specialized skill. It is no exaggeration to say that the skill has become so broad and deep that it is comparable to getting a specialized advanced degree in terms of getting the professional training and practical experience needed to excel in the job. Because of this specialization, professional training, and development it can be compared to other professional jobs, such as lawyers, doctors, and accountants. If you have to invest your time and energy into something that requires such a commitment, it only makes sense to understand what the job has to offer in return. The following sections will discuss the benefits available if you decide to pursue this as a career option. It will also cover what contribution a Basis role will deliver in an organization and discuss a typical day and week on the job.

Financial Stability

One of the reasons to pursue a professional career in SAP Basis/NetWeaver administration and architecture is that the job offers competitive salaries and a lot of financial stability compared to other IT jobs in the industry. Over the last 30 to 40 years SAP has established itself as one of the ERP standards for global organizations across the world. Most of the Fortune 500 companies, several small and medium-size businesses, federal and state government agencies, and private companies across the world use SAP as an ERP standard. Either they have already implemented the software or will be implementing and using it to run their businesses. Organizations invest a lot of financial resources into their corporate SAP systems and need a Basis/NetWeaver professional to architect, plan, build, test, deploy, and maintain the ERP application. Since the SAP application is mission-critical for conducting business transactions, organizations are willing to offer quite good compensation packages for Basis/NetWeaver professionals. In addition, this career path is stable and offers a lot of financial stability. A mid-level Basis/NetWeaver professional with three to four years' experience can earn up to $100,000 a year. Senior SAP Basis professionals with 7 to 12 years of experience can earn a lot more. Please note that salaries vary upon the geographic region and as well as the size of the company, and several other factors, such as a full-time job versus an hourly contracting opportunity.

Career Growth Opportunities

Another reason to pursue the SAP Basis/NetWeaver career is the growth opportunities it can offer. SAP Basis/NetWeaver can provide rapid career growth working for a systems integrator or for a Fortune 500 company. It can open up doors for IT roles in the organization with much broader responsibilities. This will be discussed further in a later section of this chapter.

SAP Basis/NetWeaver Role

SAP Basis/NetWeaver roles are categorized into junior-level positions, such as an entry-level junior SAP Basis administrator, to senior-level positions, such as Basis architect and SAP technical architect. Each of these roles has specific responsibilities and adds value to the organization.

Contributions of the SAP Basis Role

The SAP Basis resource ensures that the "lights are on" for the SAP system. No one can conduct any business if the system is either not available or is not delivering the expected performance. The cost of downtime per hour in some industries is so high that having a competent SAP Basis administrator on the payroll is vital to the success of the business. The Basis administrator will ensure that the organization conducts business smoothly without any interruptions. Just like you need a heart specialist in a full-fledged hospital, organizations running SAP need a SAP Basis specialist to make sure that the vital signs of the system are normal and the system is living and breathing. The following are the key contributions of the SAP Basis role:

- Plan and install the SAP systems.
- Make sure that the system is available to the project team or to the business as per the Service Level Agreement (SLA).

- Ensure good performance from the system.
- Plan and implement backup and recovery strategies for the system.
- Perform all system administration activities.
- Perform upgrades and archiving activities in the system.
- Implement software logistics and enforce the rules of moving changes in the systems.
- Perform software patching and kernel upgrades.
- Collaborate with project team members to resolve a techno-functional issue.
- Perform root cause analysis of any system problems.
- Troubleshoot and fix any system crashes.

Contributions of the SAP Technical Architect Role

The role of the SAP technical architect is more design oriented and helps in laying the broad framework of the SAP infrastructure and capabilities to serve the strategic business goals of the SAP system. SAP technical architects play a crucial role in making architecture decisions of the systems at the beginning stages of the project (blueprint phase) and will ensure that all the systems are built and integrated per the technical architecture blueprint design document approved by the organization. A well-thought-out SAP technical architecture design will ensure that the build-out infrastructure supports the current as well as the future growth needs of the organization. The following are the key contributions of the technical architect role:

- Develop the technical architecture design.
- Design development, operations, and execution architecture standards for the organization.
- Perform the SAP sizing project to procure the hardware.
- Perform capacity planning.
- Enforce technical architecture standards for the organization
- Develop designs to integrate enterprise third-party products with the SAP system.

Day in the Life of a Basis Professional in a Full-Time Job

The following is a typical day in the life of the Basis administrator working as a full-time employee for a organization:

- Arrive at work Monday morning and do some monitoring checks to make sure that all the systems are available.
- Notice that you received an alert in your inbox saying that one of the backups of your systems failed.
- You do a root cause analysis of the issue and fix the problem.
- Reschedule the backup job.

- A project team member shows up at your cube and lets you know that one of the systems is performing slowly. You will let him know that you will look into the issue.
- You take a look into the issue and kill a hanging job that was taking up lot of system resources and send an e-mail to the person who reported the issue.
- Time to attend the weekly meeting with the Basis team.
- Go for lunch with your team members after the meeting.
- Discuss shop or the latest basketball game during lunch.
- It is little slow after lunch. Around 2 P.M. you get a call from your remote location notifying you that they cannot access the system.
- You do a root cause analysis and find out it is a network issue.
- You ask the end user to open a ticket and assign it to the network team with high priority.
- Take a quick coffee break.
- You notice a coworker in the break room and chat for few minutes before heading back to your office.
- You get an e-mail from the project team functional lead saying that they are getting an ABAP dump in the system. They are not able to figure out the root cause of the issue.
- You take a look into the issue and realize that it is a functional data issue and not a Basis issue, but they need your help to resolve it. Welcome to the Basis world!
- In the spirit of collaboration and teamwork you talk to an experienced functional team member you respect and share the information that you find in the system.
- The functional team member understands the issue as being data-related. He works with another functional team member and a conversion team member to fix the data issue.
- You provide support to the functional team and conversion team. The issue is fixed.
- You wrap up your day with feeling of accomplishment and plan to take off for the day.
- Tomorrow is another day!

A Week in the Life of a Road Warrior Basis Professional

A road warrior is a traveling SAP Basis consultant with several years of experience under their belt. They usually work for one of the leading systems integrators, such as IBM, Accenture, or Deloitte. There is another group of SAP Basis consultant road warriors that work as independent consultants, either working on their own or subcontracting for the leading systems integrators. Some of them have been working so long that they have their own client base and contract directly with end clients. The road warrior lifestyle and job role can be better explained by taking a weekly view, since they are away from home for most of the working week. The most important drawback of the road warrior professional is the time away from the family or significant others. Most of the road warriors make the sacrifice so that they can work in demanding consulting projects where they make higher hourly rates than full-time salaried Basis professionals and enhance their work experience and résumés with the most current SAP technology. The following is an example of a road warrior working for a typical systems integrator:

- Make your travel arrangements at least two weeks in advance if you are an experienced road warrior.
- Pack your bags on Sunday night and get ready for the week ahead on the road.
- Get up early in the morning around 4:30 A.M. and take the first flight out to the client site.
- Endure the travel lines and security clearance, and finally make it to the client site in another city.
- Grab your lunch on the way to work and reach the client site by noon.
- Catch up with your e-mails and make plans for your deliverables for the week.
- Attend a meeting with the client technical team and Basis team.
- Address any open issues that cannot wait until the next day.
- Take off to dinner with your fellow road warriors and retire early to bed on Monday.
- Wake up and be at the client site bright and early on Tuesday, Wednesday, and Thursday.
- Most work gets done on Tuesdays and Wednesdays. Long hours are common, such as 10- to 12-hour days.
- Most deliverables such as new installs, database copies, and patching are completed.
- One of the weeknights you might visit a local brewery with your co-workers and have a beer and dinner.
- It is Thursday and time to wrap up for the week and head back to airport around 2 to 3 P.M.
- Reach home around 7 to 8 PM. Work remotely on Fridays.
- Spend time with the family on the weekend, and the cycle continues.
- The advantages of being a road warrior are that you deepen your SAP technical experience, are on the cutting edge of SAP skills, earn top dollars, and visit lot of new places.
- The disadvantages of being a road warrior are sacrificing family time, missing kids' school activities, and struggling with work-life balancing issues.
- Everything comes with a price!

SAP Basis Skill Development and Learning Resources

This section of the chapter will provide development and learning resources to start learning SAP Basis/NetWeaver skills. It will cover topics such as SAP Basis/NetWeaver training classes, free online learning resources, technical education conferences, and online SAP career advice resources.

Necessary Background for the Basis Administrator

The following background will provide a good foundation for the SAP Basis/NetWeaver career path. It does not mean that other backgrounds will not be able to pick up the skill. Resources with other backgrounds would have to work a little harder to learn the foundation skills before mastering the Basis skill.

- Any prior administration experience in operating systems such as UNIX and Windows Server. Knowledge of UNIX is particularly helpful, as large SAP shops use UNIX a lot.
- Any prior database administration experience in relational databases such as Oracle, SQL Server, and DB2 will be extremely useful.
- An academic background in computing is helpful.
- Analytical thinking and an ability for troubleshooting and problem solving will help.
- Any development experience will be helpful as well.
- Soft skills, such as inter- and intrapersonal skills, will be extremely helpful.

An introduction to all of these skills can be acquired either in a university academic program or targeted training classes.

SAP Basis Training Curriculum

SAP Education (www.sap.com/index.epx#/training-and-education/index.epx) offers training classes with a structured curriculum. Generally, the training courses are fairly expensive, and ideally you should get your employer to pay for your training courses. For new graduates, there are less expensive ways to get hands-on experience, which will be discussed in later sections of this chapter. The following table will provide all the needed information for training curriculums. The same links have scheduling and cost information as well.

SAP Training Resource Link	Training Focus Area
https://training.sap.com/us/en	General link for SAP training. You can change the country page by clicking the change option at the top of the page.
https://training.sap.com/us/en/courses-and-curricula	Courses and curriculum overview
https://training.sap.com/us/en/curriculum/intro_tech_overview_us-technical-overviews-us/	SAP technology overview
https://training.sap.com/us/en/courses-and-curricula/netweaver	NetWeaver curriculum
https://training.sap.com/us/en/courses-and-curricula/solution-manager	Solution Manager curriculum

SAP Basis Apprenticeship

One of the most effective ways to learn SAP Basis/NetWeaver skills is to join an organization as an entry-level Basis administrator and then do an apprenticeship and job shadowing, working closely with senior SAP Basis administrators. SAP Basis concepts can be picked up by going through a training class or sometimes just by reading help documentation. However, to understand the practice of Basis in real-life situations it is best to be an apprentice.

SAP SDN

One of the free SAP Basis/NetWeaver learning opportunities is studying the vast amount of community-generated content and SAP documentation in the SAP SDN (SAP Developer Network) website. The website can be accessed at www.sdn.sap.com/irj/sdn/index. This is one of the best free SAP knowledge areas to improve your Basis skills. There are countless blogs, technical articles, how-to guides, and e-learning material hosted by the site.

SAP SDN Career Center

SAP has developed a career center portal in SDN to cater to the needs of job seekers and employers looking for SAP talent. The career center can be accessed at www.sdn.sap.com/irj/scn/careers. It covers areas such as job postings, career blogs, and certification information.

SAP University Alliance Community

SAP has developed a University Alliance Community (UAC) linking universities, students, SAP, and customers for the purpose of educating the new crop of talent for tomorrow's SAP workforce requirements. The UAC can be accessed at www.sdn.sap.com/irj/uac.

SAP Conferences, User Groups, and Network Opportunities

The following are the leading SAP conferences and user groups where you can not only learn new SAP technology but also network with members of the SAP community.

SAP TECHED

SAP TECHED is the best conference to get an overview of the new SAP technology. There are sessions that give hands-on experience on some of the newer SAP technology. SAPTECHED information around the world can be accessed at www.sdn.sap.com/irj/scn/sapteched. SAPTECHED information for the United States can be accessed at www.sapteched.com/usa.

SAP User Groups

There are a number of SAP user groups around the world. Different user groups are listed at www.sapusergroups.com. The SAP user group for North America is called asug and can be accessed at www.asug.com.

SAPPHIRE NOW

SAPPHIRE NOW is the leading SAP conference event that connects SAP customers with new SAP capabilities. The event is more general in nature with a business focus. New SAP product capabilities are showcased so that the business value of the products and services SAP offers is communicated to the customers. Global SAPPHIRE NOW conference information can be accessed at www.sap.com/about-sap/events/sapphire/index.epx. SAPPHIRE NOW information for the United States can be accessed at www.sapphirenow.com/login.aspx?ReturnUrl=%2fdefault.aspx.

SAP Online Career Advice Sites

The following sites provide valuable information for both new and experienced SAP professionals.

Jon Reed

Jon Reed has been writing about SAP technology trends and doling out career advice to SAP professionals for well over a decade. Countless SAP professionals have benefited from Jon's well-thought-out career advice. You can access his site at www.jonerp.com.

Enterprisegeeks

This site was started by a group of SAP professionals (mostly SAP employees) interested in enterprise technology that can be leveraged to add business value. The blogs published are quite informative and will help even experienced SAP technical professionals learn about new capabilities and developments and, in turn, plan their own SAP career. It is because of this reason this site is included in this appendix. It can be accessed at http://enterprisegeeks.com/blog.

SAP Basis/NetWeaver Certification

SAP has invested considerable resources recently in improving the SAP certification options and quality. SAP certification is recommended for prospective professionals who would like to start a career in SAP and for new SAP professionals who have a couple of years of experience and would like to become SAP consultants or independent contractors. SAP certification may not help professionals who already have a lot of experience (more than seven years). SAP professionals in this category will either be looking into branching out into leadership roles or further specializing their SAP skills. SAPTECHED and specialized training from SAP Academy are better options for experienced professionals seeking further specialization in areas such as Solution Manager and virtualization expertise.

SAP Certification

At this time, SAP certification is grouped into two main levels. Basic certification is referred to as the associate certification level, and advanced certification is referred to as the professional certification level. In each of the levels there are focus areas for application, development, and technology tracks. SAP Basis/NetWeaver certification will fall under the technology focus areas. The following table lists the URLs that will provide more information on SAP certification, levels, and focus areas.

SAP Certification URL	Description
www.sap.com/services/education/certification/index.epx	This link will provide general certification information.
www.sap.com/services/education/certification/levels/index.epx	Provides more information on the certification levels and focus areas.

www.sap.com/services/education/certification/certificationfinder.epx	This provides a tool to search for the certification that best fits your needs. For SAP Basis/NetWeaver professionals, you have to choose SAP NetWeaver, Administration - General and Technology as a focus area to get a list of available certifications.
www.sap.com/index.epx# www.sap.com/training-and-education/visit-country-sites.epx	SAP training country sites link. Select the country you live in and get specific information such as training centers and how to register for certification.
www.vue.com/sap	SAP registration for certification exam. This service is offered by Pearson Vue and provides certification centers throughout the world.
https://training.sap.com/us/en/certification/	Online shop for certification and training.

SAP Corporate Master's Program

SAP has collaborated with certain educational institutions to establish a corporate master's program. Upon completing this program, you will receive an academic degree such as MBA or MSc from the participating university. The following URL will provide more information regarding this program.

www.sap.com/services/education/certification/corporate-master-program/index.epx

SAP Basis/NetWeaver Career Trends

In this section we will discuss SAP Basis career trends and related issues, such as how SAP skills have evolved, what skills are hot right now, the impact of outsourcing on Basis jobs, and emerging SAP Basis skills in areas such as virtualization and cloud computing environments.

Evolution of Basis/NetWeaver Skills

The SAP Basis skill set has evolved over time as the technology changed from being centered on mainframes to the client-server model, and later on to the web infrastructure and now moving toward virtualization, cloud computing, and in-memory database environments. Also the complexity of the SAP Basis job has increased over a period of time. In the client-server environments with SAP R/3 (the old name for current SAP ECC/ERP system) as the core product, the SAP Basis skill set was focused on installing and providing support to one product. In large implementations and project teams, the Basis team used to consist of resources specializing in performing transports, setting up printers and background jobs, installing the systems, applying OSS Note corrections manually, troubleshooting ABAP dumps, and improving system performance. Over time SAP has embraced Internet technologies and introduced Internet Transaction Server (ITS) and Web Application Server (WAS). The Basis skill set has evolved from supporting SAP R/3 running on client-server technologies to supporting ITS environments running on Windows and WAS integrated with a traditional Basis layer. Also, SAP started introducing new products, such as SAP BW, APO, and portals. Some of the newer products such as Portal introduced Java skills along with traditional ABAP skills. The SAP Basis administrator was expected to support multiple products based on ABAP and Java stacks. It was at this time the Basis job became more and more specialized.

The Basis team now has resources specializing in supporting BW, APO, XI (PI), portals, and other products. One Basis resource might start specializing in each of the product areas, and another would back him up. Cross-training in the Basis team, with a primary and secondary for each of the SAP products, became standardized. SAP consultants and independent contractors started specializing in newer areas, such as SAP SCM, CRM, and Business Objects. Because of the increased specialization of newer SAP products, organizations had a hard time finding professionals with these skill sets; usually these positions were filled by contractors.

The SAP skill set is now moving toward virtualization, cloud computing, and in-memory database technologies, and the Basis/NetWeaver skill set will gradually evolve to support this infrastructure. Some skills will be commoditized as a result, and newer skills will emerge to support the systems in a cloud computing environment.

Hot and Emerging SAP Basis/NetWeaver Skills

A "hot" skill is one that is in demand and considered valuable to businesses. The term "emerging" is used in the sense that the skill has the promise of becoming valuable to businesses in future. The following list does not rank these skills in any particular order; their importance or relevance depends on a whole range of criteria.

Hot SAP Basis/NetWeaver Skills

The following skills are valuable in the SAP Basis market at this time:

- **SAP ERP Enhancement Package Skills** SAP ERP skills related to the new enhancement package installer, switch framework, and integration of ERP solution to other SAP products such as BI, PI, and MDM are valued.
- **SAP ABAP and Java Administration Skills** SAP Basis resources start out in the ABAP world and pick up Java skills on the job, or start out with SAP Java skills such as portal administration and pick up ABAP skills. It takes a long time to develop Basis skills in both ABAP and Java administration. Since SAP products can be based on ABAP, Java, and sometimes dual stack (Example: Solution Manager), a Basis administrator who is proficient in both stacks is valuable.
- **SAP Solution Manager Skills** SAP Solution Manager is gaining traction and is becoming a valuable skill for Basis administrators. Capabilities in Solution Manager, such as DBA Cockpit, System Landscape Directory (SLD), CTS Plus, Test Management, SAP Landscape monitoring, and diagnostic capabilities of Solution Manager Diagnostic and Wily Introscope are valuable.
- **SAP BI/BW Skills** SAP Business Intelligence and Business Warehouse (BW)–specific Basis skills are also valuable. This skill set requires not only the traditional Basis skills but also BW skills, such as understanding the BW data model, integration with other systems such as ERP, and performance tuning skills for BW data loading and query execution.
- **SAP Business Objects Administration Skills** SAP has purchased Business Objects and is integrating it into the SAP BW environments because of its superior

dashboarding and reporting capabilities with tools such as Xcelsius and web intelligence. Architecting, installing, and integrating Business Objects into the SAP Landscapes are valuable skills.

- **SAP Technical Architecture Skills** SAP design skills, such as designing the development architecture, operations architecture, and execution architecture, are valuable. These design documents will provide the architecture approach and standards for the entire SAP infrastructure. Skills such as sizing and capacity planning are valuable as well.
- **SAP Process Integration Skills** SAP Process Integration 7.1 architecture and administration skills are unique and specialized. SAP Basis administration skills in message troubleshooting, architecting and integrating SLD, planning and implementing software logistics for the PI repository and directory objects, performance tuning of message flow through the integration server, and end-to-end message monitoring and troubleshooting failed messages are valuable skills.
- **SAP SRM Skills** SAP Supplier Relationship Management (SRM) started using the Master Data Management (MDM) catalog, and we are seeing more implementations in this area. Basis skills such as installing and administering the SRM portal and MDM catalog are valuable skills.
- **SAP GRC Skills** SAP GRC (Governance Risk and Compliance) administration skills are gaining in importance as more and more organizations are automating the SAP role provisioning to end users and meeting the audit and compliance requirements of the SAP systems.
- **SAP SCM Skills** SAP Supply Chain Management (SCM) skills such as Live Cache and Optimizer administration skills are valuable. SAP SCM integration with ERP is an important skill as well.
- **SAP CRM Skills** SAP Customer Relationship Management (CRM) with specific CRM middleware setup and administration experience is valuable.
- **uPerform Skills** uPerform is the leading SAP training third-party software integrated into SAP systems. More organizations are using uPerform for their end-user training needs; therefore, uPerform administration skills are valuable.
- **SAP Database Administration Skills** SAP developed database management tools such as BRTOOLS and recommends their use instead of native database management tools. One of the main reasons for this is the tools are "application aware" and some degree of automation is built into them. Since this set of tools is SAP proprietary, a resource with both native database administration skills such as Oracle DBA and deep experience in BRTOOLS is valuable.
- **SAP UNIX System Administration Skills** SAP Basis skills in the UNIX system administration area, such as storage technologies, high-availability systems setup, and virtualization skills, are very valuable.

Emerging SAP Basis/NetWeaver Skills

The following emerging skills should be added to the ones discussed in the previous section. Organizations are gradually moving in the direction of virtualization, cloud computing, and in-memory database applications, and developing the needed skills in this area will keep you relevant and valuable.

- **Virtualization Skills** More and more businesses are adopting virtualization. Architecting, building, and administering SAP solutions in the virtual environments such as VMware will become more important.
- **SAP HANA Skills** One of the most exciting new technologies developed by SAP recently is the High Performance Analytic Appliance (HANA) and in-memory resident database. Architecture and administration skills in this area will be very valuable in the future.
- **SAP Cloud Computing Skills** SAP is making a push for cloud computing infrastructures and has developed tools for provisioning system clones, testing environments, and resources to the business in a faster manner. SAP Basis skills in this area will become more important in the future.

SAP Soft Skills

End users depend heavily on the proper functioning and performance of the SAP systems. SAP Basis administrators, therefore, should develop the following soft skills to be effective in their jobs:

- **Communication Skills** With SAP systems having end users distributed throughout the world for multinational corporations, communication skills are very important. The ability to translate complex technologies so that a business executive and end users understand is valuable. This skill can be useful for project planning, end-user communication, and understanding system capabilities so that you can add business value by improving operational efficiency and finding process improvements.
- **Client-Facing Skills** The SAP Basis architect and technical architect roles are client-facing; therefore, developing good consulting, coordination, and presentation skills will help develop your role into a leadership position inside the organization.
- **Diversity Management Skills** In today's organizations, resources from different national and cultural backgrounds are hired and expected to work as a team to deliver business goals. Acquiring diversity management skills, such as managing a team consisting of people from different nationalities, cultures, and languages, is very valuable. Basis administrators and technical architects should enroll in such skills programs so that they can be effective in this area of their jobs.

SAP Basis/NetWeaver Project Management Skills

The following skills will help a Basis administrator gradually grow into senior lead roles inside the organization:

- SAP project management skills using tools such as Microsoft Project
- SAP program management skills
- Project Management Professional (PMP) certification
- SAP implementation methodology such as ASAP methodology
- SAP production support methodologies such as RUN SAP
- Information Technology Infrastructure Library (ITIL) understanding and certification

Impact of Outsourcing on Basis/NetWeaver Jobs

Outsourcing and offshoring business trends in the last decade have significantly affected IT careers. Jobs have been moved within the country and oftentimes to a remote service delivery center anywhere in the world. Fortunately, the SAP Basis/NetWeaver job has proved to be resistant to outsourcing and offshoring. Even though some routine jobs/job functions have moved to the delivery centers, most of the organizations still hire full-time SAP Basis/NetWeaver administrators and consultants to keep them onsite and address any issue immediately. This is primarily because of the need of organizations to make sure that the systems are available all the time. Unlike ABAP development work, which has been heavily outsourced or offshored, SAP Basis/NetWeaver skills are not suitable for outsourcing or offshoring to a significant extent. For instance, if the business needs someone to troubleshoot an application problem that is preventing users from posting business documents to the database, someone needs to work closely with the functional team member to understand the issue and resolve it in a timely manner. This process is difficult to write as a technical specification for a remote resource in a different time zone to complete the task. One other key reason is the job needs someone to resolve issues in real time and needs close client interaction. This can be best achieved by having resources on-site, or at least in the same time zone. SAP Basis jobs are also heavily application-dependent and datacenter-dependent and will most likely stay close to the business.

Strategies for Breaking into a Basis Career

Breaking into the SAP Basis field as a newbie, progressing from experienced Basis administrator to an IT management/executive position, and moving from a SAP Basis full-time professional to an independent consultant need certain strategies, which will be discussed in the following sections.

Strategies for a Newbie

Breaking into the SAP Basis/NetWeaver field is indeed challenging for a new graduate, but there are certain things you can do to help improve your chances for landing at entry-level SAP Basis job. The following are some strategies you can use to help break in as a newbie:

- **Download the trial version and learn the basics** SAP provides free copies of its software on a trial basis for evaluation purposes, and you can download the software and learn SAP Basis basics on your own. The software can be downloaded at the following location:

  www.sdn.sap.com/irj/scn/downloads
- **Free resources on SAP SDN** SAP SDN has a number of free e-learning courses and how-to guides. Use this information and the trial version of the software to further improve your skills by making them relevant. SAP SDN can be accessed at the following URL:

  www.sdn.sap.com/irj/sdn/index
- **Join University Alliance Programs** Join the universities that partner with SAP in the University Alliance Program. This will help you complete your undergraduate work, with a focus on SAP training, and improves your chances of getting that first job.

- **Join the SAP Corporate Masters program** Joining this and earning a MBA or MSc academic credential will help you to get a SAP Basis job in your chosen industry.
- **Take entry-level jobs with a systems integrator** Systems integrators, such as IBM, Accenture, and Deloitte, do campus recruitments, hiring new analysts for entry-level SAP positions. Once you join a systems integrator, they will further help you in your career needs.
- **Take an IT job in an organization using SAP heavily** Research and network and find out the organizations that use SAP a lot and join them either as an intern or as an entry-level IT position. Once inside the organization, network and make a lateral move into any SAP positions that become open.
- **Participate in an internship in SAP** Look for any internship opportunities with a systems integrator, Fortune 500 company, or SAP, which you could later use to get a full-time position.
- **Explore the SAP Career Center** The SAP Career Center publishes entry-level jobs. Apply for those positions using your SAP training and academic experience.

Strategies for a IT Management/Executive Role

The next group of professionals has worked as SAP Basis administrators and technical architects for several years and would like to break into leadership positions, such as SAP technology manager, SAP technology director, or SAP infrastructure manager. The following set of strategies will help you to break into the next level:

- **Learn project management skills** Organizations usually have learning programs that help people get trained in project management skills. Enroll in such programs and learn project and program management skills.
- **Accept increased responsibility** Ask for more responsibility every year, and deliver results. Seek feedback and apply lessons learned every year and improve your performance year on year. This will gain more visibility for you and will gradually earn you a role with more responsibility.
- **Seek a mentor** Find someone inside your organization who is in leadership position, and seek advice on ways you can contribute more to the organization and over time get promoted to positions with more responsibility.
- **Get an executive MBA** Get an executive MBA if your organization helps you with the tuition. If they do not support you in this, consider getting one with your own resources. This will pay off in the long run.
- **Get certifications** Get certified in programs such as PMP and ITIL.
- **Leave dead-end jobs** Sometimes there will be no growth inside an organization despite your best efforts. The reasons could be political, or maybe you work for an organization that is small and is not catering to your needs. If you are in this kind of situation, it is best to seek another opportunity outside the organization and then quit your current position.

- **Join a systems integrator** Joining a systems integrator such as IBM, Accenture, or Deloitte can help accelerate your career growth. Systems integrators usually have faster career paths than the typical Fortune 500 company.
- **Make a lateral move** Once you make it to a senior IT role with a systems integrator you can consider making a lateral move into a senior-level position in a Fortune 500 company. For example, once you reach a senior manager position with a leading systems integrator, it is more practical to seek a position as an IT director in a Fortune 500 company.

Strategies for the Basis Independent Consultant

The most difficult role to break into in the SAP market is the independent contractor role—especially one that pays good hourly rates. It has become more difficult in recent years because of economic slowdown. However, there are strategies you can use to break into the SAP independent contractor role. Consider the following strategies:

- **Become specialized** With the increased complexity of the SAP Basis role, organizations look for SAP Basis specialists in certain areas such as SAP SRM, SAP SCM, and SAP CRM. Organizations do not have trouble finding general Basis administrators, but specialists are hard to find. Specializing in such areas will therefore help improve your chances of getting a contract.
- **Develop cutting-edge skills** Be on top of your game, and acquire cutting-edge skills and difficult skills, such as setting up high availability, performing SAP migrations, performing upgrades with Unicode conversion, server consolidations, virtualization infrastructures, cloud computing, archiving, and HANA.
- **Network** Develop a network of SAP professionals in the industry. This will not only help you to keep yourself informed, but also will help you line up your next contract.
- **Contribute and publish** Contribute and publish blogs, etc., to SAP SDN and other related sites. This will not only allow you to help the community, but will also demonstrate your expertise and land your next gig.
- **Acquire references** SAP is a small world. Word gets around fairly quickly regarding the quality of your services. It is in your best interest to focus on doing an outstanding job at your current contract so that you can get references and land the next contract.

SAP Basis Career Path Options

You current SAP Basis job can lead you in senior IT roles in the organization. Some of the career path options are discussed in the following sections.

Basis Architect

After working as a SAP Basis administrator for few years, you can move into Basis lead or a Basis architect role. This will allow you to gradually move from being an individual contributor to a lead role. Usually, you will be leading a team of Basis administrators and will be leading the work planning efforts and contributing toward some of the architectural decisions.

Technical Architect

The next step in the career ladder is the SAP technical architect. SAP technical architects usually come from a SAP Basis background. These professionals will lay out the design guidelines and framework for any new SAP solutions and make sure that they comply with the enterprise standards and mesh well with the corporate datacenter. Being a SAP technical architect is a much broader responsibility than the Basis administrator or Basis architect role, and gives you exposure to senior IT management in your organization.

Enterprise Architect

SAP technical architects who like working in the technical areas and do not have much interest in IT management can branch out into a much broader role of an enterprise architect. This role involves all enterprise business applications and not just SAP. Your SAP technical architecture background will help you transition into this role and add value to your organization. This role will also leave you an option of moving into more general IT management roles if you change your mind and want to move in that direction at a later time.

Process Integration Architect

One other area a SAP Basis administrator can branch out is to become a process integration architect. This role will allow you to take the lead in the entire end-to-end development of interfaces, and will give lot of exposure to business process understanding. This, in turn, can help you to move into a more business-focused role in your organization. This role is a strategic career choice in the sense that it adds significant business value.

IT Management Career Path

Progressing from a SAP Basis role to SAP Basis architect/lead and SAP technical architect will open up opportunities for IT management roles in your organization. Over time you can demonstrate your management and people skills and get promoted into a SAP technology manager role and then into a general IT management role. In addition to this, if you get an executive MBA and invest in understanding finance and how businesses make money, you can progress rapidly into a senior IT management role such as IT director and vice president. There are several success stories of SAP professionals who have made it into senior IT management roles all the way to the CTO and CIO levels.

Entrepreneurship Career Path

For SAP Basis administrators and technical architects who do not like working as a full-time employee for a Fortune 500 company or a systems integrator, there is another exciting option of entrepreneurship. This option involves risk and is not for everyone. The SAP ecosystem is so broad that there are several opportunities to pursue your own business. There are opportunities in product development, service delivery, third-party integration, and training opportunities.

Work-Life Balance Issues

Organizations spend a lot of financial resources implementing and managing SAP projects. SAP work, therefore, can be stressful for the professionals working on such projects, with tight deadlines and quality goals. If a SAP professional does not handle the work-life balance issues that come with the stress, he will find himself not meeting either career goals or personal goals. Even though it is difficult to achieve a perfect balance, there are few strategies you can use to mitigate the issue and make it more manageable.

- **Work remotely** Working remotely from your home office once in a while can help you to manage work-life balance in terms of getting your work done and at the same time attend to your other responsibilities, such as parent-teacher meetings. Remote technologies such as Microsoft OC (Office Communicator), AIM (AOL Instant Messenger), and NetMeeting have allowed organizations to manage employees' accountability while working remotely. The same set of technologies allows the teleworker to collaborate with his co-workers in an effective manner.
- **Use comp time** In SAP projects, performing job activities over a weekend is common. In such instances work with your supervisor and get some comp time (compensatory time) so that you can better balance your work and personal life.
- **Take vacations** Take vacations so that you can get recharged before starting a major initiative. Accumulating a lot of vacation time and not taking it in the pursuit of career goals at the expense of personal life will catch up and will either lead to burnouts or relationship issues.
- **Attend training** Attend professional training events once a year. This will allow you to learn the latest skills and also will build your network outside your company. In addition, this will give you an opportunity to spend some time outside your work environment.
- **Use flexible work schedules** Work with your supervisor and HR departments to negotiate a flexible work schedule when possible.
- **Consider your choice of employer** Consider working for employers who value work-life balance and target employment in those organizations. Best Buy and SAS (www.sas.com/) are a couple of employers with good work-life balance initiatives.

Summary

- SAP Basis/NetWeaver administration and architecture is a financially stable career option and offers excellent career progression opportunities.
- The SAP Basis/NetWeaver professional adds a lot of value to organizations by making sure the systems are available and perform well for business use.
- SAP Education offers training classes to learn SAP Basis skill sets.
- SAP SDN is a great free online learning resource for prospective and experienced professionals.

- SAP offers several certification options to demonstrate your credentials to prospective SAP employers and to keep your skills current.
- SAPTECHED is the leading technical conference that will help SAP professionals to stay informed and trained in the most current technologies.
- SAP Basis/NetWeaver career path options include becoming a technical architect, independent consultant, or IT manager.
- Work-life balance issues are important and need to be managed to better grow your SAP career over the long term.

Additional Resources

- **Worldwide SAP University Alliance members list** http://uaaroundtheworld.informatik.tu-muenchen.de/overview(bD1lbiZjPTEwMQ==)/start.htm
- **SAP SDN e-learning** www.sdn.sap.com/irj/scn/elearn
- **SAP EcoHub** http://ecohub.sap.com

Index

D

I

J

K

L

M

N

O

P

U

V

W

X

Y

www.ingramcontent.com/pod-product-compliance
Lightning Source LLC
Chambersburg PA
CBHW080118220326
41598CB00032B/4885